Joomla!® BIBLE

Second Edition

Ric Shreves

WILEY

John Wiley & Sons, Inc.

Joomla!® Bible, Second Edition

Published by
John Wiley & Sons, Inc.
10475 Crosspoint Boulevard
Indianapolis, IN 46256
www.wiley.com

Copyright © 2013 by John Wiley & Sons, Inc., Indianapolis, Indiana

Published by John Wiley & Sons, Inc., Indianapolis, Indiana

Published simultaneously in Canada

ISBN: 978-1-118-47491-4

10 9 8 7 6 5 4 3 2 1

For general information on our other products and services or to obtain technical support, please contact our Customer Care Department within the U.S. at (877) 762-2974, outside the U.S. at (317) 572-3993 or fax (317) 572-4002.

Library of Congress Control Number: 2013932112

Trademarks: Wiley and the Wiley logo are trademarks or registered trademarks of John Wiley & Sons, Inc., in the United States and other countries, and may not be used without written permission. Joomla! Is a registered trademark of Open Source Matters, Inc. All other trademarks are the property of their respective owners. John Wiley & Sons, Inc. is not associated with any product or vendor mentioned in this book.

Wiley publishes in a variety of print and electronic formats and by print-on-demand. Some material included with standard print versions of this book may not be included in e-books or in print-on-demand. If this book refers to media such as a CD or DVD that is not included in the version you purchased, you may download this material at http://booksupport.wiley.com. For more information about Wiley products, visit www.wiley.com.

Credits

Senior Acquisitions Editor
Stephanie McComb

Project Editor
Jade L. Williams

Technical Editor
Ed Ventura

Copy Editor
Marylouise Wiack

Editorial Director
Robyn Siesky

Business Manager
Amy Knies

Senior Marketing Manager
Sandy Smith

Vice President and Executive Group Publisher
Richard Swadley

Vice President and Executive Publisher
Barry Pruett

Project Coordinator
Patrick Redmond

Graphics and Production Specialist
Carrie A. Cesavice
Jennifer Mayberry

Quality Control Technician
Lauren Mandelbaum

Proofreading
Lisa Young Stiers

Indexing
BIM Indexing & Proofreading Services

About the Author

Ric Shreves is a partner at water & stone (www.waterandstone.com), a web development agency focused on open source content management systems, or CMS. He has been building websites professionally since 1999 and writing about technology for almost as long. He has published several books on open source content management systems, including titles on Mambo, Joomla!, and Drupal. This is his fifth title with Wiley, having previously released Visual Blueprint titles on Mambo and Ubuntu Linux, as well as *Drupal 7 Bible* and the first edition of *Joomla! Bible.*

Ric is an American who has lived in Asia since 1995. He currently resides in Bali, Indonesia. You can learn more about Ric and his most recent work by visiting his website at http://ricshreves.net/.

Contents at a Glance

Contents

Contents

Contents

Contents

Contents

Contents

Acknowledgments

I would like to thank Wiley for asking me to return as the author of the second edition of *Joomla! Bible*. We worked together to produce the first edition three years ago. In the intervening years, much has changed with both the web CMS landscape in general and with Joomla! in particular. Much of my excitement for this revision text stems from the fact that the newest version of Joomla! is a major step for the project — one that I hope receives the broad audience that it deserves. Having the chance to dig into Joomla! 3 in depth while researching and writing this title has been a brilliant learning experience and has left me with a very positive view of the newest version of Joomla! — something that I hope I have communicated adequately in the pages of this book.

This project ran on an incredible schedule, largely due to the measured guidance of my project editor Jade Williams. We had a very aggressive deadline to meet and without Jade's experience and ability to prioritize, I never would have made it. I also want to say thank you to Stephanie McComb, a Senior Acquisitions Editor at Wiley. She's the person responsible for pushing through both the Joomla! and Drupal Bible titles at Wiley, and has been a steady champion for these projects internally.

Introduction

Welcome to *Joomla! Bible*. As with all books in the Bible series, you can expect to find both hands-on tutorials and real-world applications, as well as references and background information that provide a context for what you are learning. This book is a comprehensive resource on the Joomla! open source content management system. After you have read *Joomla! Bible,* you will be well prepared to build and maintain a Joomla!-based website.

Joomla! is in the forefront of one of the most dynamic trends in open source software: the rise of open source content management systems. Historically, a web CMS was a very expensive investment. Open source has changed all that. There are now a number of options that allow website developers and website owners to tap into the power of CMS-based websites.

Of all the web CMS options that exist in the market today, perhaps none is more popular than Joomla! — certainly none is growing more quickly. The Joomla! system powers millions of websites and is one of the dominant forces shaping the way people interact with information online. It has empowered developers and website owners around the world to build the websites that allow them to express themselves, to sell their products, to publicize their news, and to build communities. With the arrival of Joomla! 3, the system moves into new ground with expanded functionality and support for mobile devices.

If you are a designer looking to build functional websites for your clients, Joomla! is an excellent tool. If you are a developer looking for a framework upon which to develop custom functionality, Joomla! can meet your needs. And if you are simply a website owner wanting to take control of your website, then you need look no further than Joomla!. Whatever your goals, welcome to *Joomla! Bible.*

In keeping with the comprehensive theme of the Bible series, this book seeks to provide a range of information suitable to a wide variety of potential readers. While I have strived to present information that is relevant to the largest possible group of users, certain sections of this book are logically more relevant to certain categories of users.

If you are looking to take your first steps with an open source content management system, the book progresses logically from the first section of introductory materials through the final sections on customization and website maintenance.

If you are already familiar with Joomla!, the opening sections will probably add little to your understanding of the system, but the sections that follow will help you unlock its full potential. Joomla! is a complex system, and the middle sections of this book explore in depth how to get the most out of it.

If you are a designer or developer, the middle and final sections will be your focus, as they take you through creating and configuring a Joomla! website and cover the basics of customizing the appearance and functionality of the system.

Finally, if you are a website owner or administrator, this book should serve as a reference, providing you with an easy-to-use guide to the ongoing ownership of a Joomla! website.

Is This Book for You?

This second edition of *Joomla! Bible* has been extensively updated to focus on coverage of the Joomla! 3 series of releases. With the arrival of Joomla! 3, the system has seen a complete change in the administration interface, new functionality, and numerous changes in the work process.

This book provides new users with all the information they need to install and configure a Joomla! website. Thereafter, the book stands as a reference for the various content management and component functionalities, all of which are documented and explained in detail. New users will also find the sections on maintaining and securing the system particularly helpful.

If you are familiar with Joomla! but ready to move up to the new Joomla! 3, this book provides all the information you need to get up to speed with the new interfaces quickly. If you are familiar with the first edition of this book, you will find the organizational schema to be very similar, but the contents have been almost completely refreshed and in many cases, expanded.

How This Book Is Organized

This book is divided into six parts, including an Appendix with useful resources.

Part I: Getting Started with Joomla!

Part I covers the basics of getting started with Joomla!. It assumes you do not know anything about the system. I introduce you to Joomla! and open source and content management systems and then walk through obtaining and installing Joomla!. The third chapter takes you on a guided tour of the front end and back end of the default Joomla! installation. The final chapter in this section covers getting the most out of Joomla's many configuration options.

Part II: Working with Content and Users

In Part II, you learn how to work with content and users, the heart of the Joomla! CMS. I cover creating, editing, and managing content items in great detail. I include a separate discussion on advanced content management techniques, including managing content from the front end of your Joomla! website. Chapter 8 is dedicated to Joomla's menu system, with a comprehensive review of all the menu item types included in the default installation. Chapter 9 looks at various techniques for creating an effective home page and managing the content on your home page. Managing users is the subject of Chapter 10, with an extended look at user groups, and how you can manage user permissions and privileges in Joomla! The final chapter in this sessions deals with creating a multilingual website and a look at all the language management tools in Joomla! 3.

Part III: Working with Components, Modules, and Plug-Ins

Part III focuses on the functionality that is included in the default system. I've included separate chapters for the default components in order to take an in-depth look at how to use and configure each component. The various Joomla! modules are also detailed in two chapters, one focused on the Site Modules, the other on the Administrator Modules. The modules chapters not only detail the purpose of each of the modules, but they also include examples of uses and complete coverage of the configuration options available for the modules. The final chapter covers the default Joomla! Plug-ins and the options they give website owners.

Part IV: Customizing and Extending the System

Part IV moves into how to customize the appearance and functionality of the system. The first chapter in this section takes an in-depth look at Joomla! templates. I explain how the templates work, how to customize their appearance, and even how to create your own templates from scratch. There is also discussion of template frameworks and examples of using Twitter Bootstrap in Joomla! 3. The next chapter looks at the core components, modules, and plug-ins, with an eye towards explaining the underlying MVC architecture, and how the elements work. Customization of the components and modules is also covered. The final chapter in this section looks at extending your Joomla! website. In that chapter, I also look at a set of extensions you can add to Joomla! 3 to address common website issues.

Part V: Overseeing Website Maintenance and Management

Part V covers the ongoing maintenance of a Joomla! website. This final section of the book is focused more on website ownership issues and will be of more interest to webmasters and website owners. The first chapter in the section looks at implementing a security regimine and at the related topic of patch management. The second chapter looks at how you can enhance the performance of your website and how to improve accessibility of your content. The final chapter in this section looks at techniques for enhancing the search engine friendliness of your Joomla! website.

Part VI: Appendixes

Part VI contains the Appendixes, which provide supplemental information, including a look at all the sample data installation options, and a guide to finding all the key files in your Joomla! installation. I also cover how to install the XAMPP and MAMP server packages on your computer, thereby allowing you to create a local development installation. In the final appendix, I look at using the VirtueMart extension to add e-commerce functionality to your website.

How to Use This Book

To get the most out of this book, you need access to an installation of the Joomla! CMS. Typically, this requires a server running a combination of the Apache web server, the MySQL database, and PHP. Website management is handled through a browser with a connection to the server. Full technical requirements and recommendations for optimal versions are discussed in Chapter 2.

In Part IV, where the topics focus on working with the Joomla! code, you want to have access to your favorite code editor. In this part and elsewhere in the book, having access to an FTP client is also useful.

> **NOTE**
> This book focuses on version 3.x of the Joomla! CMS. These releases are significantly different from the previous series.

About the Icons

Many different organizational and typographical features appearing throughout this book are designed to help you get the most from the information.

Whenever I want to bring something important to your attention, the information appears in a Tip, Note, Caution, or Cross-Reference.

> **CAUTION**
> The Caution icon means that you should pay special attention to the information or instructions so that you do not experience a problem.

 The Cross-Reference arrow refers you to a related topic elsewhere in the book. Because you may not read this book straight through from cover to cover, you can use the cross-references to find the information you need quickly.

NOTE

A Note icon alerts you to some important point that requires special attention, or additional information that may be helpful.

TIP

A Tip shows you a way to accomplish a task more efficiently or quickly.

Where to Go from Here

It is my hope that you will take away from this book an increased awareness of the capabilities of the Joomla! system and a higher comfort level when working with websites based on Joomla!.

If you spend some time around open source software, you will quickly discover that the rate of change in these systems can be impressive (sometimes even a bit daunting). Joomla! is a community–driven, open source system. The community behind it is large, dynamic, and ever changing. New features are developed at a rapid pace, and new extensions, tips, tricks, and tools arise even more quickly.

If you want to get the most out of Joomla!, I strongly suggest you make an effort to keep up with the project. In Chapter 1, I list the official Joomla! project websites. You should bookmark those websites and visit them regularly. The Joomla! Forum is a great place to visit and learn what is new and of interest. Several of the official websites also provide RSS feeds and other easy ways to stay up to date with project developments.

If you want to send me feedback on this book, you can reach me directly by visiting my personal website, `http://ricshreves.net/`; there is a contact form on that website that is sent directly to me. You can also provide feedback by visiting the official John Wiley & Sons website (`www.wiley.com`).

Part I

Getting Started with Joomla!

P art I covers the basics of getting started with Joomla!. It assumes you do not know anything about the system. I introduce you to Joomla! and open source and content management systems and then walk through obtaining and installing Joomla!. The third chapter takes you on a guided tour of the front end and back end of the default Joomla! installation. The final chapter in this section covers getting the most out of Joomla's many configuration options.

Introducing the Joomla! Content Management System

IN THIS CHAPTER

Understanding open source content management

Discovering the Joomla! CMS and what it can do

Reviewing Joomla! functionality and basic architecture

Exploring the Joomla! community and how you can get involved

J oomla! is an award-winning content management system that brings powerful website creation and management tools to the masses. You don't have to be a programmer to use Joomla! because you don't need to work with the code to install, set up, or manage your site. To get started, all you need is access to a web-hosting service to install Joomla! and a web browser to create and manage your site. Moreover, the Joomla! content management system is open source, and therefore free of licensing fees and restrictions on use.

Joomla! is one of the most popular content management systems in use today, with millions of successful implementations. With the arrival of Joomla! 3, the system entered a new era, with greatly enhanced usability, extended compatibility, and an emphasis on the ability to create mobile-friendly, responsive websites. You can also use Joomla! as a framework for the development of powerful web applications, via the Joomla! Platform.

This introductory chapter explores the advantages of using both Joomla! and open source, and provides you with the big picture of how Joomla! works and how you can use it to build or manage your own website.

Discovering Open Source Content Management

A *content management system*, or CMS, is a software tool that you install on a server. The software enables you to publish pages on a website and to manage the website's features, content, and users through an easy-to-use browser-based interface. Historically, full-featured CMS products were expensive, and dominated by major brand names such as BroadVision, Vignette, and

Microsoft. Over the last decade, however, the market shifted as robust open source products arrived on the scene, supplementing, and in some cases supplanting, their commercial brethren.

The appearance of viable open source content management solutions has had a significant impact on the market, essentially democratizing the content management space. Small businesses and individuals that could never before afford a proper CMS can now implement an open source solution and create a web presence that is competitive with much larger firms. As open source systems increased in stability and functionality, they started to find a place in larger firms. Today you can find open source CMS products at every level of business, both public and private.

Deciding to use a CMS

Content management systems make maintaining a website more practical and affordable. In the past, if you wanted to build a website; you created a set of static HTML pages — that is, you hard-coded each page with your text and images. The old approach suffered from numerous limitations, particularly in terms of scalability and ease of management; with hard-coded pages, you are forever working with the code on each page whenever you want to make a change. Modifying the contents of a page by manually changing the code is both time consuming and labor intensive. Owning a static site also locks you into hiring people with coding skills to perform content management tasks.

In contrast, if you use a CMS to power your website, anyone with basic skills can make changes to the site. You do not need a programmer to change the text or the images on a page. Most systems, including Joomla!, use a content management interface that is similar to what you see in common word processing programs, such as Microsoft Word.

With a CMS, you gain significant advantages, including

- Increased control over your website
- Improved time to market with content changes
- Lower cost per page
- Decreased total cost of ownership for your site

A CMS typically enables you to:

- Identify key users and their roles
- Assign roles and responsibilities
- Define workflow
- Schedule and publish content
- Limit access to content and functionality
- Administer the system
- Take the site offline to perform maintenance tasks
- Add components

> **NOTE**
>
> Numerous types of content management systems are available; some focus on particular specialties. Systems such as Joomla! are typically labeled *web content management systems* because they focus primarily on managing a website, its content, and users. Other systems focus on document management, catalog management, or digital asset management. If you are looking for a specialized system, such as a document management system, then you should research the alternatives available to find the best match for your needs.

Deciding to use open source

Open source is about freedom; not simply the ideal of freedom, but the commercial reality of freedom. Open source software does not carry licensing or subscription fees. Although the initial attraction of open source software may be the fact that it is free of charge, you are likely to find very quickly that the long-term advantage of open source lies in two other characteristics. First, the code is accessible. Unlike many commercial products that not only hide their code but also forbid you from modifying it, open source code is visible and you are free to modify the code of an open source product to suit your specific needs. Second, open source protects you from being tied to a specific vendor. If you adopt an open source solution, you can partner with the developer of your choice to assist you. If you deploy a system such as Joomla!, which is based on popular and common technologies, you need not dread having to change vendors in the future, as it is relatively easy to find people who are familiar with the system and have the skills needed to work on it. Taken together, the initial cost advantage plus the long-term benefits of having access to the code and your choice of vendors create a compelling argument in favor of open source.

While the positive attributes of open source make it a great choice for many organizations, no solution is completely without disadvantages, and those negative aspects need to be a part of your decision process as well. If your firm has existing software deployed on a proprietary system, a change to open source will (at least initially) bring added complexity and you will want to look closely at compatibility, the costs of change, and whether open source is the right fit for your business needs.

Support can also be an issue. Like most open source products, Joomla! does not provide a support package. If your firm demands a high level of support, you will need to find an open source vendor that offers an appropriate service level agreement. If you have internal resources, or are a do-it-yourselfer, Joomla! does provide a number of community-based support options that can be of assistance, including

- Online documentation
- Community forums
- Online tutorials
- Mailing lists
- RSS feeds
- Developer wiki

Do not lose sight of the fact that while the actual Joomla! software is free, there are costs to implementing and owning any website. Common costs include

- Design services
- Consulting services
- Custom development
- Deployment
- Support
- Hosting services
- Domain names
- Licenses for other related software, for example, certain extensions
- Maintenance

While all of these expenses may not be applicable to your project, you should consider them when calculating the total cost of ownership of an open source system. Even if you plan to manage and maintain the site yourself, don't forget that there is a cost associated with your time. It is a common mistake to underestimate the amount of time it can take to maintain a site. A CMS is a complex piece of software and it can be a target for hackers and others with bad intent. You cannot just build your site and forget it. Across the life of the site you will need to install patches and security releases. The more complicated your site is, the more time you will require for maintenance and patch management.

Determining whether open source is right for you

Although open source provides a welcome alternative to commercial software and it will work for the vast majority of people, it is not necessarily the right answer for everyone. Whether open source is right for you depends upon your situation and your tolerance for business risk. The advantages are as follows:

- **Open source is cheaper to obtain.** Studies also show that implementation costs can be significantly less than for closed source solutions.
- **Open source can be vendor agnostic.** You are not tied to a single vendor and cannot be held hostage by that vendor.
- **Open source presents less risk.** Studies consistently show that the open source development process produces better code and that many eyes make for more secure applications. Moreover, when problems are detected, open source produces patches at an extremely fast rate.
- **Open source is easier to install.** It's also typically easier to configure and customize, not requiring a legion of highly paid consultants.
- **Open source promises more rapid innovation.** A large community working on a product stimulates innovation.

If you are still not sure, start small. Roll out an open source solution in a limited role in your firm. Try it out. Six months from now, evaluate the results and decide whether open source is the right path for you. If you are like many others, you will find that it is not only a viable option, but also an attractive one!

Discovering Joomla!

Joomla! started life in 2005 as a fork of the already popular Mambo open source content management system. The Joomla! community came together around the new project very quickly and helped create prominence and excitement around the new brand. Over the years, the project has gone from success to success and has grown to become one of the largest and most active open source projects.

> **NOTE**
> The Joomla! name derives from a phonetic spelling of a Swahili word meaning "all together" or "as a whole."

The features included with the core system are

- **WYSIWYG content editor.** Edit articles with the ease of use of a word processor.
- **Content scheduling.** Set start and stop dates for the publication of your content.
- **Content archiving.** Store old articles for ease of reference.
- **User management.** Create users and assign them to groups.
- **Access control.** Control the users' access to content and functionality.
- **Media manager.** Upload and organize your media files.
- **Language manager.** Add new language packs to enable multilingual interfaces for your site.
- **Banner manager.** Upload and run advertisements.
- **Contact manager.** Store contact details of your users and enable contact forms for them.
- **Search.** Search the site's content.
- **Weblinks management.** Create pages containing links to other websites.
- **Content syndication.** Syndicate your content items with RSS feeds.
- **Newsfeed aggregation and display.** Bring external RSS content into your site.
- **Integrated help system.** View help files from within your admin system.
- **Multiple template management.** Add new templates and assign them to the pages of your site.
- **Cache management.** Manage site performance by controlling the caching of information.

- **Responsive design.** Gain compatibility with a wide range of mobile devices and browser platforms.
- **Multilingual site support.** Offer your content in multiple languages with the built in Language Manager.
- **Search engine–friendly URLs.** Create search engine–friendly URLs to make your site more competitive on the search engines.

In addition to the core functionalities, Joomla! is extendable. With over 10,000 open source extensions available for little or no charge, you can customize the site to include the functionalities you need.

Deciding to use Joomla!

For most people, deciding to use Joomla! is a relatively easy step to take. Joomla! is comprehensible, affordable, and flexible enough to grow with you over time. Joomla! is, in short, an easy-to-use option for creating and managing a full-featured website.

Although Joomla! is an excellent solution for many needs, it is not suited to every conceivable use. There are areas where the system excels, and others that present challenges. If you want to be more analytical about Joomla!, then you should consider the pros and the cons.

Here are some of the best arguments for using Joomla!:

- **Tens of millions of downloads.** This is a healthy and growing project with a large fan base.
- **Over 10,000 extensions available.** The large number of extensions means you can tailor Joomla!'s functionality for your site.
- **Uses the popular LAMP stack.** It is easy to find hosting and help.
- **Presentation layer is very easy to work with.** You can customize the appearance of the site to match your brand. You aren't restricted to creating a "cookie cutter" website.
- **Decent e-commerce options.** If you want to sell products online, low and no cost extensions are available that add to Joomla! all the most common e-commerce functionalities as well as providing useable catalog management.
- **Wide developer support.** It is easy to find help for your Joomla! site. Developers, designers, and other third-party services are readily available.
- **Decent documentation.** The online documentation provided by Joomla! is some of the best in open source. You can also find commercial documentation in a variety of formats.
- **Very active community.** An active and dynamic community means that you can get support in the forums and you can be assured of the ongoing vitality of the project.
- **Affordable development costs.** Competition and a common platform make for a wide range of vendor choices and price points. Given the large number of people providing Joomla! services, you can probably even find someone in your area.

Who Uses Joomla!

Because Joomla! is so popular, you can find a large number of example sites live on the web. The system supports everything from small marketing sites to large e-commerce sites. Here's a roundup of some of the better-known companies and brands that use Joomla!.

Name	URL
Citibank	`Intranet — not publicly accessible`
The Guggenheim Museum	http://guggenheim.org
Harvard University, The Graduate School of Arts and Sciences	http://gsas.harvard.edu/
IHOP Restaurants	www.ihop.com/
Oklahoma State University	http://osu.okstate.edu
Outdoor Photographer Magazine	www.outdoorphotographer.com

If you'd like to see more examples, visit the Joomla! Community Showcase, where you will find a browsable collection of Joomla! sites organized by category. Go to http://community.joomla.org/showcase/.

Here are some of the drawbacks you should consider before committing to Joomla!:

- **No workflow.** If your site needs to replicate your offline workflow, Joomla! may not be the answer for you. The system does not include a workflow engine.

- **Possible difficulty maintaining customized sites.** If you need to customize the code of your site, you have to be careful with upgrades in order to avoid losing your customizations. So, the more customization you need, the more work is involved in upgrades.

- **SEO is mixed.** Joomla! includes a search engine–friendly (SEF) URLs option, but the default system's configuration options are quite limited. There are, however, a number of third-party extensions you can add to the site to improve this.

- **Extensions vary widely in quality.** While a lot of extensions are available for the system, they are not of equal quality. Do your homework and check extensions carefully before committing to them.

- **A number of extensions are commercial.** The Joomla! core is free of charge, but a number of extensions for the system are commercial, often charging recurring "subscription" fees.

TIP

If you'd like to try it out before you download it, you can find a fully functional version of Joomla! at http://demo. joomla.org. The demo installation lets you view the front end as well as log into the back-end admin system and try out the system. Note, however, that you do have to register to use the demo.

Complying with the Joomla! open source license

The Joomla! system is released under the GNU General Public License, commonly known as the GNU GPL. Joomla! is governed by Version 2.0 of the license. The GNU General Public License grants all users of software released under the license four freedoms:

The freedom to run the program for any purpose.

The freedom to study how the program works and adapt it to your needs.

The freedom to redistribute copies so you can help your neighbor.

The freedom to improve the program and release your improvements to the public, so that the whole community benefits.

As a site owner, this means that the software is free of licensing fees and that you are able to use it for any purpose or any type of site. The only significant restriction is on your ability to resell the system; though it is permissible to sell products that include the code, you must release those products under licensing terms that are consistent with the GNU GPL v.2. This provision essentially takes away the motivation to turn the code into a commercial product because the terms of the license mean that the person who buys the code can distribute it to the public without paying you further for that privilege.

The user's freedom extends to the right to modify the code. You are not only free to use the system however you see fit, but you are also free to customize the code to suit your needs. Although your customizations are modifications of the GPL code, the license does not force you to disclose that modified code to others, unless you decide to release and redistribute the code. In other words, you cannot be forced to release code you have developed but do not want to release to the public.

The majority of the extensions available for the Joomla! system are also released under the GNU GPL. While some of the extensions are commercial, and a few are even encrypted, a growing impetus exists within the Joomla! community to make sure that extensions are fully GPL-compliant and that users can access and modify the code for the extensions.

NOTE

View the full text of the GNU GPL version 2 at www.gnu.org/licenses/old-licenses/gpl-2.0.html .

Understanding the Joomla! Architecture

At birth, Joomla! was focused solely on the development of a world-class content management system and, accordingly, the Joomla! CMS was the focus of the project. Behind the scenes, however, there was a lot more going on than was visible to most users; there was another layer that provided a lot of the power and functionality for the CMS product. In 2011, that second layer took on a life of its own with the release of the Joomla! Platform, a web applications development platform based on the routines and protocols that powered the Joomla! CMS. Today two products bear the Joomla! name: the well-known Joomla! CMS and the lesser-known Joomla! Platform. While the two products are closely related, they serve different purposes and are intended for different audiences.

NOTE

The Joomla! Platform is also sometimes referred to as JPlatform.

Working with the Joomla! CMS

The Joomla! CMS product is the focus of this book, and by far the more commonly deployed of the two Joomla! products. The CMS is what powers the many websites deployed on Joomla! worldwide. The content management functionalities most in demand by website owners and web developers are supplied by the CMS.

In broadest terms, the Joomla! CMS works like this: When a site visitor requests a page by clicking a link, Joomla! assembles that page by retrieving the contents from the database; it then uses the Joomla! template files for guidance in how to present that information on the page. The merged information (the content plus the presentation layer) is then sent to the user's browser where it is rendered for the visitor to see.

Unlike other systems that store rendered pages, almost all information in Joomla! is kept in the database and displayed on the visitor's screen on demand. The text, images, usernames, and passwords are all kept in the database. Use of caching can change this to a limited extent, but generally speaking, everything is dynamically generated. When you are editing content in Joomla!, you are editing information in the database. The Joomla! template files provide the formatting and layout that the site visitors see on their screens. A template is actually a collection of files typically containing a mix of CSS, PHP, HTML, XML, and image files. If you want to change the underlying layout of the site's page, then you need to edit the template files.

NOTE

With the arrival of Joomla! 3, the presentation layer relies heavily on the use of Twitter Bootstrap, an interface development framework that provides developers with a number of tools that make creating responsive, consistent interfaces easier. You can learn more about Bootstrap by visiting http://twitter.github.com/bootstrap/.

Working with the Joomla! Platform

In contrast to the Joomla! CMS, which is aimed at a broad audience of website owners, the Joomla! Platform is aimed squarely at developers. The Platform is an enabling tool, allowing developers to go to market with their own web applications more quickly than they would if they did not have the suite of helpful tools and protocols included in the Platform.

Using the Platform, developers can do almost anything, even build their own CMS! The Platform is, essentially, the contents of the /libraries directory in your Joomla! distribution. That directory contains a large number of classes and methods that you can access via the command line; there is no GUI interface for the Platform. Though the Platform is a part of the CMS product, it is a completely independent set of libraries that do not require the Joomla! CMS application.

> **NOTE**
> You can find the home of the Joomla! Platform at https://github.com/joomla/joomla-platform.

Appreciating the underlying technologies

An open source product like Joomla! is only possible due to the existence of a number of supporting technologies. The system relies on a mix of programming languages, databases, and web servers. The technologies at the heart of Joomla! are also open source — a classic example of a complex system enabled by the existence of a large number of smaller parts. Joomla! not only includes some supporting technologies in the actual files that are part of the installation, but also relies on the presence of compatible technologies in the hosting environment.

The key components at work here include

- **Programming languages.** Joomla! is primarily written in PHP, though you will find a number of file types inside the system, including CSS, HTML, JavaScript, Ajax, JSON, and XML.
- **Databases.** The database is key in the Joomla! architecture. The system relies on the database for a wide range of tasks, including the storage of all content and user data. Joomla! was originally built to use the MySQL database but now supports both Microsoft SQL and T4 PostgreSQL.
- **Web servers.** Web servers are responsible for processing the requests received from the users and then routing the proper information to those users. Joomla! is tailored for use with the Apache web server, but can also use nginx or Microsoft IIS.

> **NOTE**
> The programming languages, the database, and the web server are not actually part of Joomla!; rather, they reside in the hosting environment. Nonetheless, they are necessary and must be compatible with Joomla! for things to work properly.

For a full list of technical requirements for running Joomla!, see Chapter 2.

1

Making sense of the Joomla! release schedules

Joomla! follows a release schedule that some users find confusing. The schedule isn't that hard to grasp, however, if you understand a couple of key distinctions. The first thing to remember is that the Joomla! CMS and the Joomla! Platform are not on the same release schedule and that they do not share the same version numbering. Don't confuse the two.

- The Joomla! Platform releases every 3 months.
- The Joomla! CMS releases every 6 months.

> **NOTE**
>
> When I talk about releases, I am referring to scheduled releases; if there is a need to publish a patch (typically due to a security issue that needs to be urgently addressed), then an interim release occurs to address that issue.

The second thing you need to understand is specific to the CMS. The Joomla! CMS maintains two streams of releases: One stream is called the Long Term Support release (also known as the LTS release), and the second is the Standard Term Support release (also known as the STS release). Here are some key points to keep in mind:

- New Joomla! CMS releases will appear every 6 months.
- All LTS releases are numbered as x.5 (for example, Joomla! 2.5).
- LTS releases have a lifespan of approximately two years.
- STS releases have a lifespan of approximately one year.

The key concept to grasp here is that after the lifespan of any release passes, you cannot count on support via additional patches and updates. To put this into a meaningful framework for making decisions: If you want to adopt the version with the lowest risk and the longest lifespan, stick to LTS releases. If, on the other hand, you want the most cutting edge release, then grab the most current release, which is often an STS release.

Engaging with the Joomla! Community

Joomla! is an example of a community-driven open source project. Unlike corporate-sponsored projects, Joomla! is the work of a loosely affiliated group of individuals working together as a community. It is, in other words, a volunteer effort. The community supports not only the software, but also the users. As a future user of Joomla!, you should be aware of the resources that exist within the community and how you can tap into the wealth of knowledge that exists there. In this section, I look at the structure of the Joomla! community, the key resources available, and how you can get involved with the Joomla! project by participating in this rich and varied community.

Official Joomla! Sites

The Joomla! team maintains a number of official sites. Some sites are informational, others provide a way to distribute the code, and others help promote and market Joomla!

Name	URL
Joomla! (main site)	www.joomla.org/
JoomlaCode	www.joomlacode.org/
The Joomla! Developer Network	http://developer.joomla.org/
The Joomla! Extensions Directory	http://extensions.joomla.org/
Joomla! Official Documentation	http://docs.joomla.org/
The Joomla! Forum	http://forum.joomla.org/

Understanding the structure of the community

Support for Joomla! and the administration of the project is provided by a not-for-profit organization named Open Source Matters. The foundation holds the intellectual property rights to the brand name and related assets and provides legal shelter for the project. The foundation accepts donations of cash and services. The donations go to cover the basic overhead and operating costs, like the servers, the hosting infrastructure, and promotional expenses. People are not directly paid to work on Joomla!

Open Source systems like Joomla! are offered free of charge for users. Often, people ask how this is possible. How is it that they can afford to give something valuable away for free? That is a complex question and in the case of a community-driven Open Source project, the answer is not always obvious. Community members work for free largely out of a desire for recognition, status, and access to expertise. Some are even more idealistic and participate for the pleasure of being part of something bigger than themselves and to feel like they have given something back to a group that has helped them in some fashion.

The Joomla! Team is divided into two working groups: Production and Community. Each group has a set of leaders who together make up the Joomla! leadership team. These groups help direct development and provide structure for the community efforts.

Becoming a part of the community

Volunteers are the lifeblood of Joomla! If you are inclined to get involved with the project, do so. The easiest way to start is by registering on the Joomla! Forum site and then contributing by helping others in the forums. Many users come to the forums with very basic questions; others have more complex technical issues. The forums always need people who are willing to take the time to answer these questions and help others work their way through problems. The success of the forums hinges on shared knowledge; therefore, it's essential for those with experience to assist others.

After you have participated in the forums for a while, you will be more familiar with the team members and how things work in general. If you want to do more, you can then approach a team member or the leader of a working group and ask to become involved on a more official level.

Open source projects that are the size and scope of Joomla! need all sorts of people. Don't worry about whether you have sufficient technical skills or the right type of knowledge. The most important requirements are a willingness to donate your time and a sincere desire to help others. Opportunities exist for everyone who is interested in helping.

Summary

In this introductory chapter, you looked at the basics of the Joomla! CMS and at open source in general. The chapter covered

- Appreciating the advantages of using open source and what open source means to you as a user of open source software.
- Assessing the pros and cons of using Joomla! and how they impact your decision to choose the system.
- Understanding how Joomla! works, from the system architecture to the role of underlying technologies.
- Learning how the Joomla! community is organized and how you can get involved with the project.

In the next chapter, I explain how to obtain the Joomla! installation files and how to set up Joomla! on your server.

Obtaining and Installing Joomla!

IN THIS CHAPTER

Obtaining the files necessary to install the Joomla! CMS

Using the resources of JoomlaCode.org

Installing Joomla! on your local computer or in-house server

Installing Joomla! on a web host, either manually or through the use of an automated installer

Getting started with Joomla! couldn't be easier. Because Joomla! is open source software, it is freely available for download on the web, and in some cases you may find that it is already available as part of your web-hosting package. In either case, once you have access to the installer package, you will go through a simple installation process to get Joomla! up and running on your server.

The Joomla! installer employs a wizard-style interface that allows you to simply click through a short series of steps. While you do not need any technical knowledge, you are prompted to provide some basic information to complete the process. The installer also includes an option to populate your new site with sample contents that can help you learn your way around Joomla!. Once the installer does its magic, you can immediately start working on the contents and appearance of your website.

This chapter looks at the basics of obtaining the Joomla! files and installing them on your server. Follow the steps in this chapter, and by the end, you will have a complete Joomla! installation up and ready to go.

Getting the Installation Files

Before you can begin, you need to obtain the Joomla! installer files. The official Joomla! installation files come bundled in a single, compressed archive file. Although you can download the Joomla! installation package from a variety of sources, I strongly recommend that you obtain the Joomla! installer from the official Joomla! site, for the following reasons:

- By going to the official site, you are assured of downloading the most recent version.
- The official archives are trustworthy and highly unlikely to contain dangerous or malicious code.
- You can be assured that the archive contains a complete set of the official components.

To obtain the files, go to www.joomla.org and look for the download button; it always appears prominently on the home page, as shown in Figure 2.1. Clicking the button takes you to a page where you can select the version of the installer that best suits your needs. Note that while the download link is on the main Joomla! site, the actual archive files for the installation are kept at `JoomlaCode.org`, so don't be alarmed if you are re-directed to that site; it is the official repository of the project's code.

TIP

Some web hosts provide their clients with access to installers via the web-hosting control panel. The automated installers offer a number of packages to choose from. The most popular automated installers are Fantastico, Installatron, and Softaculous; look for those names as part of your hosting package and if they exist, then you already have access to the Joomla! installer via those systems.

FIGURE 2.1

The home page of `Joomla.org`, prominently displaying the download link

Exploring the JoomlaCode site

JoomlaCode is one of the most important of the official Joomla! sites. You can visit the site by pointing your browser to www.joomlacode.org. The site is a *code forge* — that is, a repository of code for developers and other users to download.

JoomlaCode includes a significant number of resources. First and foremost, it serves as the central storehouse for the official Joomla! files. On the site, you find not only the most recent full release of Joomla!, but also patches and upgrades that allow users running older versions of Joomla! to upgrade to the most recent version. In addition to offering the official Joomla! project files, the site also functions as a distribution point for non-English language editions of Joomla! and some of the many extensions to the Joomla! core. You should take some time to browse and explore the site. As you work more with Joomla!, you are very likely to use the JoomlaCode site as a resource to identify and download additional extensions for your site.

At first glance, you may find the site difficult to navigate. JoomlaCode uses an organizational structure that is common to code forges but is not terribly intuitive. If you are not familiar with forge-type sites, you may find it confusing at first. Clicking the Home link in the top-right corner, for example, does not return you to the Home page of JoomlaCode, but instead takes you to a completely different site, Joomla.org. Moreover, browsing by Project can be rather time-consuming unless you already know the name of the extension you seek. The search functionality is also somewhat limited.

Your best bet for browsing the JoomlaCode site is to use the section labeled Browse Project Topics, which is located in the right column about halfway down the page. Click the name of the category you are interested in, and a page appears, displaying a tree-type file directory with a list of files at the bottom, as shown in Figure 2.2.

Click the link labeled Show, next to a directory, to display the contents of the directory. Click the link labeled Add Filter to restrict the projects that appear on the page to only those that fall within the category. For example, clicking the Gallery & Multimedia option takes you to a page showing a directory tree that has three options: Gallery, Podcasting, and Streaming Media. Below the tree directory is a list of all the projects in the Gallery & Multimedia category. If you then click the Add Filter link next to the option labeled Gallery, the page reloads, showing you only those projects that are included in the Gallery subcategory. Now, if you click the Add Filter link next to the Streaming Media option, the page reloads, showing you only those projects that are included in both the Gallery and the Streaming Media subcategories.

> **TIP**
>
> The Joomla! Extensions Directory website, http://extensions.joomla.org, provides a much more accessible directory of Joomla! extensions. The site also includes comments, ratings, and both commercial and noncommercial extensions. For most users, the Joomla! Extensions Directory site is a much friendlier option for browsing and searching.

FIGURE 2.2

Browsing by project topic shows you a list of projects as well as a list of subcategories.

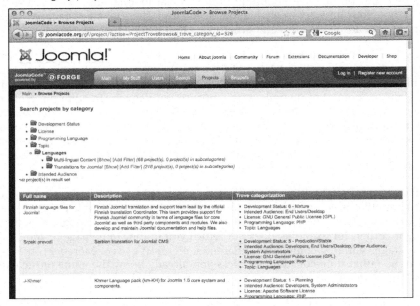

Determining which files you need

Before you start downloading files, you need to make sure that you are getting exactly what you need. The JoomlaCode site contains several versions of the Joomla! files, and you have to make sure you grab the version that is suitable for your needs. If you get the wrong files, you are likely to waste time, effort, and energy.

Identifying exactly which set of core files you need in order to install Joomla! involves first answering two questions:

> Is this a fresh installation of Joomla! or an upgrade to an existing Joomla! installation?
>
> Which archive file type is appropriate for your server?

If this is a fresh installation, you simply need to obtain the current full release from the JoomlaCode site. If this is an upgrade of an existing Joomla! site, you need to identify the Joomla! version you are running now and then look closely through the list of upgrades on the JoomlaCode site to find the installation package that is intended to upgrade to the current version. You can find a complete list of releases, both full versions and upgrades, at http://joomlacode.org/gf/project/joomla/frs/?action=index.

Patching and upgrading your site is discussed in more detail in Appendix E.

The second question, which archive file type is appropriate for your server, is simply intended to help you find an appropriate archive file format that is compatible with your server. The official Joomla! releases come in a variety of archive formats, including .zip, .tar.gz, and .tar.bz2, as you can see in Figure 2.3. Download the version of your choice; they all contain the same files. The various formats are simply provided as a convenience. The correct choice for you depends on your extraction software.

FIGURE 2.3

The JoomlaCode site is the home to all the official files.

Meeting the Technical Requirements

The technical requirements for Joomla! are quite basic. The system is very tolerant of variations in server settings and, generally speaking, runs on the vast majority of commercial web-hosting services that employ Linux, Unix, or even Windows; this makes installing Joomla! on most commercial web hosts a straightforward matter.

Many hosts even provide a way for one-click installation of Joomla! on your hosting account. This can be an easy way for beginners to install Joomla! and create the database without actually having to upload files.

Once the system is in place, visitors can access the front end to your Joomla! site by using virtually any computer and any browser. For site administrators, the back end supports the most recent versions of all the common browsers.

Understanding the server requirements

The preferred server setup for Joomla! includes the Apache web server with the MySQL database, though other configurations are possible. Table 2.1 shows the minimum and preferred technical system requirements for running Joomla! 3.x on your web server.

> **NOTE**
> You can find a current list of server requirements, as well as requirements for previous versions of Joomla!, at www.joomla.org/technical-requirements.html.

TABLE 2.1 **Server Configuration Options for Joomla! 3.x**

Software	Minimum Version	Recommended Version
PHP (Magic Quotes GPC off)	5.3.1 (or higher)	5.3.1 (or higher)
Supported Databases	Minimum Version	Recommended Version
MySQL Database (InnoDB support is required)	5.1 (or higher)	5.1 (or higher)
Microsoft SQL	10.50.1600.1 (or higher)	10.50.1600.1 (or higher)
PostgreSQL	8.3.18 (or higher)	8.3.18 (or higher)
Supported Web Servers	Minimum Version	Recommended Version
Apache web server (with mod_mysql, mod_xml, and mod_zlib)	2.x (or higher)	2.x (or higher)
nginx	1.0 (or higher)	1.1 (or higher)
Microsoft IIS	7 (or higher)	7 (or higher)

> **TIP**
> Although the requirements outline the general configuration, if you want to use search engine–friendly URLs, you need to install the mod_rewrite extension on the Apache web server, or if using Microsoft IIS, the Microsoft URL Rewrite Module. These extensions are typically installed on most web hosts, but you should always double check to be sure they are in place.

TIP

If you are a Microsoft IIS user, you should know about a dedicated Joomla! discussion forum. Visit the Joomla! IIS Forum at http://forum.joomla.org/viewforum.php?f=717.

Providing access for site visitors and administrators

Your site visitors and administrators will interact with Joomla! through their browsers. Both the front end and the back end of the site are intended to be accessed with a web browser. A wide variety of platforms and browsers, including mobile devices, can use the front end of Joomla!. Indeed, the display of the front end is impacted more by the way the site template is coded than by anything inherent in the actual system. Support for JavaScript is recommended, but not required for the default site.

NOTE

The installation of certain third-party extensions may bring with them additional requirements. You should always check whether the extensions that you install are compatible with the systems you require for your website visitors.

To administer a Joomla! site, you literally need nothing more than a connection to the Internet and a web browser. The back-end admin system is compatible with the recent versions of the most common browsers, including Internet Explorer, Firefox, Safari, and Chrome.

Installing Joomla!

Once you have obtained the installation files, your attention turns to getting the files on the server and running the installer. After you have the Joomla! system installed on your server you will be able to begin to customize your site and add the contents. Installation is a necessary part of your site setup and is relatively fast and easy to accomplish.

You can install Joomla! on either a local server or a remote web host. Installing Joomla! locally allows you to create a testing or development site that can greatly ease your development efforts. Installing Joomla! on a remote web host allows you to create a publicly accessible site that others can see and use. In either event, the process is roughly the same.

TIP

One forum is dedicated to helping people with issues installing Joomla! 3; you can view it by visiting http://forum.joomla.org/viewforum.php?f=707.

Creating a local development site

Installing Joomla! on your local computer or in-house server is typically done for testing and development purposes. A local installation makes it faster and easier to create a new site. It is a great way to develop a site prior to deploying it on a live public server as you can see the impact of your changes immediately without having to move files back and forth from a remote web server. Moreover, if you have only a slow or unreliable Internet connection, a local development installation can save huge amounts of time and frustration.

You can create a local installation on any system, Windows, Mac, or Linux. However, you need to make sure that your machine can function as a server and that it meets the technical requirements outlined in the preceding section. If you want to obtain and install each of the various server components independently, you can, but I recommend that you acquire one of several packages that allow you to install all the required software in one click.

> For Windows users, the XAMPP and WampServer packages provide an easy way to install Apache, MySQL, PHP, and related tools.
>
> Mac users can use either XAMPP or MAMP.
>
> Linux users can install XAMPP (though this is probably unnecessary as your Linux installation is likely to have all the necessary components already in place; you simply need to activate them).

NOTE

You can download XAMPP at www.apachefriends.org, WampServer at www.wampserver.com, and MAMP at www.mamp.info.

 To install MAMP, see Appendix D.

After you have installed the underlying package containing all the necessary server components, you are ready to set up Joomla! on your local machine. Installing Joomla! on any of the -AMP packages involves the following steps:

1. **Download the Joomla! core files.**
2. **Open the** `htdocs` **directory inside the** `-AMP` **folder on your machine.**
3. **Create a new directory for your Joomla! site.** Keep the name simple because you use it for the address in your browser; for example, "joomla3."
4. **Unzip the Joomla! files and place them inside the new directory.**
5. **Start the servers for your -AMP package; follow the directions that came with the application.** When the servers start, your browser opens and displays the home page of the -AMP package. What you see should be similar to Figure 2.4.
6. **Point your browser to the directory where you placed your Joomla! files.** The Joomla! installation wizard appears.

24

From this point, you can follow the steps outlined in the "Running the Joomla! installer" section.

FIGURE 2.4

The start page of MAMP, typical of the -AMP packages

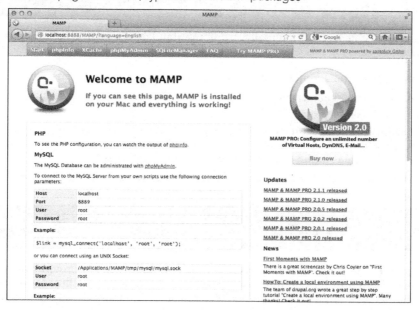

Installing on a web-hosting service

Joomla! installation on a remote server typically takes one of two approaches: either automatic installation via a web-hosting company's installer, or manual installation through your own efforts. Automated installers, such as Fantastico, Softaculous, and Installatron, allow you to set up Joomla! or other popular systems directly from your web-hosting account's control panel. If you want to use an automated installer, follow the directions of your web host. Should you need assistance, contact your web host for support.

> **NOTE**
>
> Occasionally, the use of an automated installer can result in permissions problems in the final site. For most users, these issues are not really a problem, but if you intend to extensively customize your site, you can avoid possible problems by installing the site files manually, rather than relying on an automated installer.

If you want to install Joomla! manually, using the standard Joomla! installation package, follow these steps:

1. **Download the Joomla! core files.** I discuss this earlier in the chapter.

2. **Access your web server.** You typically use FTP or your web-hosting account's file manager.

3. **Create a new directory for your Joomla! site.** Keep the name simple because you use it for the address in your browser (for example, "joomla"). If you want to install Joomla! in the root directory, you can skip this step.

4. **Move the archive containing the Joomla! files to the server.** Place the files in the directory where you want the site to appear.

> **NOTE**
>
> Appendix B shows a listing of the Joomla! files and directories as they should appear on your server.

5. **Extract the Joomla! file archive.** If your web host does not provide the option to extract archive files on the server, you need to extract the archive locally and then move the files up to the server manually. Note that this can take significantly longer because the number and size of the files are substantial!

6. **Point your browser to the directory where you placed your Joomla! files.** The Joomla! installation wizard appears.

From this point, you can follow the steps outlined in the section, "Running the Joomla! installer."

> **NOTE**
>
> The name of the root directory varies from web host to web host. If you're not sure which directory on your web server is the root directory, contact your web-hosting support team.

Running the Joomla! installer

Joomla! includes a step-by-step installer with an interface that is similar to that found in other software installation packages. The installer does most of the work for you. In most cases, you only need to supply information when prompted to do so, and then click the "next" button.

Before you can run the installer, you must follow the steps outlined in the previous two sections, depending on whether you are installing Joomla! locally or on a web host, and then you must point your browser to the address of the Joomla! files on your server. After you load the page in the browser, the installation wizard starts automatically; if your server meets the installation requirements, Step 1 of the installer, shown in Figure 2.5, appears on your screen.

If your server is not properly configured to run Joomla!, you do not see Step 1 of the installer, but rather you are shown a system status page that indicates the requirements that must be met for Joomla! to install. If your server fails to support any of the requirements, a bright-red No appears next to the item. You must fix these issues before you can install Joomla!.

Once you've made the necessary adjustments, either reload the page or click the Check Again button. Repeat as necessary. After all of the required items show a green Yes, you are allowed to proceed.

Step 1 is the Main Configuration screen, as shown in Figure 2.5. Follow these steps to complete the information needed on this screen:

1. **To install Joomla! in a language other than American English, choose your preferred option from the Select Language combo box at the top of the page.** To use the default language, no change is necessary.

2. **In the field marked Site Name, enter the name you want to use for your Joomla! site.**

3. **In the field marked Description, enter a brief description for your Joomla! site.**

> **NOTE**
> The text you enter in the Description field becomes your site's default description metadata.

4. **In the field marked Admin Email, enter a valid e-mail address for the site's Super Administrator.**

5. **(Optional) In the Admin username field, change the default username.**

6. **In the field marked Admin Password, enter a password.**

7. **Confirm the admin password by entering it again in the box provided.**

8. **To install your site in Offline mode, which is invisible to others, change the Site Offline control from No to Yes.** If you don't care if it is immediately visible, there is no need to change this option.

9. **Click the Next button in the upper-right corner of the page to move on.**

> **TIP**
> Much of the information you enter on the Main Configuration screen during installation can be changed after installation via the Joomla! Global Configuration Manager.

FIGURE 2.5

Step 1 of the installation wizard prompts you for basic global configuration information.

Step 2 of the installation wizard is the Database Configuration screen, shown in Figure 2.6. Provide the following information in order to complete this step:

1. **Select the type of database your server is using from the combo box.**

> **TIP**
> If you are trying to install Joomla! on Microsoft SQL and you do not see the option in the combo box, you need to make sure you have enabled Microsoft SQL support in your PHP installation; this may require you to download and install the Microsoft drivers for PHP for SQL Server. You can obtain the drivers, and learn more at www.microsoft.com/en-us/download/details.aspx?id=20098.

2. **In the field marked Host Name, enter the host name for your database.** This is often simply "localhost."

3. In the field marked Username, enter the username for the database.

4. In the field marked Password, enter the password associated with the user-name you entered in Step 3.

5. In the field marked Database Name, enter the name you gave to the database when you created it.

6. **You can probably leave the field marked Table Prefix unchanged.** This field already contains a default value. You do not need to change it, as the value is randomly generated for security purposes.

7. **If you are replacing an existing Joomla! installation, decide whether to replace or back up those tables by selecting an option from the control marked Old Database Process.** If you are not replacing an old Joomla! installation, this control has no effect.

8. **Once you have completed all the information required, click the Next button in the upper-right corner.**

2

NOTE

In previous versions of Joomla!, it was necessary to manually create the database, prior to running the installer; this is no longer the case. The Joomla! 3 installer can create the database for you during the installation process, giving it the name you specify in the steps above. You must, however, make sure that you have entered the proper database user-name and password and that the user account exists and has sufficient privileges to create a new database.

FIGURE 2.6

Step 2 of the installation wizard involves providing the information necessary for Joomla! to connect to your database.

Step 3 of the installation wizard is the last screen, labeled Finalisation, as shown in Figure 2.7. This screen serves two purposes: It allows you to select whether to install the Joomla! sample data and provides you with a chance to check the accuracy of the information you entered on the previous screens. Simply review the data on this page and decide whether you want to use the sample data, and if so, which set you want to use. Once you have verified the data and chosen the sample data, click the Install button; the software attempts to complete the installation.

FIGURE 2.7

Step 3 of the installation wizard provides a chance to review the information you have entered, as well as select whether you want to install the sample data.

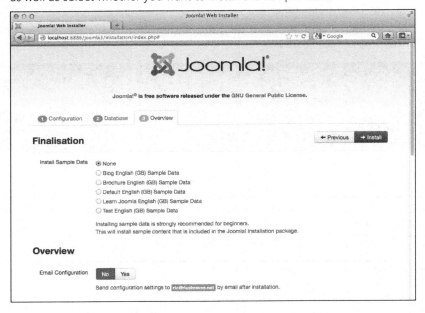

TIP

If this is your first time working with Joomla!, I highly recommended that you install the sample data. The Joomla! sample data includes a variety of useful information as well as examples of common site-building techniques. Additionally, when you elect to install the sample data, the system also creates a number of menus and modules that help speed your initial development of the site. Many experienced site developers actually choose to install the sample data because it saves them time creating the most common menus and modules; it's faster to delete what you don't need than to create all the basic parts from scratch. There are several different versions of the sample data to choose from; the most helpful is the one marked "Learn Joomla." The other versions are less detailed and more focused on specific applications, as their names imply. Note that while you can always delete the sample data, you cannot easily install it later, so if you think you might want it, install it now! See Appendix A for information on each of the different sample data sets.

Once you click the Install button, the Joomla! installer runs and you see a status screen, as shown in Figure 2.8.

FIGURE 2.8

The status screen appears as the installation wizard sets up your site — you're almost done!

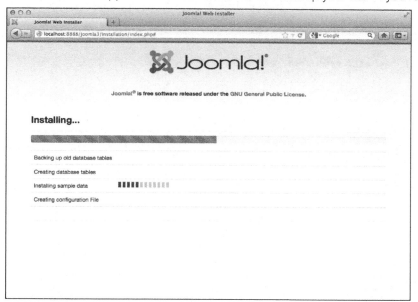

Once the installation wizard completes its work, you see the final Congratulations screen, shown in Figure 2.9. One important step is left before you can finalize things: removing the installation folder. The installation folder should not be left on the server, as it can pose a security threat to your site. To delete it, simply click the button labeled Remove Installation Folder. After you click the button, you should see a confirmation message; if not, then delete it manually.

You can click the Site button to see the front end of your new site, or you can click the Administrator button to go directly to the Admin login screen. Either way, you're ready to move on to configuring and populating your new Joomla! site.

FIGURE 2.9

The Congratulations screen. Remove the installation folder and you're ready to go!

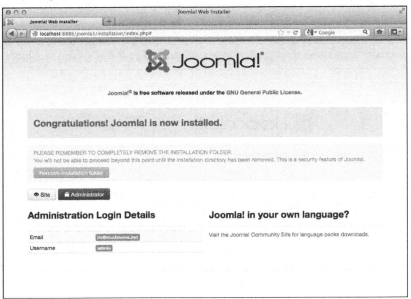

Summary

In this chapter, I covered the acquisition and installation of Joomla!. The information included the following:

- Obtaining the proper files to start installing Joomla!.
- Navigating the JoomlaCode website for file downloads and resources.
- Meeting Joomla! 3's installation requirements.
- Installing Joomla! either locally or on a web-hosting service.
- Using the system's built-in sample data.

In the next chapter, I take you on a guided tour of the front end and the back end of your new Joomla! installation.

Taking a First Look at Joomla!

IN THIS CHAPTER

Introducing the front end of the default Joomla! installation

Understanding how the default content is structured for administrators and site visitors

Introducing the back end of the default Joomla! installation

Reviewing the controls located in the Joomla! admin system

I f you worked through the previous chapter, you should have a complete Joomla! installation, ready to explore. This chapter goes through the front end and back end interfaces of Joomla! and explains what you see on screen. This chapter also provides a quick orientation and tour of the Joomla! system. At the end of this chapter, you should be familiar enough with the interfaces to start configuring and customizing Joomla! efficiently and with a clear understanding of the impacts of your decisions. The references and figures in this chapter all refer to the default site with the sample data set installed.

Exploring the Front End

The front end of your Joomla! installation is the interface that visitors see when they go to your site. The front end is the target for your output and the place where the public can access the site's content and functionality. By default, access to the front end of a Joomla! site is unrestricted; however, you can restrict the visibility of content and functionality to users who are registered and logged in to the system.

> **NOTE**
> Access controls and user privileges are covered in detail in Chapter 10.

Visitors to the site should be able to see and use the front end content and functionality with a wide range of browsers, both current and older editions. The site should also be usable by most common mobile devices.

> **NOTE**
> Accessibility to the front end is largely a function of the template for the site, so if you install a different template, it may have an impact on the usability of the front end.

In terms of the structural functionality of the front end, the key elements you see on screen and in Figure 3.1 are

- **Template.** This is the container for all the output on the page. The template defines the look and feel of each page.
- **Articles.** These are your content items.
- **Modules.** You place these elements in pre-defined positions in the template to provide output and functionality; for example, you use a module to add a menu at the top of the template, or to place a list of articles or a login form in the sidebar.
- **Components.** These provide major elements of discrete functionality, such as site search.

FIGURE 3.1

The front end of the default Joomla! 3 site with the sample data installed. Note the key output areas.

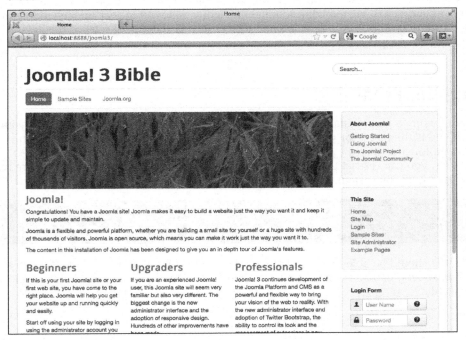

Developing Your Joomla! Vocabulary

Throughout this text I have, with a few exceptions, strived to use terminology consistent with that used by the Joomla! team on the documentation site and in the online help files. A quick orientation to Joomla! terms can help you develop a clear understanding of discussions both in this book and in Joomla! documentation resources.

- **Access Level.** Access levels provide a way for the site administrator to control access to articles or functionality. Joomla! provides three access levels: Public, Registered, and Special. Setting an item's access level to Public means that anyone can see it. Setting the access level to Registered or Special restricts visibility to the users assigned to specific user groups.

- **Archives.** You can remove articles in Joomla! from the general content areas of your site and place them in an archive. You can make archives publicly accessible or hide them from public view. This is most often used with blog-type sites because the archived articles can be used to organize old articles according to the month and year they were posted.

- **Article.** An article is a page of content created with the New Article functionality in Joomla!. Articles are collected inside the Article Manager interface, and you can create, edit, delete, publish, unpublish, and archive them. Certain classes of users can also create articles from the front end of the website.

- **Component.** Components are major units of functionality that provide output in the main content area of a page. Components are the most complex individual units in the system, sometimes constituting complete applications in themselves. Each component in the system has its own management interface inside the admin system. The default system includes a number of components, and you can add more to the system.

- **Core.** The term *core* in this context refers simply to the files included in the default Joomla! distribution.

- **Extensions.** *Extension* is a generic term that refers to any component, module, plug-in, or template that is added to the default system. You can install, delete, or manage extensions through the admin system's Extension Manager. Note that because Joomla! requires some extensions, these cannot be deleted. It's probably a good practice to only delete extensions that you have installed.

- **Menus.** Menus hold the navigation choices for your site. You create, edit, and delete them from within the Menu Manager; however, you manage menu display from the Module Manager via the Menu modules. Menus contain menu items.

- **Menu Items.** Menu items are the choices (the links) on a menu. You create, edit, and delete menus from within each of the system's Menu Item Managers. Each menu in the system has one Menu Item Manager.

- **Menu Item Types.** Each item on a menu is of a specific Menu Item Type. The creation of a new menu item requires the selection of a Menu Item Type for that item. Menu Item Types are very important in Joomla! because they dictate aspects of the appearance of the page that the menu item links to.

continued

3

continued

- **Module.** Modules typically provide output in the secondary areas of the page, that is, not inside the main content area. Modules are sometimes simply containers that hold text or pictures; at other times, they provide limited functionality, like a login box. Modules are often paired with components to provide an alternative means of displaying output from the component. Modules are collected inside the Module Manager where you can edit them and assign them to various pages and positions. The default system includes a number of different module types. You can add modules to the system through the Extensions Manager, or the site administration can create them from within the Module Manager.

- **Module Positions.** Module positions are places on the page where you can assign a module to appear. Module positions are created by the template designer who codes into the template the Module Position Holders that define each of the module positions.

- **Module Type.** Each module in the system is of a particular module type. When you create a new module manually, you must select a type for the module. The module type dictates aspects of the functionality of the module.

- **Newsfeeds.** In Joomla!, the term *newsfeed* refers to RSS or similar syndication formats. Joomla! can display newsfeed data inside the site by using either the Newsfeed component or the Feed Display module. The site can also provide syndication links for your site visitors, turning your content into a newsfeed for others to view. Do not confuse newsfeeds with the newsflash functionality; though the names are similar, they are not related in any way.

- **Newsflash.** The Newsflash module displays one or more short items of content on the screen. Do not confuse this functionality with the Newsfeed component; they are not related in any way.

- **Plug-in.** Plug-ins are helper applications that enable additional functionality in the site's components, articles, or modules. Plug-ins are collected in the Plug-in Manager. You can install new plug-ins through the Extension Manager, or they can be created by the site administrator through the Plug-in Manager.

- **Template.** Templates control the presentation layer of your Joomla! site. They define the interfaces of the site. When you change a template, you change the way the site looks for either visitors or the administrators. You can add templates to the system through the Extension Manager. The installed templates are collected inside the Template Manager where you can edit them.

- **Translations and Language Packs.** Translations are the language files of your Joomla! site. In this book, the collection of translated language files for a single language is called a *Language Pack*, as that name is more descriptive and less confusing than the generic term *Translations*. You can add new Language Packs through the Extension Manager, and installed Language Packs are collected inside the Language Manager.

- **Trash.** The trash functionality in Joomla! provides a temporary holding area for items that have been removed from use on the site and are pending permanent deletion. You can view the items in the trash by filtering the list of items to view only those that have been trashed.

Understanding the content organizational structure

Joomla! organizes content items into a configurable hierarchy of categories and articles. You can create and nest categories; that is, they support parent/child relationships. You can either assign articles to categories or segregate them from the hierarchy and group them into a generic collection called *uncategorized content*.

By way of example, let's look at the default Joomla! 3 site with the sample data installed to see how the categories have been used to create a logical set of containers for the site's content. Table 3.1 shows how the sample content is organized.

TABLE 3-1   The Category Hierarchy of the Sample Data in Joomla! 3

Category (top level)	Category (2nd tier)	Category (3rd tier)	Category (4th tier)	Category (5th tier)
Sample Data-Articles				
	Joomla!			
		Extensions		
			Components	
			Modules	
				Content Modules
				User Modules
				Display Modules
				Utility Modules
				Navigation Modules
			Templates	
				Beez3
				Protostar
			Languages	
			Plug-ins	
	Park Site			
		Park Blog		
		Photo Gallery		
			Animals	
			Scenery	
	The Fruit Shop Site			
		Growers		
		Recipes		
Uncategorized				

3

Within each of the categories above, you will find one or more articles. As the sample data installation demonstrates, it is possible to create multiple categories and nest them into complex hierarchies.

TIP

You can view the category structure of a site at any time by going to the Category Manager in the Joomla! Administration interface. To see which articles are assigned to which categories, visit the Article Manager.

A key point to note here: The category structure that the administrator implements does not translate automatically into the organizational structure that visitors see on the front end of the website. The content hierarchy is a reflection of how the articles and categories have been created on the back end of the site; it is, in other words, an organizational tool for the site's content creators. In contrast, the structure of the menus is primarily responsible for the way visitors experience the content on the site. Menus are discussed in more detail in the next section.

 For more information on working with categories and articles, see Chapter 5.

Understanding the menu structures

The default Joomla! installation, with the sample data in place, contains a large number of menu items, organized into six menus. The menus are visible in the Menu Manager, and you can find the menu items in the Menu Item Manager of each menu. Table 3.2 shows a list of all the menus in the default system with the sample data installed, including the number of menu items in each menu and the access level settings.

TABLE 3.2 Summary of the Default Menu Structure

Menu Name	Number of Items	Access Level
User Menu	3	Registered & Special
Top Menu	3	Public
About Menu	86	Public
Australian Parks	7	Public & Special
Main Menu	11	Public
Fruit Shop	8	Public & Customer Access Level

The access levels for the various menu items dictate their visibility to various classes of users. Public items are visible to all site visitors, while restricted items only show if a visitor is both registered and authenticated (logged into) the site. The site administrator is able to control the visibility of items at the time the menu items are created, or subsequently by editing the items.

 Working with users and permissions is covered in Chapter 10.

By creating multiple menus, you are able to assign various menus to different pages and to different positions on the page, as you can see in Figure 3.2. You control menu placement on the page through the assignment of the Menu modules to specific module positions, via the Module Manager, a topic discussed in the following section.

FIGURE 3.2

The front end of the default Joomla! 3 site with the various menus highlighted. Note that in this screenshot, the site visitor is authenticated as a site administrator, giving the user privileges to add and edit the content on the front end of the website.

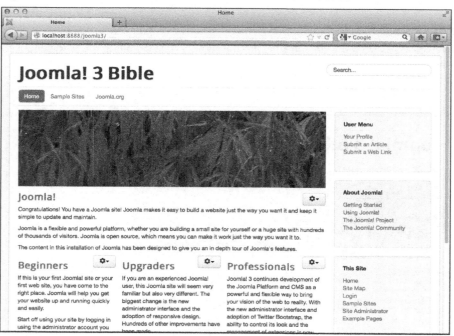

Working with menus and menu items is covered in Chapter 8.

Exposing the role of modules

The default Joomla! installation with the sample data installed includes a large number of modules. Some of the modules are published and visible, while others are not. Module visibility depends upon:

1. Whether the module is enabled, that is, whether it is published

2. Whether the module is assigned to the page you are viewing

3. Whether the viewer has sufficient access privileges to view the page and the module.

You set the module assignment, visibility, and access levels by editing the module from the Module Manager (see Figure 3.3). You place modules on the page by assigning them to module positions. The module positions are coded into the template by the template designer. Figure 3.3 shows the same page you saw in Figure 3.1, but with the names of the module positions overlaid.

FIGURE 3.3

A typical page from the default site with the sample data installed, showing various modules as they appear to front end site visitors.

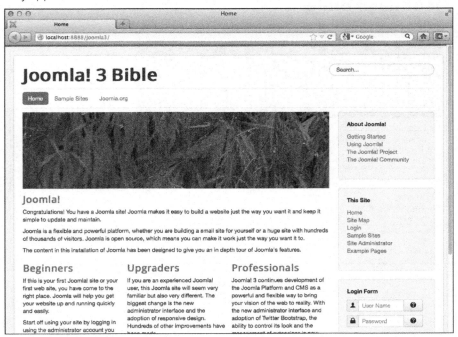

> **NOTE**
>
> Joomla! classifies modules into two categories: Site modules and Administrator modules. The Site modules are only visible on the front end of the site. The Administrator modules are only visible on the back end of the site.

To view and manipulate the modules, you need to access the Module Manager.

 Site modules are discussed in Chapter 17. Administrator modules are covered in Chapter 18.

Exploring the Back End

The back end of your Joomla! site is the administration (or admin) interface where the majority of your site management activities will occur. Using the admin interface, you can create, edit, and delete content and users, as well as modify the site configuration and appearance. The admin interface also allows you to view activity and usage statistics, and includes utilities that can help you optimize the performance of your site and keep it patched and secure.

Access to the admin system is controlled by a login form and is restricted to only those users who are assigned to user groups that have been granted the Access Administration Interface permission. In the default installation, only the Administrator and SuperUser groups have access to the admin interface. You can change this via the Users Configuration screen inside the Configuration Manager.

In a standard installation, the admin login page is located at /administrator, for example, www.yourdomain.com/administrator. To log in, a user simply points her browser to that address, and then enters her username and password into the fields. Figure 3.4 shows the login screen for the admin interface.

> **NOTE**
>
> Back end users should only access the system with more recent versions of Internet Explorer, Firefox, Chrome, or Safari to assure maximum accessibility to all the admin functions. Older or more obscure browsers may not function optimally.

Understanding the various admin interfaces

The layouts used by the admin interfaces can be grouped into three types, and each type is designed to provide slightly different functionality:

- **Control Panel.** This is a Big Picture page that serves as your landing page in the admin system. This interface is designed to give you a quick snapshot of activity and easy access to common tools.
- **Manager pages.** These are summary pages with lists of all the items in that particular category. When you click an item, you get the workspace for that item.

- **Workspace pages.** This is where most of the work occurs, such as editing, deleting, and modifying items; the interface provides all the tools you need to accomplish those tasks.

I cover each of these interfaces in the following sections.

FIGURE 3.4

The login screen for the admin interface

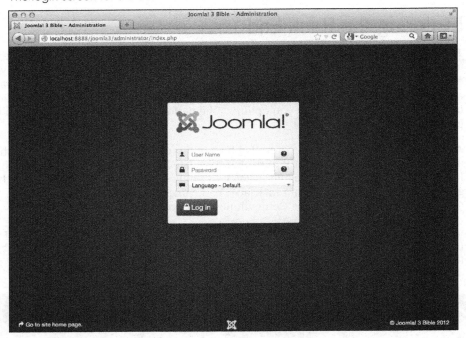

Getting an overview from the Joomla! Control Panel

The first page you see when you log in to the admin system is the Control Panel, as shown in Figure 3.5. You can also return to this page at any time by selecting the Control Panel option under the site menu.

The Control Panel is designed to provide administrators with quick access to the most frequently used tasks and tools, as well as a summary of useful information.

FIGURE 3.5

The Control Panel is the first page you see when you log in to the back end admin system.

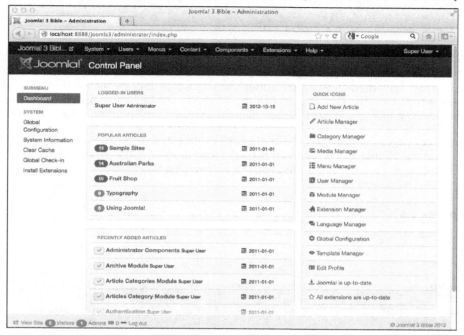

Here's a quick look at what you're seeing on this page:

- At the very top of the page, running across the length of the screen, is the main navigation menu. Clicking any of the menu choices displays additional functionality via drop-down lists.

- On the left side, underneath the Joomla! logo, is a submenu containing links to a set of key global functionalities.

- On the right side is a column labeled Quick Icons; this contains shortcuts to all the most common functionality.

- The center column shows information about activity on the site.

TIP

The output you see on the Control Panel page is created by various Administrator modules. You can customize the appearance of this page somewhat to suit your needs by reordering or disabling modules.

> **NOTE**
>
> The default admin template in Joomla! 3 uses responsive design to help keep the layout intact, regardless of browser or screen resolution. The admin interface also works very well on mobile devices.

Using the manager pages

All of the various manager-type interfaces in the admin system are similar. The manager pages are structured consistently, though the data that appears may vary. Click any of the manager links in the Quick Icons column on the Control Panel or use the links under the main admin navigation bar to see a manager similar to the one shown in Figure 3.6.

Manager pages are designed to handle large numbers of items and to display key information. In the chapters that follow, this book looks at each of the managers and explains the controls and the information that you see on each manager page.

FIGURE 3.6

A typical manager page interface — in this case, the Article Manager

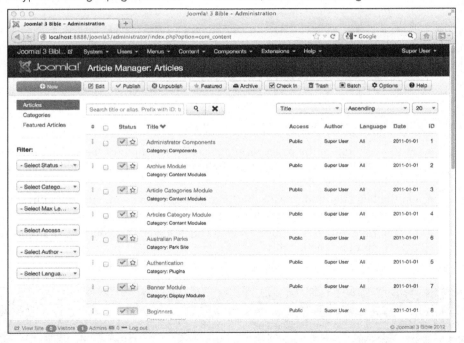

The manager interface shown in Figure 3.6 is typical and includes the following key features:

- At the top, below the blue title bar, is a set of controls running across the width of the page. These icons allow you to quickly add new items, edit items, control publication, and so on. In short, it is a list of the most common tasks.

- The left column provides two sets of controls: a set of shortcuts to related managers (in Figure 3.6 those are Articles, Categories, and Featured Articles), and below that a list of filters that you can apply to the list of items in the manager, thereby enabling you to find items more quickly.

- The primary focus of the manager interface is the list of items, which takes up the majority of the page. Each item is listed with basic information lined up in columns. Each column is sortable. Above this list of items is a search functionality and additional sort keys — all extremely useful tools for managing large or complex lists of items.

TIP

Joomla! 3 supports drag-and-drop functionality for reordering items on the manager pages. To enable drag and drop, you first have to click the reordering icon — the vertical double arrows on the far left of the column of items.

Creating with the workspace pages

Once you click through from the manager page to a specific item, or click an icon to perform a specific task, you are taken to a page with a workspace layout. All workspace pages are similar, with elements laid out consistently. The workspace layout is very task-oriented. The purpose of these pages is to give you an easy-to-use interface with all the necessary tools you need to complete the task successfully.

Typically a workspace page displays the key elements you see in Figure 3.7, including the following:

- Similar to the manager interface, there's a list of common task icons immediately below the blue title bar.

- Beneath the list of common task icons is a set of tabs that let you switch between the various options that are relevant to the task at hand.

- In the right column is a list of some of the most important functionality related to the item. In the case of articles, this column gives you the publishing controls, access controls, the ability to feature the article, and the language switches.

- The heart of this interface is the main content area, where you find all the necessary fields for accomplishing the primary task, which typically involves creating (or editing) the item. In the case of articles, this is where you enter your content and format it.

- The very bottom of the interface includes additional functionality related to the primary task. In the case of articles, this is where you will find additional fields for image and link management.

FIGURE 3.7

A typical workspace page interface — in this case, the Article Workspace Page

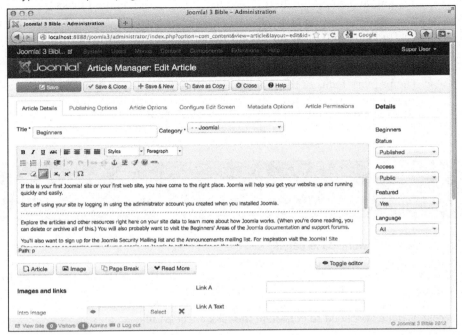

Workspaces vary according to the primary task they are designed to facilitate. The following chapters look at each of the various workspaces and explain the controls and the information that you see on each workspace page.

> **TIP**
>
> Although the Joomla! admin interface is designed to work well on a wide variety of screen display settings, bigger typically is better. The workspace pages really benefit from having your display set to a resolution greater than 1024 x 768.

Touring the main admin navigation menu

With Joomla! 3, the main navigation menu in the admin system was reworked, both to improve access to key functionality and to impose a more rational grouping on the functions. The result is quite an improvement over previous versions of the system, with items now grouped more intuitively.

In this section, I take a quick look at the contents and purpose of each menu. In subsequent chapters, you will look at the menus in more detail.

The System menu

The System menu contains links to functionality that control how the site, as whole, operates. As the options on this menu are focused on configuration settings and maintenance features, you are likely to access this menu less frequently than other menus concerned with content management.

To view the contents of the menu, click the System option on the main navigation. You will see the following options:

- **Control Panel.** Click to return to the Control Panel.
- **Global Configuration.** Click to open the Global Configuration Manager.
- **Global Check-in.** Click to force all articles that are open for editing to be closed. This is useful when someone has left an item open for editing and is blocking someone else from working with the item.
- **Clear Cache.** Click to flush the site cache. The system will rebuild the cache thereafter. This is useful when you have updated content and it is not showing up.
- **Purge Expired Cache.** Click to dump the expired cache files. This helps reclaim disk space used by the expired cache files.
- **System Information.** Click to view detailed information about the Joomla! version you have installed as well as key server configuration details.

The Users menu

As the name implies, the Users menu contains links to functionality related to the users of your website. The choices on this menu allow you to add new users, to manage existing users, and to send mass mail to your registered users.

Clicking the Users option on the main navigation menu displays the following options:

- **User Manager.** Click to open the User Manager. Move your mouse over this option to get a shortcut to add a new user.
- **Groups.** Click to open the Groups Manager. Move your mouse over this option to get a shortcut to add a new user group.
- **Access Levels.** Click to open the Access Levels Manager. Move your mouse over this option to get a shortcut to add a new access level.
- **User Notes.** The User Notes feature allows you to add notes about your users. This feature is intended to help the administrators manage large groups of users and the information entered will not be published on the front end of the website.
- **User Note Categories.** This option allows you to create categories for grouping user notes.
- **Mass Mail Users.** Click to launch the Mass Mail functionality, which you can use to send e-mail to all users of the system.

3

The Menus menu

The Menus option on the main navigation gives you quick access to all of the menus and menu items on your site. Using the options here, you can create new menus and add links to those menus for your front end site visitors.

Clicking the Menus option on the main navigation menu displays the following options:

- **Menu Manager.** Click to open the Menu Manager. Move your mouse over this option to get a shortcut to create a new menu.
- **Menus.** Following the Menu Manager option is a list of all the menus on your site. Clicking the name of any menu takes you to the Menu Item Manager for that menu. This varies from site to site.

The Content menu

The options under the Content menu lie at the heart of Joomla!'s content management functionality. You will use this menu frequently as you add new content items, modify existing articles, and manage the way they are grouped and displayed.

Clicking the Content option on the main navigation menu displays the following options:

- **Article Manager.** Click to open the Article Manager. Move your mouse over this option to get a shortcut to create a new article.
- **Category Manager.** Click to open the Category Manager. Move your mouse over this option to get a shortcut to create a new category.
- **Featured Articles.** Click to open the Featured Articles Manager.
- **Media Manager.** Click to open the Media Manager.

The Components menu

All of the site's components are grouped under the Components menu. The core components and third party components will appear here. Many times each component has submenus that allow you to jump to specific functionality included with that component.

Clicking the Components option on the main navigation menu displays the following options:

- **Banners.** Click to go to the Banner component. Submenu choices here let you jump directly to the Banner Manager, the Banner Client Manager, and the Banner Category Manager and Banner Tracks.
- **Contacts.** Click to access the Contacts component. Submenu choices here let you jump directly to the Contacts Manager and the Contacts Category Manager.
- **Joomla! Update.** Click to run the Joomla! update feature, which checks for new software updates for your system.

- **Messaging.** Click to open the Messaging component. Move your mouse over this option to access quick links to create a new private message or to open the reading screen.

- **Newsfeeds.** Click to access the Newsfeed component. Submenu choices here let you jump directly to the Newsfeed Manager and the Newsfeed Category Manager.

- **Redirect.** Click to open the Redirect component.

- **Search.** Click to access the Search Statistics.

- **Smart Search.** Click to access the Smart Search functionality, including the ability to index the site.

- **Weblinks.** Click to access the Weblinks component. Submenu choices here let you jump directly to the Links Manager and the Weblinks Category Manager.

The Extensions menu

The Extensions menu contains the links that allow you to add and manage extensions to your Joomla! site. Using the choices here, you can install, activate and publish new extensions. This menu also includes the primary links for accessing your themes, plug-ins, modules, and language packs.

Clicking the Extensions option on the main navigation menu displays the following options:

- **Extension Manager.** Click to open the Extension Manager, where you can add, manage, or remove extensions from your system.

- **Module Manager.** Click to open the Module Manager, where you can view all the modules in the system and control and configure them.

- **Plug-in Manager.** Click to open the Plug-in Manager. As the name implies, the Plug-in Manager provides the interface for dealing with all the plug-ins installed on your site.

- **Template Manager.** Click to open the Template Manager. Using the controls on this page, you can select the site's primary template and assign secondary templates to specific pages.

- **Language Manager.** Click to open the Language Manager, where you can add new languages to your site and create custom overrides of specific language strings.

The Help menu

The Help menu provides a set of links to various resources designed to help you make the most of your Joomla! site. The choices all link to official Joomla! sites, from forums to directories of service providers.

3

Clicking the Help option on the main navigation menu displays the following options:

- **Joomla Help.** Click to open an index of the help topics available from the Joomla! help system.
- **Official Support Forum.** Click to go to the Joomla! forums website.
- **Documentation Wiki.** Click to visit the Joomla! documentation wiki website.
- **Joomla Extensions.** Click to visit the Joomla! Extensions Directory website.
- **Joomla Translations.** Click to go to the languages page on the Joomla! Community Portal website.
- **Joomla Resources.** Click to go to the Joomla! Resources directory, a listing of companies and individuals around the world that provide Joomla! support, development, and extensions.
- **Community Portal.** Click to go to the home page of the Joomla! Community Portal website.
- **Security Center.** Click to visit the security center on the Joomla! Developer Network website.
- **Developer Resources.** Click to go to the Joomla! Developer Network website.
- **Joomla Shop.** Click to go to the Joomla! Shop site, where you can load up on Joomla! swag.

Summary

In this chapter, I have taken a quick tour of both the front end and the back end of the default Joomla! installation. I looked at each of the following areas, which should give you a good orientation to how the default site is laid out and where to find key controls and features:

- Understanding how the default content is organized using the categories functionality.
- Understanding how the menus and menu items are used to structure content for site visitors.
- Gaining access to the admin system.
- Reviewing the organization of the admin interfaces.
- Understanding the choices available on the main admin navigation bar.

In the next chapter, I dive into the process of configuring a Joomla! site.

Getting the Most from Site Configuration

IN THIS CHAPTER

Understanding the role of the Global Configuration Manager

Understanding and configuring site settings

Configuring the Joomla! system settings

Managing the server settings

The first task most users undertake after installing Joomla! is setting the site's global configuration options. To assist with this important process, Joomla! provides the Global Configuration Manager, which enables you to set many of the site's configuration options in one place. As the name implies, the Global Configuration Manager applies the options you set to your entire site. Although you adjust many of the settings contained in the Global Configuration Manager once and do not touch them again, you can override some of the settings on a case by case basis using the parameter options for individual items.

With Joomla! 3, the Global Configuration Manager has been reorganized to help consolidate the many configuration options of the various components and to provide easy access to user permissions management. Before Joomla! 3 you had to visit each of the individual component managers to configure the components, which tended to cause confusion and impair usability. Now, you can easily manage not only the configuration options that apply to the entire site, but also the options specific to particular components.

In this chapter, I explain the options that are available in the Global Configuration Manager and provide tips on how you can set the configuration options to achieve the best results.

> **NOTE**
> This chapter focuses on the site-wide options. I deal with component configuration in the chapters specific to each component, and the user permissions management in the chapters focused on the individual components.

Exploring the Global Configuration Manager

The Global Configuration Manager is one of the key Joomla! administration interfaces. Understanding how to configure the options presented in this interface is important to you as a site owner. Through the Global Configuration Manager, you can control fundamental elements of your site's behavior, security, performance, and even some aspects of its appearance. You need to be fluent with the controls located in the manager in order to get the most out of your Joomla! installation.

In this section, I take you on a tour of the Global Configuration Manager interface, with a special emphasis on how the navigation choices allow you to find your way through the many controls that are in this section. Indeed, of all the interfaces in the system, the Global Configuration Manager is perhaps the most complex. The good news is that it is organized logically and it is not an interface you will likely use very often after you complete the initial site configuration process.

Navigating the Global Configuration Manager

The Global Configuration Manager is located inside the Joomla! admin system. After you log in to the admin system, you access the Global Configuration Manager in either of two ways: Click the Global Configuration option on the System menu in the left column, or select Global Configuration under the System option on the main navigation menu. Figure 4.1 shows the Global Configuration landing page that loads in your browser.

Located at the top of the page, underneath the blue page title area, is a toolbar. You can access the controls on this toolbar for all the various screens in the Global Configuration Manager. As you scroll down the page, the toolbar remains visible at the top of the page, giving you easy access to key controls you need to complete your tasks. The toolbar contains the following functions:

- **Save.** Click to save any changes without exiting the Global Configuration Manager.
- **Save & Close.** Click to save any changes and then exit the Global Configuration Manager; you return to the Control Panel.
- **Cancel.** Click to exit the Global Configuration Manager without saving your changes.
- **Help.** Click to access the online help files related to the active screen.

Below the toolbar and above the workspace are five tabs used for accessing the five primary workspaces of the Global Configuration Manager.

- **Site.** Click this tab to visit the Site configuration workspace. This is the default active tab; whenever you click the Global Configuration link in the menus, you land on this tab. This tab contains some very basic functions, such as your site name and descriptive data. The controls on this tab are discussed in detail in the next section.

FIGURE 4.1

The Global Configuration landing page. Note that the active tab is the Site tab.

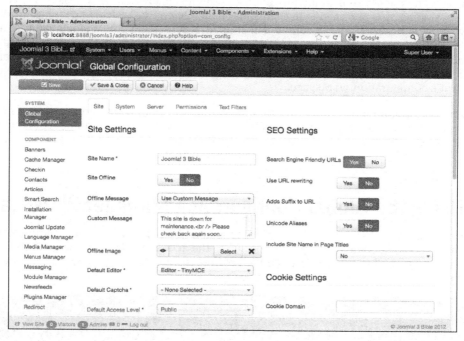

- **System.** Click this tab to visit the System configuration workspace. You manage your caching, debugging, and session options here. The controls in this tab are discussed later in this chapter.

- **Server.** Click this tab to visit the Server configuration workspace. As the name implies, the controls on this page relate to the way Joomla! interacts with your server. This tab is discussed in detail later in this chapter.

- **Permissions.** Click this tab to visit the Permissions configuration workspace. The controls on this tab allow you to set global permissions for your various user groups.

- **Text Filters.** Click this tab to visit the Text Filters configuration workspace. The controls on this page allow you to automatically filter out potentially harmful strings from the content contributed by your site members.

 Because the Permissions and Text Filters workspaces focus exclusively on user permissions, they are covered in Chapter 10.

Configuring components

Each component installed in your Joomla! system is likely to have at least some configuration settings that are specific to that component. One of the welcome changes in Joomla! 3 was the grouping of all the component configuration screens into a single point of access. In Figure 4.1, you can see an additional navigation menu in the left column. The links underneath the Component heading take you to the configuration options of the various components installed in the system; click any of these links to jump directly to the component's configuration workspace.

As the configuration options vary from component to component, and because some users may not use all the components on their site, I do not discuss the component configuration options in this chapter; instead, I deal with each component's configuration options in the later chapters that focus on each individual component.

Using the Global Configuration Manager Workspaces

Underneath the five tabs is the workspace area of the page, where you will find all the controls and configuration options specific to the active tab. Though the controls vary, you always use the toolbar discussed in the previous section to apply, save, or cancel your changes.

> **CAUTION**
>
> You must always save your changes before exiting a tab or your changes will be lost. Note that when you click the Save or the Save & Close buttons, a confirmation message, "Configuration successfully changed," should appear at the top of the page; this indicates that your choices have been applied to the system.

Each of the workspaces is different. In this chapter, I look at the Site, System, and Server workspaces in turn, reviewing the controls in each one. I start with the Site Settings workspace, in the next section.

Working with the Site tab

The Site tab is the default tab for the Global Configuration Manager. Clicking the Global Configuration link on any of the admin menus, or clicking the Site tab inside the Global Configuration Manager, takes you to the Site configuration workspace. The workspace contains basic site options, such as the site name, the site metadata, and URL structures used by the system. Figure 4.2 shows the Site configuration workspace.

The workspace is divided into four areas: Site Settings, Metadata Settings, SEO Settings, and Cookie Settings. I detail each area in the following sections.

Controlling the Site Settings

The Site Settings area of the Site tab workspace contains a mix of options that relate to the basic characteristics of your site. Two of the most important controls on this tab relate to your ability to take the site offline and to set the name of the site.

FIGURE 4.2

The Site configuration workspace inside the Global Configuration Manager

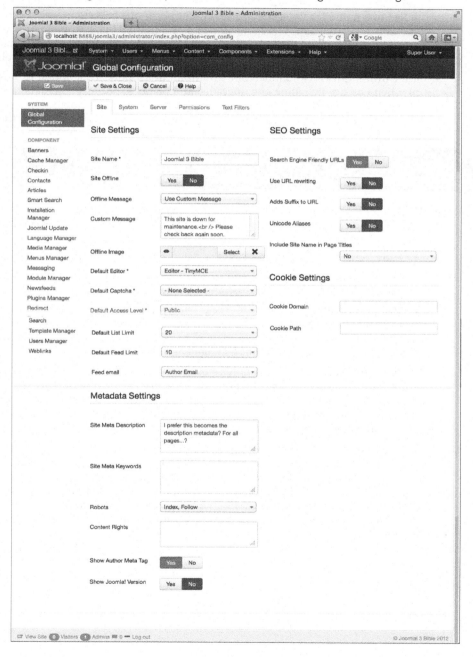

Here's a breakdown of all the options you can see in the workspace:

- **Site Name.** In this field, you can type the name you want to use for the site. The choice of a name for your site has several implications beyond merely acting as a label for the actual site. The name appears in numerous places, including in e-mails and RSS feeds generated by the site, so choose something appropriate and practical. Note that you can override the from e-mail name on the Server tab.

- **Site Offline.** Click Yes to hide your site from public view. This option is most useful when you are installing site upgrades and patches, because it avoids the possibility of visitors seeing your site in an incomplete or nonfunctional state. You can control what people see when the site is offline by making a choice from the Offline Message control, discussed next.

NOTE

Taking the site offline means that only the front end is blocked from access; the admin system remains accessible.

- **Offline Message.** This combo box control allows you to configure what visitors will see when you take the site offline via the Site Offline control. Select from the following options:
  - **Hide.** Select this option to show the visitors nothing but an empty page.
  - **Use Custom Message.** Select this option if you want to create your own message for visitors, using the Custom Message field.
  - **Use Site Language Default Message.** Select this option to display the default message, "(Site Name) This site is down for maintenance. Please check back again soon." Visitors also see a login box and an image, if you have added an Offline Image using the Offline Image control.

- **Custom Message.** This field is only relevant if you select the Use Custom Message option in the Offline Message combo box. You use the field to add your custom message, and format it with HTML. Figure 4.3 shows the result of using this field to add a custom message with HTML formatting, together with a custom offline image, uploaded using the Offline Image field.

- **Offline Image.** If you want to add an image to the page that users see when the site is offline, you can add it here. The image appears, regardless of whether you are using the custom offline message or the default message. To use this control, you simply click the Select button. In the popup window that appears, you can either upload an image or select an image that you have already added to the site's Media Manager. Figure 4.3 shows a custom offline image that has been added using this control.

FIGURE 4.3

You can use the controls on the Site Settings workspace to create a custom site offline message and image.

- **Default Editor.** Use this control to select a default editor for the use of the content contributors to your site. By default, your options in the combo box are

  - **Editor — TinyMCE.** This is the default option, which makes available to your users the popular TinyMCE WYSIWYG editor.

  - **Editor — CodeMirror.** Select this option to enable to CodeMirror editor. This editor is intended for those who prefer a full-featured code editor, rather than a word processor type interface.

  - **Editor — None.** Select this option to display no WYSIWYG editor. If you select this option, your content contributors are presented with a plain text editor, which forces them to enter the text formatting using HTML tags.

 Note that the list of WYSIWYG editors is determined by which editors are installed and enabled. See Chapter 19 for information on enabling additional WYSIWYG editors.

- **Default Access Level.** Select a value from the combo box to set the default access level for new items on your site; this includes not only new articles, but also new menu items. Note that you can always override this setting on an item-by-item basis during item creation or editing.

- **Default List Limit.** Select a value from the combo box to set the default length of lists of items that appear in the admin system. The default value is 20.

> **NOTE**
> Setting the control to a higher value results in more options appearing on the page and less use of the pagination controls, but may also result in the admin system being slightly slower due to the increased page loading times.

- **Default Feed Limit.** Select a value from the combo box to set the number of items displayed in the RSS feeds. The default value is 10.
- **Feed email.** The RSS feeds generated by your Joomla! site include the name of the author and an e-mail address with each item. Use the combo box to select the e-mail address that you want to appear. Author Email uses the e-mail address that the author has on file with the site. Site Email uses the site's e-mail address. No email does exactly what it says and does not display an e-mail address. The default is Author Email.

> **CAUTION**
> You may not want to select either the Author Email or Site Email option as they publicize e-mail addresses, potentially making them accessible to spammers.

Configuring Metadata Settings

The metadata for your website appears in the head area of the page code. Metadata is not visible to your visitors, but it is indexed by search engines. Metadata has implications for search engine optimization, and so the ability to set the metadata without having to edit the code of the site is desirable. The Global Configuration Manager provides a way to set metadata for the entire site.

> **NOTE**
> You can override the Description, Keywords, and Robots options on individual articles by specifying different values in each article's Metadata Information Parameters field. You can add third-party extensions to the site to further enhance your ability to generate appropriate metadata.

This area of the workspace enables you to specify metadata options that are applied to the entire site. You can override some of these options for individual articles or by installing third-party extensions. The following options are available:

- **Site Meta Description.** In this text field, you type the information you want to appear in the description metadata field of your pages. Doing this sets the default description metadata for the entire site.

> **TIP**
> The Description field is very important. Many search engines, including Google, use the Description field as the description for the page when the page appears in search results.

- **Site Meta Keywords.** In this text field, you type the information you want to appear in the keywords metadata field of your pages. Doing this sets the default keywords metadata for the entire site.
- **Robots.** You can select one of the options from the combo box to tell the various bots and spiders how to handle your site.
  - **Index, follow.** If you want to index all the pages on your site and follow all the links, select this option. For most site owners who are interested in generating traffic from the search engines, this is the best option.
  - **No index, follow.** If you want the search engine to follow the links but not index the pages, click this option.
  - **Index, no follow.** If you want your pages to be indexed by the search engine, but you don't want the links to be followed, select this option.
  - **No index, no follow.** If you want to block the search engines completely and keep your pages out of the search engine results, select this option.
- **Content Rights.** Use this field to specify the rights you want to claim in the site and its contents. Typically this is used to add a copyright notice, as opposed to placing it visibly on each of the site's pages.
- **Show Author Meta Tag.** Click Yes to include the author metadata field in your pages. The contents of the field are taken from the name of the author you specify in the article's metadata field.
- **Show Joomla! Version.** Click Yes to include the Joomla! version information in the metadata set. The default setting is No, as some people consider displaying version information to be a potential security risk, giving hackers information about their site software.

Modifying SEO Settings

The default URLs generated by Joomla! are not considered to be optimal for search engine marketing purposes. These URLs frequently include query strings and additional characters that may cause problems for the search engine spiders. Additionally, the URLs tend to be hard to remember and unfriendly for humans as well.

For example, a default system URL may look like this:

```
http://www.yoursite.com/index.php?option=com_
content&view=article&id=27:the-joomla-community&catid=30:
the-community&Itemid=30
```

The SEO settings on the Site tab allow you to toggle options that enable search engine–friendly URLs that help overcome this problem. In contrast with the preceding example, if you enable the search engine–friendly URLs options, the page URL can look like this:

```
http://www.yoursite.com/the-community.html
```

4

The following options are available:

- **Search Engine Friendly URLs.** Click Yes to enable the system to display search engine-friendly URLs. The default setting is Yes, assuming the installer detected support for this feature on your server during installation. With this option enabled, you can create your own URL aliases at the time you create or edit new content items; if you do not specify an alias, the system creates one automatically, based on the title of the article.

- **Use URL rewriting.** Click Yes to use the Apache `mod_rewrite` function in the creation of search engine-friendly URLs. The default setting is No. Note that this is only applicable if you are using the Apache web server and only relevant if you have set the Search Engine Friendly URLs control to Yes.

> **NOTE**
>
> To use the Apache `mod_rewrite` option, you must use the `.htaccess` file supplied with your Joomla! site. The default Joomla! distribution includes a file named `htaccess.txt` in the root directory of your Joomla! installation. You need to locate this file and rename it to `.htaccess` for this feature to work properly.

If you are using the Apache web server, you can enable search engine-friendly URLs by following these steps:

1. **Access the root of your web server.**
2. **Find the file htaccess.txt and rename it to .htaccess.**
3. **Log in to the admin system of your site.**
4. **Click the Global Configuration option under the Site menu.** The Global Configuration Manager loads in your browser.
5. **Set the Search Engine Friendly URLs option to Yes.**
6. **Set the Use Apache mod_rewrite option to Yes.**
7. **Click the Save icon on the toolbar.** Your system now displays search engine-friendly URLs.

On some servers, when you change the name of the file from `htaccess.txt` to `.htaccess`, the file seems to disappear. Don't be alarmed if this occurs; the file does not actually disappear, but rather some servers automatically hide from view files that start with a period as a security precaution.

- **Adds Suffix to URL.** Click Yes to add the suffix `.html` to the end of all URLs. The default setting is No.

> **TIP**
>
> For security, it is best to set this option to add the suffix `.html` instead of leaving the URL open-ended.

- **Unicode Aliases.** Click Yes if your site will be using non-Latin characters in the URL aliases. If you do not intend your site to use non-Latin characters in the URLs, then leave this set to the default value, No.

- **Include Site Name in Page Titles.** In this context, a page title refers to the page name that you see at the top of the browser window (or in the browser tab) when you view a page. By default, the system shows only the article title in the page title. If you want to add the site name to the page titles, then select either Before or After from the combo box. The choice you make determines the position of the site name relative to the article title.

Configuring Cookie Settings

Joomla! uses cookies to keep track of user activity for a variety of purposes, such as user registration, breadcrumbs, and so on. The controls in the Cookie Settings section of the workspace allow you to tailor those cookies. There are two configuration options in this section:

- **Cookie Domain.** This is the domain for which the site's cookies will be valid. If you want them to be valid for just the primary domain, then enter www.your domain.com. Note that for security purposes, the cookie must belong to the issuing domain. In other words, you can't set cookies for another domain. If you leave this field blank, the system defaults to the full domain of the document setting the cookie.

- **Cookie Path.** This is the URL path for which the site's cookies will be valid. Pages outside of the specified path cannot read or use the cookie. If you want the cookie to be valid for the entire site, simply enter '/'. The default value is the current directory setting the cookie.

> **TIP**
> If you have users who live in jurisdictions that regulate the use of cookies, such as the United Kingdom, you may want to install a third-party extension to enhance cookie handling and bring your site into compliance with the regulations.

4

Configuring the System tab options

The System tab includes controls relating to cache and session management; it's also the place where you can enable the debugging mode for your Joomla! installation. You can access these settings by clicking the System tab in the top-left corner of the Global Configuration Manager window. Figure 4.4 shows the workspace of the System tab.

The workspace of the System tab is divided into four areas; each area is discussed in the following sections.

FIGURE 4.4

The System tab of the Global Configuration Manager

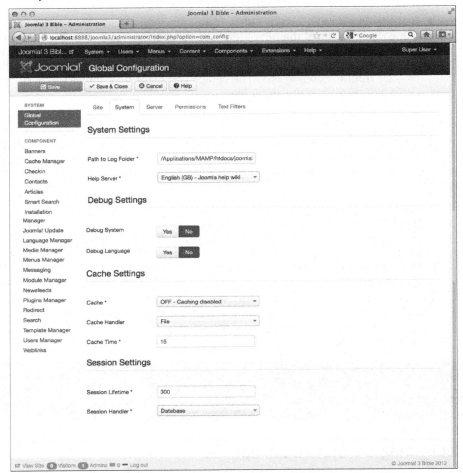

Customizing System Settings

The system settings are initially populated automatically by your Joomla! system. You probably don't want to change either of the values specified here.

- **Path to Log folder.** This field shows the location of the log files on your server. Joomla! automatically supplies this information during installation.

- **Help Server.** This is the URL of the site used to supply the information your administrators see when they click the Help icons in the admin interface. By default, this is set to the official Joomla! site.

Enabling Debug Settings

You can use the Debug settings during development or if you are having problems with your site. The settings should not be enabled for a live site, because the output will be visible to site visitors at the bottom of the pages. This section only includes two options:

- **Debug System.** Click Yes to enable the debugging system. This control provides you with diagnostic information as well as language translations and the output of SQL errors. By default, this is set to No.

- **Debug Language.** Click Yes to enable debugging of language files. This control does not work unless the Debug System option is set to Yes. By default, this is set to No.

Configuring Cache Settings

You can use these controls to enable and configure the system-wide caching. The options available here include the following:

- **Cache.** Though by default this is set to Off and disabled, once your site is live, you will probably want to enable caching as it can significantly improve your site's performance. Choose ON — Conservative caching to enable basic caching of your pages and content. If your site does not change often, or if it is experiencing heavy loads, you may want to choose the other alternative: ON — Progressive caching, which can deliver better load management for your web server.

- **Cache Handler.** This setting has only two options, File and XCache. The default setting is File, which results in the system using a directory on the site as a temporary storage space for cached files. XCache is a more aggressive setting that focuses on enhancing PHP performance.

- **Cache Time.** You can type an integer value to set the number of minutes that the cache contents are kept before being dumped and refreshed. The default value is 15 minutes. This setting requires that you set the Cache Handler control to one of the ON settings.

Working with Session Settings

The Session settings enable you to choose how to handle a logged-in, but inactive, user. The two controls are

- **Session Lifetime.** You set an integer value to specify the number of minutes the user can be inactive before the system forces him to log out. The default value is 15 minutes.

- **Session Handler.** You select from the combo box how the session data will be maintained. The default setting is Database, but you can also select XCache as an alternative. To disable the Session Handler, select None.

4

> **NOTE**
>
> Longer session values are more convenient for the users and the administrator, but excessively long values can be a security threat to your site, as they open up the possibility that a user who does not log out properly will leave an active open session which might be used by an unauthorized user. During development, however, very long session times are extremely convenient when working on the site contents.

Modifying the Server tab options

The Server tab provides a collection of settings that relate to the way your system interacts with the server upon which it is hosted. Settings here cover not only the web server, but also the Database, FTP, and Mail systems. Figure 4.5 shows the workspace.

The workspace of the Server tab is divided into five areas; each area is discussed in the following sections.

Customizing Server Settings

These settings relate to your general server configuration:

- **Path to Temp Folder.** This field shows the path to the directory where the system's temporary files are kept. Joomla! automatically creates the value for this field during installation. Don't change this without good reason, and make sure the new value is valid to avoid problems.

- **Gzip Page Compression.** Click Yes if your server supports Gzip page compression. Doing this improves site performance, but note that it only works if your server provides this feature.

- **Error Reporting.** Select a value from the combo box to set the level of error reporting you want the system to use. The options available are System Default, None, Simple, and Maximum, Development. The default setting is System Default, which allows the level of error reporting to be determined by the settings in the server's `php.ini` file.

> **NOTE**
>
> The output from the error reporting appears at the bottom of all pages and is visible to both front-end and back-end users.

- **Force SSL.** Choose from the combo box to select whether the system requires the use of SSL for connections. The options are None, Administrator Only, and Entire Site. The default is None. Note that this control depends upon whether your server supports SSL.

Adding Location Settings

The Location settings allow you to adjust the time settings to suit your site, regardless of the server's default time setting. Use the combo box to select your preferred time zone.

FIGURE 4.5

The Server tab of the Global Configuration Manager

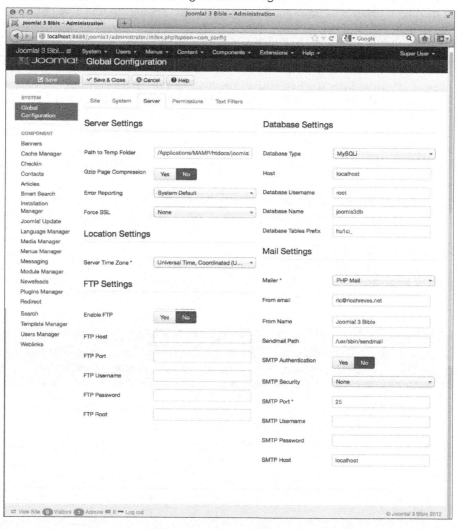

TIP

The Time Zone settings are based on Coordinated Universal Time, also known as UTC. UTC time zone offsets are interchangeable with the old standard, GMT.

Enabling FTP Settings

Joomla! has a built-in FTP function that assists you with moving files to the server without having to resort to a third-party application. The settings in this area of the workspace allow you to set up this feature. If you want to use traditional FTP or your website file manager, there is no reason to enable the following options:

- **Enable FTP.** Click Yes to use the Joomla! FTP function.
- **FTP Host.** Type the FTP URL of the host server. There may already be a value in this field; it is the best guess that Joomla! can make at the proper FTP URL and is likely to be correct.
- **FTP Port.** Type an integer value for the port number where FTP is accessed. The default value is 21.
- **FTP Username.** Type the username that Joomla! can use to access the server via FTP.
- **FTP Password.** Type the password that goes with the FTP username.
- **FTP Root.** Type the name of the directory where the files should be uploaded.

Modifying Database Settings

The values in the fields in the Database Settings area are initially created during the installation of your site. You should only modify the information in this section under exceptional circumstances, for example, when moving your site to a new server. The fields provided are

> **CAUTION**
>
> The default values for all of the Database settings are determined during the installation of your site. Changing any of these values can result in your site crashing and becoming inaccessible.

- **Database Type.** This field shows the type of database that your system is using.
- **Host.** This field shows the hostname for your database.
- **Database Username.** This field shows the username required to access your database.
- **Database Name.** This field shows the name of your database.
- **Database Tables Prefix.** This field shows the prefix used by your database tables.

> **NOTE**
>
> If you are running multiple Joomla! installations on one database, you need to make sure you have set unique database prefixes for each site.

Designating Mail Settings

Your Joomla! site can send e-mails to users under a variety of circumstances. The settings in this section of the workspace control the mail server configuration, as shown in the following list:

- **Mailer.** Select from the combo box the mailer you want to use. This is normally determined during installation. The Joomla! system supports PHP Mail, Sendmail, and SMTP. If you want to modify this value, first ensure that your server supports the protocol you select.

- **From Email.** This field contains the e-mail address that will show in the e-mails sent by the system. The value in is set during installation but you can alter it at any time in this field.

- **From Name.** This field contains the name that will show in the Mail from field of e-mail sent by the system. By default, this is the site name, taken from the Site tab.

- **Sendmail Path.** Enter in this field the path to the server's Sendmail program. This is only used if the Mailer control is set to Sendmail.

- **SMTP Authentication.** Click Yes if the SMTP server requires authentication. This is only used if the Mailer control is set to Sendmail.

- **SMTP Security.** Select the appropriate SMTP security protocol used by your mail server.

- **SMTP Port.** This field contains an integer value representing the port number of your SMTP server. The value depends on your server setup.

- **SMTP Username.** This field contains the username for the SMTP server. This is only used if the Mailer control is set to Sendmail.

- **SMTP Password.** This field contains the password for the SMTP server. This is only used if the Mailer control is set to Sendmail.

- **SMTP Host.** This field contains the hostname of the SMTP server. This is only used if the Mailer control is set to Sendmail.

Summary

In this chapter, I reviewed the system's Global Configuration options, located in the Joomla! Global Configuration Manager. Though the Global Configuration Manager includes five workspaces, I covered only three of them; I cover the other two in detail in later chapters. The three workspaces that I reviewed here enable you to do the following:

- Configure the Site tab options, which cover basic settings such as the site name, default global metadata fields, URL aliases, and cookie management.

- Configure the Joomla! System configuration options, which include debugging, caching, and session management.

- Configure the Server configuration options, which include key server, database, FTP, and mail settings.

This is the last chapter of Part 1, which is concerned with fundamental topics, including installation and basic configuration. In the next chapter, I begin Part 2, with a focus on content creation and management.

Part II

Working with Content and Users

In Part II, you learn how to work with content and users, the heart of the Joomla! CMS. I cover creating, editing, and managing content items in great detail. I include a separate discussion on advanced content management techniques, including managing content from the front end of your Joomla! website. Chapter 8 is dedicated to Joomla's menu system, with a comprehensive review of all the menu item types included in the default installation. Chapter 9 looks at various techniques for creating an effective home page and managing the content on your home page. Managing users is the subject of Chapter 10, with an extended look at user groups, and how you can manage user permissions and privileges in Joomla! The final chapter in this sessions deals with creating a multilingual website and a look at all the language management tools in Joomla! 3.

IN THIS PART

Managing Content

IN THIS CHAPTER

Creating new articles

Managing existing articles

Working with content hierarchies

Using categories to impose structure on your content

Managing global article settings

The creation and management of content items is at the very heart of any content management system, and Joomla! is no exception. Not surprisingly, the content management options in Joomla! are full-featured and include a wide variety of options. Joomla! 3 made a number of significant changes to the content management interfaces, introducing improved usability and easier access to the wide range of choices in the system.

In this chapter, I take you through the all-new content management interface in detail. In addition to content creation and editing basics, I focus on how you can use the tools to impose a logical structure on your content, both for the site's administrators and for your site visitors. Logical structuring of your content items not only makes the site easier to use for your visitors, but also promotes the efficient management of the site. Along the way, I cover the most common approaches to handling content management challenges as well as the various system parameters that enable you to enhance your site's search engine effectiveness and keep content creation overhead to a minimum.

If you can't wait, let's start with content management 101: How to create your first article in Joomla!.

Creating Articles

If you are like most Joomla! users, articles are the essence of your site. Articles hold your text content, often together with pictures or other media. Articles are a key point of user engagement and often the center for comments and social media interactions. Of course, article content is also one of the keys to your success with search engines. Given the primary role articles play on most sites, your fluency with the article creation tools in Joomla! has a direct relation to your ability to translate content ideas into a successful web presence.

In this section, I dive deeply into the Article Manager and the Add New Article workspace. I also look at the various parameters and options that affect article creation, with the goal of helping you to create more effective content items and to get the most out of the powerful Joomla! content creation tools.

You can add new articles to your site at any time. Article creation can occur from either the admin system or from the front end of the site, assuming the user has sufficient privileges to access the functionality. Most of the time, article creation is likely to occur via the admin system and, depending on the template being used on the front end, article creation may be easier from the admin system due to a more suitable interface with better access to tools. In this section, I take you through article creation from within the admin system.

To create a new article, follow these steps:

1. **Log in to the admin system of your site.**

2. **Access the Article Manager by clicking the Article Manager option under the Content menu on the main admin navigation bar.** The Article Manager loads in your web browser.

3. **Click the New button on the toolbar at the top of the Article Manager interface.** The Add New Article dialog box opens, as shown in Figure 5.2.

4. **In the Title field, type a name for the article.** This field is required.

5. **From the Category combo box, select either a category for the article or the Uncategorized option.** This field is required.

6. **Type some text for the article.** This field is required.

7. **Complete any other fields you want; all other fields are optional.**

8. **Click the Save & Close button on the toolbar in the top-right corner to save your new article.** The dialog box closes, and you return to the Article Manager.

TIP

By default, your article is published immediately. If you want to publish it later, or to save it as a draft that needs to be reviewed before publication, click the Publishing Options tab and set the Start Publishing date in the future.

In the sections that follow, I take a close look at each of the screens that make up the Article Manager and the article creation and editing workspaces.

Introducing the Article Manager

The Article Manager gives you access to all the articles in your system, together with the tools you need to create and manage your articles. The Article Manager is one of the most powerful and important screens in your Joomla! system; it's also likely to be the admin interface that you see the most frequently during the life of your site. In the pages that follow, I take you on a tour of the Article Manager interface and explain the various options that are available to you.

To view the Article Manager, log in to your Joomla! admin system and then either click the Article Manager link in the Quick Icons menu in the right column of the dashboard, or select Article Manager under the Content option on the main admin navigation bar. In either event, the Article Manager opens in your web browser, as shown in Figure 5.1.

FIGURE 5.1

The Article Manager interface, showing Joomla! 3 with sample data installed

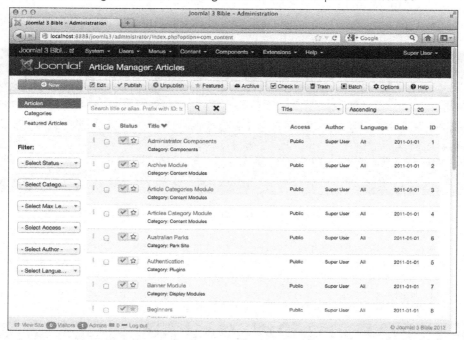

The toolbar at the top of the Article Manager provides quick access to the following functions:

- **New.** Click to add a new article. I discuss creating new articles in detail in the next section.
- **Edit.** Select an article from the list and then click this button to edit the article's details.
- **Publish.** Select one or more articles from the list and then click this button to publish them.

- **Unpublish.** Select one or more articles from the list and then click this button to unpublish them.

- **Featured.** Select one or more articles from the list and then click this button to designate the articles as featured and make them available in the Featured Articles Manager. I discuss working with featured articles in detail later in this chapter.
- **Archive.** Select an article from the list and then click this button to move the article to the archive.
- **Check In.** Select an article and then click this button to force the article's editing workspace to close and thereby "check in" the article.

- **Trash.** Select an article from the list and then click this button to move that article to the trash.
- **Batch.** Select multiple articles, then click this button to batch-apply processes to those articles. The pop-up window that appears enables you to copy or move multiple articles in one simple operation.
- **Options.** Click to open the Article Manager Options interface, where you can configure the parameters that affect the Article Manager.

- **Help.** Click to access the Help files related to the active screen.

Below the toolbar and above the list of articles are a search tool and three sorting tools to help you manage long lists of articles:

- Type a word or phrase into the field marked Search and then click the magnifying glass icon. The system searches your list of articles for the query and then displays the results of the search. To clear the screen and return to a full listing, click the button marked with the X.

- The combo box to the right of the search field allows you to specify which column of the article display is used for the sort order.

- The combo box with the word Ascending determines whether the articles appear in ascending or descending order.
- The combo box on the far right controls the number of articles that appear on the page. You can alter the default value by changing the List Length parameter in the Global Configuration Manager.

The main content area of the screen contains a list of all the articles in your Joomla! site. The columns provided are

- **Sort Order (vertical double arrows).** Click the arrows to change the sort order, or click and hold any of the icons immediately to the left of an article's title and drag the article to change its order position in the Category Manager.
- **Article Selection (unlabeled check box).** Click a check box to select an article; this is needed if you want to use several of the toolbar options. You can make multiple selections by clicking the check box next to multiple articles. Click the check box at the top of the column to select all articles on the page.
- **Status.** A green arrow indicates that an article is published. Click this check box to toggle the state of the article between published and unpublished. The star icon is highlighted only when an article is featured.
- **Title.** This field displays the full name of the article. Click the name to edit the article's details.
- **Access.** This shows the access level set for that article.
- **Author.** This displays the name of the author of the article.
- **Language.** This shows the languages in which the article is available.
- **Date.** This shows the creation date of the article.
- **ID.** This shows the system-generated user ID number. This is used internally by the system and cannot be changed by the user.

At the top of the left column are a set of links that let you jump quickly between the Article Manager, the Categories Manager, and the Featured Articles Manager. Below those links is a set of filters that can help you manage long lists of articles:

- **Select Status.** The options in this combo box allow you to filter and display the articles according to whether they are published, unpublished, archived, or trashed. This provides an easy way to identity all articles that are currently active on the site. To reset this filter, change the combo box back to the default setting, Select Status.

5

- **Select Category.** The options in this combo box allow you to filter and display the articles according to the category to which they are assigned. To reset this filter, change the combo box back to the default setting, Select Category.

- **Select Max Levels.** The options in this combo box control the number of levels of articles that appear. If your site has a complex hierarchy, this can greatly simplify the view of the list of articles in the Article Manager. To reset this filter, change the combo box back to the default setting, Select Max Levels.

- **Select Access.** The options in this combo box let you filter the list of articles by access level. To reset this filter, change the combo box back to the default setting, Select Access.

- **Select Author.** The options in this combo box allow you to filter the list of articles by author. To reset this filter, change the combo box back to the default setting, Select Author.

- **Select Language.** This combo box lets you filter the list of articles by language. To reset this filter, change the combo box back to the default setting, Select Language.

Exploring the Add New Article workspace

One of the major changes in Joomla! 3 was the reworking of the article creation interfaces. If you are familiar with the old Joomla!, you will quickly realize that things have changed significantly. The new interface does a much better job of grouping all essential tools in one place, though at the cost of increased complexity. In this section, I go through the new interface in detail, examining each of the tabs and explaining their role in content creation.

You create new articles by clicking the New button on the toolbar at the top-right corner of the Article Manager interface. Clicking the New button opens the Add New Article workspace, as shown in Figure 5.2.

The toolbar at the top of the Add New Article workspace provides quick access to the following functions:

- **Save.** Click to save your work without exiting from the Add New Article workspace.

- **Save & Close.** Click to save your work and exit the Add New Article workspace.

- **Save & New.** Click to save your work, close the current Add New Article workspace, and open another Add New Article workspace.

- **Cancel.** Click to cancel the task and exit the Add New Article workspace.

- **Help.** Click to access the online Help files related to the active screen.

FIGURE 5.2

The Add New Article workspace. Note that the default landing tab is Article Details.

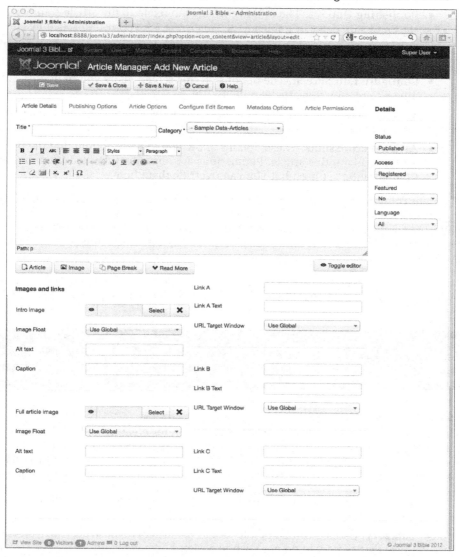

Below the toolbar you can see a set of tabs. These tabs provide you with access to secondary functionality associated with articles.

- **Article Details.** This is the crucial tab needed for creating new articles. The fields on this tab are detailed in the following section.

- **Publishing Options.** The options on this tab relate to the article's author and the start and stop dates of publication. This is the tab you use to schedule content.

- **Article Options.** Choices here allow you to change the layout of secondary information on the article's front-end display.

- **Configure Edit Screen.** The options on this screen allow you to limit the ability of others to modify this article in the future.

- **Metadata Options.** The fields on this page allow you to override the global metadata settings for this article.

- **Article Permissions.** These options allow you to view and modify the permissions associated with this article. Permissions are normally inherited from the Global Configuration settings, but you can override them here.

The right column of the workspace also includes a group of combo boxes, under the heading Details. This column contains some of the commonly used article controls, including publishing status, access controls, featured, and language. This column remains visible regardless of which tab you select, keeping these key article controls at your fingertips for fast access.

The majority of the screen in this workspace is used for the contents of the six article tabs. I will go through each of these tabs, beginning with the most important one, Article Details.

> **NOTE**
>
> Many of the options in the secondary tabs are also related to the Article Manager options specified in the Global Configuration Manager. Adjusting the global settings in the Article Manager is the topic of the last section in this chapter.

Using the Article Details tab

The Article Details tab workspace is the primary tab for creating and editing your article. This workspace is divided into two areas. The first area, located at the top of the workspace, immediately below the title, contains the fields you need to give your article a title and then enter the content that will appear on the page; all of the fields are required.

- **Title.** Type a name for the article here. The value in this field will be used as the article's title.

- **Category.** Use the combo box to assign the article to a category, or you can choose Uncategorised if you do not wish to assign it to a category.

- **Text field (no label).** Enter your content for the article in this field. If one of the system's WYSIWYG editors is enabled, you see across the top of the text field an assortment of icons that allow you to control the formatting of the text and to add media to the article. This box supports HTML and advanced formatting, allowing you to create attractive article layouts.

See Chapter 6 for more information on using the Joomla! WYSIWYG editors.

The second area is located below the large text field, and contains a set of buttons that help to simplify common tasks associated with article creation.

- **Article.** Click to view a list of all the articles in your site; select an article, and a link to the article is automatically placed inside the article. Use your cursor to control placement of the link, or cut and paste it where you want it to appear.

- **Image.** This button provides an alternative to the Add Image icon that appears at the top of the WYSIWYG editor interface. You can use either tool to add images, but the Image button is probably easier to use, as it not only allows you to upload images, but also displays all the images in the Media Library on your site. The Add Image tool in the WYSIWYG editor is not integrated with the Media Library.

- **Page Break.** Click to break your article into multiple pages. The break occurs wherever you place your cursor in the primary text field.

- **Read More.** Click to add a Read more link wherever you place your cursor in the primary text field. You use this feature to control the length of the introductory text for the article, and so it may not always be necessary. In Figure 5.4, you can see the Read More link under the Demo Article.

- **Toggle editor.** Click to show or hide the WYSIWYG editor.

Below the buttons is a group of fields under the heading Images and links. You use these fields to display images and links inside your article using preset layout formats. Using these fields, you can specify an introductory image, a main article image, and a set of links. In the default Joomla! configuration, the layout appears as shown in Figure 5.3.

The two image groups, Intro Image and Full Article Image, have the same sets of fields and buttons, as shown at the bottom of Figure 5.2:

- **Select.** Click to open the insert image pop-up menu. You can either select an image already uploaded or upload an image from your local computer.

- **Image Float.** Choose an option from the combo box to set the position of the image relative to the introductory text.

- **Alt text.** Use this field to add descriptive text that is used primarily by accessibility tools; it is only visible on the front end of the site when a visitor moves her mouse over the image.

- **Caption.** Use this field to enter a caption for your image. You can see the caption field in action in both Figures 5.3 and 5.4.

The intro image appears alongside the article's introductory text on pages where the article introductory text appears. This is typically used on sites where the page layout shows a short excerpt of posts, and requires users to click the article to see the full text. In Joomla!, this layout appears in a number of places, notably on the category landing pages and in home page layouts. Figure 5.4 shows a home page layout that uses excerpts. On that page, you see the demo article. The article uses a short excerpt, whose length is set using the Read More button, along with an intro image. The intro image does not appear on the page containing the full article.

5

FIGURE 5.3

The present article layout achieved by using the Images and links options. Note the full article image, and the set of links at the top of the article.

The full article image appears at the top of the full text of the article, as shown in Figure 5.4. This image does not appear with the introductory text.

In the right column, next to the image controls, are fields for adding three links, named Link A, Link B, and Link C. In Figure 5.3, you can see these links in action, appearing above the text of the article. The links only appear on the page displaying the full text of the article. The styling depends on the template you are using.

Each of the links has the same fields:

- **Link.** You enter the full path to the link here. It must start with "http:".
- **Link Text.** You add the text to this field that you want visitors to see; whatever text you put here appears on the page. It is hyperlinked to the value you type into the Link field.
- **URL Target Window.** This field enables you to set the target for where the web page will appear.

FIGURE 5.4

The home page of the site, showing the demo article employing the intro image functionality and the Read More link

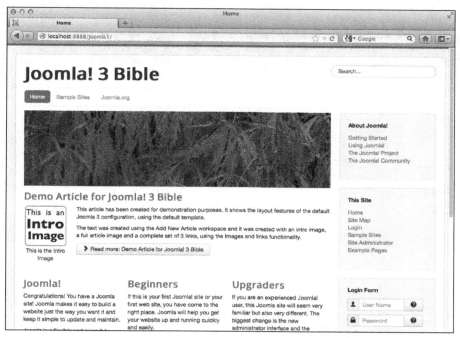

Using the Publishing Options tab

The Publishing Options tab contains a set of controls relating to the article author, creation date, and publishing controls. This workspace also allows you to specify the alias, which is used by the system for the search engine–friendly URL for the article. Figure 5.5 shows the Publishing Options tab.

The Publishing Options tab contains the following fields:

- **Alias.** Enter an alias for the system to use internally for this article. Note that this field only accepts lowercase letters without spaces. If you leave this field blank, the system modifies the article's title for use as the alias. Note that in some cases the alias may appear as part of the URL strings when SEF URLs are enabled.

- **ID.** This is a system-generated value and cannot be changed.

- **Created by.** The combo box next to this field contains a list of users; select a user to specify the author of the article and override the default setting.

- **Created by alias.** This field is normally left blank; enter text here if you want to display a name other than the name associated with the user in the system.

FIGURE 5.5

The workspace for the Publishing Options tab

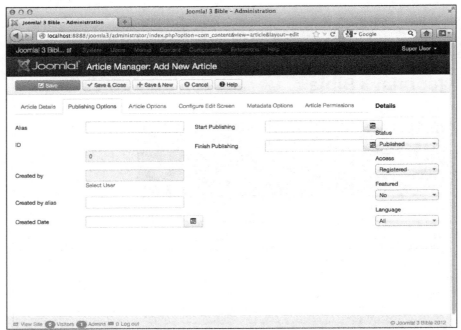

- **Created Date.** The default value is the date and time the article is created. Click the calendar icon to the right of the field to override the default date and specify one of your choosing.

- **Start Publishing.** By default, articles are scheduled to begin publishing immediately; you can use this field to specify a publication date in the future. If you set a value in the future here, the article will remain unpublished until that date, and will then appear on the site automatically without the need for further intervention by the site administrators.

- **Finish Publishing.** You can click the calendar icon to the right of this field to select a stop date for the publication of this article. If left blank, the article never expires.

Using the Article Options tab

The Article Options tab contains a number of parameters that affect the presentation of the article. These parameters are primarily concerned with the display of secondary elements, such as the author name, publication date, and so on. The choices you select on this tab override any settings in the Global Configuration Manager and are applied only to the specific article you are editing.

To access the article parameters, simply click the Article Options tab on the Add New Article page, or in the Edit Article workspace. The tab appears, as shown in Figure 5.6.

The parameters included on this page are the same as those under the Article tab of the Article Manager inside the Global Configuration Manager, with only two exceptions:

- **Read More Text.** You can use this field to specify the text that appears with the Read more link.

- **Alternative Layout.** If your template provides for alternative layouts, you can select one from this combo box; otherwise, the default layout is applied.

Using the Configure Edit Screen tab

The Configure Edit Screen tab contains four controls that allow you to restrict the ability of others to change aspects of your article. Using the settings on the tab, you can hide some of the options that appear on the article's editing screen, thereby limiting access to those options. The choices you make on this tab override the global configuration settings as they pertain to the specific article you are editing.

5

FIGURE 5.6

The workspace for the Article Options tab

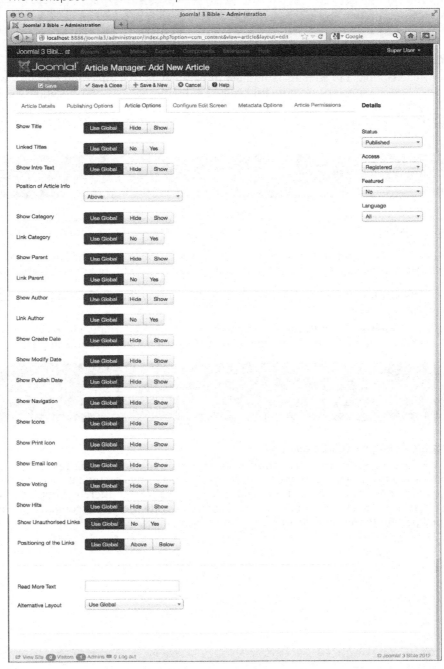

To access the parameters, click the Configure Edit Screen tab on the Add New Article page or on the Edit Article workspace. Figure 5.7 shows the Configure Edit Screen tab's contents.

FIGURE 5.7

The workspace of the Configure Edit Screen tab

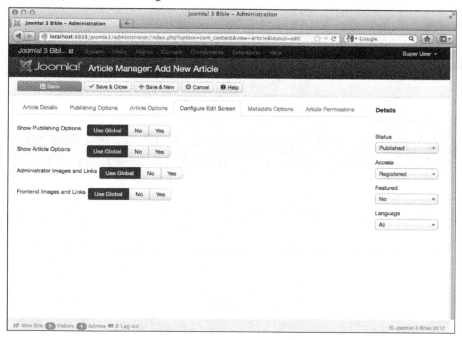

The options on this tab are a subset of the options contained on the Article Manager's Editing Layout tab, in the Global Configuration Manager.

Using the Metadata Options tab

In addition to the global site metadata, Joomla! allows you to set metadata specific to individual articles. The Metadata Options tab provides access to the metadata fields for the article. Information that you enter into any of these fields overrides and replaces any values specified in the Global Configuration Manager.

To access the parameters, click the Metadata Options tab on the article creation or editing screens. The Metadata Options fields are shown in Figure 5.8.

FIGURE 5.8

The workspace for the Metadata Options tab

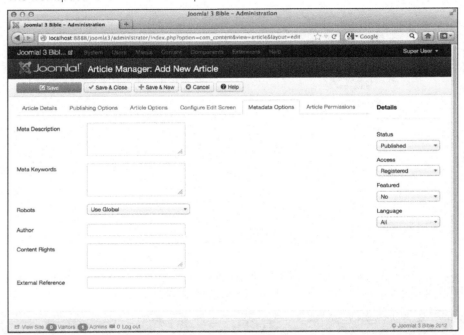

- **Meta Description.** Enter into the text field any information you want to appear in the Meta Description field for this article.

- **Meta Keywords.** Enter into the text field any keywords that you want to appear in the Meta Keyword field for this article. Separate multiple keywords with commas.

- **Robots.** Select one of the options from the combo box to tell the various bots and spiders how to handle your site:

- **Index, follow.** Select this option if you want to index all the pages on your site and follow all the links. For most site owners, interested in generating traffic from the search engines, this is the best option.

- **No index, follow.** Select this option if you want the search engine to follow the links but not index the pages.

- **Index, no follow.** Select this option if you want your pages to be indexed by the search engine, but don't want the links to be followed.

- **No index, no follow.** Select this option if you want to block the search engines completely and keep your pages out of the search engine results.

- **Author.** Enter into this text field the information you want to appear in the Meta Author field for the article.

- **Content Rights.** Use this field to specify the rights you want to claim in the site and its contents. You typically use this feature to add a copyright notice, as opposed to placing it visibly on each of the site's pages.

- **External Reference.** Use this field to add a reference to an external resource that is relevant to this specific article. Note that there is no global value for this field, as it must be specific to each particular article.

Using the Article Permissions tab

The Article Permissions tab allows you to set specific access conditions on an individual article. Configuration decisions you make here override any other settings relating to this article.

> **TIP**
>
> It is possible to set different permissions for menu items, which can create some logical problems. If, for example, you have granted access to the article, but have not granted access to the menu item leading to the article, the settings will block someone from accessing the article due to their lack of sufficient privileges to access the menu item linking to the article.

To access the parameters, click the Article Permissions tab on the article creation or editing screens. The contents of the tab are shown in Figure 5.9.

The controls on this page are the same as the global user permissions. These options are somewhat complex and I discuss them in detail in Chapter 10.

Controlling introductory text

Teasers are short excerpts of text that provide users with a small sample of a larger content item. Many sites use teasers as a way to expose multiple articles inside a small space and to inspire users to click and explore the site further. In Joomla!, introductory text is used to provide a teaser view of an article.

5

FIGURE 5.9

The workspace for the Article Permissions tab

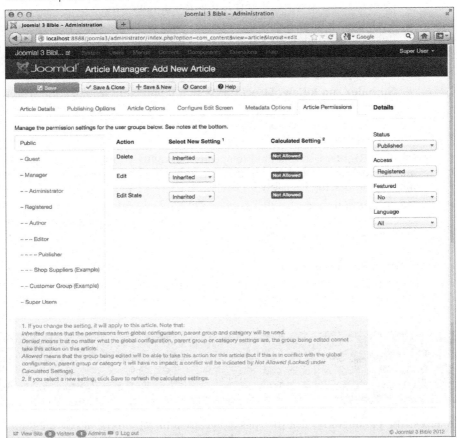

Designating the introductory text section of an article simply involves inserting a Read more break in the text. The Read More button, located at the bottom of the article editing text box, automatically segregates the article into introductory text and the main body, and automatically adds a link to the introductory text, inviting users to "read more." When the user clicks the Read more link, she is taken to the full article. You can see the introductory text functionality in action in Figure 5.10.

To set the introductory text for an article, follow these steps:

1. **Open the Edit Article workspace.**
2. **Type the full article text.**

3. **Place the cursor wherever you want the introductory text to end and the main article to begin.**

4. **Click the Read More button at the bottom of the article editing text box.** A dotted red line appears, as shown in Figure 5.10.

FIGURE 5.10

The Edit Article screen showing the introductory text divider in the text area

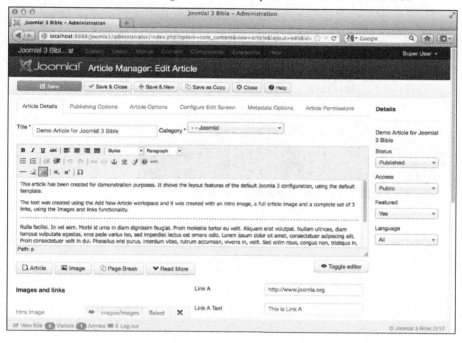

Creating multipage articles

By default, an article created in Joomla! appears as a single page, regardless of length. However, multipage articles are just a click away. The Page Break button located at the bottom of the Edit Article window is used to divide a single-page article into multiple pages. Breaking an article into multiple pages also results in the automatic creation of a table of contents. The table of contents provides links to all the pages in the article and appears on each of the new pages. Figure 5.11 shows how this looks in practice.

FIGURE 5.11

This Joomla! article from the sample data has been split into multiple pages. Note the table of contents to the right of the article and the text navigation links below the article.

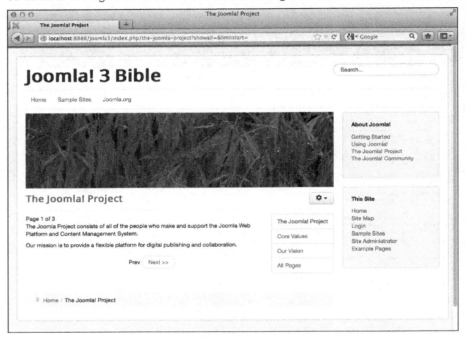

Clicking the Page Break button opens a pop-up window containing two text fields: Page Title and Table of Contents Alias, as shown in Figure 5.12. Anything you type in the Page Title field appears at the top of the visitor's browser when he views the article. The table of contents alias serves as the text for the link to the individual pages of the article in the automatically created table of contents.

FIGURE 5.12

The Page Break pop-up window

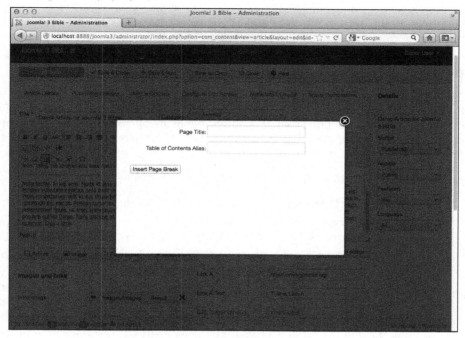

To split a single-page article into multiple pages, follow these steps:

1. **Access the Edit Article workspace.**
2. **Place the cursor where you want to split the article.**
3. **Click the Page Break button.** The Page Break pop-up window opens.
4. **Type a page title for the new page.**
5. **Type a table of contents alias for the page.**
6. **Click Insert Page Break.** The window closes and you return to the Edit Article workspace, where you see a gray, dashed line in the article at the location where you clicked.

NOTE

The display of the table of contents is controlled by the Content - Pagebreak plug-in. The plug-in contains several parameters that allow you to alter the display or to completely hide the table of contents. I discuss the plug-in in more detail in Chapter 19.

5

Managing Existing Articles

If your site is large or active, article management can take up a considerable amount of your time. In this section, I look at each of the most common tasks you are likely to perform in the course of maintaining your existing content.

Publishing and unpublishing articles

Publication is a prerequisite for article visibility and the most common method for controlling access to content. Though access controls can be set to restrict the visibility of articles, if the article is not published, it is not visible to anyone other than the content creators. Similarly, unpublishing an article operates to remove the article from the front end of the website for all but the content creators.

Articles can be published and unpublished in any of five ways:

- From the Article Manager, execute one of the following commands:
  - Click the icon in the Status column; clicking the icon toggles between published (a green check mark) and unpublished (a red circle with an X in it).
  - Click the check box next to the article's name in the Article Manager and then click the Publish or Unpublish button on the toolbar at the top.
  - Move your mouse over the title of the article you want to change. When the arrow icon appears, click it and select the command from the menu that appears.
- From the Edit Article or Add New Article workspaces, perform one of the following actions:
  - Modify the value in the combo box in the right column marked Status.
  - Click the Publishing Options tab and set a new start or stop publishing date.

If you want to publish or unpublish more than one item at a time, you can do so by clicking the check box next to each article in the Article Manager and then clicking the Publish or Unpublish button on the main toolbar.

Publication normally begins immediately and lasts indefinitely. You can, however, set an article to start and stop publication on specific dates. The start and stop publishing controls are located on the Publishing Options tab inside the Add New Article and Edit Article workspaces.

> **NOTE**
>
> The ability to publish an article depends on the user's privileges. Unless you have modified the default permissions settings, users belonging to user groups below the level of Publisher have no say in publication. Articles created by lower-level users must be published by higher-level users.

I discuss publishing articles from the front end of the website in Chapter 7.

Featuring articles

The Featured Articles functionality in Joomla! has been designed to make it easy for you to designate and display particular articles on the front page of your site. By creating a menu item with the Front Page layout option selected, you create a page to receive featured articles. Each article you designate as featured is automatically promoted to display on the Front Page layout menu item, regardless of the age or contents of the article. In this section, I look at how you can create and manage your featured articles using the Featured Articles Manager.

The Featured Articles Manager gives you access to all the featured articles in your system in one place. It also gives you the ability to change the ordering of your featured articles, thereby impacting their display on the front end of the website.

To view the Featured Articles Manager, log in to your Joomla! admin system and then either click the Featured Articles Manager link in the Quick Icons menu in the right column of the dashboard, or select Featured Articles Manager under the Content option on the main admin navigation bar. In either case, the Featured Articles Manager opens in your web browser, as shown in Figure 5.13.

FIGURE 5.13

The Featured Articles Manager interface

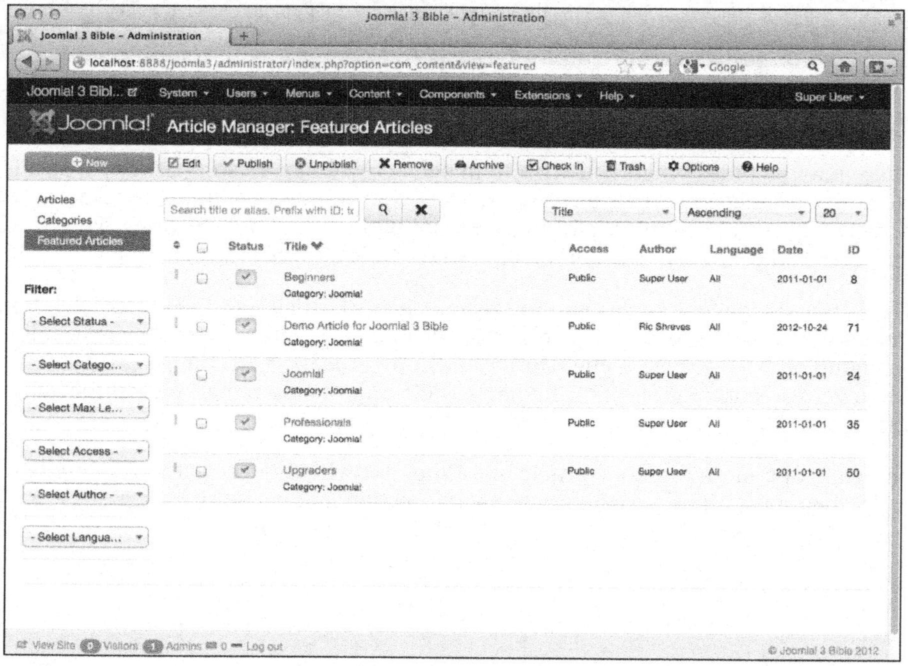

The two functions available in the Featured Articles Manager are removing items from the list of featured articles and reordering the articles. To remove an item from the featured list, simply click the check box next to the name of the article, and then click the Remove button on the top toolbar.

To reorder the articles, click the Sort Table by combo box and select Ordering; you can then simply click and drag the articles into the order you desire. Any changes you make here are reflected in the ordering of the articles on the front end of the site as well.

Modifying articles

You can edit an existing article at any time by accessing the Article Manager and by either clicking the article name, or clicking the check box next to the article name and then clicking the Edit button on the Article Manager toolbar. Changes that you make to articles are applied to the article immediately when you click any of the Save buttons inside the Edit Article workspace.

Copying and moving articles

There may be times when you wish to make a copy of an existing article, typically to create a new article using the same layout or portions of the content. Other times, you may want to re-organize your articles by re-grouping them within categories. The Article Manager makes it easy to accomplish both of these administrative tasks.

The Article Manager enables you to create copies of articles and move articles from one category to another. When you copy an article, the system makes an exact duplicate, changing only the article name. During the copy process, you can assign the new article to whatever category you desire. The new article inherits the old article's publication state and access level.

You can copy more than one article at a time, but when you select multiple articles to copy, they must all be assigned to the same section and category.

To copy an article, follow these steps:

1. **Access the Article Manager.**
2. **Select the article you want to copy by clicking the check box next to the article's title.**
3. **Click the Batch button on the Article Manager toolbar.** A dialog box appears, as shown in Figure 5.14.
4. **Assign the article to the section and category you desire.**
5. **Click the Save icon on the toolbar to save your new article.** The dialog box closes and returns you to the Article Manager.

FIGURE 5.14

The Batch process dialog box

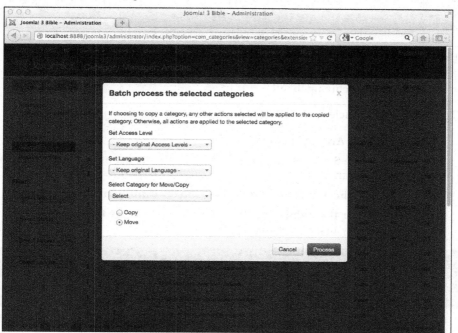

Moving articles follows exactly the same workflow, but instead of selecting the Copy option in the dialog box, you select Move.

Archiving articles

If you want to remove an article from the primary content area of your site, but you do not want to delete it, you can move it to the Article Archive. By default, archived articles are not shown in the front end of the website. You can, however, make archived articles accessible by publishing the Archived Articles module.

To archive an article, follow these steps:

1. **Access the Article Manager.**
2. **Click the check box next to the articles you want to archive.**
3. **Click the Archive button on the top toolbar.** The system immediately moves the article to the archive and removes it from the general content area of the site.

> **NOTE**
>
> You cannot edit archived articles. If you want to modify the content of an archived article, you must unarchive it, edit it, and then archive it again.

Unarchiving articles

Articles that have been moved into the archive can be restored to the general content area of your site by unarchiving them.

To unarchive an article, follow these steps:

1. **Access the Article Manager.**
2. **Change the Select Status filter to Archived.** The list of articles reloads to display only those articles in the archive.
3. **Click the check box next to the article you want to unarchive.**
4. **Click either the Publish or Unpublish button on the top toolbar.** The system immediately unarchives the article.

> **TIP**
>
> You can also unarchive an article by moving your mouse over the article title, clicking the arrow that appears, and selecting Unarchive from the options on the menu that opens.

Displaying article archives on your site

Articles that have been archived are not accessible to front-end site visitors unless the Archived Articles module is published. The Archived Articles module contains links to the articles, organized for view by date. The Archived Articles module is, by default, unpublished. You need to publish the module and assign it to the position and pages you desire before site visitors can use it. This module is most often used in blog layouts where you want to group articles chronologically, according to the month they were published. Figure 5.15 shows the output of the Archived Articles module.

FIGURE 5.15

The Archived Articles module in action

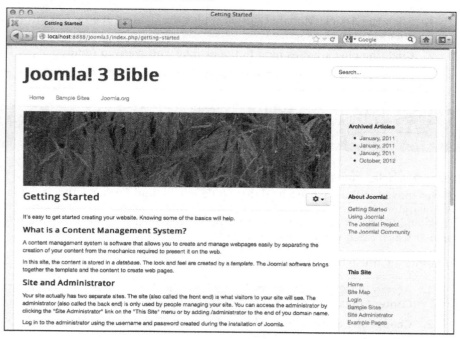

 I discuss the Archived Articles module in more detail in Chapter 17.

Deleting articles

The deletion of articles in Joomla! is a two-step process. The first step involves moving the article to the trash, where it is held until you take a second step to permanently delete the article. Articles held in the trash can be restored at any time prior to deletion. The Trash feature of Joomla! provides you with a way to clean up and remove articles from the general admin areas of the site while still retaining copies of them in case you need them in the future.

When you move articles to the trash, they are held there indefinitely. The items can be restored or deleted at the option of the administrator. Restored items are moved back to their original locations, but deleted items are permanently removed from the system and cannot be restored.

5

> **NOTE**
> Though articles can be left in the trash indefinitely, the trash is distinctly different from the Archive Manager, and you should not confuse the two. See the following section for more information.

To move an article to the trash, follow these steps:

1. **Click the Article Manager option under the Content menu.** The Article Manager opens in your browser.
2. **Click the check boxes next to the articles you want to remove.**
3. **Click the Trash button on the top toolbar.** The system moves the articles to the trash.

> **NOTE**
> Any articles moved to the trash are instantly unpublished and not visible to site visitors.

Restoring articles from the trash

Articles moved to the trash are held there indefinitely until further action is taken by the administrator. Any article can be restored at any time. The process of restoring an item is simple and the result instantaneous: the article is removed from the trash and returned to where it was located when it was moved to the trash.

To restore an article from the trash, follow these steps:

1. **Access the Article Manager by clicking the Article Manager option under the Content menu.**
2. **Change the Select Status filter to Trashed.** The list of articles reloads to display only those articles in the trash.
3. **Click the check box next to the article you want to restore.**
4. **Click either Publish or Unpublish on the toolbar**. The system removes the article from the trash, restoring it to its previous location.

> **TIP**
> You can also restore an article by moving your mouse over the article title, clicking the arrow that appears, and selecting Untrash from the options on the menu that appears.

Permanently deleting articles

Articles held in the trash can be removed from the system by deleting them. Deleting an item from the trash results in the item's permanent removal from the system; it cannot be restored once deleted.

To permanently delete an article from the trash, follow these steps:

1. **Access the Article Manager by clicking the Article Manager option under the Content menu.**

2. **Change the Select Status filter to Trashed.** The list of articles reloads to display only those articles in the trash.

3. **Click the check box next to the article you want to delete.**

4. **Click the Empty Trash button on the top toolbar.** The system immediately deletes the item and displays a message indicating that the deletion has been executed.

CAUTION

There is no confirmation dialog box; deletion is instantaneous and permanent!

Understanding Content Hierarchies in Joomla!

Like most content management systems, Joomla! allows you to organize your content into a hierarchy. Joomla! was built with the capacity to handle large and complex sites, which can be good and bad. The capacity is an advantage when you need the flexibility to manage large amounts of content, but it can be a challenge where you have a small amount of content, as improper use of the system can result in a site that is confusing to manage and needlessly complex.

NOTE

Content in Joomla! can take many forms, but for purposes of this chapter, I will focus on the most common content item, Articles. While a number of components can create output on the pages of a Joomla! site, virtually all sites include at least some articles, and many sites are composed largely, or even entirely, of articles. The flexibility of articles makes them key to site construction and while articles are most commonly used for text, they can also be containers that hold media or forms.

To get the most out of the system's content organization capabilities, you need to understand the relationship between two items: articles and categories.

- The most basic level of the content hierarchy is the article.
- Articles can either stand alone as *uncategorized content*, or be grouped together inside of categories.
- Categories can be nested into a hierarchy of parent-child relationships.

NOTE

The organization of articles inside of categories has no bearing on the actual URL display of the website. It is simply an organization of your articles in the back end.

5

Joomla! includes dedicated management tools for handling both articles and categories; you can find these tools under the Content heading on the main admin navigation menu. I discuss each of these interfaces in this section, but first, I want to look at some practical examples of the creation of content hierarchies.

Using Categories to Create Content Hierarchies

In all but the most basic sites, you are likely to need sets and subsets of content, that is, a content hierarchy. In Joomla!, you use categories to create these sets and subsets. The category functions as a container to hold your articles. Without the use of categories, you can only create a flat (one-tier) structure composed of uncategorized content. With the use of categories, however, you can create a logical structure that supports complex relationships involving parent, child, and peer groups.

The number of categories you can create is theoretically limitless though, as a practical matter, you will want to limit this to keep it manageable in the admin system. It is important to remember that the imposition of the hierarchy creates sets and subsets of your articles and that this can significantly impact the display of information, the ease of navigation, and the ease of administration. Sloppy use of the hierarchy can result in sites that are both hard for visitors to navigate and hard to administer. It is best to plan before building as it can be a time-consuming exercise to have to move things around later (though not impossible, if the need arises).

You can create and manage categories using the Joomla! Category Manager, discussed in the next section.

Introducing the Category Manager

Joomla! provides a dedicated tool for managing the categories on your site. The Category Manager is located under the Content menu on the main admin navigation bar. Clicking this navigation choice brings up a screen containing a list of all the categories in your site. You can accomplish a number of tasks directly from the Category Manager. The interface is shown in Figure 5.16.

NOTE
If you've installed the Joomla! sample data, you can already see a number of categories in the system.

FIGURE 5.16

The Category Manager interface

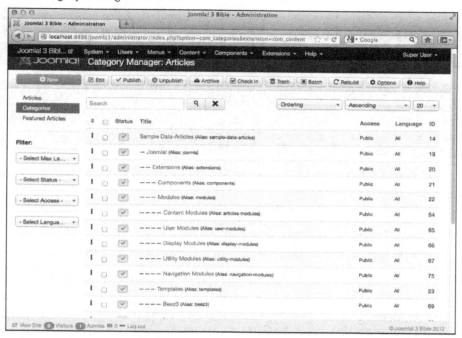

The Category Manager toolbar, located below the blue title bar, provides quick access to the following functions:

- **New.** Click to add a new category. Creating new categories is discussed in detail in the next section.

- **Edit.** Select a category from the list and then click this button to edit the category's details.

- **Publish.** Select one or more categories from the list and then click this button to publish them.

- **Unpublish.** Select one or more categories from the list and then click this button to unpublish them.

TIP

You can also use the Publish and Unpublish buttons to unarchive and restore items from the trash.

- **Archive.** Select a category from the list and then click this button to move the category to the archive.

- **Check In.** Select a category and then click this button to force the category's editing workspace to close and thereby "check in" the category.

NOTE

A category that is open for editing is blocked from use by other administrators. If you want to perform operations on a category that is currently open, then you must first close that category. This is known as *checking in* the category.

CAUTION

The Check-in feature is necessary, but it also presents the possibility for problems. If your site has multiple administrators, be careful with this command. If someone else is working on the category when you execute this command, it can cause her to lose her unsaved work.

- **Trash.** Select a category from the list and then click this button to move that category to the trash.
- **Batch.** Select multiple categories, and then click this button to batch-apply processes to those categories. The dialog box that appears enables you to copy or move multiple categories in one simple operation.
- **Rebuild.** Click to rebuild the content category table. You should not normally need to do this, but if your site is large, or you have made a number of changes to the category structure, clicking this option can help optimize the site and improve performance.
- **Options.** Click to open the Article Manager Options, where you can configure the parameters that affect the Category Manager.

TIP

Clicking the Options button lands you on the Article Manager Options interface. Once there, you need to click the Categories tab to modify the parameters relating to the Categories Manager.

- **Help.** Click to access the online Help files related to the active screen.

Below the toolbar and above the list of categories are three sorting and searching tools to help you manage long lists of categories:

- You can type a word or phrase into the field marked Search and then click the magnifying glass icon. The system searches your list of categories for the query and then displays the results of the search. To clear the screen and return to a full listing, click the button marked with the X.
- The Ordering combo box determines which column of the category display is used for the sort order.

TIP

You can also sort any column by clicking the column header.

- The Ascending combo box determines whether the categories appear in ascending or descending order.

- The combo box on the right controls the number of categories that appear on the page. You can alter the default value by changing the List Length parameter in the Global Configuration Manager.

The main content area of the screen contains a list of all the categories in your Joomla! site. The columns provided are

- **Sort Order (vertical double arrows).** Click the arrows to change the sort order, or click and hold any of the icons immediately to the left of a category title and drag the category to change its order location in the Category Manager.

- **Article Selection (unlabeled check box).** Click a check box to select a category; this is needed if you want to use several of the toolbar options. You can make multiple selections by clicking the check box next to multiple categories. Click the check box at the top of the column to select all categories on the page.

- **Status.** A green arrow indicates that a category is published. Click this check box to toggle the state of the category between published and unpublished.

- **Title.** This column displays the full name of the category. Click the name to edit the category's details.

- **Access.** This column shows the access level set for the category.

- **Language.** This column shows the languages in which the category is available.

- **ID.** This column shows the system-generated user ID number. This is used internally by the system and cannot be changed by the user.

At the top of the left column are a set of links that let you jump quickly between the Article Manager, the Categories Manager, and the Featured Articles Manager. Below those links is a set of filters that can help you manage long lists of categories:

- **Select Max Levels.** This combo box controls the number of levels of categories that appear. If your site has a complex hierarchy, this can greatly simplify the view of the list of categories in the Category Manager. To reset this filter, change the combo box back to the default setting, Select Max Levels.

- **Select Status.** This combo box allows you to filter and display the categories according to whether they are published, unpublished, archived, or trashed. This provides an easy way to identity all categories that are currently active on the site. To reset this filter, change the combo box back to the default setting, Select Status.

- **Select Access.** This combo box lets you filter the list of categories by access level. To reset this filter, change the combo box back to the default setting, Select Access.

- **Select Language.** This combo box lets you filter the list of categories by language. To reset this filter, change the combo box back to the default setting, Select Language.

5

Adding a new category to your site

You can add new categories to your site at any time by using the New button on the toolbar of the Category Manager. Clicking the New button opens the Add a New Articles Category workspace, as shown in Figure 5.17.

FIGURE 5.17

The workspace of the Add a New Articles Category

The toolbar at the top of the Add a New Articles Category workspace provides quick access to the following functions:

- **Save.** Click to save your work without exiting from the Add a New Articles Category workspace.
- **Save & Close.** Click to save your work and exit the workspace.
- **Save & New.** Click to save your work, close the current workspace, and open another New Articles Category workspace.
- **Cancel.** Click to cancel the task and exit the workspace.
- **Help.** Click to access the online Help files related to the active screen.

Below the toolbar you can see a set of tabs. The tabs provide you with access to secondary functionality associated with categories:

- **Details.** This is a crucial tab for creating new categories. The fields on this tab are discussed in the following section.
- **Options.** This tab allows you to change the layout of the category landing page on the front end of the site, associate an image with the category, and add notes for use by the administrators.
- **Metadata Options.** This tab allows you to override the global metadata settings for this category page.
- **Category Permissions.** This tab allows you to view and modify the permissions associated with this category. Permissions are normally inherited from the Global Configuration settings, but you can override them here.

The Details tab workspace is the primary tab for creating and editing the details associated with your category. This workspace is divided into two areas. The first area is located at the top of the workspace, immediately below the title, and contains the following fields:

- **Title.** You can type a name for your category in this field. This is the only required field.
- **Alias.** This field holds the machine-friendly name that Joomla! uses for the category. If you leave it blank, the system converts the category's title into a useable format. This field only accepts lowercase letters and the hyphen (dash) character. No spaces are allowed. In some situations, the alias may appear as part of the URL string when the category page is viewed on the front end of the site.
- **Description.** Any text you add into this field appears on the category page that is visible to site visitors. Note that this field includes access to the system's default WYSIWYG editor, including the Article and Image link tools.

5

TIP

If you do not provide site visitors with access to the category page on the front end of the website, there's no reason to put anything into the Description field.

The second area of the workspace, located in the bottom half of the page, is labeled Details. It contains the following fields:

- **Parent.** Select the value No parent if you want this category to be at the top of the category hierarchy; otherwise, select another category from the combo box to make the new category the child of one of your existing categories.
- **Status.** Select your publishing controls in this combo box. You can also select Archive or Trash if you want.
- **Access.** Select the access level you want the system to associate with this category.
- **Language.** If you want this category to be tied to a single specific language, select it from the combo box, or else select All to make this category accessible to all language users.
- **ID.** This field is populated automatically by the system and you cannot modify it.
- **Created by.** If you want to tie this category to a specific user, select the user's name by clicking the Select User link, and then choose the user from the pop-up window that appears.

To create a new category, follow these steps:

1. **Log in to the admin system of your site.**
2. **Access the Category Manager by clicking the Category Manager option under the Content menu on the main admin navigation bar.** The Category Manager loads in your browser.
3. **On the Category Manager interface, click the New button on the toolbar at the top of the Category Manager.** When you click that button, the Add a New Articles Category workspace opens, as shown in Figure 5.17.
4. **In the Title field, enter a name for the category.** This is the only required field.
5. **Complete any other fields you want; all other fields are optional.**
6. **Click the Save button on the toolbar to save your new category.** The dialog box closes and you return to the Category Manager.

Copying and moving categories

The Joomla! Category Manager allows you to create new categories by making copies of existing categories. Making a new category by creating a copy of an existing category can be a time saver, as the copy will retain the settings and content you have already put in place. The new category will be an exact copy of the original category with all of its articles and settings.

To copy a category, follow these steps:

1. **Open the Category Manager.**
2. **Click the check box next to the category you want to copy.**

3. **Click the Batch button on the toolbar.** The Batch process pop-up window opens, as shown in Figure 5.14.

4. **Select the options you want to apply to the copy.**

5. **Click the Copy radio button.**

6. **Click the Process button.** The system creates a copy of the selected category and returns you to the Category Manager.

Moving one or more categories entails exactly the same process, the only difference being the options you select on the Batch process pop-up window.

Editing categories

You can edit existing categories from the Category Manager. To edit a category, either click the category name in the Category Manager, or select the category and then click the Edit button on the Category Manager toolbar. Regardless of which method you use, the system opens the Edit Category dialog box.

The Edit Category dialog box is identical to the New Category dialog box, with the same fields and requirements as discussed in the previous section. To make changes to a category, you simply alter the desired fields in the Edit Category dialog box and then click the Save button on the toolbar.

Archiving and unarchiving categories

If you want to stop a category from being used on the site, but do not want to delete it, you can move it to the Category Archive. By default, archived categories do not appear in the front end of the website. You can, however, make archived articles accessible by publishing the Archived Articles module.

Archiving categories

To archive a category, follow these steps:

1. **Access the Category Manager.**

2. **Click the check box next to the categories you want to archive.**

3. **Click the Archive button on the toolbar.** The system immediately moves the categories to the archive.

Unarchiving categories

You can unarchive categories that have been moved into the archive by changing the status of the categories to either Published or Unpublished. To unarchive a category, follow these steps:

1. **Access the Category Manager.**

2. **Change the Select Status Filter to Archived.**

5

3. **Click the check box next to the categories you want to unarchive.**

4. **Select either Publish or Unpublish from the toolbar.** The system immediately unarchives the category.

> **TIP**
>
> You can also unarchive a category by moving your mouse over the article title, clicking the arrow that appears, and selecting Unarchive from the options on the menu that opens.

Deleting categories

The deletion of categories in Joomla! is a two-step process. The first step involves moving the category to the trash, where it is held until you take the second step and permanently delete the category. Categories held in the Trash Manager can be restored at any time prior to deletion. You can view the contents of the trash at any time by selecting the Status filter in the Category Manager.

Categories moved to the Trash Manager are held there indefinitely. The administrator has the option to restore or delete the items. Restored items move back to their original locations, but deleted items are permanently removed from the system and cannot be restored.

> **NOTE**
>
> Though you can leave categories in the Trash Manager indefinitely, the trash is distinctly different from the Archive Manager. You should not confuse moving categories to the Trash Manager with archiving categories.

To move a category to the trash, follow these steps:

1. **Click the Category Manager option under the Content menu.** The Category Manager opens in your browser.

2. **Click the check boxes next to the categories you want to remove.**

3. **Click the Trash button on the toolbar.** The system moves the categories to the trash.

> **NOTE**
>
> Any category that you move to the trash is instantly unpublished and not visible to site visitors.

Restoring categories from the trash

Categories moved to the trash are held there until the administrator takes further action. You can restore any category at any time. The process of restoring an item is simple and the result instantaneous: the category is removed from the trash and returned to where it was located before it was moved to the trash.

To restore a category from the trash, follow these steps:

1. **Access the Category Manager by clicking the Category Manager option under the Content menu.**

2. **Change the Select Status filter to Trashed.** The list of categories reloads to display only those categories in the trash.

3. **Click the check box next to the category you want to restore.**

4. **Click either Publish or Unpublish on the toolbar.** The system removes the category from the trash, and restores it to its previous location.

> **TIP**
>
> You can also restore a category by moving your mouse over the article title, clicking the arrow that appears, and selecting Untrash from the menu that opens.

Permanently deleting categories

Categories held in the Trash Manager can be removed from the system by emptying the trash. Emptying the trash results in the permanent removal of the categories from the system; they cannot be restored once you delete them.

To permanently delete a category from the trash, follow these steps:

1. **Access the Category Manager by clicking the Category Manager option under the Content menu.**

2. **Change the Select Status filter to Trashed.**

3. **Click the check box next to the category you want to delete.**

4. **Click the Empty Trash button on the toolbar.** The system immediately deletes the category.

> **CAUTION**
>
> There is no confirmation dialog box — deletion is instantaneous and permanent!

Creating common content structures

How you choose to use categories determines the structure of your site's contents, at least from the administrators. Joomla! permits a great deal of flexibility in this area. You can create very simple structures or complex ones, depending on how many categories you create and how you group the articles and sub-categories. Three of the most common content structures are flat sites, multilevel sites, and blog sites. In this section I look at ways to efficiently organize content in Joomla! to create all three of these structures.

5

Creating a flat site structure

A *flat site structure* is an organizational structure that does not rely upon multiple levels of nested categories, and is most appropriate for smaller sites. If you are planning to build a basic site that has little content, then a flat structure may be right for you.

> **TIP**
>
> During the creation of a new article, you have the option to either assign the article to an existing category or leave it uncategorized. As the name implies, an article that is uncategorized is outside the system's hierarchy. Uncategorized articles are, however, like any other article. Technically speaking, the "uncategorized" grouping is simply another container for your articles.

You can create flat site structures with or without using the category structure to hold your articles. You have the choice to either build the entire site out of uncategorized articles (the simplest option), or create only one category into which you place all the articles. Although you can always create multiple categories and segregate your articles into those categories, there is likely to be little advantage to that approach and it may, in fact, simply complicate administration of your site.

Creating a multilevel content structure

The Joomla! system makes it easy to create multilevel content structures. In the admin system, you create the content hierarchy by adding multiple categories, and then imposing a parent-child relationship on those categories. For the front end of the site, you use the menu items to create an organizational hierarchy for your site visitors. You are able to create parent-child relationships between menu items, or through the creation of menus and submenus.

 Menus, menu items, and menu item types are discussed in detail in Chapter 8.

Creating a blog site structure

Blog sites typically have a home page that contains numerous articles that span the width of the page. Articles are traditionally ordered chronologically, with the newest items first. Joomla! makes it easy to achieve a blog organizational structure, complete with archives, which are a common feature of many blogs.

A Content Hierarchy in Action

Perhaps the best way to grasp the creation of a multilevel content hierarchy is by looking at an example. Let's say you want to create an organizational scheme for the articles on your Recipes website. Your site lists recipes by their place in the order of a meal, so you have decided to organize recipes into three courses that reflect a typical meal. The three courses are:

- Entrées
- Main Courses
- Desserts

And let's say that within the Entrées area of the site, you want to cover two different types of recipes:

- Appetizers
- Salads

Within the Main Courses area of the site you want to organize the recipes into four different groups:

- Fish
- Meat
- Fowl
- Vegetarian

Inside the Desserts area of the site you want to cover three different types of desserts:

- Cookies
- Cakes
- Pastries

Here's how this translates into a Joomla! content hierarchy.

First, inside the administration system, follow these steps:

1. **Access the Category Manager.**
2. **Click the New button.** The New Category workspace loads.
3. **Create a new category named Entrees.**
4. **Repeat these steps for the other two main content divisions, Main Courses and Desserts.**

Next, create the second tier of content structure:

1. **Click the New button.** The New Category workspace loads.
2. **Create a new category named Appetizers.**
3. **Assign the Appetizers category to the parent category named Entrees.**
4. **Repeat the process to create a new category named Salads, and assign it to the Entrees category.**

continued

continued

5. Repeat the process to create four new categories named Fish, Meat, Fowl, and Vegetarian, assigning each to the Main Courses category.

6. Repeat the process one more time to create three new categories named Cookies, Cakes, and Pastries, assigning each to the Desserts category.

Your categories structure should now look something like this:

1. Entrées
    a. Appetizers
    b. Salads
2. Main Courses
    a. Fish
    b. Meat
    c. Fowl
    d. Vegetarian
3. Desserts
    a. Cookies
    b. Cakes
    c. Pastries

Now to complete the process, create the articles for specific recipes and group them into the appropriate categories. Create individual articles with recipes for Beef Brisket and Lamb Shank and assign them to the Meat category. When you assign them to the Meat category, they also become part of the Main Courses category, as it is the parent of the Meat category.

Logically then, your hierarchy all fits together neatly like this:

1. Main Courses (a Category)
    a. Meat (a Category)
        I. Beef Brisket (an Article)
        II. Lamb Shank (an Article)

Now when you create your site navigation, you have many options. You can

-   Create a link to the Main Courses category, which pulls up everything in the Main Courses category.
-   Create a link to the Meat category, which pulls up everything in the Meat Category.
-   Create a link to an individual article, like the Beef Brisket page or the Lamb Shank page.

The net result of an organized approach like this is that you have a logical structure on the front end for clients to navigate, and on the back end you have an organizational scheme for your content that is intuitive and easy for your administrators to use.

To achieve a traditional blog layout for your site, follow these steps:

1. **Log in to the admin system of your site.**

2. **Select the Main Menu option from under the main admin navigation option labeled Menus.** The Main Menu's Menu Item Manager opens in your web browser.

3. **Click the name of the menu item labeled Home.** The Edit Menu Item workspace opens.

4. **Click the Select button next to the field labeled Menu Item Type.**

5. **In the pop-up window that opens, click Articles.** The pop-up window closes and returns you to the Edit Menu Item workspace, where you see a new option: Choose a Category.

6. **Using the Choose a Category combo box, select the category you want to use for your blog articles (or select Uncategorized if you are using uncategorized articles for your blog).**

7. **To configure the layout, click the Advanced Options tab on the Edit Menu Item workspace.**

8. **Click Layout Options to see the available options for controlling the layout.**

9. **After you have made your choice, click Save.** The system saves the changes, closes the Menu Item Editing dialog box, and returns you to the Menu Item Manager.

Working with the Global Article Manager

The Components section of the Global Configuration Manager includes an entire section dedicated to articles. The various configuration screens are grouped together under the title Article Manager Options, as you can see in Figure 5.18. The options provided on the tabs inside the Article Manager apply global default values to the articles and categories throughout the system. While these options can always be overridden on a per-item basis, you want to try to set preliminary values here that make sense and save you some time, effort, and energy later. There are no right and wrong settings here; what's right for you is largely subjective and reflects your goals for the site and the look and feel you want to achieve.

The default values set by Joomla! are fine for many people. Nonetheless, in this section I go through all the various tabs in the Article Manager to help you understand what each control does and its implications for your site. Though there are ten tabs, I have grouped the functionality together where logical.

5

FIGURE 5.18

The Article Manager Options section of the Global Configuration Manager. Note that the default landing tab is the Articles tab.

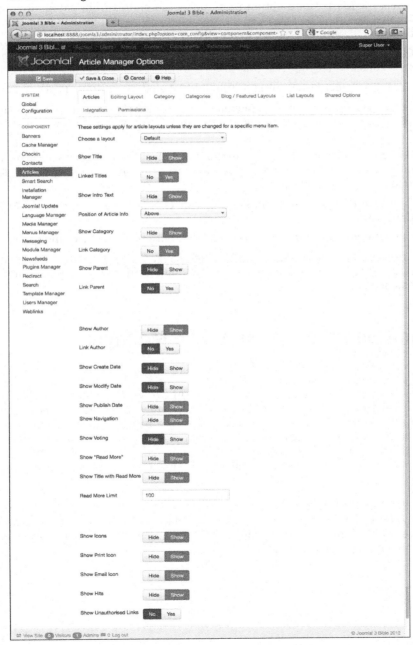

Configuring default article formatting

The Articles tab, shown in Figure 5.18, is the default landing tab for the Articles Manager Options. The tab includes a number of configuration controls, discussed below, but primarily provides access to options affecting the formatting of your articles, including the information displayed with each article and the intro text.

Here's an overview of the options on the Articles tab:

- **Choose a layout.** Select the default layout to be used for all new articles.
- **Show Title.** Select whether the article title appears along with the content.

> **TIP**
>
> If you want to use special formatting for some of the article titles on your site, you can create the titles within the body of the article, using the WYSIWYG editor to control the formatting; that approach gives you more control on an article-by-article basis. Use the Show Title parameter to hide the output of the article's title field; that way, the site visitors only see the title you have created inside the text body. This technique is also useful in situations where you want the title that appears in the admin system to be different from the title that appears on the front end of the site; the only way to make that happen is to use the article body to hold the front-end title, and then set the Show Title parameter to No.

- **Linked Titles.** Set this parameter to Yes if you want the article title to be hyperlinked to the full article.
- **Show Intro Text.** Specify whether introductory text, if any, is displayed both as a teaser and with the full article. Set this option to Hide to display the full article without the introductory text; as a result, the teaser will not appear in the full article view.
- **Position of Article Info.** Specify whether the article details appear above the article body, below the body, or are split between the two positions. Note that when the article is split, the article category, parent category, and publishing date appear above the body, and the creation date, date last modified, and hits statistic appear below the body.

> **NOTE**
>
> The Article Info appears on the articles under the heading Details and can include each article's category, parent category (if any), creation date, publishing date, date last modified, and number of views of the article (called *hits* by Joomla!). What actually appears in the Article Info is affected by the choices you make on the related parameters on the Article Manager Options tab. In the default Joomla! configuration, the only information that appears is the article category, the publishing date, and the hits statistic.

- **Show Category.** Specify whether the category name appears.
- **Link Category.** Set this parameter to Yes to hyperlink the category title to a list of the category's contents.

> **NOTE**
>
> The Link Category functionality is only relevant if you have set Show Category to Show.

5

- **Show Parent.** Specify whether the parent category appears. This is only applicable in cases where you place the article in a category that is the child of another category.
- **Link Parent.** Set this parameter to Yes to hyperlink the parent category.

> **NOTE**
> The Link Parent functionality is only relevant if you have set Show Parent to Show and there is, in fact, a parent category to display.

- **Show Author.** Set this parameter to Show if you want the name of the author to appear on the article.
- **Link Author.** Set this parameter to Yes to hyperlink the author name to the author's contact page.

> **NOTE**
> For the Link Author functionality to work properly, you must set the Show Author parameter to Show and there must also be a contact page for the author.

- **Show Create Date.** Set this parameter to Show when you want the article's creation date to appear on the article.
- **Show Modify Date.** Set this parameter to Show when you want the date and time the article was last modified to appear on the article.
- **Show Publish Date.** Set this parameter to Show when you want the article's publication date to appear on the article.
- **Show Navigation.** Specify whether navigation options, that is, the next and previous controls, appear on the article.
- **Show Voting.** Set this parameter to Show to display the rating option on the articles.
- **Show "Read More".** Set this parameter to Show to display the Read more link when needed.
- **Show Title with Read More.** Set this parameter to Show to display the article's title along with the Read more link.
- **Read More Limit.** Set this parameter to limit the amount of introductory text.
- **Show Icons.** Specify whether the print and e-mail options appear on articles as either icons or text.

> **NOTE**
> The Show Icons functionality can be overridden by the Show Print Icon and Show Email Icon parameters.

- **Show Print Icon.** Show or hide the print page functionality on the articles.
- **Show Email Icon.** Show or hide the e-mail functionality on the articles.
- **Show Hits.** Show or hide the hits statistic for each article; the hits value that appears represents an approximation of the number of times the article has been viewed by site visitors.

- **Show Unauthorized Links.** Specify whether users can view links to content for which they lack sufficient access privileges to view. If set to Yes, the links appear, but when a user without sufficient privileges clicks the link, he is prompted to log in; if he does not log in, he can't view the article. The default state is No.
- **Positioning of the Links.** Control the placement of the Links feature that is included below the Add New Article editing window.

Modifying the layout of the article editing page

The Editing Layout tab, shown in Figure 5.19, provides configuration options that impact the Add New Article and Edit Article workspaces. Some of the options hide certain features from your content creators, so be careful that you don't disable something they need. Other options relate to how links and images are handled. To access this screen, you simply click the Editing Layout tab on the Article Manager.

Here are all the Editing Layout options:

- **Show Publishing Options.** Click No to hide the Publishing Options tab from view.
- **Show Article Options.** Click No to hide the Article Options tab from view.
- **Frontend Images and Links.** Click No to remove the Images and Links option from the front-end article creation and editing interfaces.
- **Administrator Images and Links.** Click No to remove the Images and Links option from the admin system's article creation and editing interfaces.
- **URL A, B, C Target Window.** These three options relate to the introductory links functionality on the Add New Article and Edit Article workspaces. Select from the combo box where you want links to open when site visitors click them.
- **Intro Image Float.** This control relates to the images' functionality on the Add New Article and Edit Article workspaces. Click to configure the default positioning of the small introductory image relative to the introductory text.
- **Full Text Image Float.** This control relates to the images' functionality on the Add New Article and Edit Article workspaces. Click to select the positioning of the large-sized image relative to the full article text.

> **NOTE**
>
> Any restrictions you make on the Configure Edit Screen tab in the Article Manager do not apply to Super Users, who can always see all options available in the system.

Configuring category options

Two of the tabs on the Article Manager relate to categories: the Category tab and the Categories tab. Though the names are a bit confusing at first glance, they do make sense; the Categories tab configuration options apply to all categories, while the Category tab configuration options relate to what happens to items in a specific category.

5

FIGURE 5.19

The Editing Layout tab of the Article Manager

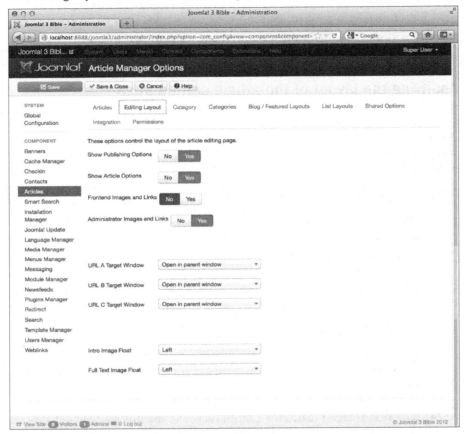

The options on the Category tab, shown in Figure 5.20, concern what a site visitor sees when she clicks a link to a category.

FIGURE 5.20

The Category tab of the Article Manager

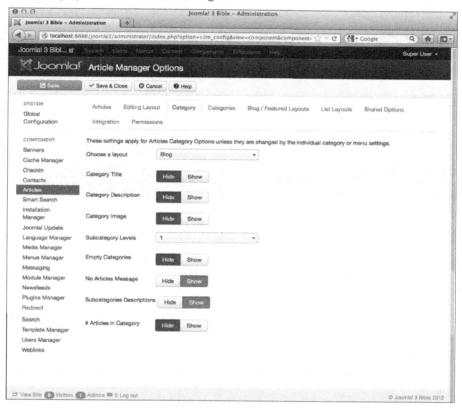

You can use the options on the Category tab to perform the following functions:

- **Choose a layout.** Select an option from this combo box to control the layout of the articles listed on the category page.
- **Category Title.** Hide or show the category title on the category page.
- **Category Description.** Hide or show the category description on the category page.
- **Category Image.** Hide or show the category image on the category page.
- **Subcategory levels.** Select the number of subcategory levels to display.
- **Empty Categories.** Hide or show empty categories on the category page.
- **No Articles Message.** Hide or show a standardized message ("There are no articles in this category.") when a category is empty. This control is only applicable if you have set Empty Categories to Show.

- **Subcategories Descriptions.** Hide or show the category title on the category page.
- **# Articles in Category.** Hide or show the number of articles per category on the category page.

To modify the display options of the categories pages, you use the Categories tab, shown in Figure 5.21.

FIGURE 5.21

The Categories tab of the Article Manager

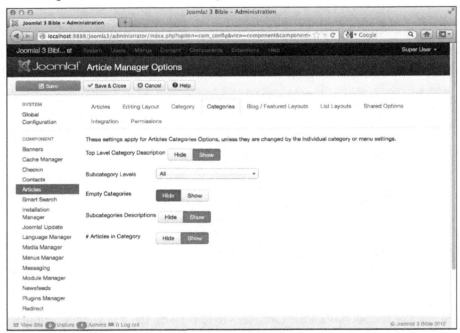

You can use the options on this tab to perform the following functions:

- **Top Level Category Description.** Show or hide the description of the top-level category.
- **Subcategory Levels.** Select how many subcategory levels you want to display on the page.
- **Empty Categories.** Show or hide empty categories.
- **Subcategories Descriptions.** Show or hide the descriptions of the subcategories.
- **# Articles in Category.** Show or hide the number of articles in each category.

Tailoring the blog and list layouts

The default Joomla! installation includes both blog and list layouts. Additionally, there are special controls for the featured articles layout. Using the tabs in the Article Manager, you can set global preferences for how pages using those layouts appear. Three of the tabs on the Article Manager relate to layouts: the Blog/Featured Layouts tab, the List Layouts tab, and the Shared Options tab. Figure 5.22 shows the Blog/Featured Layouts tab.

> **NOTE**
> Like other settings in the Article Manager, these settings can be overridden by specific menu items or articles.

FIGURE 5.22

The Blog/Featured Layouts tab of the Article Manager

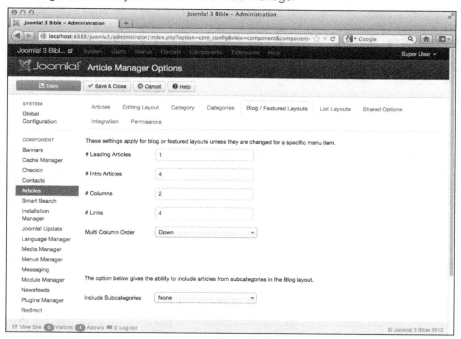

The options on the Blog/Featured Layouts tab affect all pages whose layout is set to either Blog or Featured layouts. The configuration options are

- **# Leading Articles.** Leading articles in this layout span the full width of the content area of the page. Use this field to specify how many articles appear in this format.

- **# Intro Articles.** Intro articles are the articles that follow the leading articles. These are laid out in columns, according to the setting in the # Columns field. Use this field to specify how many articles appear in this format.

- **# Columns.** Set how many columns are used to display the intro articles.
- **# Links.** Links are shown below the intro articles. Set how many you want to display with this field.
- **Multi Column Order.** This combo box controls the ordering of the items in the columns; select either Down or Across.
- **Include Subcategories.** If you want to include in the blog layout articles from the subcategories, select the number of levels here.

List layout parameters are included under the List Layouts tab, shown in Figure 5.23.

FIGURE 5.23

The List Layouts tab of the Article Manager

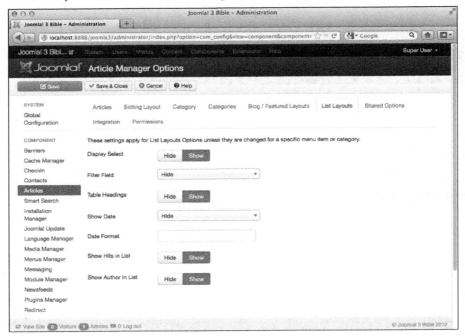

The options on the List Layouts tab affect all pages whose layout is set to List layout. The configuration options are

- **Display Select.** Show or hide the Display Select drop-down list.
- **Filter Field.** Show or hide a filter field for your site visitors to use to filter the list.
- **Table Headings.** Show or hide the headings of the table used for the list layout.

- **Show Date.** If you want to display date information on the list, select the type of information from the combo box.
- **Date Format.** You can either set a date format here or you can rely on the default format. Note that this option is only relevant if you have selected the Show option in the Show Date field.

NOTE

Date formats use a standardized notation. To learn how to use the date strings, visit www.php.net/manual/en/function. date.php.

- **Show Hits in List.** Show or hide the number of times the article has been viewed.
- **Show Author in List.** Show or hide the author of each article in the list view.

The Shared Options tab contains configuration parameters that affect all of the layouts: Blog, Featured, and List. Figure 5.24 shows the contents of the tab.

FIGURE 5.24

The Shared Options tab of the Article Manager

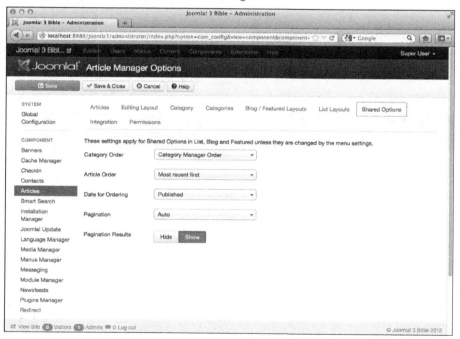

The choices on the Shared Options tab affect all layouts. The configuration options are

- **Category Order.** Set the order in which categories appear.
- **Article Order.** Set the order in which articles appear.
- **Date for Ordering.** If ordering by date, select which date to use.
- **Pagination.** Show or hide pagination at the bottom of articles.

> **TIP**
> Select Auto to let the system determine when you need to show or hide pagination.

- **Pagination Results.** Show or hide in the pagination the total number of pages in the article. This option is not relevant if you chose Hide for the Pagination option.

Managing integration and permissions

The last two tabs on the Article Manager are labeled Integration and Permissions. The Integration tab of the Article Manager specifies how feeds appear for your categories. The Permissions tab allows you to change from the global settings the user permissions that relate to the article functionality. Figure 5.25 shows the Integration tab of the Article Manager.

FIGURE 5.25

The Integration tab of the Article Manager

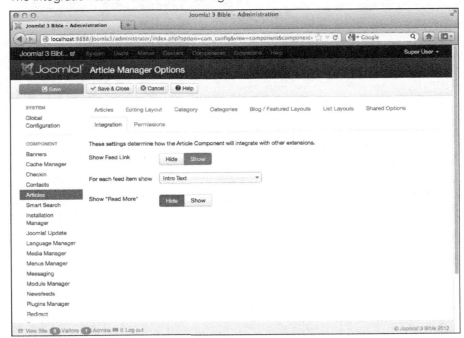

Text Filters

A concept closely related to permissions, and relevant to content creation, is the protective text filters included in the Global Configuration Manager. Any time you provide an opportunity for users to input HTML into your site, you create the possibility that harmful, or even malicious, code can find its way into your system. In order to help prevent this from happening, Joomla! has added content filtering to the Global Configuration Manager, under the tab named Text Filters.

Text filtering works by assessing the HTML that the users input, and checking it against a black list to see if the code is permitted. Joomla! provides content filtering in the default system and applies it to all users except for the Super Administrator. The default settings can be overridden by the filter parameters contained in the global article parameters, discussed earlier in the chapter.

The default Joomla! system includes a pre-determined Black List that contains the following tags: `applet, body, bgsound, base, basefont, embed, frame, frameset, head, html, id, iframe, ilayer, layer, link, meta, name, object, script, style, title,` and `xml`. The Black List also excludes the following attributes by default: `action, background, codebase, dynsrc,` and `lowsrc`.

Through the Text Filters tab of the Global Configuration Manager, you can either add new terms to the Black List or create a White List that specifically allows certain elements to be used. The system also permits you to have different lists for different user groups. The parameters also give you a way to specify which users are subject to the controls. Note that setting a control for one user group automatically sets that control for all child-level user groups.

Despite its rather broad name, all the choices on the Integration tab relate solely to how feeds are formatted.

- **Show Feed Link.** Show or hide a link to the feed for the content on the screen.
- **For each feed item show.** Use this option to control how much of the article appears in the feed.
- **Show "Read More".** Show or hide a Read more link for items appearing in the feed.

The last tab, Permissions is not dealt with in this chapter. The fields mirror those of the global permissions settings. Because this is a more complicated topic, I cover it in depth in Chapter 10.

CAUTION

Note that if you provide your own filters, the default filters provided by Joomla! are overridden and your filters are used in their place. Accordingly, don't mess with this unless you really know what you are doing, and do not create lesser protection than the system gives; otherwise, it is simply a waste of time and an open door to compromising your site.

Summary

This chapter covered a lot of ground. In addition to the basic skills needed to create and edit your articles, it also dealt with the following topics:

- Controlling publication of articles
- Featuring articles
- Archiving and deleting articles and categories
- Creating content hierarchies using a combination of categories and articles
- Configuring global article preferences and how to change from the global settings at the article level

In the next chapter, I go further into content management, with a focus on using the WYSIWYG editors and on managing media.

Working with Editors and Media

To create attractive and useable articles in Joomla!, you need to have an understanding of the various editor and media management options. Joomla! provides several article-editing tools to facilitate content creation. The system is bundled with a very good WYSIWYG editor, TinyMCE, but if you prefer to work without an editor, you can also create content directly in HTML with only a text editor interface.

In addition to the editing tools, Joomla! is also bundled with a Media Manager that enables you to easily add and manage the media files on your website directly from your browser. By using the editors in conjunction with the Media Manager, you can add images or other files to your articles quickly and easily, as I explain later in this chapter.

Working with the Editor Options in Joomla!

Joomla! comes with three content editor options: the TinyMCE WYSIWYG editor, the CodeMirror code editor, and a plain text editor. The editors range in functionality, from a Microsoft Word–type environment with buttons to speed up common tasks, to a simple text field where users can manually enter their own formatting commands. Different choices are right for different types of users. In this section I discuss the various editor options and the use for which each is best suited.

WYSIWYG is an acronym for *What You See Is What You Get*. The term is used to describe content-editing tools that let you view your text formatting as you work, and apply formatting with the simple click of a button, all without having to enter a line of code. The interface for WYSIWYG editors will be familiar to most users as it is very similar to what you might find in a typical desktop word processing program. WYSIWYG editors are easy to use and are one of the most popular features of content management systems.

I will first look at TinyMCE, including its various modes, and then explore other options.

Using the TinyMCE editor

TinyMCE is a full-featured WYSIWYG editor with a number of configuration options that enable the site administrator to customize the interface to suit the particular needs of the content creators. As you can see in Figure 6.1, the interface, with its multiple toolbars above the content window, is similar to what you might see in Microsoft Word or Apache OpenOffice.

The editor has three different modes: Simple, Advanced, and Extended. The default configuration is Advanced mode. Simple mode has far fewer controls than Advanced, while Extended has a lot more controls. I look at the formatting tools provided by each mode in the following sections.

FIGURE 6.1

The TinyMCE editor interface. In the default configuration, the editor is in Advanced mode.

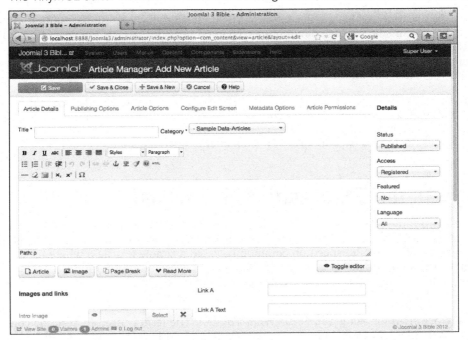

Reviewing the TinyMCE controls

In the default configuration, the top row of the editor bar includes a set of controls that focus on font formatting, styles, and alignment. The top row includes some of the most commonly used tools, which provide simple text formatting. Figure 6.1 shows the icons that represent these tools.

The top row of buttons on the editor includes the following controls:

- **Bold.** Click to format selected text as bold.
- **Italic.** Click to format selected text as italic.
- **Underline.** Click to format selected text as underline.
- **Strikethrough.** Click to format selected text as strikethrough.
- **Align Left.** Align the selected paragraph to the left.
- **Align Center.** Align the selected paragraph to the center.
- **Align Right.** Align the selected paragraph to the right.
- **Align Fully.** Set the paragraph alignment to fully aligned.
- **Styles.** Click to view and apply any of the existing styles available in the system.
- **Format.** Click to view and select preset HTML formatting.

In Advanced mode, the middle row of the TinyMCE editor bar includes a set of controls that focus on inserting and formatting various elements. The middle row includes the following controls:

- **Bullet List.** Click to convert selected text to a bulleted list.
- **Numbered List.** Click to convert selected text to a numbered list.
- **Decrease Indent.** Click to decrease paragraph indentation.
- **Increase Indent.** Click to increase paragraph indentation.
- **Undo.** Click to undo the last action.
- **Redo.** Click to re-apply the previous action.
- **Link.** Select the text you want to link, and then click to open a pop-up window where you can input a URL and set parameters and attributes.
- **Unlink.** Select text that already has a link attached to it, and then click this button to remove the link.
- **Insert/Edit Anchor.** Click to insert an anchor point in the text. This opens a pop-up window that allows you input parameters and attributes.

> **NOTE**
>
> Anchors are used to mark places that can be hyperlinked inside an article. This allows you to add accelerators to an article, providing a way for the user to jump to a specific place in the article by clicking a link.

- **Insert/Edit Image.** Click to open the Insert Image pop-up window, where you can add an image to the article.

> **TIP**
>
> Upload images to the Media Manager before you begin working on your article and note the path to the image in the Media Manager; this will save you time when you are inserting images using the button on the WYSIWYG editor. Another, even easier option is to use the Image button Joomla! provides below the text field.

- **Clean Up Messy Code.** Click this button and the system attempts to clean up the HTML code for the text in the window. You can use this when you have copied the code into the window from another source, such as Microsoft Word.

> **TIP**
>
> Copying formatted text from other applications often leads to unnecessary code appearing in your article; this tool helps avoid that problem by eliminating the unnecessary code.

- **Help.** Clicking this button opens a pop-up window with information about the version of TinyMCE that is installed on your site.
- **Edit HTML Source.** Click to open a plain text editor, which allows you to edit the content and formatting in plain HTML.

> **TIP**
>
> Edit HTML Source is most useful for viewing the code behind an existing article so that you have access to the HTML formatting that's been applied. You can use this technique to troubleshoot layout and formatting problems inside the article. If you really want to input your articles in HTML, you are better off to use the Toggle editor button located below the text field, as it does not use a pop-up window, or to explore the CodeMirror editor option explained later in this chapter.

The bottom row of the editor bar includes a set of controls focused on tables and other miscellaneous tools. The bar includes the following formatting options:

- **Insert Horizontal Rule.** Click to insert a horizontal rule at the location of the cursor in the text. The rule is created with the HTML tag HR and can be controlled by the styling set for that tag.
- **Remove Formatting.** Highlight a segment of text and then click this icon to clear all formatting associated with that text.
- **Toggle Guidelines.** If your article is using any invisible elements, such as multiple layers, click this icon to make the boundaries of the object visible and allow you to work with the object more easily.
- **Subscript.** Select text and click this icon to transform the text into lowered subscript.

- **Superscript.** Select text and click this icon to transform the text into raised super-script.

- **Insert a Custom Character.** Click to open a pop-up window containing a list of the custom characters available in the system. Click a character in the pop-up window to insert it into the article.

Enabling Extended mode in TinyMCE

The TinyMCE editor is powered by a Joomla! plug-in named Editor – TinyMCE 2.0. The plug-in includes a number of parameters that dictate in part what controls are visible to the users of the editor. One of the configuration options allows you to switch the editor into one of three modes: Simple, Advanced, or Extended. Switching between modes simply changes what options appear on the toolbar, with Extended being the richest feature set. In this section, I look at the additional controls that appear in the editor interface when you set the plug-in to Extended. Figure 6.2 shows how the TinyMCE editor interface appears in Extended mode.

FIGURE 6.2

The TinyMCE editor, configured for Extended mode

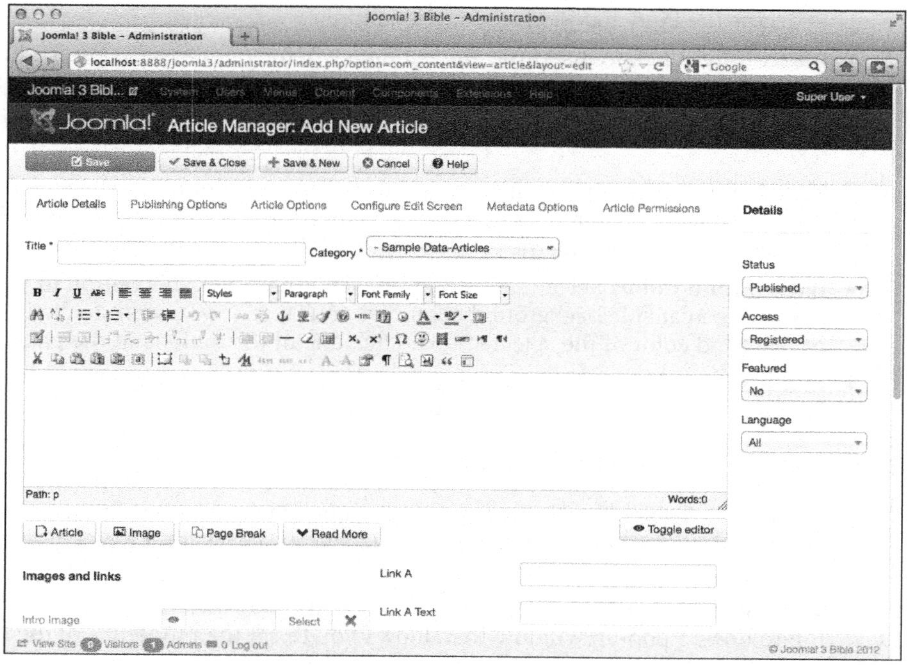

With the plug-in configured for Extended mode, additional buttons appear on the editor interface. All three of the existing rows have new options, and there is now a completely new fourth row.

The top row includes the items discussed in the previous section, plus two additional controls:

- **Font Family.** Select part of the text, and then click this combo box to view a list of the available font definitions. If you want to change the font of the selected text, click one of options in the combo box.

- **Font Size.** Select part of the text, and then click this combo box to view a list of the available font sizes. If you want to change the size of the selected text, click one of options in the combo box.

The second row includes the items discussed in the previous section, plus the following additional controls:

- **Find.** Click to open a window containing the Find tab and the Replace tab. This control opens on the Find tab.

- **Find and Replace.** Click to open a window containing the Find tab and the Replace tab. This control opens on the Find tab, but you can click the Replace tab to access the Find and Replace functionality.

- **Insert Date.** Click to insert the current date where your cursor is placed in the text box.

- **Insert Time.** Click to insert the current time where your cursor is placed in the text box.

- **Text Color.** Select part of the text, and then click this button to view a palette of the available text colors. If you want to change the color of the selected text, click one of options in the palette.

- **Background Color.** Select part of the text, and then click this button to view a palette of the available background colors for your text. If you want to change the background color of the selected text, click one of the options in the palette.

- **Full Screen.** Click to open the editor in full screen mode; click this button again to return to the original editing window.

The third row includes the items discussed in the previous section, plus the following:

- **Insert/Edit Table.** To add a new table to your article, click this button to open a pop-up window, where you can select the specifications for a new empty table. If you want to edit an existing table, select the table and then click the button.

- **Table Row Properties.** Select one or more cells in a row, and then click this button to open a pop-up window that allows you to set the properties of the entire row.

- **Table Cell Properties.** Select a cell in your table, and then click this button to open a pop-up window that allows you to set the properties of the cell.

- **Insert Row Before.** Select one or more cells in a row, and then click this button to insert a new row before the one where your cursor is located.

- **Insert Row After.** Select one or more cells in a row, and then click this button to insert a new row after the one where your cursor is located.

- **Delete Row.** Select one or more cells in a row, and then click this button to delete the entire row.

- **Insert Column Before.** Select one or more cells in a column, and then click this button to insert a new column before the one where your cursor is located.

- **Insert Column After.** Select one or more cells in a column, and then click this button to insert a new column after the one where your cursor is located.

- **Delete Column.** Select one or more cells in a column, and then click this button to delete the entire column.

- **Split Merged Table Cells.** Click inside a cell that has been merged, and then click this button to split the cell.

- **Merge Table Cells.** Select two or more neighboring cells in your table, and then click this button to merge the cells into one cell.

- **Insert Emoticon.** Click to view a pop-up window containing the available emoticons; then click an emoticon to insert it into the article.

> **NOTE**
>
> The emoticons shown under the WYSIWYG editor's Insert Emoticon control are not managed with Joomla's Media Manager; instead, they are located at `/plugins/editors/tinymce/jscripts/tiny_mce/plugins/emoticons/images`.

- **Insert/Edit Embedded Media.** Use this button to add a video or audio file to your article. Click the button to open a pop-up window with the configuration options. Note that you can also add embedded media code directly by clicking the Source tab on the pop-up window, but don't forget that any code that you enter has to comply with the Joomla! Text Filter settings.

> **NOTE**
>
> The supported media types include HTML5 Video, HTML5 Audio, Flash, QuickTime, Shockwave, Windows Media, and RealMedia.

- **Insert Horizontal Line.** Click to add a horizontal line to your article. Note that this control is very similar to the other control with the same name on this line; however, this control is much more flexible. Clicking the button opens a pop-up window that allows you to specify the size and weight of the line.

- **Direction Left to Right.** Click to set the text direction of a paragraph from left to right.

- **Direction Right to Left.** Click to set the text direction of a paragraph from right to left.

In Extended mode, there is also a completely new fourth row of controls. The options here are

- **Cut.** Select part of the text, and then click to cut the text from the article.
- **Copy.** Select part of the text, and then click to copy the text to the clipboard.
- **Paste.** Click to paste text from the clipboard.
- **Paste as Plain Text.** Click to paste text from the clipboard with all formatting removed.
- **Paste from Word.** Click to paste text copied from a Microsoft Word document.

> **TIP**
> The Paste from Word option removes some of the extraneous formatting that comes from copying text directly from Microsoft Word; however, to get the best result, either paste the Word text as plain text, using the Paste as Plain Text button, or after you have pasted the text, select it and then click the Clean Up Messy Code button.

- **Select All.** Click to select all content in the article.
- **Insert New Layer.** Click to add a new layer to the article.

> **TIP**
> Layers can be used as containers for content within your article. You can define the size and shape by clicking the visual guides for the layer and then dragging them to the shape you desire. Layers are automatically subjected to absolute positioning to fix their place in the article. Layers can overlap, where you control visibility by managing their position relative to each other using the Move Forward and Move Backwards buttons.

- **Move Forward.** Click the layer you want to move forward, and then click this button.
- **Move Backwards.** Click the layer you want to move backwards, and then click this button.
- **Toggle Absolute Positioning.** Click a layer, and then click this button to remove absolute positioning.
- **Edit CSS Class.** If you want to vary the formatting from the default CSS definition, you can do so. Highlight the text you want to modify, and then click this button; a pop-up window appears with the various options available for the selector. Any changes you make to the selector only apply to this selection.
- **Citation.** Select some text, and then click to apply styling for a citation.
- **Abbreviation.** Select some text, and then click to apply styling for an abbreviation.
- **Acronym.** Select some text, and then click to apply styling for an acronym.
- **Insertion.** Select some text, and then click this button to mark a change to the article as an insertion and add a date and other relevant information.
- **Deletion.** Select some text, and then click this button to mark a change to the article as a deletion and add a date and other relevant information.

- **Insert/Edit Attributes.** Select some text or an object, and then click to add attributes to an object or text.

- **Show/Hide Visual Control Characters.** Click to display formatting characters that would normally be invisible inside the editing field, such as spaces, paragraphs, and so on.

CAUTION

This control may not work with the most recent versions of many browsers.

- **Show/Hide Block Elements.** Click to display formatting that is normally invisible inside the editing field; in this case, it displays how items are grouped into blocks, such as paragraphs.

- **Insert Non-breaking Space Character.** Click to insert a non-breaking space character where your cursor is placed.

- **Block Quote.** Click to apply block quote formatting to a paragraph.

- **Insert Predefined Template Content.** Choose from a set of predefined content templates for use in the article. Note that no default templates are in the system, so if you want to use this feature, you must also define the templates.

TIP

TinyMCE comes with two sample templates: Simple Snippet and Layout. Of the two, only Layout has any real functionality. If you want to add more templates for your content managers to use, you need to create them. The easiest way to do this is to modify the Layout template. If you need more than one template, copy it and then modify it. The templates are located in /plugins/editors/tinymce. After you have created the templates, you need to add them to the template_list.js file for them to display inside the editor. To learn more about how to use syntax to create templates, visit the TinyMCE website at www.tinymce.com/wiki.php/Plugin:template.

 There are a number of parameters associated with the TinyMCE Plug-in. See Chapter 19 for more information about how you can further customize the editor by modifying the plug-in's settings.

Using the editor in Simple mode

The third mode for TinyMCE is called Simple mode. In Simple mode, the editor interface includes only nine buttons: Bold, Italic, Underline, Strikethrough, Undo, Redo, Clean Up Messy Code, Bullet List, and Numbered List. There are no unique controls in this mode; the buttons perform the same functions as in the other two modes.

Setting the plug-in to Simple mode not only dramatically reduces the number of options available to the content creators, but also moves the controls to the bottom of the editor window. While Simple mode may be appropriate in some situations, such as where you are allowing your site visitors to create content and you want to restrict the options available to them, for most sites this may offer too little functionality. Figure 6.3 shows the Simple mode interface.

FIGURE 6.3

The TinyMCE editor interface in Simple mode

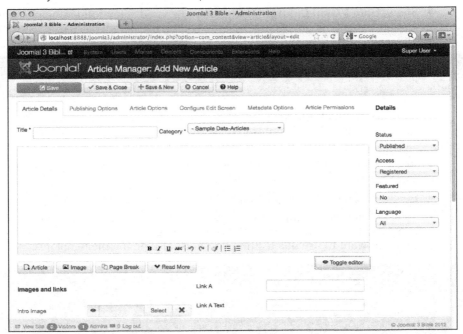

Creating content without a WYSIWYG editor

You don't have to use a WYSIWYG editor to create content. If you prefer, you can work in a plain text environment and add any styling by entering HTML tags. The plain text editor is always available. Even if the site is set to display a WYSIWYG editor automatically, you can always click the HTML button on the editor interface, or you can click the Toggle editor button located below the text box on the article creation and editing interface. In either event, the result is a plain text-editing window that enables you to type HTML formatting tags directly into the window, as shown in Figure 6.4.

TIP

Administrators who do not want to grant access to a WYSIWYG editor can force all users to use the plain text editor by setting the Editor parameter in the Global Configuration Manager to None.

FIGURE 6.4

The article-editing interface shown with the Editor field set to None in the Global Configuration Manager

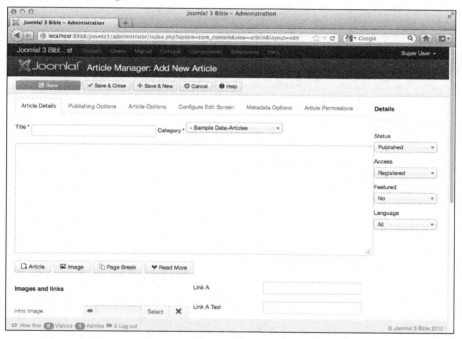

The choice to work with or without the WYSIWYG tool is largely a matter of personal preference. Although a slight performance improvement can be seen when working without the WYSIWYG controls, it is not an issue for the vast majority of users. For most, the convenience of having the easy-to-use WYSIWYG formatting options far outweighs the inconvenience of a slight delay in loading times.

CodeMirror is another editor supplied in the default Joomla! installation. CodeMirror was specifically created for coding; it is designed to make working without a WYSIWYG editor easier by displaying your code with tabs, line numbers, and color highlights. If you plan to create your article contents without using a WYSIWYG editor, you may want to enable CodeMirror as an alternative to using the plain No Editor option. You can enable

CodeMirror from the Global Configuration Manager. Figure 6.5 shows the article creation workspace with CodeMirror enabled.

NOTE
You can learn more about CodeMirror by visiting `http://codemirror.net/`.

FIGURE 6.5

The article-editing interface shown with CodeMirror designated as the editor

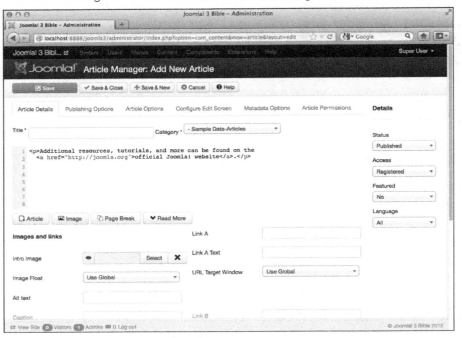

TIP
If you have multiple content contributors, I recommend that you have available for your contributors at least one WYSIWYG editor and that it is set as the default. Those users who prefer to work with the HTML code can always toggle the view to show the HTML editing window. Also, it is possible to allow registered users to select which editor they can use, and therefore it may be desirable to enable more than one. This ability only applies to users assigned to the Authors group or higher.

 Allowing users to select their preferred editor is discussed in Chapter 10.

Introducing the Joomla! Media Manager

The Media Manager component provides Joomla! site administrators with the tools to easily add media files to the system and then help keep those files organized. A built-in upload feature allows you to add files to the site in bulk. The organization tools let you group files into folders and create a logical structure that makes finding things on a big site much easier. The Media Manager is also integrated with the Image button functionality included in the article creation workspace; this greatly simplifies adding media to your articles. Figure 6.6 shows the Media Manager workspace.

FIGURE 6.6

The Media Manager in the default Thumbnail view. Note the list of folders to the left, and the list of files to the right.

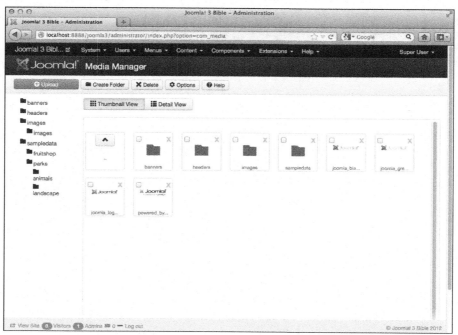

The toolbar at the top of the Media Manager provides quick access to the most commonly used functions:

- **Upload.** Click to open an upload interface for adding new files to your site.
- **Create Folder.** Click to add a new folder for storing media.
- **Delete.** Select one or more items from the list and then click this button to delete the items permanently.

- **Options.** Click to access the Media Manager's configuration options in the Global Configuration Manager.
- **Help.** Click to access the online help files related to the active screen.

Below the toolbar and above the list of items are two text links used for changing the view shown in the Media Manager. The default view is Thumbnail view, which shows a larger image and less information. The Detail view, in contrast, shows a much smaller image but more information about each file, as shown in Figure 6.7.

FIGURE 6.7

The Media Manager interface shown in Detail view

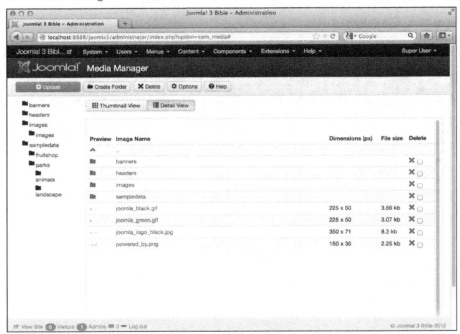

The Folders area on the left of the workspace displays a directory tree that shows all the directories associated with the Media Manager. By default, the folders shown are the contents of the /images directory on your server.

> **NOTE**
>
> If you wish the Media Manager to display the contents of another directory you can do so by modifying the value in the Media Manager configuration for Path to files folder and Path to images folder, but be aware that changing the path will break the link to existing images and files.

Clicking the names of any of the directories in the Folders area displays the contents of the directory in the Files area on the right side of the workspace. Where the thumbnails indicate image files, you can click the thumbnail to open and view the image. Where the thumbnail represents other types of media files, for example, a PDF or a PowerPoint document, you cannot open a view of the file, and the thumbnail that appears is a generic image used to represent the file type.

> **TIP**
>
> You can modify the permissible file types and the maximum file sizes via the Media Manager configuration options in the Global Configuration Manager.

Above each thumbnail, you can see a check box and an x. Clicking the x deletes that file. Clicking inside the check box selects the file, which enables you to select multiple items and delete them all simultaneously by clicking the Delete button on the toolbar. Below each item is the name of the file or directory. You can click the name to view the file or, in the case of a directory, to open the directory and view the contents.

Clicking the Detail View button changes the view of the Media Manager, as shown in Figure 6.7. This view option changes the format of the files area to display the following columns:

- **Preview.** Click this link to open a view of the image. Note this only happens if the file is an image file.

- **Image Name.** The name of the file. Though the column is labeled Image Name, it shows the name of all media files, regardless of their type.

- **Dimensions.** The width and height of the image in pixels. This is only relevant where the file is an image.

- **File size.** The size of the file. This is expressed in bytes (B) or kilobytes (KB).

- **Delete.** Either click the blue x to delete that particular file immediately, or click the check box and then click the Delete button on the top toolbar.

Working with Media Files

Media files take many forms, from common images to video to a variety of document and slide show file types. Site owners are increasingly turning to media as a way to enrich the content of their sites and enhance engagement with site users. Media can be stored locally and added directly to your pages, or they can be stored remotely with only a bit of code embedded on your page. Though articles are the most common place to display media, there's no reason why you can't display media in your modules as well.

The primary tool for working with media files in Joomla! is the Media Manager, which provides the functionality for uploading and organizing files. You can insert media into your articles via the WYSIWYG editor, via the Joomla! Image button, manually, or even through a variety of extensions specifically suited to media display.

In this section I look at the basics of working with the functionality in the Media Manager and show you how to add various types of media to your site.

Uploading files

While it is possible to add media files to your site manually, once you get used to working with the Media Manager, it is likely to become your preferred tool. Not only are the uploading and organizational tools in the Media Manager very useful, but the integration with the Image button in the Joomla! content creation/editing workspace is also a true time saver.

> **TIP**
>
> In addition to the default uploader, the Media Manager also includes an optional Flash uploader that you can enable through the Global Configuration Manager. The Flash uploader is designed to facilitate uploading multiple files simultaneously. If you are looking to move large numbers of files into your system, or if you plan to frequently upload more than one file at a time, you should consider enabling the Flash uploader because it will save you time over the default uploader. To enable the Flash uploader, visit the Media Manager configuration page in the Global Configuration Manager and change the value of the Enable flash uploader parameter to Yes.

To add a new file to your system using the Media Manager, follow these steps:

1. **Log in to the admin system of your site.**
2. **Click the Media Manager option under the Content menu.** The Media Manager opens in your browser.
3. **Click the Upload button at the top of the Media Manager interface.** An upload field appears above the list of files in the center of the page.
4. **Click the Browse button.** A pop-up window appears, showing the contents of a directory on your local computer.
5. **Navigate through the pop-up window to locate the file you want to upload and then click the Open button in the pop-up window.** The name of the file appears in the text field to the left of the Browse button.
6. **Click the Start Upload button.** The system uploads the file to the active directory and returns to the Media Manager. A confirmation message and a thumbnail for the file appear in the Media Manager.

> **TIP**
>
> Another option for adding images is to do it manually, using FTP. If you want to add media files via FTP, place the files inside the /images directory on your server. Any files placed inside the directory appear in the Media Manager. Similarly, if you use FTP to create any subdirectories inside /images, your new directories appear in the Media Manager. Files and directories that you upload via FTP to those locations can thereafter be managed by the Media Manager without limitation.

Organizing files

By default, the files included in the default system are organized into the directories you see in the Folders area of the Media Manager. You can create new subdirectories and upload new files to any of the directories in the Media Manager. It is also possible to delete files and directories from within the Media Manager.

Unfortunately, files in the system cannot be easily moved from one directory to another. The only way around this limitation is to download the file and then upload it again to the directory of your choosing. Although a download option is not included in the Media Manager, you can easily download image files in the system by following these steps:

1. **Access the Media Manager and find the image file you want to download.**
2. **Click the file's name.** The file appears alone in the Files area of the Media Manager.
3. **Right-click the file.** A menu appears.
4. **Select the Save Image As option.** A dialog box opens.
5. **Navigate to where you want to save the file on your local computer and then click Save.** The system downloads the file to your local machine and then returns you to the Media Manager.

After the file is on your local machine, you can upload it to the directory of your choice either by using the uploader in the Media Manager or by using FTP, as discussed in the preceding section.

Deleting one or more files is easy to do. To delete files one at a time, simply click the x that appears on each file. To delete multiple files, click the check box next to each file and then click the Delete button on the top toolbar.

> **Caution**
>
> Be careful when deleting files. Deletion is instantaneous, and there is no confirmation or warning dialog box. Deletion is also permanent; files are removed from the system, not moved to the trash.

You can add new directories to the system using the Create Folder button on the Media Manager. Each new directory is a subdirectory of the /images folder. To create a new subdirectory to hold your media files, follow these steps:

1. **Access the Media Manager.**
2. **In the Folders area of the Media Manager, click the name of the directory you want to be the parent directory.** The contents display in the Files area.
3. **Click the Create Folder button.** A new field appears on the page, above the list of files.
4. **Type a name for the new subdirectory in the text field next to the Create Folder button.**
5. **Click Create Folder.** The system creates a new directory. The new directory appears in the Folders area of the Media Manager.

Viewing file information

You can preview files, find the filenames, or discover the file paths in either Thumbnail or Detail view. If you need the file dimensions or size, you can find that information easiest with the Media Manager set to Detail view. To obtain the path to a file in the system, simply right-click the file's name in the Media Manager and copy the link. Typically, the easiest way to find the path is by right-clicking the file and selecting the Copy Link Location option from the menu that appears. You can now paste the link either into the appropriate place in the WYSIWYG editor or into an external document for later reference.

Displaying media on your site

The most common reason for adding media files to your system is to make them available for use in the site's articles. Although getting files into the Media Manager takes care of one important task, that is, adding files to your Joomla! system, you still need to take additional steps to display those files inside your site's articles.

Depending on what you are trying to accomplish, you want to either insert the file into the article or simply display a link to the file. To make an image visible, for example, you want to insert it into the article. The easiest route for inserting images is to use the Image button found below the text box in the article creation and editing workspaces. The Image button is integrated with the Media Manager. Anything you have added to the Media Manager shows up when you click the Image button; you simply select what you want to display. You can also upload files and add them to the Media Manager using the dialog box that appears when you click the Image button. Figure 6.8 shows the dialog box that results from clicking the Image button.

Another option for adding images is to use the Add Image functionality found in the TinyMCE editor. Unfortunately, the Add Image feature is not integrated with the Media Manager, so to add an image in this way, you must first determine the path to the image, copy that path, and then paste it into the Add Image pop-up window.

> **TIP**
>
> If you have configured TinyMCE to use Extended mode, you also see a button labeled Insert/Edit Embedded Media, which provides additional options for adding media to your articles. The control is discussed earlier in this chapter.

Similarly, adding a download link to an article requires you to first identify the proper path to the file. After you have found the path, you simply need to paste it into the article, either directly, or by adding a link to a word or phrase using the WYSIWYG editor's Add Link functionality.

FIGURE 6.8

The Joomla! Image button is integrated with the Media Manager.

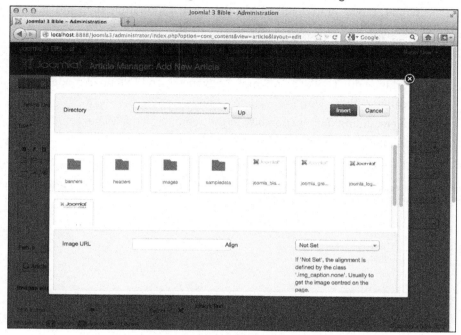

Though adding media to an article is the most common technique for displaying media on your site, it is not the only way: You can also display media or add links to media in your modules and then publish those modules on your site. To add media inside a module, you can use either the Random Image module or the Custom HTML module; both modules are discussed in Chapter 7.

> **TIP**
>
> Embedding media hosted off your site sometimes causes you to run up against restrictions created by the Joomla! Text Filters. The filters are designed to block the use of certain tags and scripts on your site. For example, in the default configuration, embedding a YouTube video is impossible because the embed code supplied by YouTube employs the `<iframe>` tag, which is a prohibited tag in the default Text Filter configuration. To work around this restriction, you can either install an extension that enables embedding via the extension, or modify the settings of the Text Filters in the Global Configuration Manager. The Text Filters are discussed in Chapter 5.

Summary

In this chapter, I took an in-depth look at the content formatting tools provided by Joomla! and how the various editors work. I also looked at how you can manage media in Joomla!. The discussion included

- Understanding the controls in the TinyMCE editor interface
- Working with TinyMCE in Simple, Advanced, and Extended modes
- Creating content with the plain text editor
- Understanding the functionality in the Joomla! Media Manager
- Adding media files to your site
- Inserting media files into your content

In the next chapter, I look further at advanced content management techniques, including using your modules to present content.

Employing Advanced Content Management Techniques

In previous chapters, I discussed the basics of Joomla! content management. In this chapter, I take a look at some of the more advanced techniques that you can use to create a richer content experience for your visitors, and I look at the tools that enable content contribution and management from the front end of your Joomla! site.

While my focus up to this point has been on using the Joomla! content management tools to create articles and display them inside the main content area of your site, there are other ways to display content on your site's pages. The modules included with the default system, for example, provide numerous content display options. Additionally, functions like the Newsfeed component and the Feed Display module allow you to bring external content into your site. This chapter discusses how to integrate these options into your site and make them part of the content mix.

Joomla! can also be configured to allow users to submit articles to your site and to create a workflow around content contributed from the front end. The system provides a number of tools to enable this functionality, thereby giving you another way to add interactivity to your site and expand your pool of potential content creators. The last part of this chapter looks at how you can set up efficient front-end content management.

Using Content Display Modules

The modules included with your Joomla! site provide additional resources for displaying your content. Although a number of the modules only provide links to your articles, such as the Latest News or the Article Category module, others can be used to actually display text or images on the page.

You typically place modules outside the main content area of the page, for example, in the sidebars, or the header or footer. Module positioning and visibility can be managed, and you can place the same module on multiple pages, or in different positions based upon rules you impose; this makes content modules highly valuable to the content manager. You can use module placement strategically to highlight related content and to display images or messages that complement whatever is in the main content area of the page.

 Module management is discussed at length in Chapter 17.

This section looks at the Joomla! content modules and how you can use them to enhance your site's content display. Later in this chapter I look at how you can bring in external content to supplement your own content creation efforts.

Creating custom content in modules

One of the most useful of the content-related modules is the Custom HTML module. Think of this module as a blank canvas. You can use the Custom HTML module to hold text, images, or other media, and you can format it exactly to suit your needs by including HTML and CSS styling.

The Custom HTML module provides no content of its own; rather, it presents you with an empty text box and a WYSIWYG editor so you can create and tailor the content as you see fit. You can either copy and paste content into the module or you can create the content from scratch, complete with the formatting you desire. Figure 7.1 shows one potential use for the Custom HTML module.

 You can find a full list of the options available in the Custom HTML module workspace in Chapter 17.

One of the most common uses for this module is to create a short excerpt or synopsis of an article or another feature on your site, together with a link to the full article or feature. When used in this fashion, the module functions as a teaser that encourages people to click and explore your site further. Although it is not possible to automatically display an article or its introductory text inside of the module, the Custom HTML module enables you to manually create a teaser that suits your needs. Simply copy and paste part of the article into a module, add a link to the full article, and then publish the module where you want the teaser to appear.

FIGURE 7.1

The Fruit Shop demo site, included in the Joomla! sample data, displays this example of the Custom HTML module. In the left column is a module named About Fruit Shop; this module was created with the Custom HTML module.

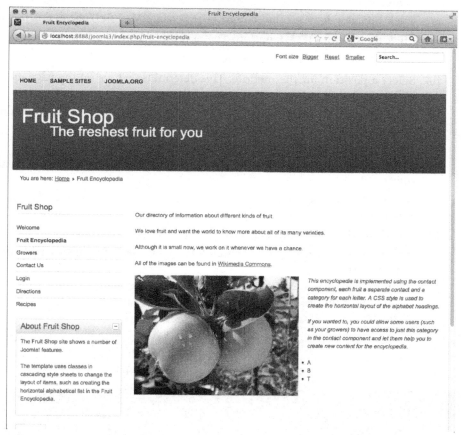

To make your own teaser using the Custom HTML module, follow these steps:

1. **Log in to the admin system of your site.**

2. **Click the Article Manager option, under the Content menu.** The Article Manager loads in your browser.

3. **Click the name of the article you want to promote with your teaser module.** The Article Editing dialog box opens.

4. **Copy the section of the text that you want to use for the teaser content in the module.**

5. **Click the Close icon.** The Article Editing dialog box closes and returns you to the Article Manager.

6. **Go to the Extensions menu and click the Module Manager option.** The Module Manager opens.

7. **Click the New icon on the toolbar.** The Select a Module Type dialog box opens.

8. **Click the Custom HTML option.** The new module workspace opens.

9. **Enter a title for your new module.** This is a required field.

10. **Select a position for the module.** This determines where on the page the module will appear.

11. **Click the Custom output tab.** The tab comes to the front, displaying a content creation text field with a WYSIWYG editor.

12. **Paste the text you copied from the article into the text box.**

13. **Enter a hard return at the end of the text and then add the words, "Read more. . .".**

14. **Apply a hyperlink to the words "Read more. . ." leading to the URL of the full article you are promoting.**

15. **Click the Menu Assignment tab.** The tab comes to the front.

16. **Use the Module Assignment combo box to choose which pages will show the new module.**

17. **Click the Save icon on the toolbar.** The system creates and saves your new module and exits the Module editing workspace, returning you to the Module Manager.

The process for creating Custom HTML modules with images is the same. The WYSIWYG editor and the Image button option below the text box on the Custom output tab give you all the options you would see in the Add New Article workspace.

> **TIP**
>
> The Custom HTML module is also a great container for displaying video, or content from sites like Twitter, Facebook, or Flickr. Note that you may have to adjust your Text Filters in order to add this content, as the default Joomla! blacklist may block the inclusion of some code on security grounds.

Displaying the most recent content

While you can easily show the latest articles on the home page via the Featured Articles functionality, you may want a way to keep a list of the latest articles accessible to visitors on the interior pages of the site. The Latest News module in Joomla! enables you to keep the most recent articles visible throughout the site. The module produces a list of the most recent articles, selected from the category of your choice. Figure 7.2 shows an implementation based on the Joomla! sample data.

FIGURE 7.2

The Parks site included in the Joomla! sample data displays in the right column a module with the title Latest Park Blogs; this is an example of the Latest News module in action.

To add a new Latest News module to your site, follow these steps:

1. **Log in to the admin system of your site.**
2. **Go to the Extensions menu and click the Module Manager option.** The Module Manager opens.
3. **Click the New icon on the toolbar.** The Select a Module Type dialog box opens.
4. **Click the Latest News option.** The new module workspace opens.

5. **Enter a title for your new module.** This is a required field.

6. **Select a position for the module's placement, via the Position combo box.** This determines where on the page the module will appear.

7. **Click the Basic Options tab.** The tab comes to the front.

8. **Use the Category combo box to select the category you want the module to use for the list of most recent content.**

9. **Use the Count field to specify how many articles you want to show.**

10. **Use the Featured Articles combo box to specify whether to show Featured Articles in the module's list of most recent content.**

11. **Use the other fields on the Basic Options tab to further filter your display, if so desired.**

12. **Click the Advanced Options tab and set any appearance preferences you may have.**

13. **Click the Menu Assignment tab.** The tab comes to the front.

14. **Use the Module Assignment combo box to choose which pages will show the new module.**

15. **Click the Save icon on the toolbar.** The system creates and saves your new module and exits the Module editing workspace, returning you to the Module Manager.

The module configuration options give you the ability to filter and control the display of the articles within certain bounds. You can select articles from specific categories and restrict them to a specific author, or to only featured articles. You can also control the number of articles that appear. Other configuration options allow you to control the styling of the module.

 See Chapter 17 for a complete overview of the options available in the Latest News module.

Displaying the most popular content

A popular feature on many sites these days is the ability to provide users with a list of the most popular articles on the site. Joomla! includes a module specifically dedicated to meeting this demand, the Most Read Content module. In this section, I show how you can add this module to your site's pages. Figure 7.3 shows the output of the Most Read Content module.

FIGURE 7.3

The Most Read Content module on this page is located at the top of the right column.

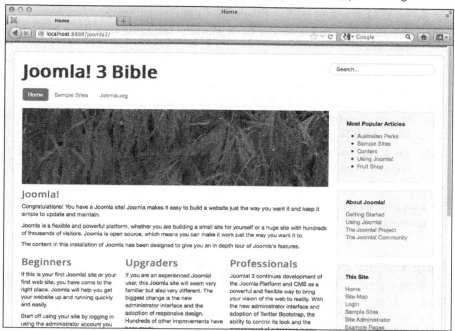

To display the Most Read Content module, follow these steps:

1. **Log in to the admin system of your site.**

2. **Go to the Extensions menu and click the Module Manager option.** The Module Manager opens.

3. **Click the New icon on the toolbar.** The Select a Module Type dialog box opens.

4. **Click the Most Read Content option.** The new module workspace opens.

5. **Enter a title for your new module.** This is a required field.

6. **Select a position for the module's placement, via the Position combo box.** This determines where on the page the module will appear.

7. **Click the Basic Options tab.** The tab comes to the front.

8. **Use the Category combo box to select the category you want the module to use for the list of most popular content.**

TIP

If you want to show the most popular content on the site, select the All Categories option.

9. Use the Count field to specify how many articles you want to show.

10. Use the Featured Articles combo box to specify whether to show Featured Articles in the module's list of most popular content.

11. Use the other fields on the Basic Options tab to further filter your display, if so desired.

12. Click the Advanced Options tab and set any appearance preferences you may have.

13. Click the Menu Assignment tab. The tab comes to the front.

14. Use the Module Assignment combo box to choose which pages will show the new module.

15. Click the Save icon on the toolbar. The system creates and saves your new module and exits the Module editing workspace, returning you to the Module Manager.

 A full list of the options available in the Most Read Content module workspace can be found in Chapter 17.

Giving visitors access to related content

One of the keys to building page views lies in your ability to help your visitors discover related content. For example, if your visitor has clicked an article about baseball, it's reasonable to assume that he might be interested in your other articles about baseball. Joomla! includes several tools that help you display related content items and thereby make your site more useful to your visitors — and increase your page views.

There are three primary modules you can use to help users discover related content: the Articles Related Items module, the Newsflash module, and, to a lesser extent, the Articles Category module. All three are part of the default Joomla! package. I cover each module in the following pages.

Using the Articles Related Items module

The Articles Related Items module is the most powerful tool for assisting users to find related articles. The module works automatically, finding related articles based on the metadata keywords associated with each article. If this module is published, it looks to the metadata keywords in the article on the screen and then lists in the module other articles that share the same keywords. Figure 7.4 shows the output as it appears on the default Joomla! site.

For this module to work, you must assign keywords specific to your articles using the Metadata Options tab in the Add New Article or Edit Article workspace. Setting global keyword metadata will not suffice.

FIGURE 7.4

The Articles Related Items module in action, in the top of the right column

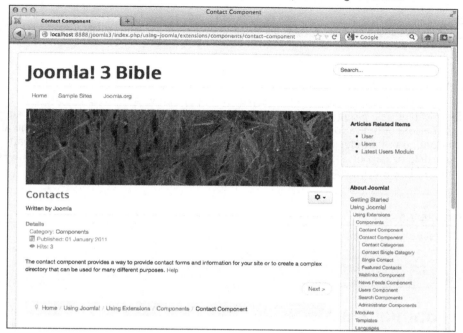

To display a list of related articles, follow these steps:

1. **Log in to the admin system of your site.**

2. **Go to the Extensions menu and click the Module Manager option.** The Module Manager opens.

3. **Click the New icon on the toolbar.** The Select a Module Type dialog box opens.

4. **Click the Articles - Related Articles option.** The new module workspace opens.

5. **Enter a title for your new module.** This is a required field.

6. **Select a position for the module's placement, via the Position combo box.** This determines where on the page the module will appear.

7. **Select any other options you want on this tab; all other fields are optional.**

8. **Use the Basic Options tab and the Advanced Options tab to configure the appearance of the module.**

9. **Click the Menu Assignment tab.** The tab comes to the front.

10. **Use the Module Assignment combo box to choose which pages will show the new module.**

11. **Click the Save icon on the toolbar.** The system creates and saves your new module and exits the Module editing workspace, returning you to the Module Manager.

 See Chapter 5 for a discussion of the Metadata Options tab and article creation workspaces.

Using the Newsflash module

You use the Newsflash module to display a fixed number of articles drawn from one or more categories, along with the first few sentences in the articles. This module supports a number of configuration variables that you can use to add interest, including the ability to randomize the articles displayed. You can also configure the module to show part of a single article or part of a group of articles drawn from a specific category. Figure 7.5 shows one possible output configuration of the Newsflash module.

FIGURE 7.5

The Newsflash module in action

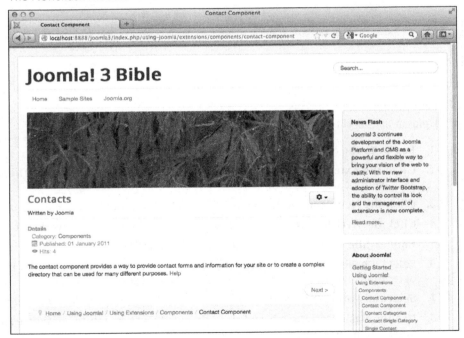

You configure the module through the Basic and Advanced Options tabs in the module's workspace. You can set the parameters to display any of the following:

- The introductory sentences from articles chosen at random from one or more categories. The article shown changes each time the page is reloaded.

- The introductory sentences from one or more articles from one or more categories, with a read more link to the full article. This configuration is similar to the teaser module used as an example in a previous section.

- The introductory sentences from one or more articles from one or more categories, without a read more link.

If you decide to use the randomization feature, you only see one article at a time, in a fixed layout. However, if you want to show multiple articles, you can do so, though without randomization. The module options allow you to set the number of articles shown and whether they appear in a horizontal or a vertical layout.

> **NOTE**
> There is one important limitation that you need to keep in mind when using this module: You cannot set the amount of text that is shown; this is set by the system.

 See Chapter 5 for a discussion on setting the metadata for articles.

To add a Newsflash module to your site, follow these steps:

1. **Log in to the admin system of your site.**

2. **Go to the Extensions menu and click the Module Manager option.** The Module Manager opens.

3. **Click the New icon on the toolbar.** The Select a Module Type dialog box opens.

4. **Click the Articles - Newsflash option.** The new module workspace opens.

5. **Enter a title for your new module.** This is a required field.

6. **Select a position for the module's placement, via the Position combo box.** This determines where on the page the module will appear.

7. **Click the Basic Options tab.** The tab comes to the front.

8. **Use the Category combo box to select the category you want the module to use for the articles displayed by the module.**

9. **Use the Number of Articles field to specify how many articles you want to show.** The other choices on this tab are optional.

10. **Click the Advanced Options tab to configure the appearance of the module, if so desired.**

11. **Click the Menu Assignment tab.** The tab comes to the front.

12. **Use the Module Assignment combo box to choose which pages will show the new module.**

13. **Click the Save icon on the toolbar.** The system creates and saves your new module and exits the Module editing workspace, returning you to the Module Manager.

Using the Articles Category module

Joomla! provides the Articles Category module to allow you to display a list of articles from one or more categories. Though its name and basic description make it sound as though this module does very little, it is actually quite powerful. There are a large number of configuration options for this module, making it possible for you to display either very specific lists of articles, or broad selections of articles drawn from a variety of categories. Figure 7.6 shows the module in a basic configuration.

FIGURE 7.6

The Articles Category module in action

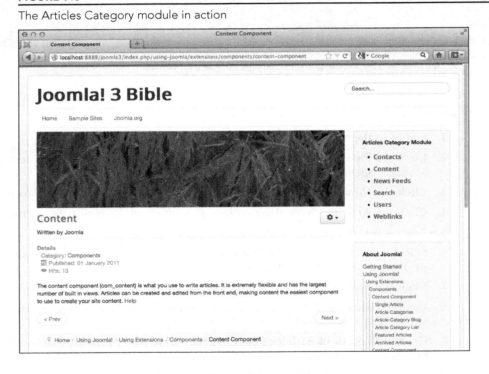

To add an Articles Category module to your site, follow these steps:

1. **Log in to the admin system of your site.**

2. **Go to the Extensions menu and click the Module Manager option.** The Module Manager opens.

3. **Click the New icon on the toolbar.** The Select a Module Type dialog box opens.

4. **Click the Articles Category option.** The new module workspace opens.

5. **Enter a title for your new module.** This is a required field.

6. **Select a position for the module's placement, via the Position combo box.** This determines where on the page the module will appear.

7. **Click the Filtering Options tab.** The tab comes to the front.

8. **Use the Category combo box to select the category you want the module to use for the list of articles.**

9. **Use the options in the other tabs to further customize the module, if so desired.**

10. **Click the Advanced Options tab to configure the appearance of the module, if so desired.**

11. **Click the Menu Assignment tab.** The tab comes to the front.

12. **Use the Module Assignment combo box to choose which pages will show the new module.**

13. **Click the Save icon on the toolbar.** The system creates and saves your new module and exits the Module editing workspace, returning you to the Module Manager.

 See Chapter 17 for more information about the three modules discussed in this section.

Displaying random images

As the name implies, the Random Image module in Joomla! lets you display a randomly selected image in a module position. The contents of the module will be drawn from the directory you designate when you create or edit the module. Used selectively, the module is an easy way to add some visual fun to your site. Figure 7.7 shows the module in use on the site.

FIGURE 7.7

The Random Image module in action

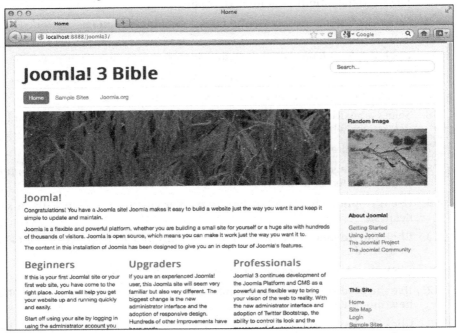

To display random images in your site, follow these steps:

1. **Log in to the admin system of your site.**

2. **Go to the Extensions menu and click the Module Manager option.** The Module Manager opens.

3. **Click the New icon on the toolbar.** The Select a Module Type dialog box opens.

4. **Click the Random Image option.** The new module workspace opens.

5. **Enter a title for your new module.** This is a required field.

6. **Select a position for the module's placement, via the Position combo box.** This determines where on the page the module will appear.

7. **Click the Basic Options tab.** The tab comes to the front.

8. **In the Image Folder field, specify the path to the directory where the images you want to display are located.**

9. **To add a hyperlink that will be applied to all the images that appear, enter a link in the Link field.**

10. **Set the Width and Height to make sure the image doesn't break your template.**

11. **Click the Advanced Options tab and set any appearance preferences you may have.**

12. **Click the Menu Assignment tab.** The tab comes to the front.

13. **Use the Module Assignment combo box to choose which pages will show the new module.**

14. **Click the Save icon on the toolbar.** The system creates and saves your new module and exits the Module editing workspace, returning you to the Module Manager.

TIP

If you have an image gallery on your site, add a link to the Random Image module and use it as a way to drive traffic into the gallery.

 For a more complete discussion of the Random Image module, see Chapter 17.

Placing modules inside articles

Ordinarily, module output is confined to the module placeholders that are defined in the code of the site's template. In some cases, however, you may want to place a module inside of the content area of a page. If that page contains an article, you can do so. Joomla! makes it possible to put a module directly inside an article; all you need to do is type some code into the text of the article.

 See Chapter 20 for more information on working with the Module Position Holders inside template files.

To insert a module inside the content area of an article, open the Edit Article workspace for the article where you want the module to appear and then follow these steps:

1. **Place the cursor in the content text box where you want the module output to appear.**

2. **Type the following code into the text box: {loadposition modulepositionname}, where "modulepositionname" is the name you want to use for this specific Module Position Holder.**

3. **Click the Save icon on the toolbar.** The system saves the article with the new Module Position Holder in place and exits the Edit Article workspace, returning you to the Article Manager.

4. **Click the Module Manager option, under the Extensions menu.** The Module Manager loads.

5. **Click the name of the module you want to place inside the article.** The Edit Module workspace opens.

6. **Click the Position combo box, and in the empty field that appears, type the name you gave the Module Position inside the article.** In this example, that name would be modulepositionname.

7. **Click the Save icon.** The system saves your changes, the Module Editing dialog box closes, and you return to the Module Manager.

NOTE

Take special note of the syntax used by the code: {loadposition xxx}, where xxx is the name of the Module Position Holder. You can use any name you want for the Module Position Holder, as long as the name is unique.

As a general rule, it is better not to use a common name for Module Position Holders placed inside of articles. A unique and distinctive name for the Module Position Holder avoids confusion with traditional Module Position Holders and avoids the need to make sure that there is a menu selection for the page; you can simply set the module's Menu Assignment to All, without fear that the module will appear in undesirable pages or positions.

TIP

The capability to place modules inside articles is enabled by the Joomla! plug-in named Content - Load Module. By default, the Content - Load Module plug-in is enabled, but if for some reason it is not, then you need to enable it from the Plug-in Manager before you can use this technique.

 The Plug-in Manager and the Content - Load Module plug-in are discussed in more detail in Chapter 19.

Bringing External Content into Your Site

Creating content for a site and then keeping that content current and compelling is one of the biggest challenges of site ownership. Joomla! provides tools that enable you to bring external content into your site, thereby providing you with fresh and updated content created by others. The various tools and techniques available in the default system are covered in the following sections.

Using iframe wrappers

A wrapper is an iframe that allows you to display the contents of a URL inside of either a module or the content area of a page. The wrapper essentially creates a page within a page, where the embedded page can be either from your own site, or from an external source. The page that is being wrapped maintains all its functionality, including navigation and other features.

Wrappers are used most frequently to perform one of the following tasks:

- Display another page from your Joomla! site, for example, a form
- Display a non-Joomla! page that is located on your server
- Display a page that is located on a different server
- Display output from an application that is located on your server

CAUTION

Although wrappers provide an easy way to display third-party content inside your site, you must be careful to avoid infringing on the intellectual property rights of others. Unless you have the permission of the site owner, displaying the content of another site inside your site is not appropriate, especially if doing so gives others the impression that the content is yours.

7

To create a wrapper inside of the content area of a page, you use the Wrapper Menu Item Type. To wrap a web page and display it inside of a module position, you use the Wrapper module. In either case, you can use the configuration options to gain limited control over the appearance of the wrapper. Note, however, that you generally have very little control over what happens within a wrapper unless you also control the web page that is being wrapped.

To create a wrapper that is displayed in the content area of your site, you will probably want to create a menu item using the Wrapper menu item type. Follow these steps to do so:

1. **Log into the admin system.**
2. **Under the Menu option on the main admin menu, click the name of the menu where you want to add the link to the wrapped content.** The Menu Manager opens.
3. **Click the New icon.** The New Menu Item workspace appears.
4. **From the Menu Item Type combo box, select Wrapper.**
5. **Enter a name for the new menu item in the Menu Title field.**
6. **Click the Advanced Options tab.** The tab comes to the front.
7. **In the URL field, enter the URL you want to display inside the wrapper.** This is a required field.
8. **Customize other fields as you desire; all other fields are optional.**
9. **Click the Save icon.** The new page is created; when viewed, the contents of the wrapper will be fetched from the external server and displayed inside the content area of the page.

 See Chapter 8 for details on the Wrapper Menu Item Type, and go to Chapter 17 for more information on the Wrapper module.

To create a wrapper that is displayed in a module position, you need to create a Wrapper module. Follow these steps:

1. **Log in to the admin system of your site.**

2. **Go to the Extensions menu and click the Module Manager option.** The Module Manager opens.

3. **Click the New icon on the toolbar.** The Select a Module Type dialog box opens.

4. **Click the Wrapper option.** The new module workspace opens.

5. **Enter a title for your new module.** This is a required field.

6. **Select a position for the module's placement, via the Position combo box.** This determines where on the page the module will appear.

7. **Click the Basic Options tab.** The tab comes to the front.

8. **In the URL field, enter the URL you want to display inside the wrapper.** This is a required field.

9. **Set the Width and Height to make sure the iframe doesn't break your template.**

10. **Click the Advanced Options tab and set any appearance preferences you may have.**

11. **Click the Menu Assignment tab.** The tab comes to the front.

12. **Use the Module Assignment combo box to choose which pages will show the new module.**

13. **Click the Save icon on the toolbar.** The system creates and saves your new module and exits the Module editing workspace, returning you to the Module Manager.

Displaying syndicated content

Syndication, which includes RSS feeds, Atom feeds, and the like, provides a convenient source of ready-to-use content. Joomla! gives you two methods for bringing syndicated content into your site: the Newsfeed component and the Feed Display module.

To display newsfeed content within the content area of the page, you use the Newsfeed component in conjunction with one of the Newsfeed Menu Item Types. Though the Newsfeed component is most commonly used to aggregate multiple syndicated newsfeeds and display them based upon categories, you can also use the Menu Item Type named Single Newsfeed to display the contents of a single feed within the content area of a page, as shown in Figure 7.8.

FIGURE 7.8

Output generated by the Newsfeed component

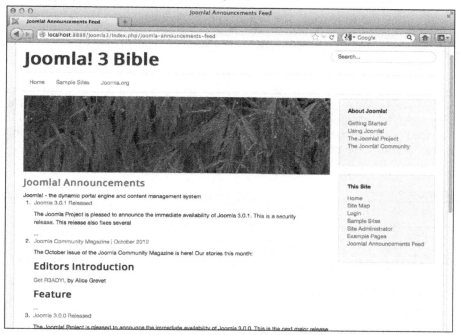

To display the output of an RSS feed in the content area of a page, follow these steps:

> **NOTE**
> This example assumes that you have already added the feeds into your Newsfeed component.

1. Log into the admin system.
2. Under the Menu option on the main admin menu, click the name of the menu where you want to add the link to the RSS content. The Menu Manager opens.
3. Click the New icon. The New Menu Item workspace appears.
4. From the Menu Item Type combo box, select Newsfeed and then choose the variation you want to employ. For this example, select Single Newsfeed.
5. From the Feed combo box, select the feed you want to display. The contents of the combo box come from the feeds you have already added to the Newsfeed component.
6. Enter a name for the new menu item in the Menu Title field.
7. Click the Advanced Options tab. The tab comes to the front.

8. **In the URL field, enter the URL of the feed.** This is a required field.

9. **Customize any other fields you want; all other fields are optional.**

10. **Click the Save icon.** The system creates the menu item.

 See Chapter 14 for a detailed discussion of how to use the Newsfeed component.

Alternatively, if you want to display feed content in a module position, you can use the Joomla! Feed Display module. The Feed Display module is independent of the Newsfeed component. Instead of drawing content from one of the newsfeeds contained in the Newsfeed component, you input the URL of the newsfeed into the module parameters. Figure 7.9 shows the Feed Display module in action.

FIGURE 7.9

Output generated by the Feed Display module

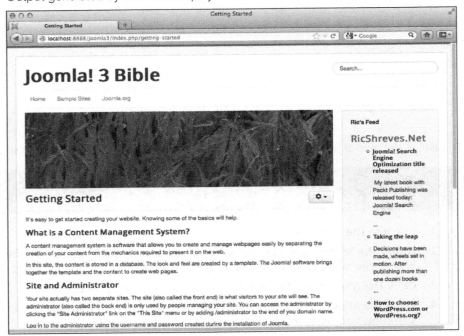

To create a module displaying an RSS feed, follow these steps:

1. **Log in to the admin system of your site.**

2. **Go to the Extensions menu and click the Module Manager option.** The Module Manager opens.

3. **Click the New icon on the toolbar.** The Select a Module Type dialog box opens.

4. **Click the Feed Display option.** The new module workspace opens.

5. **Enter a title for your new module.** This is a required field.

6. **Select a position for the module's placement, via the Position combo box.** This determines where on the page the module will appear.

7. **Click the Basic Options tab.** The tab comes to the front.

8. **In the Feed URL field, enter the URL of the feed.** This is a required field.

9. **Click the Advanced Options tab and set any appearance preferences you may have.**

10. **Click the Menu Assignment tab.** The tab comes to the front.

11. **Use the Module Assignment combo box to choose which pages will show the new module.**

12. **Click the Save icon on the toolbar.** The system creates and saves your new module and exits the Module editing workspace, returning you to the Module Manager.

 Turn to Chapter 17 to find out more about the Feed Display module.

Managing Content from the Front End

While the vast majority of site administrators manage their site content exclusively through the Joomla! admin interface, the system does provide the option to manage content from the front end. The technique has limitations, but it is a useful option that you may find attractive. In the following sections, I discuss the advantages and limitations of using this option.

Understanding the advantages and the limitations

One of the more under-used and under-documented features of Joomla! is the front-end content management functionality. The system is set up by default to allow certain classes of users to be able to submit, edit, and publish content from the front end of the website. This functionality is intended to give administrators the option to open up the site for community contribution without having to give all the users access to the admin system of their website.

> **TIP**
> As a matter of site security, you want to restrict access to the admin system to the smallest number of users possible.

Front-end content management has several significant limitations:

- It is not possible to create or manage categories or menu items from the front end.
- Authors cannot edit their own articles prior to publication.
- You must consider carefully the suitability of the site template. While the administrator template is tailored to handling the content-editing window and the WYSIWYG editor, front-end content management has to be done inside a site template.
- The system lacks a proper alert system to automatically notify higher-level users when content has been added to the system or is waiting to be edited or published.

NOTE

While there is no active notification system for new content, newly created articles do appear on the admin dashboard, under the heading Recently Added Articles. This gives users with access to the admin system the ability to easily see new articles that have been submitted and require review or publication.

Though submitting content from the front end is useful for providing your site users with a way to contribute to your site, as a site administrator you are unlikely to want to manage your content from the front end. Front-end content management is generally slower and more difficult than working from within the admin system because when you work from the front end of the site, you don't have access to the full range of the admin system's content management tools. For the same reason, the users that you assign to edit the articles may prefer to work through the admin system. You can decide whether your site security concerns outweigh the practical advantages of granting back-end access.

TIP

You may want to consider installing a clean and fast template with a wide content area on your site. You can then assign that template specifically to the Submit an Article Menu Item. Doing this gives your content contributors a suitable workspace. Note, however, that although this technique provides a suitable interface for article creation, it does not help you with editing content from the front end; published articles use the template to which the articles are assigned. See Chapter 20 for a discussion of installing and assigning templates.

Enabling user-created content

The first step to setting up front-end content management is to create users with the necessary privileges. To contribute or edit content on the front end, a user must have privileges higher than a Registered User (Author status or higher). Joomla! comes with three user groups that are tailored to facilitate content creation from the front end: Author, Editor, and Publisher. I will now discuss each group in more detail.

Using the Author group for content creation

Of all the user groups that are useful for front-end content management, Authors enjoy the fewest privileges and the most restrictions. An author can perform a limited set of front-end content management tasks, including the following:

- Create new articles
- Assign the article to a category
- Schedule an article (though it will not publish until approved by someone with at least Publisher access)
- Assign the article to the front page
- Create article metadata
- Change the category assignment of her published articles
- Edit her published articles

Authors cannot publish their articles, nor can they edit the work of others. Also, unlike Editors and Publishers, Authors cannot edit unpublished articles — not even their own.

CAUTION

Because Authors lack the ability to edit unpublished articles, once an Author clicks the Save icon on his article, he loses the ability to edit the article! This problem can be significant because it means that the Author must create the article and do any revisions on it before he clicks the Save icon. When it is saved, it goes into the queue where it has to be approved by a higher-level user. After the article is approved and published, the Author can edit it.

Providing the Editor group for editorial review

The second user group relevant to front end content management is the Editor group. Members of this group enjoy more privileges than Authors, but are still unable to control publication. Editors are able to perform the following tasks:

- Create new articles
- Assign the article to a category
- Schedule the article (though it will not be published until approved by someone with at least Publisher access)
- Assign the article to the front page
- Create article metadata
- Change the category assignment of articles
- Edit any article, published or unpublished

The key difference between an Author and an Editor is that an Editor can make changes to any article, regardless of who wrote it or its publication state.

Using the Publisher group to manage publication

The Publisher user group is by far the most useful of the three dedicated front-end content management user groups. Publishers can perform all the key functions necessary to create and publish content on a site:

- Create new articles
- Assign an article to a category
- Schedule the article
- Assign the article to the front page
- Create article metadata
- Change the category assignment of articles
- Edit any article, published or unpublished
- Publish or unpublish an article

Although the Publisher user group has significant privileges, there are several key content management functions that they lack. Publishers cannot perform the following tasks:

- Create new categories
- Copy, move, or delete categories
- Create, modify, or delete menus
- Create, modify, or delete menu items

All the tasks listed immediately above require back-end admin system access.

> **TIP**
>
> The Manager user group is another option to consider. Managers are the lowest-level user that is granted back-end admin system access. The privileges they enjoy are greater than those enjoyed by Publishers. Not only can they manage categories and menu items, but they also have access to the more powerful and easy-to-use content management tools located in the admin system. As a result, you may want to consider granting one or more users Manager level access as an alternative to Publisher access.

> **NOTE**
>
> You can tailor the permissions granted to these groups, or to specific users. You can also create your own groups if you prefer. Working with users and user groups are discussed in detail in Chapter 10.

Providing access to the tools

In addition to making sure that you have users with the proper permissions, you must also make sure that all the tools your users need are set to the appropriate access level. The access level named *Special* is intended to help enable front-end content management. Only users assigned to the Author group or higher are able to view items that have been set to Special; therefore you want to set the access levels of the menu items intended for your content contributors to Special in order to limit their access. Figure 7.10 shows the page as it looks to a user with permission to add new content.

FIGURE 7.10

The site as it appears to an authenticated user with permission to contribute content. Note the User Menu in the top-right corner and the gear-shaped editing icons next to the article titles.

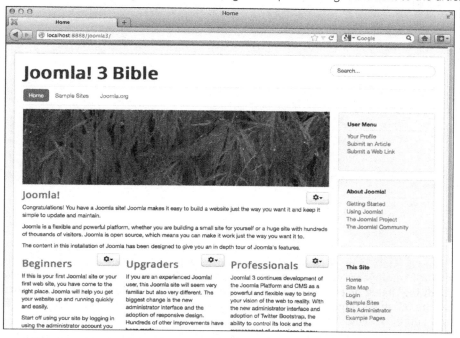

The article submission form is the key to front end content creation. By default, the system has included in the User Menu a menu item named Submit an Article, as shown in Figure 7.10. Clicking the Submit an Article link takes the user to a page containing a blank article form, thereby allowing the user to create a new article and assign it to a category. Figure 7.11 shows the Add New Article workspace as it appears from the front end of the site.

FIGURE 7.11

The Add New Article workspace on the front end of the site

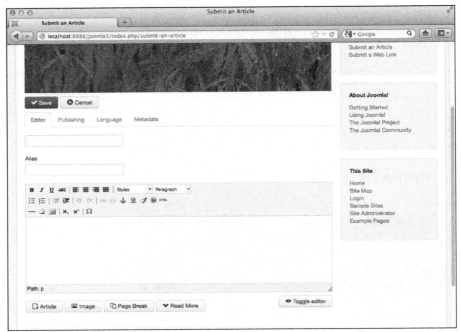

Editing is enabled by default; whenever a user with appropriate access levels is logged in, an edit icon appears on each article, as shown in Figure 7.10. Clicking the edit icon opens an editing dialog box inside the current template, thereby allowing the user to make and save her changes. Figure 7.12 shows the Edit an Article workspace as it appears from the front end of the site.

> **TIP**
>
> If you do not want to use the default user menu, you need to provide some other way for users to access the content submission form. There is a dedicated Menu Item Type that provides this functionality: Create Article.

 Managing menus and creating new menu items are covered in Chapter 8.

FIGURE 7.12

The Edit an Article workspace on the front end of the site

Summary

In this chapter, I looked at a variety of advanced content management tools and features that you can use to enhance and enrich your site. I discussed the following topics:

- Creating custom content modules
- Displaying a list of the site's newest articles
- Displaying a list of the site's most popular content
- Displaying a random image on your site
- Helping visitors discover related content items
- Placing modules inside your articles
- Bringing external content into your site using wrappers and newsfeeds
- Setting up and using front-end content management

In the next chapter I focus on the menu system and how you can use it to reveal site content to your users and create a useable, easily navigable website with Joomla! 3.

Working with the Menu System

Menus are used to create the principal navigation links on the pages of your website. The way you structure access to your content through the use of menus has a tremendous effect on the usability of your site and how your site visitors perceive the site. A hard-to-use menu structure makes a hard-to-use site.

Joomla! provides a number of tools for creating and controlling menus. There are three constituent parts to the Joomla! menu system: *menu items* are the links the users see on the site; these menu items are grouped together into containers called *menus*; menus are displayed on the page through the use of *menu modules*. Mastering the menu system means gaining an awareness of how to create and manage these three parts.

In this chapter, I go through the creation and management of menus and menu items and I explain the role played by menu modules.

Introducing the Menu Manager

The Menu Manager is a standard Joomla! component included with the default system. You use the Menu Manager to create and manage all the menus on your site. The Menu Manager displays not only a list of the menus in the system but also information about the contents of the menus, including the number of items on each menu, the publication state of those items, and which modules are associated with the menus. The interface also provides access to utilities and tools that allow you to edit existing menus and to adjust configuration settings common to all menus.

In Joomla!, the creation of a menu is only the first step you need to take to set up the site navigation. Because a menu is simply a container, after you have created it, you need to populate it with the links your visitors will use to navigate the site; those links are called *menu items*. Additionally, you need to create a *menu module*, which is used to control the placement of the menu on the pages of your site.

NOTE

I cover working with menu items in the next section.

To begin, I will look first at the Menu Manager, as it is the key interface for creating and managing the site's menus.

To access the Menu Manager, you select the Menus option on the admin navigation bar, and then select the Menu Manager option. The Menu Manager interface loads in your browser. Figure 8.1 shows the Menu Manager as it appears in Joomla! 3 with the sample data installed.

FIGURE 8.1

The Menu Manager

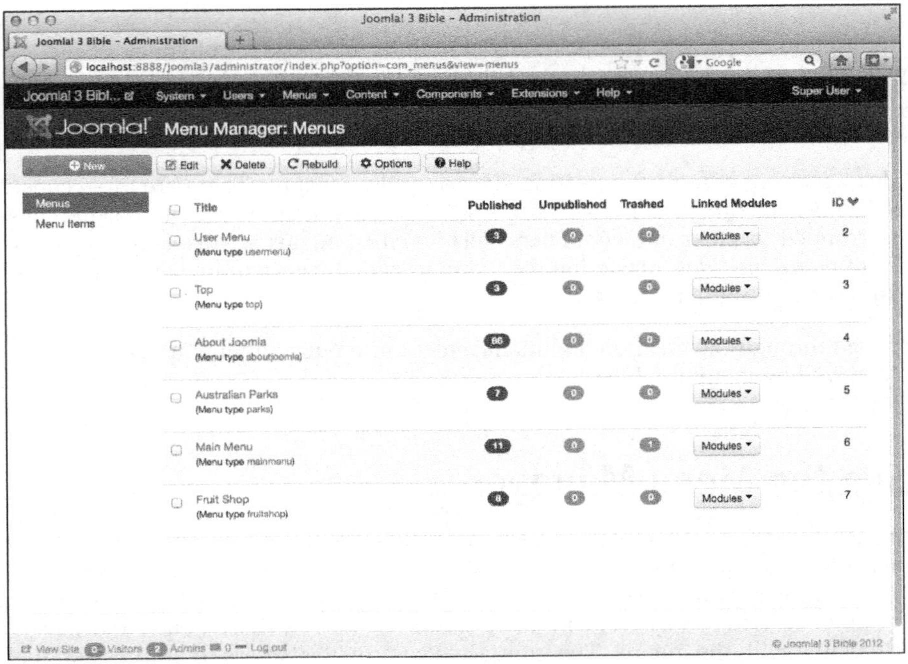

The toolbar at the top of the Menu Manager provides quick access to the following functions:

- **New.** Click to add a new menu.
- **Edit.** Select a menu from the list and then click this button to edit the menu details.
- **Delete.** Select a menu from the list and then click this button to delete the menu.
- **Rebuild.** Click if you are experiencing problems with your menus. Clicking this button forces the system to rebuild the menu tables in the database. You should not normally need this tool; use it sparingly.
- **Options.** Click to open the Menu Manager Configuration workspace in the Global Configuration Manager. Use the options on Menu Manager Configuration workspace to control global parameters relating to your site's menus.

- **Help.** Click to access the online Help files related to the active screen.

The main content area of the screen contains a list of all the menus in your Joomla! site. The columns provided are

- **Check box (no label).** Click to select a menu; you use this feature in conjunction with several of the toolbar options referenced in the previous list.
- **Title.** Shows the full name of the menu. Click to jump to the menu's Menu Item Manager. Note that the type of each menu also appears in smaller letters; click the menu type name to jump to the menu's editing workspace.
- **Published.** Shows the number of menu items published on the menu.
- **Unpublished.** Shows the number of menu items unpublished on the menu.
- **Trashed.** Shows the number of menu items currently in the trash.

8

- **Linked Modules.** Indicates which menu module is associated with this menu. Clicking the Modules button opens a display that shows you the name of the module, the access level, and the position it is assigned to.
- **ID.** Indicates the system-generated user ID number.

Creating and Managing Menus

In Joomla!, menus act as containers for the actual links that your site visitors use to navigate the site. The first step to creating a navigation structure for your site is to create a menu, which you will later populate with links. You can create as many menus as you like, or you can run your site off a single menu; the choice is yours. Each menu can hold a large number of items, and those items can be arranged into parent-child relationships to create hierarchies that reflect the content structure of the site.

In this section, I look at how you can create new menus for your site and manage existing menus. I also look at the supporting menu module that is needed to display your new menu.

Adding a new menu to your site

To create a new menu, click the New button on the toolbar at the top of the Menu Manager. When you click that button, the Add Menu workspace opens in your browser. Figure 8.2 shows the Add Menu workspace.

The toolbar at the top of the Menu Manager provides quick access to the following functions:

- **Save.** Click to save your work without exiting from the Add New Menu workspace.
- **Save & Close.** Click to save your work and exit the Add New Menu workspace.
- **Save & New.** Click to save your work, close the current Add New Menu workspace, and open another Add New Menu workspace.
- **Cancel.** Click to cancel the task and exit the Add New Menu workspace.
- **Help.** Click to access the online Help files related to the active screen.

FIGURE 8.2

The Add Menu workspace

The fields in the workspace are

- **Title.** Enter a name for the menu; this field is required. The name you enter here will be used to identify your menu in the Menu Manager.

- **Menu type.** Enter a machine-friendly name for the menu, that is, numbers and letters only with no spaces. This field is required. The system will use this name to identify the menu, and it will also be displayed with the menu's title in the Menu Manager. This name must be unique.

- **Description.** Use this optional field to enter a short description of the menu. This is particularly useful if your site has a large number of menus, or where you rarely access your admin system and are prone to forget which menu fulfills which function on the site.

To create a new menu, follow these steps:

1. **Log in to the admin system of your site.**

2. **Click the Menu Manager option under the Menus heading on the admin navigation bar.** The Menu Manager loads in your browser.

3. **On the Menu Manager interface, click the New button on the toolbar at the top of the Menu Manager.** The Add Menu workspace opens, as shown in Figure 8.2.

4. **In the Title field, type a name for the menu.** This field is required.

5. **In the Menu type field, enter a machine-readable name for the menu.** This field, which is required, permits only lowercase letters and numbers with no spaces.

6. **Add a Description if you want; this is optional.**

7. **Click the Save & Close button on the toolbar.** The workspace closes and returns you to the Menu Manager.

Once you have created the menu, you need to associate it with a menu module in order to be able to display the menu on the front end of the site. After you create your menu and return to the Menu Manager, you see that the Module column for that menu has a reminder note: Add a module for this menu type. Though you do not need to do this immediately after you create your new menu, at some point you will need to follow these next steps to complete adding a module to your menu for display:

1. **On the Menu Manager interface, click the text, Add a module for this menu type.** The new Module Menu workspace opens, as shown in Figure 8.3.

2. **Enter a name for the module in the Title field; this field is required.**

3. **From the Position combo box, select a position where you want the menu to appear.**

4. **Click the Menu Assignment tab.** The tab comes to the front.

5. **Select the pages where you want this menu to appear.**

TIP

If you want this menu to be visible throughout the site, select the On all pages option.

6. **Complete any other fields you desire; all other fields are optional.**

7. **Click Save, and your new module is created.**

NOTE

All menu modules are of the module type mod_mainmenu. It is possible to create multiple menu modules for a single menu. This technique is used primarily to create submenus, as discussed later in this chapter.

 Creating and managing site modules is discussed in Chapter 17.

FIGURE 8.3

The workspace for adding a new menu module

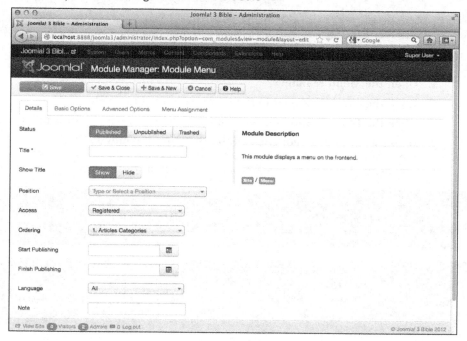

Editing and deleting menus

You can edit existing menus from the Menu Manager. To edit a menu, either click the menu type in the Title column of the Menu Manager, or select the check box next to the menu and click the Edit button on the Menu Manager toolbar. Regardless of which method you use, the system opens the Edit Menu workspace. The Edit Menu workspace is identical to the New Menu workspace, with the same fields and requirements as discussed in the preceding section.

To make changes to a menu, you simply alter the desired fields in the Edit Menu workspace, and then click Save on the toolbar. Any changes you make are applied immediately.

You can delete a menu by using the Menu Manager. Menu deletion does not use the Trash function; rather, it deletes all the elements immediately. Deleting a menu results in the removal of the actual menu, the items assigned to the menu, and the menu's module.

> **NOTE**
> While it is possible to delete a menu module without deleting the related menu, it is not possible to delete a menu without deleting the associated module.

To delete a menu, follow these steps:

1. **Open the Menu Manager.**
2. **Click the check box next to the menu you want to delete.**
3. **Click the Delete button on the toolbar.** A confirmation pop-up window opens.
4. **If you want to proceed, click OK on the pop-up window.** The system deletes the menu, the menu items, and the related menu module and then returns you to the Menu Manager. You can click Cancel to abort this process.

> **CAUTION**
> Deleting a menu also deletes the menu items associated with that menu and the related menu module. Note that the menu items are not moved to the trash — they are deleted completely!

> **CAUTION**
> Do not delete the menu containing your site's default menu item! In the default configuration, this is the Main menu, which includes the home page. In the default configuration, the home page link is the default menu item. If you delete the menu containing the default menu item, your site does not function.

Working with the Menu Item Manager

Where the Joomla! Menu Manager is designed for handling the site's menus, the Menu Item Manager provides the interface for managing the items on each of the site's menus. Each menu has its own Menu Item Manager, and that manager contains all the items on that menu.

Unlike the Menu Manager, there is no link on the administrator menus to an option labeled Menu Item Manager. You access each Menu Item Manager by clicking on the name of the menu you want to edit under the Menus option on the main administration menu. Figure 8.4 shows a typical Menu Item Manager.

FIGURE 8.4

The Menu Item Manager interface, showing the Main menu in Joomla! 3 with the sample data installed

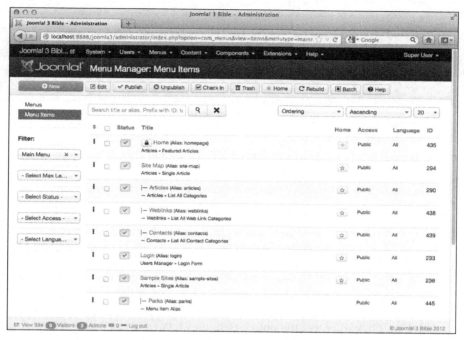

The toolbar at the top of the Menu Item Manager provides quick access to the following functions:

- **New.** Click to add a new menu item. Creating new menu items is discussed in detail in the next section.

- **Edit.** Select a menu item from the list and then click this button to edit the menu item's details.

- **Publish.** Select one or more menu items from the list and then click this button to publish them.

- **Unpublish**. Select one or more menu items from the list and then click this button to unpublish them.

TIP

You can also use the Publish and Unpublish buttons to unarchive and restore items from the trash.

- **Check In.** Select a menu item and then click this button to force the menu item's editing workspace to close and thereby "check in" the menu item.

> **NOTE**
> A menu item that is open for editing is blocked from use by other administrators. If you want to perform operations on a menu item that is currently open, then you must first close that menu item. This is known as *checking in* the menu item.

> **CAUTION**
> The Check-in feature is necessary, but it can also cause problems. If your site has multiple administrators, be careful with this command. If someone else is working on the menu item when you execute this command, it can cause her to lose her unsaved work.

- **Trash.** Select a menu item from the list and then click this button to move that menu item to the trash.
- **Home.** Select a menu item from the list and then click this button to designate that item as your site's home page.

 See Chapter 9 for an extended discussion of managing the home page of your website.

- **Rebuild.** Click to rebuild the menu table in the database. You should not normally need to do this, but if your site is large, or you have made a number of changes to the menu item structure, then using this option can help optimize the site and improve performance.
- **Batch.** Select multiple menu items, and then click this button to batch-apply processes to those menu items. The dialog box that appears enables you to copy or move multiple menu items in one simple operation.
- **Help.** Click to access the online Help files related to the active screen.

Below the toolbar and above the list of menu items are a search tool and three sorting tools to help you manage long lists of menu items:

- When you type a word or phrase into the Search field and then click the magnifying glass icon, the system searches your list of menu items for the query and then displays the results of the search. To clear the screen and return to a full listing, you click the button marked with the X.
- The Ordering combo box determines which column of the menu item display is used for the sort order.

> **TIP**
> You can also sort any column by clicking the column header.

- The Ascending combo box determines whether the menu items appear in ascending or descending order.
- The combo box on the far right controls the number of menu items that appear on the page. You can alter the default value by changing the List Length parameter in the Global Configuration Manager.

The main content area of the screen contains a list of all the items on the menu. The columns provided are

- **Sort Order (vertical double arrows).** Click the arrows to change the sort order, or click and hold any of the icons immediately to the left of a menu item title and drag the menu item to change its location on the menu.

- **Article Selection (unlabeled check box).** Click a check box to select a menu item; this is needed if you want to use several of the toolbar options. You can make multiple selections by clicking the check box next to multiple menu items. Click the check box at the top of the column to select all menu items on the page.

- **Status.** A green arrow indicates that a menu item is published. Click this check box to toggle the state of the menu item between published and unpublished.

- **Title.** This column displays the full name of the menu item. Click the name to edit the menu item's details.

- **Home.** This column shows a list of menu items eligible for use as the site's home page, with a yellow star indicating the active home page item. You can click the star to toggle the state between active and inactive.

- **Access.** This column shows the access level set for the menu item.

- **Language.** This column shows the languages in which the category is available.

- **ID.** This column shows the system-generated user ID number. This is used internally by the system and cannot be changed by the user.

At the top of the left column are two links that let you jump quickly between the Menu Manager and the Menu Items Manager. Below those links is a set of filters that can help you manage long lists of categories:

- **Main Menu.** This combo box lets you jump quickly between menus; it mirrors the choices under the Menu option on the main admin navigation bar at the top of the page.

- **Select Max Levels.** This combo box controls the number of levels of menu items that appear. If your site has a complex hierarchy, this can greatly simplify the view of the list of menu items in the Menu Item Manager. To reset this filter, change the combo box back to the default setting, Select Max Levels.

- **Select Status.** This combo box allows you to filter and display the menu items according to whether they are published, unpublished, archived, or trashed. This provides an easy way to identity all menu items that are currently active on the site. To reset this filter, change the combo box back to the default setting, Select Status.

- **Select Access.** This combo box lets you filter the list of menu items by access level. To reset this filter, change the combo box back to the default setting, Select Access.

- **Select Language.** This combo box lets you filter the list of menu items by language. To reset this filter, change the combo box back to the default setting, Select Language.

8

Creating and Managing Menu Items

From the perspective of your site visitors, Joomla! menu items are nothing more than the choices that are listed on the menus. For the site administrator, however, menu items are far more important. The decisions made during the process of creating menu items will affect how the resulting page appears on the screen.

You create new items from within the Menu Item Manager. You edit existing items from the same location, either by clicking the name of the menu item or by selecting Edit from the Menu Item Manager toolbar. The Menu Item Manager also provides controls to copy items or to move them to the trash for later deletion.

Adding new menu items to a menu

The Menu Item Manager includes a wizard-type process for creating new menu items. You start the wizard by clicking the New button on the top toolbar. During the process of creating a new item, you must select a menu item type, specify the name and target of the item, and configure the various parameter options.

Numerous menu item types are included in the Joomla! system. The various options are detailed in the following list. Adding other extensions into your Joomla! installation may result in more menu item types being available to you.

> **NOTE**
> Take a moment to become familiar with the various menu item types, as they vary widely according to the content and functionality with which they are associated. Remember that the choice to use one type over another will have a significant impact on the layout of the resulting page.

Before I take you through creating new menu items, let's take a quick look at the New Menu Item workspace, as there are a number of options here that you need to understand. To access the New Menu Item workspace, you click the New button on the Menu Item Manager toolbar. The New Menu Item workspace is shown in Figure 8.5.

The toolbar at the top of the New Menu Item workspace provides quick access to the following functions:

- **Save.** Click to save your work without exiting from the New Menu Item workspace.
- **Save & Close.** Click this button to save your work and exit the New Menu Item workspace.
- **Save & New.** Click to save your work, close the current New Menu Item workspace, and open another New Menu Item workspace.
- **Cancel.** Click to cancel the task and exit the New Menu Item workspace.
- **Help.** Click to access the online Help files related to the active screen.

FIGURE 8.5

The New Menu Item workspace

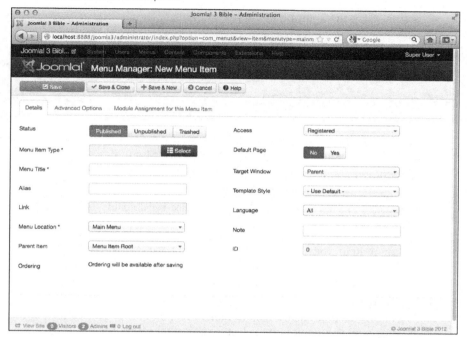

Below the toolbar you can see a set of tabs. These tabs provide you with access to secondary functionality associated with menu items:

- **Details.** This is the crucial tab for creating new menu items. I discuss the fields on this tab later in this section.

- **Advanced Options.** The options in this tab allow you to modify link attributes, page display options, and metadata options for this specific menu item.

- **Module Assignment for this Menu Item.** This tab displays a list of modules in the system. You use this tab to determine which modules will be visible on the page that is the target of this menu item.

TIP

You can also manage module assignment by editing individual modules from the Module Manager.

I will now go through each of the tabs on the New Menu Item workspace and review the options they contain.

The Details tab is the primary workspace for creating and editing the menu item, and it is divided into two areas. The left column of the workspace contains the following fields:

- **Status.** Click the appropriate button to Publish, Unpublish, or Trash the menu item.
- **Menu Item Type.** Click the Select button to open a pop-up window containing a complete list of the available menu item types; I discuss these in the next section.

NOTE

Your selection of menu item type determines which fields are visible on this tab and the contents of some of them.

- **Menu Title.** Enter the name of the item as you want it to appear on the menu as an option for your site visitors and on the Menu Item Manager.
- **Alias.** Enter an alias to use as the URL for the target; this option assumes that you have search engine–friendly URLs enabled on your site.

 See Chapter 25 for a discussion of enabling search engine–friendly URLs.

- **Link.** Enter a link that the system attaches to the menu item. When visitors click the menu item, they are taken to the linked page. Note that the value for this field is often supplied automatically, depending on the menu item type you selected.
- **Menu Location.** Select the menu where this menu item appears.
- **Parent Item.** Set the level of the menu item, that is, whether it is a top-level item or a submenu item. Select Top to make this item a top-level item. If you want to create a new submenu item, select a parent item from the list.
- **Ordering.** Set the order of this item relative to others on the same menu.

NOTE

The Ordering controls are not available until after you save your menu item for the first time.

The right column of the workspace contains the following fields:

- **Access.** Specify the access level for the menu item. The options shown here reflect the user groups that exist in the system.
- **Default Page.** Select Yes to make the target of this menu item the home page of your site.
- **Target Window.** Use this field to specify where the link will open when it is clicked. Select Parent to open the target in the same window.
- **Template Style.** Use this control to assign the target of the link to a specific template.
- **Language.** Assign a language to this menu item, or select All to make it available to all languages on your site.

- **Note.** Enter reminder or descriptive notations in this field for yourself or your fellow site administrators.

- **ID.** The value of this field is set automatically by the system and cannot be edited by you.

Click the Advanced Options tab to view additional fields for the configuration of the menu item. The options on this tab can vary widely, depending on the menu item type you select.

NOTE

The next section includes a discussion of the parameters for each menu item type.

The final tab on this workspace is titled Module Assignment for this Menu Item. Click this tab to view all the modules on the site. Figure 8.6 shows the tab.

FIGURE 8.6

The Module Assignment for this Menu Item tab of the New Menu Item workspace

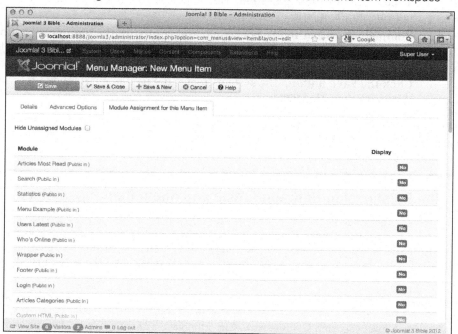

This list of modules shows you which modules will appear on the target of the menu item. Each module is marked as Yes, No, or All. Yes indicates that the module will appear on the target page. No means it will not appear. All means it will appear on all pages, including the menu item you are viewing. To modify any of the module assignments, click the name of the module; the system opens a pop-up window containing the module editing controls, where you can change the module's visibility settings.

To create a new menu item, follow these steps:

1. **Under the admin menu option labeled Menus, select the name of the menu to which you want to add a new item.** The Menu Item Manager opens.

2. **Click the New button on the toolbar.** The New Menu Item workspace opens in your browser. Figure 8.5 shows the interface.

3. **Select the desired menu item type.** This field is required.

> **NOTE**
>
> Later in this chapter I review all the Joomla! menu item types.

4. **Type a title for the menu item.** This field is required and provides the label that appears on the menu.

5. **Complete the other fields as needed, and configure the parameter options as you desire.** These options vary by menu item type, as I describe in the following section.

6. **Click the Save button.** The system creates the new menu item and returns you to the Menu Item Manager.

In the next section, I look in depth at the various menu item types and document their specific uses as well as the parameters associated with each type.

The Relationship Between Article and Menu Item Parameters

In addition to the parameters contained in the menu item types, the articles in your Joomla! system are also subject to two other groups of parameters: Article Manager parameters, and the Advanced parameters section of the Article Editing workspace. It is important to understand the hierarchical relationship between these three sets of parameters to avoid undesirable results caused by entering contradictory settings.

The Joomla! system works as follows: First, it examines the settings in the Advanced parameters of the Article Editing workspace. If a specific Yes/No, Show/Hide value is set, then those values are applied to the article and no further checking is done. However, if the values are set to Use Global, then the system looks next to the Component parameters set in the menu item type. If a specific Yes/No, Show/Hide value is set, then those values are applied to the article and no further checking is done. However, if the values are set to Use Global, then the system finally looks to the Article Manager parameters.

Understanding the various menu item types

In Joomla!, every menu item you create has to be associated with a *menu item type*. Menu item types are essentially preset page layouts. When you choose one menu item type over another, you affect the presentation of the content on the page. Some menu item types are narrowly tailored to fit certain types of content, while others are more general. In addition, each of the menu item types includes parameters that allow you to optimize the output to better suit your needs.

Each menu item type is intended for a specific use. You should try to match the type you select to the content you intend to display. A Login Form menu item type, for example, can never be used to hold an article. If you want to display an article, it is more appropriate to use the Single Article menu item type. Put another way, the menu item types are purpose-built: By selecting the menu item type that best matches the content, you find that the resulting layout tends to address the most common issues associated with that type of content. Additionally, most menu item types provide for some customization options via the Advanced Options tab in the menu item type workspace.

> **TIP**
>
> If you need more customization than is provided by the Advanced Options tab, then you might want create a custom template to handle your content.

The menu item types are grouped into nine categories:

- **Contacts.** Choices designed to display output from the Contact component.
- **Articles.** Layouts suitable for articles and archives.
- **Smart Search.** A layout specially designed for the search form.
- **Newsfeeds.** Layouts to handle the output of the Newsfeed component.
- **Search.** A layout tailored to search results.
- **Users Manager.** Layouts to handle various user-focused forms.
- **Weblinks.** Layouts suitable for use with the Weblinks component.
- **Wrapper.** A layout specifically for the iframe wrapper.
- **System Links.** Utility formats that allow you to perform common menu tasks, like adding dividers, or providing a link to an external URL.

> **TIP**
>
> You must select a menu item type when you create the menu item, but you can change it later by editing the menu item.

The menu item types within a group tend to share a number of common parameters, but they also frequently have at least a few unique parameters. In the following sections, I go through all the various menu item types in the default Joomla! 3 system, show you what they look like, and note the parameters involved.

8

Reviewing the Contacts group of menu item types

The menu item types in the Contacts group relate to the display of the output from the Contact component. The options here allow you to display contacts either individually or by category, and you can also provide contact forms that allow site visitors to send a message directly to a contact.

The group contains four menu item types, with each tailored to display a particular output:

- **List All Contact Categories.** Display in list format all the categories of contacts in the system.

- **List Contacts in a Category.** Display in list format all the contacts from a specific category.

- **Single Contact.** Display a single predetermined contact.

- **Featured Contacts.** Display a list of contacts marked as featured in the Contact component.

 You create and edit contacts through the Contact Manager component. Working with Contacts is discussed in Chapter 13.

The menu item types for this group share a number of common parameters. The Advanced Options tab on the menu item type workspace contains the following options, which are common to all four menu item types:

- **Contact Display Options.** The choices you make here establish what information about the contact is shown on the page.

- **Mail Options.** The first parameter here determines whether you show or hide a contact form from your site visitors; this is the contact form that is used to allow people to send a message to a specific contact. If you elect to show the form, the other options here are used to specify the parameters relating to the form.

- **Link Type Options.** The options in this section control the appearance of the links that appear as part of the contact's listing.

- **Page Display Options.** The options here are used to specify the page title, page heading, and any custom styling you want to use on the page.

- **Metadata Options.** The controls here allow you to specify metadata specific to the target of the menu item. The data that you input here overrides the global metadata for the target page only.

Next, I will look at each of the menu item types in the Contacts group and examine the unique aspects of each menu item type.

List All Contact Categories

This menu item type enables you to display on a page all the contact categories in the system, as shown in Figure 8.7.

FIGURE 8.7

Example showing the output of the List All Contact Categories menu item type

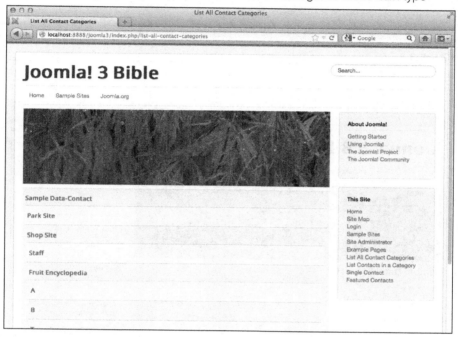

The List All Contact Categories menu item type contains several unique options.

- **On the Details tab:**
  - **Select a Top Level Category.** The value you select here determines which categories appear on the page. Select the value Root to display all the categories in the system. This is a required field.
- **On the Advanced Options tab:**
  - **Categories Options.** The options here control the layout of the categories listed on the first page (the top level).
  - **Category Options.** The options here control the layout when visitors click a specific category. The choices relate to the display of the category data.

- **List Layouts.** The options here control the layout when visitors click a specific category. The choices relate to the list display of the contacts.
- **Integration Options.** This option shows or hides an RSS feed link for the target of this menu item.

List Contacts in a Category

This menu item type enables you to display on a page all the published contacts from a given category, as shown in Figure 8.8.

FIGURE 8.8

The output of the List Contacts in a Category menu item type

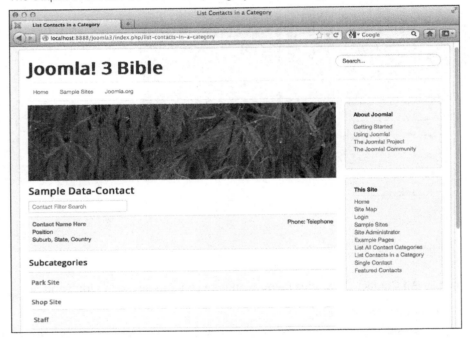

The List Contacts in a Category menu item type contains several unique options.

- **On the Details tab:**
  - **Select a Category.** The value you select here determines which category the list of contacts will be drawn from. This is a required field.

- **On the Advanced Options tab:**
  - **Category Options.** The options here control the layout when visitors click a specific category. The choices relate to the display of the category data.
  - **List Layouts.** The options here control the layout when visitors click a specific category. The choices relate to the list display of the contacts.
  - **Integration Options.** These options show or hide an RSS feed link for the target of this menu item.

Single Contact

This menu item type shows a single contact's details on a page, as shown in Figure 8.9. The Single Contact menu item type contains only one unique field, located on the Details tab. Select the name of the contact that you want to display. The options in this combo box come from the Contacts component. This is a required field.

FIGURE 8.9

An example of the Single Contact menu item type

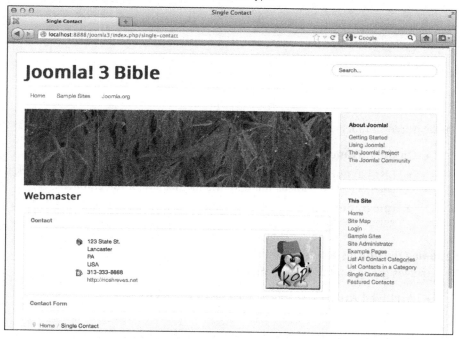

Featured Contacts

Use this menu item type to display a list of all the contacts marked as featured in the Contacts component, as shown in Figure 8.10.

FIGURE 8.10

Example showing the output of the Featured Contacts menu item type

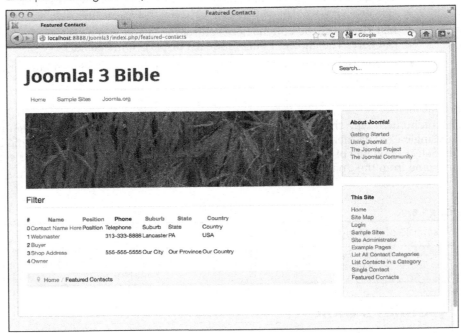

The Featured Contacts menu item type contains several unique options.

- **On the Advanced Options tab:**
  - **List Layouts.** The options here control the layout when visitors click a specific category. The choices relate to the list display of the contacts.
  - **Integration Options.** These options show or hide an RSS feed link for the target of this menu item.

Reviewing the Articles group of menu item types

The Articles group contains seven menu item types:

- **Archived Articles.** Displays a list of archived articles.
- **Single Article.** Displays a single predetermined article.
- **List All Categories.** Lists all the article categories on a page.
- **Category Blog.** Displays article introductions from a category, with multiple layout options.

- **Category List.** Displays a list of the articles in a predetermined category.
- **Featured Articles.** Shows a list of articles marked as featured, with multiple layout options.
- **Create Article.** A special purpose menu item type used for the creation of articles from the front end of the site.

The menu item types for this group share only a few common parameters. The Advanced Options tab on the menu item type workspace contains the following options, which are common to all of the Articles menu item types:

- **Link Type Options.** The options in this section control the appearance of the links on the page.
- **Page Display Options.** The options here are used to specify the page title, page heading, and any custom styling you want to use for the page.
- **Metadata Options.** The options here allow you to specify metadata specific to the target of the menu item. The data that you input here overrides the global metadata for the target page only.

Next, I will look at each of the menu item types in the Articles group and examine the unique aspects of each menu item type.

Archived Articles

You can use the Archived Article List format to create a page containing a list of the site's archived articles, as shown in Figure 8.11. The articles are organized by date, and the layout includes a handy set of filters to allow your site visitors to sort the articles by date.

 I discuss the process of archiving articles in Chapter 5.

The Advanced Options tab on Archived Articles menu item type contains several unique options:

- **Archive Options.** The options here control the ordering of the articles that appear on the page, as well as the number of articles displayed, the introductory text word count, and the visibility of any filters.
- **Article Options.** The Article Options relate to the display of the articles inside the archive. You use the choices here to control the information shown about each article.

FIGURE 8.11

Example of the Archived Articles menu item type in action

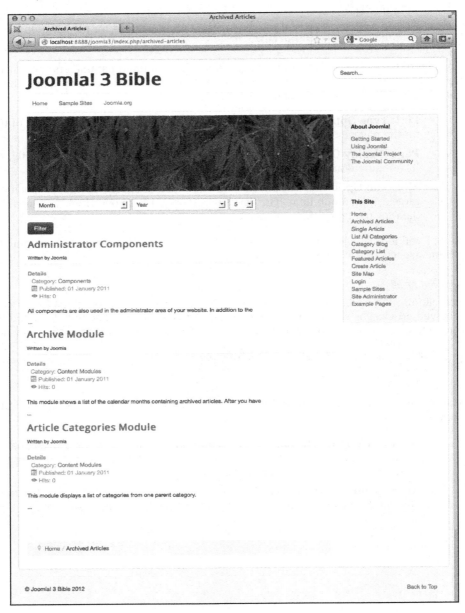

Single Article

You can use the Article Layout menu item type to display a single article on a page, as shown in Figure 8.12. This is probably the most commonly used menu item type, as it is the basis for the display of most of a typical site's content items.

FIGURE 8.12

Example of the output of the Single Article menu item type

The Single Article menu item type contains several unique options.

- **On the Details tab:**
  - **Select Article.** You must select an existing article for display on the page. This is a required field.
- **On the Advanced Options tab:**
  - **Article Options.** The Article Options relate to the display of the articles inside the archive. Use the choices here to control the information shown about each article.

Category Blog

This menu item type displays all of the articles in a category, laid out in a blog-type format. In Joomla!, a blog-type layout divides the content area of the page into three sections. At the top are one or more lead articles. Below the lead articles are the introductory articles, which you have the option to display in multiple columns. At the bottom of the content area of the page is a links area that shows a list of links to additional articles. You can control the number of articles, the number of columns, and the number of links through the parameters of this menu item type.

Figure 8.13 shows a Category Blog layout in the default configuration.

The Category Blog menu item type contains several unique options.

- **On the Details tab:**
  - **Choose a Category.** The value you select here determines which category the list of articles will be drawn from. This is a required field.
- **On the Advanced Options tab:**
  - **Category Options.** The options here control the layout of the category information on the page. You can see this information at the top of the content area in Figure 8.13.
  - **Blog Layout Options.** The options here allow you to customize the layout of the resulting page. You can specify the number of leading and introductory articles, and control the number of columns and the ordering of the articles.
  - **Article Options.** The Article Options relate to the display of the articles inside the blog. Use the choices here to control the information shown about each article.
  - **Integration Options.** These options show or hide an RSS feed link for the target of this menu item.

Category List

The Category List menu item type displays a list of all the articles in a particular category, as shown in Figure 8.14.

FIGURE 8.13

Example of the Category Blog menu item type in action

FIGURE 8.14

Example of the Category List menu item type layout

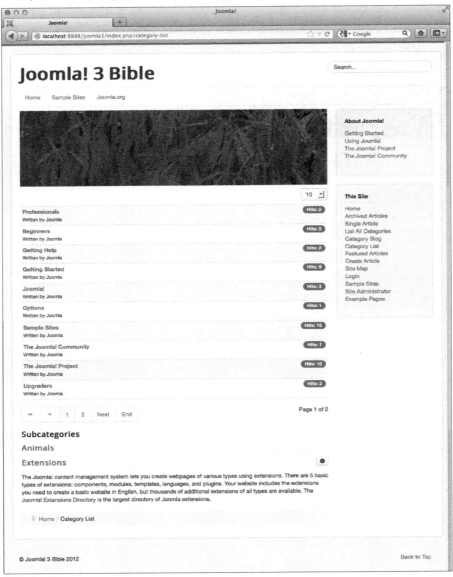

The Category List menu item type contains several unique options.

- **On the Details tab:**
  - **Choose a Category.** The value you select here determines which category to display. This is a required field.
- **On the Advanced Options tab:**
  - **Category Options.** The options here control the layout when visitors click a specific category. The choices relate to the display of the category data.
  - **List Layouts.** The options here control the layout when visitors click a specific category. The choices relate to the list display of the articles.
  - **Article Options.** The Article Options relate to the display of the articles inside the category. You use the choices here to control the information shown about each article.
  - **Integration Options.** These options show or hide an RSS feed link for the target of this menu item.

Featured Articles

This menu item type displays articles that are designated as featured. This menu item type is used by the default system for the front page of the site. At the top of the page are one or more lead articles, which span the width of the page. Below the lead articles are the introductory articles, which are typically displayed in multiple columns. You can control the number of articles and the number of columns through the Advanced Options tab.

Figure 8.15 shows a Featured Articles layout in the default configuration, that is, with one leading article and the introductory articles displayed in two columns.

The Featured Articles menu item type contains formatting parameters on the Advanced Options tab:

- **Layout Options.** The options here allow you to customize the layout. You can specify the number of leading and introductory articles, and control the number of columns and the ordering of the articles.
- **Article Options.** These options relate to the display of the articles. You use the choices here to control the information shown about each article.
- **Integration Options.** These options show or hide an RSS feed link for the target of this menu item.

8

FIGURE 8.15

Example of the Featured Articles layout

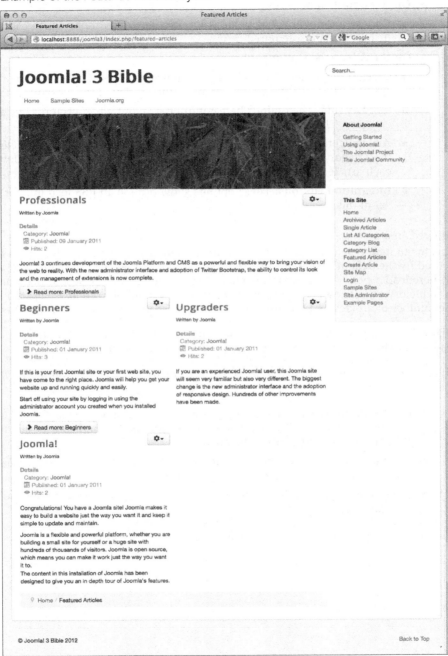

Create Article

The Create Article menu item type is used to create a page specifically for the purpose of allowing front-end users to add articles to the site, as shown in Figure 8.16. You do not assign content to this menu item type; rather, when you add a menu item of this type, an article creation form is automatically displayed.

> **NOTE**
>
> This menu item type is designed to be used only by those users assigned to the Author group or higher.

FIGURE 8.16

Example of the Create Article menu item type in action

The only unique parameters available for customization are found on the Advanced Options tab, under the Basic Options heading. If you want to add a default category where all new articles will be assigned, click Yes next to Default category, and then select the category from the combo box below.

TIP

If your site does not employ the front-end content creation process, there is no reason to create items of this menu item type.

Displaying the Smart Search form

The Smart Search group contains only one menu item type, named Search. This item type makes it possible to display the smart search form. It can also be configured to display a set of search results based on a predetermined query. In Figure 8.17, you see the output resulting from the use of this menu item type, configured to return results for the "iframe." Note that a search form also appears above the search results. The parameters allow some control over these features.

FIGURE 8.17

Example of the Search menu item type in action; in this case configured to display a predetermined query.

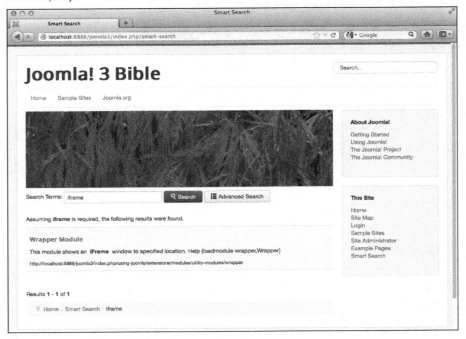

The Search menu item type has a number of parameters.

- **On the Details tab:**
  - **Search Query.** The text phrase you enter here is used to produce the search results on the page.
- **On the Advanced Options tab:**
  - **Basic Options.** The options here control the visibility of filters and the Advanced Search button, together with basic parameters relating to the description shown on the page.
  - **Advanced Options.** These options relate primarily to pagination and sorting. You can also find some of the RSS feed options here.
  - **Integration Options.** These options show or hide an RSS feed link for the target of this menu item.
  - **Link Type Options.** These options control the appearance of the links.
  - **Page Display Options.** The options here are used to specify the page title, page heading, and any custom styling you want to use on the page.
  - **Metadata Options.** These options allow you to specify metadata specific to the target of the menu item. The data that you input here overrides the global metadata for the target page only.

Reviewing the Newsfeed group of menu item types

The Newsfeed group contains three menu item types, all related to displaying the output of the Newsfeed component:

- **List All Newsfeed Categories.** Provides a link to a listing of all designated categories.
- **List Newsfeeds in a Category.** Displays a list of all newsfeeds in a specific category.
- **Single Newsfeed.** Shows the output of a single newsfeed.

The menu item types for this group share four sets of parameters. The Advanced Options tab on the menu item type workspace contains the following options, which are common to all three menu item types:

- **Feed Display Options.** Contains options relating to the display of the feeds, including the feed image, description, ordering, and length.
- **Link Type Options.** Contains options that control the appearance of the links.
- **Page Display Options.** Contains options that specify the page title, page heading, and any custom styling you want to use on the page.
- **Metadata Options.** Contains options that allow you to specify metadata specific to the target of the menu item. The data that you input here overrides the global metadata for the target page only.

8

Next, I will look at each of the menu item types in the Newsfeed group and examine the unique aspects of each one.

List All Newsfeed Categories

This menu item type enables the display of a list of the newsfeed categories in the site's Newsfeed component. Figure 8.18 shows how the output might look on a page. Each of the listed category names is hyperlinked to a separate page that shows a list of the feeds in the category.

FIGURE 8.18

Example of the List All Newsfeed Categories menu item type

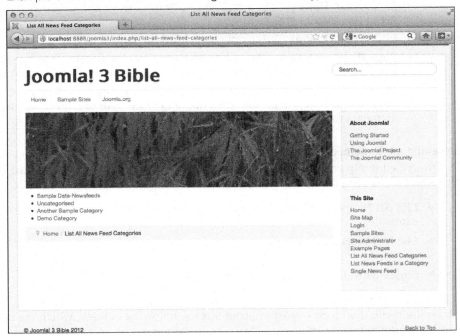

The List All Newsfeed Categories menu item type contains several unique options.

- **On the Details tab:**
    - **Select a Top Level Category.** The value you select here determines which category appears. This is a required field.

- **On the Advanced Options tab:**
  - **Categories Options.** The options here control the layout of the categories listed on the first page (the top level).
  - **Category Options.** The options here control the layout when visitors click a specific category. The choices relate to the display of the category data.
  - **List Layouts.** The options here control the layout when visitors click a specific category. The choices relate to the list display of the articles.

List Newsfeeds in a Category

This menu item type enables you to display on a page the list of newsfeeds from a specific category, as shown in Figure 8.19.

FIGURE 8.19

The output of the List Newsfeeds in a Category menu item type

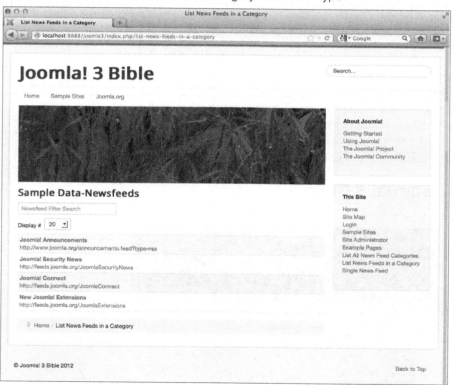

The List Newsfeeds in a Category menu item type contains several unique options.

- **On the Details tab:**
  - **Category.** The value you select here determines which category appears. This is a required field.
- **On the Advanced Options tab:**
  - **Category Options.** The options here control the layout when visitors click a specific category. The choices relate to the display of the category data.
  - **List Layouts.** The options here control the layout when visitors click a specific category. The choices relate to the list display of the articles.

Single Newsfeed

This menu item type displays the contents of a single newsfeed on a page, as shown in Figure 8.20.

The Single Newsfeed menu item type contains only one unique field, the Feed field. Located on the Details tab, this is a required field. You first click the Select button to view a list of the newsfeeds in the Newsfeed component; you then select the feed you want to display on the page.

FIGURE 8.20

Example of the Single Newsfeed menu item type in action

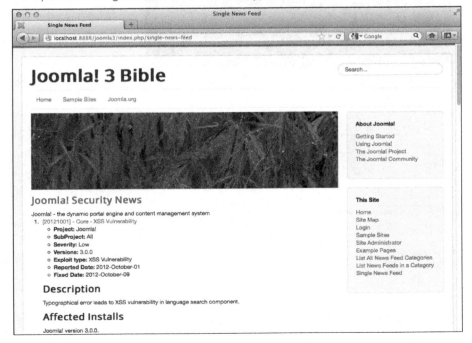

Using the Search Form or Search Results menu item type

The Search group contains only one menu item type, named Search Form or Search Results. This menu item type provides a way to display a link to a search form page, or a set of search results from a predetermined query. Figure 8.21 shows the output of this menu item type, without specifying a preset search query.

FIGURE 8.21

Example of the Search Form or Search Results menu item type being used to provide a search form only

The Search Form or Search Results menu item type has a number of parameters.

- **On the Details tab:**
  - **Search Query.** The text phrase you enter here is used to produce the search results on the page. This is an optional field.
- **On the Advanced Options tab:**
  - **Basic Options.** The options here control the visibility of filters and the Advanced Search button, together with basic parameters relating to the description shown on the page.
  - **Page Display Options.** The options here are used to specify the page title, page heading, and any custom styling you want to use on the page.
  - **Metadata Options.** The options here allow you to specify metadata specific to the target of the menu item. The data that you input here overrides the global metadata for the target page only.

Reviewing the Users Manager group of menu item types

The Users Manager group contains six menu item types, all designed to provide form output that your site visitors can use:

- **Login Form.** Displays the login form in the content area of the page.
- **User Profile.** Displays a user's profile.
- **Edit User Profiles.** Displays the editing interface for a user's profile.
- **Registration Form.** Displays Joomla's user registration form.
- **Username Reminder Request.** Displays the forum used to request a username reminder.
- **Password Reset.** Displays a form allowing users to request that their password be reset.

A majority of the parameters for these menu item types are shared. The Advanced Options tab on the menu item type workspace contains the following options, which are common to all the menu item types in this group:

- **Link Type Options.** The options in this section control the appearance of the links.
- **Page Display Options.** The options here are used to specify the page title, page heading, and any custom styling you want to use on the page.
- **Metadata Options.** The options here allow you to specify metadata specific to the target of the menu item. The data that you input here overrides the global metadata for the target page only.

Next, I will look at each of the menu item types in the Users Manager group and examine the unique aspects of each menu item type.

Login Form

The Login Form menu item type enables you to display the standard Joomla! login form for the front end of the site. Unlike the Login module, the Login Form menu item type displays the form in the content area of a page, as shown in Figure 8.22. Note that this page is used both for logging in and logging out; accordingly, the parameters for this menu item type allow you to tailor the output for either function.

FIGURE 8.22

The output of the Login Form menu item type

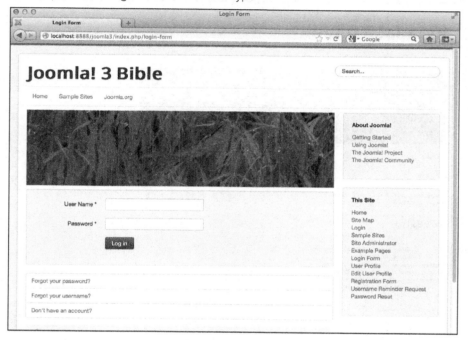

The Login Form menu item type contains several unique options, all located on the Advanced Options tab. You must click the Basic Options group to see parameters that allow you to set redirects for both login and logout and for options related to the appearance of the form.

User Profile

The User Profile menu item type displays to an authenticated user her profile information, together with a link to edit the profile. Note that this menu item type is only useful to an authenticated user and is a duplicate of the link that already exists on the default user menu. Figure 8.23 shows the output of this menu item type.

For more information on managing users and related functions, see Chapter 10.

FIGURE 8.23

The output of the User Profile menu item type

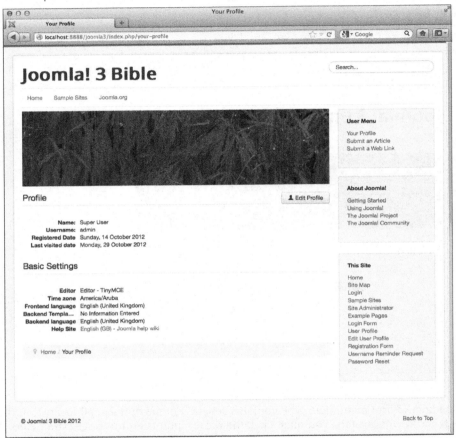

There are no unique parameters for this menu item type.

Edit User Profile

The Edit User Profile menu item type provides users with a page where they can manage their account details and set options for their use of the site, including the language and time zone settings, as shown in Figure 8.24. Note that a user must be authenticated to see this form.

FIGURE 8.24

The Edit User Profile menu item type

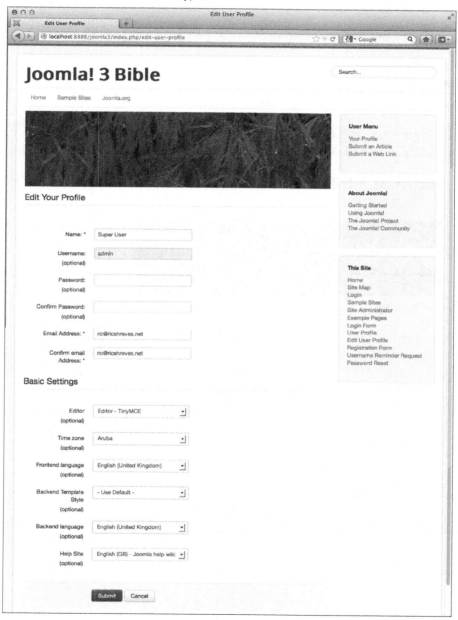

There are no unique parameters for this menu item type.

Registration Form

You use this menu item type to assign the User Registration Form to its own page, as shown in Figure 8.25.

FIGURE 8.25

Example of the Registration Form menu item type in action

There are no unique parameters for this menu item type.

Username Reminder Request

This menu item type enables you to place the Forget Your Username? form on a page, as shown in Figure 8.26.

FIGURE 8.26

Example of the default Username Reminder Request menu item type in action

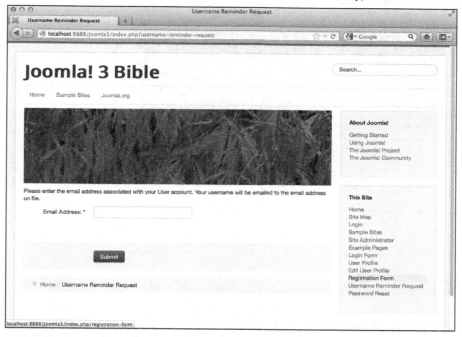

There are no unique parameters for this menu item type.

Password Reset

This menu item type enables you to place the Forgot Your Password? form on a page, as shown in Figure 8.27.

FIGURE 8.27

Example of the default Password Reset menu item type in action

There are no unique parameters for this menu item type.

Reviewing the Weblinks group of menu item types

The Weblinks group contains three menu item types. All three types are concerned with the display of content from the Weblinks component. The three menu item types are

- **List All Weblink Categories.** Displays a listing of all the weblinks categories in the system.
- **List Weblinks in a Category.** Displays a list of all the weblinks from a predetermined weblink category.
- **Submit a Weblink.** A specialty menu item type that displays a form where a user can submit a weblink for inclusion on your site.

 The Weblinks component is covered in Chapter 16.

The menu item types for this group share a number of common parameters. The Advanced Options tab on the menu item type workspace contains the following options, which are common to all three menu item types:

- **Link Type Options.** The options in this section control the appearance of the links.

- **Page Display Options.** The options here are used to specify the page title, page heading, and any custom styling you want to use on the page.

- **Metadata Options.** These options allow you to specify metadata specific to the target of the menu item. The data that you input here overrides the global metadata for the target page only.

Next, I will look at each of the menu item types in the Weblinks group and examine the unique aspects of each one.

List All Weblink Categories

You can use this menu item type to display a list of the weblink categories on a page. The category names are clickable and display a list of all links in the category, as shown in Figure 8.28.

FIGURE 8.28

Example of the List All Weblink Categories output

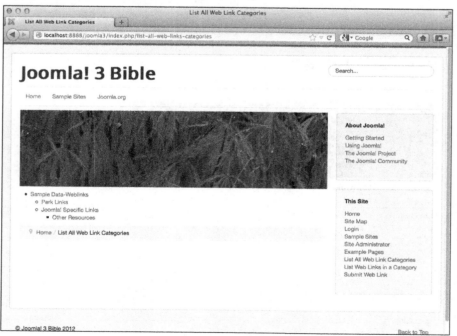

The List All Weblink Categories menu item type contains several unique options.

- **On the Details tab:**
  - **Select a Top Level Category.** The value you select here determines which categories appear on the page. Select the value Root to display all the categories in the system. This is a required field.
- **On the Advanced Options tab:**
  - **Categories Options.** The options here control the layout of the categories listed on the first page (the top level).
  - **Category Options.** The options here control the layout when visitors click a specific category. The choices relate to the display of the category data.
  - **List Layouts.** The options here control the layout when visitors click a specific category. The choices relate to the list display of the links.

List Weblinks in a Category

This menu item type displays on a page a list of all the weblinks in a single category, as shown in Figure 8.29.

FIGURE 8.29

The output of the List Weblinks in a Category menu item type

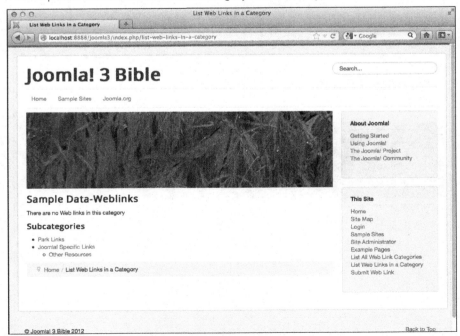

The List Weblinks in a Category menu item type contains several unique options.

- **On the Details tab:**
  - **Select a Category.** The value you select here determines which category appears. This is a required field.
- **On the Advanced Options tab:**
  - **Category Options.** The options here control the layout when visitors click a specific category. The choices relate to the display of the category data.
  - **List Layouts.** The options here control the layout when visitors click a specific category. The choices relate to the list display of the links.

Submit Weblink

You can use this menu item type when you want to enable front-end users to submit weblinks to your site, as shown in Figure 8.30. This privilege is only available to users with an access level of Special, that is, authors and above. If this menu item is shown to users who lack the proper permissions, they see an error message when they click the menu item.

FIGURE 8.30

Example of the Submit Weblink menu item type in action

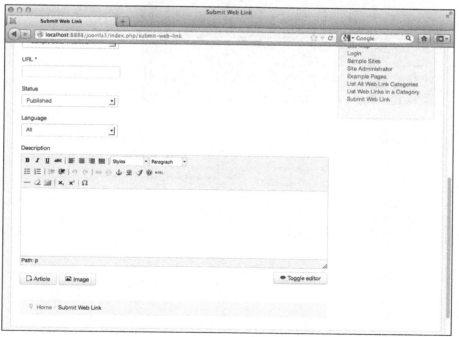

There are no unique parameters for this menu item type.

Using the Wrapper menu item type

The Wrapper group contains only one menu item type, named fIrame Wrapper. This type enables you to create a link to an iframe, which you can use to display a page inside your site that shows external content, as shown in Figure 8.31.

FIGURE 8.31

Example of the Wrapper menu item type in action, in this case, wrapping the Joomla! Extensions Directory

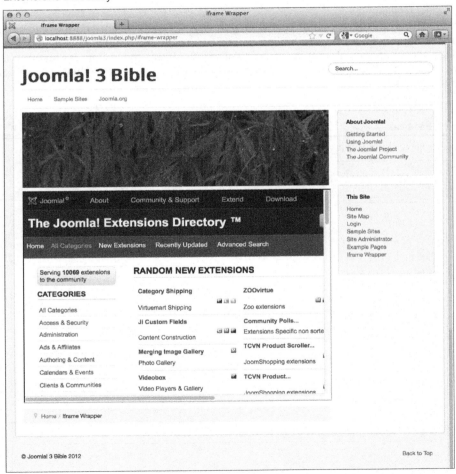

The Wrapper menu item type has a number of configuration parameters, located on the Advanced Options tab:

- **Basic Options.** The only field located here is a required field: the URL of the page you want to display inside the wrapper.

- **Scroll bars parameters.** You can set basic dimensions and specify whether you want to show scroll bars on the iframe if the page exceeds the stated dimensions.

- **Advanced Options.** This section contains additional options relating to how the wrapper responds to content larger than the available area.

- **Link Type Options.** The options in this section control the appearance of the links.

- **Page Display Options.** The options here are used to specify the page title, page heading, and any custom styling you want to use on the page.

- **Metadata Options.** The options here allow you to specify metadata specific to the target of the menu item. The data that you input here overrides the global metadata for the target page only.

Reviewing the System Links group of menu item types

The System Links group contains three menu item types:

- **External URL.** Adds a link to an external URL to a menu.

- **Menu Item Alias.** Is useful for creating a menu item that links to an existing menu item's target.

- **Text Separator.** Adds a text separator to a menu; this is useful for adding titles to groupings of menu items on a menu.

Next, I will look at each of the menu item types in the System Links group and examine each one in more detail.

External URL

You can use the External URL menu item type to add to your Joomla! site a link to an external page. The menu item types you should note include the following.

- **On the Details tab:**
    - **Link.** Enter the URL of the page you want to link to in this field.
- **On the Advanced Options tab:** Customize the styling of the menu item.

Menu Item Alias

The Menu Item Alias menu item type is designed to allow you to create duplicates of menu items when you want to have a menu item appear on more than one menu on the page. For example, if you want to have a choice on both the header and the footer of the page, you could either create two standard menu items and place one on each of the menus at the top and bottom of the page or you could create one standard menu item that you assign to one menu and then create a menu alias that you assign to the other menu. The alias mirrors the settings of the original menu item. If you change the original item, then the alias is modified as well; this simplifies menu item management.

There is only one parameter you should note with this menu item type: Menu Item. The Menu Item field is required and is located under the Required Settings heading on the Advanced Options tab. Select one of your site's existing menu items from the combo box to create the alias.

Text Separator

You can use this menu item type to add a visual separator to a menu. Separators provide a break in long lists of menu items and enable you to group menu items visually. There is no other functionality associated with this type.

This menu item type contains only one parameter of note: Link Image. The parameter is located on the Advanced Options tab; it allows you to select an image to display with the menu item.

Creating multi-tier menus

The default Joomla! 3 system makes it easy to create menus that contain multiple levels of menu items. You can do all the necessary work from within a menu's Menu Item Manager. All you need to do is add all the items to the menu, and then create parent-child relationships between different items to establish the hierarchy.

> **Tip**
> You can see a great example of using this technique to create a complex menu by viewing the About Joomla menu in the sample data.

To create one menu with multiple levels of items, follow these steps:

1. **Access the menu you want to modify by clicking the name of the menu under the Menus option on the main admin navigation bar.** The Menu Item Manager opens in your browser.

2. **Click the New button to create a new menu item or click the name of an existing menu item.** The Menu Item Editing workspace opens.

3. **In the Parent field, select a menu item to be the parent of the item you are editing.**

4. **Complete any other fields you want to modify.**

> **Tip**
> If you want the styling of the second- or third-tier links to be different than the top level, add a custom style to the link using the Link CSS Style field under the Link Type Options on the Advanced Options tab of the menu item's workspace.

5. **Click the Save button.** The system saves your changes to the item and returns you to the Menu Item Manager.

You can repeat this process as needed to create multiple levels of menu items, where each child item is attached to a parent. In this case, all the parents and their children appear inside one menu.

 See Chapter 20 for a discussion of menu styling. See Chapter 22 for a discussion of extensions that you can add to your site to enhance the menu functionality.

Editing and deleting menu items

You can edit existing menu items from the Menu Item Manager. To edit a menu item, either click the menu item name in the Menu Item Manager, or select the menu item and then click the Edit button on the Menu Item Manager toolbar. Regardless of which method you use, the system opens the Edit Menu Item workspace.

The Edit Menu Item workspace is identical to the New Menu Item workspace, with the same fields and requirements as previously discussed.

To make changes to a menu item, you simply alter the desired fields in the Edit Menu Item workspace, and then click the Save button on the toolbar. Any changes you make are applied immediately.

Deleting a menu item is a two-step process: First, send the item to the trash, and then empty the trash. Sending a menu item to the trash results in the menu item being removed from the Menu Item Manager.

Menu items moved to the trash are held there indefinitely. The items can be restored or deleted at the option of the administrator. Restored items move back to their original locations; deleted items are permanently removed from the system and cannot be restored.

To move a menu item to the trash, follow these steps:

1. **Access the Menu Item Manager containing the menu items you want to remove.** To do this, go to Menu option on the admin navigation bar and click the name of the menu where the items are located. The Menu Item Manager opens in your browser.

2. **Click the check boxes next to the items you want to remove.**

3. **Click the Trash button on the toolbar.** The system moves the items to the trash.

8

> **NOTE**
> Any menu items moved to the trash are instantly unpublished and not visible to site visitors.

Restoring items from the trash

Menu items moved to the trash are held there indefinitely until further action is taken by the administrator. You can restore any menu item at any time. The process of restoring an item is simple and the result instantaneous: The item is removed from the trash and returned to where it was located when it was moved to the trash.

To restore a menu item from the trash, follow these steps:

1. **Access the Menu Item Manager by clicking the menu's name under the Menu option on the main admin navigation bar.** The Menu Item Manager loads in your browser.

2. **Change the Select Status filter to Trashed.** The list of menu items reloads to display only those menu items in the trash.

> **NOTE**
> The menu items shown are only those that were originally located on this specific menu. Each menu has its own trash; there is no global trash.

3. **Click the check box next to the menu item you want to restore.**

4. **Click either Publish or Unpublish on the toolbar.** The system removes the menu item from the trash, and restores it to its previous location.

Deleting items permanently

You can remove menu items held in the Trash Manager from the system by deleting them. Deleting an item from the Trash Manager results in the item's permanent removal from the system; it cannot be restored once deleted.

To permanently delete a menu item from the trash, follow these steps:

1. **Access the Menu Item Manager by clicking the menu's name under the Menu option on the main admin navigation bar.** The Menu Item Manager loads in your browser.

2. **Change the Select Status filter to Trashed.** The list of items reloads to display only those items in the trash.

3. **Click the check box next to the menu item you want to delete.**

4. **Click the Empty Trash button on the top toolbar.** The system immediately deletes the item and displays a success message.

> **CAUTION**
> There is no confirmation dialog box prior to emptying the trash — deletion is instantaneous and permanent!

Controlling Access to Menus and Menu Items

Both menus and menu items are subject to access level controls; that is, you can specify which user groups are able to see and use the menus and their items. Access controls allow you to restrict the visibility of your site's contents and limit the use of certain features of your site. For many sites, access controls play a role not only in site security, but also in site marketing; by selectively showing links that require registration to view, you motivate users to join the site and become registered users.

> **TIP**
>
> As a general rule, where there is a conflict between the access level settings of a menu and those of an item on that menu, the more restrictive access level is applied.

Access to menus and the items on those menus can be controlled either in tandem or individually, given certain logical constraints. For example, if the access level of the items on a particular menu are set to Public, but the access level of the actual menu containing the menu items is set to Registered, unauthenticated users (Public users) cannot see either the menu or the individual menu items. In contrast, if the access level of the menu is set to Public, but the access levels of the items on that menu are set to Registered, the menu is visible to unauthenticated users, but the menu items are not. In either situation, authenticated users have access to both the menu and the items.

You can set menu access levels via the relevant menu module. To set access to an entire menu, follow these steps:

1. **Click Module Manager, under the Extensions menu.** The Module Manager loads.

2. **Identify the menu module that provides the menu you want to modify.**

3. **Click the name of the relevant menu module.** The Module Editing workspace opens in your browser.

4. **Use the Access combo box to set the permissions for the entire menu handled by this module.**

5. **Click the Save button.** The system saves the changes and returns you to the Module Manager.

Access to menu items is handled differently. You can set menu item access levels inside the Menu Item Edit workspace. To set access to a menu item, follow these steps:

1. **Under the Menus option on the admin navigation bar, select the name of the menu that contains the item you want to edit.** The Menu Item Manager opens in your browser.

2. **Click the name of the item you want to edit.** The Menu Item Editing workspace appears in your browser.

8

3. **Use the Access combo box to set the permissions for the entire menu.**

4. **Click the Save button.** The system saves the changes and returns you to the Menu Item Manager.

> **NOTE**
>
> You can also set the access levels for articles and many other functionalities via the parameters specific to those articles or functionalities. This means that you may sometimes have a third level of access controls that you must consider. Regardless, the general rule remains the same: Where there is a conflict, the more restrictive access level applies.

Summary

In this chapter, I introduced the Joomla! menu management system and covered the key functionalities related to creating and managing your site's menus. I covered the following key concepts:

- Understanding the relationship between menus, menu items, and menu modules
- Working with the Menu Manager
- Working with the Menu Item Manager
- Creating, editing, and deleting menus
- Creating, editing, and deleting menu items
- Creating and editing a menu module
- Creating multi-tier menus
- Controlling access to menus and menu items

In the next chapter, I focus on a narrower, but no less important area: managing the front page of your Joomla! site.

Managing the Home Page of Your Site

IN THIS CHAPTER

Selecting a page to be your home page

Identifying appropriate menu item types for your home page

Managing the layout of your home page

Using articles on your home page

Publishing component output to your home page

Assigning modules to your home page

In Joomla! terms, the front page of your site is known as the *home page*. Your home page gives visitors their first impression of your website. Because the home page has such an important role, Joomla! provides special tools for managing its contents and layout. Gaining command of the tools and techniques that can help you create a positive first impression is the goal of this chapter.

The tools built into the admin system give you a great deal of control over the home page of your site. You can assign articles to your home page, as well as component output and module output. Although optimizing the contents that appear on the home page is the easiest way to make it more effective, you should also consider the layout of the page. The parameters associated with your menu items and articles give you a measure of control over the layout, but if you want to do even more, you can assign a unique template to provide the home page with its own distinct look and feel. In the pages that follow, I look at the various options for the home page, including the role of featured articles, how to use components and modules on the home page, and how to tailor the layout to achieve more variety and better usability.

Creating the Home Page of Your Site

In Joomla!, the concept of a home page is a fluid one. There is no predetermined home page; rather, it is whatever page you specify as the home page, and it displays whatever content you designate. Accordingly, there is no single definitive home page layout. The layout of the home page depends largely on the menu item type that you select for the page and on how you configure the menu item type.

In the default Joomla! site, home page status is assigned to a page named Home and located on the Main Menu. Figure 9.1 shows how you can identify which page in your system is designated as the home page.

FIGURE 9.1

Icons show you which menu holds the site's home page and which item on the menu is currently designated as the home page.

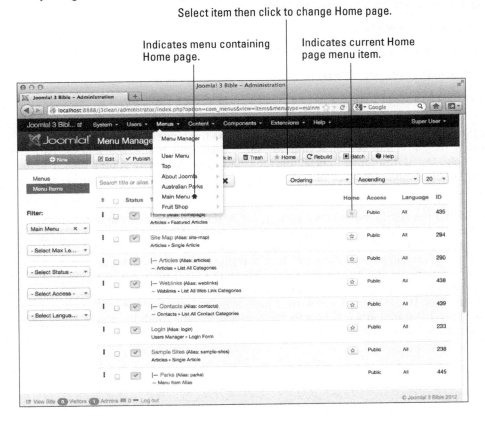

The home page in the default Joomla! 3 site has been created with the Articles — Featured Articles menu item type. The menu item type has been configured to create the layout you see on the front end, that is, one leading article spanning the page and three introductory articles arranged in three columns. Figure 9.2 shows the default home page with the sample data installed.

FIGURE 9.2

The default Joomla! front page in Joomla! 3, with the sample data installed

Of course, the menu item type is not the only factor that affects home page display. The template that you use for the page has a significant impact, particularly in regards to the placement of modules and decorative items outside the content area. The layout used in the articles also has an impact, though this may be nominal, depending on the limitations imposed on content display by the menu item type. Understanding the roles these various elements play is key to gaining command over your home page layout.

In this section, I focus on the default menu item types that Joomla! provides to facilitate home page layout and then I look at how to go farther and set a special template for use by your home page. In the sections that follow, I show you how to work with various types of content for your home page.

Working with the default content layout options

The default Joomla! installation comes with several menu item types that are well suited for use as the front page of your site. While the default configuration uses the Articles — Featured Articles menu item type, there's no reason why you can't select something else. The key to making the right decision lies in understanding your choices and identifying which menu item type addresses your needs the best. Here are some of the factors you want to consider in making your selection:

- **Your need for a particular layout.** Each menu item type exhibits varying levels of flexibility in its layout.

- **The nature of your site.** A blog site is likely to use a different menu item type than a marketing-oriented brochure site.

- **How much content you want to show on the home page.** Some menu item types are designed to handle multiple articles; others, only one.

> **TIP**
>
> Remember, the menu item type only affects what happens inside the content area of the page. What appears in the module positions is not a factor in selecting your menu item type.

There are three menu item types that are well suited for use as the home page of a site:

- **Articles — Featured Articles.** If you select this menu item type for your home page, articles marked as featured are displayed on the home page. This menu item type is used for the home page in the default configuration. It works very well for sites with regularly changing content and can also be used for blog sites. The Advanced Options tab for this menu item type allows you to control the number of leading and introductory articles and to use a multi-column layout for your introductory items.

- **Articles — Category Blog.** This is a traditional blog layout that shows the introductions of articles drawn from a category. The Advanced Options tab for this menu item type allows you to control the number of leading and introductory articles and to use a multi-column layout for your introductory items.
- **Articles — Single Article.** This menu item type displays a single article on the page. It is suitable for marketing or brochure sites where the home page displays a single piece of content, for example, a welcome message.

I look at the Featured Articles menu item type in more detail next, and I discuss the Category Blog and Single Article menu item types in Chapter 8.

 To see how each of the menu item types appears on the front end of the site, refer to Chapter 8.

As noted earlier in this chapter, the home page you see in the default Joomla! installation is created from the menu item type named Article — Featured Articles, as shown in Figure 9.2. This menu item type has several options that allow you to customize the appearance of the content layout. To view the parameters that contribute to the layout you see in the default site, you can access the menu item that controls the front page by following these steps:

1. **On the main admin navigation bar, click the Main Menu option under Menus.** The Menu Item Manager for the Main menu opens in your browser.
2. **Click the menu item named Home.** The Menu Item Editing dialog box opens in your browser.
3. **Click the Advanced Options tab.** The tab moves to the front.

The key options that impact the layout are found under the Layout Options heading. You can use the parameters here to set the number of items displayed, the number of columns used to hold the articles, the ordering of the items, and the pagination controls shown at the bottom of the screen.

In the default configuration, the front page is configured to show featured articles from all categories. The layout shows one leading article and three introductory articles in three columns. Figure 9.3 shows the Advanced Options tab of the Home menu item's workspace.

9

FIGURE 9.3

The Advanced Options tab of the Home menu item in the default installation

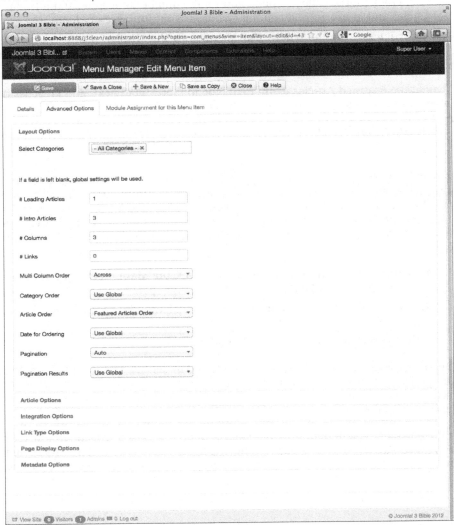

The fields on the Advanced Options tab have the following functions:

- **Select Categories.** You can choose the categories from which the articles will be displayed. Note that with this menu item type, this refers to only those articles marked featured within the categories. Choosing a parent category will include articles from the child categories.

- **# Leading Articles.** A leading article appears at the top of the content area and spans the width of the content area. In the default configuration, the value of this parameter is set to 1. The leading article is not impacted by the setting of the Columns parameters. If you set this value to zero, then a leading article is not used and the first articles that appear are the introductory articles.

- **# Intro Articles.** The value in this parameter sets the number of articles that appear after the leading articles. Note that the introductory articles are subject to the settings in the Columns parameters. If you set this value to zero, then introductory articles are not shown.

- **# Columns.** This option controls the number of columns used to display the introductory articles. Note that you need to set the value between 1 and 3.

- **# Links.** This option controls the number of links that appear at the bottom of the content area of the page. Set the value to zero if you do not want to use this feature.

- **Multi Column Order.** This option controls the ordering of articles among columns. The options are across or down.

- **Category Order.** If more than one category is included, this control sets the ordering for the categories.

- **Article Order.** This option controls the ordering of the articles that appear.

- **Date for Ordering.** If you have chosen to display articles by date, this control lets you specify which date to use, such as creation date, modification date, and so on.

- **Pagination.** This option shows or hides pagination controls at the bottom of the page.

- **Pagination Results.** If you show the pagination controls, this parameter lets you specify whether the total number of pages is shown, as opposed to just showing previous and next buttons.

Creating a single-column layout

If you prefer your home page to use a single-column layout instead of the default layout, you can easily do this with either the Articles — Featured Articles or the Articles — Category Blog menu item type. There are two different methods to achieve a one-column layout with these menu item types; both methods involve modifying the layout parameters on the Advanced Options tab. One approach is to set the Columns parameter to a value of 1. Another approach involves setting the # Intro Articles parameter to the value zero and using only the # Leading Articles parameter to control the articles that are displayed. No matter which option you choose, the visual output on the front page is the same.

9

Creating multi-column layout variations

The default system uses a hybrid layout, with a single-column leading article followed by the introductory articles displayed in three columns. Common variations to this layout include applying one or more of the following modifications to the parameters:

- Using more than one leading article
- Changing the number of introductory articles
- Changing the Columns parameter to more or fewer than three columns

Alternatively, if you want to create a multi-column layout throughout the home page content area, you can do so by setting the value of the # Leading Articles parameter to zero; this configuration results in only the introductory articles being displayed. You can then set the Columns parameter to display the introductory articles in either two or more columns.

Using a distinct template for the home page

Although the default Joomla! system uses only one template to display all the pages on the site, you can easily change this and assign a distinct template to serve as your front page. Many sites employ more than one template, often for the purpose of providing a unique look and feel for the front page. Because the front page of your website sets the tone and provides the first impression for your visitors, it is a good idea to create a template that is specifically designed to present the first page that visitors see in the most optimal fashion. You can then use a separate template, or templates, for the internal pages.

> **TIP**
>
> Using a distinct home page layout is an effective design technique. If you look around at different websites, you will see this technique is widely used. Marketing sites often want a splash page for brand or product identity or to help create a particular mood for their site. News sites often need to display large amounts of information on the home page, yet want a simpler, easier-to-read layout on the interior pages. Community sites often display personalized information on the home page. In all of these situations, the use of a different template for the home page is a simple way to achieve their design goals.

You set the template for the site globally via the Template Manager. You can assign a different template to specific pages either via the Template Manager or by editing the menu item pointing to the page; the latter technique is often the easiest, as you can select the template at the same time you create or edit the menu item. To set a separate template for the front page, follow these steps:

1. **Log in to the admin system of your Joomla! site.**
2. **On the admin navigation bar, click the Menus option and then select the name of the menu containing your home page.** The Menu Item Manager loads in your browser.

3. **Click the name of the home page.** The Edit Menu Item workspace opens.

4. **Select the template option you desire from the Template Style combo box.**

5. **Click the Save button on the top toolbar.** The system now associates the template with the home page, closes the Edit Menu Item workspace, and returns you to the Menu Item Manager.

 To find out more about working with the templates in Joomla!, see Chapter 20.

Publishing Articles on the Home Page

Articles are the most commonly displayed content on Joomla! home pages. Whether your home page uses a blog format, a categories format, or the default featured articles format, the displayed content comes from the articles located in your Articles Manager. Accordingly, the decisions you make when you create new articles can directly impact your home page. Article titles, category assignments, decisions to make an article featured (or not), and any parameters you adjust can all play a role. In this section, I look at how you can control the article output on your site's home page.

> **TIP**
>
> Note that the article display settings on the home page are controlled by the Article Options you have selected on the Advanced Options tab of the menu item type's workspace. If you want to have the flexibility to vary settings for individual articles, set the Article Options combo boxes to Use Article Settings; this allows you to create unique settings for specific articles.

Displaying featured articles

If you are using the Articles — Featured Articles menu item type, the main content area of the page is populated entirely with featured articles. As discussed earlier, you can limit this display to particular categories, or it can display all articles marked as featured, regardless of their category assignment. Featured articles are marked clearly in the Articles Manager with a gold star, but you can also view them separately, via the Featured Articles Manager, as shown in Figure 9.4.

9

FIGURE 9.4

The Featured Articles Manager

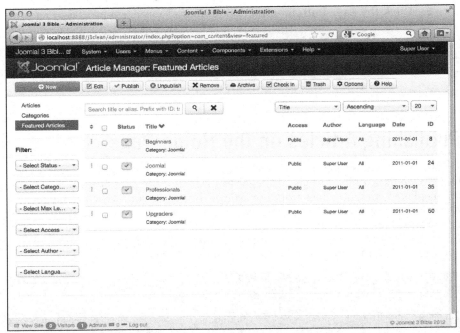

The Article — Category Blog menu item type also allows you to use featured articles as part of the display priorities. The option to prioritize featured articles is not selected by default in this menu item type, and so you must take the following steps to create this ordering:

1. **Log in to the admin system of your Joomla! site.**
2. **On the admin navigation bar, click the Menus option, and then select the name of the menu containing your home page.** The Menu Item Manager loads in your browser.
3. **Click the name of the home page.** The Edit Menu Item workspace opens.
4. **Click the Advanced Options tab.** The tab comes to the front.
5. **Click Layout Options.** The Blog Layout Options section expands to reveal the fields inside.
6. **In the Article Order combo box, select the Featured Articles Order option.**
7. **Click the Save button.**

The change you've just made to the menu item type now means that you can use the Featured Articles Manager to handle your home page articles.

TIP

Default article sort orders can be defined globally via the parameters in the Articles component section of the Global Configuration Manager. However, the options offered there do not include using featured articles for the sort order. Therefore, if you want to use featured articles for your ordering criteria of a page, you need to select a menu item type for the page that supports this option.

The only purpose of the Featured Articles Manager is to provide fast access to all the articles marked as featured in your system; it is, in essence, a filtered view of the articles contained in the Articles Manager. Though it does not bring any unique functionality, the Featured Articles Manager does make several tasks easier. First, and most obvious, it gives you a quick look at all the featured articles, making managing their publication status easier. Second, you can change the ordering of the featured articles here by clicking and dragging the articles to reorder them.

 Working with articles and the Article Manager are discussed in Chapter 5. Article Archives are also covered in Chapter 5.

Building a page without featured articles

You are not forced to use featured articles for your home page. Though some people find it more convenient to use featured articles due to the existence of the Featured Articles Manager, the choice is yours. Other menu item types discussed earlier do not use featured articles for the home page display.

If you elect not to use featured articles, the issue of exactly which articles will appear on the home page depends primarily on two factors: the number of articles you have elected to display in your menu item type, and the sorting criteria for the display. If, for example, you have chosen to display three articles and the sorting criteria is set to creation date, the system shows the three most recently created articles, with the most recent appearing first.

The simplest option to control is the Articles — Single Article menu item type. If you elect to use a single article for the home page, you designate the specific page to be used via the menu item editing workspace. Any display parameters you want to use are also set from the Advanced Options tab in the menu item editing workspace.

In the next section, I look at creating home pages without the use of articles — that is, by displaying component output on the home page.

9

Publishing Component Output on the Home Page

Many components in your Joomla! system are capable of displaying output either through the peripheral module positions or in the primary content area of a page. Third-party extensions added to your site may also bring with them new menu item types, allowing you to link those new components to your menu items. Displaying component output on the home page can be desirable, particularly with certain types of specialty sites. If, for example, you run a community site, you may want output from a forum component to appear on the home page. Or maybe you've built a site for a photographer and he wants to display a gallery on the home page. In either case, the home page contents would come from a component, not from your Articles Manager. In this section, I look at how to set up a home page that shows component output.

In the default system, it is possible to use the output of the following components as the site's home page: Contacts, Newsfeeds, and Weblinks. If you have added additional components to your site, you may have additional options. In any case, the process is exactly the same as discussed in previous sections of this chapter — that is, you create an appropriate menu item type and then set the menu item to be the site's home page.

> **NOTE**
>
> Technically speaking, articles are also the result of a component, that is, the Article component. However, because this component is so closely integrated with the system, and has its own set of dedicated management interfaces, I have added this section to talk about the output from the other content-producing components in the system.

If you want to mix component output with articles, things start to get interesting. The way the system is engineered, each page is the result of a single menu item type, and a single menu item type cannot display output from two different sources. A hybrid home page, that is, one showing both articles and component output, can be rendered by the default system by using a different approach: Use your content area for one type of output, via the appropriate menu item type, and then use modules to supply the other output you desire. I explore the options for displaying the output on the home page through the use of modules in the following section.

> **TIP**
>
> If you must show both an article and component output in the main content area of the page, place a module inside your article and display one of the outputs using the module. I cover adding modules to articles in Chapter 7.

Publishing Modules on the Home Page

Modules can be published on any page, including the home page, assuming that module positions are available in the active template. In the default system, modules provide much of the output you see on the top, bottom, and right side of the home page. Within a home page, modules are particularly useful, as they give you a way to expose deep content on the home page without distracting from the main message you want to display in the primary content area. Modules also offer a great deal of flexibility, not only in their positioning on the page, but also in their contents. Modules can contain text, images, forms, or even the output of some components, making the strategic use of modules a very effective tool at driving engagement with site visitors. In this section, I look at how you can add modules to your home page.

Modules can either be managed across the entire site, via the modules' workspace in the Module Manager, or they can be managed in the context of a single page, via the page's menu item workspace. The option you use depends on what you want to do: If your focus is on managing a module's visibility throughout the site as a whole, then you want to access that specific module's workspace via the Module Manager. On the other hand, if you are trying to manage multiple module assignments on a single page, then you want to work from within the page's menu item workspace, where you can see all the modules available for that page.

In the context of managing module assignment on your home page, the more logical work-flow is to access the menu item you have designated as home, and then click the tab labeled Module Assignment for this Menu Item. The page that loads shows you all the modules in the system and whether they are assigned to the home page. Sometimes the list is quite long. To narrow the list to only those items currently assigned to the home page, click the check box labeled Hide Unassigned Modules. In the default system with the sample data installed, you will see something like Figure 9.5.

FIGURE 9.5

The modules assigned to the home page in the default installation

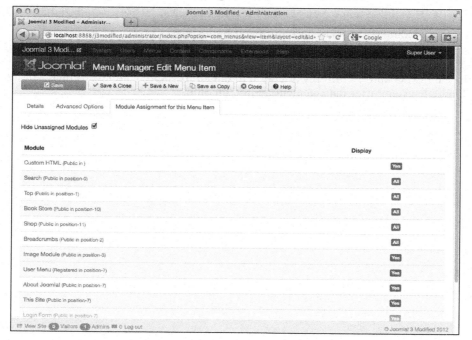

You can adjust the settings for any of these modules by clicking the name of the module, which opens a pop-up window containing the module's parameters. If you want to add a module, then deselect the Hide Unassigned Modules check box, find the module you want on the list, and click its name to open the module's parameters, which you can adjust to include the home page.

 I cover modules in more detail in Chapter 17.

Summary

In this chapter, I covered various tools and techniques that help you manage the home page of your Joomla! site. I covered the following topics:

- Designating any page on your site as the home page
- Deciding which menu item type to use for your home page
- Managing the menu item type parameters to affect home page layout
- Creating a home page in blog layout
- Creating a home page in multi-column layout
- Using a dedicated template for your home page to give it a unique look and feel
- Working with featured articles for home page content
- Creating a home page without featured articles
- Adding component output to your home page
- Controlling module assignment to your home page

In the next chapter, I turn my attention to one of the more complex elements of the Joomla! system: user management and permissions.

Managing Your Site's Users

IN THIS CHAPTER

Working with the Joomla! User Manager

Understanding the system's user hierarchy

Adding new users to the system

Managing your existing users

Working with user groups

Setting up user registration

Specifying what users can see

Specifying what users can do

U sers are the lifeblood of any site. Proper user management is needed both to inspire repeat visitors and to protect the integrity of a site. Whether your site is large or small, fluency with the Joomla! tools for user registration, user management, and access control is essential for good website management. Joomla! makes it possible for you to offer site membership to your visitors while also protecting your security. You can create multiple users and multiple groups of users, and control what they can see and do while on the site.

In this chapter, I take a detailed look at the Joomla! User Manager and how you can use it to create and manage the registered users on your website. I also examine the connections between users, user groups, access levels, and permissions and how they relate to the management of your site's many content items, components, modules, and plug-ins.

Introducing the User Manager

The User Manager handles the creation and management of all registered users in the Joomla! system. If you want to add a new user to your system, or manage the details associated with any existing users, you can perform these tasks with the tools located in the User Manager. If you have a large site with many members, the User Manager will be one of your key site management interfaces. You can see all the registered users at a glance, identify their group membership, and see basic information like the date of their last visit. The interface also gives you the ability to block problem users or adjust user permissions to grant, or deny, access to protected areas of your site. In this section, I take you on a quick tour of the User Manager interface, explaining the information shown and the various tools and their uses.

The User Manager is located inside the Joomla! admin system. After you have logged in to the admin system, you can access the User Manager in two ways: either by clicking the User Manager link in the right column of the dashboard or by selecting the User Manager option from the main admin menu. Figure 10.1 shows the default User Manager.

The toolbar at the top of the User Manager provides quick access to the following functions:

- **New.** Click to create a new user account.
- **Edit.** Select a user from the list and then click this button to edit the user's account details.
- **Activate.** Select one or more users from the list and then click this button to activate the user accounts.

FIGURE 10.1

The User Manager interface, showing the default administrator account and one front-end user

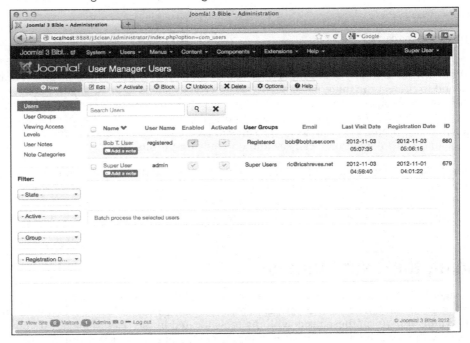

- **Block.** Select a user from the list and then click this button to block the user's access to the system.

- **Unblock.** Select a user from the list and then click this button to unblock the user's access to the system.

- **Delete.** Select one or more users from the list and then click this button to delete the user accounts.

- **Options.** Click to access the User Manager parameters, located in the Global Configuration Manager.

- **Help.** Click to access the Help files related to the active screen.

Below the toolbar and above the list of users is a search form. You can type a word or phrase into the Search Users field and then click the magnifying glass icon. The system searches your list of users for the query and then displays the results of the search. To clear the screen and return to a full listing, click the button marked with the X.

At the top of the left column is a set of links that lets you jump quickly between the User Manager, the User Groups Manager, the Access Levels Manager, the User Notes Manager, and the User Note Categories Manager. Below those links is a set of filters that can help you manage long lists of users:

- **State.** The options in this combo box allow you to filter and display the users according to whether they are enabled or disabled. To reset this filter, change the combo box back to the default setting of State.

- **Active.** The options in this combo box allow you to filter and display the users according to whether they are activated or unactivated. To reset this filter, change the combo box back to the default setting of Active.

- **Group.** The options in this combo box allow you to filter and display the users according to their user group. These options reflect the user groups that exist on the site. To reset this filter, change the combo box back to the default setting of Group.

- **Registration Date.** The options in this combo box allow you to filter and display the users according to their registration date. To reset this filter, change the combo box back to the default setting of Registration Date.

The main content area of the screen contains a list of all the registered users in your Joomla! site. The columns provided are

- **Check box (no label).** You can click a check box to select a user account; this is necessary if you want to use several of the toolbar options.

- **Name.** This field displays the full name of the user. Click the name to edit the user's details.

- **User Name.** The name displayed in this field is the username needed for login.

- **Enabled.** A green check mark in this column indicates that the account is active. The field shows a red X when the user account is disabled. A user account may be

10

disabled for one of two reasons: Either the user has been blocked by an administrator, or the user has failed to confirm and activate a new account. Administrators can toggle between the two settings by clicking the button shown.

- **Activated.** The check box in this column indicates whether the account has been activated after registration.

NOTE

Whether a new account requires administrator activation after registration depends upon how the site is configured. The User Manager parameters give you control over this setting.

- **User Groups.** This column displays the group to which the user is assigned.
- **Email.** This column displays the e-mail address associated with this user account.
- **Last Visit Date.** This column displays the date and time the user last logged in to the site.
- **Registration Date.** This column displays the date and time the user account was created.
- **ID.** This column displays the system-generated user ID number.

TIP

You can also sort any column by clicking the column header.

Finally, at the bottom of the screen, below the content area, is one additional control: Batch process the selected users. You can select one or more users, and then click this link to open a control that allows you to modify the users' group membership.

Understanding the Default User Hierarchy

In Joomla!, all users must be assigned to at least one user group. Access permissions in the system are attached to the groups, and each member of a group inherits those privileges. The Joomla! system provides a flexible hierarchy of user groups but also includes a set of pre-defined groups for your use. Many people find that the default user groups work just fine for their sites; other people may want to either modify the default groups or add new groups, or both. To determine what is right for your site, you first need to understand the default user hierarchy. In this section, I look at the default structure and then use this as the foundation for the discussion in the following sections, where I talk about adding and managing users to your system.

The default user groups are divided between users with only front-end access, and those with access to both the front end and the back end of the site. Each group has different privileges in the system. Higher-level groups always include all the privileges of lower-level groups. You can view the user groups in your site at any time by visiting the User Groups Manager, shown in Figure 10.2.

FIGURE 10.2

The User Groups Manager, showing the default user groups, without the sample data installed

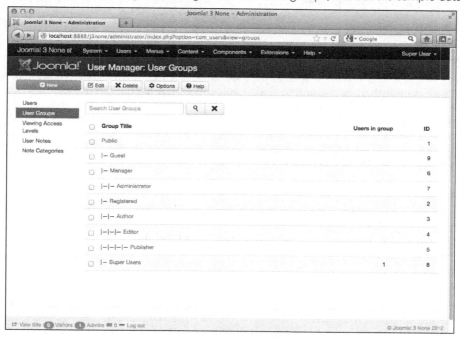

In the following sections, I discuss each of the default user groups.

Classifying front-end users

Seven different groups are restricted to front-end access only. The groups are named Public, Guest, Manager, Registered, Author, Editor, and Publisher. The users assigned to these groups have varying levels of access to only the front end of the site. Although they can log in to the front end and perform tasks, they cannot log in to the back end of the site. This limited form of access is useful both for providing control over access to content and for setting up a workflow that allows users to add content to the site.

10

Public

The Public user group is no different in permissions than the Guest group. The Public group is provided as a utility group for site administrators. Because the group is located at the top level of the hierarchy, it is the parent of all other groups. By not putting any restrictions on this group, Joomla! has given site administrators a parent group they can use to create new groups without complications.

> **TIP**
>
> Any restrictions you place on the Public group are inherited by all other groups on the site, as all other groups are children of the Public group.

Guest

The Guest access level is a special purpose group created for use as an access control device, rather than as a group to which you can assign users. The designation is designed to allow you a tool for displaying certain content to non-authenticated users only. In other words, if you designate the access level of an article as Guest, that article will only be visible to non-authenticated users; it will be hidden from view of authenticated users. You will not normally assign any users to this group, rather you will simply use it to control the visibility of specific content.

Manager

In terms of privileges, the Manager user group is more concerned with content management than with system administration. Users assigned to the Manager group enjoy rights very similar to those of Publishers, but with the added ability to delete items.

Registered

Registered users are the most limited access group. A user in this group can view pages and menus where the access level has been set to either Public or Registered, but he cannot add or edit content items. This group allows the site administrator to recognize and distinguish certain users from general public viewers of the website; it also allows the administrator to allow Registered site visitors to see more items and do more things than a general public visitor. Registered is generally the default group for new users who register through the front end of the site.

Author

The Author group is one step up in the hierarchy from the Registered group. Authors not only have access to restricted content items and menus, but can also access pages and menus where the access level has been set to Special. The most important privilege that users in this group enjoy is the ability to add content from the front end.

Administrators typically use the Author group to create a front-end content management workflow. Authors can add content to pages and edit content they have created. Authors cannot, however, edit the pages of other users. Additionally, Authors cannot schedule or publish content items and they cannot create content structures, such as sections or categories. As such, this group is typically part of a larger workflow process that includes other user groups that complete the publication cycle. In the default configuration, members of the Author group are also able to submit weblinks from the front end of the site, though the site administrator can modify this configuration.

 See Chapter 7 for an extended discussion of setting up front-end content management workflow.

Editor

Users assigned to the Editor group enjoy the same privileges as Authors, plus the ability to edit the content items created by other users. Editors are part of a front-end content management workflow, but because they are unable to schedule or publish pages, Editors are normally part of a larger schema involving other user groups.

Publisher

Publishers enjoy the same privileges as Editors, plus they can create pages, edit the pages of other users, and schedule and publish pages.

Classifying back-end users

Two groups are classified as back-end users: Administrator and Super Administrator. Users assigned to these groups are able to log in to the back-end administration system of your site; accordingly, you should only grant this level of access to trusted users.

Administrator

The Administrator group has significant system administration privileges. Users in this group enjoy all the rights of a Manager, plus the ability to work with the site's users, modules, and components.

Super Administrator

The Super Administrator group is the Joomla! equivalent of a Super User. This is the most powerful user group in the system, with no limits on the user's ability to perform tasks within the system. Key privileges, such as access to the Global Configuration Manager and the ability to take the site offline, make this group suitable for only the most trusted users. As a general rule, you can restrict membership in this group to as few users as possible.

> **TIP**
> A Super Administrator account cannot be directly deleted, but it can be downgraded to a lower level group and then deleted.

10

Adding Users to the System

There are different reasons for adding users to your site. Offering users access to restricted areas on the front end of a website is one way to encourage loyalty and repeat visits. Commercial sites typically offer membership as a means of restricting content to either paying customers or those who have given up some information about themselves in exchange for greater access to content. In cases where you also allow front-end content creation, membership can serve a broader, almost hybrid role, that is, front-end members who have access to both greater content and extended functionality. In contrast, access to the back end of the site is focused on spreading the burden of site administration and is typically open to a much smaller group of trusted users.

New users can be added to a site in one of two ways: by a site administrator via the User Manager, or by the users themselves via the front-end user registration process. In this section, I discuss adding users through the admin system, because this is the most powerful approach to user creation. Later in this chapter, I discuss enabling user registration in order to allow users to create their own accounts.

Creating a new user

In the default configuration, only Administrators and Super Administrators have the ability to add new users to your Joomla! system from inside the User Manager.

NOTE

While the ability of the Super Administrator is unrestricted, Administrators are not able to create new Super Administrators.

To create a new user, follow these steps:

1. **Log in to the back-end admin system.**
2. **Click the User Manager option under the Users menu.** The User Manager loads in your browser window.
3. **Click the New button on the User Manager toolbar.** The Add New User workspace opens.
4. **Type the user's name in the Name field.**
5. **Assign a username by typing it in the Login Name field.**
6. **Assign the user a password in the Password field.**
7. **Type the password again in the Confirm Password field.**
8. **Type the user's e-mail address in the Email field.**
9. **Click the Assigned User Groups tab.** The tab comes to the front.
10. **Assign the user to a group by clicking the check box next to one or more user groups in the list.**

11. **Set any additional parameters you want on the Basic Settings tab; all settings here are optional.**

12. **Click Save.** The system creates the new user account and returns you to the User Manager.

> **CAUTION**
>
> Note that the system allows you to create a user account without a password; however, the user will not be able to access the account. So, although the system does not prompt you for a password, it is essentially a required field and should always be set.

Working with the New User workspace

Users can be created from within the administration system through the use of the Add New User workspace. The workspace is purposely built for user creation and includes all the tools you need to create new users and assign them to the group of your choice.

When you click the New button on the User Manager toolbar, the Add New User workspace loads in your browser window, as shown in Figure 10.3.

At the top of the page, the Add New User toolbar includes the following buttons:

- **Save.** Click to save your work without exiting from the Add New User workspace.
- **Save & Close.** Click to save your work and exit the Add New User workspace.
- **Save & New.** Click to save your work, close the current Add New User workspace, and open another Add New User workspace.
- **Cancel.** Click to cancel the task and exit the Add New User workspace.
- **Help.** Click to access the online Help files related to the active screen.

The Add New User workspace is divided into three tabs: Account Details, Assigned User Groups, and Basic Settings

I cover each tab in more detail in the following sections.

Populating the Account Details

The Account Details section of the Add New User workspace includes the following fields, some of which are required to create a new user account:

- **Name.** You typically enter the user's real name here. This field is required.
- **Login Name.** You enter a name for the user to log in to the system. This field is required.
- **Password.** The user creates a password for his user account in this field.
- **Confirm Password.** This field is to confirm the password. The value typed into this field must be identical to the value typed into the Password field.

10

- **Email.** You enter a valid e-mail address for contacting the user in this field. All system e-mails, including the Username Reminder and Password Reset notifications, are sent to this address. This field is required.
- **Registration Date.** Once you save the user, this field is automatically populated.
- **Last Visit Date.** The system automatically populates this field.
- **Last Reset Date.** The system automatically populates this field.
- **Password Reset Count.** The system automatically populates this field.
- **Receive System emails.** You select Yes if the user is to receive administrative notifications from the Joomla! system. Note that this is really only appropriate for users with an administrative role on the site.
- **Block this User.** You select Yes to prevent the user from accessing the system.
- **ID.** The system automatically populates this field.

FIGURE 10.3

The Add New User workspace

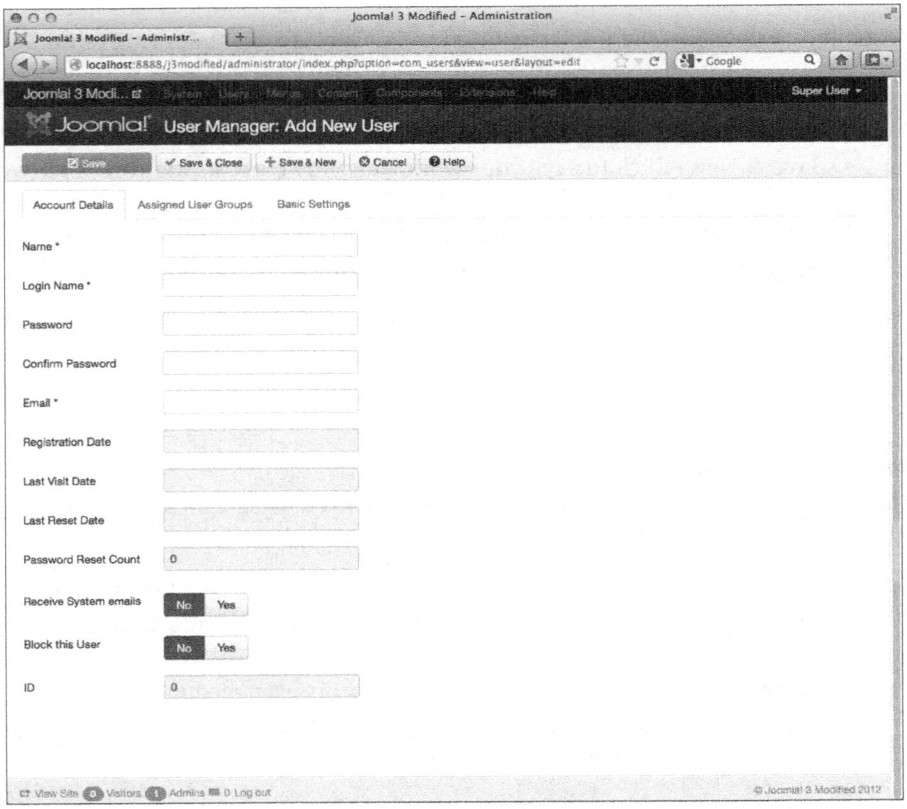

Managing Account Notification E-Mails

By default, the Joomla! system automatically sends e-mail notifications to users in several circumstances. When a new account is created, the system sends a new account notification e-mail to the user at the e-mail address that is input into the New User workspace. Similarly, when the user clicks the Username Reminder or Password Reset links, the system sends an e-mail to the user with details about how to regain access to her account.

The text for the various notification e-mails is contained in the system's language files. The specific file for handling the user e-mail notification ends with _users.ini; for example, if you are using the default language settings, you will find the desired language in the file language>en-GB>en-GB. com_user.ini. You can modify the wording in the e-mail notifications by downloading the file, locating the appropriate line in the file, and then changing the parts you want. After you have made your changes, you upload the file to your server, overwriting the original.

Specifying the Assigned User Groups

The Assigned User Groups tab allows you to associate the user with one or more user groups. You can set the default value in the Global Configuration Manager preferences. If you want to change this value, you can do so by selecting from the list of user groups on this page. Note that the user groups you see on this page represent all user groups currently in existence on the site. You can add new user groups from the User Groups Manager, discussed later in this chapter.

Configuring the Basic Settings

The Basic Settings tab contains a set of optional fields that you can use to tailor the user's account to her language and locale preferences. The fields are

- **Backend Template Style.** If you want the user to see a template other than the default template, select it from the combo box. Note that this field is not relevant if the user does not have access to the back end of your site.

- **Backend language.** Select the language you want this user to see when he accesses the back end of the system. By default, this is set to the language you have specified in the Global Configuration Manager. The choices in the combo box are limited to the Language Packs you have installed in your system. Also note that if this user is assigned to a group that does not have access to the back end, the settings for this field do not affect the user.

- **Frontend language.** Select the language you want this user to see when she accesses the front end of the system. By default, this is set to the language you have specified in the Global Configuration Manager. The choices available in the combo box reflect the Language Packs you have installed in your system.

- **Editor.** Select an editor for this user to work with during article creation. By default, this is set to the editor you have designated in the Global Configuration Manager. Note that the choices in the combo box reflect the editors you have installed in your system.

10

- **Help site.** Specify where the user is directed when he clicks the Help button. You can direct the user to a specific Help site. The default setting is the Help site selected in the Global Configuration Manager.

- **Time zone.** Specify the time zone for the user. The default setting is the time zone specified in the Global Configuration Manager.

Managing Existing Users

In addition to enabling the creation of new user accounts, the User Manager provides an interface for managing your existing users. You can update user details, create new passwords, or change a user's Group affiliation, giving him more or fewer privileges. If your site is small, or does not offer a membership option, you may not use this interface very often, but if you have a large site with many members, you will use the tools in this section a lot.

The following sections look at the most common tasks associated with managing your existing users, including editing, deleting, and blocking users.

Editing user accounts

You can edit the accounts of existing users from the User Manager. To edit a user account, either click the user's name in the User Manager, or select the account and then click the Edit button on the User Manager toolbar. Regardless of which method you use, the system opens the Edit User workspace, which is identical to the Add New User workspace (refer to Figure 10.3).

To make changes to a user's account, you simply alter the desired fields in the Add Edit User workspace and then click the Save button on the toolbar. The system applies your changes immediately.

Deleting users

To delete one or more users, follow these steps:

1. **Open the User Manager.**
2. **Select the accounts of one or more users.**
3. **Click the Delete button.**

CAUTION

Deleting a user account is permanent and cannot be undone. Moreover, the system does not display a confirmation dialog box prior to deletion. Clicking the Delete button immediately deletes the user account!

Blocking users

Administrators can block the access of any user. If you have a problem user or you simply need to shut down an account temporarily, blocking access is the only certain way of keeping the user out of the system.

> **NOTE**
> Blocking a user only denies the user access to his account; it does not prevent him from visiting or viewing the site.

To block access, follow these steps:

1. **Access the User Manager.**
2. **Click the check box next to the user's name.**
3. **Click the Block User button on the toolbar.** The Enabled field changes from a green check mark to a red X.

Blocking a user does not delete the user's account. If the issue with the user is resolved, you need only select the user and then click the Unblock button, and the user's account becomes fully active.

> **CAUTION**
> Blocking a user effectively can be difficult if your site allows user registration, because blocking one account does not prevent the user from obtaining a new account by re-registering under a new name or e-mail address.

Adding and Editing User Groups

You can add new user groups to your site freely. Similarly, you can edit your existing user groups at any time. Adding, editing, and deleting user groups are handled via the User Groups Manager. The User Groups Manager has a relatively simple interface with very little functionality. Basically, the User Groups Manager lets you create a user group, give it a name, set its place in the user group hierarchy — and not much else. Other tasks, like establishing permissions and assigning members to the group, are handled elsewhere.

> **NOTE**
> I discuss adding users to a group through the User Manager earlier in this chapter. I cover managing user access and permissions later in this chapter.

You can access the User Groups Manager from either the Users menu or from the left column links inside any of the User Manager interfaces. Figure 10.4 shows the User Groups Manager, with the Learning Joomla! sample data installed.

10

FIGURE 10.4

The User Groups Manager, showing additional user groups added by the sample data

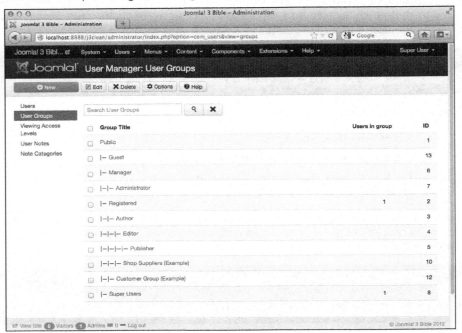

As noted, there's little functionality in the manager. The choices on the toolbar let you create, edit, or delete a user group. You can also click the Options button to jump to the User Component configuration workspace in the Global Configuration Manager, or click the Help button to see the help files.

To create a new user group, follow these steps:

1. **Log in to the back-end admin system.**

2. **Click the Groups option under the Users menu.** The User Groups Manager loads in your browser window.

3. **Click the New button on the User Manager toolbar.** The Add New User workspace opens.

4. **Enter a name for the new group in the Group Title field.** This is a required field.

5. **Assign the group a place in the user group hierarchy by selecting a value from the Group Parent combo box.**

6. **Click Save.** The system creates the new group.

You can also edit new groups via the User Groups Manager. To edit a group, either click the group's name in the User Groups Manager, or select the check box next to the group name and then click the Edit button on the User Groups Manager toolbar. Regardless of which method you use, the system opens the Edit Group workspace, which is identical to the Add New Group workspace. In the Edit Group workspace, you can alter either the group title or the parent group. Once you've made your changes, click the Save button on the toolbar.

To delete one or more user groups, follow these steps:

1. **Open the User Groups Manager.**
2. **Click the check box next to the name of the groups you want to delete.**
3. **Click the Delete button.** The system deletes the groups you selected.

Enabling Front-End User Registration

You can set up Joomla! to allow new users to register from the front end of the website, with or without the need for administrator approval. By default, front-end user registration is active in the Joomla! system. A site visitor can register and create his own account by clicking the Create an Account link on the Login Form. The Login Form appears on the pages of the site as a result of enabling and assigning the Login module to a position on the page. There are also alternatives to the default approach. The User Registration settings can be manipulated by the administrator via the Global Configuration Manager and new menu items can be created to handle user registration chores. In this section, I look at the various options for providing front-end user registration and at the configuration options that allow you to tailor the registration process to suit your needs.

I will start by looking at the configuration options for user registration, and then I will look at the methods you can use to make registration available to the site visitors.

10

Configuring user registration

Although your Joomla! site has front-end user registration enabled by default, you can modify this feature by adjusting the configuration settings. The default setting allows casual visitors to register, but access to the site is not automatic. After the user registers, the system sends a confirmation e-mail to the address that she entered during the registration process. The new user must then click a link in that confirmation e-mail to validate and activate the account. Only after successful validation does the username and password grant access to the site.

> **NOTE**
> The confirmation e-mail process only occurs when a user registers from the front end; it does not occur when a new user is created via the back-end User Manager.

This default approach to user registration is commonly used, and for many sites it is sufficient. However, if you are concerned about security, you can — and should — require a more rigorous registration process. There are two easy ways to do this: First, implement Captcha on the user registration form; second, require administrator approval as an additional step in registration.

Captcha forces a user to type in a code that appears on the screen before she can submit the form. If she enters the code incorrectly, the form is not submitted. Captcha is designed to block bots and scripts from automatically submitting forms, and is a reasonably effective way to make sure that a human being is submitting the form. To enable Captcha on your user forms, follow these steps:

1. **Log in to the back-end admin system.**
2. **Click the Global Configuration option under the System menu.** The Global Configuration Manager loads in your browser window.
3. **Click the Users Manager link under the Components heading in the left column.** The Users Configuration workspace loads in your browser.
4. **Find the Captcha field, and select the Captcha - ReCaptcha option.**
5. **Click the Save & Close button on the toolbar.**
6. **Select the Plug-in manager option, under the Extensions menu.** The Plug-in Manager loads in your browser.
7. **Click the Captcha - ReCaptcha module.** The module opens for editing.
8. **Click the Basic Options tab.** The tab comes to the front.
9. **Enter your ReCaptcha Public Key in the field provided.** This is a required field.
10. **Enter your ReCaptcha Private Key in the field provided.** This is a required field.
11. **Click Save.**

While Captcha is useful at reducing the number of invalid form submissions, if you want to improve the integrity of the process, you should involve the administrator. There are two alternatives for involving the administrator in new account creation: Either remove front-end registration completely, or require that the administrator approve all new accounts.

Blocking front-end user registration is the most effective way of making sure that inappropriate users are blocked, but it is also less convenient for both the administrators and the users.

To disable front-end user registration, follow these steps:

1. **Log in to the back-end admin system.**

2. **Access the Global Configuration Manager by clicking the Global Configuration button on the Control Panel, or by clicking the Global Configuration option on the System menu.** The Global Configuration Manager loads in your browser window.

3. **Click the Users Manager link under the Components heading in the left column.** The Users Configuration workspace loads in your browser.

4. **Change the Allow User Registration setting from Yes to No.**

5. **Click the Save button on the toolbar when you are finished.**

The less intrusive alternative is to require administrators to activate new accounts. If you apply this configuration option, new users register via the front-end registration feature, but they cannot access the site until an administrator activates the account. This approach ensures the integrity of the user accounts, at the cost of increased administration overhead. To set up this process, you need to configure the system to both require administrator activation and to send registration notifications to the administrators.

To set up the workflow for administrator activation, follow these steps:

1. **Log in to the back-end admin system.**

2. **Access the Global Configuration Manager by clicking the Global Configuration button on the Control Panel, or by clicking the Global Configuration option on the Site menu.** The Global Configuration Manager loads in your browser window.

3. **Click the Users Manager link under the Components heading in the left column.** The Users Configuration workspace loads in your browser.

10

4. **Find the New User Account Activation field, and select the Admin option.**

5. **Set the value of the Notification Mail to Administrators parameter to Yes.**

6. **Click the Save button on the toolbar when you are finished.**

If, on the other hand, you feel that your site can operate safely with a less secure user registration process, you can allow user registration without the user having to first receive and click a link in a validation e-mail; this approach allows the user to access the site immediately after registration.

To enable registration without confirmation, follow these steps:

1. **Log in to the back-end admin system.**

2. **Access the Global Configuration Manager by clicking the Global Configuration button on the Control Panel, or by clicking the Global Configuration option on the Site menu.** The Global Configuration Manager loads in your browser window.

3. **Click the Users Manager link under the Components heading in the left column.** The Users Configuration workspace loads in your browser.

4. **Find the New User Account Activation field, and select the None option.**

5. **Click the Save button on the toolbar when you are finished.**

> **TIP**
>
> Though it is possible to configure your site to use a less secure registration process, you probably do not want to disable the default e-mail confirmation process. The confirmation e-mail may slow down registration, but it helps protect your site from automated registration routines, or from people who try to register without giving a valid e-mail address.

Assuming that you have a front-end registration process set up with the security levels and workflow you desire, you need to decide how to display the registration form to users. In the following sections, I look at the two alternatives: using the Login module and creating a login page.

Using the Login module

The Login module is the default method that Joomla! uses for enabling user registration. The module is part of the standard system and appears in all default configurations. The module contains quite a bit of functionality, only some of which is employed in the default setup. Visually, the module displays a login form, a link that leads to the user registration form, a username reminder link, a password reminder link, and a Remember Me option that helps a browser to remember a user by setting a cookie, as shown in Figure 10.5.

FIGURE 10.5

In the Default Login Form module, the question mark icons lead to the various reminder functions.

Once a user logs in, the Login module still serves a function as it remains on the screen displaying a welcome message and a Log out button.

As you can see in Figure 10.5, the module is pretty minimalist. If you would like to include instructions or other information with the form, you can do so by accessing the Basic Options tab of the Login Module workspace. There are two fields on the tab, Pre-text and Post-text, where you can enter text or HTML that you want to appear either immediately above or below the login form fields. Other controls on the Basic Options tab allow you to adjust the greeting displayed to logged-in users.

Later in this chapter, I discuss using the redirection functions associated with this module.

 For a complete discussion of the parameters and options available with the Login module, see Chapter 17.

Creating a login page

While the Login module is the most commonly used method for providing login functionality for your site visitors, it is not the only method available; the login form can also be displayed as a page with the form fields and controls located in the main content area of the page, rather than in a module position. Using a login page instead of the module offers the advantage of added flexibility. You have more space to work with in the content area and you can provide additional information with the form, information that may not fit neatly into a module. Additionally, while the Login module is useful, it does take up screen space that you may want to use for other purposes. If you use the page approach to displaying the login form, you only need to supply a link to it on one of your menus.

10

TIP

Of course, you can always use both options. You may want, for example, to make the Login form prominent on the home page through the use of the module, but on interior pages where you want to use the sidebars for different purposes, you can hide the module and use a link to the login page on one of your menus.

To create a login page, use the Menu Manager to create a menu item of the appropriate type. Follow these steps:

1. **Log in to the back-end admin system.**

2. **On the menu named Menus, select the menu where you want the link to the login page to appear.** After you click the menu, the Menu Item Manager loads in your browser window.

3. **On the Menu Item Manager, click the New button on the toolbar.** The New Menu Item workspace opens in your browser.

4. **Click the Select button next to the Menu Item Type field.** A pop-up window appears.

5. **Click the Users Manager option.** The option expands to list several choices.

6. **Select the Login Form option.** The pop-up window closes.

7. **Type a name for the link in the Menu Title field.** This is a required field.

8. **Click the Save button on the toolbar when you are finished.**

 See Chapter 8 for a detailed discussion of the Parameters and other options available for menu items.

Redirecting users after login or logout

Normally in Joomla!, after a user logs in or logs out, he is left on the same page. It is possible, however, to automatically redirect users to particular pages upon login or logout. This is a useful system feature that helps you channel users into particular content, or allows you the option to set up landing pages with content tailored to a user who is entering or exiting the restricted areas of your site. One of the most effective uses of this feature is to create a landing page that greets members upon login. The page usually carries a welcome message to site members and highlights what is new or being featured on the site.

If you are using the Login module, the Login and Logout Redirection Page options are located on the Basic Options tab of the Login Module Editing workspace. To set the Login Redirection Page for the Login module, follow these steps:

1. **Log in to the back-end admin system.**

2. **On the Extensions menu, click the Module Manager option.** The Module Manager loads in your browser window.

3. **In the Module Manager, click Login.** The Login module editing workspace opens in your browser.

4. **Click the Basic Options tab.** The tab comes to the front.

5. **To set redirection after login, use the Login Redirection Page combo box.** Select from the list the page that you want the users to see.

6. **To set redirection after logout, use the Logout Redirection Page combo box.** Select from the list the page that you want the users to see.

7. **Click the Save button on the toolbar.**

If, on the other hand, you are using the login page rather than the Login module, you must set it up in a different fashion:

1. **Log in to the back-end admin system.**

2. **On the menu named Menus, click the name of the menu that contains the link to your login page.** The Menu Item Editing workspace loads in your browser window.

3. **Click the Advanced Options tab.** The tab comes to the front.

4. **To set redirection after login, enter the URL of the destination page in the Login Redirect field.**

5. **To set redirection after logout, enter the URL of the destination page in the Logout Redirect field.**

6. **Click the Save button on the toolbar.**

> **CAUTION**
> The URL must not be located outside your site.

Creating a user registration page

While the Login module contains a link for site visitors to register, you can also link directly to a user registration page by creating a new menu item of the appropriate type. The page supplied by the menu item type is exactly the same as the page that appears when a visitor clicks the Create an account link on the Login module, so you will probably only use this option when you do not use the Login module.

To create a user registration page, use the Menu Manager to create a menu item of the appropriate type. Follow these steps:

1. **Log in to the back-end admin system.**

2. **On the menu named Menus, select the menu where you want the link to the login page to appear.** After you click the menu, the Menu Item Manager loads in your browser window.

10

263

3. **On the Menu Item Manager, click the New button on the toolbar.** The New Menu Item workspace opens in your browser.

4. **Click the Select button next to the Menu Item Type field.** A pop-up window appears.

5. **Click the Users Manager option.** The option expands to list several choices.

6. **Select the Registration Form option.** The pop-up window closes.

7. **Type a name for the link in the Menu Title field.** This is a required field.

8. **Click the Save button on the toolbar when you are finished.**

 See Chapter 8 for a detailed discussion of the parameters and other options available for menu items.

Enabling the Username Reminder function

As a convenience to users, Joomla! comes with a built-in Username Reminder function. If a user wants to log in but has forgotten her username, she can click the question mark icon that appears next to the User Name field on the Login module. A new page loads, prompting the user for her e-mail address. If she enters the correct e-mail address, the system sends the user her username by e-mail. The process is entirely automatic.

> **NOTE**
> The Login form displayed on the Login Form menu item type does not rely on the question mark icons; rather, it uses links displayed below the form. However, the function is the same.

As an alternative to relying on the link, you can create a direct link to the Username Reminder page by using the Menu Manager. To link directly to the Username Reminder page, follow these steps:

1. **Log in to the back-end admin system.**

2. **On the menu named Menus, select the menu where you want the link to the login page to appear.** After you click the menu, the Menu Item Manager loads in your browser window.

3. **On the Menu Item Manager, click the New button on the toolbar.** The New Menu Item workspace opens in your browser.

4. **Click the Select button next to the Menu Item Type field.** A pop-up window appears.

5. **Click the Users Manager option.** The option expands to list several choices.

6. **Select the Username Reminder Request option.** The pop-up window closes.

7. **Type a name for the link in the Menu Title field.** This is a required field.

8. **Click the Save button on the toolbar when you are finished.**

Note that the Username Reminder link is hard-coded into the Login Form module. If you display the Login Form module, you must also display the link. The only way to remove this link is to edit the module code to remove or otherwise hide the link.

 Modifying the default modules is discussed in Chapter 17.

Enabling the Password Reset function

Joomla! offers a similar feature to the Username Reminder function, called the Password Reset function. An existing user who has forgotten his password can request help from the system. Unlike the Username Reminder feature, which simply sends the data to the user, the Password Reset process requires additional steps. When a user clicks the question mark icon on the Login module, or the Forgot your Password? link on a login form page, a new page opens and prompts the user to input his registered e-mail address. If he inputs the address correctly, the system sends him a verification e-mail. The e-mail contains a token and a link to a page on the website. The user must copy the token, and then visit the web page. On the web page, the user pastes the token into the space provided and clicks the Submit button. The system opens yet another page where the user enters a new password that can then be used to access the site.

To create an alternative to the Password Reset function in the Login module, you can create a direct link to the Password Reset page with the Menu Manager. To create a direct link to the Password Reset page, follow these steps:

1. **Log in to the back-end admin system.**
2. **On the menu named Menus, select the menu where you want the link to the login page to appear.** After you click the menu, the Menu Item Manager loads in your browser window.
3. **On the Menu Item Manager, click the New button on the toolbar.** The New Menu Item workspace opens in your browser.
4. **Click the Select button next to the Menu Item Type field.** A pop-up window appears.
5. **Click the Users Manager option.** The option expands to list several choices.
6. **Select the Password Reset option.** The pop-up window closes.
7. **Type a name for the link in the Menu Title field.** This is a required field.
8. **Click the Save button on the toolbar when you are finished.**

> **NOTE**
> The Password Reset link is hard-coded into the Login Form module. If you display the Login Form module, you also display the link. The only way to remove this link is to edit the module code to remove or otherwise hide the link.

10

See Chapter 17 for more information on modifying the default modules.

Working with the User Profile Page

All Joomla! system users have their own user profile page. The page contains basic information about the user, including her name, username, registration date, and basic settings. The page can be viewed and edited from the front end of the website. In the default configuration, authenticated users can access the profile via the Your Profile link on the User menu. Figure 10.6 shows a typical user profile page. Publishing the page is a useful way to encourage your users to keep their information current, and it allows them to perform basic tasks like updating their passwords.

FIGURE 10.6

A typical user profile page

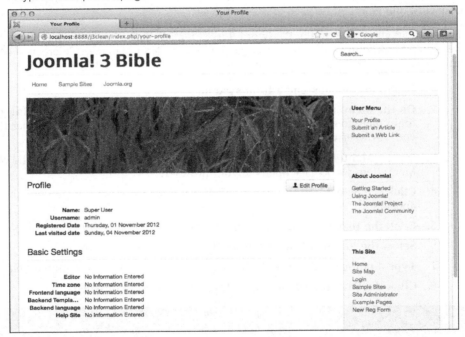

NOTE

The options that appear under the Basic Settings heading vary, depending on which group the user is assigned to; groups with more privileges display more options.

The menu item types included in the system give you a way to create links to both the user profile page and the editing page for the user profile. This allows you to create your own links rather than having to rely solely on the visibility of the User menu.

To create a direct link to the user profile page, follow these steps:

1. **Log in to the back-end admin system.**
2. **On the menu named Menus, select the menu where you want the link to the login page to appear.** After you click the menu, the Menu Item Manager loads in your browser window.
3. **On the Menu Item Manager, click the New button on the toolbar.** The New Menu Item workspace opens in your browser.
4. **Click the Select button next to the Menu Item Type field.** A pop-up window appears.
5. **Click the Users Manager option.** The option expands to list several choices.
6. **Select the User Profile option.** The pop-up window closes.
7. **Type a name for the link in the Menu Title field.** This is a required field.
8. **Click the Save button on the toolbar when you are finished.**

The User Profile page includes a link to the edit page, but if you prefer to create a link to the edit page manually, you can do so by following these steps:

1. **Log in to the back-end admin system.**
2. **On the menu named Menus, select the menu where you want the link to the user profile page to appear.** After you click the menu, the Menu Item Manager loads in your browser window.
3. **On the Menu Item Manager, click the New button on the toolbar.** The New Menu Item workspace opens in your browser.
4. **Click the Select button next to the Menu Item Type field.** A pop-up window appears.
5. **Click the Users Manager option.** The option expands to list several choices.
6. **Select the Edit User Profile option.** The pop-up window closes.
7. **Type a name for the link in the Menu Title field.** This is a required field.
8. **Click the Save button on the toolbar when you are finished.**

Controlling Access to Content and Functionalities

The main reason for creating user groups is to control access to content and functionalities. As discussed at the outset of this chapter, the Joomla! system's user groups are designed to give you varying levels of privileges; however, it's best not to equate user groups with access. A better framework for thinking about access in Joomla! is to split the topic of access into two areas: deciding what users can see and controlling what users can do. This two-part framework is useful in that it mirrors the way Joomla! handles access. Deciding what users can see is governed by what Access level has been assigned to the item. Controlling what users can do is dictated by the Permissions associated with the functionality. In this section I look in detail at how you can control what users can see and do on your site.

Deciding what users can see

In Joomla!, you control what people can see by assigning *access levels* to items. When you create a menu item, or a new article, the system expects you to set a value for the access parameter. Each access level permits certain user groups to have access to the item. Therefore, when you set the access level for an item, you define which groups of users are able to see it.

The system comes with a set of four predefined access levels: Guest, Public, Registered, and Special. You can add more access levels, or adjust the settings for the existing levels, via the Access Levels Manager. Figure 10.7 shows the Access Levels Manager.

FIGURE 10.7

The Access Levels Manager

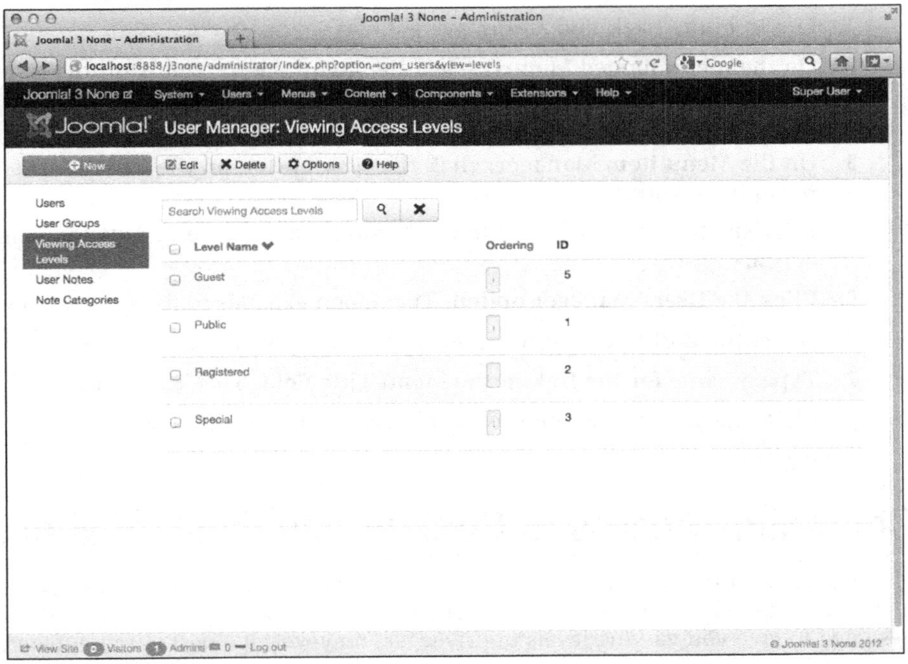

Table 10.1 shows how the default access levels translate into default user group privileges.

TABLE 10.1 How the Default Access Levels Relate to the Default User Groups

Access Level	Is Visible to the Following User Groups
Guest	Guest
Public	All
Registered	Manager, Administrator, Registered, Author, Editor, Publisher, and Super Users
Special	Manager, Administrator, Author, Editor, Publisher, and Super Users

TIP

The Guest access level was designed to give you a way to hide things from authenticated users. In other words, if a user is logged in, he won't see items set to the Guest access level. The Special access level was designed to facilitate front-end content management workflow.

 Working with front-end content management workflow is discussed at length in Chapter 5.

You can set access at various levels in the content hierarchy. There are access parameters for categories and articles, as shown in Table 10.2. By limiting access to a category, you limit access to the articles and subcategories within that category. Although access levels for individual articles can be set to create exceptions, they can only be used to create more restricted access, not less restricted access. In other words, if you set a category's access levels to Registered, then if you set the subcategories or articles in that section to Public, this will have no effect — the more restricted access of the parent grouping (the category) prevails. In contrast, if you set the parent grouping to Public access, then you can make access to any child items more restricted. For example, you can set access to a category to Public and set access to an article in that category to Registered with no problem.

TABLE 10.2 Managing Content Access

Item	To Change Access Levels, Go To...
Category	Category item editing workspace, Details tab.
Article	Article editing workspace, Details tab.

Joomla! allows you to control access to both entire menus and individual menu items. Limiting access to a menu also limits access to the items on that menu, as shown in Table 10.3.

10

TABLE 10.3 Managing Menu Access Levels

Item	To Change Access Levels, Go To...
Menu	Module Manager and edit the module's Details tab.
Menu Item	Edit Menu Item workspace and edit the Details tab.

It is possible to add new access levels to your site. To do so, follow these steps:

1. **Log in to the back-end admin system.**
2. **On the menu named Users, select the Access Levels option.** After you click the option, the Access Levels Manager loads in your browser window.
3. **Click the New button on the toolbar.** The New Access Level workspace opens in your browser.
4. **Type a name for the access level in the Level Title field.** This is a required field.
5. **Select one or more user groups.**
6. **Click the Save button on the toolbar when you are finished.**

The new access levels now appear throughout the site as an option on the Access control combo boxes.

Controlling what users can do

In Joomla!, you control what users can do by setting *permissions* to perform actions. Typically you find permissions parameters associated with components, modules, and plug-ins, but not content items. You can set permissions globally, via the Permissions tab in the Global Configuration Manager, and you can also set them on a per-item basis, using the various permissions options associated with the components.

> **TIP**
> The simplest way to manage permissions is to first set them globally, via the Global Configuration Manager, and then vary them as needed for individual items.

To set the permissions for the entire site, access the Permissions tab in the Global Configuration Manager. Figure 10.8 shows the Permissions tab.

On the left side of the Permissions tab, you can see a list of all the user groups in the system. As you select each user group, you can see the settings for each of the actions listed. There are three options in the Select New Setting combo box: *Inherited*, *Allowed*, and *Denied*. The column on the far right, labeled Calculated Setting, shows you the permissions inherited by this group from its parent group (if any).

FIGURE 10.8

The Permissions tab of the Global Configuration Manager, showing the global permissions for the Registered user group

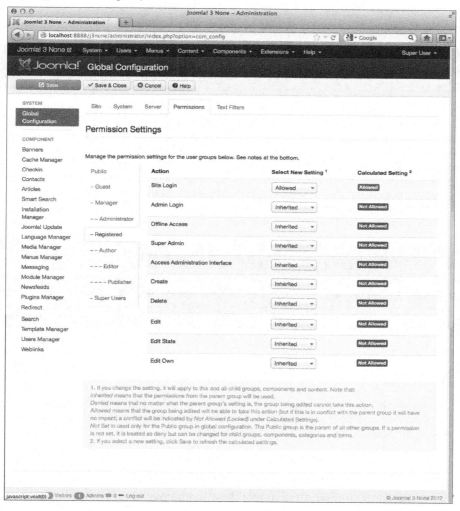

Here's what the options in the Select New Setting combo box mean:

- **Inherited.** The permissions from the parent group are used.
- **Allowed.** The group is allowed to take the action.
- **Denied.** The group is denied permission, regardless of the parent group's setting.

> **TIP**
>
> If a conflict in settings occurs, you see the note, Not Allowed (Locked), in the Calculated Setting column.

In addition to the global settings, you can customize permissions for individual components, modules, and plug-ins. The settings for these items are all grouped together in the Global Configuration Manager. For example, if you wanted to set the permissions for the Banner component, you would visit the Global Configuration Manager and click the Banners link under the Components heading in the left column. The Permissions tab that appears gives you the chance to tailor the settings specific to that component. The Permissions tabs for the varying components function the same way as the Global Configuration Permissions tab, but note that the setting on the Permissions tab of the Global Configuration Manager are considered to be the parent permissions.

> **NOTE**
>
> Settings are inherited; that is, the permissions attached to the parent are applied to the children. Similar to the structures used to control access, inheritance only applies to more restrictive settings. In other words, if the parent group is set to Denied, the children cannot be set to Allowed. If, in contrast, the parent permissions are set to Allowed, it is possible to configure the children group permissions to Denied.

Summary

This chapter is concerned with user management in Joomla! and the related topic of access control. I looked in depth at the tools that enable user management and how you can use the Joomla! system to do the following:

- Add new users to your site from the back end of your site
- Enable user registration for the front end of your site
- Configure user registration workflow to improve security
- Work with the system's user groups
- Control what users can see and do on your site

In the next chapter, I turn my attention to working with the Language Manager in Joomla! and how it can help you implement a fully multilingual website.

Creating a Multilingual Website

IN THIS CHAPTER

Creating a multilingual interface for your site

Enabling support for presenting articles in multiple languages

Creating content structures that support a multilingual site

Implementing tools that support multilingual content

By its very nature, the web is multilingual. Huge audiences exist for content in English, Spanish, Brazilian Portuguese, and Chinese, in particular. While the default Joomla! installer comes in British English, you can find officially maintained installers in a wide variety of other languages. If you want to offer your site in multiple languages, other issues arise. Joomla! provides Language Packs that allow you to present the site interface in any number of languages, but that still leaves the issue of presenting your content in different languages. While Joomla! language management doesn't translate the content for you, it can provide a logical structure for maintaining multilingual content, as well as provide your site visitors with the tools they need to choose their preferred language.

In this chapter, I look at both sides of the translation issue, that is, providing the site interfaces in additional languages and managing multilingual content.

Introducing the Language Manager

The Language Manager is at the heart of the language management capabilities of Joomla!. It has two important functions: First, it enables you to add and customize multiple translations of the interface, and second, it serves an enabling function by maintaining the connections between the language of the interface and the language of your content items. The various elements of the Language Manager handle the interface language shown on the front end, the interface language shown on the back end, and the languages available for the content.

All the words and phrases used by the Joomla! interface are collected into *Language Packs*, each of which provides support for a single language. Language Packs are a type of extension for the Joomla! system. As the site administrator, you must install a Language Pack for each language you want the site to display. You can administer and edit the Language Packs through the Joomla! Language Manager.

273

> **TIP**
>
> If you plan to offer the site in only one language, you are unlikely to need many of the Language Manager's capabilities, aside from the ability to customize the words and phrases used by the interface. If you installed Joomla! using the local language installer you need for your preferred language, then you do not need to worry about adding Language Packs. You can find a complete list of the local language installers on the JoomlaCode site, under the Languages category.

To access the Language Manager, you need to log in to the admin system of your website, go to the Extensions menu, and click the Language Manager option. The Language Manager loads in your browser window, as shown in Figure 11.1.

FIGURE 11.1

The Language Manager interface, shown with additional Language Packs installed and the default language set to British English

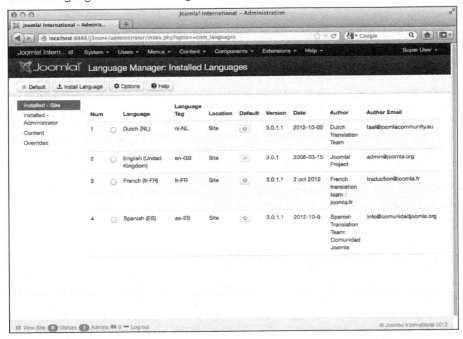

The toolbar at the top of the Language Manager contains the following buttons:

- **Default.** Select a language from the list and then click this button to set the language as the site's default language.

- **Install Language.** Click to view a list of available Language Packs and then select and install one.
- **Options.** Click to open the Language Manager options in the Global Configuration Manager.

- **Help.** Click to access the online Help files related to the active screen.

Below the toolbar in the left column are four text links that allow you to jump to the different workspaces in the Language Manager. They are:

- **Installed - Site.** Click to view a list of installed Language Packs for the front-end interface.
- **Installed - Administrator.** Click to view a list of installed Language Packs for the back-end interface.
- **Content.** Click to view a list of the available content languages. You can also add new content languages from the content language workspace.
- **Overrides.** Click to open the overrides workspace, where you can create exceptions to the text strings in your Language Packs.

The content areas of the screen for the Installed - Site and the Installed - Administrator workspaces are identical. From these screens you can see the Language Packs installed for the site, as well as information about them, at a glance. The columns provided are

- **Num.** This is an indexing number assigned by Joomla!. You cannot change this number.
- **Radio Button (no label).** You can click a radio button to select a language; you need to do this if you want to use the default option on the toolbar, referenced previously.
- **Language.** This column displays the full name of the Language Packs installed on the site.
- **Language Tag.** This is the abbreviation code used for the language.
- **Location.** This indicates whether the Language Pack applies to the front end or the back end of the site.
- **Default.** A yellow star in this column indicates that the language is selected as the site's default language.

- **Version.** This is the version number of the Language Pack.
- **Date.** This is the creation date of the Language Pack.
- **Author.** This is the name of the author of the Language Pack.
- **Author Email.** This is a contact e-mail for the author of the Language Pack.

Installing New Language Packs

If your Joomla! site does not use your preferred language, or you want to add an additional translation for the site's interface, then you can download and install one or more additional Language Packs. You can add new Language Packs directly from inside the Language Manager. Typically, each pack contains complete translations of all the various text strings used for both the front end and the back end of the site; you do not need to download two Language Packs to cover both the site and the administration interfaces, unless of course you want to display the front end and back end in different languages.

To install a new Language Pack, follow these steps:

1. **Log in to the admin system of your website.**
2. **Click the Language Manager option on the Extensions menu of the main admin navigation bar.** The Language Manager loads in your browser window.
3. **Click the Install Language button on the toolbar.** The Install Accredited Language Translations workspace opens in your browser.
4. **Scroll down the list to find the language you desire.** Click once to select the Language Pack.

5. **Click the Upload File & Install button.** The system attempts to install the Language Pack; if successful, it displays a confirmation message on the screen.

After you have installed the Language Pack, you see it listed in the Language Manager.

Modifying a Language Pack

The system's Language Packs specify the language strings that are used throughout the site. The strings cover everything from basics such as Read more, to error messages, to instruction text for common core functionalities. If you want to change the wording used in any of these strings, you can do so by using the Language Overrides workspace in the Language Manager. In this section, I show you how to customize the text in the interface to suit your needs.

Let's start with an example: Assume that you want to change the Password Reminder text that appears on the Login module. In the default installation, this text reads, "Forgot your password?" You can change it to the more conversational, "Have you forgotten your password?" To do so, follow these steps:

1. **Log in to the admin system of your Joomla! installation.**
2. **Click the Language Manager option on the Extensions menu of the main admin navigation bar.** The Language Manager loads in your browser window.
3. **Click the Overrides link in the left column.** The Language Overrides workspace opens.
4. **Use the filter combo box at the bottom of the left column to select the Language Pack you want to modify.**
5. **Click the New button on the toolbar.** The Edit Override workspace opens, as shown in Figure 11.2.
6. **In the Search field, on the bottom right, type *forgot your password.*** This is the string you want to modify.
7. **Click the Search button.** A list appears of results matching your query.
8. **Click the result you want to modify.** The system updates the values on the screen to reflect the choice you made.
9. **Change the text as you see fit.**
10. **Click the Save button.** The system saves your modified text as the new string, replacing the old one throughout the site.

As you create overrides, the system displays all of them so that you can easily access them inside the Edit Override workspace.

FIGURE 11.2

The Edit Override workspace lets you modify the text strings in your Language Packs.

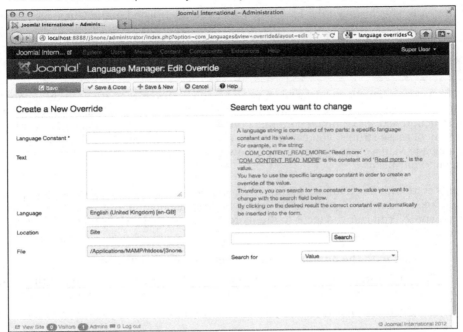

Enabling Multilingual Content

In the first part of this chapter, I showed you how to enable a multilingual interface for your Joomla! site. Adding Language Packs and providing the ability to display the interface in multiple languages is, however, only part of what is needed to create a fully multilingual site. You need to do more work if you want to offer your contents in multiple languages and if you want to give site visitors the tools to switch between the languages.

Multilingual content management imposes on the site administrators a significant and ongoing amount of work. For example, if you want to offer your Joomla! content in three different languages, you need to create and then maintain three parallel content structures. Each menu and every menu item has to exist in three different versions. Each article also has to exist in three different versions.

In this part of the chapter, I look at what it takes to configure the site to provide visitors with a full multilingual experience and how to create the content structures you need. At the end of the chapter, I also look at some of the helper tools the system provides.

Configuring the site to support a fully multilingual presentation

Configuring your site to support multilingual content is a two-step process. First, you have to install the appropriate Language Pack, and then you need to create a *Content Language*. Creating a Content Language is necessary to make a connection between the existing Language Pack and the language used for the categories, articles, and menu items. Without a Content Language, you will not be able to assign a category, article, or menu item to a language, and the system will not know what interface language to show to the users viewing the item.

NOTE

It's not necessary to install the Language Pack before you create the Content Language, but it does seem to make more sense, given that one of the pieces of information required during creation of the Content Language (that is, the Language Tag setting) has to match the Language Pack.

Earlier in this chapter I looked at installing Language Packs, so in this section, I am going to look at the second step: creating a Content Language. By way of example, assume you want to give your site visitors the option to view contents in either English or Spanish. Because English is already part of the default installation, you need only create a Content Language for Spanish. Here's how to add a new Content Language:

1. **Log in to the admin system of your Joomla! installation.**
2. **Click the Language Manager option on the Extensions menu of the main admin navigation bar.** The Language Manager loads in your browser window.
3. **Click the Content link in the left column.** The Content Languages workspace opens.
4. **Click the New button on the toolbar.** The New Content Language workspace opens in your browser, as shown in Figure 11.3.
5. **In the Title field, enter a name for the language.** The name will appear in the lists where people select the language, so you should keep it short and straightforward. This is a required field.

TIP

Because the value in the title field may appear as a choice for users, you probably want to use the name as it appears in the language; for example, instead of Spanish, you would use Espanol.

6. **In the Title Native field, enter a name for the language in your own language.** This is a required field.
7. **In the URL Language Code field, add whatever you want to appear in the URL strings for the content in this language.** This value must be unique among your languages. This is a required field.

TIP

It's best to keep this short, typically the two-letter code for the language. For example, for Spanish, you might want to use "es."

8. **In the Image Prefix field, add whatever you want to appear as the name of the image file used for the language flag for the language switcher.** This is a required field.

9. **In the Language Tag field, enter the 5-digit code for the language you want to use.** This is a required field.

TIP

Language tags follow a set format and your input must match this format. The format is two lowercase letters, followed by a dash, followed by two uppercase letters; for example, es – ES, which is the language tag for Spanish.

CAUTION

The value you enter in the Content Language's Language Tag field must match the language tag of the related Language Pack.

10. **Click the Site Name tab.** The tab comes to the front.

11. **In the Custom Site Name field, enter a name for your site in the appropriate language.**

TIP

This field is optional, but for many people the site name may vary, if only slightly, from language to language. This is common if you have appended a tagline or slogan to your site name for SEO purposes.

12. **Click Save.** All other fields on this tab and the others are optional.

Once you save your work, the new Content Language will appear on the list of items in the Content Languages Manager. Make sure the language is published, or else it will not appear on the various lists in the interface. The content language is necessary for you to take the next steps: the creation of the content structures to support multilingual content.

Creating the content structures to support multiple languages

The Joomla! multilingual content system works best when you create parallel content structures for the various languages. Use one structure for each language and place inside it all the content items for that language. If you follow this approach, the site is easier to maintain and features like the Joomla! breadcrumbs work without any problems.

For example, if you want to provide your contents in both English and Spanish, you need to create parallel categories and content items in both languages. You also need to create menus and menu items for each language. In this section I take you through setting up the structures that you need.

FIGURE 11.3

The New Content Language workspace

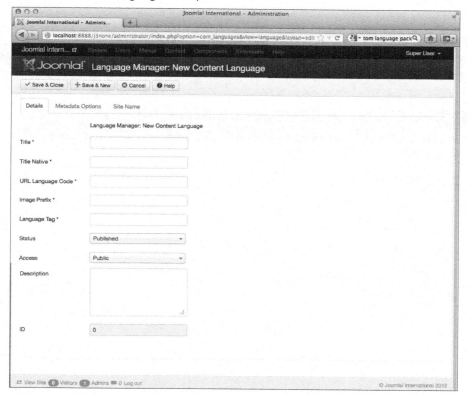

Structuring your categories

Start by creating parallel categories as containers for the articles in each of your languages. As you create the articles for a particular language, you will assign them to the relevant category for that language.

> **NOTE**
>
> You can, of course, create all the subcategories you want, but in each case make sure the subcategories are nested inside the parent category for the relevant language.

To continue the example from earlier in this chapter, you need to create three parent categories: one for English content, one for Spanish content, and a catch-all category called ALL; the latter is used for any items that are shared across languages and is a useful device for holding the generic home page that I discuss in the next section. As you create each category, you must set the language option for the category to the proper language.

Figure 11.4 shows how the category structure of a bilingual English/Spanish site might look.

FIGURE 11.4

A sample multilingual category structure. Note the Language column values for the categories.

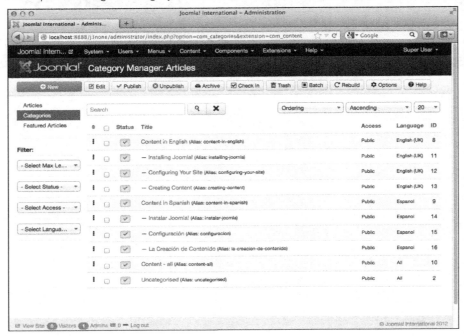

Setting up the menus

Like the categories, the menus and the menu items of your multilingual site must demonstrate a parallel structure. Also, like the categories, the menu items must be configured to use the proper language. There is one unique issue that relates to the menus, and it is important: Each language needs a menu with a default page set and, in addition, there must be a generic default page set on a neutral menu and that menu must be unpublished. That sounds a bit confusing, so let me continue with the previous example to illustrate how to set up these menus.

 For detailed instructions on creating menus and menu items, see Chapter 8.

Access your site's Menu Manager and then follow these steps:

1. **Rename the site's default main menu.** Call it something generic like Main Menu - ALL.

2. **Access the menu's module and rename it to match Main Menu - ALL.**

3. **Create a new menu to hold the English language content items.** Call it Main Menu - EN.

4. **Create a menu module to go with it.** Name it consistently; call it Main Menu - EN and set the language of the module to English.

5. **Create a new menu to hold the Spanish language content items.** Call it Main Menu - ES.

6. **Create a menu module to go with it.** Name it consistently; call it Main Menu - ES and set the language of the module to Espanol.

Figure 11.5 shows how the sample menu structure looks.

FIGURE 11.5

The Menu Manager showing the three menus necessary to support the multilingual content structure

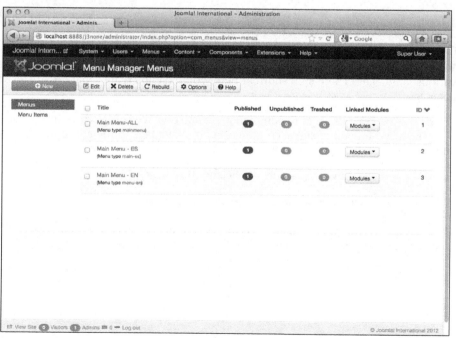

Creating the menus is just the first step; you also need to make sure each of the menus has a default page. The Main Menu - ALL should already contain a default page, so all you need to do is add default pages to the other two menus. Access each menu's Menu Item Manager and create a default page for each one. Select an appropriate menu item type, like Featured Articles, and make sure to set the language of the default page of the Main Menu - EN menu to English and the language of the default page of the Main Menu - ES menu to Espanol.

> **NOTE**
>
> As you set up each local language menu with a default page, you see a flag representing the language appear next to the menu item in the Home column and also next to the name of the menus on the main admin navigation bar.

The last step in this part of the process is to go to the Module Manager and unpublish the Main Menu - ALL module. Don't delete it, just unpublish it.

Your menus are now ready to use. Now it is time to create your articles. As you add your articles to the menus, make sure you always set the language to match the menu.

> **NOTE**
>
> All of these discussions about parallel structure assume you want to show the same categories, articles, or menu items to visitors in each language. If you do not want to show them the same things, there is no need to strictly adhere to a parallel structure.

Creating the articles

With your categories and menus in place, you are ready to start creating the articles in the various languages. There's no shortcut here; you have to create separate articles for each language.

To see the example through to completion, create one Welcome article in English and one in Spanish. When you create each article, set the language to the appropriate language and assign the article to a category inside the proper language category.

Figure 11.6 shows how the sample article structure looks.

 See Chapter 5 for more information on creating and editing articles.

The final step in the process is to publish the enabling tools that help the users choose their language and help the system filter content by language.

FIGURE 11.6

The Article Manager showing the parallel structure of the articles created. Note the Categories and the Language column.

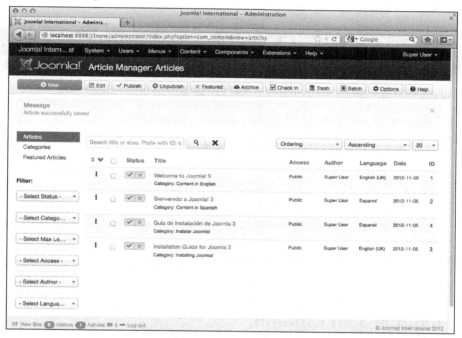

Enabling the supporting plug-ins

You need to enable two additional items to complete the process of creating a fully multilingual website. One of the items is the Language Switcher module, and the other is the System - Language Filter plug-in.

The Language Switcher is a site module. It is designed to display flags on the front end of the site that represent each of the published site languages so that users can select a language by clicking a language flag. This module is necessary for your site visitors to be able to see the available languages and choose from the list of options. You can view this module published in the right column in Figure 11.7.

See Chapter 17 for more information on working with Site modules.

TIP

If you want to display this module, or any module, in multiple languages, simply create multiple instances of the Language Switcher module, set the language preference, add any local language text content, and then assign the appropriate module to the appropriate language menu items.

Joomla! needs the System - Language Filter plug-in to display content in the language selected. The System - Language Filter plug-in should only be enabled when the Language Switcher module is published. There is no visible output from this plug-in; it is simply an enabling tool needed by the system.

CAUTION

Publish the Language Switcher module before you enable the Language Filter plug-in.

While the Language Switcher module and the Language Filter plug-in are the only additional items you need to complete your multilingual site configuration, you may want to add two other items to the list, one module and one plug-in.

 See Chapter 19 for more information on working with plug-ins.

FIGURE 11.7

The front end of the sample multilingual website. Note the Language Switcher module in the right column, customized to the appropriate language. Note also the various interface pieces in Spanish.

The system includes a utility module designed to help out the site administrator; it's called the Multilanguage Status module. This module monitors your multilingual content items and notifies you if it detects any errors or anomalies. The Multilanguage Status module is an Administrator module, so when you access the Module Manager, you will need to filter the list of modules to show only the Administrator modules. When you publish the module, a new item appears on the bottom status bar: Multilanguage Status. If any errors are found, a warning message appears.

 See Chapter 18 for more information on working with Administrator modules.

The final optional item is a plug-in named System - Language Code. You can use this plug-in to remove the language code from the site's URLs. Though it is not necessary to use this plug-in, it does tend to improve the URL structures for search engine optimization purposes.

Summary

In this chapter, I covered the various tasks associated with enabling multilingual support for your site. I looked at the following:

- Understanding the role of the Language Manager
- Installing new Language Packs
- Modifying the text strings that appear on the interface of your site
- Adding support for multilingual content
- Creating the content structures needed to support multiple languages
- Enabling supporting modules and plug-ins

In the next chapter, I move into the third part of the book, where I look in detail at the default site's components, modules, and plug-ins. I start with a look at the Banner component.

Part III

Working with Components, Modules, and Plug-Ins

P art III focuses on the functionality that is included in the default system. I've included separate chapters for the default components in order to take an in-depth look at how to use and configure each component. The various Joomla! modules are also detailed in two chapters, one focused on the Site Modules, the other on the Administrator Modules. The modules chapters not only detail the purpose of each of the modules, but they also include examples of uses and complete coverage of the configuration options available for the modules. The final chapter covers the default Joomla! Plug-ins and the options they give website owners.

Using the Banner Manager

IN THIS CHAPTER

Understanding how the Banners component and Banner module work together

Creating new banners

Associating banners with clients

Grouping banners into categories

Tracking banner performance

Creating new Banner modules

Enabling conditional display of banners

The Banner Manager component in Joomla! is responsible for handling the advertising space on your website. Although the name implies that it is only suitable for banner ads, you can use it to display graphical content in any shape or size; the only limitation you face comes from what fits comfortably into your page layout. The component is quite powerful. It can handle multiple types of ads, manage multiple clients, enable conditional banner display, and generate reports on banner performance.

The Banner Manager works in conjunction with the Banner module. The Banner Manager component handles the management of the banners and the clients, while the Banner module handles the actual display of the banners. The Banner Manager component serves as an interface that lets you organize banners into categories and associate them with clients, as well as set the limitations on display. The Banner module, in contrast, enables you to control the placement of the banners by page and by position on the page.

In this chapter, I look at how the Banner Manager component works in harmony with the Banner module to allow you to manage banners across your site, as well as manage ads and ad campaigns.

Introducing the Banner Manager

To start placing ads on your site, you must first create *banners,* which, in Joomla! terminology, means any item that can be published by the site's Banner module and managed via the Banner Manager. That sounds like a broad definition, and it is. The Banners component, despite the name, can handle much more than simple banner ads. The component is flexible enough to allow you to use it as a vehicle for displaying virtually anything you like — an advertising graphic, a simple decorative picture, a text message, or even an ad sourced from a third-party site or advertising network. Regardless of the content, the item you want to display is called a banner and managed via the Banner Manager.

> **TIP**
>
> While most people use the Banner Manager component strictly for managing the advertising space on their site, you can do much more with it; it's really up to you to define how you want to use this component.

To access the Banner Manager, you can go to the Components menu and select the Banners option. The Banner Manager interface loads in your browser. Figure 12.1 shows the Banner Manager as it appears with the Learning Joomla! sample data.

FIGURE 12.1

The Banner Manager interface

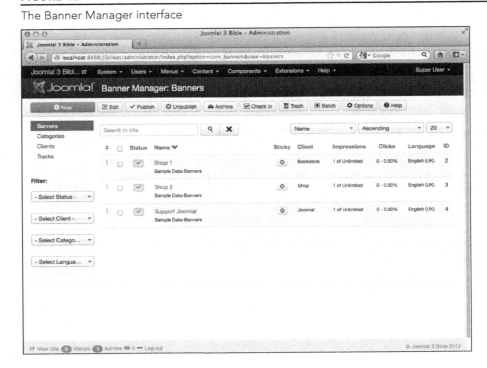

The toolbar at the top of the Banner Manager provides quick access to the following functions:

- **New.** Click to add a new banner.

- **Edit.** Select a banner from the list and then click this button to edit the banner details.

- **Publish.** Select one or more banners from the list and then click this button to publish them. You publish a banner to make it visible on the front end of the website.

- **Unpublish.** Select one or more banners from the list and then click this button to unpublish them. You unpublish a banner to hide it from the front end of the website.

- **Archive.** Select one or more banners from the list and then click this button to move the banner to the archive.

- **Check In.** Select one or more banners and then click this button to force the banner's editing workspace to close and thereby "check in" the banner.

- **Trash.** Select one or more banners from the list and then click this button to delete the banners.

- **Batch.** Select multiple banners and then click this button to batch-apply processes to them. The pop-up window that appears enables you execute changes to multiple banners in one simple operation.

- **Options.** Click to open the Banner Manager Options, where you can configure the parameters that affect the Banner Manager.

- **Help.** Click to access the online Help files related to the active screen.

Below the toolbar, in the left column, are four links: Banners shows you the Banner Manager, Categories shows you the Banner Categories Manager, Clients shows you the Banner Clients Manager, and Tracks opens the Banner Tracks workspace. Each of these options is discussed in the sections that follow.

Below the four links in the left column are four sorting tools to help you manage long lists of banners:

- **Select Status.** The options in this combo box allow you to filter and display the banners according to whether they are published, unpublished, archived, or trashed. This provides an easy way to identity all banners that are currently active on the site.

- **Select Client.** The options in this combo box allow you to filter and display the banners according to the client with whom they are associated.

- **Select Category.** The options in this combo box allow you to filter and display the banners according to the category to which they are assigned.

- **Select Language.** The options in this combo box let you filter the list of banners by language.

12

> **TIP**
> You can apply more than one filter at a time to get even more granular results.

Below the toolbar and above the list of banners are four sorting and searching tools to help you manage long lists of banners:

- Type a word or phrase into the Search field and then click the magnifying glass button. The system searches your list of banners for the query and then displays the results of the search. To clear the screen and return to a full listing, click the button marked with the X.
- Use the combo box to the right of the Search field to specify which column of the banner display is used for the sort order.
- Use the Ascending combo box to specify whether the banners appear in ascending or descending order.
- Use the combo box on the far right to control the number of banners that appear on the page. You can alter the default value by changing the List Length parameter in the Global Configuration Manager.

The main content area of the screen contains a list of all the banners in your Joomla! site. The columns provided are

- **Sort Order (vertical double arrows).** Click the arrows to change the sort order. You can also click and hold any of the buttons immediately to the left of a banner's title, and then drag the banner to change its order location in the Banner Manager.
- **Banner Selection (unlabeled check box).** Click a check box to select a banner; this is useful if you want to use several of the toolbar options.
- **Status.** A green check mark indicates that the banner is published. A red x indicates that it is unpublished.
- **Name.** This field displays the full name of the banner. Click the name to edit the banner's details.
- **Sticky.** This column indicates whether the banner has been marked as 'sticky.' A green checkmark indicates the banner is selected as sticky. A red x indicates it is not sticky. You can toggle between the two states by clicking the box in this column.

> **TIP**
> You can use your Banner module settings to prioritize sticky banners. Sticky banners always show in the position to which they are assigned; they do not rotate impressions with other banners.

- **Client.** This field shows the name of the client to whom the banner is assigned.
- **Impressions.** This field provides two pieces of information: First, it shows the number of times the banner has appeared on the site (known as "impressions"); second, it indicates whether the administrator has set a limit on the number of

impressions of the banner. If a limit has not been set on the impressions, the field shows "Unlimited."

- **Clicks.** This field indicates the number of times the banner has been clicked by visitors to your site.
- **Language.** This field shows the language designated for the banner.
- **ID.** This field shows the system-generated user ID number.

Configuring the Banner Component

You can customize global configuration options for the Banner component through the Banner Manager Options workspace in the Global Configuration Manager. You can view and modify the parameters by clicking the Banners link under the Components heading in the Global Configuration Manager, or by clicking the Options button on the Banner Manager toolbar. Figure 12.2 shows the Banner Manager Options workspace. The options you specify here are applied to all banners, but you can override them by modifying the specific parameters of individual banners.

The Banner Manager Options workspace includes a very limited number of parameters:

- **Purchase Type.** Use the combo box to choose a period to be used for calculating the basis of banner subscriptions. The options include Daily, Weekly, Monthly, Yearly, and Unlimited. Choose Unlimited if you do not want to sell impressions based on time.
- **Track Impressions.** Set the option to Yes to track the number of impressions per banner.
- **Track Clicks.** Set the option to Yes to track the number of clicks on each banner.
- **Meta Keyword Prefix.** Set a prefix to be used if you are employing the meta-tag matching function to control banner display. This improves the performance of the Banner module.

After you have set the parameters you desire, click the Save button in the top-left corner to save your changes, or click Cancel to close the parameters window without saving the changes.

FIGURE 12.2

The Banner Manager Options workspace in the Global Configuration Manager

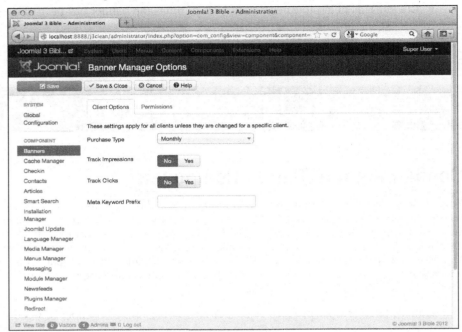

Managing Clients

Clients are created by the administrator for the purpose of grouping banners. Though you do not have to assign banners to clients, the client functionality is most useful if you are accepting advertising on your site. By creating clients, you are able to group all the ads from one client in one place and you are also able to capture contact and contract term details, all in one place.

To view the clients in your system, you can click the Clients link at the top of the Banner Manager.

> **TIP**
> If you do not need multiple clients, you can simply create a single client and assign all your banners to that client.

Exploring the Banner Client Manager

The Banner Client Manager displays a list of all the clients that exist in the system. You can use this interface to add new clients and to review and edit existing clients. Figure 12.3 shows the Banner Client Manager.

FIGURE 12.3

The Banner Client Manager with the Learning Joomla! sample data installed

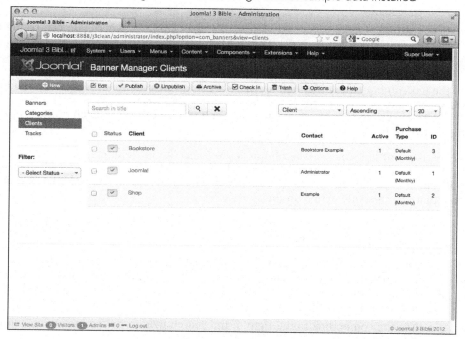

The toolbar at the top of the Banner Client Manager provides quick access to the following functions:

- **New.** Click to add a new client.

- **Edit.** Select a client from the list and then click this button to edit the client's details.

- **Publish.** Select one or more clients from the list and then click this button to publish them. Publishing a client means that the client's banners can be viewed on the front end of the website, assuming the banners are also published.

- **Unpublish.** Select one or more clients from the list and then click this button to unpublish them. Unpublishing a client means that the client's banners will not be available on the front end of the website.
- **Archive.** Select one or more clients from the list and then click this button to move the client to the archive.
- **Check In.** Select one or more clients from the list and then click this button to force the client's editing workspace to close and thereby "check in" the client.
- **Trash.** Select one or more clients from the list and then click this button to delete the clients.
- **Options.** Click to open the Banner Manager Options, where you can configure the parameters that affect the Banner Manager.
- **Help.** Click to access the online Help files related to the active screen.

In the left column below the toolbar, there are four links: Banners shows you the Banner Manager, Categories shows you the Banner Categories Manager, Clients shows you the Client Manager, and Tracks opens the Banner Tracks workspace. Each of these options is discussed in the sections that follow.

Below the four links in the left column is the Select Status Filter combo box. The options in this combo box allow you to filter and display the clients according to whether they are published, unpublished, archived, or trashed. This provides an easy way to identify all clients that are currently active on the site.

Below the toolbar and above the list of clients are four sorting and searching tools to help you manage long lists of clients:

- Type a word or phrase into the Search field and then click the magnifying glass button. The system searches your list of clients for the query and then displays the results of the search. To clear the screen and return to a full listing, click the button marked with the X.
- Use the combo box to the right of the Search field to determine which column of the client display is used for the sort order.

TIP
You can also sort any column by clicking the column header.

- Use the Ascending combo box to specify whether the clients appear in ascending or descending order.
- Use the combo box on the far right to control the number of clients that appear on the page. You can alter the default value by changing the List Length parameter in the Global Configuration Manager.

The main content area of the screen contains a list of all the banner clients in your Joomla! site. The columns provided are

- **Client Selection (unlabeled check box).** You can click a check box to select a client; this is useful if you want to use several of the toolbar options.
- **Status.** A green check mark indicates that the client is published. A red x indicates that it is unpublished.
- **Client.** This is the name given to the client.
- **Contact.** This is the Joomla! contact associated with the client. The contacts come from the system's Contacts component.
- **Active.** This is the number of banners associated with the client.
- **Purchase Type.** This indicates the type of purchase subscription associated with the client. Unlimited means that banner display is not restricted by time.
- **ID.** This is the system-generated user ID number.

Creating clients

You can create clients from the New Banner Client workspace, as shown in Figure 12.4. To access the New Banner Client workspace, you click the New button on the toolbar at the top of the Banner Client Manager.

FIGURE 12.4

The New Banner Client workspace

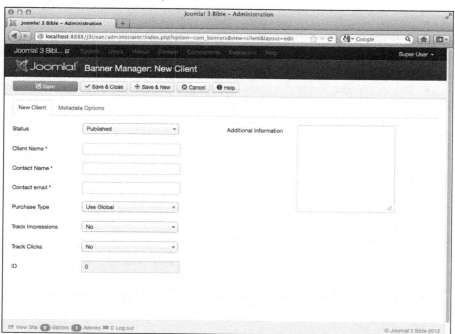

The toolbar at the top of the New Banner Client workspace provides quick access to the following functions:

- **Save.** Click to save your work and create a new client without leaving the workspace.
- **Save & Close.** Click to save your work, create a new client, and exit the New Client workspace.
- **Save & New.** Click to save your work, close the current New Client workspace, and open another New Client workspace.
- **Cancel.** Click to cancel the task and exit the New Client workspace.
- **Help.** Click to display the Help files related to the active screen.

There are two tabs at the top of workspace:

- **New Client.** This tab contains the key fields needed to create a new banner client. The fields are discussed in the following bulleted list.
- **Metadata Options.** This tab contains the fields needed to override the global metadata settings for this client's banners as a group. If you are using the keyword-matching feature to help control display of banners, you should use the Meta Keywords field, which is useful for adding relevant keywords that can trigger the display of banners from this client.

The New Client tab of the New Banner Client workspace includes the following fields:

- **Status.** Specify the status of the client: Published, Unpublished, Archived, or Trashed.
- **Client Name.** Enter a name for the client as you want to see it in the administration system. This is a required field.
- **Contact Name.** Enter the name of your contact person for this client. This is a required field.
- **Contact email.** Enter an e-mail address for the contact person for this client. This is a required field.
- **Purchase Type.** Specify the term for the impressions or click calculations. The options are Daily, Weekly, Monthly, Yearly, or Unlimited.
- **Track Impressions.** Select Yes to count the impressions and display the number of impressions in the Banner Tracks.
- **Track Clicks.** Select Yes to count the clicks and display the number of clicks in the Banner Tracks.
- **ID.** The value in this field is assigned automatically by the Joomla! system and is used internally by the system.
- **Additional Information (optional).** Add notes or descriptive information. This is provided for the benefit of the administrators and does not appear on the front end of the site.

The Metadata Options tab contains the following fields, which relate to the functionality to display banners based upon meta keywords matching:

- **Meta Keywords.** Enter the keywords you want to associate with the client's banners. These apply to all the client's banners, unless overridden at the banner level.
- **Use Own Prefix.** Select Yes to implement the keyword-prefix option. This improves system performance as it only matches keywords that include the specified prefix.
- **Meta Keyword Prefix.** If you set the Use Own Prefix option to Yes, then you can enter the prefix here.

NOTE

To learn more about using keyword matching to control banner display, see the discussion of the Banner module later in this chapter.

To create a new banner client, follow these steps:

1. **Log in to the admin system.**
2. **Go to the Components menu and select the Clients option from the Banners submenu.** The Banner Client Manager loads in your browser.
3. **Click the New button on the toolbar at the top of the Banner Client Manager.** The New Banner Client Workspace opens (refer to Figure 12.4).
4. **In the Client Name field, type the name of the client.** This field is required.
5. **In the Contact Name field, type the name of the person who will be your contact for this client.** This field is required.
6. **In the Contact email field, type the e-mail address for the contact person.** This field is required.
7. **Click the Save button on the toolbar to save your new banner client.** All other fields, including those in the Metadata Options tab, are optional.

TIP

Make sure your client's status is set to Published if you want the client's banners to be visible on the front end of the website.

Editing clients

You can edit existing banner clients from the Banner Client Manager. To edit a client, either click the client name in the Banner Client Manager, or select the client and then click the Edit button on the Banner Client Manager toolbar. Regardless of which method you use, the system opens the Edit Banner Client workspace. The Edit Banner Client workspace is identical to the New Banner Client workspace, with the same fields and requirements as discussed in the previous section.

To make changes to a client, you simply alter the desired fields in the Edit Banner Client workspace and then click the Save button on the toolbar. Any changes you have made are applied immediately.

Archiving clients

If you want to remove a client from use on the site, but do not want to delete the client record, you can move the client to the Client Archive. By default, archived clients are not shown on the front end of the website.

To archive a client, follow these steps:

1. **Log in to the admin system.**
2. **Go to the Components menu and select the Clients option from the Banners submenu.** The Banner Client Manager loads in your browser.
3. **Click the check box next to the client or clients you want to archive.**
4. **Click the Archive button on the toolbar.** The system immediately moves the selected clients to the archive.

> **NOTE**
> Archiving a client does not archive that client's banners. You must archive banners separately.

A client that has been moved into the archive can be unarchived by changing the status of the client to either Published or Unpublished. To unarchive a client, follow these steps:

1. **Log in to the admin system.**
2. **Go to the Components menu and select the Clients option from the Banners submenu.** The Banner Client Manager loads in your browser.
3. **Change the Select Status Filter to Archived.**
4. **Click the check box next to the client or clients you want to unarchive.**
5. **Select either Publish or Unpublish from the toolbar.** The system immediately unarchives the selected clients.

Deleting clients

The deletion of clients in Joomla! is a two-step process. The first step involves moving the client to the trash, where the client is held until you take the second step and permanently delete it. Clients held in the trash can be restored at any time prior to deletion. You can view the contents of the trash at any time by selecting the Trashed option from the Select Status Filter in the Banner Client Manager.

Clients that you move to the trash are held there indefinitely. The clients can be restored or deleted at the option of the administrator. Restored clients return to their original locations, but deleted clients are permanently removed from the system and cannot be restored.

Though clients can be left in the trash indefinitely, the trash is distinctly different from the archive. Moving banners to the trash should not be confused with archiving clients.

To move a client to the trash, follow these steps:

1. **Log in to the admin system.**
2. **Go to the Components menu and select the Clients option from the Banners submenu.** The Banner Client Manager loads in your browser.
3. **Click the check boxes next to the client or clients you want to move to the trash.**
4. **Click the Trash button on the toolbar.** The system moves the selected clients to the trash.

NOTE
Any client that you move to the trash is instantly unpublished and not visible to site visitors. Trashing a client, however, has no impact on the banners associated with that client.

Restoring clients from the trash

Clients that you move to the trash are held there until the administrator takes further action. Any client can be restored at any time. The process of restoring a client is simple and the result instantaneous: the client is removed from the trash and returns to where it was located before it was moved to the trash.

To restore a client from the trash, follow these steps:

1. **Log in to the admin system.**
2. **Go to the Components menu and select the Clients option from the Banners submenu.** The Banner Client Manager loads in your browser.
3. **Change the Select Status Filter to Trashed.** The list of clients reloads to display only clients that are in the trash.
4. **Click the check box next to the client or clients you want to restore.**
5. **Click either Publish or Unpublish on the toolbar.** The system removes the selected clients from the trash, and restores them to their previous location.

TIP
You can also restore a client by moving your mouse over the client name, clicking the arrow that appears, and selecting Untrash from the options on the menu that opens.

Deleting clients permanently

Clients held in the trash can be removed from the system by emptying the trash. Emptying the trash results in the client's permanent removal from the system; it cannot be restored once deleted.

To permanently delete a client from the trash, follow these steps:

1. **Log in to the admin system.**
2. **Go to the Components menu and select the Clients option from the Banners submenu.** The Banner Client Manager loads in your browser.
3. **Change the Select Status Filter to Trashed.**
4. **Click the check box next to the client or clients you want to delete.**
5. **Click the Empty Trash button on the toolbar.** The system immediately deletes the selected clients.

CAUTION

Deleting a banner client is permanent and cannot be undone. Moreover, there is no confirmation dialog box — clicking the Delete button immediately deletes the client!

NOTE

Deleting a client does not delete the banners associated with the client; the client field of the banners reverts to No Client.

Managing Categories

Categories, like clients, are an organizational tool for grouping banners. Every banner must be assigned to a category or labeled as uncategorized. Categories are independent of the client's grouping — that is, a banner can belong to any combination of the category and client fields. Categories can also be nested into subcategories.

Categories are most useful for grouping banners that will appear in particular sections of your site or for the management of advertising campaigns. As you will see later in this chapter, you can create Banner modules that show only the banners from specific categories; this means that strategic use of categories can help you run more effective advertising campaigns and keep your management overhead down.

In this section, I cover how to create and manage your site's banner categories.

TIP

If you do not need multiple banners in your system, you can simply create a single category and assign all your banners to that category, or you can leave them all marked as uncategorized. For purposes of Joomla!, the uncategorized designation functions just like any other category for grouping banners.

Exploring the Banner Categories Manager

You can create and edit banner categories through the Banner Categories Manager. You access the Banner Categories Manager directly from the Banners submenu on the Components menu, or by clicking the Categories link in the left column of the Banner Manager. Figure 12.5 shows the Banner Categories Manager as it appears with the sample data installed.

FIGURE 12.5

The Banner Categories Manager

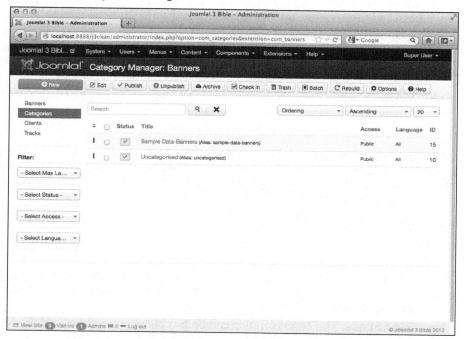

The toolbar at the top of the Banner Categories Manager provides quick access to the following functions:

- **New.** Click to add a new banner category.

- **Edit.** Select a category from the list and then click this button to edit the banner category details.

- **Publish.** Select one or more banner categories from the list and then click this button to publish them. You publish a category to make it visible on the front end of the website.

- **Unpublish.** Select one or more banner categories from the list and then click this button to unpublish them. You unpublish a category to hide it from display on the front end of the website.

- **Archive.** Select one or more categories from the list and then click this button to move the category to the archive.

- **Check In.** Select one or more categories and then click this button to force the category's editing workspace to close and thereby "check in" the category.

- **Trash.** Select one or more categories from the list and then click this button to delete the selected categories.

- **Batch.** Select multiple categories and then click this button to batch-apply processes to those categories. The pop-up window that appears enables you to copy or move multiple categories in one simple operation.

- **Rebuild.** Click if you are experiencing problems with your banner categories. Clicking this button forces the system to rebuild the banner category tables in the database. You should not normally need this tool; use it sparingly.

- **Options.** Click to open the Banner Manager Options, where you can configure the parameters that affect the Banner Manager.

- **Help.** Click to access the online Help files related to the active screen.

In the left column, below the toolbar, are four links: Banners shows you the Banner Manager, Categories shows you the Banner Categories Manager, Clients shows you the Banner Clients Manager, and Tracks opens the Banner Tracks workspace. I discuss each of these options in the sections that follow.

Below the four links in the left column are four sorting tools to help you manage long lists of categories:

- **Select Max Levels.** This combo box controls the number of levels of categories that are displayed. If your site has a complex hierarchy, this can greatly simplify the view of the list of categories. To reset this filter, change the combo box back to the default setting, Select Max Levels.

- **Select Status.** The options in this combo box allow you to filter and display the categories according to whether they are published, unpublished, archived, or trashed. This provides an easy way to identity all categories that are currently active on the site. To reset this filter, change the combo box back to the default setting, Select Status.

- **Select Access.** This combo box lets you filter the list of categories by access level. To reset this filter, change the combo box back to the default setting, Select Access.

- **Select Language.** This combo box lets you filter the list of categories by language. To reset this filter, change the combo box back to the default setting, Select Language.

Below the toolbar and above the list of categories are four sorting and searching tools to help you manage long lists of categories:

- Type a word or phrase into the Search field and then click the magnifying glass button. The system searches your list of categories for the query and then displays the results of the search. To clear the screen and return to a full listing, click the button marked with the X.

- Use the combo box to the right of the Search field to determine which column of the display is used for the sort order.

- Use the Ascending combo box to specify whether the categories appear in ascending or descending order.

- Use the combo box on the far right to control the number of categories that appear on the page. You can alter the default value by changing the List Length parameter in the Global Configuration Manager.

The main content area of the screen contains a list of all the banner categories in your Joomla! site. The columns provided are

- **Sort Order (vertical double arrows).** You can click the arrows to change the sort order. You can also click and hold any of the buttons immediately to the left of a category's title, and then drag the category to change its order location in the Banner Category Manager.

- **Category Selection (unlabeled check box).** You can click a check box to select a category; this is necessary if you want to use several of the toolbar options.

- **Status.** A green check mark indicates that the category is published. A red x indicates that it is unpublished.

- **Title.** This field displays the full name of the category. Click the name to edit the category's details.

- **Access.** This field indicates the access level assigned to the category.

- **Language.** This field shows the language designated for the category.

- **ID.** This field indicates the system-generated user ID number.

Tip

You can also sort any column by clicking the column header.

Creating categories

You can create new categories from within the Banner Categories Manager. Categories are used as containers to hold banners; they are purely organizational in nature. Figure 12.6 shows the Add A New Banners Category workspace.

12

FIGURE 12.6

The Add A New Banners Category workspace

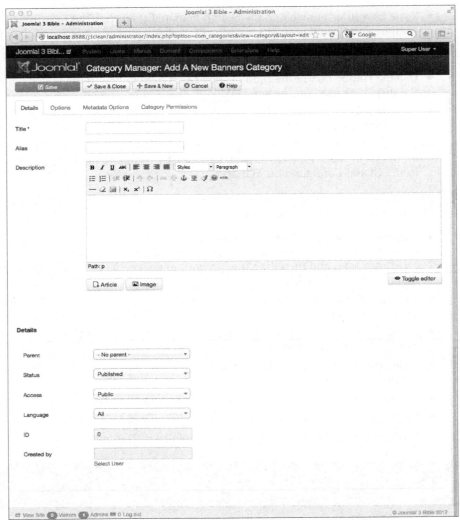

The toolbar at the top of the Add A New Banners Category workspace provides quick access to the following functions:

- **Save.** Click to save your work and create a new category without leaving the workspace.

- **Save & Close.** Click to save your work, create a new category, and exit the Add A New Banners Category workspace.

- **Save & New.** Click to save your work, close the current Add A New Banners Category workspace, and open another Add A New Banners Category workspace.

- **Cancel.** Click to cancel the task and exit the Add A New Banners Category workspace.

- **Help.** Click to display the Help files related to the active screen.

Note the four tabs at the top of the workspace. These tabs provide you with access to secondary functionality associated with categories, as follows:

- **Details.** This is the crucial tab needed for creating new categories. The fields on this tab are described in the following bulleted list.

- **Options.** The choices on this tab allow you to change the layout of the category landing page on the front end of the site, associate an image with the category, and add notes for use by the administrators.

- **Metadata Options.** The fields on this tab allow you to override the global metadata settings for this category's page. If you are using the keyword-matching feature to help control the display of banners, you can use the Meta Keywords field to add relevant keywords that can trigger the display of banners in this category.

TIP

The controls on the Options and Metadata Options tabs are carry-overs from other parts of Joomla!, but are not very useful in relation to banner categories, as you will probably never link to a banner categories page on the front end of your site!

- **Category Permissions.** This tab allows you to view and modify the permissions associated with this category. Permissions are normally inherited from the Global Configuration settings, but you can override them here.

The Details section of the Add A New Banners Category workspace includes the following fields:

- **Title.** This field is used to assign the category a name. This is the only required field.

- **Alias.** The alias is the internal name for the category. If you leave this field blank, the system automatically uses your title for the alias, with any spaces converted to hyphens. Note that if you want to add a value to this field, it only accepts lowercase letters without any spaces.

- **Description.** This is an optional field into which you can add a description of the banner category. Note that this is provided for the benefit of the administrators and does not appear on the front end of the site.

- **Parent.** If you want to nest the banner categories, you can select a parent category from the combo box.

- **Status.** This field allows you to set the status of the category: Published, Unpublished, Archived, or Trashed.

- **Access.** This field allows you to select the access level needed to view the banner category.

- **Language.** This field allows you to select the language of the banner category. This control is key if you are running a multilingual site and want to show specific banners to users who have selected specific languages.

 See Chapter 11 for an explanation of how parallel language banners relate to the display of content; the same concepts apply here.

- **ID.** The value in this field is assigned automatically by the Joomla! system and is used internally by the system.

- **Created by.** You can specify the creator of the category by clicking the Select User link below this field.

To create a new banner category, follow these steps:

1. **Log in to the admin system.**

2. **Go to the Components menu and select the Categories option from the Banners submenu.** The Banner Category Manager loads in your browser.

3. **Click the New button on the toolbar at the top of the Banner Category Manager.** The Add A New Banners Category workspace opens (refer to Figure 12.6).

4. **In the Title field, type the name you want to use for the category.** This is the only required field.

5. **Select and complete any other fields you want; all other fields are optional.**

6. **Click the Save button on the toolbar.** The workspace closes and returns you to the Banner Category Manager.

Editing categories

You can edit existing banner categories from the Banner Category Manager. To edit a banner, you either click the banner title in the Banner Category Manager or select the banner and then click the Edit button on the Banner Category Manager toolbar. Regardless of which method you use, the system opens the Edit Banner Category workspace.

The Edit Banner Category workspace is identical to the Add A New Category workspace, with the same fields and requirements as discussed in the previous section.

To make changes to a category, you simply alter the desired fields in the Edit Banner Category workspace and then click the Save button on the toolbar. Any changes you make are applied immediately.

Archiving categories

If you want to remove a category from use on the site, but do not want to delete it, you can move it to the archive. By default, archived categories are not shown in the front end of the website.

To archive a category, follow these steps:

1. **Log in to the admin system.**

2. **Go to the Components menu and select the Categories option from the Banners submenu.** The Banner Category Manager loads in your browser.

3. **Click the check box next to the banner category or categories you want to archive.**

4. **Click the Archive button on the toolbar.** The system immediately moves the selected categories to the archive.

Categories that have been moved into the archive can by unarchived by changing the status of the category to either Published or Unpublished. To unarchive a category, follow these steps:

1. **Log in to the admin system.**

2. **Go to the Components menu and select the Banners option from the Banners submenu.** The Banner Category Manager loads in your browser.

3. **Change the Select Status Filter to Archived.**

4. **Click the check box next to the category or categories you want to unarchive.**

5. **Select either Publish or Unpublish from the toolbar.** The system immediately unarchives the selected categories.

Deleting categories

The deletion of banner categories in Joomla! is a two-step process. The first step involves moving the category to the trash, where it is held until you take the second step and permanently delete the category. Categories held in the trash can be restored at any time prior to deletion. You can view the contents of the trash at any time by using the Select Status filter in the Banner Category Manager.

Categories moved to the trash are held there indefinitely. The categories can be restored or deleted at the option of the administrator. Restored categories return to their original locations, but deleted categories are permanently removed from the system and cannot be restored.

NOTE

Though categories can be left in the trash indefinitely, the trash is distinctly different from the archive. Moving categories to the trash should not be confused with archiving categories.

To move a category to the trash, follow these steps:

1. **Log in to the admin system.**
2. **Go to the Components menu and select the Categories option from the Banners submenu.** The Banner Category Manager loads in your browser.
3. **Click the check box next to the category or categories you want to remove.**
4. **Click the Trash button on the toolbar.** The system moves the selected categories to the trash.

NOTE

Any categories moved to the trash are instantly unpublished and not visible to site visitors.

Restoring categories from the trash

Categories moved to the trash are held there until the administrator takes further action. Any category can be restored at any time. The process of restoring a category is simple and the result instantaneous: the category is removed from the trash and returns to where it was located before it was moved to the trash.

To restore a category from the trash, follow these steps:

1. **Log in to the admin system.**
2. **Go to the Components menu and select the Categories option from the Banners submenu.** The Banner Category Manager loads in your browser.
3. **Change the Select Status Filter to Trashed.** The list of categories reloads to display only those categories in the trash.
4. **Click the check box next to the category or categories you want to restore.**
5. **Click either Publish or Unpublish on the toolbar.** The system removes the selected categories from the trash, and restores them to their previous location.

> **TIP**
> You can also restore a category by moving your mouse over the category title, clicking the arrow that appears, and selecting Untrash from the options on the menu that opens.

Deleting categories permanently

Categories held in the trash can be removed from the system by emptying the trash. Emptying the trash results in the category's permanent removal from the system; it cannot be restored once deleted.

To permanently delete a category from the trash, follow these steps:

1. **Log in to the admin system.**
2. **Go to the Components menu and select the Categories option from the Banners submenu.** The Banner Category Manager loads in your browser.
3. **Change the Select Status Filter to Trashed.**
4. **Click the check box next to the category or categories you want to delete.**
5. **Click the Empty Trash button on the toolbar.** The system immediately deletes the selected categories.

> **NOTE**
> Deleting a banner category is permanent and cannot be undone. Moreover, there is no confirmation dialog box — clicking the Delete button immediately deletes the category! Note, however, that you cannot delete a category if there are banners assigned to that category. If you want to delete the category, you must first delete or reassign any banners assigned to that category.

Managing Banners

Creating, copying, editing, and deleting banners are all tasks that you can perform from within the confines of the Banner Manager. The only additional resource you need is the content for the actual banner. Joomla! supports two banner types, *image banners* and *custom code banners*. As the names imply, an image banner displays a graphic, while a custom code banner is comprised of lines of code. You typically use the image banner type where you have your own ad graphics; the custom code banner is typical of third-party or affiliate ad networks.

The system supports ad display by impression, by click, or by time. Regardless of which type of banner you prefer, or which display criteria you want to employ, you will use the Banner Manager to create and manage the banners.

In this section, I look at how to create and manage the banners for your site.

> **NOTE**
>
> If your goal is to display a graphical banner ad, keep in mind that the graphics must be created outside the Joomla! system. Typically these files are in GIF, JPEG, or other artwork formats. You cannot actually create the graphical ads inside Joomla!; you can only add existing graphic files to Joomla!.

Creating banners

Adding banners to the Joomla! system is called creating banners, although in most cases, you are not actually creating the content inside Joomla at all, but rather you are simply adding already existing content to the system.

To get started, click the New button on the toolbar at the top of the Banner Manager. Figure 12.7 shows the New Banner workspace.

FIGURE 12.7

The New Banner workspace

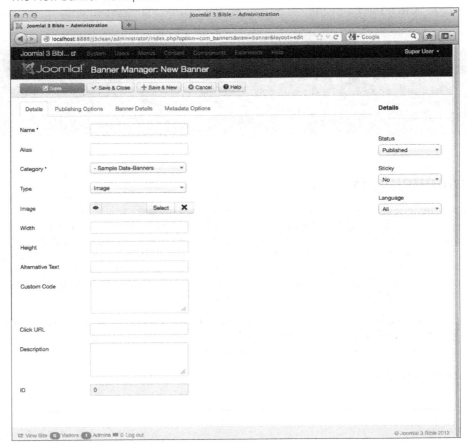

The toolbar at the top of the New Banner workspace provides quick access to the following functions:

- **Save.** Click to save your work and create a new banner without exiting the workspace.
- **Save & Close.** Click to save your work, create a new banner, and exit the New Banner workspace.
- **Save & New.** Click to save your work, close the current New Banner workspace, and open another New Banner workspace.
- **Cancel.** Click to cancel the task and exit the New Banner workspace.
- **Help.** Click to display the Help files related to the active screen.

Note the four tabs at the top of the workspace. These tabs provide you with access to secondary functionality associated with banners, as follows:

- **Details.** This is the crucial tab needed for creating new banners. The fields on this tab are described in the following bulleted list.
- **Publishing Options.** The fields on this tab allow you to track the banner's creation and modification dates and, more importantly, the start and stop publishing dates.
- **Banner Details.** This tab allows you to set the impressions and click limits for the banner, if any. You can also associate the banner with a contract period and a client.
- **Metadata Options.** The fields on this tab allow you to override the global metadata settings for this banner page. If you are using the keyword-matching feature to help control the display of banners, you should use the Meta Keywords field to add relevant keywords that can trigger the display of the banner.

The Details tab of the New Banner workspace includes the following fields, some of which are required to create a new banner:

- **Name.** You can enter a name for the banner here. This field is required.
- **Alias.** The alias is the internal name for the banner. If you leave this field blank, the system automatically uses your title for the alias, with any spaces converted to hyphens. Note that if you want to add a value to this field, it only accepts lower-case letters without any spaces.
- **Category.** This field allows you to assign the banner to a category or to mark it as uncategorized, and is required.
- **Type.** To upload and use a graphic file for your banner display, select Image. If you wish to enter your own code in the Custom Code field, select Custom.
- **Image.** If you selected Image in the Type combo box, you can use the Select button to find and upload the graphic you want to use for the banner. You can also select an image from the Media Library.

12

- **Width.** This field specifies the width of the banner.
- **Height.** This field specifies the height of the banner.
- **Alternative Text.** If you selected Image in the Type combo box, you can type text in the Alternative Text field; your text appears when a user moves her mouse over the banner image.
- **Custom Code.** You can use this field to add additional code to the banner, for example, if the banner is part of an affiliate scheme and you need to add an affiliate tracking code.
- **Click URL.** This field associates a URL with the banner. If the user clicks on the banner, they will be taken to the URL you enter here.
- **Description.** Administrators use this field to add notes or comments for their internal use. The contents of this field do not appear on the front end of the website.
- **ID.** This is an automatically generated number used internally by the Joomla! system.

The Publishing Options tab does not contain any required fields, but there are some useful controls here you should be aware of, including the start and stop dates for the banner display:

- **Created Date.** This field is automatically populated by the system and shows the creation date and time for the banner.
- **Created by.** You can specify the creator of the banner by clicking the Select User link below the field. The options that appear reflect the users in your Joomla! system.
- **Created by alias.** You can create an alias for the banner creator by entering it here. If you supply a value here, it appears instead of the user's name.
- **Modified Date.** This is the date the banner was last modified. The system automatically populates this field.
- **Modified by.** This is the name of the last user to modify the banner. The system automatically populates this field.
- **Revision.** This is a count of the number of times the banner has been revised. The system automatically populates this field.
- **Start Publishing.** Though optional, you can use this field to set a specific starting date for the publication of the banner. If you leave this field blank, the system assumes that you want to start publishing immediately.
- **Stop Publishing.** Though optional, you can use this field to set a specific ending date for the publication of the banner. If you leave this field blank, the system assumes that you want the banner to remain published indefinitely, or until any display limitations are realized.

The Banner Details tab does not include any required fields, but if you are managing banners for clients, you will find the options here to be especially useful:

- **Max. Impressions.** You can use this field to set a limit on the number of times the banner will appear. Click the Unlimited check box to remove the restrictions. The default value is Unlimited.

- **Total Impressions.** This field indicates how many times the banner has been displayed on the site. For a new banner, this value is 0. Use the Reset Impressions button to return the value of this field to 0.

- **Total Clicks.** This field indicates how many times site visitors have clicked this banner. For a new banner, this value is 0. Use the Reset Clicks button to return the value of this field to 0.

- **Client.** This field allows you to assign the banner to a client.

- **Purchase Type.** This field allows you to set the term for the impressions or click calculations. The options are Daily, Weekly, Monthly, Yearly, or Unlimited.

- **Track Impressions.** You can select Yes to count the impressions and display the number of impressions in the Banner Tracks.

- **Track Clicks.** You can select Yes to count the clicks and display the number of clicks in the Banner Tracks.

The Metadata Options tab contains the following fields, which relate to the functionality of displaying banners based upon meta keywords matching:

- **Meta Keywords.** You can enter the keywords you want to associate with the banner.

- **Use Own Prefix.** Set this to Yes to implement the keyword-prefix option. This improves system performance as it only matches keywords with the specified prefix.

- **Meta Keyword Prefix.** If you set the Use Own Prefix option to Yes, then you can enter the prefix here.

> **NOTE**
>
> To learn more about using keyword matching to control banner display, see the discussion of the Banner module later in this chapter.

To create a new banner, follow these steps:

1. **Log in to the admin system.**

2. **Select the Banners option under the Components menu.** The Banner Manager loads in your browser.

3. **Click the New button on the toolbar of the Banner Manager.** The New Banner workspace opens (refer to Figure 12.7).

4. **In the Name field, type the name you want to use for the banner.** This field is required.

5. **Select a category for the banner or leave it as uncategorized.** This field is required.

6. **Select a type for the banner.**

7. **If you selected the Image banner type, then add an image using the field of the same name; if you selected Custom, then enter the code you desire in the Custom Code field.**

8. **Click the Save button on the toolbar at the top left to save your new banner.** All other fields are optional.

> **NOTE**
>
> Like the articles workspace, this banner workspace also includes a column on the right side of the Details tab. This column is designed to give you quick access to the most common tasks associated with banners, that is, your publishing controls and language association.

> **TIP**
>
> Note the Sticky option in the right column. Select Yes to give a banner preference in the rotation of multiple banners. A sticky banner appears more often than a nonsticky banner. The default value is No. This is only applicable where the Banner module is set to give preference to sticky banners.

Editing banners

You can edit existing banners from the Banner Manager. To edit a banner, either click the banner name in the Banner Manager, or select the banner and then click the Edit button on the Banner Manager toolbar. Regardless of which method you use, the system opens the Edit Banner workspace.

The Edit Banner workspace is identical to the Add A New Banner workspace, with the same fields and requirements as discussed in the previous section.

To make changes to a banner, you simply alter the desired fields in the Edit Banner workspace, and then click the Save button on the toolbar. Any changes you make are applied immediately.

> **TIP**
>
> The Batch button on the toolbar offers several editing options and can save you time if you are trying to modify multiple banners. Select one or more banners, and then click the Batch button. In the pop-up window that appears, you can change the client or language assignment of all the banners simultaneously. The Batch feature also supports moving banners between categories and copying banners.

Archiving banners

If you want to remove a banner from use on the site, but you do not want to delete it, you can move it to the Banner Archive. By default, archived banners are not shown in the front end of the website. You can, however, make archived banners accessible by publishing the Archived Banners module.

To archive a banner, follow these steps:

1. **Log in to the admin system.**
2. **Select the Banners option under the Components menu.** The Banner Manager loads in your browser.
3. **Click the check box next to the banner or banners you want to archive.**
4. **Click the Archive button on the toolbar.** The system immediately moves the selected banners to the archive.

Banners that have been moved into the archive can be unarchived by changing the status of the banner to either Published or Unpublished. To unarchive a banner, follow these steps:

1. **Log in to the admin system.**
2. **Select the Banners option under the Components menu.** The Banner Manager loads in your browser.
3. **Change the Select Status Filter to Archived.**
4. **Click the check box next to the banner or banners you want to unarchive.**
5. **Select either Publish or Unpublish from the toolbar.** The system immediately unarchives the selected banners.

Deleting banners

The deletion of banners in Joomla! is a two-step process. The first step involves moving the banner to the trash, where it is held until you take the second step and permanently delete the banner. Banners held in the trash can be restored at any time prior to deletion. You can view the contents of the trash at any time by using the Select Status filter in the Banner Manager.

Banners moved to the trash are held there indefinitely. The banners can be restored or deleted at the option of the administrator. Restored banners return to their original locations, but deleted banners are permanently removed from the system and cannot be restored.

> **NOTE**
> Though banners can be left in the trash indefinitely, the trash is distinctly different from the archive. Moving banners to the trash should not be confused with archiving banners.

To move a banner to the trash, follow these steps:

1. **Log in to the admin system.**
2. **Select the Banners option under the Components menu.** The Banner Manager loads in your browser.
3. **Click the check box next to the banner or banners you want to remove.**
4. **Click the Trash button on the toolbar.** The system moves the selected banners to the trash.

> **NOTE**
>
> Any banner moved to the trash is instantly unpublished and not visible to site visitors.

Restoring banners from the trash

Banners moved to the trash are held there until the administrator takes further action. Any banner can be restored at any time. The process of restoring a banner is simple, and the result instantaneous: the banner is removed from the trash and returns to where it was located before it was moved to the trash.

To restore a banner from the trash, follow these steps:

1. **Log in to the admin system.**
2. **Select the Banners option under the Components menu.** The Banner Manager loads in your browser.
3. **Change the Select Status Filter to Trashed.** The list of banners reloads to display only those banners in the trash.
4. **Click the check box next to the banner or banners you want to restore.**
5. **Click either Publish or Unpublish on the toolbar.** The system removes the selected banners from the trash, and restores them to their previous location.

> **TIP**
>
> You can also restore a banner by moving your mouse over the banner name, clicking the arrow that appears, and selecting Untrash from the options on the menu that opens.

Deleting banners permanently

Banners held in the trash can be removed from the system by emptying the trash. Emptying the trash results in a banner's permanent removal from the system; it cannot be restored once deleted.

To permanently delete a banner from the trash, follow these steps:

1. **Log in to the admin system.**
2. **Select the Banners option under the Components menu.** The Banner Manager loads in your browser.

3. **Change the Select Status Filter to Trashed.**

4. **Click the check box next to the banner or banners you want to delete.**

5. **Click the Empty Trash button on the toolbar.** The system immediately deletes the selected banners.

CAUTION

Deleting a banner is permanent and cannot be undone. Moreover, there is no confirmation dialog box — clicking the Delete button immediately deletes the banner!

Tracking banner performance

The Joomla! Banner Manager includes a feature that allows you to track the performance of all the banners contained in the Banner component. The feature is called Tracks and you can use it not only to monitor banner performance but also to generate reports for your banner clients. To access Tracks, click the Access Tracks option under Banners on the Components menu or click the Tracks link in the left column of the Banner Manager workspace. Figure 12.8 shows example output from the Tracks feature.

FIGURE 12.8

The Tracks feature of the Banner Manager

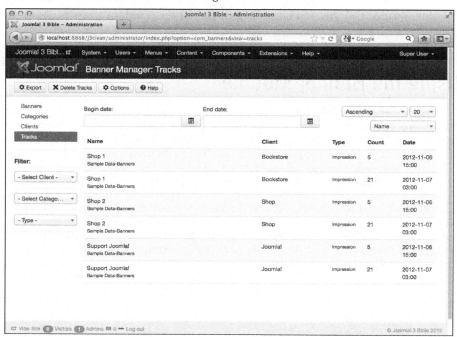

Tracks is a simple system that counts impressions and clicks, and then displays that data for you on the screen. It includes some basic filters to help you manage long lists of results, but the functionality is limited to basic filtering by client, category, type, and date range. One feature that is unique to Tracks is the ability to export reports. Reports are exported in CSV format and contain whatever data is on the screen at the time. In other words, to export a global report, you need to display all banners from all clients and categories. To generate a report for a specific client, you can filter by client and then export. Here's how to export a Tracks report:

1. **Log in to the admin system.**

2. **Select the Tracks option from the Banners submenu on the Components menu.** The Tracks workspace loads in your browser.

3. **Filter the results to display only the banners and the time period you want to include in the report.**

4. **Click the Export button on the toolbar.** The export pane opens.

5. **Specify whether you want to compress the output file.** Because reports are generated as CSV files, they are typically quite small.

6. **Enter a filename for the export file.**

7. **Click the Export button.** A pop-up window appears, asking you to confirm a location for the download. When you confirm the location, the pop-up window closes and the file downloads.

The downloaded CSV file can be opened by any of the standard spreadsheet or database programs.

Using the Banner Module

The Banner module works hand-in-hand with the Banners component to control the display of ads on your website. Although the Banners component is used to set up your clients and organize your banners, it is the Banner module that is responsible for the placement of the ads on the page. The component and the module work together to control campaigns, and the settings in one can affect the other. Appreciating the interaction between these two features is key to running ads effectively on your site.

Like all other modules in your system, you can access the Banner module from the Module Manager. To reach your Banner module, click the Module Manager option under the Extensions menu. Find the Banners link in the Title column and click it to view the settings for the Banner module. Figure 12.9 shows a standard Banner module.

FIGURE 12.9

The Banner module interface

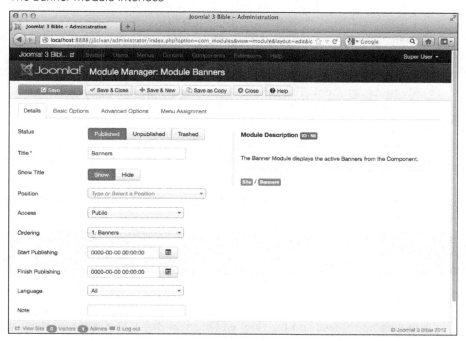

The toolbar at the top of the Banner module workspace provides quick access to the following functions:

- **Save.** Click to save your work and create a new module without exiting the workspace.

- **Save & Close.** Click to save your work, create a new module, and exit the Banner module workspace.

- **Save & New.** Click to save your work, close the current Banner module workspace, and open another Banners module workspace.

- **Save as Copy.** Click to save your changes to a copy of the current module, and exits the Banner module workspace.

- **Close.** Click to cancel the task and exit the Banner module workspace.

- **Help.** Click to display the Help files related to the active screen.

There are four tabs at the top of workspace:

- **Details.** This tab contains the key fields needed to create a new Banner module. The fields are discussed in the following bulleted list.
- **Basic Options.** This tab contains various fields related to client, category, and banner tagging.
- **Advanced Options.** This tab contains options relating to layout and caching.
- **Menu Assignment.** This tab contains settings that determine where the module will appear, by associating the module with the site's menu items.

 For a full discussion of the options available with this module, see Chapter 17.

The Details tab of the Banners module workspace is the key tab for creating a new banner module. It includes the following fields:

- **Status.** Set this control to Published if you want the module to appear on the front end of your site.

> **NOTE**
> The Start Publishing field can override this setting.

- **Title.** Enter a name for the module.
- **Show Title.** Set this control to Yes if you want the module title to appear wherever the module appears on the front end of the website. Generally speaking, for a Banner module, you want to set this control to No.
- **Position.** Use this combo box to assign the module to one of the template's module position holders.
- **Access.** Use this combo box to determine which user groups you want to be able to see the module.
- **Ordering.** Only use this field if there is more than one module assigned to the same module position; you use this to control the ordering of the modules.
- **Start Publishing (optional).** Use this field to set a specific starting date for the publication of the module. If you leave this blank, the system assumes that you want to start publishing immediately.
- **Finish Publishing (optional).** Use this field to set a specific end date for the publication of the module. If you leave this blank, the system assumes that you want to publish the module indefinitely.
- **Language.** Select the language of the Banner module. This control is key if you are running a multilingual site and you want to show specific banners to users who have selected specific languages.

 See Chapter 11 for an explanation of how parallel language banners relate to the display of content; the same concepts apply here.

- **Note.** The system supplies this description text and you cannot edit it.

Creating a new Banner module

You need at least one Banner module to display the output of the Banners component. If you installed the sample data, you can choose to either modify an existing Banner module, or create a new one. Banner module creation occurs from inside the Module Manager.

> **TIP**
>
> Running multiple Banner modules is a common solution when you need to show more than one ad on a page, or to show ads in different positions on different pages. Clever use of multiple Banner modules, coupled with appropriate configuration of the modules and the Banner component, allow you to give your site variety and make your available advertising space more flexible and effective.

To create a new Banner module, follow these steps:

1. **Access the Module Manager by clicking the selection of the same name under the Extensions menu.** The Module Manager loads in your browser window.

2. **Click the New button on the toolbar.** The Select a Module Type page opens in your browser.

3. **Select the Banners option.** The Banner Module workspace opens.

4. **Type a name for the module in the Title field.** This is a required field.

5. **For the Show Title field, select the No option.**

6. **Select the position where you want the banner to appear.**

7. **Click the Basic Options tab.** The tab comes to the front.

8. **Select a client, a category, or both to determine which banners will display.** The default value displays all published banners in the system, without regard to client or category.

9. **Select other options as you see fit; all other settings are optional.**

10. **Click the Save button to create your module and return to the Module Manager.**

Enabling context-sensitive banner display

Joomla! supports the conditional display of banners. If you use this option, you can relate the banner display to the articles, using the meta keywords. The keyword-matching functionality only displays the banner on articles where there are matching keywords on both the article and the banner. This is a very useful tool that provides you with basic contextual targeting.

> **TIP**
>
> While you can target the banners using keywords that relate to the content, there's no reason why you can't use other criteria; for example, if you know the article is popular with gamers, then you might want to tag it to reflect the audience, rather than only the content.

Implementing keyword targeting requires you to take several steps. You need to first enable the Banner module to use keyword tagging, then you need to make sure that the banners and the articles have the appropriate meta keywords. To enable your Banner module to support conditional display, follow these steps:

1. **Click Module Manager under the Extensions menu.** The Module Manager loads in your browser window.

2. **Click the name of the Banner module you want.** The Module editing workspace opens in your browser.

3. **Click the Basic Options tab.** The tab comes to the front.

4. **Select Yes in the Search by Tag field.**

5. **Click the Save button.**

Tagging the articles and the banners is a simple matter: You simply add matching keywords into the Metadata Options tabs for both.

Keyword matching does increase the load on your server. If you are running a lot of banners, or you have a very busy site, then you should consider employing the Keyword Prefix option. This option is designed to ease the performance burden by only searching for matches on keywords that carry a specific prefix, rather than searching the entire keyword data set. This is enabled via the Metadata Options tabs in either the Banner Clients workspace or the Banners workspace, as discussed earlier in this chapter. After you enable the option, you need to use the prefix for the meta keywords on both the banners and the articles, or this feature will not be of any use. For example, if you specify the prefix "ads_" then you need to create meta keywords using the prefix (for example, ads_watches, ads_hamilton, and so on). If those keywords appear on both an article and a banner, then the banner appears on that article.

Summary

In this chapter, I have covered the use of both the Banner component and the Banner module, two tools that work hand-in-hand to help you display advertisements or other messages on your site. I covered the following topics in this chapter:

- Creating, editing, and deleting banners
- Working with banner clients to tie banners to specific owners
- Using banner categories to group your banners
- Configuring the Banner Manager to work in concert with the Banner module
- Managing banner display with the Banner module
- Tracking banner performance and exporting reports
- Enabling conditional display of banners

In the next chapter, I look at another of the core Joomla! components, the Contacts component.

Working with the Contacts Component

The default Joomla! system includes a directory system called the Contacts component. Although the Contacts component was initially created to provide a simple directory of a site's users, it has evolved to take on a more generic role. While you can still use it to create a listing of your users, each with their own contact form, you can also use it as a basic directory for almost any type of text information. If your site allows membership, the Contact Manager becomes an essential tool for enabling communication with site members. If you want your site to contain a directory of information about particular people, places, or items, you can use the Contact Manager to creatively achieve that goal. The Contact Manager is also the key to creating contact forms in Joomla!.

In this chapter I go through the creation of contacts, how to group contacts, how to display the information in a directory structure, and how to use the Contacts component to enable the creation of contact forms.

Introducing the Contact Manager

The Contact Manager is the essential tool for working with the directory entries you create inside the Contacts Component. It is also your central workspace for creating, grouping, editing, and deleting user contact information. The entries you create with the Contact Manager form the basis of your directory, whether it is a directory of users or other items. How you deliver the information in those entries to your site visitors depends largely on your configuration settings, what you enter into the various fields, and how you link it all together with your menu items. In this section I introduce the Contact Manager workspace to help you become oriented with the layout and tools needed to manage all your entries.

You access the Contact Manager by going to the Components menu and clicking the Contacts option. The Contact Manager interface loads in your browser, as shown in Figure 13.1.

FIGURE 13.1

The Contact Manager, showing the Learning Joomla! sample data installed

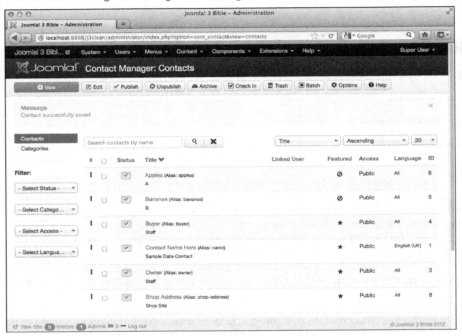

The toolbar at the top of the Contact Manager provides quick access to the following functions:

- **New.** Click to add a new contact.
- **Edit.** Select a contact from the list and then click this button to edit the contact details.
- **Publish.** Select one or more contacts from the list and then click this button to publish them. You publish a contact to make it visible on the front end of the website.

- **Unpublish.** Select one or more contacts from the list and then click this button to unpublish them. You unpublish a contact to hide it from the front end of the website.

- **Archive.** Select one or more contacts from the list and then click this button to move the contact to the archive.

- **Check In.** Select one or more contacts from the list and then click this button to force the contact's editing workspace to close and thereby "check in" the contact.

- **Trash.** Select one or more contacts from the list and then click this button to delete them.

- **Batch.** Select multiple contacts and then click this button to batch-apply processes to those contacts. A pop-up window appears, where you can modify multiple contacts in one simple operation.

- **Options.** Click to open the Contact Manager Options, where you can configure the parameters that affect the Contact Manager. I discuss configuring the Contacts component in the next section.

- **Help.** Click to access the online Help files related to the active screen.

Below the toolbar, in the left column, are two links: Contacts shows you the Contacts Manager, and Categories shows you the Contacts Categories Manager. I discuss each of these options in the sections that follow.

Below the four links in the left column are four sorting tools to help you manage long lists of contacts:

- **Select Status.** The options in this combo box allow you to filter and display the contacts according to whether they are published, unpublished, archived, or trashed. This provides an easy way to identify all contacts that are currently active on the site. To reset this filter, change the combo box back to the default setting, Select Status.

- **Select Category.** The options in this combo box allow you to filter and display the contacts according to the category to which they are assigned. To reset this filter, change the combo box back to the default setting, Select Category.

- **Select Access.** The options in this combo box let you filter the list of contacts by access level. To reset this filter, change the combo box back to the default setting, Select Access.

- **Select Language.** The options in this combo box let you filter the list of contacts by language. To reset this filter, change the combo box back to the default setting, Select Language.

Below the toolbar and above the list of contacts are four sorting and searching tools to help you manage long lists of contacts:

- Type a word or phrase into the field marked Search contacts by name, and then click the magnifying glass button. The system searches your list of contacts for the query and then displays the results of the search. To clear the screen and return to a full listing, click the button marked with the X.

- Use the combo box to the right of the Search field to specify which column of the contacts display is used for the sort order.

- Use the Ascending combo box to specify whether the contacts appear in ascending or descending order.

- Use the combo box on the far right to control the number of contacts that appear on the page. You can alter the default value by changing the List Length parameter in the Global Configuration Manager.

The main content area of the screen contains a list of all the contacts in your Joomla! site. The columns provided are

- **Sort Order (vertical double arrows).** Click the arrows to change the sort order. You can also click and hold any of the buttons immediately to the left of a contact's title and drag the contact to change its order location in the Contacts Manager.

- **Contact Selection (unlabeled check box).** Click a check box to select a contact; this is necessary if you want to use several of the toolbar options.

- **Status.** A green check mark indicates that the contact is published. A red x indicates that it is unpublished.

- **Title.** This field displays the full name of the contact. Click the name to edit the contact's details.

- **Linked User.** If this contact has been linked to a user, the user's name appears here.

- **Featured.** This field indicates whether a contact has been featured. Featured contacts are designated with a black star symbol. You can click the icon in this column to toggle between featured and not featured.

- **Access.** This field indicates the access level assigned to the contact.

- **Language.** This field shows the language designated for the contact.

- **ID.** This field shows the system-generated user ID number.

> **TIP**
> You can also sort any column by clicking the column header.

Configuring the Contacts Component

You can configure global options for the Contacts component using the Options button located on the toolbar of the Contacts Manager. Clicking this button takes you to the Contacts component's workspace in the Global Configuration Manager. You use this workspace to set the global parameters available to this component. You can override the parameters for individual contacts by setting alternative values in an individual contact's workspace (which I discuss later in this chapter), or by overriding them in the menu item settings. The configuration options are designed to help you control the formatting of the contacts and their categories, as well as set permissions for the use of the component. In this section, I review the numerous options that are available for configuring the Contacts component.

Figure 13.2 shows the landing tab of the Contacts component configuration workspace.

There are eight tabs leading to eight workspaces for the Contacts component's configuration:

- **Contact.** This tab contains settings relating to the display of single contacts. The choices on this tab determine what information appears along with the contact.

- **Icons.** You can use this tab to assign icons to appear as field labels shown on a single contact page.

- **Category.** This tab sets the options for the display of a single contact category page.

- **Categories.** This tab sets the options for the display of pages containing multiple contact categories.

- **List Layouts.** This tab controls the layout of contacts in list format.

- **Form.** This tab sets the parameters for the contact forms associated with contacts.

- **Integration.** This tab allows you to show or hide a feed link on the page.

- **Permissions.** This tab determines the extent to which the various user groups are able to perform actions with the Contacts component.

The Contact tab, shown in Figure 13.2, is the landing tab. The settings on this tab are applied to single contact display. The options are

- **Choose a layout.** You can use this combo box to select from the available layouts for the contacts.

- **Contact Category.** You can show or hide the name of the contact's category. Choose the option Show with Link to link the contact category name to the category page.

- **Show Contact List.** If you set this value to Show, a combo box containing all the contacts appears on the page; visitors can jump to another contact by selecting it from the combo box list.

- **Display format.** You can choose a style for displaying the sections of the contact form.

Several of the remaining options on this tab relate to which details are displayed about the contact. You can show or hide a wide variety of information, from the contact's name to her full address.

FIGURE 13.2

The Contacts component configuration workspace

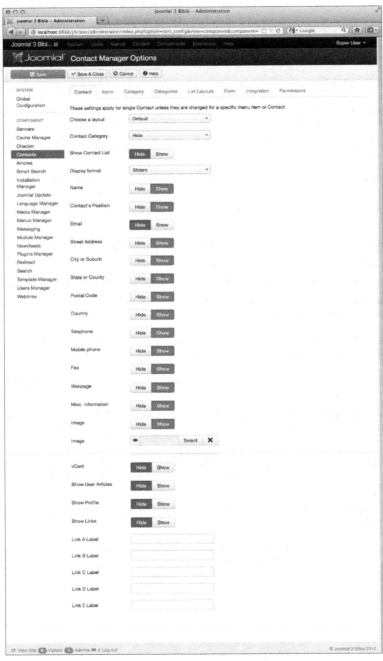

There are several additional fields on this tab that you should be aware of:

- **vCard.** If you set this value to Show, site visitors see a link to download a vCard with the contact's details.

- **Show User Articles.** If you map a contact to a user in the system, you can show on the contact's page links to the articles submitted by the user.

- **Show Profile.** If you map a contact to a user in the system, you can show the user's profiles on the contact.

- **Show Links.** If you want to display additional links along with the contact, you can set this value to Show.

The Category tab includes the following options:

- **Choose a layout.** Use this combo box to control the layout of the contacts listed on the category page.

- **Category Title.** Show or hide the category title on the category page.

- **Category Description.** Show or hide the category description on the category page.

- **Category Image.** Show or hide the category image on the category page.

- **Subcategory Levels.** Select the number of subcategory levels to display.

- **Empty Categories.** Show or hide empty categories on the category page.

- **Subcategories Descriptions.** Show or hide the descriptions of the subcategories.

- **# Contacts in Category.** Show or hide the number of contacts per category on the category page.

The Categories tab includes the following options:

- **Top Level Category Description.** Show or hide the description of the top-level category.

- **Subcategory Levels.** Select how many subcategory levels you want to display on the page.

- **Empty Categories.** Show or hide empty categories.

- **Subcategories Descriptions.** Show or hide the descriptions of the subcategories.

- **# Contacts in Category.** Show or hide the number of contacts in each category.

13

The List Layouts tab includes the following options:

- **Display Select.** Show or hide the display select combo box.
- **Table Headings.** Show or hide the table headings of the table used for the list layout.
- **Position.** Show or hide the contact's position.
- **Email.** Show or hide the contact's e-mail address.
- **Phone.** Show or hide the contact's phone number.
- **Mobile.** Show or hide the contact's mobile phone number.
- **Fax.** Show or hide the contact's fax number.
- **City or Suburb.** Show or hide the contact's city or suburb.
- **State or County.** Show or hide the contact's state or county.
- **Country.** Show or hide the contact's country.
- **Pagination.** Show or hide the pagination controls.
- **Pagination Results.** Show or hide the total page count on the pagination controls. This is only applicable if you set Pagination to Show.
- **Sort by.** Set the default sort criteria for the list of contacts.

The Form tab includes the following options:

- **Allow Captcha on Contact.** Select from the options here to choose whether Captcha is used on the user contacts forms.
- **Show Contact Form.** Choose Show to display a contact form for the user on the user's contact page.
* **Send Copy to Submitter.** If you choose Show, it gives the person submitting the contact form the option to have the form output mailed to the user, with a copy being emailed to the sender.
- **Banned e-mail.** To control spam, enter any terms you want to be banned from the e-mail form. If any e-mail address includes any of the banned terms, the form submission is blocked. Separate multiple terms with semicolons. This is only applicable if you set the E-mail Form parameter to Show.
- **Banned subject.** To control spam, enter any terms you want to be banned from the e-mail form subject lines. If any e-mail subject line includes any of the banned terms, the form submission is blocked. Separate multiple terms with semicolons. This is only applicable if you set the E-mail Form parameter to Show.
- **Banned text.** To control spam, enter any terms you want to be banned from the e-mail form text. If any e-mail form text includes any of the banned terms, the form submission is blocked. Separate multiple terms with semicolons. This is only applicable if you set the E-mail Form parameter to Show.
- **Session check.** Set this control to Yes to force the system to check whether the user has cookies enabled for session management. If cookies are not, enabled, the user will be blocked from sending email. This control is largely used as an added

measure of protection against automated robots and other agents that may try to use the form to generate spam or try to find vulnerabilities in your site.

- **Custom reply.** Set to No to turn off the system's auto replies. This is typically used to allow you to integrate an external mail management tool without causing conflicts.

- **Contact redirect.** If you want the user to be directed to a specific page after they submit the form, enter the URL here.

The Integration tab contains only one control, which allows you to specify whether to show or hide the feed link.

The Permissions tab works consistently with the Global Configuration permissions tab. Here you can dictate the extent to which the various user groups on your site can use the functionality of Contacts component.

 See Chapter 10 for a discussion of how permissions relate to user groups.

After you have set the parameters you desire, click the Save button in the top-left corner to save your changes or click Cancel to close the Parameters window without saving the changes.

Managing Contacts

Contacts are essentially specialty content items. How you use them is up to you, but the original purpose of the Contacts component was for use as a directory of the users of your website. Typical alternative uses of the Contacts component include

- Creation of a set of contacts to display on the Contact Us page of a corporate site
- A directory of the members of a community site
- A listing of items for a glossary, as shown in the sample Fruit Site included with the Learning Joomla! sample data
- A listing of store or office locations

Each of the uses cited above depends on the creation of individual contacts that contain the necessary information for a single item, be it a person, place, or thing. The contacts are then grouped into one or more categories for display on the site.

In this section, I discuss the creation of new contacts and how to manage them.

Adding a new contact

As the site administrator, you can add new contacts to the Contacts component at any time from the back end of your website. To add a new contact to your site, you must visit the Contact Manager and click the New button on the toolbar. The New Contact workspace opens in your browser, as shown in Figure 13.3.

FIGURE 13.3

The New Contact workspace

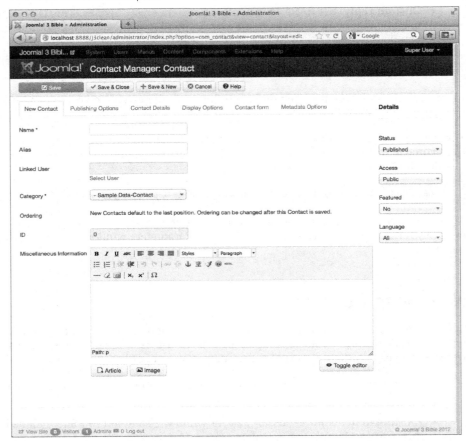

The toolbar at the top of the New Contact workspace provides quick access to the following functions:

- **Save.** Click to save your work and create a new contact without exiting the workspace.
- **Save & Close.** Click to save your work, create a new contact, and exit the New Contact workspace.
- **Save & New.** Click to save your work, close the current New Contact workspace, and open another New Contact workspace.
- **Cancel.** Click to cancel the task and exit the New Contact workspace.
- **Help.** Click to display the Help files related to the active screen.

The workspace is divided into six tabs:

- **New Contact.** This is the basic tab containing all the required fields for creating a new contact.

- **Publishing Options.** This tab contains fields for author alias and start and stop dates for publication.

- **Contact Details.** This tab contains a set of fields where you can add detailed information about the contact.

- **Display Options.** This tab contains controls that affect the display of the contact.

- **Contact form.** This tab contains parameters relating to the contact form for the contact.

- **Metadata Options.** This tab contains metadata fields for the contact.

The New Contact tab of the workspace contains the following fields:

- **Name.** You can enter the full name of the contact into this field, which is required.

- **Alias.** The Alias field is an internal identifier for your contact. This is used in some cases to create search engine–friendly URLs for the item. You can specify the contents of this field if you want, but note that it only accepts lowercase letters without any spaces. If you do not specify the contents of this field, the system automatically creates the alias based on the contact's name.

- **Linked User.** If this contact is to be associated to an existing user in the system, you can click the Select User link and then match the contact to the specific user.

- **Category.** You can assign the contact to a category using this combo box. This field is required.

- **Ordering.** Note that this control is not available for a new contact. New items are placed by default in the last position on the list. After you add your contact, you can adjust the list position either from the Contact Manager or by editing the contact item.

- **ID.** This value is automatically created by the system for internal use.

- **Miscellaneous Information.** You can use this text field to enter a wide variety of content, from additional details about the contact to complex formatting of extensive data. Whatever you put in this field appears on the front end of the website.

The Publishing Options tab contains the following fields (none of which are required):

- **Created by.** You can specify the creator of the contact by clicking the Select User link below the field.

- **Created by alias.** You can create an alias for the contact creator by entering it here. If you supply a value here, it appears instead of the user's name.

- **Created Date.** This field is automatically populated by the system and shows the creation date and time for the contact.

13

337

- **Start Publishing.** Though optional, you can use this field to set a specific starting date for the publication of the contact. If you leave this field blank, the system assumes that you want to start publishing immediately.
- **Stop Publishing.** Though optional, you can use this field to set a specific ending date for the publication of the contact. If you leave this field blank, the system assumes that you want the contact to remain published indefinitely.

The Contact Details tab of the workspace contains detailed information about the contact, including:

- **Image.** Use this field to add an image of the person, place, or thing that is the subject of the contact. Click the Select button to either choose an image from the Media Library or upload a new image.
- **Position.** Enter the contact's position into this field.
- **Email.** Enter the contact's e-mail address into this field.
- **Address.** Enter the contact's street address into this field.
- **City or Suburb.** Enter the contact's city or suburb into this field.
- **State or Province.** Enter the contact's state or province into this field.
- **Postal/ZIP Code.** Enter the contact's postal code or ZIP code into this field.
- **Country.** Enter the contact's country into this field.
- **Telephone.** Enter the contact's phone number into this field.
- **Mobile.** Enter the contact's mobile phone number into this field.
- **Fax.** Enter the contact's fax number into this field.
- **Website.** Enter the contact's website address into this field.
- **First Sort Field.** Specify one of the contact's populated fields to use as the primary sort criterion.
- **Second Sort Field.** Specify one of the contact's populated fields to use as the secondary sort criterion.
- **Third Sort Field.** Specify one of the contact's populated fields to use as the tertiary sort criterion.

The Display Options, Contact form, and Metadata Options tabs include controls that you can use to show or hide various data about the contact, customize the contact form, and supply the contact metadata. If you leave the default settings in place, the preferences set in the Contacts component configuration workspace in the Global Configuration Manager are applied. You can override the global settings by altering the values on any of these three tabs.

> **NOTE**
> Like the articles workspace, this workspace also includes a column on the right side of the interface, under the Details heading. The column is designed to give you quick access to the most common tasks associated with contacts, that is, your publishing controls, access settings, and language association.

To add a new contact, follow these steps:

1. **Log in to the admin system on your site.**

2. **Go to the Components menu and select the Contacts option.** The Contact Manager loads in your browser.

3. **Click the New button on the toolbar.** The New Contact workspace opens (refer to Figure 13.3).

4. **In the Name field, type a name for the contact.** This is a required field.

5. **Select a category for the contact from the Category combo box.** This is a required field.

6. **Select any additional options you want; all other fields are optional.**

7. **Click the Save button on the toolbar to save your new contact.**

Editing contacts

You can edit existing contacts from the Contacts Manager. To edit a contact, you either click the contact name in the Contacts Manager or select the contact and then click the Edit button on the Contact Manager toolbar. Regardless of which method you use, the system opens the Edit Contact workspace.

The Edit Contact workspace is identical to the New Contact workspace, with the same fields and requirements as discussed in the previous section. To make changes to a contact, you simply alter the desired fields in the Edit Contact workspace, and then click the Save button on the toolbar. Any changes you make are applied immediately.

TIP

The Batch button on the Contact Manager toolbar offers several editing options and can save you time if you are trying to modify multiple contacts. Select one or more contacts and then click the Batch button. In the pop-up window that appears, you can change the access level, the language, or the linked user of all the contacts simultaneously. The Batch feature also supports moving contacts between categories and copying contacts.

Archiving contacts

If you want to remove a contact from use on the site, but do not want to delete it, you can move it to the archive. By default, archived contacts are not shown on the front end of the website.

To archive a contact, follow these steps:

1. **Log in to the admin system on your site.**

2. **Go to the Components menu and select the Contacts option.** The Contact Manager loads in your browser.

3. **Click the check box next to the contact or contacts you want to archive.**

4. **Click the Archive button on the toolbar.** The system immediately moves the selected contacts to the archive.

13

Contacts that have been moved into the archive can be unarchived by changing their status to either Published or Unpublished. To unarchive a contact, follow these steps:

1. **Log in to the admin system on your site.**
2. **Go to the Components menu and select the Contacts option.** The Contact Manager loads in your browser.
3. **Change the Select Status Filter to Archived.**
4. **Click the check box next to the contact or contacts you want to unarchive.**
5. **Select either Publish or Unpublish from the toolbar.** The system immediately unarchives the selected contacts.

Deleting contacts

The deletion of contacts in Joomla! is a two-step process. The first step involves moving the contact to the trash, where it is held until you take the second step and permanently delete the contact. Contacts held in the trash can be restored at any time prior to deletion. You can view the contents of the trash at any time by selecting the Trashed option from the Select Status Filter in the Contact Manager.

Contacts moved to the trash are held there indefinitely. The contacts can be restored or deleted at the option of the administrator. Restored contacts move back to their original locations, but deleted contacts are permanently removed from the system and cannot be restored.

> **NOTE**
> Though contacts can be left in the trash indefinitely, the trash is distinctly different from the archive. Moving contacts to the trash should not be confused with archiving contacts.

To move a contact to the trash, follow these steps:

1. **Log in to the admin system on your site.**
2. **Go to the Components menu and select the Contacts option.** The Contact Manager loads in your browser.
3. **Click the check box next to the contact or contacts you want to move to the trash.**
4. **Click the Trash button on the toolbar.** The system moves the selected contacts to the trash.

> **NOTE**
> Any contact moved to the trash is instantly unpublished and not visible to site visitors.

Restoring contacts from the trash

Contacts moved to the trash are held there until the administrator takes further action. Any contact can be restored at any time. The process of restoring a contact is simple and the result instantaneous: the contact is removed from the trash and returns to where it was located before it was moved to the trash.

To restore a contact from the trash, follow these steps:

1. **Log in to the admin system on your site.**

2. **Go to the Components menu and select the Contacts option.** The Contact Manager loads in your browser.

3. **Change the Select Status Filter to Trashed.** The list of contacts reloads to display only those contacts in the trash.

4. **Click the check box next to the contact or contacts you want to restore.**

5. **Click either Publish or Unpublish on the toolbar.** The system removes the selected contacts from the trash, and restores them to their previous locations.

TIP

You can also restore a contact by moving your mouse over the contact's title in the Contact Manager, clicking the arrow that appears, and selecting Untrash from the menu that opens.

Deleting contacts permanently

Contacts held in the trash can be removed from the system by emptying the trash. Emptying the trash results in the contact's permanent removal from the system; it cannot be restored once deleted.

To permanently delete a contact from the trash, follow these steps:

1. **Log in to the admin system on your site.**

2. **Go to the Components menu and select the Contacts option.** The Contact Manager loads in your browser.

3. **Change the Select Status Filter to Trashed.**

4. **Click the check box next to the contact or contacts you want to delete.**

5. **Click the Empty Trash button on the toolbar.** The system immediately deletes the selected contacts.

CAUTION

Deleting a contact is permanent and cannot be undone. Moreover, there is no confirmation dialog box — clicking the Empty Trash button immediately deletes the contact!

13

Managing Categories

Categories are created by the administrator for the purpose of grouping contacts. Categories can also be nested into subcategories to create groups and subgroups. Through the use of the menu item types, a site administrator can create links to go directly to various levels in the hierarchy, making it possible to build a proper directory using the Contacts component.

> **NOTE**
> The Fruit Shop sample site contained in the Learning Joomla! sample data shows how the creative use of the Categories feature can turn your contacts into a directory of terms or items. The Fruit Encyclopedia section of the Fruit Shop site is created with the Contacts component, where each fruit is a separate contact and the contacts are grouped into categories, with each category being a different letter of the alphabet. You can see the structure used in Figure 13.4. The layout is achieved by using the List All Contact Categories menu item type and then adding a custom class (categories-list alphabet) via the Page Display options on the Advanced Options tab of the menu item type workspace.

In this section, I cover how to create and manage your site's contact categories.

To view the contact categories, click the Categories submenu under Contacts on the main admin menu, or click the Categories link in the left column of the Contacts Manager. Whichever option you select, the Contacts Category Manager loads in your browser, as shown in Figure 13.4.

The toolbar at the top of the Contacts Category Manager provides quick access to the following functions:

- **New.** Click to add a new contact category.
- **Edit.** Select a category from the list and then click this button to edit the contact category details.
- **Publish.** Select one or more contact categories from the list and then click this button to publish them. You publish a category to make it visible on the front end of the website.
- **Unpublish.** Select one or more contact categories from the list and then click this button to unpublish them. You unpublish a category to hide it from display on the front end of the website.
- **Archive.** Select one or more contact categories from the list and then click this button to move the category to the archive.
- **Check In.** Select one or more contact categories and then click this button to force the category editing workspaces to close and thereby "check in" the categories.
- **Trash.** Select one or more categories from the list and then click this button to delete them.

342

FIGURE 13.4

The Contacts Category Manager with the Learning Joomla! sample data installed

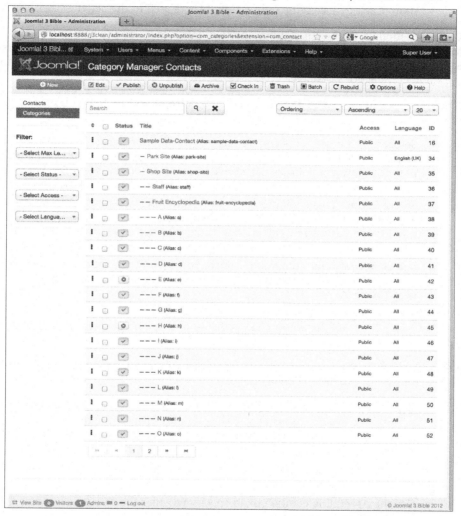

- **Batch.** Select multiple categories and then click this button to batch-apply processes to them. The pop-up window that appears enables you to copy or move multiple categories in one simple operation.

- **Rebuild.** Click if you are experiencing problems with your contact categories. Clicking this button forces the system to rebuild the contacts category tables in the database. You should not normally need this tool; use it sparingly.

- **Options.** Click to open the Contact Manager Options, where you can configure the parameters that affect the Contact Manager.
- **Help.** Click to access the online Help files related to the active screen.

Below the toolbar, in the left column, are two links: Contacts shows you the Contacts Manager, and Categories shows you the Contact Categories Manager. The Contacts Manager is discussed earlier in this chapter; below I go through the options available in the Contact Categories Manager.

Below the four links in the left column are four sorting tools to help you manage long lists of categories:

- **Select Max Levels.** This combo box allows you to control the number of levels of categories that appear. If your site has a complex hierarchy, this can greatly simplify the view of the list of categories in the Contact Manager. To reset this filter, change the combo box back to the default setting, Select Max Levels.
- **Select Status.** This combo box allows you to filter and display the categories according to whether they are published, unpublished, archived, or trashed. This provides an easy way to identify all categories that are currently active on the site. To reset this filter, change the combo box back to the default setting, Select Status.
- **Select Access.** This combo box allows you to filter the list of categories by access level. To reset this filter, change the combo box back to the default setting, Select Access.
- **Select Language.** This combo box allows you to filter the list of categories by language. To reset this filter, change the combo box back to the default setting, Select Language.

Below the toolbar and above the list of categories are four sorting and searching tools to help you manage long lists of categories:

- Type a word or phrase into the Search field and then click the magnifying glass button. The system searches your list of categories for the query and then displays the results of the search. To clear the screen and return to a full listing, click the button marked with the X.
- Use the combo box to the right of the Search field to determine which column of the display is used for the sort order.
- Use the Ascending combo box to specify whether the categories appear in ascending or descending order.
- Use the combo box on the far right to control the number of categories that appear on the page. You can alter the default value by changing the List Length parameter in the Global Configuration Manager.

The main content area of the screen contains a list of all the contact categories in your Joomla! site. The columns provided are

- **Sort Order (vertical double arrows).** You can click the arrows to change the sort order. You can also click and hold any of the buttons immediately to the left of a category's title and then drag the category to change its order location in the Contacts Category Manager.

- **Category Selection (unlabeled check box).** You can click a check box to select a category; this is necessary if you want to use several of the toolbar options.

- **Status.** A green check mark indicates that the category is published. A red x indicates that it is unpublished.

- **Title.** This field displays the full name of the category. Click the name to edit the category's details.

- **Access.** This field shows the access level assigned to the category.

- **Language.** This field shows the language designated for the category.

- **ID.** This field shows the system-generated user ID number.

TIP

You can also sort any column by clicking the column header.

Creating a new category

You can create categories from within the Contacts Category Manager by clicking the New button on the toolbar. Category data is entered into the Add A New Contacts Category workspace, shown in Figure 13.5.

The toolbar at the top of the Add A New Contacts Category workspace provides quick access to the following functions:

- **Save.** Click to save your work and create a new category without exiting the workspace.

- **Save & Close.** Click to save your work, create a new category, and exit the Add A New Contacts Category workspace.

- **Save & New.** Click to save your work, close the current Add A New Contacts Category workspace, and open another Add A New Contacts Category workspace.

- **Cancel.** Click to cancel the task and exit the Add A New Contacts Category workspace.

- **Help.** Click to display the Help files related to the active screen.

FIGURE 13.5

The Add A New Contacts Category workspace

Note the four tabs located at the top of the workspace. These tabs provide you with access to secondary functionality associated with categories:

- **Details.** This is the crucial tab needed for creating new categories. The fields on this tab are detailed in the following bulleted list.

- **Publishing Options.** The tab displays information relating to the categories, ID, creator, creation date and number of views.

- **Options.** The choices on this tab allow you to change the layout of the category landing page on the front end of the site, associate an image with the category, and add notes for use by the administrators.

- **Metadata Options.** The fields on this tab allow you to override the global metadata settings for this category's page.

- **Category Permissions.** This tab allows you to view and modify the permissions associated with this category. Permissions are normally inherited from the Global Configuration settings, but you can override them here.

The Details tab of the Add A New Contacts Category workspace includes the following fields:

- **Title.** You can use this field to assign the category a name. This is the only required field.

- **Alias.** The alias is the internal name for the item. If you leave this field blank, the system automatically uses your title for the alias, with any spaces converted to hyphens. Note that if you want to add a value to this field, it only accepts lower-case letters without any spaces.

- **Description.** This is an optional field in which you can add a description of the contact category.

- **Parent.** If you want to nest the contact categories, you can select a parent category from this combo box.

- **Status.** You can set the status of the category: Published, Unpublished, Archived, or Trashed.

- **Access.** You can select the access level needed to view the contact category.

- **Language.** You can select the language of the contact category. This control is key if you are running a multilingual site and want to show specific contacts to users who have selected specific languages.

 See Chapter 11 for an explanation of how parallel language contacts relate to the display of content; the same concepts apply here.

- **ID.** The value in this field is assigned automatically by the Joomla! system and is used internally by the system.

- **Created by.** You can specify the creator of the category by clicking the Select User link below the field.

The Publishing Options tab contains a set of data that is primarily informational. The tab displays the system ID for the category, the creator, the creation date, and the number of times the contact has been viewed, called Hits in the system. None of the options on this page can be edited once the contact has been created, as the values are specified automatically by the system.

The Options tab of the Add A New Contacts Category workspace includes the following fields:

- **Alternative Layout.** If your template provides for alternative layouts, you can select one from this combo box; otherwise, the default layout is applied.

- **Image.** If you want to associate an image with this category, you can click the Select button and choose one from the Media Library, or upload one of your own. If you are displaying the category on the front end of the site, the image appears on the page.

- **Note.** This is an optional field for use by the administrator.

The Metadata Options tab of the Add A New Contacts Category workspace includes the following fields:

- **Meta Description.** Enter into the text field any information you want to appear in the meta Description field for this category.

- **Meta Keywords.** Enter into the text field any keywords that you want to appear in the meta Keyword field for this category. Separate multiple keywords with commas.

- **Author.** Enter into this text field the information you want to appear in the meta Author field for this category.

- **Robots.** Select one of the options from this combo box to tell the various bots and spiders how to handle your site:

  - **Index, follow.** Select this option if you want to index all the pages on your site and follow all the links. For most site owners, who are interested in generating traffic from the search engines, this is the best option.

  - **No index, follow.** Select this option if you want the search engine to follow the links but not index the pages.

  - **Index, no follow.** Select this option if you want your pages to be indexed by the search engine, but don't want the links to be followed.

  - **No index, no follow.** Select this option if you want to block the search engines completely and keep your pages out of the search engine results.

The Category Permissions tab allows you to set specific permissions for the category. Settings that you make here override the global user permissions.

To create a new category, follow these steps:

1. **Log in to the admin system on your site.**

2. **Go to the Components menu and select the Categories option from the Contacts submenu.** The Contacts Category Manager loads in your browser.

3. **Click the New button on the toolbar at the top of the Contacts Category Manager.** The Add A New Contacts Category workspace opens (refer to Figure 13.5).

4. **In the Title field, type a name for this category.** This is the only required field.

5. **Add additional information or optional settings as you see fit.**

6. **Click the Save button on the toolbar.**

Editing categories

You can edit existing contact categories from the Contacts Category Manager. To edit a category, either click the category name in the Contacts Category Manager or select the category on the list and then click the Edit button on the Contacts Category Manager toolbar. Regardless of which method you use, the system opens the Edit Category workspace.

The Edit Category workspace is identical to the New Category workspace, with the same fields and requirements as discussed in the previous section.

To make changes to a category, you simply alter the desired fields in the Edit Category workspace and then click the Save button on the toolbar. Any changes you make are applied immediately.

> **TIP**
> The Batch button on the toolbar offers several editing options and can save you time if you are trying to modify multiple contacts. Select one or more categories and then click the Batch button. In the pop-up window that appears, you can change the access level or language assignment of all the contacts simultaneously. The Batch feature also supports moving and copying categories.

Archiving categories

If you want to remove a category from use on the site, but do not want to delete it, you can move it to the archive. By default, archived categories are not shown on the front end of the website.

To archive a category, follow these steps:

1. **Log in to the admin system.**

2. **Go to the Components menu and select the Categories option from the Contacts submenu.** The Contacts Category Manager loads in your browser.

3. **Click the check box next to the category or categories that you want to archive.**

4. **Click the Archive button on the toolbar.** The system immediately moves the selected categories to the archive.

> **NOTE**
> Moving a contact category to the archive has no impact on the contacts assigned to the category. If you want to archive the contacts, you have to do that separately.

Categories that have been moved into the archive can unarchived by changing the status of the category to either Published or Unpublished. To unarchive a category, follow these steps:

1. **Log in to the admin system.**
2. **Go to the Components menu and select the Categories option from the Contacts submenu.** The Contacts Category Manager loads in your browser.
3. **Change the Select Status Filter to Archived.**
4. **Click the check box next to the category or categories that you want to unarchive.**
5. **Select either Publish or Unpublish from the toolbar.** The system immediately unarchives the selected categories.

Deleting categories

The deletion of contact categories in Joomla! is a two-step process. The first step involves moving the category to the trash, where it is held until you take the second step and permanently delete the category. Categories held in the trash can be restored at any time prior to deletion. You can view the contents of the trash at any time by using the Select Status Filter in the Contacts Category Manager.

Categories moved to the trash are held there indefinitely. The items can be restored or deleted at the option of the administrator. Restored items move back to their original locations, but deleted items are permanently removed from the system and cannot be restored.

> **NOTE**
> Though categories can be left in the trash indefinitely, the trash is distinctly different from the archives. Moving categories to the trash should not be confused with archiving categories.

To move a category to the trash, follow these steps:

1. **Log in to the admin system.**
2. **Go to the Components menu and select the Categories option from the Contacts submenu.** The Contacts Category Manager loads in your browser.
3. **Click the check box next to the category or categories that you want to move to the trash.**
4. **Click the Trash button on the toolbar.** The system moves the selected categories to the trash.

Restoring categories from the trash

Categories moved to the trash are held there until the administrator takes further action. Any category can be restored at any time. The process of restoring a category is simple and the result instantaneous: the category is removed from the trash and returns to where it was located before it was moved to the trash.

To restore a category from the trash, follow these steps:

1. **Log in to the admin system.**

2. **Go to the Components menu and select the Categories option from the Contacts submenu.** The Contacts Category Manager loads in your browser.

3. **Change the Select Status Filter to Trashed.** The list of categories reloads to display only those categories in the trash.

4. **Click the check box next to the category or categories that you want to restore.**

5. **Click either Publish or Unpublish on the toolbar.** The system removes the selected categories from the trash, and restores them to their previous locations.

> **TIP**
>
> You can also restore a category by moving your mouse over the category title in the Contacts Category Manager, clicking the arrow that appears, and selecting Untrash from the menu that opens.

Deleting categories permanently

Categories held in the trash can be removed from the system by emptying the trash. Emptying the trash results in the category's permanent removal from the system; it cannot be restored once deleted.

To permanently delete a category from the trash, follow these steps:

1. **Log in to the admin system.**

2. **Go to the Components menu and select the Categories option from the Contacts submenu.** The Contacts Category Manager loads in your browser.

3. **Change the Select Status Filter to Trashed.**

4. **Click the check box next to the category or categories that you want to delete.**

5. **Click the Empty Trash button on the toolbar.** The system immediately deletes the selected categories.

> **NOTE**
>
> Deleting a contact category is permanent and cannot be undone. Moreover, there is no confirmation dialog box — clicking the Empty Trash button immediately deletes the category! Note, however, that a category cannot be deleted if there are contacts assigned to that category. If you want to delete the category, you must first delete or reassign any contacts assigned to that category.

13

Creating Contact Forms

The Contact Manager is the key to setting up contact forms to gather feedback from site visitors or to generate leads. Creating a contact form for your site is a two-stage process, though there are several options along the way. You can create one or more contact forms for the site and publish them either collectively or individually. By linking the form to a specific contact, you can also present additional information about the contact and easily manage the routing of the form to the desired person.

In this final section, I take you through setting up a primary contact form for your website.

> **NOTE**
> There are several extensions designed to provide more flexibility in form creation and management; several of those extensions are discussed in Chapter 22.

The first step to complete is to create a specific contact to receive the output of the form. I discuss creating a new contact earlier in this chapter. If you want to use an existing contact, you can; however, be aware that you may want to publish specific information on the contact page that is not part of that contact's profile, for example, a company address or a company website address. You need to configure this contact by editing the contact and making the following selections on the Contact Form tab:

- Set the Show Contact Form option to Yes.
- If you want to offer the option to send the form output to the submitters, as well as to the contact, select Yes in the Send Copy to Submitter field.

> **TIP**
> You may also want to use the Miscellaneous Information text field on the Edit Contact tab to add additional information, such as a link to a Google Map for a company or store location.

The second step is to create a new menu item linking to your contact. You use the Single Contact menu item type. For the Select Contact field, you choose the contact you created in step one. Make sure that your Show Contact Form parameter is set to Yes. Once you save your changes, your site has a new menu item leading to the contact, with a form option for your site visitors. Figure 13.6 shows one possible implementation.

 I discuss creating a new menu item as well as the Single Contact menu item type in Chapter 8.

FIGURE 13.6

The creation of a simple Contact Us page using a contact from the Contacts component and the standard form

> **TIP**
>
> If you have installed the Learning Joomla! sample data, you can see an alternative implementation in the Fruit Shop site. The Contact Us link on the Fruit Shop menu contains a link to a contacts category and uses this technique to present multiple contacts, each with a form, on a single page. This is a good solution for a company that wants to route contact forms to multiple departments or multiple store locations.

Summary

In this chapter, I looked at how to use the Contacts component included in Joomla!. I covered the following topics:

- Configuring the Contacts component
- Adding contacts to the component
- Creating categories to hold your contacts
- Managing your contacts and categories
- Using the component to create a directory
- Creating a basic Contact Us page using the component's contact form functionality

In the next chapter, I look at another of the default components: the Newsfeed component.

Using the Newsfeed Component

The Newsfeed component is an RSS aggregation tool. This component allows you to add syndicated RSS and Atom feeds (referred to in Joomla! by the generic name "newsfeeds") to your site and to group them into categories. You can then display the content on your pages by creating menu items that link to the component's output.

The Newsfeed component provides all the parameters needed to manage the aggregation of multiple feeds and, to a lesser extent, the individual feed items. You can control the number of items gathered and the frequency of the updates. The feed items gathered by the Newsfeed component can then be channeled into the site to display in a variety of ways.

The Newsfeed component makes it very easy to bring external content into your site and to manage it all from one interface. Because the feeds update automatically, there's never been an easier way to bring current information into your site to enhance your site's relevance and value to your visitors.

> **NOTE**
>
> The Joomla! interface switches back and forth between "Newsfeeds" and "News Feeds." I've tried to standardize usage here in this text to "Newsfeeds," but regardless of which term you see, we're all talking about the same thing.

Introducing the Newsfeed Manager

The Newsfeed Manager is your central point of contact with the functionality of the Newsfeed component. The manager is the dashboard that provides access to all the tools you need to aggregate feed content into your site. Using the features inside the Newsfeed Manager, you can add new feeds, group them together into categories, and even customize their display. The tools provided by this component are relatively easy to use, and with a short orientation on how it all works, you will be using the Newsfeed component with confidence in no time at all.

I will begin by taking a quick tour of the Newsfeed Manager interface to explain what you can find there and how you can use the manager to achieve your goals. You can access the Newsfeed Manager by going to the Components menu and selecting the Newsfeeds option, which loads the Newsfeed Manager interface in your browser. Figure 14.1 shows the Newsfeed Manager as it appears with the Joomla! sample data installed.

> **NOTE**
>
> On the Components menu, the option labeled Newsfeeds leads to the same screen as the Newsfeeds submenu option labeled Feeds. Despite having different names, these two navigation choices lead to the same page — the Newsfeed Manager.

FIGURE 14.1

The Newsfeed Manager, with the Learning Joomla! sample data installed

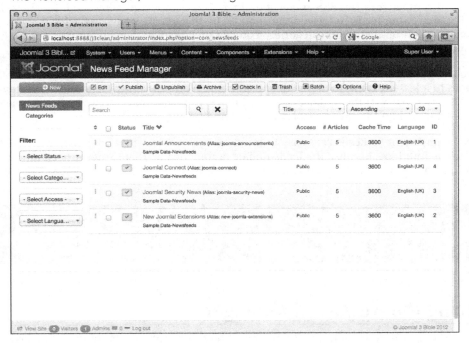

The buttons on the toolbar at the top of the Newsfeed Manager provide quick access to the following common tasks:

- **New.** Click to add a newsfeed.

- **Edit.** Select a newsfeed from the list and then click this button to edit the newsfeed's details.

- **Publish.** Select one or more newsfeeds from the list and then click this button to publish them. You publish a newsfeed to make it visible on the front end of the website.

- **Unpublish.** Select one or more newsfeeds from the list and then click this button to unpublish them. You unpublish a newsfeed to hide it from the front end of the website.

- **Archive.** Select one or more newsfeeds from the list and then click this button to move the newsfeeds to the archive.

- **Check In.** Select one or more newsfeeds from the list and then click this button to force the newsfeed editing workspaces to close and thereby "check in" the newsfeeds.

- **Trash.** Select one or more newsfeeds from the list and then click this button to delete the selected newsfeeds.

- **Batch.** Select multiple newsfeeds and then click this button to batch-apply processes to those newsfeeds. The pop-up window that appears enables you to modify multiple newsfeeds in one simple operation.

- **Options.** Click to open the Newsfeed Manager Options, where you can configure the parameters that affect the Newsfeed Manager. I discuss configuring the Newsfeed component in the next section.

- **Help.** Click to access the online Help files related to the active screen.

Below the toolbar, in the left column, are two links: Newsfeeds shows you the Newsfeed Manager, and Categories shows you the Newsfeeds Categories Manager. I discuss each of these options in the sections that follow.

Below the two links in the left column are four sorting tools to help you manage long lists of newsfeeds:

- **Select Status.** The options in this combo box allow you to filter and display the newsfeeds according to whether they are published, unpublished, archived, or trashed. This provides an easy way to identify all newsfeeds that are currently active on the site. To reset this filter, change the combo box back to the default setting, Select Status.

- **Select Category.** The options in this combo box allow you to filter and display the newsfeeds according to the category to which they are assigned. To reset this filter, change the combo box back to the default setting, Select Category.

14

- **Select Access.** The options in this combo box allow you to filter the list of news-feeds by access level. To reset this filter, change the combo box back to the default setting, Select Access.
- **Select Language.** The options in this combo box allow you to filter the list of newsfeeds by language. To reset this filter, change the combo box back to the default setting, Select Language.

Below the toolbar and above the list of newsfeeds are four sorting and searching tools to help you manage long lists of newsfeeds:

- Type a word or phrase into the Search newsfeeds by name field, and then click the magnifying glass button. The system searches your list of newsfeeds for the query and then displays the results of the search. To clear the screen and return to a full listing, click the button marked with the X.
- Use the combo box to the right of the Search field to specify which column of the newsfeeds display is used for the sort order.
- Use the Ascending combo box to specify whether the newsfeeds appear in ascending or descending order.
- Use the combo box on the far right to control the number of newsfeeds that appear on the page. You can alter the default value by changing the List Length parameter in the Global Configuration Manager.

The main content area of the screen contains a list of all the newsfeeds in your Joomla! site. The columns provided are

- **Sort Order (vertical double arrows).** You can click the arrows to change the sort order, or click and hold any of the buttons immediately to the left of a newsfeed's title and drag the newsfeed to change its order location in the Newsfeed Manager.
- **Newsfeed Selection (unlabeled check box).** You can click a check box to select a newsfeed; this is necessary if you want to use several of the toolbar options.
- **Status.** A green check mark indicates that the newsfeed is published. A red x indicates that it is unpublished.
- **Title.** This field displays the full name of the newsfeed. You can click the name to edit the newsfeed's details.
- **Access.** This field indicates the access level assigned to the newsfeeds.
- **# Articles.** This field shows how many items have been gathered from this feed and are available for display.
- **Cache Time.** This field shows how long the contents of the newsfeed are kept locally before the list is refreshed.
- **Language.** This field shows the language designated for the newsfeeds.
- **ID.** This field shows the system-generated ID number.

TIP
You can also sort any column by clicking the column header.

Configuring the Newsfeed Component

You can configure global options for the Newsfeed component by using the Options button located on the toolbar of the Newsfeed Manager. Clicking the button takes you to the Newsfeed component's workspace in the Global Configuration Manager. The workspace is used to set the global parameters available to this component. You can override the parameters for individual newsfeeds by setting alternative values in an individual newsfeed's workspace (discussed later in this chapter), or by overriding them in the menu item settings. The configuration options are designed to help you control the formatting of the newsfeeds and their categories, as well as set permissions for the use of the component. In this section, I review the numerous options that are available for configuring the Newsfeed component.

Figure 14.2 shows the landing tab of the Newsfeed component's configuration workspace.

FIGURE 14.2

The Newsfeed component's configuration workspace

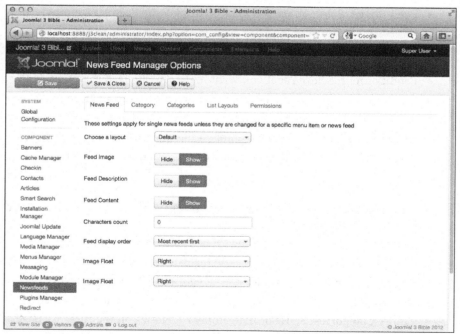

There are five tabs leading to five workspaces for the Newsfeed component's configuration:

- **Newsfeed.** This tab contains settings relating to the display of single newsfeeds. The choices on this tab determine what information appears along with the newsfeed.
- **Category.** This tab allows you to set the options for the display of a single newsfeed category page.
- **Categories.** This tab allows you to set the options for the display of pages containing multiple newsfeed categories.
- **List Layouts.** This tab controls the layout of newsfeeds in list format.
- **Permissions.** This tab allows you to specify the extent to which the various user groups are able to perform actions with the Newsfeed component.

The Newsfeed tab, shown in Figure 14.2, is the landing tab. The settings on this tab are applied to the display of single newsfeeds. The options are

- **Choose a layout.** Use this combo box to select from the available layouts for the newsfeeds.
- **Feed Image.** Select Yes if you want to display the Feed Image provided by the source of the feed.
- **Feed Description.** Select Yes if you want to display the Feed Description set by the source of the feed.
- **Feed Content.** Select Yes if you want to display the feed's content on the page.
- **Characters count.** Set the number of characters to display from each feed article.
- **Feed display order.** Set the order of display for the articles from the feed.
- **Image Float.** Control the positioning of the first image associated with the feed.
- **Image Float.** Control the positioning of additional images associated with the feed.

The Category tab includes the following options:

- **Choose a layout.** Use this combo box to control the layout of the newsfeeds listed on the category page.
- **Category Title.** Show or hide the category title on the category page.
- **Category Description.** Show or hide the category description on the category page.
- **Category Image.** Show or hide the category image on the category page.
- **Subcategory levels.** Select the number of subcategory levels to display.
- **Empty Categories.** Show or hide empty categories on the category page.
- **Subcategories Descriptions.** Show or hide the descriptions from the subcategories.
- **# Feeds in Category.** Show or hide the number of newsfeeds per category on the category page.

The Categories tab includes the following options:

- **Top Level Category Description.** Show or hide the description of the top-level category.
- **Subcategory Levels.** Select how many subcategory levels you want to display on the page.
- **Empty Categories.** Show or hide empty categories.
- **Subcategories Descriptions.** Show or hide the descriptions of the subcategories.
- **# Feeds in Category.** Show or hide the number of newsfeeds in each category.

The List Layouts tab includes the following options:

- **Display Select.** Show or hide the display select combo box.
- **Table Headings.** Show or hide the table headings of the table used for the list layout.
- **# Articles.** Show or hide the newsfeed's position.
- **Feed Links.** Show or hide the newsfeed's e-mail address.
- **Pagination.** Show or hide the pagination controls.
- **Pagination Results.** Show or hide the total page count on the pagination controls. This is only applicable if you set Pagination to Show.

The Permissions tab works consistently with the Global Configuration permissions tab. Here you can dictate the extent to which the various user groups on your site can use the functionality of the Newsfeed component.

 See Chapter 10 for a discussion of how permissions relate to user groups.

After you have set the parameters you desire, click the Save button in the top-left corner to save your changes, or click Cancel to close the Parameters window without saving the changes.

Managing Your Newsfeeds

You can add newsfeeds to your site through the Newsfeed Manager. The manager provides a single point of contact where you can see all feeds coming into your site and then manage them. Using the Newsfeed Manager, you can group newsfeeds into categories and subcategories, set the publishing options, and alter the configuration options relating to the display of the feeds. If you plan to publish a large number of feeds on your site, the Newsfeed Manager greatly simplifies keeping up with the feeds and controlling their publication.

In this section I look at how to add newsfeeds and how to manage them once they are in the system. Later in this section, I also look briefly at your publication options. After that, I turn my attention to managing newsfeed categories, as these are optional.

Adding a newsfeed

Administrators can add newsfeeds to the Newsfeed component at any time through the admin system. Newsfeeds are added to the system through the Newsfeed Manager, so you need to point your browser to the Newsfeed Manager and click the New button on the toolbar. The Add A Newsfeed workspace opens in your browser, as shown in Figure 14.3.

> **NOTE**
> Before you begin, make sure you have a valid newsfeed URL. Supported feed formats include RSS 0.91, RSS 1.0, RSS 2.0, Atom 0.3, and Atom 1.0.

The toolbar at the top of the Add A Newsfeed workspace provides quick access to the following functions:

- **Save.** Click to save your work.
- **Save & Close.** Click to save your work and exit the Add A Newsfeed workspace.
- **Save & New.** Click to save your work, close the current Add A Newsfeed workspace, and open another Add A Newsfeed workspace.
- **Cancel.** Click to cancel the task and exit the Add A Newsfeed workspace.
- **Help.** Click to display the Help files related to the active screen.

The workspace is divided into four tabs:

- **New.** This is the basic tab containing most of the required fields for creating a newsfeed.
- **Publishing Options.** This tab contains fields for author alias, start and stop dates for publication, and fields relating to article display and caching. Several of the fields on this tab are required.
- **Display Options.** This tab allows you to control how a newsfeed appears.
- **Metadata Options.** This tab contains metadata fields for the newsfeed.

The New tab of the workspace contains the following fields:

- **Title.** Use this field to name your newsfeed. This is a required field.
- **Link.** Enter the URL for the source of the newsfeed. This field is required. Note that the URL should normally begin with `http://`.
- **Category.** Assign the newsfeed to a category using this combo box. This field is required.
- **Description.** Enter the text that you want to appear at the top of the page where the newsfeed's output appears on the front end of the website.

- **Images.** Use these fields if you want an image to appear on the same page as the newsfeed's output.

FIGURE 14.3

The Add A Newsfeed workspace

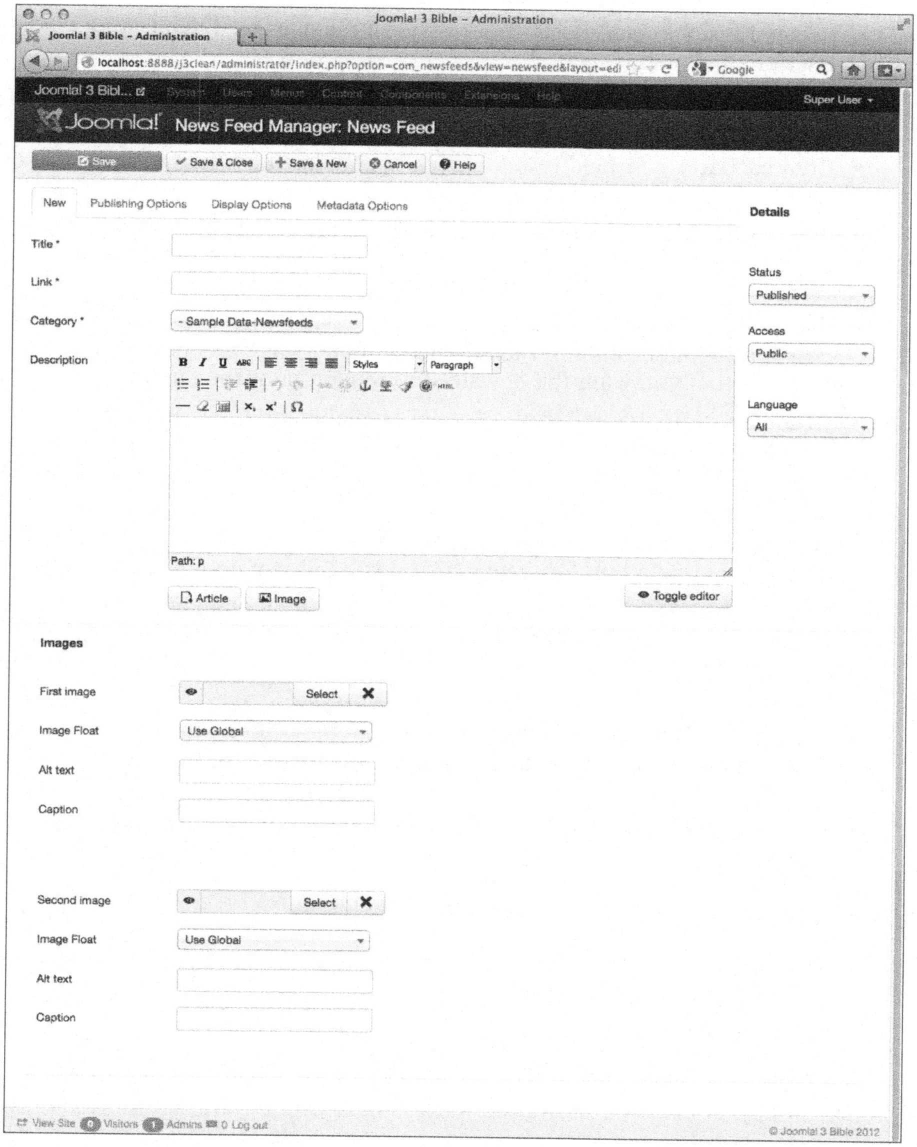

The Publishing Options tab contains several required fields, as well as controls affecting the output and publication of the newsfeed:

- **Alias.** You can specify the URL to be used for the page in this field. This is typically used as a means of optimizing the URL for the search engines. If you leave it blank the system will fill it in automatically.

- **ID.** This value is automatically created by the system for internal use.

- **Created by.** You can specify the creator of the newsfeed by clicking the Select User link below this field.

- **Author's Alias.** You can create an alias for the newsfeed creator by entering it here. If you supply a value here, it appears instead of the user's name.

- **Created Date.** This field is automatically populated by the system and shows the creation date and time for the contact.

- **Start Publishing.** Though optional, you can use this field to set a specific starting date for the publication of the newsfeed. If you leave this field blank, the system assumes that you want to start publishing immediately.

- **Finish Publishing.** Though optional, you can use this field to set a specific ending date for the publication of the newsfeed. If you leave this field blank, the system assumes that you want the newsfeed to remain published indefinitely.

- **Ordering.** Note that this control is not available for a new newsfeed. New items are placed by default in the last position on the list. After you add your newsfeed, you can adjust the list position either from the Newsfeed Manager or by editing the newsfeed.

- **Number of Articles.** You can specify how many articles you want to appear. This is a required field but the system defaults to 5 if you do not specify otherwise.

- **Cache Time.** The value in this field represents how often your system checks the original feed source for new content. The integer value here is in minutes. This is a required field, though the system defaults to 3,600 minutes if you do not specify a value.

- **Language Direction.** If your feed content is in a different text orientation than your other text, you can use this combo box to tell the system to display it differently.

- **External Reference.** You can use this field to add a cross-reference to an external data source.

The Display Options tab includes the following fields:

- **Feed Image.** You can show or hide the image supplied by the feed, if any.

- **Feed Description.** You can show or hide the description supplied by the feed, if any.

- **Feed Content.** You can show or hide the content supplied by the feed.

- **Character Count.** You can set the feed length by entering in this field the number of characters to display from the feed.
- **Alternative Layout.** If your template provides for alternative layouts, you can select one from this combo box; otherwise, the default layout is applied.
- **Feed Display Order.** You can set the order of display for the items from the feed.

The Metadata Options tab of the Add A New Newsfeed workspace includes the following fields:

- **Meta Description.** Enter into the text field any information you want to appear in the meta Description field for this newsfeed.
- **Meta Keywords.** Enter into the text field any keywords that you want to appear in the meta Keyword field for this newsfeed. Separate multiple keywords with commas.
- **External Reference.** Use this field to add a link to any relevant external references.
- **Robots.** Select one of the options from this combo box to tell the various bots and spiders how to handle your site:
  - **Index, follow.** Select this option if you want to index all the pages on your site and follow all the links. For most site owners, who are interested in generating traffic from the search engines, this is the best option.
  - **No index, follow.** Select this option if you want the search engine to follow the links but not index the pages.
  - **Index, no follow.** Select this option if you want your pages to be indexed by the search engine, but don't want the links to be followed.
  - **No index, no follow.** Select this option if you want to block the search engines completely and keep your pages out of the search engine results.
- **Content Rights.** Use this field to declare any restrictions on use of the contents.

> **NOTE**
>
> Like the articles workspace, this newsfeed workspace also includes a column on the right side under the Details heading. The column is designed to give you quick access to the most common tasks associated with newsfeeds, that is, your publishing controls, access settings, and language association.

14

To add a newsfeed, follow these steps:

1. **Log in to the admin system on your site.**
2. **Go to the Components menu and select the Newsfeeds option.** The Newsfeed Manager loads in your browser.
3. **Click the New button on the toolbar.** The Add A Newsfeed workspace opens (refer to Figure 14.3).

4. **In the Title field, type a name for the feed.** This field is required.

5. **Type the address for the feed source in the Link field.** Normally this begins with `http://`. This field is required.

6. **Select a category for the feed from the Category combo box or leave the feed classified as uncategorized.** This field is required.

7. **Select any additional options you want; all other fields are optional.**

8. **Click the Save button on the toolbar in the top-left corner to save your newsfeed.**

DISPLAYING NEWSFEEDS ON YOUR SITE

After you bring newsfeeds into your system with the Newsfeed Manager, the question becomes how to display the newsfeeds on your site. Adding feeds to the Manager does not automatically translate into displaying feed output on your site.

There are two common ways to display newsfeed content on your site: using either a page or a module.

By linking your menu items to the Newsfeed component, you can display feeds or categories of feeds as content items on your site. For a discussion of how to add newsfeeds to the pages on your site through the creation of menu items, see Chapter 8.

Alternatively, you can bypass the Newsfeed component completely and create a new module to hold a single newsfeed. You can use modules to aggregate and display individual newsfeeds, and these modules are not dependent in any way upon the Newsfeed component. Chapter 17 covers adding newsfeed content inside a module on your site.

Editing a newsfeed

The details relating to an existing newsfeed can be edited from the Newsfeed Manager. To edit a newsfeed, you can either click the newsfeed's name in the Newsfeed Manager or select the newsfeed and then click the Edit button on the Newsfeed Manager toolbar. Regardless of which method you use, the system opens the Edit Newsfeed workspace.

NOTE

Because the feed is provided by an external source, when I talk about editing, I am referring to editing your settings for the display of the newsfeed; it is not possible to edit the actually content of a newsfeed originating from an external source.

The Edit Newsfeed workspace is identical to the Add A Newsfeed workspace, with the same fields and requirements as discussed in the previous section. To make changes to a newsfeed, you simply alter the desired fields in the Edit Newsfeed workspace, and then click the Save button on the toolbar. Any changes you make are applied immediately.

TIP

The Batch button on the toolbar offers several editing options and can save you time if you are trying to modify multiple contacts. Select one or more newsfeeds and then click the Batch button. In the pop-up window that appears, you can change the access level, the language, or the linked user of all the contacts simultaneously. The Batch feature also supports moving newsfeeds between categories and copying newsfeeds.

Archiving a newsfeed

If you want to remove a newsfeed from use on the site, but do not want to delete it, you can move it to the archive. By default, archived newsfeeds are not shown on the front end of the website.

To archive a newsfeed, follow these steps:

1. **Log in to the admin system on your site.**
2. **Go to the Components menu and select the Newsfeeds option.** The Newsfeed Manager loads in your browser.
3. **Click the check box next to the newsfeed you want to archive.**
4. **Click the Archive button on the toolbar.** The system immediately moves the newsfeed to the archive.

A newsfeed that has been moved into the archive can be unarchived by changing the status of the newsfeed to either Published or Unpublished. To unarchive a newsfeed, follow these steps:

1. **Log in to the admin system on your site.**
2. **Go to the Components menu and select the Newsfeeds option.** The Newsfeed Manager loads in your browser.
3. **Change the Select Status Filter to Archived.**
4. **Click the check box next to the newsfeed you want to unarchive.**
5. **Select either Publish or Unpublish from the toolbar.** The system immediately unarchives the newsfeed.

Deleting a newsfeed

The deletion of newsfeeds in Joomla! is a two-step process. The first step involves moving the newsfeed to the trash, where it is held until you take the second step and permanently delete the newsfeed. Newsfeeds held in the trash can be restored at any time prior to deletion. You can view the newsfeeds in the trash at any time by selecting the Trashed option from the Select Status Filter in the Newsfeed Manager.

Newsfeeds moved to the trash are held there indefinitely. The newsfeeds can be restored or deleted at the option of the administrator. Restored newsfeeds move back to their original locations, but deleted newsfeeds are permanently removed from the system and cannot be restored.

> **NOTE**
> Though newsfeeds can be left in the trash indefinitely, the trash is distinctly different from the archive. Moving newsfeeds to the trash should not be confused with archiving newsfeeds.

14

To move a newsfeed to the trash, follow these steps:

1. **Log in to the admin system on your site.**
2. **Go to the Components menu and select the Newsfeeds option.** The Newsfeed Manager loads in your browser.
3. **Click the check box next to the newsfeed you want to remove.**
4. **Click the Trash button on the toolbar.** The system moves the newsfeed to the trash.

> **NOTE**
>
> Any newsfeed moved to the trash is instantly unpublished and not visible to site visitors.

Restoring a newsfeed from the trash

Newsfeeds moved to the trash are held there until the administrator takes further action. Any newsfeed can be restored at any time. The process of restoring a newsfeed is simple and the result instantaneous: the newsfeed is removed from the trash and returned to where it was located before it was moved to the trash.

To restore a newsfeed from the trash, follow these steps:

1. **Log in to the admin system on your site.**
2. **Go to the Components menu and select the Newsfeeds option.** The Newsfeed Manager loads in your browser.
3. **Change the Select Status Filter to Trashed.** The list of newsfeeds reloads to display only those newsfeeds in the trash.
4. **Click the check box next to the newsfeed you want to restore.**
5. **Click either Publish or Unpublish on toolbar.** The system removes the newsfeed from the trash, and restores it to its previous location.

> **TIP**
>
> You can also restore a newsfeed by moving your mouse over the newsfeed title in the Newsfeeds Manager, clicking the arrow that appears, and selecting Untrash from the menu that opens.

Deleting a newsfeed permanently

Newsfeeds held in the trash can be removed from the system by emptying the trash. Emptying the trash results in the newsfeed's permanent removal from the system; it cannot be restored once deleted.

To permanently delete a newsfeed from the trash, follow these steps:

1. **Log in to the admin system on your site.**
2. **Go to the Components menu and select the Newsfeeds option.** The Newsfeed Manager loads in your browser.
3. **Change the Select Status Filter to Trashed.** The list of newsfeeds reloads to show only those newsfeeds in the trash.
4. **Click the check box next to the newsfeed you want to delete.**
5. **Click the Empty Trash button on toolbar.** The system immediately deletes the newsfeed.

CAUTION

Deleting a newsfeed is permanent and cannot be undone. Moreover, there is no confirmation dialog box — clicking the Empty Trash button immediately deletes the newsfeed!

Managing Newsfeed Categories

Categories can be created by the administrator for the purpose of grouping newsfeeds. You can create multiple categories and arrange them into a hierarchy of parent-child relationships. While categories are not necessary — you can leave your newsfeeds uncategorized if you like — they are helpful if you have a large number of newsfeeds, or if you want to have more alternatives for displaying your newsfeeds. Joomla! provides menu item types that allow you to link directly to newsfeed categories, a technique you can see demonstrated if you have installed the sample data.

In this section I look at how to create and manage newsfeed categories.

NOTE

If you are already familiar with category management in other areas of Joomla!, you will be happy to know that the system is very consistent and the category functions and features are very similar throughout the site.

14

To view the categories available in your system, click the Categories link at the top of the Newsfeed Manager. The Newsfeeds Category Manager loads in your browser, as shown in Figure 14.4.

FIGURE 14.4

The Newsfeeds Category Manager, shown with the Learning Joomla! sample data installed

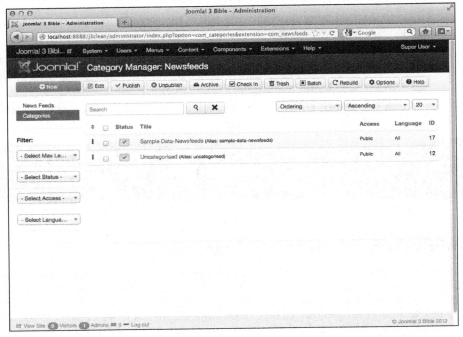

The toolbar at the top of the Newsfeeds Category Manager provides quick access to the following functions:

- **New.** Click to add a newsfeed category.
- **Edit.** Select a category from the list and then click this button to edit the newsfeed category details.
- **Publish.** Select one or more newsfeed categories from the list and then click this button to publish them. You publish a category to make it visible on the front end of the website.
- **Unpublish.** Select one or more newsfeed categories from the list and then click this button to unpublish them. You unpublish a category to hide it from display on the front end of the website.
- **Archive.** Select one or more newsfeed categories from the list and then click this button to move the category to the archive.
- **Check In.** Select one or more newsfeed categories from the list and then click this button to force the category editing workspaces to close and thereby "check in" the categories.

- **Trash.** Select one or more categories from the list and then click this button to delete them.

- **Batch.** Select multiple categories and then click this button to batch-apply processes to them. The pop-up window that appears enables you to copy or move multiple categories in one simple operation.

- **Rebuild.** Click if you are experiencing problems with your newsfeed categories. Clicking this button forces the system to rebuild the newsfeed category tables in the database. You should not normally need this tool; use it sparingly.

- **Options.** Click to open the Newsfeeds component configuration workspace, where you can configure the parameters that affect the Newsfeed Manager.

- **Help.** Click to access the online Help files related to the active screen.

Below the toolbar, in the left column, are two links: Newsfeeds shows you the Newsfeed Manager, and Categories shows you the Newsfeeds Categories Manager. The Newsfeed Manager is discussed earlier in this chapter. I discuss the Newsfeeds Categories Manager in the section that follows.

Below the four links in the left column are four sorting tools to help you manage long lists of categories:

- **Select Max Levels.** Use this combo box to control the number of levels of categories that appear. If your site has a complex hierarchy, this can greatly simplify the view of the list of categories in the Newsfeeds Category Manager. To reset this filter, change the combo box back to the default setting, Select Max Levels.

- **Select Status.** Use this combo box to filter and display the categories according to whether they are published, unpublished, archived, or trashed. This provides an easy way to identify all categories that are currently active on the site. To reset this filter, change the combo box back to the default setting, Select Status.

- **Select Access.** Use this combo box to filter the list of categories by access level. To reset this filter, change the combo box back to the default setting, Select Access.

- **Select Language.** Use this combo box to filter the list of categories by language. To reset this filter, change the combo box back to the default setting, Select Language.

Below the toolbar and above the list of categories are four sorting and searching tools to help you manage long lists of categories:

- Type a word or phrase into the Search field and then click the magnifying glass button. The system searches your list of categories for the query and then displays the results of the search. To clear the screen and return to a full listing, click the button marked with the X.

- Use the combo box to the right of the Search field to determine which column of the display is used for the sort order.

14

- Use the Ascending combo box to specify whether the categories appear in ascending or descending order.

- Use the combo box on the far right to control the number of categories that appear on the page. You can alter the default value by changing the List Length parameter in the Global Configuration Manager.

The main content area of the screen contains a list of all the newsfeed categories in your Joomla! site. The columns provided are

- **Sort Order (vertical double arrows).** You can click the arrows to change the sort order. You can also click and hold any of the buttons immediately to the left of a category's title and drag the category to change its order location in the Newsfeeds Category Manager.

- **Category Selection (unlabeled check box).** You can click a check box to select a category; this is necessary if you want to use several of the toolbar options.

- **Status.** A green check mark indicates that the category is published. A red x indicates that it is unpublished.

- **Title.** This field displays the full name of the category. You can click the name to edit the category's details.

- **Access.** This field indicates the access level assigned to the category.

- **Language.** This field shows the language designated for the category.

- **ID.** This field shows the system-generated user ID number.

TIP

You can also sort any column by clicking the column header.

Creating a new category

You can create categories from within the Newsfeed Category Manager, by clicking the New button on the toolbar. Category data is entered into the Add A New Newsfeeds Category workspace, shown in Figure 14.5.

The toolbar at the top of the Add A New Newsfeeds Category workspace provides quick access to the following functions:

- **Save.** Click to save your work and create a new category without exiting the workspace.

- **Save & Close.** Click to save your work, create a new category, and exit the Add A New Newsfeeds Category workspace.

- **Save & New.** Click to save your work, close the current Add A New Newsfeeds Category workspace, and open another Add A New Newsfeeds Category workspace.

FIGURE 14.5

The Add A New Newsfeeds Category workspace

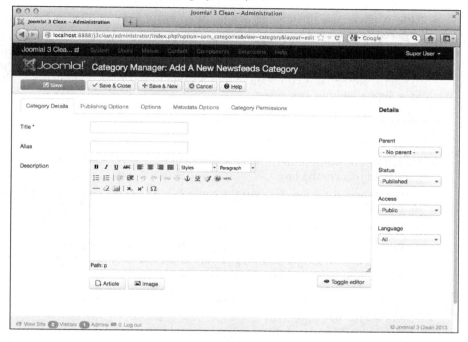

- **Cancel.** Click to cancel the task and exit the Add A New Newsfeeds Category workspace.
- **Help.** Click to display the Help files related to the active screen.

Note the five tabs located at the top of the workspace. These tabs provide you with access to secondary functionality associated with categories:

- **Category Details.** This is the crucial tab needed for creating new categories. The fields on this tab are detailed in the following bulleted list.
- **Publishing Options.** This tab allows you to change the layout of the category landing page on the front end of the site, associate an image with the category, and add notes for use by the administrators.
- **Options.** This tab allows you to select an alternative layout for the category page and associate an image with the category as well.
- **Metadata Options.** The fields on this tab allow you to override the global metadata settings for this category's page.
- **Category Permissions.** This tab allows you to view and modify the permissions associated with this category. Permissions are normally inherited from the Global Configuration settings, but you can override them here.

14

The Category Details section of the Add A New Newsfeeds Category workspace includes the following fields:

- **Title.** You can use this field to assign the category a name. This is the only required field.
- **Alias.** The alias is the internal name for the item. If you leave this field blank, the system automatically uses your title for the alias, with any spaces converted to hyphens. Note that if you want to add a value to this field, it only accepts lower-case letters without any spaces.
- **Description.** This is an optional field in which you can add a description of the newsfeed category. If you are displaying the category on the front end of the site, the description appears on the page.
- **Parent.** If you want to nest the newsfeed categories, you can select a parent category from this combo box.
- **Status.** You can set the status of the category: Published, Unpublished, Archived, or Trashed.
- **Access.** You can select the access level needed to view the newsfeed category.
- **Language.** You can select the language of the newsfeed category. This control is key if you are running a multilingual site and want to show specific categories to users who have selected specific languages.

 See Chapter 11 for an explanation of how parallel language categories relate to the display of content; the same concepts apply here.

The Publishing Options tab of the Add A New Newsfeeds Category workspace includes the following fields:

- **ID.** The value in this field is assigned automatically by the Joomla! system and is used internally by the system.
- **Hits.** The value in this field is automatically generated by Joomla! and indicates the number of times the category has been viewed on the front end of the site.
- **Created by.** You can specify the creator of the category by clicking the Select User link below this field.

The Options tab of the Add A New Newsfeeds Category workspace includes the following fields:

- **Alternative Layout.** If your template provides for alternative layouts, you can select one from this combo box; otherwise, the default layout is applied.
- **Image.** If you want to associate an image with this category, you can click the Select button and choose one from the Media Library, or upload one of your own. If you are displaying the category on the front end of the site, the image appears on the page.
- **Note.** This is an optional field used by the administrator.

The Metadata Options tab of the Add A New Newsfeeds Category workspace includes the following fields:

- **Meta Description.** Enter into this text field any information you want to appear in the meta Description field for this category.

- **Meta Keywords.** Enter into this text field any keywords that you want to appear in the meta Keyword field for this category. Separate multiple keywords with commas.

- **Author.** Enter into this text field the information you want to appear in the meta Author field for this category.

- **Robots.** Select one of the options from this combo box to tell the various bots and spiders how to handle your site.

  - **Index, follow.** Select this option if you want to index all the pages on your site and follow all the links. For most site owners, who are interested in generating traffic from the search engines, this is the best option.

  - **No index, follow.** Select this option if you want the search engine to follow the links but not index the pages.

  - **Index, no follow.** Select this option if you want your pages to be indexed by the search engine, but don't want the links to be followed.

  - **No index, no follow.** Select this option if you want to block the search engines completely and keep your pages out of the search engine results.

The Category Permissions tab allows you to set specific permissions for the category. Settings that you make here override the global user permissions.

To create a new category, follow these steps:

1. **Log in to the admin system on your site.**

2. **Go to the Components menu and select the Categories option from the Newsfeeds submenu.** The Newsfeeds Category Manager loads in your browser.

3. **Click the New button on the toolbar at the top of the Newsfeeds Category Manager.** The Add A New Newsfeeds Category workspace opens (refer to Figure 14.5).

4. **In the Title field, type a name for this category.** This is the only required field.

5. **Add additional information or optional settings as you see fit.**

6. **Click the Save button on the toolbar.**

Editing categories

You can edit existing newsfeed categories from the Newsfeeds Category Manager. To edit a category, either click the category name in the Newsfeeds Category Manager or select the category on the list and then click the Edit button on the Newsfeeds Category Manager toolbar. Regardless of which method you use, the system opens the Edit Newsfeeds Category workspace.

14

The Edit Newsfeeds Category workspace is identical to the Add A New Newsfeeds Category workspace, with the same fields and requirements as discussed in the previous section.

To make changes to a category, you simply alter the desired fields in the Edit Newsfeeds Category workspace and then click the Save button on the toolbar. Any changes you make are applied immediately.

> **TIP**
>
> The Batch button on the toolbar offers several editing options and can save you time if you are trying to modify multiple categories. Select one or more categories and then click the Batch button. In the pop-up window that appears, you can change the access level or language assignment of all the categories simultaneously. The Batch feature also supports moving and copying categories.

Archiving categories

If you want to remove a category from use on the site, but do not want to delete it, you can move it to the archive. By default, archived categories do not appear on the front end of the website.

To archive a category, follow these steps:

1. **Log in to the admin system on your site.**
2. **Go to the Components menu and choose the Categories option from the Newsfeeds submenu.** The Newsfeeds Category Manager loads in your browser.
3. **Click the check box next to the category or categories you want to archive.**
4. **Click the Archive button on the toolbar.** The system immediately moves the selected categories to the archive.

> **NOTE**
>
> Moving a newsfeed category to the archive has no impact on the newsfeeds assigned to the category. If you want to archive the newsfeeds, you have to do that separately.

Categories that have been moved into the archive can be unarchived by changing the status of the category to either Published or Unpublished. To unarchive a category, follow these steps:

1. **Log in to the admin system on your site.**
2. **Go to the Components menu and choose the Categories option from the Newsfeeds submenu.** The Newsfeeds Category Manager loads in your browser.
3. **Change the Select Status Filter to Archived.**
4. **Click the check box next to the category or categories you want to unarchive.**
5. **Select either Publish or Unpublish from the toolbar.** The system immediately unarchives the selected categories.

Deleting categories

The deletion of newsfeed categories in Joomla! is a two-step process. The first step involves moving the category to the trash, where it is held until you take the second step and permanently delete the category. Categories held in the trash can be restored at any time prior to deletion. You can view the contents of the trash at any time by using the Select Status Filter in the Newsfeeds Category Manager.

Categories moved to the trash are held there indefinitely. The categories can be restored or deleted at the option of the administrator. Restored categories move back to their original locations, but deleted categories are permanently removed from the system and cannot be restored.

> **NOTE**
>
> Though categories can be left in the trash indefinitely, the trash is distinctly different from the archive. Moving categories to the trash should not be confused with archiving categories.

To move a category to the trash, follow these steps:

1. **Log in to the admin system on your site.**
2. **Go to the Components menu and choose the Categories option from the Newsfeeds submenu.** The Newsfeeds Category Manager loads in your browser.
3. **Click the check box next to the category or categories you want to move to the trash.**
4. **Click the Trash button on the toolbar.** The system moves the selected categories to the trash.

Restoring categories from the trash

Categories moved to the trash are held there until the administrator takes further action. Any category can be restored at any time. The process of restoring a category is simple and the result instantaneous: the category is removed from the trash and returns to where it was located before it was moved to the trash.

To restore a category from the trash, follow these steps:

1. **Log in to the admin system on your site.**
2. **Go to the Components menu and choose the Categories option from the Newsfeeds submenu.** The Newsfeeds Category Manager loads in your browser.
3. **Change the Select Status Filter to Trashed.** The list of categories reloads to display only those categories in the trash.
4. **Click the check box next to the category or categories you want to restore.**
5. **Click either Publish or Unpublish on the toolbar.** The system moves the selected categories from the trash, and restores them to their previous locations.

14

Deleting categories permanently

Categories held in the trash can be removed from the system by emptying the trash. Emptying the trash results in the category's permanent removal from the system; it cannot be restored once deleted.

To permanently delete a category from the trash, follow these steps:

1. **Log in to the admin system on your site.**
2. **Go to the Components menu and choose the Categories option from the Newsfeeds submenu.** The Newsfeeds Category Manager loads in your browser.
3. **Change the Select Status Filter to Trashed.**
4. **Click the check box next to the category or categories you want to delete.**
5. **Click the Empty Trash button on the toolbar.** The system immediately deletes the selected categories.

Summary

In this chapter, I covered the use of the Joomla! feed aggregator, the Newsfeed component. This chapter addressed the following topics:

- Configuring the Newsfeed component to suit your needs
- Adding newsfeeds to your site
- Managing existing fields through the Newsfeed Manager
- Creating categories to hold your newsfeeds
- Managing newsfeed categories

In the next chapter, I look at how you can use the Joomla! Site Search component.

Using the Site Search Components

The Joomla! system comes with two search components: a basic keyword search and a more advanced indexed search system. The two systems are incompatible — you must select one or the other — and are suitable to different purposes. The basic Joomla! search is the more limited of the two, but is easier to set up. For smaller sites, it may be all you need. For larger sites, or for sites where you want to provide users with more search options, the Joomla! Smart Search is the way to go. Smart Search offers more complete indexing of your site and includes tools to manage your indexed content. Both search options have their own modules and menu items. To create an optimal search experience for your site visitors, you need to understand how these two search options work and how to configure them and present them to your visitors.

In this chapter I introduce the site search functionality and the two components that provide it. I also explain the differences between the two systems and how to implement them on your site for maximum effect.

Creating an Effective Site Search

If you own a large or complex site, then offering site search for your visitors is not an option; it's a necessity. Even smaller sites these days tend to offer a search function, because it is not only a time saver for users but also desirable for site owners, as it can help expose deep content more easily. Thoroughness and usability are key factors in site search; the search functionality should be easy to use and it should provide accurate results.

Traditionally, Joomla! has only offered a keyword-based search functionality; that is, when a user enters a search query in the search form, the system tries to match the words in the query to the site contents in real time. The basic keyword search functionality in Joomla! is provided by the Search component. Over the years, Joomla! users everywhere lobbied for a better Search component; the keyword search technique tends to be slower and less comprehensive than searching an index of a site's contents.

The arrival of Joomla! 2.5 introduced an enhanced site search. The new Joomla! feature was called Smart Search and differed significantly from the basic search. Smart Search is an index-based search tool; that is, the system periodically indexes the entire site and when a search query is submitted, it is the index that is searched. Index-based searching tends to deliver faster results to users and can be tailored to display only selected content. In this section, I look at how to set up both methods of site search.

Working with Joomla! basic search

The basic search functionality in Joomla! is supplied by the Search component and supported by a variety of plug-ins. This search feature has been present in Joomla! since the beginning, and it is limited in what it can do. In short, the Search component is designed to search the articles and selected components, as determined by the configuration of the supporting plug-ins. It is, in other words, limited in what it will return in results; it does not index the entire site. For small sites, or for sites that want only to index the articles and one or two of the core components, the basic search is an adequate solution.

The Search component and the supporting plug-ins are enabled by default. A Search module type supports the Search component, and there is also a menu item type dedicated to the component. The search box you see on the default templates is the Search module associated with the basic search.

To use this component, you simply either publish the Search module or link to the menu item type named Search Form or Search Results. In addition to the basic module and component, there are five plug-ins associated with the Search component and you should understand what they do, as you may want to configure them to suit your site's search needs. The plug-ins are

- **Search – Categories.** Enables the searching of categories on your site
- **Search – Contacts.** Enables the searching of Contacts component content
- **Search – Articles.** Enables the searching of articles on your site
- **Search – Newsfeeds.** Enables the searching of Newsfeed component content
- **Search – Weblinks.** Enables the searching of Weblinks component content

Each of these plug-ins is responsible for handling the indexing of specific components. If you do not want a particular component's output indexed, you can simply disable the plug-in.

See Chapter 19 for a discussion of all the plug-ins and the parameters associated with each plug-in.

Enhancing site search with Smart Search

Joomla! comes bundled with an additional search component called Smart Search, which is designed to provide indexing of your entire site and searching of the resulting index. If you want to provide site visitors with a richer search experience as well as provide search results from all areas of your site, then this is the option you want to use.

The Smart Search component is disabled in the default configuration. Like the basic Search component, Smart Search also includes dedicated modules and plug-ins. Six plug-ins provide the indexing functionality and allow you to select which types of contents are included in the search index. The plug-ins are

- **Content - Smart Search.** Enables the indexing by the Smart Search component. This key plug-in is disabled by default. It must be enabled to use Smart Search.
- **Smart Search – Categories.** Enables the indexing of categories on your site.
- **Smart Search – Contacts.** Enables the indexing of Contacts component content.
- **Smart Search – Articles.** Enables the indexing of the articles on your site.
- **Smart Search – Newsfeeds.** Enables the indexing of Newsfeed component content.
- **Smart Search – Weblinks.** Enables the indexing of Weblinks component content.

To run the Smart Search functionality on your site, you need to take several steps. First, you must enable the Content - Smart Search plug-in, then index your site, and finally either publish the Smart Search module or create a menu item linked to the search page. While setting up Smart Search is certainly more involved than the basic Search, the results are much richer.

15

> **NOTE**
>
> Smart Search can impose a significant load on your server resources. If your site has a large number of items, or if your site content changes frequently, Smart Search's indexing routine uses considerable server resources in an effort to keep the index up to date. Chapter 24 includes a discussion of performance management.

If you intend to implement Smart Search, you should also disable the basic Search component before you publish the Smart Search interface to your site visitors. The Smart Search component and the Search component have similar functions and are not intended to be enabled at the same time. While you can run them both, there's not a good reason to do so and you run the risk of exposing users to a confusing variety of search options. Accordingly, in the remainder of this section, I look at enabling Smart Search and disabling the basic Search function.

Enabling the Smart Search content plug-in

Before you can use Smart Search, you have to enable the Content - Smart Search plug-in. This is the plug-in that powers indexing site-wide; without it, any attempt to index the site returns an error message. To enable the plug-in, follow these steps:

1. **Log in to the admin system of your Joomla! site.**
2. **Select the Plug-in Manager option, under the Extensions heading on the main admin navigation bar.** The Plug-in Manager loads in your browser.
3. **From the list of plug-ins, find the item named Content - Smart Search.** Click the box with the red x in the Status column to enable the plug-in. The system enables the plug-in and the red x changes to a green check mark.

That's all there is to it; there are no configuration options. The plug-in is now enabled and Smart Search is ready to index your site. In the next section I explain how to run the indexer.

> **NOTE**
>
> The other Smart Search–related plug-ins are enabled by default.

Running the indexer

Now that Smart Search is enabled, it's time to generate your first index of the site. Until you generate an index, anyone searching the site using a search form provided by Smart Search will not see any results. To create the index, follow these steps:

1. **Log in to the admin system of your Joomla! site.**
2. **Select the Smart Search option, under the Components heading on the main admin navigation bar.** The Smart Search Managed Indexed Content workspace loads in your browser.

3. **Click the Index button on the toolbar.** The system begins indexing the site; as it does so, a status pop-up window appears on your screen. When the process is finished, you see a message telling you the job is done and that you can close the pop-up window. Do not close the pop-up prior to completion of the indexing.

4. **Click the gray X in the top right corner of the pop-up window to close the window.** The pop-up window hides and you can now see a listing of all the indexed content, similar to that shown in Figure 15.1.

FIGURE 15.1

A typical index generated by Smart Search

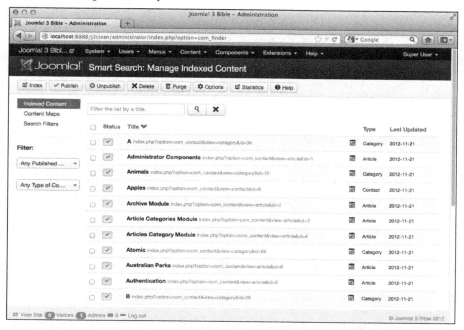

If you have not done so already, you should disable all elements of the basic Joomla! Search component. While the system works without this step, removing the basic search function reduces the possibility of confusing your site visitors and also helps keep your system lean and efficient. Make sure you take the following steps:

- Check all your menus and unpublish all menu items pointing to the Search component.

- Go to the Module Manager and unpublish all modules of the type Search.

- Go to the Plug-ins Manager and disable all plug-ins of the type beginning with the prefix "Search -".

15

> **NOTE**
>
> You may not want everything on your site to be indexed. While you can exclude entire categories of content by disabling the relevant plug-ins, if you want, instead, to be selective about specific items within a content type, the Smart Search system provides an interface for managing your indexed content; a topic that I discuss later in this chapter.

Providing visitors with the right search interface

Each of the search components has dedicated interface elements: modules, and menu item types. You need to publish the right interfaces to make your preferred search component available to your site visitors.

Joomla! includes two search modules, one for each search component. The module names reflect the component names: The Search module type matches up with the Search component, and the Smart Search module type is intended for use with the Smart Search component. The modules are purpose-built and tied to the specific components; you need to select the appropriate module to match the component you are using. The two modules are very similar visually, the only difference being that the Smart Search module includes an option to display an Advanced Search link inside the module output.

 Chapter 17 covers both the Search and Smart Search modules and includes a summary of the configuration variables available for each one.

Similarly, the Joomla! system includes two menu item types specifically designed to allow you to create menu links to pages that include search forms. The names here are a bit confusing: The Search Form or Search Results menu item type matches the Search component. The Search menu item type matches the Smart Search component. Both menu item types do the same thing, that is, provide users with a search interface. There are differences, however, between what they offer. Figure 15.2 shows the two pages generated by these menu item types, side-by-side.

 I discuss both menu item types in Chapter 8. The chapter includes figures of the resulting pages and a discussion of the configuration parameters that are available for each.

> **TIP**
>
> Don't mix the modules or the menu item types of the two components; this will only cause confusion for your site visitors!

If you are using the Smart Search option, you can add another enhancement for your site visitors: custom search filters. Search filters are a way for administrators to create search forms that search a specific section of the site. Once created, the search filters can then be used by site visitors via the Smart Search module or Search menu item type. To access the Search Filters feature, you can go to the Smart Search component and click the Search Filters link in the left column. Figure 15.3 shows the Search Filters workspace.

FIGURE 15.2

A Search Results or Search Form menu item type is on the left, and the Search menu item type is on the right.

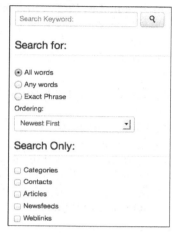
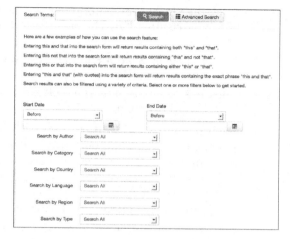

FIGURE 15.3

The Search Filters workspace, showing one filter created

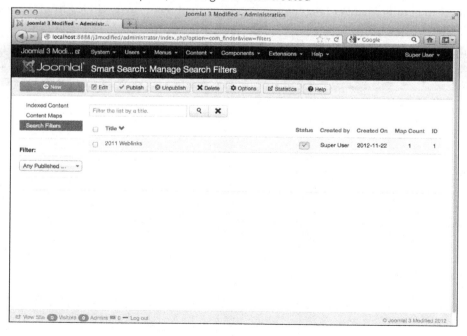

15

Creating a filter is the best way to understand what it can do. Follow these steps:

1. **Log in to the admin system of your site.**

2. **Click the Smart Search option under the Components heading on the main admin navigation bar.** The Smart Search Manage Indexed Content workspace opens.

3. **Click the Select Search Filters link in the left column.** The Search Filters workspace loads in your browser.

4. **Click the New button on the toolbar.** The Edit (new) Search Filter workspace opens, as shown in Figure 15.4.

5. **Enter a name for your filter in the Title field.** This is a required field.

6. **Set the parameters that will restrict the scope of the search.** You can do this by selecting either a date range, or one of the options at the bottom of the page, that is, Search by Author, Search by Category, and so on. You can combine as many options as you like.

7. **Select any other options you desire; all other fields are optional.**

8. **Click the Save button.** Your search filter is created.

Now that you have a search filter, you can make it available to your site visitors via either the Smart Search module or the Search menu item type. When a visitor runs a search using a search form that is restricted by a filter, the only results she sees are those that meet the requirements of the filter; all other content items are excluded from the search results.

TIP
The Search Filters option is a great way to create specialty searches that only apply to specific areas of your site.

FIGURE 15.4

The Edit (new) Search Filter workspace, showing a filter in the process of being created

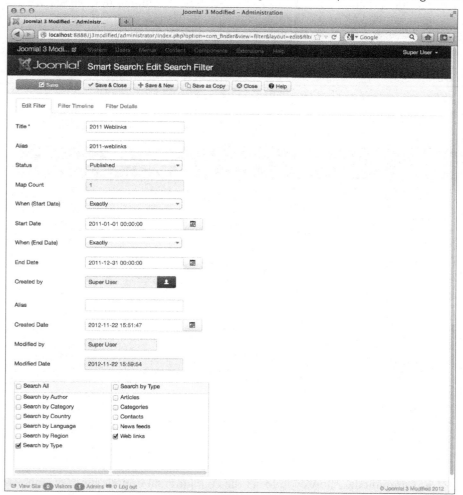

Configuring the Site Search Components

Both the Search and the Smart Search components have dedicated configuration managers. Using the parameters in each component's configuration manager, you can set various display and feature options and control which user groups have permission to use the component. In this section I look at both configuration managers and how you can use them to tailor the search functionality to your needs.

Of the two components, the Search component's configuration manager is the simplest. You can click the Options button on the toolbar of the Search component manager to open the configuration page. You can also access the configuration workspace by clicking the Smart Search link in the Components column of the Global Configuration Manager. Figure 15.5 shows the Search component's configuration workspace.

FIGURE 15.5

The Search component's configuration workspace

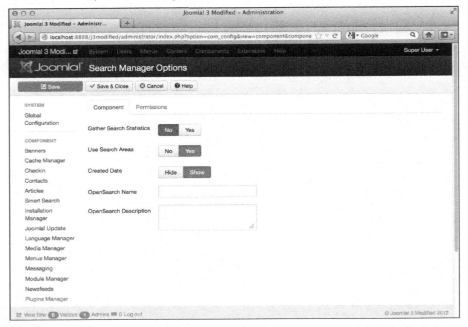

Two tabs lead to two workspaces for the Search component's configuration:

- **Component.** Allows you to set the configuration options for the component's output
- **Permissions.** Determines the extent to which the various user groups are able to perform actions with the Search component

The Component tab, shown in Figure 15.5, is the landing tab. The settings on this tab are applied to the search form displayed by the Search component. The options are

- **Gather Search Statistics.** Set to Yes to enable the system to track search queries. The gathered statistics are viewable in the Search component's workspace.

- **Use Search Areas.** Set to Yes to give users the option to filter the search results by areas, that is, Categories, Contacts, and so on.

- **Created Date.** Show or hide the created date of items that appear in the search results. When set to Show, the date appears at the end of each search result shown.

- **OpenSearch Name.** Specify the name that appears in the browser's search box. This only applies if the browser supports OpenSearch.

- **OpenSearch Description.** Enter the description that is shown for the search link when it appears in the browser's search box. This only applies if the browser supports OpenSearch.

The Permissions tab works consistently with the Global Configuration permissions tab. Here you can dictate the extent to which the various user groups on your site can use the functionality of the Search component.

In contrast, the Smart Search component's configuration manager includes more options. To access the configuration manager, you click the Options button on the toolbar of the component. You can also access the configuration workspace by clicking the Smart Search link in the Components column of the Global Configuration Manager. Figure 15.6 shows the Smart Search component's configuration workspace.

Three tabs lead to three workspaces for the Smart Search component's configuration:

- **Search.** Allows you to set the configuration options for the Smart Search component's output

- **Index.** Allows you to set the configuration options for the indexing of your site

- **Permissions.** Determines the extent to which the various user groups are able to perform actions with the Smart Search component

The Search tab, shown in Figure 15.6, is the landing tab. The settings on this tab are applied to the search form displayed by the component and to the search results. The options are

- **Gather Search Statistics.** Set to Yes to enable the system to track search queries. The gathered statistics are viewable in the Smart Search component's workspace.

- **Result Description.** Show or hide the items' descriptions in the search results.

- **Description Length.** Use this field to specify the maximum length of the description displayed, if you have set the Result Description option to Show.

- **Allow Empty Search.** Set to Yes to allow your users to submit an empty search query.

TIP

Note that if your site is larger, then allowing empty searches can create a heavy load on your server.

- **Result URL.** Show or hide the URL of the items in the search results.

15

FIGURE 15.6

The Smart Search component's configuration workspace

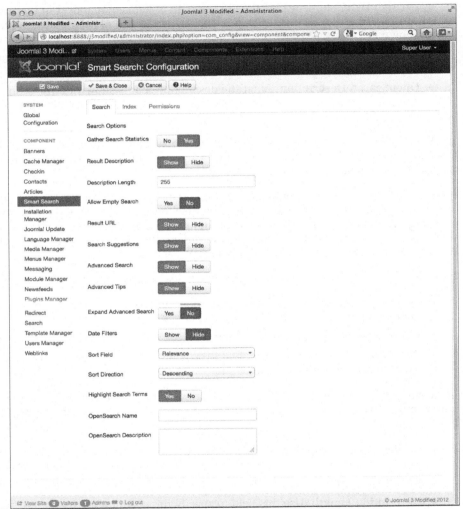

- **Search Suggestions.** Set to Yes if you want the system to suggest possible queries to users. The suggestions are based on what the user types into the search form. This is most useful in cases where the user has misspelled a word or phrase.

- **Advanced Search.** Show or hide the advanced search option.

- **Advanced Tips.** The system automatically displays search tips for the advanced search feature. If you do not want to display those tips, set this option to Hide.

- **Expand Advanced Search.** Normally, advanced search appears as a button. When the user clicks the button, the advanced search panel opens. If you want to expand that panel by default, set this option to Yes.

- **Date Filters.** Show or hide date filters for your users to apply to the search results.

- **Sort Field.** Use this combo box to select the sorting criteria for the search results.

- **Sort Direction.** Use this combo box to sort the search results in either ascending or descending order.

- **Highlight Search Terms.** Set to Yes to highlight the query string in the results set.

- **OpenSearch Name.** Specify the name that appears in the browser's search box. This only applies if the browser supports OpenSearch.

- **OpenSearch Description.** Enter the description that is shown for the search link when it appears in the browser's search box. This only applies if the browser supports OpenSearch.

The Index tab allows you to configure the indexing of your site's contents. Using the options on this tab, you can control resource usage, shape how your site index is weighted, and enable stemming. By controlling the weighting, you can help improve the search results and also emphasize the content you want to be prominent in the search results. The options are

- **Indexer Batch Size.** The system batches items for processing during indexing. You can use this option to control the size of the batch. Larger batch sizes result in faster indexing, but use up more memory and system resources. You need to watch how your site behaves during indexing to strike the right balance.

- **Memory Table Limit.** The default value here, 30,000, is designed to work for most systems. You should not change this value unless you are receiving aggregate table error messages during indexing.

- **Title Text Weight Multiplier.** You can set the weighting you want to give to the title field.

15

- **Body Text Weight Multiplier.** You can set the weighting you want to give to the body text of the item.
- **Meta Data Text Weight Multiplier.** You can set the weighting you want to give to the item's metadata.
- **Path Text Weight Multiplier.** You can set the weighting you want to give to the item's path.
- **Miscellaneous Text Weight Multiplier.** You can set the weighting you want to give to other information associated with each item.
- **Enable Stemmer.** You can set to Yes to enable the use of stemming.
- **Stemmer.** If your site is in English only, you can select the English option. If you have a non-English or multilingual site, you can select Snowball.

> **NOTE**
> The Snowball stemmer requires the Stem PHP extension and provides support for 14 languages, including Danish, German, English, Spanish, Finnish, French, Hungarian, Italian, Norwegian, Dutch, Portuguese, Romanian, Russian, and Turkish. To learn more, or to download the extension, visit http://pecl.php.net/package/stem.

- **Enable Logging.** You can set to Yes to create a log file during indexing. Use this feature if you are having problems with indexing and need a troubleshooting resource.

Managing Indexed Content

Smart Search indexes all your articles and key core components. Exactly which components are indexed depends on which Smart Search plug-ins are enabled. In the default configuration, the plug-ins provide indexing of your articles, the Contacts component, the Weblinks component, and the Newsfeed component. If you want to completely exclude any of these components, you can simply disable the appropriate plug-in. If, on the other hand, you want to eliminate specific items within a component, you need to take a different approach and use the Smart Search component's Manage Indexed Content workspace.

To access the Manage Indexed Content workspace, you click the Smart Search option under the Components menu. The toolbar at the top of the Manage Indexed Content workspace provides quick access to the following functions:

- **Index.** Click to index the site.
- **Publish.** Select one or more items from the list and then click this button to publish them. You publish an item to make it subject to search and display in the search results.
- **Unpublish.** Select one or more items from the list and then click this button to unpublish them. You unpublish an item to hide it from the search and exclude it from the search results.

- **Delete.** Select an item from the list and then click this button to delete it from the index.
- **Purge.** Click to force the system to completely dump the present index.
- **Options.** Click to open the Smart Search configuration workspace, where you can configure the parameters that affect the Smart Search component.
- **Statistics.** Click to view a brief summary of the indexed content.
- **Help.** Click to access the online Help files related to the active screen.

Below the toolbar, in the left column, are three links: Indexed Content shows you the Manage Indexed Content workspace, Content Maps shows you the Content Maps workspace, and Search Filters takes you to the Search Filters Manager. I discuss each of these options in the sections that follow.

Below the three links are two filters that can be applied to the list of indexed items. The first allows you to filter by publication state. The second allows you to filter by type of content. The two filters can be combined to further refine your view of the indexed items.

Below the toolbar and above the list of items is a search field. Type a word or phrase into the field marked Filter the list by a title, and then click the magnifying glass button. The system searches your list of items for the query and then displays the results of the search. To clear the screen and return to a full listing, click the button marked with the X.

The main content area of the screen contains a list of all the items in the index. The columns provided are

- **Item Selection (unlabeled check box).** You can click a check box to select an item; this is necessary if you want to process multiple items at once.
- **Status.** A green check mark means it is published; a red x means it is unpublished. Click to toggle the state.
- **Title.** This field displays the full name of the item. The information following the title is the path.
- **Calendar icon (no label).** You can move your mouse over the icon to view information about the publication of the item.
- **Type.** This column tells you what component produced the output.
- **Last Updated.** This field indicates the last time this item was updated in the index.

The Content Maps link in the left column of the page provides another way to view the contents of your site index. You can click this link to open the Content Maps workspace, shown in Figure 15.7.

15

FIGURE 15.7

The Content Maps workspace

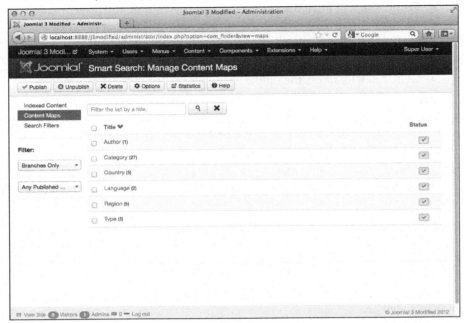

The Content Maps workspace simply displays the items in the index, grouped by a variety of classifications, including author, category, language, and other factors. You can unpublish an entire group simply by changing the publication status of that group. You can also click a group to drill down into the subcategories of the group, if any.

Tracking Site Search Activity

Joomla! includes a tool to help you keep track of the search activity on your site. The Search link on the Components menu item takes you to a page labeled Search Term Analysis. The page displays a list of all the search terms that have been input via the site search and a list of how many results were returned. This information is useful to you as a site owner, as it provides insight into what your visitors are interested in and looking for. Figure 15.8 shows the Search Term Analysis report.

The Search Term Analysis feature works for both the basic Search component and the more advanced Smart Search component. In either case, however, you must set the configuration options for the relevant component to allow the gathering of search statistics. I discuss configuring the components earlier in this chapter.

FIGURE 15.8

The Search Term Analysis report

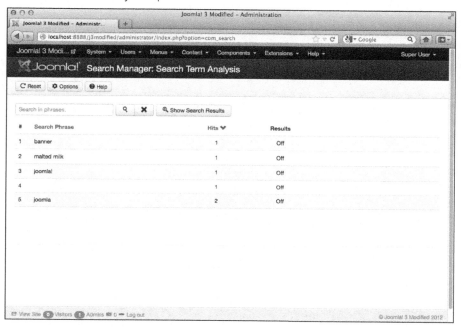

Summary

This chapter looked at two site search components from Joomla!: Search and Smart Search. The topics included

- Understanding the differences between the two components and what they provide
- Configuring the components
- Setting up the proper search interfaces for your visitors
- Enabling Smart Search
- Creating search filters
- Managing your indexed content
- Gathering site search activity reports

In the next chapter, I take a look at the Weblinks component and how you can use it to add links to your site.

15

Using the Weblinks Component

The Weblinks component enables you to accumulate URLs to other websites and online resources and then publish those links easily on your website. This component also makes it easy to organize those links and to track the number of times users have clicked them. While a links page is a common feature of many websites, the Weblinks component is much more powerful than a simple links page. Because the Weblinks component enables you to create categories and subcategories of links, you can use the Joomla! menu items to link to various levels of the hierarchy, allowing the display of link resources throughout your site, rather than simply on one single page. The Weblinks component also provides all the parameters needed to control the appearance and behavior of the links.

In this chapter, I introduce the Weblinks component, explore the available configuration options, and then show you how to add links and categories to your site.

Introducing the Weblinks Manager

The Weblinks component has a narrow range of functionality; it's all about enriching the content of your site by displaying links to external sites, and organizing those links into categories. The primary interface for interacting with the component is the Weblinks Manager, which provides quick access to the tools you need to create and manage all your links. The Weblinks Manager is your gateway to the Weblinks component and the workspace you will use most frequently as you add and manage the links on your site. Though the Weblinks Manager interface is mainly informational, allowing you to see all the links in the system and the number of clicks they have received, the interface also provides access to the tools you need to add, edit, archive, and delete the weblinks in your site.

In this section, I introduce the Weblinks Manager interface and the tools it contains. In later sections, I look at the creation and management of the links and categories. To access the Weblinks component, you must log in to the admin system, go to the Components menu, and then select the Weblinks option. The Weblinks Manager loads in your browser window.

NOTE

Joomla! uses both the terms "Weblinks" and "Web Links." To limit confusion, I am using the standard "Weblinks." Regardless of which term you see, they are referring to the same thing.

Figure 16.1 shows the Weblinks Manager as it appears with the Joomla! sample data installed.

FIGURE 16.1

The Weblinks Manager

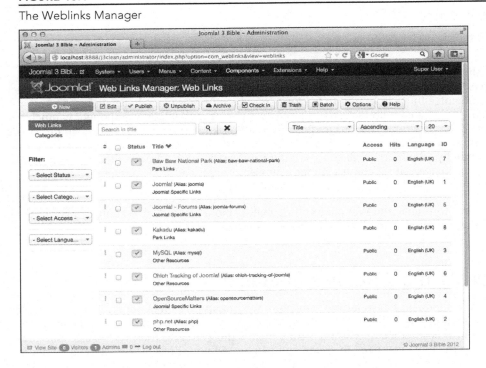

The toolbar at the top of the Weblinks Manager provides quick access to the following functions:

- **New.** Click to add a weblink.

- **Edit.** Select a weblink from the list and then click this button to edit the weblink's details.

- **Publish.** Select one or more weblinks from the list and then click this button to publish them. You publish a weblink to make it visible on the front end of the website.

- **Unpublish.** Select one or more weblinks from the list and then click this button to unpublish them. You unpublish a weblink to hide it from the front end of the website.

- **Archive.** Select one or more weblinks from the list and then click this button to move the weblink to the archive.

- **Check In.** Select one or more weblinks and then click this button to force the weblink editing workspaces to close and thereby "check in" the weblinks.

- **Trash.** Select one or more weblinks from the list and then click this button to delete them.

- **Batch.** Select multiple weblinks and then click this button to batch-apply processes to those weblinks. The pop-up window that appears enables you to modify multiple weblinks in one simple operation.

- **Options.** Click to open the Weblinks Manager Options workspace, where you can configure the parameters that affect the Weblinks component. I discuss configuring the Weblinks component in the next section.

- **Help.** Click to access the online Help files related to the active screen.

Below the toolbar, in the left column, are two links: Weblinks shows you the Weblinks Manager, and Categories shows you the Weblinks Category Manager. I discuss each of these options in the sections that follow.

Below the two links in the left column are four sorting tools to help you manage long lists of weblinks:

- **Select Status.** The options in this combo box allow you to filter and display the weblinks according to whether they are published, unpublished, archived, or trashed. This provides an easy way to identify all weblinks that are currently active on the site. To reset this filter, change the combo box back to the default setting, Select Status.

- **Select Category.** The options in this combo box allow you to filter and display the weblinks according to the category to which they are assigned. To reset this filter, change the combo box back to the default setting, Select Category.

- **Select Access.** The options in this combo box allow you to filter the list of weblinks by access level. To reset this filter, change the combo box back to the default setting, Select Access.

- **Select Language.** The options in this combo box allow you to filter the list of web-links by language. To reset this filter, change the combo box back to the default setting, Select Language.

Below the toolbar and above the list of weblinks are four sorting and searching tools to help you manage long lists of weblinks:

- Type a word or phrase into the field marked Search in title, and then click the magnifying glass button. The system searches your list of weblinks for the query and then displays the results of the search. To clear the screen and return to a full listing, click the button marked with the X.
- Use the combo box to the right of the Search field to determine which column of the weblinks display is used for the sort order.

> **TIP**
> You can also sort any column by clicking the column header.

- Use the Ascending combo box to specify whether the weblinks appear in ascending or descending order.
- Use the combo box on the far right to control the number of weblinks that appear on the page. You can alter the default value by changing the List Length parameter in the Global Configuration Manager.

The main content area of the screen contains a list of all the weblinks in your Joomla! site. The columns provided are

- **Sort Order (vertical double arrows).** You can click the arrows to change the sort order, or click and hold any of the buttons immediately to the left of a weblink's title and drag the weblink to change its order location in the Weblinks Manager.
- **Weblink Selection (unlabeled check box).** You can click a check box to select a weblink; this is necessary if you want to use several of the toolbar options.
- **Status.** A green check mark indicates that the weblink is published. A red x indicates that it is unpublished.
- **Title.** This field displays the full name of the weblink. Click the name to edit the weblink's details. The information in parentheses is the alias used for the weblink by the Joomla! system; the information below the title is the category the link is assigned to.
- **Access.** This field indicates the access level assigned to the weblinks.
- **Hits.** This field shows the number of times that users have clicked the weblink.
- **Language.** This field shows the language designated for the weblinks.
- **ID.** This field shows the system-generated ID number.

The Weblinks Manager provides an overview of all the weblinks in the system, and it also provides the tools you need to manage your weblinks. By understanding the Weblinks

Manager interface, you gain a solid grasp of what this component is all about. Before I explain how to create links and group them into categories, I want to look at some of the options that exist in the Weblinks component configuration interface.

Configuring the Weblinks Component

Like other components in the system, the Weblinks component has its own configuration interface. You can use the configuration parameters to tailor the functionality of the component to better suit your needs. The options allow you to set critical default values, like the target for the links, whether the system counts clicks on the links, and the general formatting and display of the links and their categories. You can also control which user groups have permission to use the functionality of the component.

You can view and modify the Weblinks component's configuration parameters by clicking the Options button on the Weblinks Manager toolbar, or by accessing the Global Configuration Manager and then clicking the Weblinks option in the Components column. Figure 16.2 shows the Weblinks component's configuration workspace.

FIGURE 16.2

The Weblinks component's configuration workspace

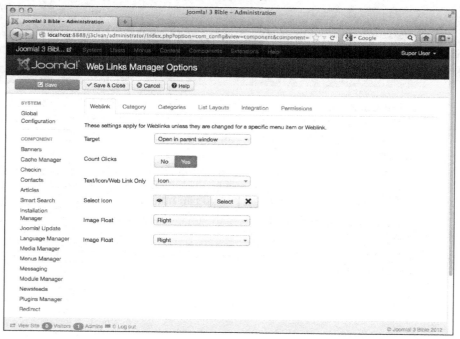

There are six tabs leading to six workspaces where you can configure the Weblinks component:

- **Weblink.** Contains settings relating to the display of a single weblink. The choices on this tab determine what information appears along with the weblink.
- **Category.** Sets the options for the display of a single weblink category page.
- **Categories.** Sets the options for the display of pages containing multiple weblink categories.
- **List Layouts.** Controls the layout of weblinks in list format.
- **Integration.** Allows you to show or hide the feed link for the component's pages.
- **Permissions.** Determines the extent to which the various user groups are able to perform actions with the Weblinks component.

The Weblink tab, shown in Figure 16.2, is the landing tab. The settings on this tab are applied to a single weblink's display. The options are

- **Target.** You can use this combo box to set the target for the weblink's URLs. This gives you control over how the browser responds when a visitor clicks the link. The options are Open in parent window, Open in new window, Open in popup, and Modal.

TIP

The parent window is the window that contains your website. If you set the target option to Open in parent window, the user is taken away from your site when she clicks the link. The Open in new window option simply opens a new window on top of your site window. Although the visitor can see the target of the link, your site remains in the browser window behind the new window. The Open in popup and Modal options also leave the visitor on your site, but give him a more limited browser interface.

- **Count Clicks.** If you want to track the number of times the links are clicked, you can set this parameter to Yes. This data appears on the Weblinks Manager.
- **Text/Icon/Weblink Only.** You can select what is shown for each link: link only, text only, or an icon.
- **Select Icon.** If you selected the Icon option in the Text/Icon/Weblink Only field, then you can choose the icon here by clicking the Select button. You can use an image from the Media Manager or you can upload one.
- **Image Float.** This combo box sets the image alignment for the first image that is displayed.
- **Image Float.** This combo box sets the image alignment for any additional images that are displayed.

16

NOTE

If your goal is to use the Weblinks component to support reciprocal link exchanges, you may be frustrated. By default, all links entered into the Weblinks component are displayed with a value hardcoded into the attribute. You cannot disable this feature without hacking the core files. As a result, links added to the Weblinks component are not indexed by search engines, and this means that potential link exchange partners are unlikely to grant a link exchange as they do not gain a search engine benefit from your link to their site.

To address this situation, you need to either bypass the Weblinks component entirely and build your links page by using an article, or use a third-party extension for links management.

The Category tab controls the layout of a page showing a single category. The tab includes the following options:

- **Choose a layout.** Use this combo box to control the layout of the weblinks listed on the category page.
- **Category Title.** Show or hide the category title on the category page.
- **Category Description.** Show or hide the category description on the category page.
- **Category Image.** Show or hide the category image on the category page.
- **Subcategory Levels.** Select the number of subcategory levels to display.
- **Empty Categories.** Show or hide empty categories on the category page.
- **Subcategories Descriptions.** Show or hide the descriptions from the subcategories.
- **# Weblinks.** Show or hide the number of weblinks per category on the category page.

The Categories tab affects the layout of pages containing multiple categories and includes the following options:

- **Top Level Category Description.** Show or hide the description of the top-level category.
- **Subcategory Levels.** Select how many subcategory levels you want to display on the page.
- **Empty Categories.** Show or hide empty categories.
- **Subcategories Descriptions.** Show or hide the descriptions of the subcategories.
- **# Weblinks.** Show or hide the number of weblinks in each category.

The List Layouts tab relates to the appearance of the page when a list of items is shown. The tab includes the following options:

- **Display Select.** Show or hide the display select combo box.
- **Table Headings.** Show or hide the table headings of the table used for the list layout.
- **Links description.** Show or hide the description for the weblink, if any.
- **Hits.** Show or hide on the front end the number of times the link has been clicked.
- **Pagination.** Show or hide the pagination controls.
- **Pagination Results.** Show or hide the total page count on the pagination controls. This is only applicable if you set Pagination to Show.

The Integration tab contains only one control, Show Feed Link, which, as the name implies, controls whether the RSS feed link is visible on the Weblink component's pages.

The Permissions tab works consistently with the Global Configuration permissions tab. Here you can dictate the extent to which the various user groups on your site can use the functionality of the Weblinks component.

 See Chapter 10 for a discussion of how permissions relate to user groups.

After you have set the parameters you desire, click the Save button in the top-left corner to save your changes, or click Cancel to close the Parameters window without saving the changes.

Managing Weblinks

You can add weblinks to your site through the Weblinks Manager. The Weblinks Manager provides a single point of contact where you can see all of the links in your site and then manage them. Using the Weblinks Manager, you can group weblinks into categories and subcategories, set the publishing options, and alter the configuration options relating to the display of the links and what happens when a visitor clicks a link. If you plan to publish a large number of links on your site, the Weblinks Manager greatly simplifies keeping up with the links and controlling their publication.

In this section I look at how to add weblinks and how to manage them once they are in the system. Later in the section, I also look briefly at your publication options. After that, I turn my attention to managing categories, as these are optional.

Adding a new link

If you are an administrator, you can add new weblinks to the Weblinks component at any time through the admin system. Before you begin, you should make sure you have a valid URL. You add weblinks to the system through the Weblinks Manager, so you need to point your browser to the Weblinks Manager and click the New button on the toolbar. The New Weblink workspace opens in your browser, as shown in Figure 16.3.

FIGURE 16.3

The New Weblink workspace

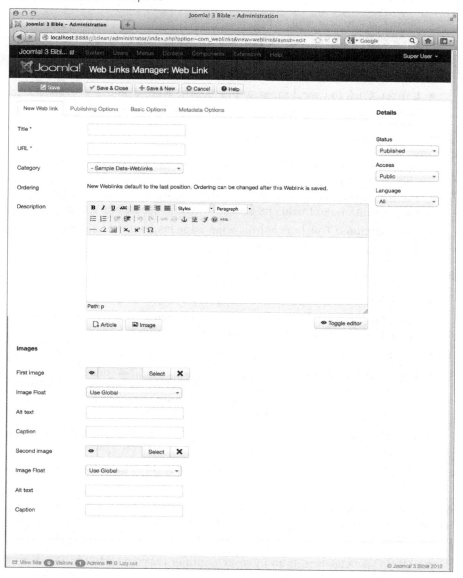

The toolbar at the top of the New Weblink workspace provides quick access to the following functions:

- **Save.** Click to save your work.
- **Save & Close.** Click to save your work and exit the New Weblink workspace.
- **Save & New.** Click to save your work, close the current New Weblink workspace, and open another New Weblink workspace.
- **Cancel.** Click to cancel the task and exit the New Weblink workspace.
- **Help.** Click to display the Help files related to the active screen.

The New Weblink workspace is divided into four tabs:

- **New Weblink.** This is the basic tab containing most of the required fields for creating a weblink.
- **Publishing Options.** This tab controls fields for author alias, start and stop dates for publication, and fields relating to weblink display and caching.
- **Basic Options.** This tab controls what happens after the user clicks a weblink.
- **Metadata Options.** This tab has impact on a weblink.

The New Weblink tab of the workspace contains the following fields:

- **Title.** Enter a name for your weblink here. This is a required field.
- **URL.** Enter the URL for the source of the weblink here. This is a required field. Note that this should normally begin with `http://`.
- **Category.** Use this combo box to assign the weblink to a category.
- **Ordering.** Use this field to change the order of your weblinks. Note that this control is not available for a new weblink. New items are placed by default in the last position on the list. After you add your weblink, you can adjust the list position either from the Weblinks Manager or by editing the weblink.
- **Description.** Use this field to enter a brief text description that appears underneath the weblink for your site visitors.
- **Images.** Use this section if you want an image to appear on the same page as the weblink.

The Publishing Options tab contains optional controls concerning the information associated with the weblink on the page and with controls that allow you to specify publication dates:

- **Alias.** The alias field is an internal identifier for your weblink. This is sometimes used to create search engine–friendly URLs for the item. You can specify the contents of this field if you want, but note that it only accepts lowercase letters without any spaces. If you do not specify the contents of this field, the system automatically creates the alias based on the item's name.

- **ID.** This value is automatically created by the system for internal use.
- **Created by.** You can specify the creator of the weblink by clicking the button next to the field.
- **Author's Alias.** You can create an alias for the weblink creator by entering it here. If you supply a value here, it appears instead of the user's name.
- **Created Date.** This field is automatically populated by the system and shows the creation date and time for the weblink.
- **Start Publishing.** Though optional, you can use this field to set a specific starting date for the publication of the weblink. If you leave it blank, the system assumes that you want to start publishing immediately.
- **Finish Publishing.** Though optional, you can use this field to set a specific ending date for the publication of the weblink. If you leave it blank, the system assumes that you want the weblink to remain published indefinitely.
- **Revision.** This field displays the number of times the link has been revised. The system automatically generates the information in this field.
- **Modified by.** This field displays the name of the user who last modified the weblink. The system automatically generates the information in this field.
- **Modified Date.** This field displays the date the weblink was last modified. The system automatically generates the information in this field.

The parameters on the Basic Options tab affect what happens after a user clicks a weblink. The tab includes the following fields:

- **Target.** You can use this combo box to set the target for the weblink's URLs. This gives you control over how the browser responds when a visitor clicks a link. The options are Use global, Open in parent window, Open in new window, Open in popup, and Modal.
- **Width.** If you selected either Open in popup or Modal for the value of the Target field, then you can use this field to specify the width of the popup or modal. You can enter an integer value, which represents the width in pixels.
- **Height.** If you selected either Open in popup or Modal for the value of the Target field, then you can use this field to specify the height of the popup or modal. You can enter an integer value, which represents the height in pixels.
- **Count Clicks.** You can specify whether you want the system to count the number of times users click the weblink.

As noted earlier, the Metadata Options tab does not apply to a single weblink. Because there is not a menu item type that allows you to link directly to a page containing a single weblink from the Weblinks component, there is not a page to hold the metadata. You can skip this tab when creating or editing a weblink.

To add a new weblink to the Weblinks component, follow these steps:

1. **Log in to the admin system on your site.**
2. **Go to the Components menu and select the Weblinks option.** The Weblinks Manager loads in your browser.
3. **Click the New button on the toolbar at the top of the Weblinks Manager.** The New Weblink workspace opens (refer to Figure 16.3).
4. **Type a name for the link in the Title field.** This is a required field.
5. **Type the address for the link source in the URL field.** Normally this begins with `http://`. This field is required.
6. **Select any additional options you want; all other fields are optional.**
7. **Click the Save button on the toolbar to save your new weblink.**

Editing a weblink

You can edit an existing weblink from the Weblinks Manager. To edit a weblink, you must either click the weblink name in the Weblinks Manager or select the weblink and then click the Edit button on the Weblinks Manager toolbar. Regardless of which method you use, the system opens the Edit Weblink workspace. The Edit Weblink workspace is identical to the New Weblink workspace, with the same fields and requirements as discussed in the preceding section.

To make changes to a weblink, you can simply alter the desired fields in the Edit Weblink workspace and then click the Save button on the toolbar. Any changes you make are applied immediately.

> **TIP**
>
> The Batch button on the toolbar offers several editing options and can save you time if you are trying to modify multiple weblinks. Select one or more weblinks and then click the Batch button. In the pop-up window that appears, you can change the access level or the language of all the weblinks simultaneously. The Batch feature also supports moving weblinks between categories and copying weblinks.

Archiving a weblink

If you want to remove a weblink from use on the site, but do not want to delete it, you can move it to the archive. Archived weblinks do not appear on the front end of the website. The archive feature is useful as it allows you to unpublish things without having to delete them and without having them clutter your Weblinks Manager interface with inactive content. Archiving basically hides the link on the front end, and moves it neatly out of site on the back end. The link remains accessible to administrators, who can simply filter the list of links on the Weblinks Manager to show those items that are archived.

To archive a weblink, follow these steps:

1. **Log in to the admin system on your site.**
2. **Go to the Components menu and select the Weblinks option.** The Weblinks Manager loads in your browser.
3. **Click the check box next to any weblinks you want to archive.**
4. **Click the Archive button on the toolbar.** The system immediately moves the selected weblinks to the archive.

Weblinks that have been moved into the archive can be unarchived by changing their status to either published or unpublished. To unarchive a weblink, follow these steps:

1. **Log in to the admin system on your site.**
2. **Go to the Components menu and select the Weblinks option.** The Weblinks Manager loads in your browser.
3. **Change the Select Status Filter to Archived.**
4. **Click the check box next to any weblinks you want to unarchive.**
5. **Select either Publish or Unpublish from the toolbar.** The system immediately unarchives the selected weblinks.

Deleting a weblink

The deletion of weblinks in Joomla! is a two-step process. The first step involves moving the weblink to the trash, where it is held until you take the second step and permanently delete it. Weblinks held in the trash can be restored at any time prior to deletion. You can view the weblinks in the trash at any time by selecting the Trashed option from the Select Status Filter in the Weblinks Manager.

Weblinks moved to the trash are held there indefinitely. They can be restored or deleted at the option of the administrator. Restored weblinks move back to their original locations, but deleted links are permanently removed from the system and cannot be restored.

NOTE

Though weblinks can be left in the trash indefinitely, the trash is distinctly different from the archive. Moving weblinks to the trash should not be confused with archiving weblinks.

To move a weblink to the trash, follow these steps:

1. **Log in to the admin system on your site.**
2. **Go to the Components menu and select the Weblinks option.** The Weblinks Manager loads in your browser.
3. **Click the check box next to any weblinks you want to move to the trash.**
4. **Click the Trash button on the toolbar.** The system moves the selected weblinks to the trash.

NOTE

Any weblink moved to the trash is instantly unpublished and not visible to site visitors.

Restoring a weblink from the trash

Weblinks moved to the trash are held there until the administrator takes further action. Any weblink can be restored at any time. The process of restoring a weblink is simple and the result instantaneous: the link is removed from the trash and returns to where it was located before it was moved to the trash.

To restore a weblink from the trash, follow these steps:

1. **Log in to the admin system on your site.**
2. **Go to the Components menu and select the Weblinks option.** The Weblinks Manager loads in your browser.
3. **Change the Select Status Filter to Trashed.** The list of weblinks reloads to display only those weblinks in the trash.
4. **Click the check box next to any weblinks you want to restore.**
5. **Click either Publish or Unpublish on the toolbar.** The system moves the selected weblinks from the trash and restores them to their previous locations.

TIP

You can also restore a weblink by moving your mouse over the weblink title in the Weblinks Manager, clicking the arrow that appears, and selecting Untrash from the menu that opens.

Deleting a weblink permanently

Weblinks held in the trash can be removed from the system by emptying the trash. Emptying the trash results in the weblink's permanent removal from the system; it cannot be restored once deleted.

To permanently delete a weblink from the trash, follow these steps:

1. **Log in to the admin system on your site.**
2. **Go to the Components menu and select the Weblinks option.** The Weblinks Manager loads in your browser.
3. **Change the Select Status Filter to Trashed.** The list of weblinks reloads to show only the ones in the trash.
4. **Click the check box next to any weblinks you want to delete.**
5. **Click the Empty Trash button on the toolbar.** The system immediately deletes the selected weblinks.

CAUTION

Deleting a weblink is permanent and cannot be undone. Moreover, there is no confirmation dialog box — clicking the Empty Trash button immediately deletes the weblink!

Managing Weblinks Categories

If you are an administrator, you can create categories for the purpose of grouping weblinks. You can create multiple categories and arrange them into a hierarchy of parent-child relationships. While categories are not necessary — you can leave your weblinks uncategorized if you like — they are helpful if you have a large number of weblinks, or if you want to have more alternatives for displaying your weblinks. Joomla! provides menu item types that allow you to link directly to weblinks categories, a technique you can see demonstrated if you have installed the sample data.

In this section I look at how to create and manage weblinks categories.

NOTE

If you are already familiar with category management in other areas of Joomla!, you will be happy to know that the system is very consistent and the category functions and features are very similar throughout the site.

You can manage the weblinks categories through the Weblinks Category Manager. To access the Weblinks Category Manager, you select the Categories submenu under the Weblinks option on the main admin navigation bar, or click the Categories link in the left column of the Weblinks Manager. Figure 16.4 shows the Weblinks Category Manager with the sample data loaded.

FIGURE 16.4

The Weblinks Category Manager

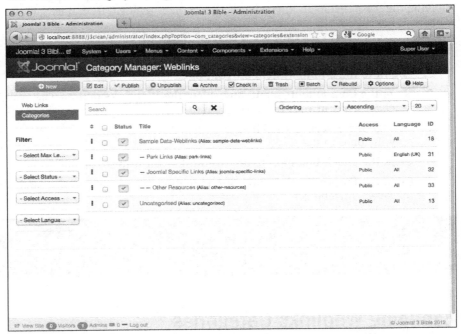

The toolbar at the top of the Weblinks Category Manager provides quick access to the following functions:

- **New.** Click to add a new weblinks category.

- **Edit.** Select a category from the list and then click this button to edit the category details.

- **Publish.** Select one or more categories from the list and then click this button to publish them. You publish a category to make it visible on the front end of the website.

- **Unpublish.** Select one or more weblink categories from the list and then click this button to unpublish them. You unpublish a category to hide it from display on the front end of the website.

- **Archive.** Select one or more weblink categories from the list and then click this button to move the category to the archive.

- **Check In.** Select one or more weblink categories from the list and then click this button to force the category editing workspaces to close and thereby "check in" the categories.

- **Trash.** Select one or more categories from the list and then click this button to move them to the trash.

- **Batch.** Select multiple categories and then click this button to batch-apply processes to them. The pop-up window that appears enables you modify multiple categories in one simple operation.

- **Rebuild.** Click if you are experiencing problems with your weblink categories. Clicking this button forces the system to rebuild the weblink category tables in the database. You should not normally need this tool; use it sparingly.

- **Options.** Click to open the Weblinks component configuration workspace, where you can configure the parameters that affect the weblinks.

- **Help.** Click to access the online Help files related to the active screen.

Below the toolbar, in the left column, are two links: Weblinks shows you the Weblinks Manager, and Categories shows you the Weblinks Category Manager. Below the two links in the left column are four sorting tools to help you manage long lists of categories:

- **Select Max Levels.** The options in this combo box allow you to control the number of levels of categories that display. If your site has a complex hierarchy, this can greatly simplify the view of the list of categories in the Weblinks Category Manager. To reset this filter, change the combo box back to the default setting, Select Max Levels.

- **Select Status.** The options in this combo box allow you to filter and display the categories according to whether they are published, unpublished, archived, or trashed. This provides an easy way to identify all categories that are currently active on the site. To reset this filter, change the combo box back to the default setting, Select Status.

- **Select Access.** The options in this combo box allow you to filter the list of categories by access level. To reset this filter, change the combo box back to the default setting, Select Access.

- **Select Language.** The options in this combo box allow you to filter the list of categories by language. To reset this filter, change the combo box back to the default setting, Select Language.

Below the toolbar and above the list of categories are four sorting and searching tools to help you manage long lists of categories:

- Type a word or phrase into the Search field and then click the magnifying glass button. The system searches your list of categories for the query and then displays the results of the search. To clear the screen and return to a full listing, click the button marked with the X.

- Use the combo box to the right of the Search field to specify which column of the display is used for the sort order.

- Use the Ascending combo box to specify whether the categories appear in ascending or descending order.
- Use the combo box on the far right to control the number of categories that appear on the page. You can alter the default value by changing the List Length parameter in the Global Configuration Manager.

The main content area of the screen contains a list of all the weblinks categories in your Joomla! site. The columns provided are

- **Sort Order (vertical double arrows).** You can click the arrows to change the sort order, or click and hold any of the buttons immediately to the left of a category's title and drag the category to change its order location in the Weblinks Category Manager.
- **Category Selection (unlabeled check box).** You can click a check box to select a category; this is necessary if you want to use several of the toolbar options.
- **Status.** A green check mark indicates that the category is published. A red x indicates that it is unpublished.
- **Title.** This field displays the full name of the category. You can click the name to edit the category's details.
- **Access.** This field indicates the access level assigned to the category.
- **Language.** This field shows the language designated for the category.
- **ID.** This field shows the system-generated user ID number.

Creating a new category

You can create categories from within the Weblinks Category Manager by clicking the New button on the toolbar. Category data is entered into the Add A New Weblinks Category workspace, shown in Figure 16.5.

The toolbar at the top of the Add A New Weblinks Category workspace provides quick access to the following functions:

- **Save.** Click to save your work.
- **Save & Close.** Click to save your work and exit the Add A New Weblinks Category workspace.
- **Save & New.** Click to save your work, close the current Add A New Weblinks Category workspace, and open another Add A New Weblinks Category workspace.
- **Cancel.** Click to cancel the task and exit the Add A New Weblinks Category workspace.
- **Help.** Click to display the Help files related to the active screen.

FIGURE 16.5

The Add A New Weblinks Category workspace

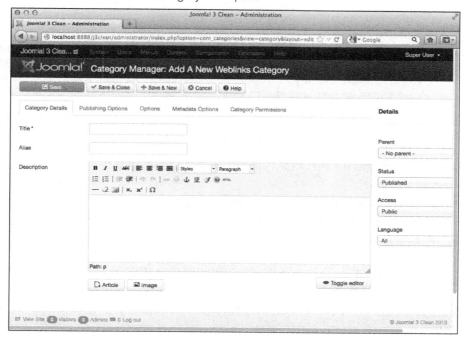

Note the five tabs located at the top of the workspace. These tabs provide you with access to secondary functionality associated with categories:

- **Category Details.** This is the crucial tab needed for creating new categories. The fields on this tab are detailed in the following bulleted list.

- **Publishing Options.** This tab contains fields for the ID, hits, and the name of the category's creator.

- **Options.** This tab allows you to change the layout of the category landing page on the front end of the site, associate an image with the category, and add notes for use by the administrators.

- **Metadata Options.** This tab allows you to override the global metadata settings for this category's page.

- **Category Permissions.** This tab allows you to view and modify the permissions associated with this category. Permissions are normally inherited from the Global Configuration settings, but you can override them here.

The Category Details section of the Add A New Weblinks Category workspace includes the following fields:

- **Title.** You can use this field to assign the category a name. This is the only required field.
- **Alias.** The alias is the internal name for the item. If you leave this field blank, the system automatically uses your title for the alias, with any spaces converted to hyphens. Note that if you want to add a value to this field, it only accepts lower-case letters without any spaces.
- **Description.** This is an optional field in which you can add a description of the weblinks category. If you are displaying the category on the front end of the site, the description appears on the page.

The Publishing Options tab of the Add A New Weblinks Category workspace includes the following fields:

- **ID.** The value in this field is assigned automatically by the Joomla! system and is used internally by the system.
- **Hits.** This field shows the number of times this category has been visited on the front end of the website.
- **Created by.** You can specify the creator of the category by clicking the button with the icon of a person.

The Options tab of the Add A New Weblinks Category workspace includes the following fields:

- **Alternative Layout.** If your template provides for alternative layouts, you can select one from this combo box; otherwise, the default layout is applied.
- **Image.** If you want to associate an image with this category, you can click the Select button and choose one from the Media Manager, or upload one of your own. If you are displaying the category on the front end of the site, the image appears on the page.
- **Note.** This is an optional field used by the administrator.

The Metadata Options tab allows you to override the global configuration metadata set for the category page. The tab includes the following fields:

- **Meta Description.** Enter into the text field any information you want to appear in the meta Description field for this category.
- **Meta Keywords.** Enter into the text field any keywords you want to appear in the meta Keyword field for this category. Separate multiple keywords with commas.
- **Author.** Enter into this text field the information you want to appear in the meta Author field for the category.

- **Robots.** Select one of the options from this combo box to tell the various bots and spiders how to handle your site:

  - **Index, follow.** Select this option if you want to index all the pages on your site and follow all the links. For most site owners, who are interested in generating traffic from the search engines, this is the best option.

  - **No index, follow.** Select this option if you want the search engines to follow the links but not index the pages.

  - **Index, no follow.** Select this option if you want your pages to be indexed by the search engines, but don't want the links to be followed.

  - **No index, no follow.** Select this option if you want to block the search engines completely and keep your pages out of the search engine results.

The Category Permissions tab allows you to set specific permissions for the category. Settings that you make here override the global user permissions.

To create a new category, follow these steps:

1. **Log in to the admin system on your site.**
2. **Go to the Components menu and select the Categories option from the Weblinks submenu.** The Weblinks Category Manager loads in your browser.
3. **Click the New button on the toolbar at the top of the Weblinks Category Manager.** The Add A New Weblinks Category workspace opens (refer to Figure 16.5).
4. **In the Title field, type a name for this category.** This is the only required field.
5. **Add additional information or optional settings as you see fit.**
6. **Click the Save button on the toolbar.**

Now that you know how to create a new category, I will now look at editing, archiving, and deleting categories.

Editing categories

You can edit existing weblinks categories from the Weblinks Category Manager. To edit a category, you either click the category name in the Weblinks Category Manager, or select the category on the list and then click the Edit button on the Weblinks Category Manager toolbar. Regardless of which method you use, the system opens the Edit Weblinks Category workspace.

The Edit Weblinks Category workspace is identical to the Add A New Weblinks Category workspace, with the same fields and requirements as discussed in the previous section.

To make changes to a category, you simply alter the desired fields in the Edit Weblinks Category workspace and then click the Save button on the toolbar. Any changes you make are applied immediately.

> **TIP**
>
> The Batch button on the toolbar offers several editing options and can save you time if you are trying to modify multiple categories. Select one or more categories and then click the Batch button. In the pop-up window that appears, you can change the access level or language assignment of all the categories simultaneously. The Batch feature also supports moving and copying categories.

Archiving categories

If you want to remove a category from use on the site, but do not want to delete it, you can move it to the archive. By default, archived categories are not shown on the front end of the website.

To archive a category, follow these steps:

1. **Log in to the admin system on your site.**
2. **Go to the Components menu and choose the Categories option from the Weblinks submenu.** The Weblinks Category Manager loads in your browser.
3. **Click the check box next to the category or categories you want to archive.**
4. **Click the Archive button on the toolbar.** The system immediately moves the selected categories to the archive.

> **NOTE**
>
> Moving a weblinks category to the archive has no impact on the weblinks assigned to the category. If you want to archive the weblinks, you have to do that separately.

Categories that have been moved into the archive can unarchived by changing the status of the category to either published or unpublished. To unarchive a category, follow these steps:

1. **Log in to the admin system on your site.**
2. **Go to the Components menu and choose the Categories option from the Weblinks submenu.** The Weblinks Category Manager loads in your browser.
3. **Change the Select Status Filter to Archived.**
4. **Click the check box next to the category or categories you want to unarchive.**
5. **Select either Publish or Unpublish from the toolbar.** The system immediately unarchives the selected categories.

Deleting categories

The deletion of weblinks categories in Joomla! is a two-step process. The first step involves moving the category to the trash, where it is held until you take the second step and permanently delete the category. Categories held in the trash can be restored at any time prior to deletion. You can view the contents of the trash at any time by using the Select Status Filter in the Weblinks Category Manager.

Categories moved to the trash are held there indefinitely. The items can be restored or deleted at the option of the administrator. Restored items move back to their original locations, but deleted items are permanently removed from the system and cannot be restored.

> **NOTE**
>
> Though categories can be left in the trash indefinitely, the trash is distinctly different from the archive. Moving categories to the trash should not be confused with archiving categories.

To move a category to the trash, follow these steps:

1. **Log in to the admin system on your site.**
2. **Go to the Components menu and choose the Categories option from the Weblinks submenu.** The Weblinks Category Manager loads in your browser.
3. **Click the check box next to the category or categories you want to move to the trash.**
4. **Click the Trash button on the toolbar.** The system moves the selected categories to the trash.

Restoring categories from the trash

Categories moved to the trash are held there until the administrator takes further action. Any category can be restored at any time. The process of restoring an item is simple and the result instantaneous: the category is removed from the trash and returns to where it was located before it was moved to the trash.

To restore a category from the trash, follow these steps:

1. **Log in to the admin system on your site.**
2. **Go to the Components menu and choose the Categories option from the Weblinks submenu.** The Weblinks Category Manager loads in your browser.
3. **Change the Select Status Filter to Trashed.** The list of categories reloads to display only those categories in the trash.
4. **Click the check box next to the category or categories you want to restore.**
5. **Click either Publish or Unpublish on the toolbar.** The system removes the selected categories from the trash and restores them to their previous locations.

> **TIP**
>
> You can also restore a category by moving your mouse over the category title in the Weblinks Category Manager, clicking the arrow that appears, and selecting Untrash from the menu that opens.

Deleting categories permanently

Categories held in the trash can be removed from the system by emptying the trash. Emptying the trash results in the item's permanent removal from the system; it cannot be restored once deleted.

To permanently delete a category from the trash, follow these steps:

1. **Log in to the admin system on your site.**

2. **Go to the Components menu and choose the Categories option from the submenu under the Weblinks heading.** The Weblinks Category Manager loads in your browser.

3. **Change the Select Status Filter to Trashed.**

4. **Click the check box next to the category or categories you want to delete.**

5. **Click the Empty Trash button on the toolbar.** The system immediately deletes the selected categories.

> **NOTE**
> Deleting a weblinks category is permanent and cannot be undone. Moreover, there is no confirmation dialog box — clicking the Empty Trash button immediately deletes the category! Note, however, that a category cannot be deleted if there are weblinks assigned to that category. If you want to delete the category, you must first delete or reassign any weblinks assigned to that category.

Summary

In this chapter, I covered the use of the Joomla! Weblinks component, a tool for adding links to external resources to your site. The topics covered included

- Configuring the Weblinks component
- Adding new weblinks to your site
- Managing your weblinks
- Creating categories to group your weblinks
- Editing, archiving, and deleting weblinks and categories

In the next chapter, I take a first look at modules, in this case, the Site modules that come with your Joomla! installation. I look at Administrator modules in the chapter that follows.

Working with the Site Modules

J oomla! uses modules to display content and functionality on areas of the page other than the
main content area. Though it is possible to embed modules inside the content area of the
page, modules most often appear in sidebars, at the top or bottom of a layout, and on the
edges of the main content area of the page. Modules are critical for designing compelling sites
with good functionality. They can be used to display content, ease navigation, highlight information, and handle advertising duties.

The system includes both front-end modules and back-end modules. The modules for the front
end of the system are called Site modules. The modules for the back end are called Administrator
modules. In this chapter, I cover the Site Module Manager and all of the Site modules available
in Joomla! 3. In the next chapter, I concentrate on the Administrator modules.

Introducing the Site Module Manager

The Site Module Manager provides an interface for controlling the Joomla! system's numerous
Site modules. The system includes 24 different Site module types. Several of the module types
are closely related to and dependent on the core components, while others are independent, self-
contained units. All types share a similar process for the creation, duplication, and deletion of
modules. The difference between the modules is largely in the parameters that are available for
each module. By mastering the parameters, you will be able to tailor the modules to your needs.

You can control all the Joomla! modules through the Module Manager. The manager contains all
the system modules, together with any third-party modules you may install. The Module
Manager provides an interface that lets you see at a glance all the modules in the system and
then perform a variety of common tasks associated with the modules. You can access the individual modules for editing, or you can create new modules. You can also control the publishing
state of any module with one click. Batch processes are available to reduce to the amount of time
you spend performing tasks on multiple modules. In this section, I introduce the Module Manager.

To access the Site Module Manager, you need to log in to the admin system, and then go to the Extensions menu and select the Module Manager option. The Module Manager loads in your browser window, as shown in Figure 17.1.

FIGURE 17.1

The Module Manager, showing the Site Module Manager with sample data installed

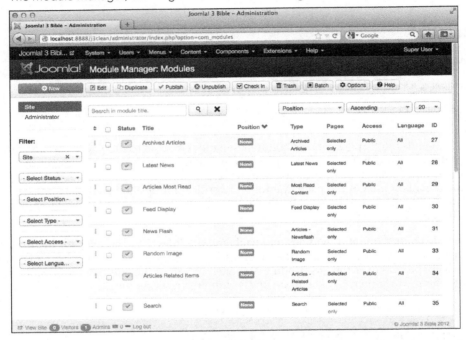

The toolbar at the top of the Module Manager provides quick access to the following functions:

- **New.** Click to create a new module.
- **Edit.** Select a module from the list and then click this button to edit the module.
- **Duplicate.** Select one or more modules from the list and then click this button to make an exact copy of the module.
- **Publish.** Select one or more modules from the list and then click this button to publish them. You publish a module to make it visible on the front end of the website.
- **Unpublish.** Select one or more modules from the list and then click this button to unpublish them. You unpublish a module to hide it from the front end of the website.
- **Check In.** Select one or more modules from the list and then click this button to force the module editing workspaces to close and thereby "check in" the modules.

- **Trash.** Select one or more modules from the list and then click this button to delete them.

- **Batch.** Select multiple modules and then click this button to batch-apply processes to them. The pop-up window that appears enables you alter multiple modules in one simple operation.

- **Options.** Click to open the Module Manager Options workspace, where you can configure the permissions to use the Module Manager.

> **NOTE**
>
> Module Manager permissions work consistently with the Permissions tab in the Global Configuration Manager. See the discussion on setting permissions in Chapter 10 to learn more.

- **Help.** Click to access the online Help files related to the active screen.

Two text links are located below the toolbar. The Site link shows you the Site Module Manager, which I discuss in this chapter. The Administrator link takes you to the Administrator Module Manager, which I discuss in the next chapter.

Located below the two text links and beside the list of modules are six sorting and searching tools to help you manage long lists of modules:

- **Site.** Use this combo box to switch between the Site Module Manager and the Administrator Module Manager.

- **Select Status.** Use this combo box to filter and display the modules according to whether they are published, unpublished, or trashed. This provides an easy way to identity all modules that are currently active on the site. To reset this filter, change the combo box back to the default setting, Select Status.

- **Select Position.** Use this combo box to filter the list of modules according to the position to which they are assigned. To reset this filter, change the combo box back to the default setting, Select Position.

- **Select Type.** Use this combo box to filter the list of modules by type. To reset this filter, change the combo box back to the default setting, Select Type.

- **Select Access.** Use this combo box to filter the list of modules by access level. To reset this filter, change the combo box back to the default setting, Select Access.

- **Select Language.** Use this combo box to filter the list of modules by language. To reset this filter, change the combo box back to the default setting, Select Language.

> **TIP**
>
> You can combine the filters to further refine the view of the list of modules.

Below the toolbar and above the list of modules are four sorting and searching tools:

- Type a word or phrase into the field marked Search in module title, and then click the magnifying glass button. The system searches your list of modules for the query and then displays the results of the search. To clear the screen and return to a full listing, click the button marked with the X.

- Use the combo box to the right of the Search field to specify which column of the modules display is used for the sort order.

- Use the Ascending combo box to specify whether the modules appear in ascending or descending order.
- Use the combo box on the far right to control the number of modules that appear on the page. You can alter the default value by changing the List Length parameter in the Global Configuration Manager.

The main content area of the screen contains a list of all the modules in your Joomla! site. The columns provided are

- **Sort Order (vertical double arrows).** You can click the arrows to change the sort order, or click and hold any of the buttons immediately to the left of a module's title and drag the module to change its location order in the Module Manager.
- **Module Selection (unlabeled check box).** You can click a check box to select a module; this is necessary if you want to use several of the toolbar options.
- **Status.** A green check mark indicates that the module is published. A red x indicates that it is unpublished.
- **Title.** This field displays the full name of the module. You can click the name to edit the module.
- **Position.** This field displays the position to which the module is assigned. A single module can only be assigned to one position.
- **Type.** This field displays the type of the module. Each module can be of only one type.
- **Pages.** This field indicates which pages the module has been assigned to. The only options here are All, which means to all pages on the site; None, which means the module has not been assigned to any pages; and Selected only, which means the module is assigned to some but not all of the pages. To change these setting, you need to edit the module.
- **Access.** This field shows the access level assigned to the module.
- **Language.** This field shows the language designated for the module.
- **ID.** This field shows the system-generated ID number.

Now that you have some idea of what information is presented by the Module Manager, and which buttons allow you to access the key functionality, I will focus on creating new modules.

Creating new modules

You can create new modules from within the Module Manager. Creating a new module is an alternative to editing or duplicating an existing module. If you have installed the sample data, you may want to use some of the sample data modules, rather than beginning from scratch. Regardless of which method you choose, the options available in the module are the same.

Creating a new module is a two-step process: First you must select the module type you want to create, and then you must set up that module type with the required information. To begin, you simply click the New button on the toolbar, and the system loads a new window in the browser, as shown in Figure 17.2. The new window requires you to select the module type you want to create.

FIGURE 17.2

The first step in creating a new module is selecting the module type.

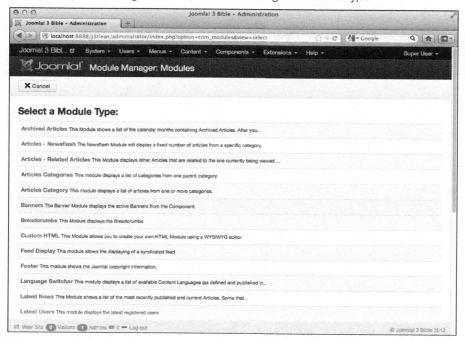

Select one of the 24 module type choices and click the Next button; the page reloads and displays the next step in the module creation process, as shown in Figure 17.3.

FIGURE 17.3

In this example, I show the second step in the module creation process for a new Newsflash module.

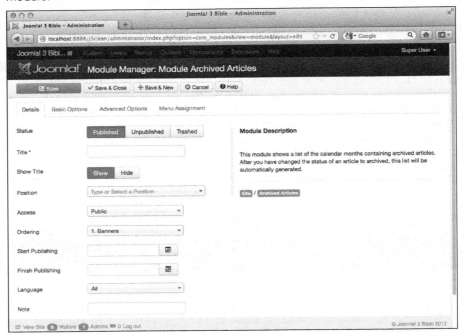

The toolbar at the top of the Module workspace provides quick access to the following functions:

- **Save.** Click to save your work.
- **Save & Close.** Click to save your work and exit the New Module workspace.
- **Save & New.** Click to save your work, close the current New Module workspace, and open another New Module workspace.
- **Cancel.** Click to cancel the task and exit the New Module workspace.
- **Help.** Click to display the Help files related to the active screen.

The Module workspace is divided into four tabs:

- **Details.** This is the basic tab containing most of the required fields for creating a module. This is the tab where you also control the publication status and position of the module on the page. This tab is the same for all modules. I discuss the fields on this tab in the following bulleted list.

- **Basic Options.** This tab provides the custom parameters that are unique to each module. The options on this tab vary from module to module. I review the specific options that are available to each module type later in this chapter.

- **Advanced Options.** This tab contains options related to layout, styling, and caching. The Site modules share a number of common fields on this tab, but there is some variation between the modules. I discuss the fields in this tab shortly.

- **Menu Assignment.** This tab (which is the same for all modules) allows you to specify the pages where the module appears. I discuss the fields in this tab shortly.

> **NOTE**
>
> Only three modules are different from the pattern I have just described: The Articles Category module and the Custom HTML module have additional tabs, and the Footer module has one less tab. I discuss the variations later in the chapter in the sections dealing with those specific modules.

Of the four tabs in the Module workspace, three of them are at least partially standardized across all module types: Details, Advanced Options, and Menu Assignment. Accordingly, I cover the fields you will find on the common tabs here.

Using the Details tab

The Details tab is the default landing tab that you see when you create a new module or open a module for editing. The tab contains the fields that set the basic parameters for a module, including the module's name and its position on the page. There are ten fields on this tab, but only two of them are essential. The fields are

- **Status.** Select from the options, Published, Unpublished, and Trashed.

- **Title.** This field displays the full name of the module. You can click the name to edit the module.

- **Show Title.** This field allows you to show or hide the title of the module on the front end of the site.

- **Position.** This combo box allows you to assign the module to a position in the template.

> **NOTE**
>
> All the templates in the system are listed in the Position combo box. Make sure you select a valid position on the active template, or you will not see the module!

- **Access.** This combo box allows you to assign the access level to the module.

- **Ordering.** This combo box allows you to specify the order of the module relative to any others assigned in the same position.

- **Start Publishing.** Though optional, this field allows you to set a specific starting date for the publication of the module. If you leave it blank, the system assumes that you want to start publishing immediately.

- **Finish Publishing.** Though optional, this field allows you to set a specific ending date for the publication of the module. If you leave it blank, the system assumes that you want the module to remain published indefinitely.

- **Language.** This combo box allows you to designate the language for the module.

- **Note.** This field allows you to add notes for use by the site administrators.

Configuring the Advanced Options

The Advanced Options tab is only partially standardized throughout the Site modules. A set of common fields appear on all modules, but there are some variations where individual modules may have more or, in a few cases, fewer of these options. The fields common to most modules are

- **Alternative Layout.** This combo box allows you to select an alternative layout, if your template provides for this; otherwise, the default layout is applied.

- **Module Class Suffix.** This field allows you to specify a suffix that is automatically appended to all CSS styles that affect this module. The use of a specified suffix makes it possible for you to style this module individually.

- **Caching.** This control allows you to exempt a specific module from the site's caching, as set in the Global Configuration Manager. Select the No Caching option to prevent the contents of this module from being cached. The default setting is Use Global.

- **Cache Time.** This field allows you to set the time, in minutes, that you want the contents to be cached. Enter an integer value here. The default value is 900 minutes, meaning that after 900 minutes the system will re-create, or refresh, this module. Note that this control is only meaningful if you have enabled the Caching option for the module.

- **Module Tag.** This option allows you to select the HTML tag to use for the module; this allows you to control the formatting of specific modules by linking them to particular styles in your stylesheet.

- **Bootstrap Size.** This combo box allows you to select a value to determine how many columns the module will span.

- **Header Tag.** This combo box allows you to select the desired HTML tag for the module title.

- **Header Class.** This field allows you to enter a special class for controlling the formatting of the module title.

- **Module Style.** This combo box gives you access to all the module styles in your system. You can select a value here to override the default formatting of your template.

Determining Menu Assignment

You can use the Menu Assignment tab of the workspace to assign the module to appear on only certain pages of your site. You have the option to assign the module to no pages, to all pages, or to only certain pages. If you want to assign the module selectively, you can choose the Only on the Pages Selected option and then select the appropriate choices from the list.

While the module types all share common elements, there are also unique parameters that you must consider. In later sections, I review each of the module types, explain how they are used, show you an example, and then explain any distinct configuration parameters that might exist on the module workspace tabs.

NOTE

If you have installed additional extensions on your site, you may also see additional module types that allow for the creation of new modules beyond the system defaults.

Creating duplicate modules

You can make exact copies of modules by using the Duplicate command in the Module Manager. This function is very useful if you need to run multiple instances of the same module type, as duplicating a module saves you several steps and fast tracks module configuration. When you duplicate a module, an exact copy of the module is placed in the Module Manager. The new module has the same configuration and name as the original, but with a number appended to the end to the name, for example, Archived Articles (2).

To duplicate a module, follow these steps:

1. **Open the Module Manager.**
2. **Select the module you want to duplicate by clicking the check box next to the module name.**
3. **Click the Duplicate button.** The system immediately makes a copy of the module and places it in the Module Manager.

NOTE

Duplicated modules are unpublished by default.

Editing modules

You can edit existing modules from within the Module Manager. Editing is limited to the name and configuration details of the module. You cannot change the module type from the editing workspace; to do this, you must create a new module of the type you desire.

To edit a module, you can either click the module name in the Module Manager, or select the module on the list and then click the Edit button on the Module Manager toolbar. Regardless of which method you use, the system opens the Edit Module workspace. The Edit Module workspace is identical to the New Module workspace, with the same fields and requirements.

To make changes to a module, you simply alter the desired fields in the Edit Module workspace and then click the Save button on the toolbar. Any changes you make are applied immediately.

> **NOTE**
>
> The Edit Module workspace does have one extra button on the toolbar: Save as Copy. You can use this button to quickly clone a module, creating a new module that is identical to the one you are editing.

Deleting modules

The deletion of modules in Joomla! is a two-step process. The first step involves moving the module to the trash, where it is held until you take the second step and permanently delete the module. Modules held in the trash can be restored at any time prior to deletion. You can view the contents of the trash at any time using the Select Status Filter in the Module Manager.

Modules moved to the trash are held there indefinitely. The modules can be restored or deleted at the option of the administrator. Restored modules move back to their original locations, but deleted modules are permanently removed from the system and cannot be restored.

To move a module to the trash, follow these steps:

1. **Log in to the admin system on your site.**
2. **Go to the Extensions menu and choose the Module Manager option.** The Module Manager loads in your browser.
3. **Click the check box next to the module or modules you want to move to the trash.**
4. **Click the Trash button on the toolbar.** The system moves the selected modules to the trash.

Restoring modules from the trash

Modules moved to the trash are held there until the administrator takes further action. Any module can be restored at any time. The process of restoring a module is simple and the result instantaneous: the module is removed from the trash and returns to where it was located before it was moved to the trash.

To restore a module from the trash, follow these steps:

1. **Log in to the admin system on your site.**
2. **Go to the Extensions menu and choose the Module Manager option.** The Module Manager loads in your browser.
3. **Change the Select Status Filter to Trashed.** The list of modules reloads to display only those modules in the trash.

4. **Click the check box next to the module or modules you want to restore.**

5. **Click either Publish or Unpublish on the toolbar.** The system removes the selected modules from the trash, and restores them to their previous locations.

Deleting modules permanently

Modules held in the trash can be removed from the system by emptying the trash. Emptying the trash results in the module's permanent removal from the system; it cannot be restored once deleted.

To permanently delete a module from the trash, follow these steps:

1. **Log in to the admin system on your site.**

2. **Go to the Extensions menu and choose the Module Manager option.** The Module Manager loads in your browser.

3. **Change the Select Status Filter to Trashed.** The list of modules reloads to display only those modules in the trash.

4. **Click the check box next to the module or modules you want to permanently delete.**

5. **Click the Empty Trash button on the toolbar.** The system immediately deletes the selected modules.

> **NOTE**
> Deleting a module is permanent and cannot be undone. Moreover, there is no confirmation dialog box — clicking the Empty Trash button immediately deletes the module!

Reviewing the Site Modules

The default Joomla! installation comes with 24 Site module types. The various module types provide a wide range of functionality, from displaying content, to providing navigation, to controlling layout and advertising. If you are the site administrator, each of the module types is available to you; you simply need to click the New button and select the type you want. There are no restrictions on how many modules of each type you can run.

In the following section, I look at each of the default Site module types. I describe what each module does and how you can use it, show you what it looks like when published, and then cover any unique configuration parameters that are available with the module.

Publishing your archives with the Archived Articles module

The Archived Articles module displays a list of months, with each month linked to the archived articles dating to that month. It is essentially a navigation menu for archived content items, as shown in Figure 17.4. When activated, clicking the name of the month takes the user to a page listing all the archived items for that time period.

FIGURE 17.4

The Archived Articles module viewed from the front end of the site

Archived Articles

- January, 2011
- January, 2012
- February, 2012

The Basic Options tab contains only one option: # of Months. The numerical value you enter in this field controls how many months are shown in the module. The default value is 10. The Advanced Options tab of this module does not contain any unique fields.

 I cover working with archived articles in Chapter 5.

Drawing attention with the Articles - Newsflash module

The Articles - Newsflash module provides a way for you to insert a fixed or rotating content item into a module position. You can draw this content from one or more article categories. This feature is useful because it enables you to place a piece of text, typically small, that rotates to display a fixed number of news items, announcements, or any other items you want to attract visitors' attention, as shown in Figure 17.5.

FIGURE 17.5

This example shows the front-end output of the default Newsflash module with the sample data loaded. Here the module is shown in the Top module position of the default template.

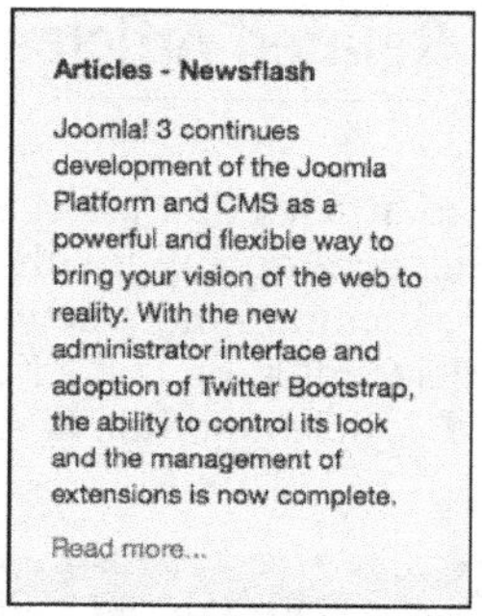

> **Articles - Newsflash**
>
> Joomla! 3 continues development of the Joomla Platform and CMS as a powerful and flexible way to bring your vision of the web to reality. With the new administrator interface and adoption of Twitter Bootstrap, the ability to control its look and the management of extensions is now complete.
>
> Read more...

17

NOTE

The system name for this module type is `mod_newsflash`.

The Basic Options tab of the Newsflash module contains a number of special fields that allow you to control the formatting of the items inside the module. The options are

- **Category.** Select a content category for display by the module. If you do not designate a specific category, the module displays items from all categories.

- **Show Images.** Specify whether the module shows images associated with the content item. The default setting is No.

- **Show Article Title.** Show or hide the articles' titles.

- **Linked Titles.** Specify whether the article title functions as a clickable hyperlink that leads to the full article.

- **Header Level.** Select the HTML header level formatting for the article title.

- **Show last separator.** Select Yes if you want to show a separator in the module immediately after the last article.

- **Read more... Link.** Show or hide the Read more link at the end of each article.

- **Number of Articles.** Specify the number of articles to be displayed. If you leave this option blank, the system displays five articles, in rotation.

- **Order Results.** Specify how you want the articles to be ordered in the rotation.

TIP

Select the Ordering option in the Order Results combo box if you want the ordering of the items in the Newsflash module to be dictated by the order in which the articles appear within the Category Manager in the Article Manager.

The Advanced Options tab of the Articles - Newsflash module does not contain any unique fields.

Connecting related content with the Articles - Related Articles module

The Articles - Related Articles module displays a list of links to articles that are related to the article the user is viewing. The criteria for determining this relationship involve keyword matching. Where two or more articles share at least one common meta keyword tag, they are considered to be related. To employ this feature, articles must be tagged with meta keywords. The front-end output of the Articles - Related Articles module is shown in Figure 17.6.

> **TIP**
>
> To get the most out of the Articles - Related Articles module, you need to not only tag your articles, but also tag them consistently and accurately. The effectiveness of this module depends solely upon the integrity of the underlying tag schema.

FIGURE 17.6

The front-end output of the Articles - Related Articles module

Articles - Related Articles

- Beginners
- The Joomla! Community

> **NOTE**
>
> The system name for this module type is `mod_related_items`.

The Basic Options tab contains only one control: Show Date. You can set this option to Show if you want to display the date of publication in the list of articles. The default setting is Hide. The Advanced Options tab of the Articles - Related Articles module does not contain any unique fields.

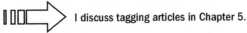 I discuss tagging articles in Chapter 5.

The Advanced Options tab of the Articles Related Articles module does not contain any unique fields.

Displaying your categories with the Articles Categories module

You can use the Articles Categories module to display a list of categories, with links to the category pages. The module serves as an alternative to using a menu for displaying navigation choices. Figure 17.7 shows typical output from this module.

FIGURE 17.7

The output of the Articles Categories module, viewed from the front end of the site

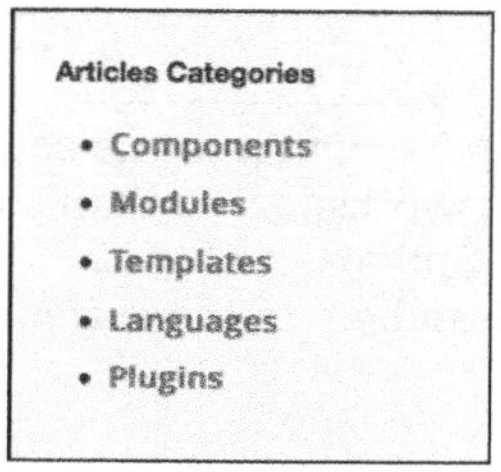

Articles Categories

- Components
- Modules
- Templates
- Languages
- Plugins

17

The Basic Options tab of the Articles Categories module contains a number of special fields, which allow you to control the display of the categories and subcategories inside the module. The options are

- **Parent Category.** Select an article category to be displayed in the module.
- **Category Descriptions.** Show or hide the descriptions for the categories.
- **Show Subcategories.** Show or hide the subcategories belonging to the parent category that you select in the Parent Category field.
- **# First Subcategories.** Specify how many first-level subcategories you want to display. The default value is All.
- **Maximum Level Depth.** Set the depth of the subcategories that you want to display. The default value is All.

The Advanced Options tab of the Articles Categories module contains one unique field: Heading style. You can use the combo box next to this control to specify the HTML formatting for the module heading.

Publishing the Articles Category module

You can use the Articles Category module to display a list of articles from a category. The parameters allow you to filter the list and to display articles from inside subcategories, making this module a useful alternative to using a menu to build navigation for your site visitors. Figure 17.8 shows the module at work.

FIGURE 17.8

The output of the Articles Category module

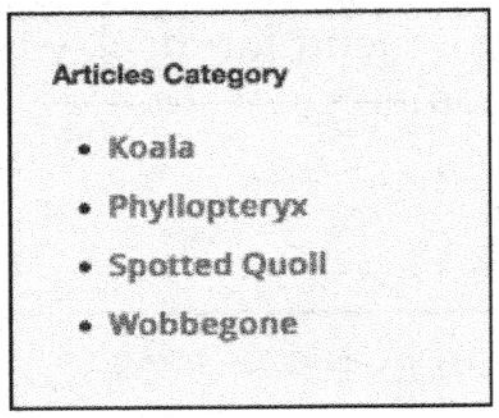

The tabs included in the Articles Category module provide an exception to the common tab structure of the other module workspaces. This module's workspace contains nine tabs, instead of the usual four. While the Details, Advanced Options, and Menu Assignments tabs remain consistent with the module tabs elsewhere in the system, the other six tabs contain unique fields. The additional tabs are

- **Basic Options.** Use this combo box, labeled Mode, to select either Normal mode or Dynamic mode for controlling the module display.

> **TIP**
>
> Use Normal mode when you want to display a static set of links to articles drawn from a specific category. In contrast, you can use Dynamic mode to display context-sensitive lists of articles. Dynamic mode automatically detects when the page is a category page and, if so, it displays in the module a list of the articles for the category. In all other cases, the module automatically hides.

- **Dynamic Mode Options.** Show or hide the module on article pages. This tab is only relevant if you have selected Dynamic mode on the Basic Options tab.
- **Filtering Options.** Use the options on this tab to determine what appears in the module. The filtering options are described in more detail in the following bulleted list.
- **Ordering Options.** Select the ordering criteria for the articles listed in the module.
- **Grouping Options.** Use the parameters on this tab to group the articles' links by date, author, or category.
- **Display Options.** Use the options on this tab to set the formatting and the amount of detail displayed inside the module. There are numerous fields here, and I look at them in more detail shortly.

The Filtering Options tab and the Display Options tab are the only two complex tabs in the set. I explain the fields you can find on each of these tabs in the following bulleted lists.

The Filtering Options tab contains several fields that you can use to filter the articles from one or more categories and display them in the module. The fields are

- **Featured Articles.** Specify how you want the module to handle featured articles. You can either show featured articles, hide featured articles, or show only features articles.
- **Count.** Set the number of articles you want to display.
- **Category Filtering Type.** Specify whether you want your category selection to be inclusive or exclusive. This option works in conjunction with the Category field.
- **Category.** Specify the category from which the articles will be selected.
- **Child Category Articles.** Choose whether to include or exclude articles from sub-categories.
- **Category Depth.** Specify the number of subcategories you want to display.
- **Author Filtering Type.** Specify whether you want the author filter to be inclusive or exclusive. This option works in conjunction with the Authors field.
- **Authors.** Select the authors and use them to filter the articles.
- **Author Alias Filtering Type.** Specify whether the author alias filter is inclusive or exclusive. This option works in conjunction with the Author Aliases field.
- **Author Aliases.** Select the author aliases and use them to filter the articles.
- **Article IDs to Exclude.** Enter article IDs in this field to exclude them from display in the module.

17

> **NOTE**
> You can find the article IDs in the list of articles in the Articles Manager.

- **Date Filtering.** Use this filter to specify articles using either a range of dates or a relative date, such as the previous 30 days.
- **Date Range Field.** Select which date will be used for the date filter.
- **Start Date Range.** Set the start date here, if filtering by the Date Range Field.
- **To Date.** Set the end date here, if filtering by the Date Range Field.
- **Relative Date.** Enter an integer value to specify the number of days; for example, entering 30 filters the last 30 days of articles.

The Display Options tab lets you define the details that display, as well as some of their formatting. The fields include

- **Heading Level.** Use this combo box to set the HTML styling for the module heading.
- **Linked Titles.** Set to Yes if you want the article title to be hyperlinked to the full article.
- **Date.** Set to Show to display article date information on the list; then use the Date Field to specify which date is used.

- **Date Field.** If you are showing the date on the list, select the date to use from this combo box.
- **Date Format.** Set a date format here, or use the default format. This is only relevant if you have elected to show a date in the Date Field.
- **Category.** Show or hide the name of the category.
- **Hits.** Show or hide the number of times each article has been viewed.
- **Author.** Show or hide the author of each article in the list view.
- **Introtext.** Show or hide an excerpt of text in addition to the article title; you can set the number of words to be displayed in the Introtext Limit field.
- **Introtext Limit.** If you have set the Introtext field to Show, set the length of the text here.
- **Show "Read More".** Show or hide a Read more link for items appearing in the module.
- **Show Title with Read More.** Set to Show to display the article's title along with the Read more link.
- **Read More Limit.** If you have set the Show Title with Read More option to Show, set this parameter to limit the length of the title text.

Managing advertising with the Banner module

The Banner module allows you to control the placement of banners on your site. The banners displayed by the module are drawn from the list of active banners in the Banners component. Figure 17.9 shows the Banner module being used to display a small ad.

> **TIP**
> Sites frequently employ more than one instance of the Banner module, as running multiple Banner modules gives you more flexibility to run ads in different positions and on different pages. With the available parameters and the ability to run multiple instances, it is possible to get a lot of variation out of this module. Duplicating an existing Banner module is the fastest way to create multiple modules.

FIGURE 17.9

The output of the Banner module is shown here using one of the banners in the sample data set.

 I discuss using the Banner component and the Banner module in Chapter 12.

The Basic Options tab includes the following fields:

- **Target.** Use the combo box to set the target for the banner URLs. This gives you control over how the browser responds when a visitor clicks a banner. The three options are Open in parent window, Open in new window, and Open in popup.
- **Count.** Set the number of banners to display in this slot; if you select multiple banners, they follow a random order inside the module, according to the filtering and randomization parameters you set in the following fields.
- **Client.** Use this filter to display only those banners from a specific client.
- **Category.** Use this filter to display only those banners from a specific category.
- **Search by Tags.** Select Yes to enable the system to match tags in content with tags assigned to banners to determine which banners are displayed. Note that you must associate tags with content items and with banners for this to work.
- **Randomise.** Specify whether banners are displayed sequentially or randomly.
- **Header Text.** Type text you want to appear on the page immediately before the banner.
- **Footer Text.** Type text you want to appear on the page immediately after the banner.

> **NOTE**
>
> The system name for this module type is `mod_banner`.

 I cover creating and managing banner clients and categories, as well as uploading banner graphics, in Chapter 12.

The Advanced Options tab of the Banners module does not contain any unique fields.

Enhancing navigation with the Breadcrumbs module

The Breadcrumbs module of your Joomla! system is responsible for the display of the breadcrumb trail on your website's pages, as shown in Figure 17.10. A *breadcrumb trail* is a position marker, in the sense that it shows users where they are in the site, and provides a way for users to navigate back or up to higher levels in the site's hierarchy.

FIGURE 17.10

The Breadcrumbs module looks like this from the front end of the site.

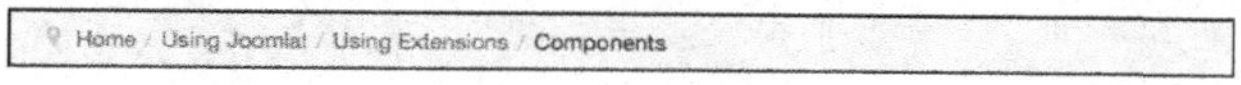

Home / Using Joomla! / Using Extensions / Components

The Basic Options tab includes the following fields:

- **Show "You are here".** Select Yes to display the phrase, "You are here," in front of the breadcrumb trail.

- **Show Home.** Specify whether the breadcrumb trail always includes a link back to the home page. The default setting is Yes.

- **Text for Home entry.** Type the label you want to appear for the home page entry in the breadcrumb trail in this field. The default Show Home setting is Yes. Note that this control is dependent upon the Show Home setting. If you set Show Home to No, then this field does not have a function.

- **Show Last.** Specify whether the breadcrumb trail always includes the current page. The default setting is Yes.

- **Text Separator.** Select a keyboard symbol to use to separate entries on the breadcrumb trail. If you leave this field blank, the system uses the default separator, " > >".

The Advanced Options tab of the Breadcrumbs module does not contain any unique fields.

TIP

While the Breadcrumbs module offers an easy way to improve the navigation and usability of your site, if you are using third-party components, you should check your Breadcrumbs module output as some components may not produce the result you expect.

This output can also be confusing if you use your menu items to link to pages deep inside your site. In that case, with one click, the user may penetrate several layers inside your site. The result is a long and complex breadcrumb trail that may be confusing to some users.

Creating content with the Custom HTML module

The Custom HTML module allows you to create modules that contain HTML code and then position those modules on your pages. This useful module not only enables you to show text and images, but also allows you to integrate outside functionality — like an affiliate link, a PayPal button, or embedded media — in a sidebar or other module position. Figure 17.11 shows the module being used as a simple text placeholder.

TIP

You can think of the Custom HTML module as simply a custom content module. Despite its name, entering custom HTML is only one thing you can do with this module type. This is a catchall module category that has a lot of functionality for a site administrator who needs to create placeholders for a variety of content that does not fit neatly into one of the other module types. If you use your site actively, you will probably use this module more than once.

FIGURE 17.11

The output from a Custom HTML module

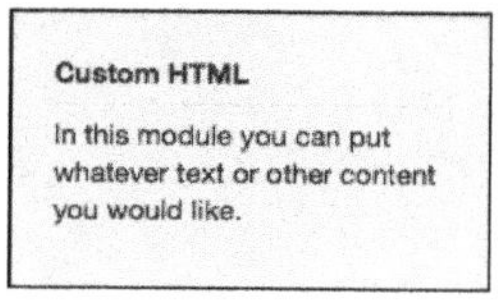

Custom HTML

In this module you can put whatever text or other content you would like.

17

The Basic Options tab includes only two fields: Prepare Content and Select a Background-Image. You can set the Prepare Content control to Yes to allow the Custom output tab to benefit from the Joomla! Content plug-ins, which give you greater control over formatting and content creation inside the module. You can use the Select a Background-Image field to add a background image to the module's content area.

The Custom HTML module workspace varies from other module types. The important difference is the presence of an additional tab on the workspace labeled Custom Output. This tab provides you with a text field where you can add whatever you want this module to display. You can display text, images, embedded media, or HTML. If you have a WYSIWYG Editor enabled on your site, the Custom Output tab displays the WYSIWYG toolbars.

 In Chapter 7, I discuss using modules to display content on a website.

The Advanced Options tab of the Custom HTML module does not contain any unique fields.

Adding external content with the Feed Display module

You can use the Feed Display module to create a module that contains content obtained from an RSS feed. The module allows you to input a feed URL and specify the output for the front end of your website. You select from the available module positions to display the contents on the front end of the site. The system automatically retrieves and refreshes the feed data. Note that this module is independent in functionality and not associated with the Newsfeed component. Figure 17.12 shows the Feed Display module in action.

FIGURE 17.12

The output from a Feed Display module

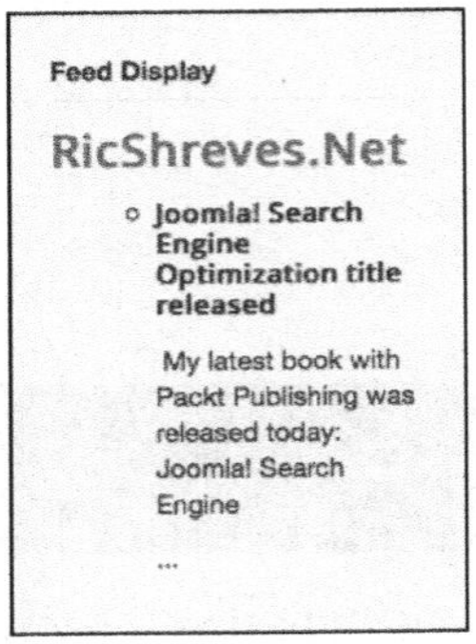

> **NOTE**
> The system name for this module type is `mod_feed`.

The Basic Options tab contains the following controls:

- **Feed URL.** Enter the address of the feed in this field. Typically the URL begins with `http://`. Though it is not marked, this field is required.
- **RTL Feed.** Select Yes if your feed reads right to left, instead of left to right.
- **Feed Title.** Specify whether you want to display the title of the feed, as supplied by the source of the feed.
- **Feed Description.** Specify whether to display the description of the feed, as supplied by the source of the feed.
- **Feed Image.** Specify whether to display the image associated with the feed, as supplied by the source of the feed.

> **TIP**
> Be careful when displaying feed images in your module positions, as large or odd-sized images can be problematic to display.

- **Items.** Specify an integer value to control the number of feed items that appear in the module. The default value is 3.
- **Item Description.** Specify whether to display the description of the feed item, as supplied by the source of the feed.
- **Word Count.** Specify an integer value to control the length of the feed item that appears. Set the value to zero to show the entire item.

I cover the use of modules to bring external content into your site in more detail in Chapter 7. I cover the Newsfeed component in Chapter 14.

The Advanced Options tab of the Feed Display module does not contain any unique fields.

Adding the Footer module

The Footer module serves no purpose other than to generate and display basic information about Joomla!, including a copyright notice, as shown in Figure 17.13. The module cannot be controlled other than to limit its display to particular positions or pages.

TIP

If you want to display your own footer content, unpublish this module and then create a new Custom HTML module containing your own content. Then assign your new module to the Footer module position.

17

FIGURE 17.13

The Footer module looks like this from the front end of the site.

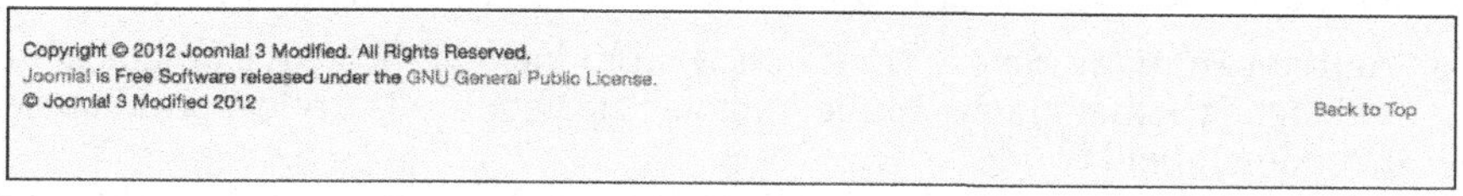

Copyright © 2012 Joomla! 3 Modified. All Rights Reserved.
Joomla! is Free Software released under the GNU General Public License.
© Joomla! 3 Modified 2012

Back to Top

NOTE

The system name for this module type is mod_footer.

There are not any additional parameters for this module type.

Language Switcher module

The Language Switcher module provides your site visitors with access to links that allow them to choose their preferred language. When published and properly configured, the module displays a list of all the language options available for your site. The module can show flags, text, or both, providing you with a necessary tool for creating a fully multilingual Joomla! site. Figure 17.14 shows the Language Switcher module's output.

 This module is only one part of what you need to implement a fully multilingual site. To learn how to set up your site to support more than one language, see Chapter 11.

FIGURE 17.14

The Language Switcher module, shown here in Spanish

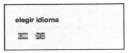

The Basic Options tab contains the following controls:

- **Pre-text.** Enter the text that you want to appear above the language flags.
- **Post-text.** Enter the text that you want to appear below the language flags.
- **Use Dropdown.** Select Yes if you want the names of the languages to appear in a drop-down menu, rather than as a list. If you select Yes, the following fields become irrelevant.
- **Use Image Flags.** Select Yes if you want to show an image of the relevant flag associated with each language. This control is irrelevant if you set the Use Dropdown field to Yes.
- **Horizontal Display.** Set the horizontal or vertical display of the list of languages. This control is irrelevant if you set the Use Dropdown field to Yes.
- **Active Language.** Select Yes if you want to include the active language in the list of languages that appear in the module. This control is irrelevant if you set the Use Dropdown field to Yes.

> **NOTE**
> The default system includes special CSS formatting for the active language. The class created for this purpose is `lang-active`.

- **Languages Full Names.** Select Yes to show the complete language name; select No to show the two-letter abbreviation for the language.

The Advanced Options tab of the Language Switcher module does not contain any unique fields.

Highlighting the most recent content with the Latest News module

The Latest News module displays a list of the most recent articles on your website, as shown in Figure 17.15. Using the module's options, you can control the content selected for display, showing, for example, only those articles belonging to a particular section, category, or author.

> **NOTE**
> Don't let the name fool you; this module has nothing specifically to do with news. A better name might be the Most Recent Articles module.

FIGURE 17.15

The front-end output of the Latest News module, in this example, shows a list of articles from the Joomla! sample data.

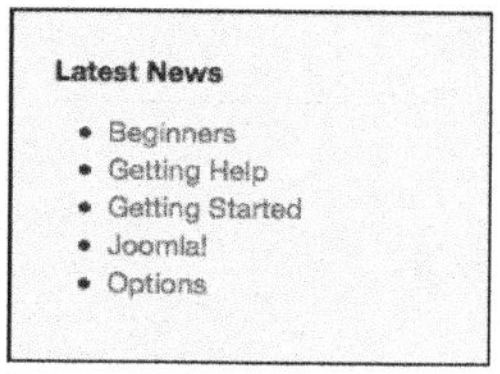

Latest News

- Beginners
- Getting Help
- Getting Started
- Joomla!
- Options

NOTE

The system name for this module type is `mod_latestnews`.

The Basic Options tab contains the following options:

- **Category.** Specify the category from which the articles are drawn.
- **Count.** Specify an integer value to control the number of items displayed by this module. The default value is 5.
- **Featured Articles.** Set this filter to determine whether the module Featured Articles.
- **Order.** Use this control to specify the criteria for selection of the articles. The module always displays the latest items, so use this combo box to control how the system defines latest — for example, most recently published, modified, added, or touched.
- **Authors.** Use this filter to select articles by author. There are three options: Anyone; Added or Modified by Me; and Not Added or Modified by Me.

The Advanced Options tab of the Latest News module does not contain any unique fields.

Publishing the Latest Users module

You can publish the Latest Users module to display a list of the newest users in the system. This module has a very narrow function, and a limited number of configuration options. You can specify the number of users listed and also restrict the output to show only those members that are part of the same user group as the viewer. The module does not provide a link to the user profile and is not integrated with the Contacts component. Figure 17.16 shows the Latest Users module's output.

TIP

The Latest Users module is most useful for community sites, where you are trying to show activity and introduce new members to the community.

FIGURE 17.16

The Latest Users module displays a list of the newest users.

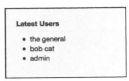

The Basic Options tab of the Latest Users module contains only two fields, one allowing you to specify the number of users shown and the other called Filter groups. When you set the Filter groups control to Yes, it restricts the display to only those users in the same user group as the person viewing the page.

The Advanced Options tab of the Latest Users module does not contain any unique fields.

Displaying the Login module

The Login module provides a form to give site users a way to log in to the system and gain access to additional articles or functionality. In addition to the standard login form functionality, this module also displays links to the password reminder and the username reminder. If you configure the site to allow user registration, the module also displays a link to the form that allows new users to create an account. Figure 17.17 shows the Login module with all of the options displayed.

> **NOTE**
>
> Once a user has logged in, this module also changes to display a Log Out link.

FIGURE 17.17

The front-end output of the Login module shows the system configured to allow user registration.

The Basic Options tab contains the following controls:

- **Pre-text.** Enter the text that you want to appear above the Login Form.
- **Post-text.** Enter the text that you want to appear below the Login Form.
- **Login Redirection Page.** If you want to redirect the user to a new page after she logs in, select the page from the combo box beside this control.
- **Logout Redirection Page.** If you want to redirect the user to a new page after she logs out, select the page from the combo box beside this control.
- **Show Greeting.** Specify whether the system displays a greeting for users upon login. The default value is Yes, which results in the greeting appearing in the module position after login. The default greeting is, "Hi, *username.*"

 See Chapter 11 for a discussion of how to override the default text strings used in Joomla!.

- **Show Name/Username.** Specify whether the greeting shows the username or the real name of the user. This control is only relevant if you set the Show Greeting parameter to Yes.
- **Encrypt Login Form.** Select Yes if you want the system to encrypt the form using SSL. The default value is No.

 I offer more detailed information about creating user registration functionality in Chapter 10.

The Advanced Options tab of the Login module does not contain any unique fields.

Creating navigation with the Menu module

Menu modules play a key role in the system and are closely tied to the Menu Manager. Each menu in the system has its own module. Menu modules are automatically created by the system each time you create a menu in the Menu Manager. Once you populate your menu with menu items, you publish the related Menu module to display the links to your site visitors. A typical Menu module output is shown in Figure 17.18.

TIP

Menu modules are among the most important in the system. Fluency in menu styling requires an awareness of not only the parameters, but also the underlying CSS styles that affect the menus. Tools like Firebug or the Web Developer Toolbar for the Firefox browser can make the task of styling menus much easier by exposing the styling and making it easy to identify exactly which styles affect which items. You can download the Firebug or Web Developer extensions from `http://addons.mozilla.org`.

 I cover the Menu Manager in detail in Chapter 8.

FIGURE 17.18

The front-end output of the Menu module

About Joomla!

Getting Started
Using Joomla!
  Using Extensions
    Components
      Content Component
        Single Article
        Article Categories
        Article Category Blog
        Article Category List
        Featured Articles
        Archived Articles
      Contact Component
      Weblinks Component
      News Feeds Component
      Users Component
      Search Components
      Administrator Components
    Modules
    Templates
    Languages
    Plugins
  Parameters
  Getting Help
The Joomla! Project
The Joomla! Community

NOTE

The system name for this module type is `mod_mainmenu`.

The Basic Options tab contains the following options:

- **Select Menu.** Select the menu you want to control from the combo box.
- **Base Item.** Select an item from the menu to be the base for controlling the module display. When you use the Base Item parameter, it tells the system to only display the module when the user is viewing that menu item, or any of the subsidiary

menu items. Use the Start Level and End Level fields to specify the range of pages where the module is visible.

- **Start Level.** Select a level to start displaying the module. Note that the Start Level menu item must be on the same level or higher than the End Level menu item.

- **End Level.** Select the level where the module ceases to display. This parameter works in conjunction with the Base Item and Start Level parameters to create a range of pages where the module is displayed. Select All to show all sublevels.

- **Show Sub-menu items.** Set the visibility of submenu items. Set this control to Yes to display all submenu items, even when the parent item is not selected. The default setting is No. This control is irrelevant if there are not any submenu items.

> **TIP**
> If you set the Start Level and the End Level to the same value and then set Show Sub-menu Items to Yes, the module only displays a single level.

 I discuss the formatting of menus and the creation of submenus in Chapter 8.

Though the Menu module's main purpose is to control menu placement, visibility, and access, it also impacts certain aspects of the menu's appearance. The Advanced Options tab includes a number of parameters to help you style the menu. Note that this module has some unique fields on the Advanced Options tab, in addition to the common fields shared with the other Site modules. The unique fields are

- **Menu Tag ID.** If you want to specify unique styling for the menu, use this field to add an ID, which will be associated with the menu's UL tag. Enter the desired ID here and then create the appropriate selectors in your CSS file.

- **Menu Class Suffix.** Another option for styling is to use a particular class suffix. Enter the desired suffix here and then create the appropriate selectors in your CSS file.

- **Target Position.** This field is only used if you are popping up the results when a user clicks the links in the menu. If you are opening a pop-up window, use this field to specify the position of the pop-up window on the user's screen.

Featuring popular content with the Most Read Content module

The Most Read Content module allows you to place on the page a list of the most popular articles on the site, as judged by the number of views each article has received. The module displays a list of the titles with links to the articles, as shown in Figure 17.19.

> **TIP**
> You can create multiple instances of this module type and then use the filters to create modules to display the most popular items in each of the various sections of your site.

FIGURE 17.19

The front-end output of the Most Read Content module

Most Read Content

- Australian Parks
- Fruit Shop
- Directions

The Basic Options tab contains the following controls:

- **Category.** Select the categories from which the articles are drawn.
- **Count.** Specify an integer value to control the number of articles that this module displays. The default value is 5.
- **Featured Articles.** Show or hide featured articles.

The Advanced Options tab of the Most Read Content module does not contain any unique fields.

Displaying images with the Random Image module

The Random Image module displays a selection of images in a module position, according to the parameters you set. Images are drawn from a single directory that you designate in the configuration parameters. The display of the images is randomized. There are few options for controlling this module. Figure 17.20 shows the module in use.

FIGURE 17.20

The front-end output of the Random Image module

Random Image

NOTE

The system name for this module type is `mod_random_image`.

The Basic Options tab contains the following options:

- **Image Type.** Enter file extensions in this field to filter the images that the module displays. You can enter multiple file types, separated by commas. Note that you do not need the leading "." as in ".jpg." The default setting for this parameter is jpg.

- **Image Folder.** Specify the address of the directory that contains the images you want to display. The path you enter here should be relative to the site's URL.

- **Link.** If you want to hyperlink the images to a specific URL, enter the full URL here.

- **Width (px).** Enter an integer value to force the image to a specific width in pixels (px). If you do not specify a value here, the system uses the original file's dimensions.

- **Height (px).** Enter an integer value to force the image to a specific height in pixels (px). If you do not specify a value here, the system uses the original file's dimensions.

The Advanced Options tab of the Random Image module does not contain any unique fields, but note that this module does not permit caching.

Providing site search with the Search module

The Search module makes it possible for you to place a site search box on any page inside a module position. This module is associated with Joomla's basic Search component, so all you need to do is enable and publish this module to allow visitors to search the site with ease. There are few configuration options; all parameters related to this module focus on the appearance of the search form. Figure 17.21 shows the module in use.

TIP

Site search in Joomla! is enabled by the search plug-ins. You can use some of the settings for the plug-ins to configure your search, for example, by specifying what is or is not included in the search results. To learn more about configuring the search plug-in, see Chapter 19. Note also that the Smart Search module provides an alternative for searching your site.

FIGURE 17.21

The front-end output of the Search module in the default Joomla! system

Search...

The Basic Options tab contains the following controls:

- **Box label.** Enter the text you want to appear as the label for the search form. If you leave this field blank, the system uses the default text.

- **Box width.** Enter an integer value here to set the size of the text field for the search form; the value is calculated in characters.

- **Box Text.** Enter the default text you want to appear in the search box. If you leave this field blank, the system uses the default text.

- **Search button.** Hide or display a search button on the form. In either case, the user can initiate the search by pressing the Return key on his keyboard, but with the button present, he also has the option to click the button to start the search.

- **Button position.** Use this option to position the button relative to the search text field. The options are Right, Left, Top, and Bottom, with the default option being to the right of the search form.

- **Search button image.** Specify whether the button is drawn using CSS or with an image.

- **Button text.** Enter the text you want to appear on the Search button. If you leave this field blank, the system uses the default search string specified in the language file.

- **OpenSearch autodiscovery.** The OpenSearch protocol is supported by Joomla!. If you set this parameter to Yes, browsers that also support OpenSearch can integrate your site search into the browser search box, giving users another way to search your site.

- **OpenSearch title.** Use this option to control the text that appears in the browser search box when a browser adds your site as a search provider using the OpenSearch protocol. This parameter is only relevant if you set OpenSearch autodiscovery to Yes.

- **Set ItemID.** If you want to target a specific page for the display of the search results, add the ItemID of that page's menu item to this field.

The Advanced Options tab of the Search module does not contain any unique fields.

Enhancing searches with the Smart Search module

Smart Search is an alternative to Joomla's basic site search, and typically more effective at finding content located outside of the Joomla! articles, weblinks, and Newsfeed components. The Smart Search module provides a search form for visitors to search your site. It is very similar to the Search module, discussed in the previous section; the real difference is in the way the site's contents are indexed. Figure 17.22 shows the output of the module.

 See Chapter 15 for a discussion of the two Joomla! search components.

FIGURE 17.22

The output of the Smart Search module is configured to display a link to an advanced search page.

The Basic Options tab contains three controls:

- **Search Filter.** Select a filter from the combo box to limit the display of the results shown by this module.

- **Search Suggestions.** Show or hide automatic search suggestions.

- **Advanced Search.** Show or hide the Advanced Search option.

Smart Search is one of the few system modules that have unique fields on the Advanced Search tab — oddly, these are some of the same fields that are on the Basic Options tab of the regular Search module. The fields are

- **Search Field Size.** Enter an integer value here to set the size of the text field for the search form; this value is calculated in characters.

- **Alternate Label.** Enter a label for the search box if you don't want to use the default label.

- **Search Field Label.** Show or hide the search field label.

- **Label position.** Set the position of the label relative to the search text field. The options are Right, Left, Top, and Bottom, with the default option being to the right of the search form.

- **Search button.** Hide or display a search button on the form. In either case, the user can initiate the search by pressing the Return key on her keyboard, but having the Search button also enables her to click the button to start the search.

- **Button position.** Position the button relative to the search text field. The options are Right, Left, Top, and Bottom, with the default option being to the right of the search form.
- **OpenSearch autodiscovery.** The OpenSearch protocol is supported by Joomla!. If you set this parameter to Yes, browsers that also support OpenSearch can integrate your site search into the browser search box, giving users another way to search your site.
- **OpenSearch title.** Enter the text that you want to appear in the browser search box when a browser adds your site as a search provider using the OpenSearch protocol. This parameter is only relevant if you have set OpenSearch autodiscovery to Yes.

Showing site information with the Statistics module

The Statistics module displays information about your site and hosting environment. The module is configurable and you can set it to display basic information about your server, your site visitor traffic, and information on the contents of your site, including the number of articles and weblinks. The Statistics module is shown in Figure 17.23.

> **TIP**
> Although the Statistics module is a convenient way to add some extra content to your site — content that you don't have to maintain — you may want to think twice before exposing information about your server configuration to the world.

FIGURE 17.23

The front-end output of the Statistics module

NOTE

The system name for this module type is `mod_stats`.

The Basic Options tab contains four controls. For the statistical data to display on your site, at least one of the first three controls must be set to Yes.

- **Server Information.** Select Yes to display basic information about your server, including the operating system, the time, whether caching or GZip are enabled, and the version number of your PHP and MySQL installations. The default setting for this control is No.

- **Site Information.** Select Yes to display basic information about your site and its contents, including the number of members, content items, and weblinks. The default setting is No.

- **Hit Counter.** Select Yes to display how many views your content items have received. The default setting is No.

- **Increase Counter.** Enter an integer value here to increase the number of hits shown on the Hits counter.

The Advanced Options tab of the Statistics module does not contain any unique fields.

Adding RSS with the Syndicate Feeds module

The Syndicate Feeds module displays an RSS feed button that is automatically linked to the RSS feed for the page on which it appears. The module is useful when you want visitors to know they can subscribe to the contents of a particular page. There are not any filters that allow you to refine this functionality; it always links to the feed for the page contents. The module is shown in Figure 17.24.

TIP

While you can assign the module to all the pages of your site, this is unlikely to be the best configuration, as not all pages will contain content appropriate for subscription. The better choice is to show the module on only those pages where it is relevant. To do so, use the Menu Assignment tab to assign the module to the desired pages.

FIGURE 17.24

The front-end output of the Syndicate Feeds module

NOTE

The system name for this module type is `mod_syndicate`.

The Basic Options tab contains three controls:

- **Display Text.** Select No to display only the RSS icon; select Yes to add text next to the icon. If you choose Yes, enter the text you desire in the Text field.

- **Text.** If you set the Display Text field to Yes, enter the text you want to display here.

- **Feed Format.** Select the format for the syndication feed. The system supports RSS 2.0 and Atom 1.0.

The Advanced Options tab of the Syndicate Feeds module does not contain any unique fields; note, however, that caching is not available for this module.

Publishing links via the Weblinks module

The Weblinks module allows you to display a set of weblinks selected from a category in the Weblinks component. Configuration options let you control the appearance of the links and what happens after a visitor clicks a link. As I discussed previously in the book, this module works in conjunction with the Weblinks component. Figure 17.25 shows the Weblinks module's output.

 See Chapter 16 for a more in-depth discussion of the Weblinks component.

FIGURE 17.25

The output of the Weblinks module

The Basic Options tab includes the following options:

- **Category.** Choose the category from which the weblinks will be chosen.

- **Count.** Specify how many weblinks you want to display.

- **Ordering.** Set the ordering for the display of the links.

- **Direction.** Display the weblinks in ascending or descending order, based on the sort criteria you chose in the Ordering field.
- **Target Window.** Specify where the page opens when a user clicks a weblink. The options are Open in New Window, Open in Pop-up, and Open in Parent Window.
- **Follow/No Follow.** Tell search engine robots whether to follow the link.
- **Description.** Show or hide the description you gave the weblink.
- **Hits.** Show or hide the number of times the link has been displayed.
- **Count Clicks.** Select Yes to have the system count the number of times the link is clicked; this information appears in the Weblinks Manager.

The Advanced Options tab of the Weblinks module does not contain any unique fields.

Showing activity with the Who's Online module

The Who's Online module offers a way to show activity levels on your site. The module displays the number of members online at any time, and you can also configure it to list their names. The module is shown in Figure 17.26.

FIGURE 17.26

This is the front-end output of the Who's Online module. The module is configured to show only the number of guests and members.

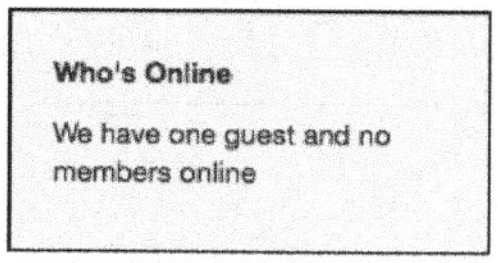

Who's Online

We have one guest and no members online

> **NOTE**
>
> The system name for this module type is `mod_whosonline`.

The Basic Options tab contains only one parameter, the Display control. You can use the combo box to select what you want the module to display. The options are # of Guests/Users, User Names, and Both.

> **NOTE**
>
> When the Who's Online module workspace says "Guests," it means "visitors who are not logged in." When the workspace refers to "Users," it means "authenticated users."

The Advanced Options tab of the Who's Online module does not contain any unique fields.

Displaying external content with the Wrapper module

The Wrapper module allows you to display external web pages inside your site. A wrapper is just another name for an iframe, and you can use it to display the contents of an external URL, as shown in Figure 17.27. The parameters associated with this module relate to the URL content, the appearance, and the size of the iframe.

> **TIP**
>
> The Wrapper module is typically used in module positions located in, above, or below the main content area, as the sidebar columns are typically too small for the wrapper to work effectively. If you intend to use the wrapper in the side columns, be aware that the scrollbars can take up a lot of space when they are active. If you have control over the web page that is being displayed, you can account for this. If, however, you do not control the web page you want to display, then the wrapper display may be more difficult to control. Conversely, placing the wrapper at the top or bottom of the content area gives you a much wider area to work with, plus the ability to expand the height without completely breaking your page layout.

FIGURE 17.27

The front-end output of the Wrapper module is wrapping an external website.

> **NOTE**
>
> The system name for this module type is `mod_wrapper`.

The Basic Options tab contains the following controls:

- **URL.** Enter the address of the web page you want to display inside the wrapper.
- **Auto Add.** Select Yes to automatically append the prefix `http://` to the URL. Set the control to No to disable this feature.
- **Scroll Bars.** Select No to hide scroll bars, and Yes to show them. Setting the control to Auto means that the system only displays scroll bars when they are needed to display the entire page.
- **Width.** Specify the width of the iframe either in pixels or as a percentage.
- **Height.** Specify the height of the iframe either in pixels or as a percentage.
- **Auto Height.** Select Yes if you want the iframe to size itself automatically to match the web page being displayed.
- **Frame Border.** Show or hide the borders of the iframe.
- **Target Name.** Specify a name for the iframe. This is optional and only needed where you are using the iframe as a target for opening a URL.

The Advanced Options tab of the Wrapper module does not contain any unique fields.

17

Summary

In this chapter, I reviewed the Joomla! Site modules, which are the modules used on the front end of the website. This chapter focused on the module options and how you can use them on your site. The topics included

- Understanding the Site Module Manager interface
- Creating new modules
- Duplicating modules to save time and effort
- Editing and deleting existing modules
- Reviewing all the system's 24 Site modules

In the next chapter, I look at the other Joomla! modules, that is, the Administrator modules used on the back end of the site.

Working with the Administrator Modules

The Joomla! system includes both Site modules and Administrator modules. Site modules provide output for the site visitors, and Administrator modules supplement the administration interface and provide the site administrators with access to useful features and information.

Because Administrator modules tend to supply critical functionality, programmers and system administrators rarely alter them, and the vast majority of Joomla! sites use only the default configuration. However, a closer examination of the modules shows that you can gain some benefits from learning how to manage your site's Administrator modules. By understanding the configuration options for the modules, you can enhance your site's admin interface and customize it to better serve your company and your users.

In this chapter I look at the tools you need to manage the Administrator modules and cover each of the individual modules' options and uses.

Introducing the Administrator Modules Manager

The Administrator Modules Manager provides the interface for controlling the Joomla! system's Administrator modules. The system includes 15 different Administrator module types. Several of the module types are closely related to and dependent on the core components; others are independent, self-contained units. All share a similar process for the creation, duplication, and deletion of modules. The difference between the modules is largely in the parameters that are available for each one. By mastering the parameters, you will be able to tailor the modules to your needs.

You can control all the Joomla! modules through the Modules Manager. The manager contains all the Joomla! modules, together with any third-party modules you may install. The Modules Manager provides an interface that lets you see, at a glance, all the modules in the system and then perform a variety of common tasks associated with modules. You can access the individual modules for editing, or you can create new modules. You can also control the publishing state of any module with one click. Batch processes are available to reduce the work required to perform tasks on multiple modules. In this section, I introduce the Administrator Modules Manager.

To access the Administrator Modules Manager, you first log in to the admin system, go to the Extensions menu, and then select the Module Manager option. Once the Modules Manager loads in your browser, you click the Administrator link in the left column. The Administrator Module Manager loads in your browser window, as shown in Figure 18.1.

FIGURE 18.1

The Modules Manager appears, showing the Administrator Modules Manager.

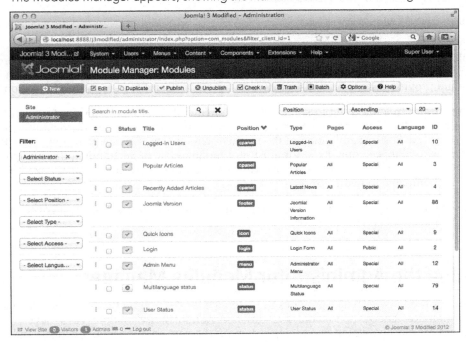

The toolbar at the top of the Module Manager provides quick access to the following functions:

- **New.** Click to create a new module.
- **Edit.** Select a module from the list and then click this button to edit the module.

- **Duplicate.** Select one or more modules from the list and then click this button to make an exact copy of the module.

- **Publish.** Select one or more modules from the list and then click this button to publish them. You publish a module to make it visible on the front end of the website.

- **Unpublish.** Select one or more modules from the list and then click this button to unpublish them. You unpublish a module to hide it from the front end of the website.

- **Check In.** Select one or more modules from the list and then click this button to force the module editing workspaces to close and thereby "check in" the modules.

- **Trash.** Select one or more modules from the list and then click this button to delete them.

- **Batch.** Select multiple modules from the list and then click this button to batch-apply processes to them. The pop-up window that appears enables you to edit multiple modules in one simple operation.

- **Options.** Click to open the Modules Manager Options workspace, where you can configure the permissions to use the Modules Manager.

NOTE

Module Manager permissions work consistently with the Permissions tab in the Global Configuration Manager. See the discussion on setting permissions in Chapter 10 to learn more.

18

- **Help.** Click to access the online Help files related to the active screen.

Two text links are located below the toolbar. The Site link shows you the Site Modules Manager, which I discuss in the previous chapter. The Administrator link takes you to the Administrator Modules Manager.

Located below the two text links and beside the list of modules are six sorting and searching tools to help you manage long lists of modules:

- **Administrator.** Use this combo box to switch between the Site Modules Manager and the Administrator Modules Manager. This performs the same function as the Site and Administrator links.

- **Select Status.** Use this combo box to filter and display the modules according to whether they are published, unpublished, or trashed. This provides an easy way to identify all modules that are currently active on the site. To reset this filter, change the combo box back to the default setting, Select Status.

- **Select Position.** Use this combo box to filter the list of modules by the position to which they are assigned. To reset this filter, change the combo box back to the default setting, Select Position.

- **Select Type.** Use this combo box to filter the list by module type. To reset this filter, change the combo box back to the default setting, Select Type.

- **Select Access.** Use this combo box to filter the list of modules by access level. To reset this filter, change the combo box back to the default setting, Select Access.

- **Select Language.** Use this combo box to filter the list of modules by language. To reset this filter, change the combo box back to the default setting, Select Language.

Below the toolbar and above the list of modules are four sorting and searching tools:

- Type a word or phrase into the field marked Search in module title, and then click the magnifying glass button. The system searches your list of modules for the query and then displays the results of the search. To clear the screen and return to a full listing, click the button marked with the X.
- Use the combo box to the right of the Search field to specify which column of the modules display is used for the sort order.

- Use the Ascending combo box to specify whether the modules appear in ascending or descending order.
- Use the combo box on the far right to control the number of modules that appear on the page. You can change the default value by changing the List Length parameter in the Global Configuration Manager.

The main content area of the screen contains a list of all the modules in your Joomla! site. The columns provided are

- **Sort Order (vertical double arrows).** You can click the arrows to change the sort order; you can also click and hold any of the buttons immediately to the left of a module's title and drag the module to change its order location in the Modules Manager.
- **Module Selection (unlabeled check box).** You can click a check box to select a module; this is necessary if you want to use several of the toolbar options.
- **Status.** A green check mark indicates that the module is published. A red x indicates that it is unpublished.
- **Title.** This field displays the full name of the module. Click the name to edit the module.
- **Position.** This field displays the position to which the module is assigned. You can only assign a single module to one position.
- **Type.** This field shows the module's type. Each module can be of only one type.
- **Pages.** This field shows which pages the module has been assigned to. The only options here are All, meaning to all pages on the site; None, which means the module has not been assigned to any pages; and Selected only, which means the module is assigned to some, but not all, of the pages. To change these setting, edit the module.

- **Access.** This field indicates the access level assigned to the module.
- **Language.** This field shows the language designated for the module.
- **ID.** This field shows the system-generated ID number.

Now that you have some idea of what information is presented by the Modules Manager, and which buttons allow you to access the key functionality, I will show you how to create new modules.

Creating new modules

You can create new modules from within the Module Manager. Creating a new module is an alternative to editing or duplicating an existing module. If you have installed the sample data, you may want to start off by modifying the sample data modules, rather than beginning from scratch and creating your own modules. Regardless of which method you choose, the options available in the module are the same.

Creating a new module is a two-step process: First you must select the module type you want to create, and then you must set up that module type with the required information. To begin, you simply click the New button on the toolbar, and the system loads a new page in the browser, as shown in Figure 18.2. The new page requires you to select the module type you want to create.

FIGURE 18.2

The first step in creating a new module is to select the module type.

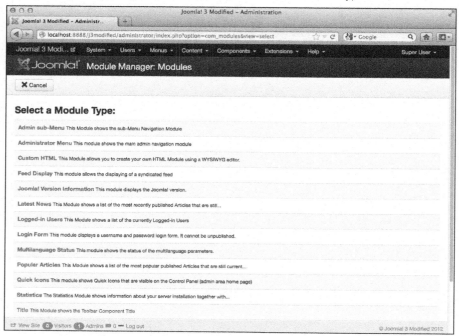

Select one of the 15 module type choices and click the Next button; the page reloads and displays the next step in the module creation process, as shown in Figure 18.3.

The toolbar at the top of the New Module workspace provides quick access to the following functions:

- **Save.** Click to save your work.
- **Save & Close.** Click to save your work and exit the New Module workspace.
- **Save & New.** Click to save your work, close the current New Module workspace, and open another New Module workspace.
- **Cancel.** Click to cancel the task and exit the New Module workspace.
- **Help.** Click to display the Help files related to the active screen.

FIGURE 18.3

The second step in the New Module creation process. In this example, you see the screen for a new Administrator Menu module.

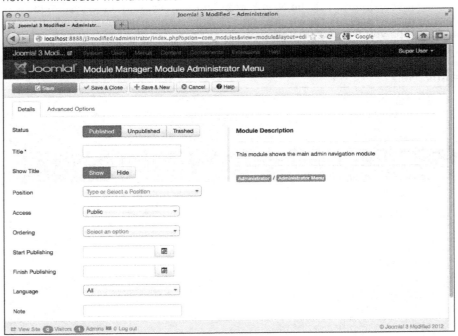

The New Module workspace is divided into tabs. The most common configuration is three tabs:

- **Details.** This is the basic tab containing most of the required fields for creating a module. It is also where you control the module's publication status and position on the page. This tab is the same for all modules. I discuss the fields on this tab in the following bulleted list.

- **Basic Options.** This tab provides the custom parameters unique to each module, and so the options on this tab vary from module to module. I review the specific options available to each module type later in this chapter.

- **Advanced Options.** This tab contains options related to layout, styling, and caching. The site modules share a number of common fields on this tab, but there is some variation between modules. I discuss these fields shortly.

> **NOTE**
>
> The modules that don't follow this pattern are highlighted later in the chapter, in the sections dealing with those specific modules.

Of the tabs in the Module workspace, two are at least partially standardized across all module types: Details and Advanced Options. Accordingly, I cover the fields you will find on the common tabs here.

Using the Details tab

The Details tab is the default landing tab that you see when you create a new module or open a module for editing. The tab contains the fields that set the basic parameters for a module, including the module's name and its position on the page. There are ten fields on this page, but only two of them are essential. The fields are

- **Status.** Select a state for the module. The options are Published, Unpublished, and Trashed.

- **Title.** This field displays the full name of the module. Click the name to edit the module.

- **Show Title.** You can show or hide the title of the module on the front end of the site.

- **Position.** You can assign the module to a position in the template. This is a critical field.

> **NOTE**
>
> All the templates in the system are listed in the Position combo box. Make sure you select a valid position on the active template, or you will not see the module!

18

> **TIP**
>
> It is possible to publish something in an inappropriate position and end up with the output blocking you from being able to access key functionality. If this happens to you and you cannot access the toolbar, unpublish the offending module. Once it is unpublished, the interface is restored and you can edit the module to correct the problem before publishing it again.

- **Access.** You can specify the access level assigned to the module.
- **Ordering.** You can specify the order of the module relative to any others assigned in the same position.
- **Start Publishing.** Though optional, you can set a specific starting date for the publication of the module. If you leave this field blank, the system assumes that you want to start publishing immediately.
- **Finish Publishing.** Though optional, you can set a specific ending date for the publication of the module. If you leave this field blank, the system assumes that you want the module to remain published indefinitely.
- **Language.** You can designate the language for the module.
- **Note.** You can add notes here for use by the site administrators.

Configuring the Advanced Options

The Advanced Options tab is only partially standardized throughout the Administrator modules. There is a set of common fields that appear on all modules, but there are some variations where individual modules may have more or, in a some cases, fewer of these options. The fields that are common to most modules are

- **Alternative Layout.** If your template provides for alternative layouts, you can select one from this combo box; otherwise, the default layout is applied.
- **Module Class Suffix.** You can specify a suffix that is automatically appended to all CSS styles that affect this module. The use of a specified suffix makes it possible for you to style this module individually.
- **Caching.** You can exempt a specific module from the site's caching, as set in the Global Configuration Manager. Select the No Caching option to prevent the contents of this module from being cached. The default setting is Use Global.
- **Cache Time.** You can set how frequently, in minutes, you want the contents to be cached. Enter an integer value here. The default value is 900 minutes, meaning that after 900 minutes the system re-creates, or refreshes, this module. Note that this control is only relevant if the caching for the module is enabled.
- **Automatic title.** Select Yes to allow the system to automatically translate the module title, if supported by the template.
- **Module Tag.** You can select the HTML tag you want to use for the module; this allows you to control the formatting of specific modules by linking them to particular styles in your stylesheet.
- **Bootstrap Size.** You can specify how many columns the module will span.
- **Header Tag.** You can select the desired HTML tag for the module title.

- **Header Class.** If you want to use a special class for controlling the formatting of the module title, you can enter it here.

- **Module Style.** You can select a value from this combo box to override the default formatting of your template. The combo box gives you access to all the module styles in your system.

While the module types all share common elements, there are also unique parameters that you must consider. In later sections, I review each of the module types, explain how they are used, show you an example, and then explain any distinct configuration parameters that might exist on the Module workspace tabs.

NOTE

If you have installed additional extensions to your site, you may also see additional module types that allow for the creation of new modules beyond the system defaults.

Creating duplicate modules

You can make exact copies of modules by using the Duplicate command in the Module Manager. This function is very useful if you need to run multiple instances of the same module type, as duplicating a module saves you several steps and fast tracks module configuration. When you duplicate a module, an exact copy of the module is placed in the Module Manager. The new module has the same configuration and name as the original, but with a number appended to the end of the name.

To duplicate a module, follow these steps:

1. **Log in to the admin system on your site.**

2. **Go to the Extensions menu and choose the Module Manager option.** The Site Modules Manager loads in your browser.

3. **Click the Administrator link in the left column.** The Administrator Modules Manager loads in your browser.

4. **Select the module you want to duplicate by clicking the check box next to the module name.**

5. **Click the Duplicate button.** The system immediately makes a copy of the module and places it in the Module Manager.

NOTE

Duplicated modules are unpublished by default.

Editing modules

You can edit existing modules from within the Module Manager. Editing is limited to the name and configuration details of the module. You cannot change the module type from the editing workspace; to do this, you must create a new module of the type you desire.

To edit a module, you either click the module name in the Module Manager or select the module on the list and then click the Edit button on the Module Manager toolbar. Regardless of which method you use, the system opens the Edit Module workspace. The Edit Module workspace is identical to the New Module workspace, with the same fields and requirements.

To edit a module, you simply alter the desired fields in the Edit Module workspace and then click the Save button on the toolbar. Any changes you make are applied immediately.

> **NOTE**
> The Edit Module workspace does have one extra button on the toolbar: Save as Copy. You can use this button to quickly duplicate a module, creating a new module identical to the one you are editing.

Deleting modules

The deletion of modules in Joomla! is a two-step process. The first step involves moving the module to the trash, where it is held until you take the second step and permanently delete the module. Modules held in the trash can be restored at any time prior to deletion. You can view the contents of the trash at any time by using the Select Status Filter in the Module Manager.

Modules moved to the trash are held there indefinitely. The modules can be restored or deleted at the option of the administrator. Restored modules move back to their original locations, but deleted modules are permanently removed from the system and cannot be restored.

To move a module to the trash, follow these steps:

1. **Log in to the admin system on your site.**
2. **Go to the Extensions menu and choose the Module Manager option.** The Site Modules Manager loads in your browser.
3. **Click the Administrator link in the left column.** The Administrator Modules Manager loads in your browser.
4. **Click the check box next to the module or modules you want to move to the trash.**
5. **Click the Trash button on the toolbar.** The system moves the selected modules to the trash.

Restoring modules from the trash

Modules moved to the trash are held there until the administrator takes further action. Any module can be restored at any time. The process of restoring a module is simple and the result instantaneous: the module is removed from the trash and returns to where it was located before it was moved to the trash.

To restore a module from the trash, follow these steps:

1. **Log in to the admin system on your site.**

2. **Go to the Extensions menu and choose the Module Manager option.** The Site Modules Manager loads in your browser.

3. **Click the Administrator link in the left column.** The Administrator Modules Manager loads in your browser.

4. **Change the Select Status Filter to Trashed.** The list of modules reloads to display only those modules in the trash.

5. **Click the check box next to the module or modules you want to restore.**

6. **Click either Publish or Unpublish on the toolbar.** The system removes the selected modules from the trash and restores them to their previous locations.

Deleting modules permanently

Modules held in the trash can be removed from the system by emptying the trash. Emptying the trash results in the module's permanent removal from the system; it cannot be restored once deleted.

To permanently delete a module from the trash, follow these steps:

1. **Log in to the admin system on your site.**

2. **Go to the Extensions menu and choose the Module Manager option.** The Site Modules Manager loads in your browser.

3. **Click the Administrator link in the left column.** The Administrator Modules Manager loads in your browser.

4. **Change the Select Status Filter to Trashed.** The list of modules reloads to display only those modules in the trash.

5. **Click the check box next to the module or modules you want to delete.**

6. **Click the Empty Trash button on the toolbar.** The system immediately deletes the selected modules.

> **NOTE**
> Deleting a module is permanent and cannot be undone. Moreover, there is no confirmation dialog box — clicking the Empty Trash button immediately deletes the module!

Reviewing the Administrator Modules

The default Joomla! installation comes with 15 Administrator module types. The various module types provide a wide range of functionality, from displaying content to providing navigation and utilities. Each of the module types is available to you as the site administrator; you simply need to click the New button and select the type you want. There are no restrictions on how many modules of each type you can run.

18

In this section, I look at each of the default Administrator module types. I describe what each module does and how you can use it, provide a figure showing what it looks like when published, and then cover any unique configuration parameters that come with the module.

Publishing the Admin Sub-menu module

The Admin Sub-menu appears on some pages of the admin system, immediately below the title, but above the filters. You can see this menu in action, for example, on the Module Manager screen where it holds the text links in the left column labeled Site and Administrator. You can see the links in Figure 18.4.

Like the Admin menu, this menu is not part of the normal Joomla! Menu Manager scheme; the module is not related to and cannot be controlled by the Menu Manager.

FIGURE 18.4

The Admin Sub-menu module in action on the Module Manager interface

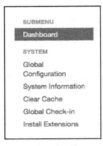

> **NOTE**
> The system name for this module type is `mod_submenu`.

This module does not include a Basic Options tab. The Advanced tab does not have any unique fields. Note that caching is not available for this module, and so the Caching field does not have a function either.

Configuring the Administrator Menu module

The Administrator Menu module is responsible for the navigation menu that appears at the top of each admin page, as shown in Figure 18.5. Unlike the Site Menu modules, the Administrator Menu are not linked to the Menu Manager. Modifying the options on the Administrator Menu is not possible (aside from hacking the core files).

> **NOTE**
> The system name for this module type is `mod_menu`.

472

FIGURE 18.5

The output of the Administrator Menu module is shown at the top of the page.

This module type does not include a Basic Options tab. The Advanced Options tab does show several unique fields, in addition to the common fields found in other modules.

- **Add New Shortcuts.** Set to Show to display the Add New Shortcut option to important screens.

NOTE

At the time of this writing, this parameter was not functioning properly.

- **Help Menu.** Show or hide the Help menu, which links to the official Joomla! help resources. If you are using the Custom Support Forum option, you will probably want to set this parameter to Hide.

- **Custom Support Forum.** You can specify a support website for your admin users by adding the URL in this field. If you choose this option, you may want to set the Help Menu option to Hide.

NOTE

Caching is not available for this module type.

Creating custom output with the Custom HTML module

The Custom HTML module is designed to allow you to display any custom content you want inside the admin interface. The module workspace provides a large text editing box and a WYSIWYG editor that enables you to enter text, images, or HTML code and then display the output in a module position in the admin system. Figure 18.6 shows an example application of this module.

TIP

Good uses for this module include instructions to administrators, branding text or images, lists of links, and special announcements you need the administrators to see.

FIGURE 18.6

The Custom HTML module in action on the Control Panel

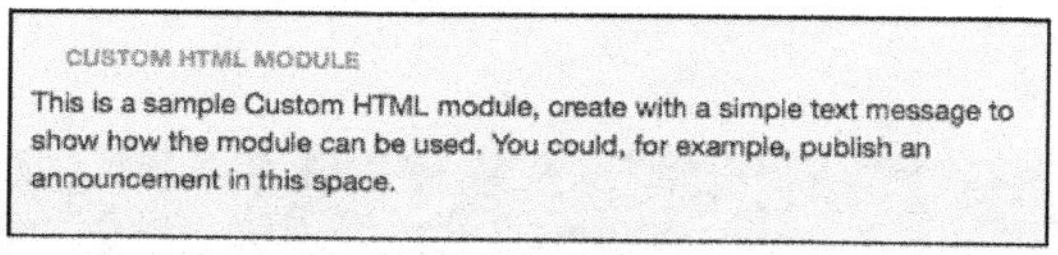

CUSTOM HTML MODULE

This is a sample Custom HTML module, create with a simple text message to show how the module can be used. You could, for example, publish an announcement in this space.

NOTE

The system name for this module type is `mod_custom`.

The Custom HTML workspace is the only Administrator module workspace with four tabs: Details, Basic Options, Advanced Options, and Custom Output. The Details and Advanced Options tabs follow the common format used in other admin module workspaces.

The Basic Options tab includes only one control: Prepare Content. This is set to Yes by default. You want to keep this option enabled, as it allows you to access all the tools and plug-ins used for normal content creation in Joomla!

The fourth tab in this workspace is the Custom Output tab. This tab provides the text box for creating the content you want to display in this module. If your site is configured to permit the use of a WYSIWYG editor, you also see it here.

Displaying external content with the Feed Display module

The Feed Display module enables the gathering of RSS feed output and the display of that output inside a module position in the admin system. This module is independent of the Newsfeed Manager, so you need to enter the full URL of the feed in the Basic Options tab of the module. Figure 18.7 shows the output of the Feed Display module.

TIP

While you can use this module for any purpose, it is particularly helpful for displaying the most recent announcements from the Joomla! Security Center. The URL for that feed is `http://feeds.joomla.org/Joomla SecurityNews`.

FIGURE 18.7

The Feed Display module

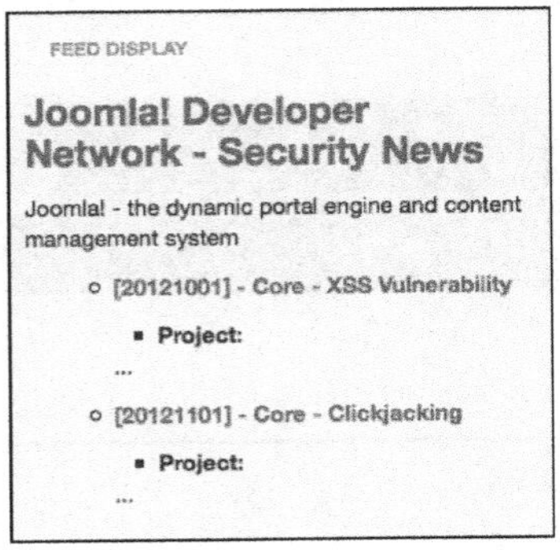

NOTE

The system name for this module type is `mod_feed`.

The Basic Options tab contains the following parameters:

- **Feed URL.** Enter the address of the feed. Typically this begins with `http://`. Though it is not noted as such, this field is required.
- **RTL Feed.** Set this option to Yes if your feed reads right to left, instead of left to right.
- **Feed Title.** Specify whether to display the title of the feed, as supplied by the source of the feed.
- **Feed Description.** Specify whether to display the description of the feed, as supplied by the source of the feed.
- **Feed Image.** Specify whether to display the image associated with the feed, as supplied by the source of the feed.

> **TIP**
>
> Be careful with displaying feed images in your module positions, as large or odd-sized images can be problematic to display.

- **Items.** Specify an integer value to control the number of feed items that appear in the module. The default value is 3.
- **Item Description.** Specify whether to display the description of the feed item, as supplied by the source of the feed.
- **Word Count.** Specify an integer value to control the length of the feed item shown. Set the value to zero to show the entire item.

18

> **NOTE**
>
> Although adding feeds to the admin system may be a useful way to keep your administrators up to date with critical information — like the Joomla! Security Newsfeed — never forget that the Feed Display module draws its content from outside your server and that sometimes waiting on the feed data may result in delays in the loading of the admin interface.

Publishing the Joomla! Version Information module

The Joomla! Version Information module has a very limited purpose: It displays the Joomla! version information for the system. The only parameters here allow you to control whether the module displays the verbose version of the information or an abbreviated version. Figure 18.8 shows the module output.

> **NOTE**
>
> The system name for this module type is `mod_version`.

This module's Basic Options tab has only two fields: Version format, which allows you to control the amount of detail shown in the version data; and Show Joomla!, which includes the Joomla! name when you select the Short option for the Version format field. The Advanced tab does not have any unique fields. Note that caching is not available for this module, and so the Caching field does not have a function either.

FIGURE 18.8

The output of the Joomla! Version Information module, set to verbose mode

> JOOMLA VERSION
>
> Joomla! 3.0.2 Stable [Ember] 08-November-2012 14:00 GMT

Displaying the latest articles with the Latest News module

The Latest News module is somewhat misnamed because it doesn't show the latest news items, but rather the most recently added articles. The module output shows a list of the most recent items, along with the creation date and time and the name of the author, as shown in Figure 18.9. The names of the articles are clickable and open the articles in editing view.

> **TIP**
>
> This module is particularly useful in sites that have multiple administrators or multiple content creators because it allows you to see at a glance what has been changed.

FIGURE 18.9

The Latest News module

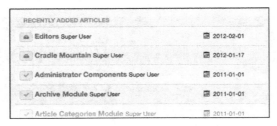

RECENTLY ADDED ARTICLES	
Editors Super User	2012-02-01
Cradle Mountain Super User	2012-01-17
Administrator Components Super User	2011-01-01
Archive Module Super User	2011-01-01
Article Categories Module Super User	2011-01-01

> **NOTE**
>
> The system name for this module type is mod_latest.

The Basic Options tab contains four controls:

- **Count.** Specify the number of items to be shown.
- **Order.** Set the order of display.
- **Category.** Select the category from which the module will access the articles for display; this combo box provides a list of the categories on your site.
- **Authors.** Use this combo box to filter the list, in this case based on the identity of the author of the articles. The options are Anyone; Added or modified by me; and Not added or modified by me.

The Advanced tab does not have any unique fields.

> **NOTE**
>
> Caching is not available for this module type.

Logged-in Users module

The Logged-in Users module displays a list of all system users that are currently logged in. The list includes a user's name with a link to her data in the User Manager, an indication of her Group membership, and the date of her last activity on the site. In the default system, the module's output appears on the Control Panel, as shown in Figure 18.10.

FIGURE 18.10

The Logged-in Users module in action is shown assigned to the cpanel module position on the Control Panel.

> **NOTE**
>
> The system name for this module type is `mod_logged`.

The Basic Options tab includes two fields:

- **Count.** Specify the number of users to list in the module.
- **Name.** Specify whether the module displays the users' real names or their usernames.

The Advanced Options tab includes one unique option: Automatic title. When set to Yes, the control automatically provides a translated title, when available.

> **NOTE**
>
> Caching is not available for this module type.

 For an extended discussion of user management, see Chapter 10.

Using the Login Form module

The Login Form module supplies the Login Form used to access the administration system. This module is essential for the system and cannot be disabled. Figure 18.11 shows the module as it appears only on the admin entry page.

CAUTION

This is one of the system's modules that is better left untouched. There are not any real options here, other than to enable SSL. Do not unpublish this module or you will be blocked from accessing the admin system!

FIGURE 18.11

The output of the Login Form module is shown on the admin entry page.

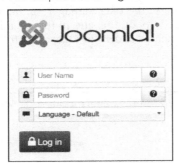

NOTE

The system name for this module type is `mod_login`.

The module parameters section contains only one field: Encrypt Login Form. The parameter allows you to enable SSL for the login process. Although this is more secure, if your server does not have SSL enabled, this option does not work.

The Advanced tab does not have any unique fields.

NOTE

Caching is not available for this module type.

Multilanguage Status utility module

The Multilanguage Status module is a utility module provided to help administrators keep track of the integrity of their multilingual content. When activated, the module appears in the footer area of the admin interface where it displays alerts when it detects potential problems with your multilingual content items. When you click the Multilanguage Status link in the footer, a dialog box appears, showing any issues that the system detected. Figure 18.12 shows the warning advice the system can provide.

FIGURE 18.12

This is a typical warning dialog box generated by the Multilanguage Status module.

> ⚠ This site is set as a multilanguage site. One or more of the Default Home pages for the published Content languages are missing although the Language Filter plugin is enabled OR/AND one or more Language Switcher modules are published
>
> ⚠ This site is set as a multilanguage site. The Languagefilter plugin is not enabled although one or more Language Switcher modules OR/AND one or more specific Content language Default Home pages are published.

Details	Status
Language Filter Plugin	Disabled
Published Language Switcher Modules	1
Published Default Home pages	1 assigned to language 'All'

Language Published Site Languages Published Content Languages Published Default Home pages

NOTE

The system name for this module type is `mod_multilangstatus`.

This module does not include a Basic Options tab. The Advanced tab does not have any unique fields.

NOTE

Caching is not available for this module type.

Displaying popular content with the Popular Articles module

The Popular Articles module displays a list of the ten most frequently viewed articles on your website. The module shows the name of the article, the date and time it was created, and the number of hits the article has received during its lifetime. You can click an article's title to open the article in editing view.

The default system includes a Popular Articles module as part of the default Control Panel display. Figure 18.13 shows the module output.

FIGURE 18.13

The output of the Popular Articles module is shown here in the default Control Panel configuration.

479

> **NOTE**
> The system name for this module type is `mod_popular`.

The Basic Options tab includes three fields:

- **Count.** Specify the number of articles you want to list in the module.
- **Category.** Select the category from which the module draws the articles for display; this combo box provides a list of the categories on your site.
- **Authors.** Specify a filter for the list, in this case based on the identity of the author of the articles. The options are Anyone; Added or modified by me; and Not added or modified by me.

The Advanced Options tab does not have any unique fields.

> **NOTE**
> Caching is not available for this module type.

Using the administrator's Quick Icons module

The Quick Icons module produces the shortcut icons that appear on the right side of the Control Panel, as shown in Figure 18.14. The module appears only on the Control Panel page and does not appear on the internal admin system pages.

FIGURE 18.14

The Quick Icons module is shown here in the default position on the Control Panel.

NOTE

The system name for this module type is `mod_quickicon`.

The Basic Options tab contains only one control, Group. The value entered in the Group field should match the value of the same name in the Quick Icons plug-in.

Viewing site stats with the Statistics module

The Statistics module displays information about your site and hosting environment. The module is configurable and you can set it to display basic information about your server, your site visitor traffic, and information on the contents of your site, including the number of articles and weblinks. The module is shown in Figure 18.15.

NOTE

The system name for this module type is `mod_stats_admin`.

The Basic Options tab contains four controls. In order to display any statistical information on your site, at least one of the first three controls must be set to Yes.

- **Server Information.** Set to Yes to display basic information about your server, including the operating system, the time, whether caching or GZip are enabled, and the version number of your PHP and MySQL installations. The default setting for this control is No.

- **Site Information.** Set to Yes to display basic information about your site and its contents, including the number of members, content items, and weblinks. The default setting is No.

- **Hit Counter.** Set to Yes to display how many views your content items have received. The default setting is No.

- **Increase Counter.** Enter an integer value here to increase the number of hits shown on the Hits counter.

FIGURE 18.15

The output of the Statistics module

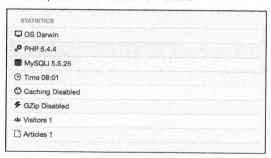

The Advanced Options tab of the Statistics module does not contain any unique fields.

Using the Title module

The Title module displays the page title that appears on many of the interior admin system pages. The default system includes one Title module, as shown in Figure 18.16.

FIGURE 18.16

The output of the Title module

> **NOTE**
>
> The system name for this module type is `mod_title`.

This module does not include a Basic Options tab. The Advanced Options tab does not have any unique fields.

> **NOTE**
>
> Caching is not available for this module type.

Enabling the Toolbar module

The Toolbar module provides the buttons that appear at the top of the admin pages. These buttons provide quick access to essential tasks throughout the system. The output of this module is essential for the site administrator. Figure 18.17 shows the module output.

FIGURE 18.17

The Modules Manager uses a typical toolbar.

> **NOTE**
>
> The system name for this module type is `mod_toolbar`.

This module does not include a Basic Options tab. The Advanced Options tab does not have any unique fields.

Configuring the User Status module

The User Status module supplies the icons that appear on the bottom toolbar of each admin system page. You can configure this module to provide the following information: a link to the preview function, the current number of visitors to the front end of the site, the number of users logged in, how many messages the user has, and a link to log out of the system. Figure 18.18 shows the module in action.

FIGURE 18.18

The output of the User Status module is shown in the default position.

The Basic Options tab provides three controls:

- **Show logged-in users.** Set to Yes to display the number of users logged in to the front end of the site.
- **Show logged-in backend users.** Set to Yes to display the number of back-end users who are logged in.
- **Show messages.** Set this option to Yes to show the current count of the user's unread messages.

The Advanced Options tab does not have any unique fields.

18

Summary

In this chapter, I reviewed the Joomla! Administrator modules, which are the modules used on the back end of the website. This chapter focused on understanding all the module options and how you can use them on your site. The topics included

- Understanding the Administrator Modules Manager interface
- Creating new modules
- Duplicating modules to save time and effort
- Editing and deleting existing modules
- Reviewing all 15 of the system's Administrator modules

In the next chapter, I discuss the plug-ins that are included in your Joomla! installation.

Working with Plug-Ins

P lug-ins are small, specialized pieces of code that typically run only when triggered by an
event. Plug-ins are used as "helper" applications, providing additional functionality or
extending existing Joomla! functions.

The default Joomla! system includes 46 plug-ins. They provide a number of significant and useful functions, including login authentication, site search, search engine–friendly URLs, and the
WYSIWYG content editor. Although not all of the 46 plug-ins are enabled in the default configuration, the system uses most of them. Several of the plug-ins are essential to the proper functioning of your Joomla! site and should only be disabled if you fully understand the implications and
have planned accordingly.

In this chapter I introduce the management interface for plug-ins and then review all of the 46
plug-ins so that you understand what they do and how you can configure them to suit your
needs.

> **NOTE**
> Plug-ins first appeared in Joomla! with the release of version 1.5. Prior to version 1.5, the system used helper exten-
> sions called mambots. Although mambots and plug-ins are similar in function, they are not identical and cannot be
> interchanged.

Introducing the Plug-in Manager

Plug-ins are a type of extension. Like modules, templates, and Language Packs, plug-ins have
their own dedicated management interface. The Joomla! plug-ins are controlled through the
Plug-in Manager. The manager contains all the system plug-ins, together with any third-party
plug-ins you may have installed. To view the plug-ins in your site, you need to log in to the
admin system and go to the Extensions menu. You then select the Plug-in Manager option, and
the Plug-in Manager loads in your browser window, as shown in Figure 19.1.

FIGURE 19.1

The Plug-in Manager, showing the plug-ins in Joomla! 3

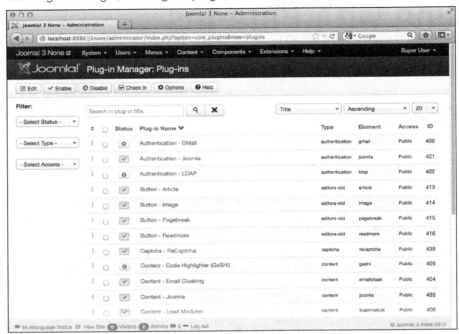

The toolbar at the top of the Plug-in Manager provides quick access to the following functions:

- **Edit.** Select a plug-in from the list and then click this button to edit the plug-in.
- **Enable.** Select one or more plug-ins from the list and then click this button to enable them. You enable a plug-in to make it active on the site.
- **Disable.** Select one or more plug-ins from the list and then click this button to disable them.
- **Check In.** Select one or more plug-ins from the list and then click this button to force the plug-in editing workspaces to close and thereby "check in" the plug-ins.
- **Options.** Click to open the Plug-in Manager Options workspace, where you can configure the permissions to use the Plug-in Manager.

NOTE

Plug-in Manager permissions work consistently with the Permissions tab in the Global Configuration Manager. See the discussion on setting permissions in Chapter 10 to learn more.

- **Help.** Click to access the online Help files related to the active screen.

Located below the toolbar in the left column, are three sorting tools to help you manage long lists of plug-ins:

- **Select Status.** Use this combo box to filter and display the plug-ins according to whether they are published, unpublished, or trashed. This provides an easy way to identify all plug-ins that are currently active on the site. To reset this filter, change the combo box back to the default setting, Select Status.

- **Select Type.** Use this combo box to filter the list by the plug-in type. To reset this filter, change the combo box back to the default setting, Select Type.

- **Select Access.** Use this combo box to filter the list of plug-ins by access level. To reset this filter, change the combo box back to the default setting, Select Access.

> **TIP**
> You can combine the filters to further refine the view of the list of plug-ins.

Below the toolbar and above the list of plug-ins are four sorting and searching tools:

- Type a word or phrase into the field marked Search in plug-in title, and then click the magnifying glass button. The system searches your list of plug-ins for the query and then displays the results of the search. To clear the screen and return to a full listing, click the button marked with the X.

- Use the combo box to the right of the Search field to specify which column of the plug-ins display is used for the sort order.

> **TIP**
> You can also sort any column by clicking the column header.

- Use the Ascending combo box to specify whether the plug-ins appear in ascending or descending order.

- Use the combo box on the far right to specify the number of plug-ins that appear on the page. You can alter the default value by changing the List Length parameter in the Global Configuration Manager.

The main content area of the screen contains a list of all the plug-ins in your Joomla! site. The columns provided are

- **Sort Order (vertical double arrows).** This column allows you to change the sort order of the plug-ins. Click the arrows to change the sort order; you can also click and hold any of the buttons immediately to the left of a plug-in's title and then drag the plug-in to change its order location in the Plug-in Manager.

- **Plug-in Selection (unlabeled check box).** This column allows you to select individual plug-ins. Click a check box to select a plug-in; this is necessary if you want to use several of the toolbar options.

19

- **Status.** This field shows the status of the plug-in. A green check mark indicates that the plug-in is enabled, while a red x indicates that it is disabled.
- **Plug-in Name.** This field displays the full name of the plug-in. Click the name to edit the plug-in.
- **Type.** This field displays the type of the plug-in. Each plug-in can be of only one type.
- **Element.** This field displays the name of the directory that holds the plug-in's files. For example, in the case of the Authentication - Joomla plug-in, the value in the Element field is "joomla." This means you can find the files for this plug-in on the server in the directory `plugins/authentication/joomla`.
- **Access.** This field indicates the access level assigned to the plug-in.
- **ID.** This field shows the system-generated ID number.

 See Chapter 22 for a discussion on adding new plug-ins, and turn to Chapter 21 to learn how to create plug-ins.

Modifying plug-ins

You can edit existing plug-ins from the Plug-in Manager. To edit a plug-in, you either click the plug-in name in the Plug-in Manager, or select the plug-in on the list and then click the Edit icon on the Plug-in Manager toolbar. Regardless of which method you use, the system opens the Edit Plug-in workspace.

To make changes to a plug-in, you simply alter the desired fields in the Edit Plug-in workspace and then click the Save button on the toolbar. Any changes you make are applied immediately.

> **NOTE**
> You can delete plug-ins from the Manage workspace of the Extensions Manager. I cover deleting extensions in Chapter 22.

Reviewing the Default Plug-ins

The workspace of each of the 46 default plug-ins follows the same general pattern: a common toolbar and two tabs. The two tabs are labeled Details and Basic Options. The Details tab is identical for all the plug-in types. The Basic Options tab holds the parameters that are unique to each plug-in. Only a handful of plug-ins break from this pattern, either because they lack a Basic Options tab, or because they have one or more additional tabs. A typical plug-in workspace is shown in Figure 19.2.

FIGURE 19.2

A typical plug-in workspace, in this case, the Authentication - LDAP plug-in. The Toolbar and Details sections are the same for all plug-in types; the Parameters section varies by plug-in type.

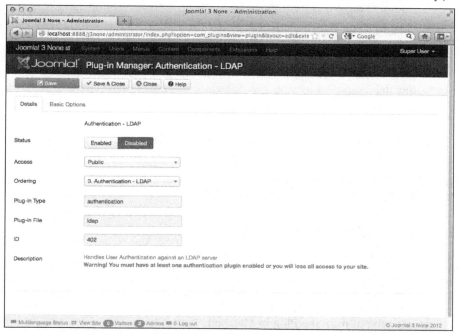

The toolbar at the top of the plug-in workspace provides quick access to the following functions:

- **Save.** Click to save your work without exiting the plug-in workspace. This option lets you save without exiting the screen, and is useful if you are interrupted or if you want to save your work but remain in this workspace.
- **Save & Close.** Click to save your work and exit the plug-in workspace.
- **Close.** Click to cancel the task and exit the plug-in workspace.
- **Help.** Click to display the Help files related to the active screen.

The Details tab of all the plug-ins carries the same set of fields:

- **Status.** This field allows you to specify the status of the plug-in. Select Enabled to make the plug-in active; select Disabled to deactivate the plug-in.
- **Access.** This field allows you to specify the access level of the plug-in. Choose from Public, Registered, or Special to set the access level. Setting the plug-in to a level higher than Public may result in some functionality working incorrectly for some site visitors.

- **Ordering.** This field allows you to specify the order of the plug-in relative to other enabled plug-ins of the same type. The order impacts the sequence in which plug-ins are activated and so may affect some functionality in limited circumstances. Do not change this from the default setting without a compelling reason.

- **Plug-in Type.** This identifier is set by the system and tells you the type of plug-in. You cannot edit this field.

- **Plug-in File.** This field allows you to specify the name of the plug-in file. Each plug-in has two files associated with it, one PHP and one XML. You cannot edit this field.

- **ID.** This field displays the system-generated ID for the plug-in. You cannot edit this field.

- **Description.** This field displays descriptive text provided by Joomla! to help users understand the purpose of the plug-in.

The Basic Options tab content varies for each plug-in. I discuss the details of the parameters for each plug-in in the sections that follow.

Using Authentication plug-ins

The Authentication plug-ins are responsible for handling the user authentication processes in Joomla!. The system offers several alternative methods for handling authentication. The default method is the system-specific Joomla plug-in. Alternatives include GMail, and LDAP. In the default configuration, only the Authentication - Joomla plug-in is active. If you want to use any of the alternative methods, you need to enable and configure the appropriate plug-in from the Plug-in Manager.

NOTE

The Authentication plug-in files are located in the `plug-ins/authentication` directory.

GMail

The GMail Authentication plug-in allows users to log in to your Joomla! site using their Gmail user ID. Although the Joomla! system includes the GMail Authentication plug-in, this plug-in is not enabled in the default system. If you want to enable your site to accept logins with Gmail credentials, then you need to enable the plug-in and follow the steps outlined in the text that follows. The plug-in's workspace is shown in Figure 19.3.

FIGURE 19.3

The Authentication - GMail plug-in workspace, showing the Basic Options tab

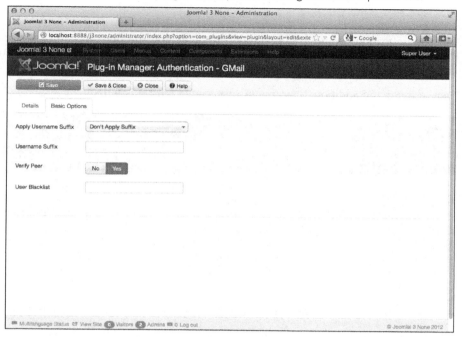

The Basic Options tab includes the following parameters:

- **Apply Username Suffix.** In the case of Gmail authentication, suffix refers to what comes after the @ sign in the user's e-mail address. Typically, this is gmail.com. If you want to support Gmail accounts that don't end with the usual @gmail.com suffix, then you need to set this parameter to add the suffix, and then enter the permitted suffix in the Username Suffix field.

- **Username Suffix.** If you want to support e-mail addresses that don't end with the usual @gmail.com suffix, enter the suffix here and set the Apply Username Suffix parameter to add the suffix.

- **Verify Peer.** If you want the system to check to make sure the certificate of the SSL connection is valid, set this option to Yes. Gmail authentication occurs over SSL.

- **User Blacklist.** If you want to block individuals from logging in, use this field to enter their usernames. Separate multiple names with commas.

19

To use the GMail plug-in for authentication on your site, the user must have an account on your site with the same username they use for Gmail.

Joomla!

The Authentication - Joomla! plug-in powers the default Joomla! authentication scheme. This plug-in is enabled in the default system and should not be disabled unless you have made provisions for alternative authentication.

There are not any additional parameters associated with this plug-in.

> **CAUTION**
>
> Do not disable this plug-in if you have not enabled an alternative Authentication plug-in. Leaving the system without active Authentication plug-ins causes problems and may block the users' ability to log into the site.

LDAP

The Authentication - LDAP plug-in allows you to configure your site to connect with an LDAP server. LDAP, or *Lightweight Directory Access Protocol*, is used in some systems to access directory systems over TCP/IP. The LDAP plug-in is bundled with the Joomla! system, but it is not enabled in the default configuration. If you want to use this plug-in, you need to enable it and set the configuration parameters. The plug-in workspace is shown in Figure 19.4.

The Authentication - LDAP plug-in offers the following parameters on the Basic Options tab:

- **Host.** Enter the URL of the LDAP server.
- **Port.** Set the Port to be used for the connection to the LDAP server. The default setting is 389.
- **LDAP V3.** Select Yes if your system is using LDAP V3.
- **Negotiate TLS.** Select Yes to employ TLS encryption for traffic to and from the server.
- **Follow Referrals.** Select Yes to set the LDAP_OPT_REFERRALS flag to Yes.
- **Authorisation Method.** Specify the authorization method you want to use in the LDAP connection. The default option is Bind Directly as User, and the alternative is Bind and Search.
- **Base DN.** Enter the Base DN of your LDAP server.
- **Search String.** Enter the query string to search for a user. This field supports multiple query strings, separated by semicolons.
- **User's DN.** Enter a string that dynamically matches the username typed by the user with the DN pattern of the user entry in LDAP. This is only used if the Authorisation Method option is set to Bind Directly as User.
- **Connect Username.** Specify the username needed to negotiate the DN phase of the connection. For an anonymous connection, leave this field blank. If you enter a value here, you also need to complete the Connect Password field.

- **Connect Password.** Specify the password needed to negotiate the DN phase of the connection. For an anonymous connection, leave this field blank. The password is related to the Connect Username.
- **Map: Full Name.** Enter the name of the LDAP attribute that contains the user's full name.
- **Map: email.** Enter the name of the LDAP attribute that contains the user's e-mail address.
- **Map: User ID.** Enter the name of the LDAP attribute that contains the user's user ID.

FIGURE 19.4

The Authentication - LDAP plug-in workspace, showing the Basic Options tab

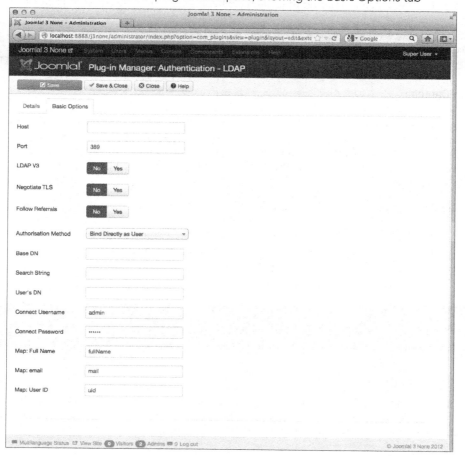

LDAP setup can be confusing, largely due to the number of options that exist on both sides of the equation — the LDAP server and the Joomla! CMS. There are also several third-party extensions that you can add to your system to make LDAP more useful with features such as Single Sign On and Kerberos support. A good place to start is with this article in the Joomla! Community Magazine: `http://community.joomla.org/ component/zine/artic`

Captcha plug-ins

Captcha is a challenge response technique for helping verify that a form is being submitted by a human being. It is used to block robots and scripts used by spammers and hackers trying to gain fraudulent access to a system. Captcha is only one of a number of methods used to help secure forms, but it is one of the most effective. It is also familiar to users and therefore a desirable approach to decreasing invalid form submissions. Joomla! incorporates the ReCaptcha variation of Captcha. There is only one plug-in in this category.

> **NOTE**
> The Captcha plug-in files are located in the `plug-ins/captcha` directory.

ReCaptcha

ReCaptcha is a free Captcha protocol from Google. The text phrases users are required to type are selected from books that have been digitized by optical character readers. The input from the users is fed back into the system to validate the text used in the digital editions of the books, thereby turning your users into a resource for helping digitize out-of-print books and old texts. This plug-in is disabled by default. The plug-in's Basic Options tab is shown in Figure 19.5.

The Basic Options tab includes the following parameters, all of which are required:

- **Public Key.** Enter the public key value from Google here.
- **Private Key.** Enter the private key value from Google here.
- **Theme.** Select the skin you want for the ReCaptcha output on the front end of the site; there are four different skins to choose from.

> **NOTE**
> To get a public key and private key for your domain, visit `www.google.com/recaptcha`.

Content plug-ins

The Content plug-ins provide various enhancements to the Joomla! articles. With the exception of the GeSHi Code Highlighter plug-in, all plug-ins are enabled and are used by the default system. Few parameters exist for this group of plug-ins.

FIGURE 19.5

The Captcha - ReCaptcha plug-in workspace, showing the Basic Options tab

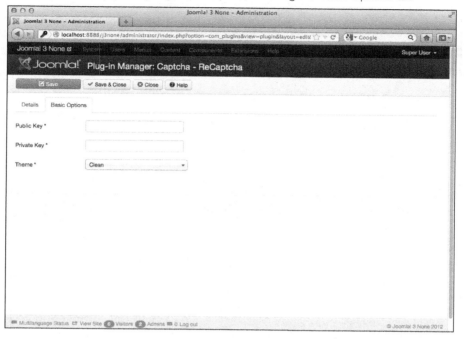

Code Highlighter (GeSHi)

The Code Highlighter plug-in adds GeSHi style formatting to any code you display to visitors on your site. This plug-in is useful when the articles on your site include samples of code displayed in the articles for site visitors to see. GeSHi makes the code more readable by adding standardized code formatting to the text. This plug-in is disabled by default; if you want to use it, you must enable it.

No parameters are associated with this plug-in.

Email Cloaking

The Email Cloaking plug-in provides your site with a measure of protection against spam spiders and bots that try to harvest unprotected e-mail addresses from websites. The plug-in works by hiding the e-mail addresses in your content items from the bots. This plug-in is enabled by default. The plug-in's workspace is shown in Figure 19.6.

FIGURE 19.6

The Content - Email Cloaking plug-in workspace, showing the Basic Options tab

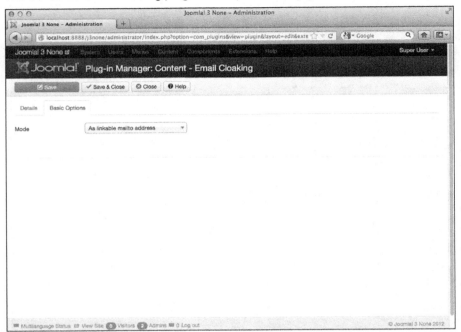

The Email Cloaking plug-in's Basic Options tab contains only one control: Mode. This parameter determines the technique used to hide the e-mail address. The default, As linkable mailto address, uses JavaScript to hide the e-mail address from spiders and bots, yet still allows the address to be functional and clickable. The other option, Non-linkable Text, simply converts the e-mail address to text and strips out any link to the e-mail functionality.

TIP

If you want to disable cloaking selectively, you can do so by inserting the following tag anywhere in the article:

```
{emailcloak=off}
```

Joomla

The Joomla plug-in handles several housekeeping tasks for your content items, for example, processing items by category and sending email notifications related to content. The plug-in is enabled by default. The plug-in's workspace is shown in Figure 19.7.

FIGURE 19.7

The Content - Joomla plug-in workspace, showing the Basic Options tab

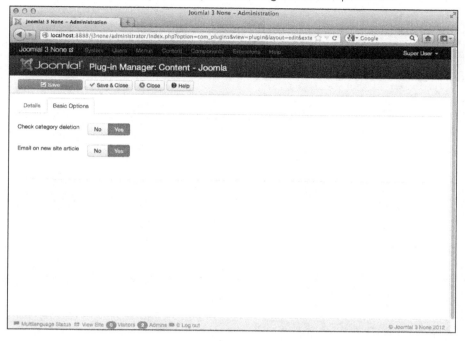

The Basic Options tab contains two settings:

- **Check category deletion.** Select Yes to have the system check that a category is empty prior to deletion. If you do not care whether the category is empty, you can set this option to No.

CAUTION

If you are working on a site with multiple administrators, setting this option to No is potentially dangerous!

- **Email on new site article.** Select Yes to have the system send an e-mail to the administrators when a new article is submitted from the front end of the site. Note that an administrator has to set her preference to accept e-mail notifications or she will not receive e-mails, regardless of how you set this parameter.

Load Modules

The Load Modules plug-in enables you to add modules inside of the content area of articles. This plug-in exists in the default system and is enabled. The plug-in's Basic Options tab is shown in Figure 19.8.

 See Chapter 7 for more on working with modules inside of articles.

FIGURE 19.8

The Content - Load Modules plug-in workspace, showing the Basic Options tab

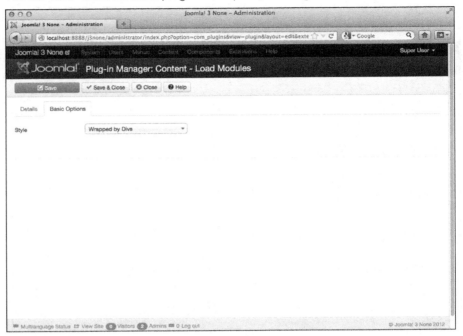

The Basic Options tab contains only one option, Style. The options in this combo box determine how the system handles the styling of the module position. The options are Wrapped by table (column); Wrapped by table (horizontal); Wrapped by Divs; Wrapped by Multiple Divs; and No wrapping (raw output).

TIP

Managing the styling of modules inserted inside of articles can be a challenge. If you are uncertain which style approach is best for your purposes, try the various options, viewing the source code of the resulting article that contains the module. In this way you can find the approach that works best for you and provides you with the selectors you need to style the module appropriately.

Page Navigation

The Page Navigation plug-in supplies the back, next, and numbered page features you see in certain content areas of the site. This plug-in is enabled by default. The plug-in's Basic Options tab is shown in Figure 19.9.

FIGURE 19.9

The Content - Page Navigation plug-in workspace, showing the Basic Options tab

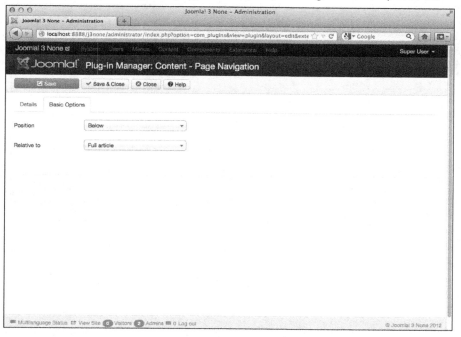

The Basic Options tab contains the following options:

- **Position.** Choose Above or Below to place the pagination controls above or below the article; the Relative to control determines how the system defines the article area.

- **Relative to.** This control determines whether the pagination is placed above or below the body text, or above or below the full article, including title or other information.

> **NOTE**
>
> If you want to hide the Page Navigation feature on your articles, it is not necessary to disable the plug-in, although that is one option. The easiest way to control this feature is through the site's Global Configuration and through the parameters associated with menu items.

Pagebreak

The Pagebreak plug-in enables the creation of multipage articles with tables of contents. This plug-in supplies the Page Break button that you see beneath the text box in the Joomla! article editing workspace. The plug-in is enabled by default. The plug-in's Basic Options tab is shown in Figure 19.10.

FIGURE 19.10

The Content - Pagebreak plug-in workspace, showing the Basic Options tab

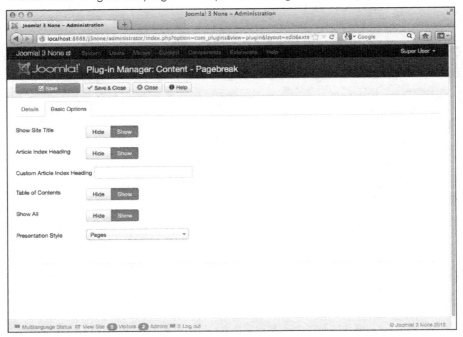

The Basic Options tab contains the following options:

- **Show Site Title.** Show or hide Title and Heading attributes as part of the title tag for the pages. This option becomes available when you use the Page Break feature.

- **Article Index Heading.** Show or hide the Custom Article Index Heading at the top of the table of contents created by the Page Break feature.

- **Custom Article Index Heading.** Specify the content if you have chosen to show the Article Index Heading.

- **Table of Contents.** Show or hide the table of contents for the multipage article.

- **Show All.** Show or hide the full text of the article.

- **Presentation Style.** Display multiple pages as pages, tabs, or sliders.

 See Chapter 5 for a more in-depth discussion on how to create multipage articles and tables of contents.

Smart Search

The Content - Smart Search plug-in powers the indexing of content for the Smart Search component. If you want to use Smart Search, you must enable this plug-in; otherwise, leave it disabled. There are no additional parameters associated with this plug-in.

Vote

The Vote plug-in enables the article ratings functionality in Joomla! This plug-in is enabled by default. There are not any parameters associated with this plug-in.

> **NOTE**
>
> If you want to hide the Vote feature in your articles, it is not necessary to disable the plug-in, although that is one option. The most flexible way to control this feature is through the site's Global Configuration Manager and through the parameters associated with menu items.

Editors plug-ins

The Editors plug-ins add various content item–editing options to the system. This family of plug-ins provides WYSIWYG editor functionality and plain text editor functionality. All three of the default editors are enabled by default.

> **CAUTION**
>
> You must have at least one of the Editor plug-ins installed to access your content items in the admin system.

The question of which editor, if any, is used throughout the site is determined by the settings in the Global Configuration Manager. The options that appear on that screen are the result of enabling the various plug-ins. A user can also select her preferred editor from her user page.

 I discuss working with the various editors to create and edit content in detail in Chapter 6.

19

> **NOTE**
>
> The Editor plug-in files are located in the `plug-ins/editors` directory.

CodeMirror

The CodeMirror plug-in is intended to make it easier to work with the articles in Code view. It provides a number of features that make editing the code easier and is an improvement over the plain text editor and over working with the HTML window of TinyMCE. The plug-in's Basic Options tab is shown in Figure 19.11.

FIGURE 19.11

The Content - CodeMirror plug-in workspace, showing the Basic Options tab

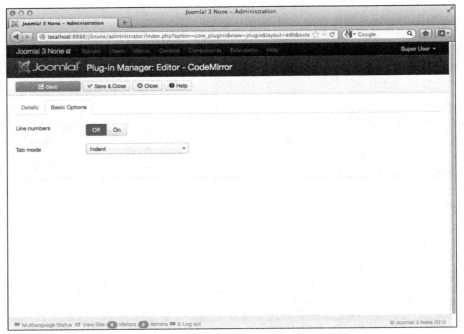

The plug-in's Basic Options tab includes only configuration parameters:

- **Line numbers.** Show or hide the line numbers in the editing window.
- **Tab mode.** Select the function that the Tab key performs. The options are either Indent or Shift.

None

The None plug-in supplies the basic text editor option for content items. There is not a WYSIWYG editor associated with this option. If the system is set to None, then content creation is done in a plain text interface, where the content creator needs to add HTML tags to achieve formatting; it is the most basic editing option in Joomla!.

No parameters are associated with this plug-in.

TinyMCE

The TinyMCE plug-in enables the powerful TinyMCE WYSIWYG editor. TinyMCE is enabled by default both in the Plug-ins section and in the Global Configuration Manager. The Content - TinyMCE plug-in is one of the few system plug-ins that have additional tabs. The plug-in has the standard Details tab as well as a Basic Options tab and another tab labeled Advanced parameters; both the Basic Options and Advanced parameters tabs are discussed next. The plug-in's Basic Options tab is shown in Figure 19.12.

NOTE

If you have the TinyMCE editor enabled, users can still edit the HTML of the article by clicking the HTML button on the TinyMCE toolbar.

FIGURE 19.12

The Editor - TinyMCE plug-in workspace, showing the Basic Options tab

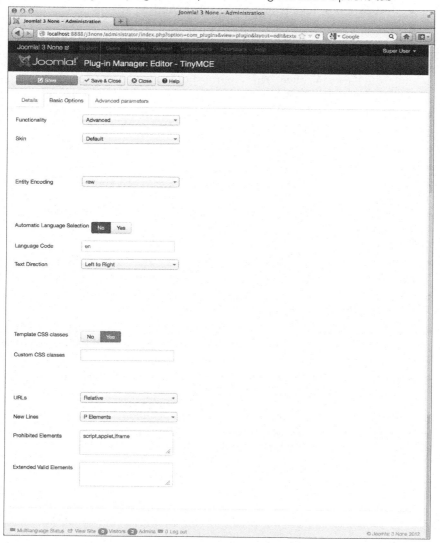

The TinyMCE plug-in offers a large number of configuration and customization options. The parameters are divided into two categories: Basic Options and Advanced parameters.

The parameters in the Basic Options tab apply to the editor in all configurations, Simple, Advanced, or Extended. The options include the following:

- **Functionality.** Select either a very basic editor or a more complex and full-featured version. The default setting is Advanced, which gives the user access to the full toolbar and all available options.
- **Skin.** Choose which skin you want the editor to use.
- **Entity Encoding.** Specify how characters are encoded. The options are
  - **Named.** Converts characters to named entities
  - **Numeric.** Converts characters to numerical entities
  - **Raw.** Stores characters in non-entity form
- **Automatic Language Selection.** Select No (the default) if there are not any Language Packs installed. This control should only be enabled where the site has multiple Language Packs installed.
- **Language Code.** Enter the default language to be used in the interface if the Automatic Language Selection parameter is set to No.
- **Text Direction.** Specify whether the text reads right-to-left or left-to-right.
- **Template CSS classes.** Select Yes to let the editor use the style selectors from the template's CSS file. Note that this can be overridden by the Custom CSS Classes parameter.
- **Custom CSS Classes.** Specify a particular Cascading Style Sheet to be used by the editor. If you enter a value in this field, it overrides the settings in the Template CSS classes parameter.
- **URLs.** Select either Absolute or Relative to control whether URLs to pages inside your site include the `http://` and primary domain prefix.
- **New Lines.** Specify whether the editor treats a new line in an article as a P (paragraph) element or a BR (line break) element.
- **Prohibited Elements.** List any HTML elements you want to be automatically cleaned out of articles. The default value for this field is applet, which prevents applets from being inserted into articles.
- **Extended Valid Elements.** Enter additional HTML tags that you want to be able to use, beyond those defined in the default editor.

The Advanced parameters tab includes a small set of elements that apply to all the editor's modes, but the majority of controls on this tab are only applicable if you set the Functionality parameter on the Basic Options tab to Extended mode.

> **TIP**
>
> A number of the options on this tab deal with advanced functionality. If you are confident that the person who is using the editor can use these tools safely, then it is helpful to have many of these options enabled. On the other hand, if you have concerns about your content editors, then you should be careful when enabling functions; some of them give the user more power to stray from the site standards, as well as the ability to introduce items or changes that may be undesirable.

The Advanced parameters include

- **Toolbar.** Specify whether the editor's toolbar appears above or below the text editing window.

- **Toolbar align.** Specify how the toolbar is aligned relative to the text editing window.

- **HTML Height.** Enter an integer value to set the height of the HTML editing pop-up window. The value is measured in pixels.

- **HTML Width.** Enter an integer value to set the width of the HTML editing pop-up window. The value is measured in pixels.

- **Resizing.** Select On to give the user the ability to drag and resize the height of the editing window.

- **Horizontal resizing.** Select On to give the user the ability to drag and resize the width of the editing window.

- **Element Path.** Select On to enable the display of the Element Path immediately below the editing window. The Element Path is an aid to accessibility and makes it simpler to navigate through the styling in the editing window, one element at a time.

- **Fonts.** Show or hide the combo box fonts on the editor toolbar.

- **Paste.** Show or hide the Paste button on the editor toolbar.

- **Search-Replace.** Show or hide the Search and Replace button on the editor toolbar.

- **Insert Date.** Show or hide the Insert Date button on the editor toolbar. Note that the Date Format parameter is related.

- **Date Format.** Specify the date format you want to use. The date format is used by the Insert Date command. The default is %Y-%m-%d, which means Year-Month-Day.

- **Insert Time.** Show or hide the Insert Time button on the toolbar. Note that the Time Format parameter is related.

- **Time Format.** Specify the time format you want to use. The time format is reflected in the time shown when you use the Insert Time command on the toolbar. The default is %H.%M.%S, which means Hour.Minute.Second.

- **Colours.** Show or hide on the editor toolbar the button that opens a color picker.

- **Smilies.** Show or hide the Smilies button on the editor toolbar.

19

- **Media.** Show or hide the Media button on the editor toolbar; this button allows the user to insert various types of embedded media.
- **Horizontal Rule.** Show or hide the Horizontal Rule button on the editor toolbar.
- **Directionality.** Show or hide the Directionality button on the editor toolbar; this button allows you to alter the text read direction.
- **Fullscreen.** Show or hide the Fullscreen button on the editor toolbar.
- **Style.** Show or hide the CSS Style button on the editor toolbar.
- **Layer.** Show or hide the Layer button on the editor toolbar.
- **XHTMLxtras.** Show or hide the additional XHTML features on the editor toolbar.
- **Visualchars.** Show or hide the Show Hidden Characters button on the editor toolbar; when clicked, this button displays any invisible characters in the editing window, such as nonbreaking spaces.
- **Visualblocks.** Show or hide the Show Blocks button on the editor toolbar; when clicked, this button shows the outline of HTML block elements in the editing window.
- **Nonbreaking.** Show or hide the button to insert nonbreaking space characters on the editor toolbar.
- **Template.** Show or hide the Template button on the editor toolbar.
- **Blockquote.** Show or hide the Blockquote button on the editor toolbar.
- **Wordcount.** Show or hide the Word Count button on the editor toolbar.
- **Advanced image.** Turn On or Off the user's ability to access the advanced features of the Insert Image dialog box.
- **Advanced link.** Turn On or Off the user's ability to access the advanced features of the Insert Link dialog box.
- **Advanced List.** Turn On or Off the user's ability to access the advanced features of the Insert List dialog box.
- **Save Warning.** Select On to warn users if they try to exit an article without saving.
- **Context menu.** Turn On or Off the context menus.
- **Inline pop-ups.** Select On if you want the system to use inline floating displays instead of pop-ups. This is useful for editors who are using browsers that have pop-up blockers.
- **Custom plug-in.** Add any custom plug-ins to TinyMCE by specifying them here.
- **Custom button.** Add any custom buttons to TinyMCE by specifying them here.

> **TIP**
>
> TinyMCE supports the addition of custom plug-ins to allow you to add your own functionality to the editor for your site. For a good discussion of what's involved in creating a TinyMCE plug-in, visit `www.tinymce.com/wiki.php/Creating_a_plug-in`.

Editors XTD plug-ins

The Editors XTD plug-ins are a set of utilities that extend the functionality of the content editors and the content items. The three plug-ins enable the three buttons that you see below the content editing window when creating or editing an article. All of these plug-ins are enabled by default. None of these plug-ins include additional configuration parameters.

> **NOTE**
>
> The Editors XTD plug-in files are located in the `plug-ins/editors-xtd` directory.

Button - Article

The Article plug-in enables you to easily insert links to other articles within the body of your articles. The plug-in is enabled by default and does not contain any additional parameters.

Button - Image

The Image plug-in displays the Image button below the editing window. Clicking this button produces a window that allows you to insert and configure images inside of content items. The plug-in does not contain any additional parameters.

> **TIP**
>
> The Image button is redundant to controls that exist on the TinyMCE and XStandard WYSIWYG editors. If you have either of these editors enabled, then you may want to disable the Image plug-in.

Button - Pagebreak

The Pagebreak plug-in enables the Pagebreak button that appears below the content editing window. Clicking this button inserts a page break into an article, thereby turning a single-page article into a multipage article. The plug-in does not contain any additional parameters.

> **TIP**
>
> The TinyMCE editor also provides page-break functionality. If you have enabled TinyMCE, you may want to consider disabling this control, as it is redundant.

Button - Readmore

The Readmore plug-in displays the Read More button below the content editing box. Clicking this button allows you to separate the first part of the article from the remainder and shows a Read more link that leads the viewer to the full article. The plug-in does not contain any additional parameters.

19

Extension plug-ins

The Extension group of plug-ins contains only one plug-in. That plug-in is named Extension -Joomla and its purpose is to monitor the various sites needed for tracking updates to your extensions. There are no configurable parameters for the plug-in. If you are using the update notifications function in the Extensions Manager, do not disable this plug-in.

Finder plug-ins

The Finder group of plug-ins enables the Smart Search component's indexing of various aspects of your site. The various plug-ins enable the indexing and searching of different types of content articles, weblinks, contacts, categories, sections, and newsfeeds. All the plug-ins in the default installation are enabled. Disabling a particular plug-in results in the related content being excluded from the Smart Search index and search results.

> **NOTE**
>
> The Search plug-in files are located in the `plug-ins/search` directory.

> **TIP**
>
> If you are using the basic Joomla! Search component instead of Smart Search, you should disable all the plug-ins in this group.

Categories

The Smart Search - Categories plug-in powers the indexing of your site's categories. Though this is enabled by default, it does not serve any function unless you have set up Smart Search. If you want to exclude your categories from being indexed, disable this plug-in. The plug-in does not contain any additional parameters.

Contacts

The Smart Search - Contacts plug-in powers the indexing of the content of your Contacts component. Though this plug-in is enabled by default, it does not serve any function unless you have set up Smart Search. If you want to exclude the Contacts component from being indexed or you are not using the Contacts component, then you should disable this plug-in. The plug-in does not contain any additional parameters.

Content

The Smart Search - Content plug-in powers the indexing of your site's articles. Though this plug-in is enabled by default, it does not serve any function unless you have set up Smart Search. If you want to exclude your articles from being indexed, disable this plug-in. The plug-in does not contain any additional parameters.

Newsfeeds

The Smart Search - Newsfeeds plug-in powers the indexing of contents of your Newsfeed component. Though this plug-in is enabled by default, it does not serve any function unless you have set up Smart Search. If you want to exclude your newsfeeds from being indexed, or you are not using the Newsfeed component, then you should disable this plug-in. The plug-in does not contain any additional parameters.

Weblinks

The Smart Search – Weblinks plug-in powers the indexing of the content of the Weblinks component. Though this plug-in is enabled by default, it does not serve any function unless you have set up Smart Search. If you want to exclude your weblinks from being indexed, or you are not using the Weblinks component, then you should disable this plug-in. The plug-in does not contain any additional parameters.

Quickicon plug-ins

The Quickicon group of plug-ins enables the update functionality for both the Joomla! core and for your extensions. You don't want to disable these plug-ins unless your site is behind a firewall and does not have a connection to either the Internet or a local update repository.

> **NOTE**
>
> The Search plug-in files are located in the `plug-ins/search` directory.

Joomla! Extensions Updates Notification

This plug-in checks for available updates to your extensions and then notifies you via an alert on the Control Panel. The plug-in's Basic Options tab contains only one control, Group. The value in the Group field tells the system where to look for the icons displayed in the updates notifications in the admin interface.

Joomla! Update Notification

This plug-in checks for available updates to the Joomla! core and then notifies you via an alert on the Control Panel. The plug-in's Basic Options tab contains only one control, Group. The value in the Group field tells the system where to look for the icons displayed in the updates notifications in the admin interface.

> **NOTE**
>
> The `mod_quickicon` value displays the default Joomla! system icons.

19

Search plug-ins

The Search group of plug-ins enables Joomla's basic site search functionality and is related to the Search component. Different plug-ins enable the searching of different types of content articles, weblinks, contacts, categories, sections, and newsfeeds. All the plug-ins in the default installation are enabled. Disabling a particular plug-in results in the related content being excluded from the search results.

> **NOTE**
> The Search plug-in files are located in the `plug-ins/search` directory.

> **TIP**
> If you are using Smart Search instead of the basic Joomla! Search component, you should disable all the plug-ins in this group.

Categories

The Categories plug-in enables the indexing and searching of the categories content. Disable this plug-in if you do not want the categories to appear in the search results. The plug-in's Basic Options tab is shown in Figure 19.13.

FIGURE 19.13

The Search - Categories plug-in workspace, showing the Basic Options tab

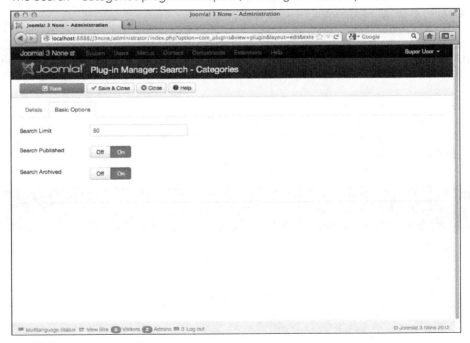

The Basic Options tab contains the following options:

- **Search Limit.** Enter an integer value in this field to specify the maximum number of search results to return.
- **Search Published.** Turn On or Off searching of published categories.
- **Search Archived.** Turn On or Off searching of archived categories.

Contacts

The Contacts plug-in enables the indexing and searching of the contacts in your site. Disable this plug-in if you do not want the contents of your Contacts component to appear in the search results. The plug-in's Basic Options tab is shown in Figure 19.14.

The Basic Options tab contains the following options:

- **Search Limit.** Enter an integer value in this field to specify the maximum number of search results to return.
- **Search Published.** Turn On or Off searching of published contacts.
- **Search Archived.** Turn On or Off searching of archived contacts.

FIGURE 19.14

The Search - Contacts plug-in workspace, showing the Basic Options tab

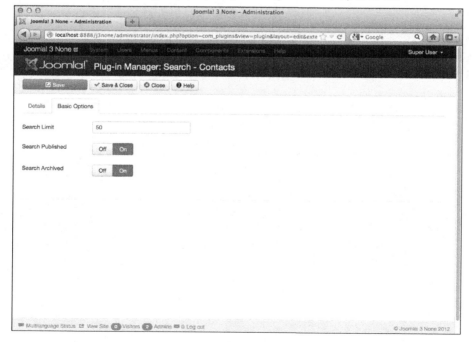

Content

The Content plug-in enables the indexing and searching of articles on your site. Disable this plug-in if you do not want the articles to appear in the search results. The plug-in's Basic Options tab is shown in Figure 19.15.

FIGURE 19.15

The Search - Content plug-in workspace, showing the Basic Options tab

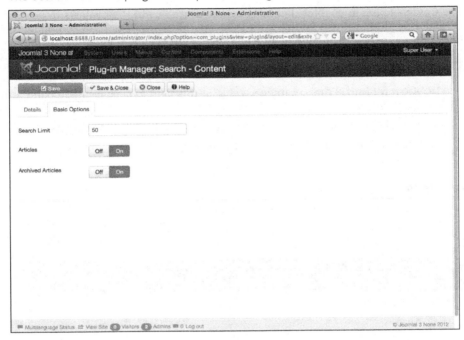

The Basic Options tab contains the following options:

- **Search Limit.** Enter an integer value in this field to specify the maximum number of search results to return.
- **Articles.** Select No to exclude articles from the search results. The default setting is Yes.
- **Archived Articles.** Select No to exclude archived articles from the search results. The default setting is Yes.

Newsfeeds

The Newsfeeds plug-in enables the indexing and searching of newsfeed items. Disable this plug-in if you do not want the content of the Newsfeed component to appear in the search results. The plug-in's Basic Options tab is shown in Figure 19.16.

FIGURE 19.16

The Search - Newsfeeds plug-in workspace, showing the Basic Options tab

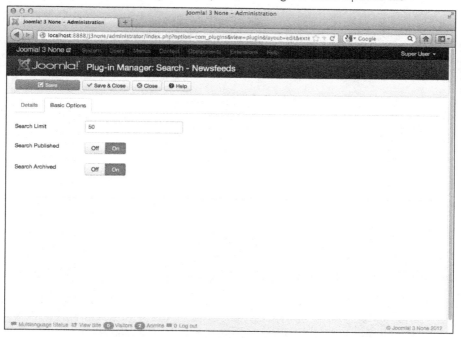

The Basic Options tab contains the following options:

- **Search Limit.** Enter an integer value in this field to specify the maximum number of search results to return.
- **Search Published.** Turn On or Off searching of published newsfeeds.
- **Search Archived.** Turn On or Off searching of archived newsfeeds.

Weblinks

The Weblinks plug-in enables the indexing and searching of weblink items. Disable this plug-in if you do not want the contents of the Weblinks component to appear in the search results. The plug-in's Basic Options tab is shown in Figure 19.17.

FIGURE 19.17

The Search – Weblinks plug-in workspace, showing the Basic Options tab

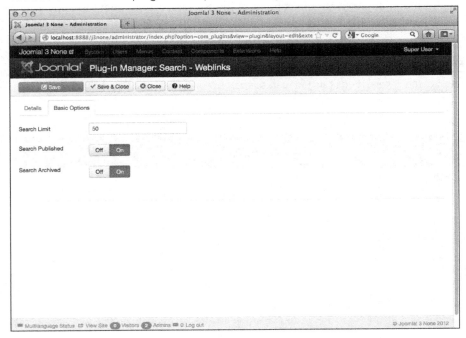

The Basic Options tab contains the following options:

- **Search Limit.** Enter an integer value in this field to specify the maximum number of search results to return.
- **Search Published.** Turn On or Off searching of published weblinks.
- **Search Archived.** Turn On or Off searching of archived weblinks.

System plug-ins

The System plug-ins provide a variety of global system functions, from caching to debugging. Of the eleven plug-ins in this category, only eight are published. The other three plug-ins (Language Filter, Language Code, and Cache) provide functions that not all users may want or need.

NOTE

The System plug-in files are located in the `plug-ins/system` directory.

Cache

The Cache plug-in enables page caching on your Joomla! site. This parameter is independent of the caching controls contained in the Global Configuration Manager. By default, this plug-in is disabled. To use it on your site, you need to enable and configure it. The plug-in's workspace is shown in Figure 19.18.

FIGURE 19.18

The System - Cache plug-in workspace, showing the Basic Options tab

The Basic Options tab contains only one parameter, Use Browser Caching. This control allows you to tap into the local caching function of the viewer's browser, assuming the browser permits this to occur.

Debug

The Debug plug-in is used to display information about the system that is intended to be of use in debugging a site. When active, the Debug plug-in outputs the information at the bottom of the screen in your browser. The Debug plug-in is disabled in the default configuration and you should only activate it during development or when you are trying to solve a problem with your site and need access to this information. Note that this plug-in is one of the few that include more than two tabs. The plug-in has a total of four tabs: the standard Details tab, a Basic Options tab, a Language Options tab, and a Logging tab; each is discussed in this section. The plug-in's Basic Options tab is shown in Figure 19.19.

FIGURE 19.19

The System - Debug plug-in workspace, showing the Basic Options tab

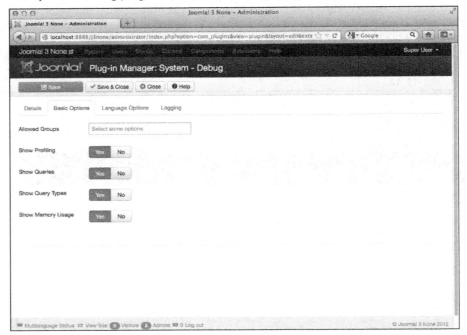

The Basic Options tab contains the following options:

- **Allowed Groups.** When this plug-in is enabled (the default setting), all user groups can see debugging output. If you want to restrict the visibility of the output to specific groups, click this field and select the user groups from the list that appears.

- **Show Profiling.** When set to Yes, this option includes the time profiling information in the debugging output.

- **Show Queries.** When set to Yes, this option includes the SQL query log in the debugging output.

- **Show Query Types.** When set to Yes, this option includes a list of the types of queries and their frequency.

- **Show Memory Usage.** When set to Yes, this option includes the memory usage data in the debugging output.

The Language Options tab contains options that are primarily relevant to multilingual websites. The configuration parameters on this tab include

- **Show errors when parsing language files.** When set to Yes, the debugging information includes a list of errors in language files, according to the Joomla! language specifications.
- **Show Language Files.** When set to Yes, this option includes information on the loaded language file(s) in the debugging output.
- **Show Language Strings.** When set to Yes, the system displays a list of untranslated strings.
- **Strip First Word.** When set to Yes, the system always strips the first word in multi-word strings.
- **Strip From Start.** When you want to instruct the system to strip words from the start of the strings, enter them in this field.
- **Strip From End.** When you want to instruct the system to strip words from the end of the strings, enter them in this field.

The Logging tab includes only one configuration option: Log deprecated API. When set to Yes, the system displays in the debugging information a notification if an API is deprecated.

Highlight

The Highlight plug-in is a utility plug-in that powers the highlighting of certain terms. There are not any configuration options for this plug-in.

Language Code

The Language Code plug-in enables page caching on your Joomla! site. This parameter is independent of the caching controls contained in the Global Configuration Manager. By default, this plug-in is disabled. To use it on your site, you need to enable and configure it. However, there are not any configuration options for this plug-in.

Language Filter

The Language Filter plug-in is a utility for use in multilingual websites. When enabled, the plug-in makes it possible to edit the language code used in the generated HTML for the pages. Once you enable and save the plug-in, a new tab, Language codes, appears. Figure 19.20 shows the plug-in's workspace with the Language codes tab visible.

To use this utility, click the Language codes tab, and then simply type in the field provided whatever code you want to use for each language.

19

FIGURE 19.20

The System - Language Code plug-in's workspace, shown enabled with the Language codes tab visible

Log

The Log plug-in provides optional system logging. When enabled, the plug-in maintains a log file of website activity. By default, this plug-in is disabled. The plug-in's workspace is shown in Figure 19.21.

The Basic Options tab of this plug-in contains only one configuration option: Log user names. Set this to Yes to add active user sessions to the log files.

> **TIP**
>
> The Log plug-in is a great aid to debugging a site; however, if you do not need it, you should disable it because it generates an additional load on the server.

Logout

The Logout plug-in serves a very narrow function: It redirects users to the home page of the site when they log out from within a restricted area of the site. If your site has front-end users, do not disable this plug-in. If your site does not allow front-end users, then feel free to disable this plug-in. There are not any configuration options for this plug-in.

FIGURE 19.21

The System - Log plug-in workspace, showing the Basic Options tab

P3P Policy

The P3P Policy plug-in is a utility used to tailor sessions management to work properly with the Internet Explorer browser. By default, this plug-in is enabled; don't disable it. The plug-in's Basic Options tab is shown in Figure 19.22.

The plug-in has only one configurable parameter on the Basic Options tab: P3P Tags. Use the field provided to add any additional P3P policy tags you require.

NOTE

To learn more about The Platform for Privacy Preferences 1.0 (P3P1.0) Specification, visit www.w3.org/TR/P3P/.

Redirect

The Redirect plug-in is a system utility that helps the Joomla! system catch missing pages and redirect users appropriately. This plug-in is enabled by default; do not disable it. No parameters are associated with this plug-in.

FIGURE 19.22

The System - P3P Policy plug-in's Basic Options tab

Remember Me

The Remember Me plug-in supplies the functionality that allows the website to remember a visitor and thereby avoid prompting her to log in again. This plug-in is enabled by default. No parameters are associated with this plug-in.

> **TIP**
>
> If site security or the preservation of personal data and identity is paramount for your site, then this plug-in should be disabled, thereby removing the possibility that the site will enable an unauthorized person to use an authorized account.

SEF

The SEF plug-in enables the use of search engine–friendly URLs in the articles on your site. This plug-in is independent from the Search Engine Friendly option in the Global Configuration Manager. The plug-in is enabled in the default installation. The plug-in's Basic Options tab is shown in Figure 19.23.

FIGURE 19.23

The System - SEF plug-in's Basic Options tab

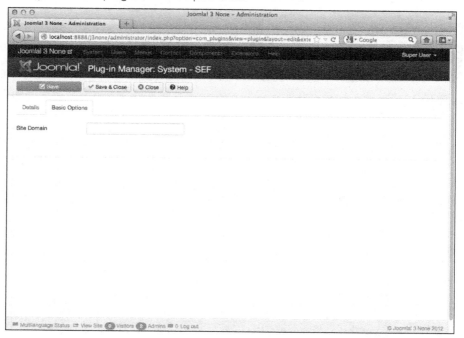

The Basic Options tab contains only one configurable parameter: Site Domain. This is a canonical URL control. You use the field to exactly specify the primary domain for the site and what formulation you want to use, such as www.yourdomain.com or simply yourdomain.com.

Enabling User plug-ins

The User plug-ins are dedicated to enabling functionality related to your site users. There are only three plug-ins in this group, and only one of them is enabled by default. Read the following summaries of these plug-ins to determine whether you want to enable the other two plug-ins on your site.

Contact Creator

When enabled, the Contact Creator plug-in automatically creates contact information for all new users. By default, this plug-in is disabled. To use it on your site, you need to enable and configure it. The plug-in's Basic Options tab is shown in Figure 19.24.

FIGURE 19.24

The User - Contact Creator plug-in workspace, showing the Basic Options tab

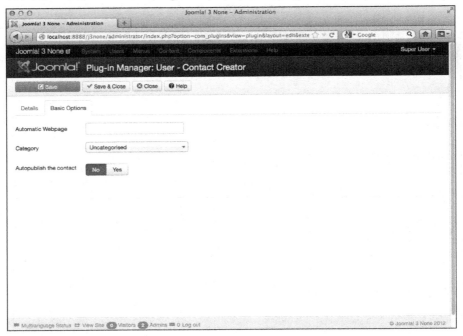

The Basic Options tab contains three options:

- **Automatic Webpage.** Specify the URL for the contact's profile page if you want the system to automatically generate a link to that page. Note that this does not actually create the page, it simply creates a link you can use for the page. You can use one or more of the following variables to create the URL, for example, http://yourdomain.com/[username].

  - **[name].** The system substitutes the user's real name.
  - **[username].** The system substitutes the user's username.
  - **[userid].** The system substitutes the user's user ID.
  - **[email].** The system substitutes the user's e-mail address of record.

- **Category.** Select the default category to which all new contacts will be assigned.

- **Autopublish the contact.** Select Yes to automatically publish the user's contact. Select No to require manual publishing by a site administrator.

Joomla!

The Joomla! plug-in is used by the system to handle user synchronization. This is an essential plug-in and is enabled in the default configuration. The plug-in's workspace is shown in Figure 19.25.

FIGURE 19.25

The User - Joomla! plug-in's workspace, showing the Basic Options tab

The Basic Options tab contains two options: Auto-create Users and Notification Mail to User. Set the Auto-create Users control to Yes to allow the system to automatically create users without administrator intervention. Set Notification Mail to User to enable the system to send a notification email to the users upon successful registration for your site.

> **Caution**
>
> Disabling this plug-in results in users being unable to log in to the site!

Profile

The Profile plug-in enables user profile functionality on your Joomla! site. The configuration parameters allow you to specify which fields are shown in the new user registration form and the editable profile page. By default, this plug-in is disabled. To use it on your site, you need to enable and configure it. The plug-in's workspace is shown in Figure 19.26.

The numerous fields on the Basic Options tab are relatively self-explanatory: For each option, you can select Required, Optional, or Disabled. These options control what is shown on the registration form and on the profile edit form. The only exception is the Select TOS Article field. This field is provided so that you can set up a Terms of Service page and then link to it for the registration form.

19

FIGURE 19.26

The User - Profile plug-in workspace, showing the Basic Options tab

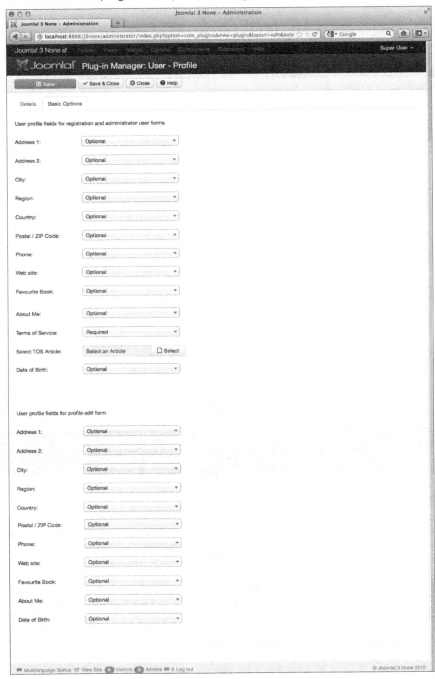

Summary

In this chapter, I covered the use of the Joomla! plug-ins. The topics included

- Using the Plug-in Manager
- Editing plug-ins
- Understanding the core plug-ins, including their optional parameters

In the next chapter, I look at how to customize the system, starting with the Joomla! templates.

19

Part IV

Customizing and Extending the System

P art IV moves into how to customize the appearance and functionality of the system. The first chapter in this section takes an in-depth look at Joomla! templates. I explain how the templates work, how to customize their appearance, and even how to create your own templates from scratch. There is also discussion of template frameworks and examples of using Twitter Bootstrap in Joomla! 3. The next chapter looks at the core components, modules, and plug-ins, with an eye towards explaining the underlying MVC architecture, and how the elements work. Customization of the components and modules is also covered. The final chapter in this section looks at extending your Joomla! website. In that chapter, I also look at a set of extensions you can add to Joomla! 3 to address common website issues.

Customizing the Appearance of Joomla!

IN THIS CHAPTER

Reviewing the default templates

Understanding the role played by templates

Customizing template styles

Duplicating styles

Assigning styles

Modifying templates

Creating new templates

Overriding module and component output

One of the joys of working with the Joomla! system is the ease with which you can create an attractive website. Unlike many other content management systems that lock you into a standardized, cookie-cutter approach to site design, Joomla! has great flexibility. The presentation layer is controlled through the use of templates. A template is a collection of files that work together to handle the layout and presentation of your site. Your default Joomla! site comes with two site templates and two administrator templates. You can work with these, add new templates, or create your own. In addition, the system uses a feature known as template styles. Using styles, you can create multiple variations of a single template and assign those styles to various pages of your site. Taken together, Joomla! templates and styles give you the freedom to create exactly the site appearance you desire.

This chapter takes you through the basics of understanding how Joomla! templates work and then digs more deeply to explain how you can customize an existing template or even go farther and build your own template from scratch.

Exploring the Default Templates

The Joomla! default distribution includes a set of templates to help you get started. These templates may be sufficient for your needs, or they may serve as a base for your customization efforts. Regardless, they offer a great set of examples of what can be done with the Joomla! system and provide you with an opportunity to learn. In Joomla! 3.x, there are two front-end templates and two back-end templates:

- Front-end templates
  - Beez3
  - Protostar
- Back-end templates
  - Hathor
  - Isis

Reviewing the site templates

The Beez template is included in the default Joomla! 1.5.x distribution. More than any of the other default templates, Beez makes heavy use of CSS formatting and provides a number of overrides. The overrides are specifically designed to replace the table-based presentation of the core's modules and components.

Beez3

Beez has been part of the Joomla! distribution for a number of years. The version included with Joomla! 3 is the latest evolution of the design. The template is part of the default installation but is not set as the default template. If you want to see Beez3 in action, you need to enable it.

If you have installed the Learn Joomla! sample data, you will find that Beez3 is offered in two styles: the Default style and an additional style called Fruit Shop. The Fruit Shop style is included to provide an example of using template styles and is assigned to the pages relating to the Fruit Shop sample site.

The template, with the Default style applied, is shown in Figure 20.1.

FIGURE 20.1

The Beez3 template, shown in the Default style with the sample data installed

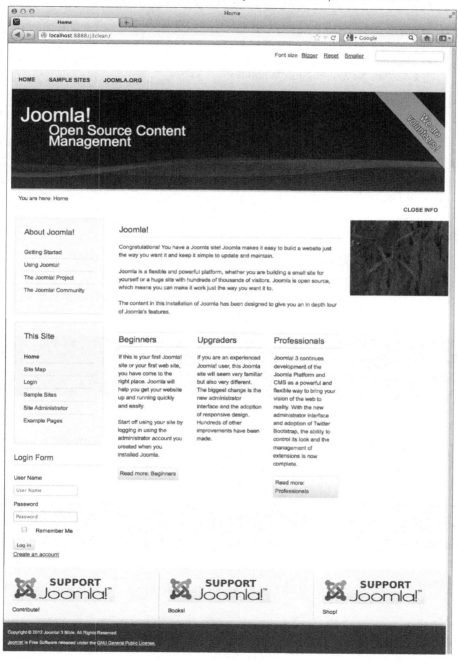

The Beez3 template includes the following attributes and features:

- The template's files are located at /templates/beez.
- The CSS files are located at /templates/beez/css.
- The overrides are located at /templates/beez/html.
- The template provides overrides for four of the core components: Contacts, Content, Newsfeed, and Weblinks.
- The template provides an override for only one module, the Breadcrumbs module.
- The template overrides the default Module chrome at /templates/beez/html/ modules.php.
- The template includes 11 module position holders, plus one additional holder intended for user with the Debug module.
- The template includes a font-sizer functionality, which you can see at the top right of Figure 20.1.

The Beez3 template also includes a number of style options that you can edit directly from the administration interface:

- Ability to configure wrapper sizes
- Ability to alter the position of the navigation menu
- Ability to change color schemes; there are five color schemes to choose from.
- Ability to change the header image

> **TIP**
>
> For additional information above the Beez3 template, including a guide to the CSS, visit the dedicated page on the Joomla! docs site at http://docs.joomla.org/Beez.

Protostar

Protostar is the new site template included with Joomla! 3. This template is also set as the default template; it's what you see the first time you look at the front end of Joomla! 3. The template uses Twitter Bootstrap extensively, as well as the elements of the Joomla! User Interface library.

> **TIP**
>
> Twitter Bootstrap is discussed in more detail later in this chapter.

In the default Joomla! installation, Protostar is bundled with only one style. The template is shown in Figure 20.2.

FIGURE 20.2

The Protostar template is shown with the sample data installed.

The Protostar template includes the following attributes and features:

- The template's files are located at /templates/protostar.
- The CSS files are located at /templates/protostar/css.
- The overrides are located at /templates/protostar/html.
- The template overrides the default Module chrome at /templates/protostar/html/modules.php.
- The template overrides the default pagination styling at /templates/protostar/html/pagination.php.
- The template includes eight module position holders, plus one additional module holder intended for use by the Debug module.

The Protostar template also includes two style options that you can edit directly from the administration interface:

- Support for Google fonts for site headings.
- Ability to select either fixed width or fluid width.

 For an evaluation of the accessibility of both Beez3 and Protostar, see Chapter 24.

Reviewing the administrator templates

Joomla! 3 comes with two administrator templates, offering your site administrators their choice of interfaces. The default template is called Isis, and the alternative template, Hathor. Each template offers a choice of configuration options through the Styles workspace of the Template Manager.

Hathor

The Hathor template is visually reminiscent of the admin interface of previous editions of Joomla!. The template supports a slightly narrower range of options than Isis, but it does provide a nice alternative if you are familiar with the old interface. Hathor is not enabled by default.

The template is shown in Figure 20.3.

The Hathor template includes the following attributes and features:

- The template's files are located at /administrator/templates/hathor.
- The CSS files are located at /administrator/templates/hathor/css.
- The template provides overrides for all the core components, which are located at /administrator/templates/hathor/html.
- The menu module has a specific override, which is located at /administrator/templates/hathor/html/mod_menu.
- The template overrides the default Module chrome at /administrator/templates/hathor/html/modules.php.
- The template overrides the default pagination styling at /administrator/templates/hathor/html/pagination.php.

The default style for the template includes the following configurable options, which you can adjust directly from the Template Manager's Style workspace:

- Select one of the four color variations, including a high-visibility option for improved accessibility.
- Set the admin interface to use bold text, thereby enhancing readability, if accessibility is a concern.

FIGURE 20.3

The Hathor administrator template

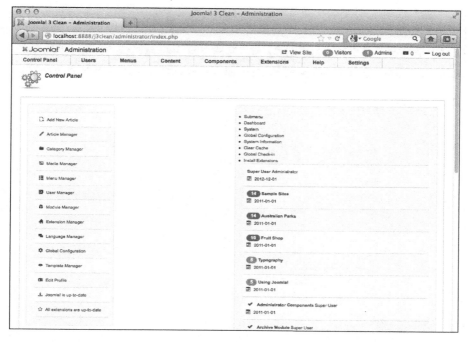

Isis

The default administrator template in Joomla! 3 is Isis. Compared to the previous Joomla! admin interface, Isis takes a completely different approach with a new layout that emphasizes responsive design. The template also includes a number of options that can be managed from the default style. The template is shown in Figure 20.4.

The Isis template includes the following attributes and features:

- The template's files are located at /administrator/templates/isis.
- The CSS files are located at /administrator/templates/isis/css.
- The overrides are located at /administrator/templates/isis/html.
- The template overrides the default Module chrome at /administrator/templates/isis/html/modules.php.
- The template overrides the messaging styling at /administrator/templates/isis/html/modules.php.
- The template overrides the default pagination styling at /administrator/templates/isis/html/pagination.php.

FIGURE 20.4

The Isis administrator template

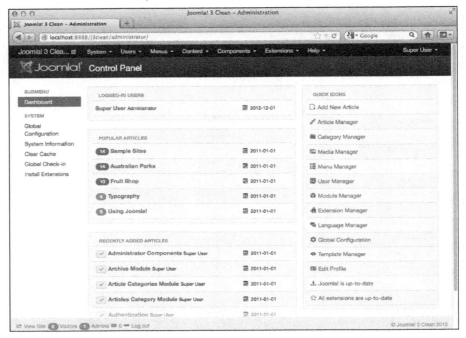

The default style for the template includes the following configurable options, which you can adjust directly from the Template Manager's Style workspace:

- You can modify the color of the navigation bar and the header.
- You can set the administrator menu to automatically collapse or be fixed to display.
- You can hide the header.
- You can assign the status module to multiple positions.
- You can fix the toolbar in place or set it to sticky to allow it to remain visible at all times.

> **TIP**
>
> Looking for more help with the default templates? There is a dedicated Joomla! 3 templates thread on the Joomla! Forum. Visit http://forum.joomla.org/viewforum.php?f=713.

Finding the Module Positions on a Page

It is sometimes useful to be able to quickly identify the module positions that are active on the page you see in your browser. Although you can always look up the names of the positions in the template's XML file, preview the template in the Template Manager, or open up the template's code and look where the module position holders have been inserted, sometimes you just want to see where they are on the rendered page with the published items in place. To do this, follow these steps:

1. Open the page in your browser and look at the URL that appears in the browser's address bar.

2. If there are not any parameters displayed at the end of the URL, append "?tp=1" to the URL and click the Refresh button. The module positions will be outlined and lightly shaded, with the name of the position appearing in red.

3. If there are parameters at the end of the URL, append "&tp=1" to the URL and click the Refresh button. The module positions will be outlined and lightly shaded, with the name of the position appearing in red.

Note that this shows you all active module positions, regardless of whether anything is published to them; the one exception is if the template has made the appearance of module positions conditional and that condition is not being met.

Understanding How Templates Work

The Joomla! template files are responsible for what your visitors see on the screen. When a visitor to your website clicks a link, it sets off a process that culminates in the production of a web page inside his browser. The final step in that process is the rendering of the page inside the template. Though some elements, such as modules and components, have their own layouts that control the look and feel of a particular bit of output, all of those various elements are brought together inside the template.

As you will see in the next section, a template is a set of files; it is not one single item. The various parts of the template work together to format the final page output. Typically the template works as a frame, providing the final layout and design that you see on the page, while the content inside that frame is produced by the various functional elements of the site. The template also controls all of the text and the colors on the screen, via the template's CSS files.

While some modules and components may influence the site's look and feel, the template has the most control over the presentation. This creates an opportunity for you; by gaining a better understanding of the template's options, you are able to tailor the site output to suit your needs.

20

> **NOTE**
>
> If you are new to Joomla! templates, one of the key concepts you need to grasp is that designing templates is very different from designing traditional web pages. Whereas in a traditional web page design you have to fix everything on each page inside a separate file, in Joomla! template design you are creating the outer shell only, and you then call other output for display inside this structure. This template is then used for multiple pages.

As I just noted, a template is actually a collection of files that work together. In this section, I outline the basic files that are needed and their roles in the system. Note that some templates are more complex than others and may include a large number of additional files. The discussion of the default templates in the next section demonstrates the variation that can occur with different approaches to template design.

Locating the template directories

All front-end templates are kept inside the `/templates` directory located at the root of the Joomla! installation. All back-end templates are kept in `/administrator/templates`. Inside the `/templates` directory, each template has its own directory named for the template. For example, the default Protostar template's files are found at `/templates/protostar`.

Inside the individual template's directory, you typically find

- **A** `/css` **directory** containing the CSS files needed by the template
- **An** `/html` **directory** containing overrides, if any
- **An** `/images` **directory** containing any images specifically needed by the template
- **A** `/javascript` **directory** containing any scripts needed by the template

The template may also have other directories, as defined by the template developer.

Reviewing the key files

At a minimum, a Joomla! template includes the following files:

- `index.php`
- `template.css`
- `templateDetails.xml`
- `template_thumbnail.png`

I discuss each of these key files in detail in the following sections.

index.php

`index.php` is the key file in the template. This file contains the HTML formatting for the page layout and the statements that include the component and module output. The file provides a standard document head and then outlines the page's `div` structure and places all the element position holders on the page. Elements are positioned on the page through the use of `jdoc:include` statements.

The `include` statements use the syntax `jdoc:include type="nameoftype"`. The available `jdoc` include types are

- **component** `<jdoc:include type="component" />` This is used only once in the template to set the placement of the main content area for the page.

- **head** `<jdoc:include type="head" />` This is used only once in the template to set the style, script, and meta elements inside the template's `<head>` area.

- **installation** `<jdoc:include type="installation" />` This is only used in the Joomla! installer template and should not appear in your site or admin template's `index.php` file.

- **message** `<jdoc:include type="message" />` This is used only once in the template. It is placed inside the `<body>` area where you want system messages to appear on the page.

- **module** `<jdoc:include type="module" name="modulename" />` This is used to place a single module on the page. Additional attributes to control the layout and appearance may be available.

- **modules** `<jdoc:include type="modules" name="modulepositionname" />` This is used to place the module position holders in the template. Additional attributes to control the layout and appearance may be available.

> **NOTE**
>
> Module position holders must not only be placed into the `index.php` file but must also be declared in the `templateDetails.xml` file, discussed shortly.

An `index.php` file may or may not use all the available types; however, it will certainly use at least the head, component, message, and module types, as these are the minimum types needed to construct a useable template.

template.css

The styling of templates is handled by Cascading Style Sheets. Although a template is very likely to have multiple CSS files, the key file is `template.css`, which is located inside the template's `/css` directory. This file is typically used to set the page width and margins, the placement of the elements on the page, as well as the look of the fonts, backgrounds, borders, and so on.

20

templateDetails.xml

This is an enabling file; it is not directly involved in the display of contents on the page. The file contains information that is needed by the Joomla! installer and the Template Manager. It also includes the definition of the template parameters for the Template Manager and the declaration of the module position holders for use by the Module Manager.

The file provides the following key information:

- The descriptive information for the installer and the Template Manager
- The declaration inside the `<files>` tags of all the files in the package for the installer
- The declaration inside the `<positions>` tags of all the module position holders for the Module Manager
- The declaration inside the `<param>` tags of the template parameters that are available in the Template Manager

template_thumbnail.png

This file is the thumbnail image of the template that is shown inside the Template Manager. It is only used in the admin system. The image file is generally 206 x 150 pixels in size. Although the system supports JPEG, GIF, and PNG, the preferred format is PNG.

Using the Joomla! Template Manager

All of the system's templates, both site templates and administrator templates, are managed from within the Joomla! Template Manager. The Template Manager gives you access to the templates and their related styles. The interface contains all the controls you need to manage the appearance of your website, and is the doorway to the workspaces where you can modify your templates and styles. To access the Template Manager, you click the option of the same name under the Extensions menu.

In this section, I look at both the Templates and Styles interfaces, and discuss what you can see there and the tools they provide.

Viewing templates and styles

The Template Manager is divided into two spaces: Templates and Styles. The default landing page is the Styles workspace of the Template Manager. Clicking the Template Manager option under the Extensions menu displays the output shown in Figure 20.5.

FIGURE 20.5

The Template Manager interface, showing the Styles landing page

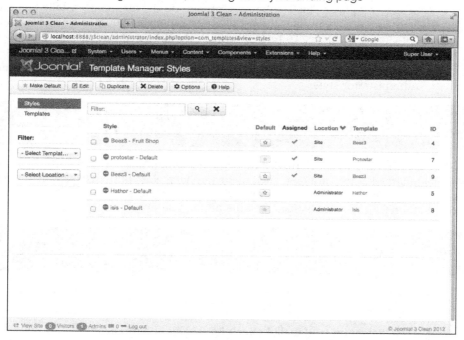

The toolbar at the top of the Template Manager: Styles workspace provides quick access to the following functions:

- **Make Default.** Select a style from the list and then click this button to set the style as the default.
- **Edit.** Select a style from the list and then click this button to edit the style's details.
- **Duplicate.** Select a style from the list and then click this button to make a copy of the style.
- **Delete.** Select a style from the list and then click this button to delete the style. Note that every template must have at least one style.

20

- **Options.** Click to access the configuration options for the Template Manager.
- **Help.** Click to access the online Help files related to the active screen.

In the left column, below the toolbar, are additional navigation tools. At the top of the column are two links: Styles shows you the Template Manager: Styles workspace, and Templates takes you to the Template Manager: Templates workspace, discussed shortly. Located below the Site and Templates links, in the left column, are two sorting tools to help you manage long lists of styles:

- **Select Template.** This combo box contains all the templates installed on the site. Select a template to filter the list of styles and display only those styles related to the chosen template. To reset this filter, change the combo box back to the default setting, Select Template.
- **Select Location.** This control simply lets you choose between Site styles and Administrator styles.

TIP
You can combine the filters to further refine the view of the list of styles.

Below the toolbar and above the list of styles is a search tool. Type a word or phrase into the field marked Filter: and then click the magnifying glass button. The system searches your list of styles for the query and then displays the results of the search. To clear the screen and return to a full listing, click the button marked with the X.

TIP
You can also sort any column by clicking the column header.

The main content area of the Template Manager: Styles workspace contains a list of all the styles in your Joomla! site. The columns provided are

- **Style Selection (unlabeled check box).** This column allows you to select a style by clicking the check box next to the style; this is necessary if you want to use any of the toolbar options, referenced in the preceding list.
- **Style.** This column displays the name of the style. Click the name to edit the style's details.
- **Default.** This column shows which style is selected as the default style. A yellow star indicates the default style. There is always one default style for the site templates, and another default style for the administrator templates.
- **Assigned.** This column shows how styles are applied. If a green check mark appears in this column, it indicates that the style is assigned to one or more specific menu items. If there is nothing in this column, it means the style is applied throughout the site.
- **Location.** This column indicates whether the template is a site template or an administrator template.

- **Template.** This column shows the name of the template to which this style applies.
- **ID.** This column shows a system-generated identification number for the style.

The second Template Manager interface you need to be familiar with is the Templates workspace. Clicking the Templates option in the left column takes you to the Template Manager: Templates workspace, shown in Figure 20.6.

FIGURE 20.6

The Template Manager: Templates interface

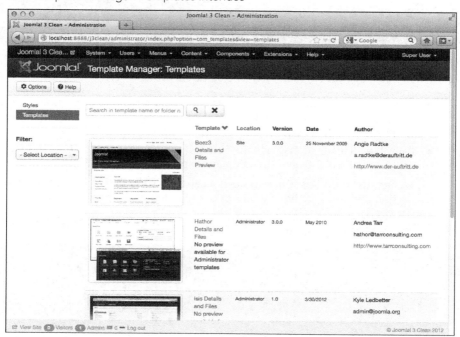

The toolbar at the top of the Template Manager: Templates workspace provides quick access to the following functions:

- **Options.** Click to access the configuration options for the Template Manager.

- **Help.** Click to access the online Help files related to the active screen.

The left column below the toolbar contains additional navigation tools. At the top of the column are two links: Styles shows you the Template Manager: Styles workspace, discussed previously. Templates takes you to the Template Manager: Templates workspace. Located below the Site and Templates links in the left column is a combo box labeled Select Location. This control simply lets you choose between Site styles and Administrator styles.

Below the toolbar and above the list of templates is a search tool. Type a word or phrase into the field marked Search in template name or folder name, and then click the magnifying glass button. The system searches your list of templates for the query and then displays the results of the search. To clear the screen and return to a full listing, click the button marked with the X.

> **TIP**
> You can also sort any column by clicking the column header.

The main content area of the Template Manager: Templates workspace contains a list of all the templates in your Joomla! site. The columns provided are

- **Screenshot (no label).** This image is supplied by the template author, so the contents will vary; it simply offers you a convenient way to distinguish between templates.
- **Template.** This field displays the name of the template. Click the name to edit the template's details. Below the template name are two links:
  - **Details and Files.** Click to open a separate page with more template information and links to the key files of the template.
  - **Preview.** Click to open a preview of the template in a new window, showing the module position holders on the page.

> **TIP**
> The Preview button does not show by default. To display this button, and thereby have an easy way to both see what the template looks like and figure out the module positions, go to the Template Manager Configuration Options, and set the Preview Module Positions control to Enabled.

- **Location.** This value indicates whether the template is a site template or an administrator template.
- **Version.** This is the version number of the template.
- **Date.** This is the date the template was created.
- **Author.** This is the author of the template, typically with contact details.

 See Chapter 22 for a discussion of how to add new extensions, including templates, to your Joomla! site.

Setting the default style

The default style appears on all pages where another style is not specifically assigned. When styles are not assigned to any pages, the default style is shown throughout the site. There can be only one default Site style and one default Administrator style. Default styles are clearly shown in the Template Manager: Styles workspace; they are marked with a gold star in the Default column, as shown in Figure 20.5.

To change the default style, follow these steps:

1. **Log in to the admin system of your site.**

2. **Access the Template Manager by selecting the Template Manager option under the Extensions menu.** The Template Manager: Styles workspace loads in your browser.

3. **Click the check box next to the style you want to make the default style.**

4. **Click the Make Default button on the toolbar.** A yellow star appears in the Default column by the style of your choice. The new style immediately becomes active as the site's default style.

Assigning styles

If you want to use more than one style on your site, you can do so by assigning styles to specific menu items on the site. This feature allows you to tailor specific styles to specific types of content. You can, for example, use different headers for different sections of the site, or use dedicated color schemes for particular sections. Simply duplicate the styles you need, modify them, and then assign them to your menu items.

> **NOTE**
> I discuss duplicating and modifying styles in the next section. If you need more flexibility than what is provided by your templates' style options, you need to either install a different template that meets your needs, or clone and modify an existing template and make your changes to the template files. I cover creating and modifying templates later in this chapter.

The Edit Style workspace provides you with the tools to assign styles. There is not a limit to the number of styles you can use; if you want, you can use a different style for each section or even each page of your site. Styles can even be applied from multiple templates. You can see this technique in action if you have installed the Learn Joomla! sample data. The sample data uses both Beez and Protostar.

To assign a template to a specific page, follow these steps:

1. **Log in to the admin system of your site.**

2. **Select the Template Manager option under the Extensions menu.** The Template Manager: Styles workspace loads in your browser.

3. **Click the name of the style you want to assign.** The Edit Style workspace opens.

20

4. **Click the Menus assignment tab.** The tab comes to the front, as shown in Figure 20.7.

5. **Click the names of the menu items where you want this style to appear.**

6. **Click the Save button on the toolbar.** The style immediately becomes active for the menu items you have selected.

TIP

If you want to make a page eligible for style assignment, the page must have a menu item associated with it; otherwise, the default style is assigned to the page.

FIGURE 20.7

The Edit Style workspace, showing the Menus assignment tab

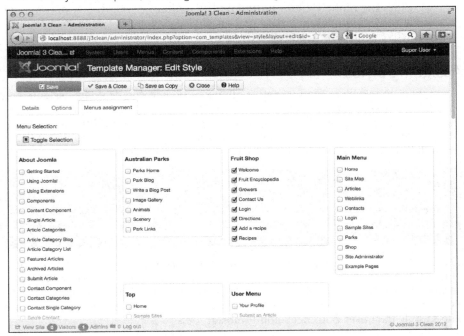

Customizing Template Styles

The easiest way to modify a template is to work with the template styles. Put simply, styles are variations on a template. Each style comes with a variety of parameters that you can use to tailor the template to your needs. The system also provides you with the ability to duplicate styles with just the click of a button, thereby allowing you to create specific styles that you can then assign to specific menu items on your site. The ability to alter style parameters, plus the ability to create duplicate styles and then assign them, makes template styles a valuable tool in managing the presentation layer of your website.

> **NOTE**
>
> The range of options presented by styles is dictated by decisions made by the template's creators. Available style options vary from template to template and may not address your specific needs. While you can count on basic options, like changing the logo or some of the colors, support for more complex customization is not consistent. Even if the template's style doesn't do everything you want it to, it is still a good place to start because if there is a style parameter that suits your needs, you can work quickly from within the admin interface, without having to alter any code.

Clicking the name of a style in the Template Manager: Styles workspace opens the Edit Style workspace, as shown in Figure 20.8. The Edit Style workspace enables you to accomplish several tasks:

- Name the style.
- Set it as the default style.
- Customize the style.
- Assign the style to menu items.

The toolbar at the top of the Edit Style workspace provides quick access to the following functions:

- **Save.** Click to save your work without exiting the Edit Style workspace. This option lets you save without exiting the screen, and is useful if you are interrupted or if you want to save your work but remain in this workspace.
- **Save & Close.** Click to save your work and exit from the Edit Style workspace.
- **Save as Copy.** Click to save the style as a copy, thereby creating a duplicate of the style.
- **Close.** Click to cancel the task and exit the Edit Style workspace.
- **Help.** Click to display the Help files related to the active screen.

20

FIGURE 20.8

The Edit Style workspace is showing the Details tab.

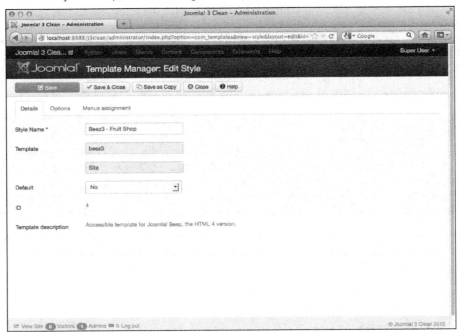

This workspace is divided into three sections: Details, Options, and Menus assignment. The Details section is standard for all styles and is the landing page when you enter the Edit Style workspace. The tab contains the following fields:

- **Style Name.** This field displays the name of the style. This is the only required field.

- **Template.** This field displays the name of the template to which the style applies. This field is not editable.

- **(no label).** This field indicates whether this is a Site or an Administrator style. This field is not editable.

- **Default.** This combo box offers two choices: Yes or No. When set to Yes, this style becomes the default style for the site.

- **ID.** This field shows a system-generated ID for the style. This field is not editable.

- **Template description.** This field displays a short description of the template. This field is not editable.

You can use the fields on the Options tab to set the configuration parameters for the style. The contents of the Options tab vary from template to template. Any choices that you have here are set by the template developer.

> **NOTE**
> Even though the Options tab fields vary, you can almost always count on the ability to set the site name and the logo.

The Menus assignment tab allows you to assign the style to one or more menu items. If the style is the default style, then you do not need to make any changes to this tab. Figure 20.7 shows an example of how this tab looks.

To modify a style, follow these steps:

1. **Log in to the admin system of your site.**
2. **Access the Template Manager by selecting the Template Manager option under the Extensions menu.** The Template Manager: Styles workspace loads in your browser.
3. **Click the name of the style you want to modify.** The Edit Style workspace opens.
4. **Make any changes you desire.**
5. **Click the Save button on the toolbar.** The changes are saved by the system.

As I noted at the outset of this section, making changes to your styles is the simplest way of customizing your template, but it suffers from a significant limitation in that the options you have are determined by the template developer. If you want to do anything beyond what the developer has made available via the Edit Style functionality, you need to work with the actual templates. In the next section, I look more closely at how you can customize the Joomla! presentation layer by working on the actual template files.

Working with Templates

The files that actually control the layout and appearance of your site are included in your templates. A template is not one single file, but rather a collection of files that combine to produce the output you see on the site. Styles, which I discussed previously, are an attribute of templates; the options you see in the Edit Style workspace come directly from one of the files contained in the template.

If you want to change the appearance of your site, and you cannot do this by editing a style, then you have three choices: find another template that meets your needs; modify an existing template; or create a new template of your own design. In this section, I look at the last two options: modifying an existing template and creating a new one.

 I cover adding new templates to your site in Chapter 22.

20

Modifying an existing template

Modifying templates means modifying the code of the template files. Most often, this means making changes to one of the CSS files to modify the styling, but it may also mean making changes to the actual page template files. While you can always download the files and modify them on your local machine, Joomla! 3 gives you the ability to directly edit the files of your template from within the admin system. In this section, I look at using the integrated editing tools to make changes to an existing template.

Before you start modifying a template, I strongly encourage you to make a copy of the template and make your changes to the copy, not the original. By working on the copy, you preserve the original template. This has several advantages:

- You have a ready reference to compare against as you work.
- You can always start fresh with a new copy if something goes horribly wrong.
- You don't lose your changes when the original is updated.

Therefore, the first step you should take before making any changes to a template is always the same: Make a copy of the template. Once you have a copy, you can modify it without worrying about the issues I just outlined. To make a copy of a template, follow these steps:

1. **Log in to the admin system of your site.**
2. **Access the Template Manager by selecting the Template Manager option under the Extensions menu.** The Template Manager: Styles workspace loads in your browser.
3. **Click the Templates link in the left column.** The Template Manager: Templates workspace loads in your browser.
4. **Click the name of the template you want to copy.** The Template Editing workspace opens.
5. **Click the Save button on the toolbar, as shown in Figure 20.9.** The Copy Template pop-up window appears.
6. **Type a unique name for the new template in the New Template Name field.**
7. **Click the Copy Template button.** The system copies the template, installs the template, closes the pop-up window, and displays a confirmation message.

The new template is identical to the original template, except for the name. You can now make your changes to the new template.

Clicking the name of a template in the Template Manager: Templates workspace opens the Customise Template workspace, as shown in Figure 20.9. The Customise Template workspace enables you to accomplish several tasks:

- Copy the template.
- Edit the various page templates.
- Edit the stylesheets.

FIGURE 20.9

The Customise Template workspace

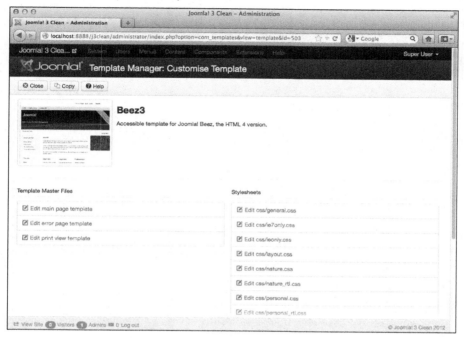

The toolbar at the top of the Customise Template workspace provides quick access to the following functions:

- **Close.** Click to cancel the task and exit the Customise Template workspace.
- **Copy.** Click to make a copy of the template.
- **Help.** Click to display the Help files related to the active screen.

The workspace is divided into two sections: Template Master Files and Stylesheets. The Template Master Files section includes links to the key template files, and the Stylesheets section includes links to the stylesheets used by the template. I will now discuss both of these sections.

Editing the template master files

Once inside the Customise Template workspace, if you click any of the links under the Template Master Files heading, you can view and edit the code of the page templates. Figure 20.10 shows a typical Edit File workspace. From this window, you can modify the code in the file and save the changes.

FIGURE 20.10

A typical Edit File workspace

The toolbar at the top of the Edit File workspace provides quick access to the following functions:

- **Save.** Click to save your work without exiting from the Edit File workspace. This option lets you save without exiting the screen, and is useful if you are interrupted or if you want to save your work but remain in this workspace.

- **Save & Close.** Click to save your work and exit the Edit File workspace.

- **Cancel.** Click to cancel the task and exit the Edit File workspace.

- **Help.** Click to display the Help files related to the active screen.

Using this workspace, you can modify the code in the Source Code window and save the changes, thereby updating the template file.

> **CAUTION**
>
> If you make a mistake editing a template on a live site, this can result in the front end of the site becoming unstable. Therefore, using this feature on a live site is not recommended. The better course of action is to download the files and edit them locally, test them, and then move them back to the live site, overwriting the original files. If you absolutely must work on the live site, take it offline while you work so you can test with lower risk.

Editing the stylesheets

The Template Manager also enables you to edit the various CSS files associated with your templates. When you are inside the Customise Template workspace, clicking the names of any of the items listed under the Stylesheets heading opens the stylesheet for editing. Figure 20.11 shows a typical example.

FIGURE 20.11

The Edit File workspace for one of the template's stylesheets

The toolbar at the top of the Edit File workspace is identical to the one used for editing the page template files. The options on the toolbar are described in the previous section.

Creating a New Template

While editing an existing template offers many people the flexibility they need, others may prefer to create their own template. Building your own template offers you the ultimate blank canvas; you build exactly what you need and you retain complete control of the result. Basic template creation is pretty straightforward, aided by the inclusion of Twitter Bootstrap support in Joomla! 3. Templates can range from quite simple or very complex, depending on how many features you implement and how much logic you build into the

20

template. Display elements are easy to insert and require only basic coding ability; conditional display logic requires more advanced PHP skills, but it is still manageable with a little practice.

In this section I look at the minimum requirements for setting up a basic template. With these basics in place, you will have a solid foundation from which you can expand the template and introduce more advanced features as needed.

Jump-starting Your Work with a Template Framework

Template frameworks can help jump-start your template building. A framework is nothing more than a base for a template. Typically, a framework includes a number of basic elements that are ready to go, and a user interface that allows you to easily customize the layout and features that will be included in the template. Some templates reduce your work to simply adding the design via CSS; others require more work on your part. With the arrival of Joomla! 3 and the inclusion of Twitter Bootstrap, frameworks are likely to become the preferred template development platforms for many people. Here's a quick look at three free frameworks you can use to build a great Joomla! 3 template in record time.

Gantry

The Gantry Framework was created by the team at RocketTheme. It has been around for a number of years but was recently revised to take advantage of Twitter Bootstrap. Gantry installs as an extension to your Joomla! site. A base template is included, which you then modify via the Styles workspace of the Template Manager. Gantry turbocharges the Styles workspace with a large number of options and a slick interface. It includes more than 75 module positions, responsive and fixed-width templates, Google font support, and much more. Learn more at `http://gantry-framework.org/`.

T3

T3 is a template framework from JoomlArt. It installs as an extension and provides a base theme, T3 Blank, as well as a greatly enhanced Style workspace. T3 provides an easy-to-use visual template editor called Theme Magic and additional menu styling. Based on HTML 5 and Twitter Bootstrap, T3 provides a great deal of flexibility and supports responsive design. Learn more at `http://t3.joomlart.com`.

Warp

Warp is a template framework from YOOtheme. Unlike T3 and Gantry, Warp is not based on Twitter Bootstrap, but is the result of a number of years of work and development from the YOO team. It does enjoy the advantage of integrating smoothly with two other products from YOO: Widgetkit and ZOO. Warp works a little differently than the other two frameworks and favors the use of child templates. Templates built with the system can support over 40 module positions, responsive or fixed-width designs, built-in social sharing, and an Ajax search. Learn more at `www.yootheme.com/themes/warp-framework`.

Creating the required structure

By way of example, in this section I am going to create a new Joomla! 3 template named *Balinese*. I will start by creating the necessary files, and then I will install it on my Joomla! site so I can see my changes and finalize the development.

> **NOTE**
>
> Given the savings in time and effort that you can gain from starting with a base template, it's hard to justify building a new template completely from scratch. Unless you plan to release the template for others to use, the additional work it takes to create everything yourself is probably not the best use of your time. In this section I show starting from scratch as a tutorial tool, a way to help you understand the template components and gain insights into how they work. Normally, I start with a base template or a template framework.

As discussed earlier in this chapter, a valid template requires only three files: an `index.php` file, a `style.css` file, and a `templateDetails.xml` file. Though only three files are required, virtually all templates use more, from additional stylesheets and templates to scripts. For this example, I will add only the basics; where you go from there is up to you.

I am going to create a Twitter Bootstrap–enabled template in this example. Twitter Bootstrap is new to the Joomla! core in version 3 and a real bonus for template developers. Bootstrap is a front-end development framework, and because it is built right into the Joomla! core, all you have to do is declare it in your template to have access to all the power it brings. You can view the included files by visiting `/media/jui` and browsing the subdirectories.

Bootstrap's CSS and JavaScript files not only help assure consistency in the Joomla! UI, but also make it very easy for you to create a responsive and full-featured template for your site. The Bootstrap CSS files contain a standardized set of selectors you can use to format your site. The CSS includes global styles for the body and support for grid systems. Also included is formatting for common elements like forms, buttons, and typography. The JavaScript files include common helper functionality that you can access as needed. The JavaScript powers features like tooltips, popovers, and more.

> **NOTE**
>
> Learn more about Twitter Bootstrap at `http://twitter.github.com/bootstrap/`.

In order to implement your template in a manner consistent with the templates in the core, I advise you to start by creating a directory to hold your template and then adding to it two additional folders:

- `css` to hold your template's stylesheet
- `images` to hold any images specific to the template

Next, create three empty files, one named `index.php`, one named `template.css`, and another named `templateDetails.xml`. Put the `template.css` file in the `/css` directory; leave the other two files in the template's directory. At the end of this process, you should have a structure that looks like Figure 20.12.

20

FIGURE 20.12

The directory structure and file placement for a template named Balinese

You will now start populating those files with code, starting with the key file, `index.php`.

index.php file

The `index.php` file is responsible for placing all the output on the page. The following code sets all the key elements in place, but relies exclusively on Twitter Bootstrap for styling. Begin your file by adding this code:

```php
<?php

    defined('_JEXEC') or die;

    $doc = JFactory::getDocument();

    $doc->addStyleSheet($this->baseurl . '/media/jui/css/bootstrap.min.
      css');
    $doc->addStyleSheet($this->baseurl . '/media/jui/css/bootstrap-
      responsive.css');
    $doc->addStyleSheet('templates/' . $this->template . '/css/
      template.css');
?>
<!DOCTYPE html>
<html lang="en">
```

Here's what's going on in this code:

- The first line of the code enhances your site security by prohibiting direct access of the code.
- The lines beginning with `$doc` connect external files to this one. Note that the first two stylesheets are Twitter Bootstrap stylesheets. These files are part of the Joomla! core and are located outside the template directory. The last stylesheet is the standard `template.css` included with each template. You will use that file for any unique styles or style overrides you may need later.
- The final two lines add the DOCTYPE and declare the language used by the site.

Next, you'll create the head of the document by adding the following lines immediately after the code:

```
<head>

    <jdoc:include type="head" />

    <meta name="viewport" content="width=device-width, initial-
    scale=1.0">

</head>
```

Note the jdoc:include statement at the top of the <head>. That include statement brings in the page title, meta information, and system JavaScript. The meta tag works with the bootstrap-responsive.css file declared earlier to enable a fully responsive template layout; both of these elements are necessary to build a responsive template with Twitter Bootstrap.

Next, you'll build the remainder of the document, the contents of the <body> tag, and the final lines. Add the following code immediately after the closing </head> tag:

NOTE

The default templates require that you use a numerical naming convention for module position holders. While that may help standardization, it's confusing for site administrators. I have used a logical name system for the module positions in this template. In this fashion, the code is easier to decipher and module assignment in the Module Manager is simpler.

```
<body>

    <!-- Bootstrap container -->
    <div class='container'>

        <!-- header modules -->
        <div class='row-fluid'>
          <div class='dark-top'>
            <div class='span9'>
              <jdoc:include type="modules" name="top nav"
style="none" />
            </div>
            <div class='span3'>
              <jdoc:include type="modules" name="search" style="none"
/>
            </div>
          </div>
        </div>

        <!-- breadcrumbs -->
        <div class='row-fluid'>
          <div class='span12'>
```

20

```
        <jdoc:include type="modules" name="breadcrumbs"
style="none" />
        </div>
    </div>

    <!-- main content area and right sidebar -->
    <div class='row-fluid'>

        <!-- main content area -->
        <div class='span9'>
            <jdoc:include type="message" />
            <jdoc:include type="component" />
        </div>

        <!-- right sidebar -->
        <div class='span3'>
            <jdoc:include type="modules" name="right column"
style="xhtml" />
        </div>

    </div>

    <!-- footer -->
    <div class='row-fluid'>
            <div class='span12'>
                <jdoc:include type="modules" name="footer"
style="none" />
            </div>
    </div>

    </div>

</body>
</html>
```

Here's what's going on in the body of the file:

- The template created here relies on the 12-column grid system that is standard in Twitter Bootstrap. This layout is invoked by adding the default Twitter Bootstrap class .container and using it to hold your page body output. Subsequently standardized class names are used to define the width of sections of the page, relative to the 12 columns.

  - .span12 runs the width of the page.

  - .span9 takes 75 percent of the screen width.

  - .span3 takes 25 percent of the screen width.

NOTE

The default Bootstrap grid system utilizes 12 columns, making for a 940 pixel-wide container without responsive features enabled. With the responsive CSS file added, the grid adapts to be either 724 pixels or 1170 pixels wide, depending on your viewport. Below 767 pixel-wide viewports, the columns become fluid and stack vertically. Note that if you change the container class to `container-fluid`, the entire content area expands to fill 100 percent of the screen, regardless of the screen size.

- The class `.row-fluid` allows the template to flex and resize as the screen size changes; this is supplied by the responsive CSS file from Twitter Bootstrap.

- The `jdoc:include` statements are used to place functionality on the page. The various types shown here are

  - **modules.** Provide module placeholders

  - **message.** Places system alerts and confirmation messages

  - **component.** Places component output

NOTE

Each of the `jdoc` statements used to place a module position holder on the page includes the attribute `style:`. The attribute is used to designate the module style to be applied. See the discussion of Module chrome later in this chapter for more information about what the values used in the attribute mean.

template.css file

This example has relied on the Twitter Bootstrap CSS files for the site styling. The `template.css` file can be used for additional styles unique to your template or to override styling. In this case, you want to add some styling to enhance the appearance of the modules in the right column. The raw output is pretty rough.

Open the `template.css` file and add the following:

```
.dark-top {
    background-color:rgb(24,74,125);
    border:1px solid #ccc;
    padding:5px;
    margin:0px 0px 10px 0px;
    height:35px;
}

.dark-top a {
  color:rgb(255,255,255);
}

.dark-top a:hover {
  color:rgb(24,74,125);
}
```

20

```
.breadcrumb {
  font-size:10px;
  padding:0px 0px 10px 0px;
  border-bottom:1px solid #ccc;
}

h3 {
  font-size:14px;
  line-height:20px;
  margin:10px 0px 5px 0px;
}

.footer1 {
  border-top:1px solid #ccc;
  padding-top:10px;
  margin:30px 0px 0px 0px;
}
```

Some of the selectors in this file, like the `.dark-top` class, are unique to this template; others are not. In the case of items like the h3 definition, or the `.breadcrumb` class, you are changing the default styling for those items. This works because Joomla! looks last at the template's CSS files, and if it finds new definitions for existing selectors, it merges them, giving preference to the definitions in the template CSS if there is a conflict. Use this technique to tailor the output without having to modify the core files.

> **NOTE**
>
> The process of modifying existing styling is called *overriding*. In this example, you are overriding the definitions for h3 and `.breadcrumb`.

templateDetails.xml file

The `templateDetails.xml` file needs to include all the data necessary for the Joomla! installer as well as the module positions. As your template does not yet include any style parameters, there are none declared in the code.

Open the `templateDetails.xml` file you created earlier and add the following specified code:

```xml
<?xml version="1.0" encoding="utf-8"?>
<!DOCTYPE install PUBLIC "-//Joomla! 2.5//DTD template 1.0//EN"
    "http://www.joomla.org/xml/dtd/2.5/template-install.dtd">
<extension version="3.0" type="template" client="site">
  <name>Balinese</name>
  <version>3.0</version>
  <creationDate>12/01/2012</creationDate>
  <author>Ric Shreves</author>
  <authorEmail>ric@ricshreves.net</authorEmail>
```

```
<description>A simple Twitter Bootstrap enabled template for Joomla
3.0</description>
<files>
  <filename>index.php</filename>
  <folder>css</folder>
  <folder>images</folder>
</files>
<positions>
      <position>debug</position>
      <position>search</position>
      <position>top nav</position>
      <position>breadcrumbs</position>
      <position>header image</position>
      <position>right column</position>
      <position>footer</position>
</positions>
<config>
</config>
</extension>
```

The template created here relies on the 12-column grid system that is standard in Twitter Bootstrap. This layout is invoked by adding the default Twitter Bootstrap class `.container` and using it to hold your page body output. Subsequently standardized class names are used to define the width of sections of the page, relative to the 12 columns.

Note that the list of module positions in this file matches up with the module position holders placed in the `index.php` file.

Packaging the template files

Templates need to be archived for installation. To package the template, you simply zip all the files. The process is really that simple. Once zipped up, it can be installed with the automated Installer from Joomla!. You can use any of the most common archive formats, including ZIP, tar.gz, and tar.bz2.

> **NOTE**
>
> In addition to the files discussed in the preceding section, you should also include a thumbnail image of the template. The image should be 206 x 150 pixels. The recommended file format is PNG, and the file should be named `template_thumbnail.png`.

> **TIP**
>
> Don't leave any empty directories in your template folder, as this can cause installation errors in some configurations.

20

Now that you have a complete template and an installable package, log into your Joomla! admin system and install the Balinese template. Once you have installed it, make it active. Go to the Template Manager: Styles workspace and set Balinese as the default style; then visit the front end of the site. I intended this template to be an internal page template — you will be making a home page template in the next section — so click any of the articles to see how the Balinese template works for your internal pages. Figure 20.13 shows a typical article page with Balinese installed.

Creating a dedicated home page template

One of the most common requests I see in template development is for a site with a distinct home page design. You are now going to take the Balinese template you have just developed, and modify it to make it suitable for use as a home page to learn how this can be easily done.

FIGURE 20.13

This article page is shown with the Balinese template

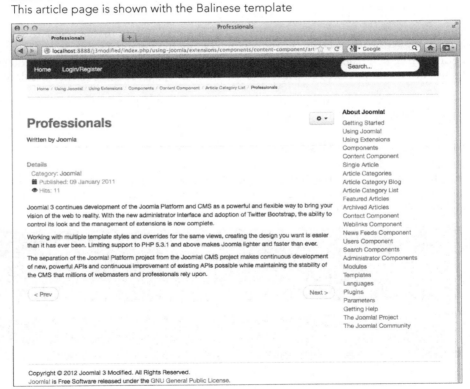

Working with Template Parameters

Adding parameters to a template can greatly enhance the flexibility of the template. Template parameters allow the site administrator to adjust the appearance or behavior of the template from within the Template Manager: Styles workspace. The templates included in Joomla! 3 provide useful examples of how this works.

Perhaps not surprisingly, template parameters are most commonly used by designers who have built their templates for sale or for general release. Parameters are rarely included in templates by developers who are building for their own uses.

If you are interested in learning more about how to add parameters to your templates, review this page on the Joomla! documentation site: `http://docs.joomla.org/Defining_a_parameter_in_templateDetails.xml`.

The first thing you have to do is to duplicate Balinese. Follow the steps included earlier in this chapter to create a copy of Balinese on your Joomla! site. Name the new template Balihome. Next, open the `template.php` file for editing and make the following changes:

```php
<?php

    defined('_JEXEC') or die;

    $doc = JFactory::getDocument();

    $doc->addStyleSheet($this->baseurl . '/media/jui/css/bootstrap.
min.css');
    $doc->addStyleSheet($this->baseurl . '/media/jui/css/bootstrap-
responsive.css');
    $doc->addStyleSheet('templates/' . $this->template . '/css/
template.css');

?>
<!DOCTYPE html>
<html lang="en">

<head>

    <jdoc:include type="head" />

    <meta name="viewport" content="width=device-width,
initial-scale=1.0">

</head>

<body>
```

20

```
                    <!-- Bootstrap container -->
                    <div class='container'>

                        <!-- header modules -->
                        <div class='row-fluid'>
                          <div class='dark-top'>
                            <div class='span9'>
                              <jdoc:include type="modules" name="top nav"
style="none" />
                            </div>
                            <div class='span3'>
                              <jdoc:include type="modules" name="search"
style="none" />
                            </div>
                          </div>
                        </div>

                        <!-- carousel -->
                        <div class='row'>
                          <div class='span12'>
                                <div id="myCarousel" class="carousel slide">
                    <!-- Carousel items -->
                    <div class="carousel-inner">
                       <div class="active item"><img src="http://localhost:8888/
j3modified/templates/Balihome/images/temple.jpg" />
                          <div class="carousel-caption">
                                    <h4>Balinese Temple</h4>
                                    <p>One of many on the island of ten
thousand temples. This example is located in the center of the
island.</p>
                                </div></div>
                       <div class="item"><img src="http://localhost:8888/j3modified/
templates/Balihome/images/surfsup.jpg" />
                          <div class="carousel-caption">
                                    <h4>Surf</h4>
                                    <p>3 of the 10 top surf breaks in the world
are located in Bali.</p>
                                </div></div>
                       <div class="item"><img src="http://localhost:8888/j3modified/
templates/Balihome/images/temple.jpg" />
                          <div class="carousel-caption">
                                    <h4>Tradition</h4>
                                    <p>The rich and distinct Balinese culture
is one of the island's charms.</p>
                                </div></div>
                    </div>
                    <!-- Carousel nav -->
                    <a class="carousel-control left" href="#myCarousel" data-
slide="prev">&lsaquo;</a>
                    <a class="carousel-control right" href="#myCarousel" data-
slide="next">&rsaquo;</a>
```

564

```
    </div>
        </div>
    </div>

    <!-- main content area and right sidebar -->
    <div class='row-fluid'>

        <!-- main content area -->
        <div class='span12'>
            <jdoc:include type="message" />
            <jdoc:include type="component" />
        </div>

    </div>

    <!-- footer -->
    <div class='row-fluid'>
            <div class='span12'>
                <jdoc:include type="modules" name="footer"
 style="none" />
            </div>
    </div>

    </div>

</body>
</html>
```

In this code, I have made only a few changes, and to only one part of the template. Specifically, I did the following:

- Deleted the breadcrumbs
- Deleted the right column
- Expanded the main content area to 12 columns
- Added a jQuery carousel, courtesy of Twitter Bootstrap

The only item that really requires any explanation is the carousel. There are not any additional extensions added here. The code that powers the carousel is built into Twitter Bootstrap. Look for the comment tagged carousel. You can see where I placed it on the page, and added the images, captions, and controls.

NOTE
When you try this for yourself, replace my image links with links to your images!

20

Access the Template Manager: Styles workspace and assign the Balihome template to your site's home page. When you visit the front page of the site, you should see something similar to Figure 20.14.

FIGURE 20.14

The Balihome template is tailored for use as a site home page.

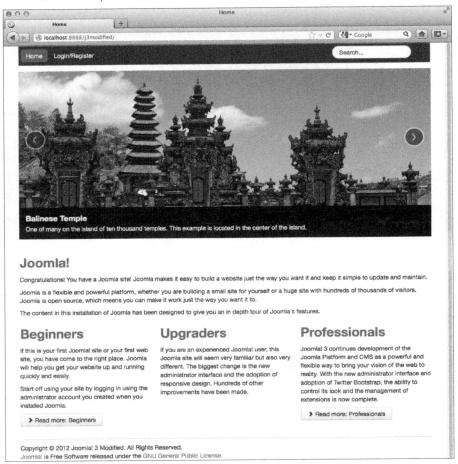

Overriding Module and Component Output

Up to this point, I have focused on working with templates and styling. While gaining mastery of template files and stylesheets is extremely useful for customizing the presentation layer of your site, those elements don't handle everything that appears on the screen. To gain control of the entire front end, you also need to be able to work with the component and module output, that is, you need to control what happens inside the containers that place the output of those elements on the page. While you can always play with the CSS to impact the appearance of the output, there will be times when you want to do more, such as customize the layout or add or delete elements. In those situations, you need another tool.

Joomla! component architecture is based on the MVC model — that is, Model, View, and Controller. Views are what you are concerned with when it comes to controlling the appearance of the output. Views rely on their own templates to control the layout of the component or module. You can override those view templates by creating new ones of your own and placing them inside your active site template directory. In this section, I show you how to apply this technique.

Customizing view templates

If a component developer has followed coding conventions, you should be able to find a /views directory inside the component's directory of your Joomla! installation. Take, for example, the Contacts component. Figure 20.15 shows the directory contents.

FIGURE 20.15

This is a partial view of the contents of the /components/com_contact directory.

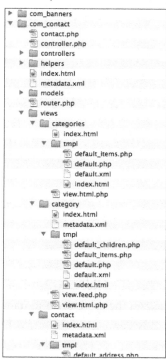

The Contacts component contains a large number of views. The templates for each view are located in the /tmpl subdirectories. You can see that the /categories/tmpl directory contains two PHP files: default_items.php and default.php. Similarly, /category/tmpl contains three PHP files. Each of these files holds part of the key to the appearance of the output of the Contacts component. If you want to change any of the output described in these files, you can do so by overriding that specific file. Again, by way of example, go the Beez3 template directory on your Joomla! installation and open the /html/com_contact directory. As you can see in Figure 20.16, the author of the Beez3 template has created customized versions of a large number of the views templates for the Contacts component.

FIGURE 20.16

This is a partial view of the contents of the /components/com_contact directory.

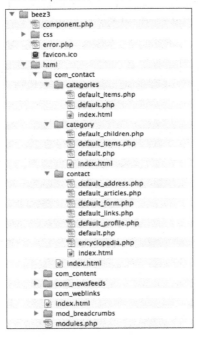

When Joomla! finds one of these files in the template directory, it uses the contents of this file instead of the contents of the original file. Note that the directory structure and file-names have been carefully maintained — they must match the structure and names of the original files in the component or this technique will fail.

To create your own override, simply follow these steps:

1. **Create a new directory in your template directory.** Name it /html.

2. **Find the view template you want to override.** Note its location and name and then make a copy of it.

3. **Place the copy inside the** `/html` **directory of your template, making sure to match the component name, directory structure, and filename.** Refer to the previous example.

4. **Make your changes to the new template file in your** `/html` **directory.**

5. **Save your changes.**

That's all there is to it; it's very straightforward and very flexible. The technique applies in the same measure to both components and modules.

By way of an example, you are going to make a very basic modification to the output of the default Joomla! Login module. You are going to override the default template controlling the output of the Login module so that you can customize the appearance of the form.

Here are the steps:

1. **Copy the file** `/modules/mod_login/tmpl/default.php`.

2. **Open your active template directory and place the copied file inside a subdirectory named** `/html/mod_login`. For example, if you are using the Balinese template, you create this: `/templates/balinese/html/mod_login/default.php`.

3. **Make your changes to the new file.**

4. **Save your changes.** The new template now overrides the original template and is displayed on the site.

Your new override takes precedence over the original view template — and, importantly, you have accomplished this without making any changes to the original module.

Creating Module Chrome

Joomla! allows for control over the output of modules via either CSS or through the use of Module chrome. The naming is a bit deceptive: Module chrome is what developers call it; for site administrators, this is simply the Module Style settings you can see in the Advanced Options tab of the Edit Module workspace. You have the option either to create your own custom Module chrome or to use a default set of module styles.

The standard Module Style options are

- **none.** Generates raw output with no styling or formatting added and no module title output
- **table.** Outputs the module in a table
- **horz.** Outputs the module as a table wrapped inside a table (a nested table)
- **xhtml.** Outputs the module wrapped in `divs`
- **rounded.** Outputs the module in nested `divs` that support the use of rounded corners
- **outline.** Outputs the module wrapped in the Module Position Preview wrapper

2 0

The Module chrome styles are applied to the module position holders inside the `index.php` file. To define the chrome, add the `style` attribute to the `jdoc:include` statement that places the module position holder. By way of example, look at the following lines of code, taken from the `index.php` file of the Balinese template that you built earlier in this chapter:

```
<!-- right sidebar -->
<div class='span3'>
    <jdoc:include type="modules" name="right column" style="xhtml" />
</div>
...
...
...
<!-- footer -->
<div class='row-fluid'>
   <div class='span12'>
         <jdoc:include type="modules" name="footer" style="none" />
   </div>
  </div>
```

These two snippets show the default Module chrome options in action. The first snippet shows the `jdoc:include` statement with the style attribute set to `xhtml`. The second shows the same attribute set to "none." As a result of these attributes, all modules assigned to the Right column module position use the XHTML style for their output. In contrast, none of the modules assigned to the Footer position have any styling added to their output.

While the default styles add a great deal of flexibility, there may be times when you need to achieve even more specific styling. In those cases where you cannot get what you need from the default Module chrome styles, you can create your own custom Module chrome.

To see a custom Module chrome in action, look at the default Beez3 template. Go to the Beez3 template directory on your server and open the file `/html/modules.php`. The file contains three custom chrome styles: `beezDivision`, `beezHide`, and `beezTabs`. Look for the functions that are named as follows: `function modChrome_styleName()`.

This function indicates a custom module style. The available properties are determined by the properties that particular module possesses. There are, however, common key output properties that you are most likely to use: `$module->content`, `$module->title`, and `$module->showtitle`. `Showtitle` is a Boolean operator, and should be set to True to display the module title. `Content` and `title` return the content of the module and the title of the module.

Using Class Suffixes

The Joomla! system provides the administrator with the option to add class suffixes to a number of items in the system. Page class suffixes, Module class suffixes, and Menu class suffixes are all examples of the Class Suffix option in action. The purpose of all these options is the same, that is, to give you the opportunity to make the styling specific to that item by appending to the existing class the suffix of your choice.

To take advantage of this feature, you need to specify the suffix for the item and then create the CSS styling that goes with it. You have two options for setting the value of the suffix. First, if you simply type a label into the provided class suffix field, the value is appended directly to the existing class, thereby removing the old class from application to the item and also creating a new class that you can style. Alternatively, if you enter a space and then type in the label, the system behaves differently: Instead of replacing the old class with a new one, the system leaves the old class and adds a new class with the same name as your label. Both the old class and the new class are applied to the item.

By way of example, if the item was originally styled with a class named "moduleheading" and you add the Module Class suffix "_blue", then the styling for the item would look like this: class="moduleheading_blue". If, instead, you add the Module Class suffix " blue" (that is, a space " " plus the word "blue"), the code would be class="moduleheading blue".

The final step to complete the process would be to add the appropriate selector to your template. css file. You can learn more about class suffixes at http://docs.joomla.org/Using_Class_ Suffixes.

> **NOTE**
> It is also possible to specify custom attributes and parameters by way of the modules.php file. Module parameters are accessed using the $params object. Additional attributes require the creation of an $attribs array. While these techniques are very powerful and add a great deal of flexibility, they also require some fluency with PHP. You can learn more at http://docs.joomla.org/Applying_custom_module_chrome.

To add custom Module chrome to your template, follow these steps:

1. **Create a new blank file, name it** modules.php, **and place it inside your template's** /html **directory.**

2. **Make sure the file has both an opening and closing PHP tag.**

3. **Add the following code at the top of the file, inside the opening tag:** defined ('_JEXEC') or die ('Restricted access').

4. **Add the following code to create your function (substituting the name of your function for the value** STYLENAME**):**

```
function modChrome_STYLENAME( $module, &$params, &$attribs )
{
  /* add the chrome for the Module output here
 must include <?php echo $module->content; ?> to output the
 content. */
}
```

5. **Save the file.**

6. **Open the template's** `index.php` **file.**

7. **For each module position where you want the custom chrome to appear, add the attribute** `style="STYLENAME"` **to the** `jdoc:include` **statements used to create the module position holder, for example,** `<jdoc:include type="modules" name="right" style="STYLENAME" />`.

8. **Save the file.** The new Module chrome appears, formatting the output of the modules in the affected module position.

Summary

In this chapter, I covered the basics of customizing the presentation layer of your Joomla! site. The topics included

- Reviewing the default templates
- Understanding how templates work
- Customizing template output through the styles
- Duplicating styles
- Assigning styles to menu items
- Customizing templates
- Building a new template
- Overriding module and component output

In the next chapter, I turn my attention to modifying the core components, modules, and plug-ins.

Customizing Joomla! Functionality

IN THIS CHAPTER

Finding the right tools for extension development

Understanding component architecture

Building your own components

Reviewing modules and how they work

Creating your own modules

Understanding the architecture of plug-ins

Creating your own plug-ins

Joomla! is extensible and customizable by design. The system's various components, modules, and plug-ins are easily identified and can be targeted for customization. Components, the system's most complex element, employ the Model-View-Controller (MVC) architecture that cleanly segregates the business logic from the presentation layer. Although the MVC architecture helps make the planning and creation of new components simpler, component creation remains a challenging and sometimes complex task suited more to experienced programmers. Modules are the most commonly modified element in the system. Managing the customization of modules is relatively easier than working with components and can be done by anyone with basic programming skills and an awareness of the system requirements and architecture. Plug-ins are used to provide narrow functionality that enables other extensions. And, although creating a plug-in may require more knowledge of the underlying Joomla! framework, the actual process of creating a plug-in is relatively easy.

In this chapter, I take you through the key elements and anatomy of components, modules, and plug-ins, and discuss how to create new versions of these extensions. The focus is on creating a basic understanding of the architecture of components, modules, and plug-ins and is not intended as a complete guide to all aspects of extension creation; that topic is broad enough for a book of its own!

Understanding the Basic Principles

Customizing the functionality of the Joomla! CMS means modifying or creating components, modules, and plug-ins. As you have seen in previous chapters, modules and components have varying roles on the front end and back end of your site. Plug-ins are enabling applications that provide extended functionality for other elements of the system.

Customization of Joomla! functionality varies from simple to complex. You are most likely to want to customize the output of a module or a component. If you only want to modify the output, you should not create new extensions; rather, you should override the output of the component or module by including new template files inside your active Joomla! template.

 Chapter 20 details how to override component and module output.

Components are by far the most complex of the extensions and often have both front-end and back-end elements that you have to consider when you are engaged in customization. Given the complexity of component architecture, and the key role that components play in the system, component customization is by far the more difficult task. Modules are often self-contained and are relatively easy to work with. Plug-ins tend to be highly specialized and more often the provenance of a developer who needs to add some enabling functionality to a new component.

As a general rule, you should avoid modifying the core files. The textbook approach is to create a new version of the component, module, or plug-in and make your modifications to that code; you can then install your new extension and manage it independently of the core. Modifications made to core files can be more difficult to maintain when you need to update or upgrade your site. Modifications made to the core can also be troublesome if someone other than the developer takes over site maintenance. In either case, unless the changes are well documented, they can be easy to miss and hard to replicate.

Finding the Right Tools

As with any type of work, customizing Joomla! is made easier with the right tools. Although the selection of an individual development tool kit is a personal and subjective decision, a few tools are clear winners.

Assembling your tool kit

In the broadest and most basic terms, customizing a Joomla! site requires access to the following tools:

- **Web browser.** You should have access to all of the most popular browsers for testing purposes, but for your work during development the Firefox browser is the tool of choice. The existence of a number of add-ons that extend the functionality of Firefox has pushed this browser into the forefront for developers. I discuss several of these add-ons in the following section. Firefox can be downloaded free of charge from `http://www.mozilla.org`.

- **Code editor.** Many editing programs are available, and everyone seems to have their own favorites. Many people use Adobe Dreamweaver, although I do not think that it is the easiest program or the best choice for working with PHP. Mac and Linux users, in particular, may prefer other choices to Dreamweaver. Among popular alternatives are Vim, eMacs, and TextWrangler, though they tend to be less friendly to those new to coding. Dreamweaver is a commercial application and, while expensive on its own, it is a good deal when purchased as part of one of the Adobe software suites.

- **FTP client.** Again, there are a multitude of choices here and many people have their own favorites. If you are using the Firefox browser, the FireFTP add-on gives you an effective FTP client that works directly from inside the browser. You can download this add-on for free at `https://addons.mozilla.org/en-US/firefox/addon/684`. Another good cross-platform choice is FileZilla.

- **IDE.** While the items listed here may technically be all that you need (a number of developers get by with just these), if you want to do more, you can use other options. A popular choice among more experienced developers is the Eclipse Integrated Development Environment (IDE). Eclipse not only provides a powerful authoring environment, but also includes professional-quality debugging tools, integration with Subversion, and a variety of utilities that can make your work easier. You can download the Eclipse IDE free of charge from `www.eclipse.org`.

TIP

If you are not familiar with Eclipse, you may want to start with the Joomla! docs article entitled "Setting up your workstation for Joomla! development," which you can find at `http://docs.joomla.org/Setting_up_your_workstation_for_Joomla!_development`.

TIP

If you are looking to do some minor work on the presentation layer — say, merely adding a bit of JavaScript to a template, or modifying the CSS — you don't need anything more than your browser. You can use the file editor built into the Template Manager to make changes to templates or their related CSS file. For a discussion of the Template Editor, see Chapter 20.

Adding extensions that aid customization

You can extend your Joomla! site, your Firefox browser, or your Eclipse workstation. Here's a list of popular add-ons and extensions that can make customization of your Joomla! site easier:

- **Firebug.** While the newest version of the Firefox browser includes some basic developer tools, the Firebug add-on goes even farther. With Firebug installed, you can click an element on the screen and view the code that produces it, the CSS that styles it, and a variety of related information. Firebug is particularly useful when working on the presentation layer of a site. The YSlow and PageSpeed add-ons discussed in this list integrate with Firebug. You can download the Firebug add-on free of charge at `https://addons.mozilla.org/en-US/firefox/addon/1843`.

- **FireFTP.** This add-on is an FTP client that runs from inside Firefox as a new tab in the browser window.

- **Phing.** This Eclipse extension is designed to ease the packaging, deploying, and testing of applications. This works very well with extension development and helps provide an easy way to manage multiple changes and versions to your custom extensions. You can download Phing for the Eclipse IDE free of charge at `http://phing.info`.

- **Web Developer.** This Firefox add-on is targeted more at web designers than programmers. It offers many of the same functions as Firebug, as well as a toolbar that gives you quick access to many options, including a window sizer that lets you view how your page will look at different screen settings and basic accessibility testing tools. You can download the Web Developer add-on for the Firefox browser free of charge at `https://addons.mozilla.org/en-US/firefox/addon/60`.

- **YSlow or PageSpeed.** These add-ons for the Firefox browser help identify performance issues on web pages. These are diagnostic tools that help you identify bottlenecks, large files, and slow spots in your pages. You can download the YSlow add-on for the Firefox browser free of charge at `https://addons.mozilla.org/firefox/addon/5369`, and PageSpeed free of charge at `http://code.google.com/speed/page-speed/download.html`.

> **TIP**
>
> The Joomla! Extensions Directory has a separate category containing a list of development tools. For more information, visit `http://extensions.joomla.org/extensions/tools/development-tools`.

> **NOTE**
>
> The Joomla! CMS is an application built on top of the Joomla! Platform, a software development framework designed to facilitate the creation of web applications. The Joomla! Platform is documented in a dedicated API, located at `http://api.joomla.org/`. If you want to create new extensions for Joomla!, or contribute to the Joomla! development efforts, you need to spend some time and become acquainted with the Joomla! API. Be aware, however, that while the Joomla! CMS is built on top of the Joomla! Platform, some code in the CMS is not part of the Platform, and hence not part of the underlying API. Additional documentation can be found at the Joomla! Documentation Wiki at `http://docs.joomla.org`. There is also a manually produced API reference at `http://docs.joomla.org/Framework`. All of these resources are worth at least a quick glance if you are interested in creating Joomla! extensions.

Customizing Components

Components are the heart of the Joomla! system. The main content output of each page is generated by a component, and many of the site's modules are dependent in some way on components for their data. Components are the most complex elements in the system and the most difficult to customize. Many issues are involved, from the presentation of data to the manipulation of the database. A complete discussion of component development is worthy of a separate book, and a full discussion of the topic is beyond the scope of this chapter.

The following sections demonstrate how to execute simple modifications to a component, and introduce the basic concepts that underlie the creation of new components.

 I cover overriding component views in Chapter 20.

Introducing Component Architecture

The system's components are divided into two categories: Site components and Administrator components. The front-end Site components are located in the /components directory. The back-end Administrator components are located in the /administrator/components directory. All components use the same naming convention: com_componentname.

With Joomla! 1.5, the project adopted the MVC component architecture; that is, components are built around the creation of models, views, and controllers. Understanding the MVC concept is key to understanding how to work with Joomla! components. Model-View-Controller is a software design pattern that helps developers plan an application and then organize the code into a consistent and logical framework. The segregation of the application into models, views, and controllers makes it easy to separate the business logic of the application from the presentation of the data. The key advantage of this approach is that you can work with the presentation of the data without having to make changes to the underlying application's logic.

Looking at each of the three elements in turn:

- **Models.** The model provides routines to manage and manipulate the data for the application. In most cases, the data is pulled from the database, although other data sources can be used. The Joomla! framework provides the abstract class JModelBase.

- **Views.** The view part of the application renders the data. The view does not modify the data; it only displays what is retrieved. The view is technically part of the site's presentation layer and includes one or more templates that provide the formatting of the data. Note that views can display data from multiple models, though this is not normally done. The Joomla! framework provides the abstract class JViewBase.

- **Controllers.** The controller reacts to actions, triggers the retrieval of data from the model, and passes the data to the view for display. The role of the controller is to associate the model with the view. The Joomla! framework provides the abstract class JControllerBase.

Understanding the anatomy of a typical component

To help understand how components are structured, I want to take a look at an example. The Contacts component, though complex, provides a good example of the typical Joomla! component architecture. The Contacts component has both a front-end and a back-end element. The component provides front-end output that appears for site visitors and a back-end admin interface that allows for the creation and management of contacts. The back-end component is located at /administrator/components/com_contact. The front-end component can be found at /components/com_contact.

Visit the /components/com_contact directory and view the structure of the subdirectories. You can see that the directory structure corresponds to the MVC architecture: There is a /models directory, a /views directory, and /controllers directory, and their contents are consistent with the directory names.

- The /models directory contains files that process the data for each of the following: Categories, Category, Contact, and Featured.
- The /views directory parallels the models, and provides views for the output of the Categories, Category, Contact, and Featured models.
- The /controllers directory contains one file, which supplies the controller logic for the component.

The key file is contact.php, located in the component's root directory. This is the first file called when the component is in use and is responsible for loading the proper controller, in this case, the controller.php file. The controller.php file defines the controller class and functions needed for this component. The controller file automatically loads the models and pushes the data to the views for each model.

The /models directory contains the model for your component. There are a number of files in this directory, each handling the task of preparing the data for a specific type of output.

- categories.php. Handles retrieving of lists of contact categories
- category.php. Handles retrieving of a list of items in a category
- contact.php. Handles the output relating to a single contact, including the contact form
- featured.php. Handles the output relating to featured contacts

The `/views` directory contains a parallel set of directories for the component's view, each containing the templates used to format the output:

- `/categories`
- `/category`
- `/contact`
- `/featured`

The key file in each of the view directories is called `view.html.php`. The file pushes the data to the template — the last piece of the puzzle.

The final formatting of the component output is done through the use of template files. Each view has a separate directory, named `/tmpl`, that contains the template files. The contents of the `/tmpl` directory for the categories view are

- `default_items.php`
- `default.php`
- `default.xml`
- `index.html`

The categories view uses two templates, `default.php` and `default_items.php`. The `default.php` file is the primary file and calls the `default_items.php` file in the course of rendering the output. These two files contain the HTML needed to format the data on the screen.

Creating a new component

Although a complete tutorial on creating new Joomla! components is beyond the scope of this book, an awareness of the basic principles can get you started and provide you with enough information to enable you to create an installable component, though I leave it up to you to include the logic you need to add your functionality to the component.

Detailing the minimum requirements for developing a component is difficult because the requirements are defined by the extent and nature of the functionality of the component you are building. Even the ideal of providing a model, a view, and a controller is merely advisory rather than compulsory. Moreover, your component may not need both a front end and a back end; many components exist in one place only. The best advice is to define what you need the component to do, and then look at the most efficient way to get it done. If the component can benefit from a proper MVC architecture, you should use it; if it cannot, then do only what is needed.

Figure 21.1 shows the directory structure and files for a basic component. This is the view of the files as they appear in the installation package, and it is how you would set up the structure in your development environment. Note the segregation of the various models, views, and controllers into site and administrator directories.

FIGURE 21.1

The directories and files needed for a simple MVC component

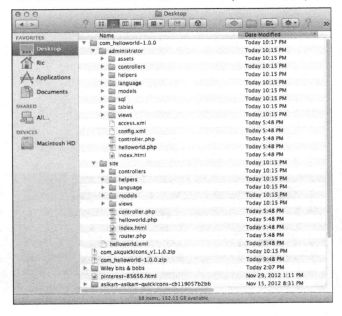

> **NOTE**
>
> The other factor to consider is whether you want to distribute the component. If you want to release the component for others to use, you should follow the MVC framework. To help get you started, the Joomla! documentation site includes an excellent tutorial called Developing a Model-View-Controller Component. Visit `http://docs.joomla.org/Developing_a_Model-View-Controller_Component/3.0/Introduction`.

While you can literally spend hours setting up your component structures and adding the basic syntax needed to support installation and the default Joomla! libraries, there is a much simpler way to fast-track development of new components: Component Creator for Joomla. Component Creator is an online service that enables you to quickly assemble a basic component by stepping through a simple wizard interface. At the conclusion of the process, you can download a fully installable component package. The basic service is free, but restricts your component to only one table. To build more complex components, you need to subscribe to their premium service. Alternatively, you can download the simple component package and add the necessary tables yourself. Even if the basic version does not meet all your requirements, the time you save by using Component Creator for the basic component shell makes this tool the easiest way to speed up your component development. To start building your first component, go to `www.notwebdesign.com/joomla-component-creator/`.

> **NOTE**
>
> You do need to register with the site to gain access to the free version of Component Creator.

Packaging a component

Proper packaging may not be a concern if your component is only intended for your own use, but if you intend to give your component to others, or you want to install it again elsewhere, you should create a proper installation package for the component. Proper packaging allows you to manage component installation through the default Joomla! Extension Installer. If you use a service like Component Creator, the installation routines are handled for you. If not, then you must set it up manually.

Component packages are archives that contain all the necessary elements of a component, including an XML file containing the information needed by the Joomla! Installer. The XML file must include the information needed to both install and uninstall the component, as well as the information needed for adding any menu items needed for the back-end admin interface for your component. The installation package must also contain any SQL scripts needed to set up the database properly.

> **CAUTION**
>
> Make sure that your XML file is created in UTF-8 format.

The sample component shown in Figure 21.1 is named Hello, World!. The necessary XML file for that component is named `helloworld.xml` and the contents look like this:

```xml
<?xml version="1.0" encoding="utf-8"?>
<extension type="component" version="1.6.0" method="upgrade">
    <name>com_helloworld</name>
    <creationDate>2012-12-02</creationDate>
    <copyright>Copyright (C) 2012. All rights reserved.</copyright>
    <license>GNU General Public License version 2 or later; see
LICENSE.txt</license>
    <author>rico</author>
    <authorEmail>ric@ ricshreves.net </authorEmail>
    <authorUrl>http://ricshreves.net</authorUrl>
    <version>1.0.0</version>
    <description>Basic demo component for Joomla! 3.</description>

    <install> <!-- Runs on install -->
        <sql>
            <file driver="mysql" charset="utf8">sql/install.mysql.
utf8.sql</file>
        </sql>
    </install>
    <uninstall> <!-- Runs on uninstall -->
        <sql>
            <file driver="mysql" charset="utf8">sql/uninstall.mysql.
utf8.sql</file>
        </sql>
    </uninstall>

    <files folder="site">
        <filename>index.html</filename>
        <filename>helloworld.php</filename>
        <filename>controller.php</filename>
        <filename>router.php</filename>
        <folder>views</folder>
        <folder>models</folder>
        <folder>controllers</folder>
        <folder>helpers</folder>
    </files>
    <languages folder="site">
        <language tag="en-GB">language/en-GB.com_helloworld.ini
        </language>
    </languages>
    <administration>
        <menu img="components/com_helloworld/assets/images/s_com_
helloworld.png" >COM_HELLOWORLD</menu>
        <submenu>
```

```
            <menu link="option=com_helloworld&amp;view=peoples"
    view="peoples" img="components/com_helloworld/assets/images/s_
    peoples.png" alt="Helloworld/Peoples">COM_HELLOWORLD_TITLE_
    PEOPLES</menu>

        </submenu>
        <files folder="administrator">
            <filename>access.xml</filename>
            <filename>config.xml</filename>
            <filename>controller.php</filename>
            <filename>index.html</filename>
            <filename>helloworld.php</filename>
            <folder>controllers</folder>
            <folder>assets</folder>
            <folder>helpers</folder>
            <folder>models</folder>
            <folder>sql</folder>
            <folder>tables</folder>
            <folder>views</folder>
        </files>
        <languages folder="administrator">
            <language tag="en-GB">language/en-GB.com_helloworld.ini
            </language>
            <language tag="en-GB">language/en-GB.com_helloworld.sys.
ini
            </language>
        </languages>
    </administration>
</extension>
```

The `helloworld.xml` file is consistent with the basic XML files you see associated with the other extensions in the system. The file not only contains basic information about the extension and the developer, but also tells the system where to find the key elements of the component.

Customizing Modules

Modules are probably the most commonly modified pieces of the Joomla! core; this is due to the fact that modules are easy to customize and are relatively easy to create from scratch. In this section, I cover the elements of a typical module and the basics of module creation.

> **NOTE**
>
> At the time this was written, the module documentation had yet to be updated for Joomla! 3. As a result, many of the official documentation resources discuss older versions of the system. Module architecture remains little changed from Joomla! 2.5, and modules written for 2.5 will work in the current version.

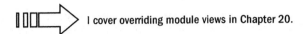 I cover overriding module views in Chapter 20.

Understanding the elements of a typical module

The system's modules are divided into two categories: Site modules and Administrator modules. The front-end Site modules are located in the /modules directory. The back-end Administrator modules are located in the /administrator/modules directory.

The easiest way to see all the elements of a typical module is to look at an example. The default system's Login module is typical of Site modules throughout the system. The Login module supplies a Login form for front-end users, along with links to the Password Reset and Username Reminder functions. If front-end user registration is enabled in the Global Configuration Manager, then the module also includes a user registration link labeled Create an account.

The Login module is located at modules/mod_login. The contents of the directory are

- helper.php
- index.html
- mod_login.php
- mod_login.xml
- /tmpl

The structure of the Login module is typical of modules throughout the system and demonstrates the key requirements for creating a module. I will now look at each of the items in the module directory in turn.

mod_modulename.php

The mod_modulename.php file is the principle functional file for a module. This is the first file called by the system when the module is needed. It contains the initialization routines and includes the helper.php file. It also calls the template that displays the module output (this template is located in the /tmpl directory).

By way of example, here is the mod_login.php file:

```php
<?php
/**
 * @package     Joomla.Site
 * @subpackage  mod_login
 *
 * @copyright   Copyright (C) 2005 - 2012 Open Source Matters, Inc.
   All rights reserved.
 * @license     GNU General Public License version 2 or later; see
   LICENSE.txt
 */
```

```php
defined('_JEXEC') or die;

// Include the login functions only once
require_once __DIR__ . '/helper.php';

$params->def('greeting', 1);

$type    = modLoginHelper::getType();
$return  = modLoginHelper::getReturnURL($params, $type);
$user    = JFactory::getUser();
$layout  = $params->get('layout', 'default');

// Logged users must load the logout sublayout
if (!$user->guest)
{
    $layout .= '_logout';
}
require JModuleHelper::getLayoutPath('mod_login', $layout);
```

Here's what's happening in this code:

- The first lines below the comments prevent direct access to the file, a simple and common security precaution used throughout the Joomla! system.
- Next, the code includes the functions specified in the `helper.php` file, discussed in the next section.
- In the next line, the module grabs the greeting parameter for use in the module.
- Immediately after that, the class `modLoginHelper` is declared; this handles many of the chores related to the login process.
- The module next gets the user information.
- If the user is logged in, the system is told to display the logout layout.

> **NOTE**
>
> `Jfactory` provides access to a group of core Joomla! objects. It is typically used to return an object associated with the current site or user condition.

helper.php

The `helper.php` file contains one or more classes that are used to retrieve the data that is displayed by the module.

The contents of the Login module's `helper.php` file are typical:

```php
<?php
/**
 * @package     Joomla.Site
 * @subpackage  mod_login
 *
```

```
 * @copyright   Copyright (C) 2005 - 2012 Open Source Matters, Inc.
   All rights reserved.
 * @license      GNU General Public License version 2 or later; see
   LICENSE.txt
 */

defined('_JEXEC') or die;

/**
 * Helper for mod_login
 *
 * @package      Joomla.Site
 * @subpackage   mod_login
 * @since        1.5
 */
class modLoginHelper
{
    public static function getReturnURL($params, $type)
    {
        $app    = JFactory::getApplication();
        $router = $app->getRouter();
        $url = null;
        if ($itemid = $params->get($type))
        {
            $db             = JFactory::getDbo();
            $query = $db->getQuery(true);

            $query->select($db->quoteName('link'));
            $query->from($db->quoteName('#__menu'));
            $query->where($db->quoteName('published') . '=1');
            $query->where($db->quoteName('id') . '=' .
$db->quote($itemid));

            $db->setQuery($query);
            if ($link = $db->loadResult()) {
                if ($router->getMode() == JROUTER_MODE_SEF) {
                    $url = 'index.php?Itemid='.$itemid;
                }
                else {
                    $url = $link.'&Itemid='.$itemid;
                }
            }
        }
        if (!$url)
        {
            // Stay on the same page
            $uri = clone JURI::getInstance();
            $vars = $router->parse($uri);
            unset($vars['lang']);
```

```
                if ($router->getMode() == JROUTER_MODE_SEF)
                {
                        if (isset($vars['Itemid']))
                        {
                                $itemid = $vars['Itemid'];
                                $menu = $app->getMenu();
                                $item = $menu->getItem($itemid);
                                unset($vars['Itemid']);
                                if (isset($item) && $vars == $item-
>query) {
                                        $url = 'index.
php?Itemid='.$itemid;
                                }
                                else {
                                        $url = 'index.php?'.JURI::build
Query($vars).'&Itemid='.$itemid;
                                }
                        }
                        else
                        {
                                $url = 'index.php?'.
JURI::buildQuery($vars);
                        }
                }
                else
                {
                        $url = 'index.php?'.JURI::buildQuery($vars);
                }
        }

        return base64_encode($url);
}

public static function getType()
{
        $user = JFactory::getUser();
        return (!$user->get('guest')) ? 'logout' : 'login';
}
}
```

The file defines the helper class modLoginHelper, which includes two functions to help set the return URL and determine the user's status for the purpose of displaying either the logout or the login button.

XML

The mod_modulename.xml file is also a required module file. The XML file helps the Joomla! Installer determine what it needs to copy to install the module properly, and it also tells the Module Manager about the module, including not only basic identification information but also which parameters, if any, are available for module configuration.

The `mod_login.xml` file looks like this:

```xml
<?xml version="1.0" encoding="utf-8"?>
<extension
    type="module"
    version="3.0"
    client="site"
    method="upgrade">
<name>mod_login</name>
<author>Joomla! Project</author>
<creationDate>July 2006</creationDate>
<copyright>Copyright (C) 2005 - 2012 Open Source Matters. All
rights reserved.</copyright>
<license>GNU General Public License version 2 or later; see
LICENSE.txt</license>
<authorEmail>admin@joomla.org</authorEmail>
<authorUrl>www.joomla.org</authorUrl>
<version>3.0.0</version>
<description>MOD_LOGIN_XML_DESCRIPTION</description>
<files>
        <filename module="mod_login">mod_login.php</filename>
        <folder>tmpl</folder>
        <filename>helper.php</filename>
        <filename>index.html</filename>                 <filename>mod_
login.xml</filename>
</files>
<languages>
        <language tag="en-GB">en-GB.mod_login.ini</language>
        <language tag="en-GB">en-GB.mod_login.sys.ini</language>
</languages>
<help key="JHELP_EXTENSIONS_MODULE_MANAGER_LOGIN" />
<config>
        <fields name="params">
                <fieldset name="basic">
                        <field
                                name="pretext"
                                type="textarea"
                                filter="safehtml"
                                cols="30"
                                rows="5"
                                label="MOD_LOGIN_FIELD_PRE_TEXT_LABEL"
                                description="MOD_LOGIN_FIELD_PRE_TEXT_
DESC" />
                        <field
                                name="posttext"
                                type="textarea"
                                filter="safehtml"
                                cols="30"
                                rows="5"
```

```
                                    label="MOD_LOGIN_FIELD_POST_TEXT_
LABEL"
                                    description="MOD_LOGIN_FIELD_POST_
TEXT_DESC" />
                        <field
                                    name="login"
                                    type="menuitem"
                                    disable="separator"
                                    label="MOD_LOGIN_FIELD_LOGIN_
REDIRECTURL_LABEL"
                                    description="MOD_LOGIN_FIELD_LOGIN_
REDIRECTURL_DESC" >
                                    <option
                                            value="">JDEFAULT</option>
                        </field>
                        <field
                                    name="logout"
                                    type="menuitem"
                                    disable="separator"
                                    label="MOD_LOGIN_FIELD_LOGOUT_
REDIRECTURL_LABEL"
                                    description="MOD_LOGIN_FIELD_LOGOUT_
REDIRECTURL_DESC" >
                                    <option
                                            value="">JDEFAULT</option>
                        </field>
                        <field
                                    name="greeting"
                                    type="radio"
                                    class="btn-group"
                                    default="1"
                                    label="MOD_LOGIN_FIELD_GREETING_LABEL"
                                    description="MOD_LOGIN_FIELD_GREETING_
DESC">
                                    <option
                                            value="0">JNO</option>
                                    <option
                                            value="1">JYES</option>
                        </field>
                        <field
                                    name="name"
                                    type="list"
                                    default="0"
                                    label="MOD_LOGIN_FIELD_NAME_LABEL"
                                    description="MOD_LOGIN_FIELD_NAME_
DESC">
                                    <option
                                            value="0">MOD_LOGIN_VALUE_
NAME</option>
```

```
                                        <option
                                                value="1">MOD_LOGIN_VALUE_
                USERNAME</option>
                                </field>
                                <field
                                        name="usesecure"
                                        type="radio"
                                        class="btn-group"
                                        default="0"
                                        label="MOD_LOGIN_FIELD_USESECURE_
                LABEL"
                                        description="MOD_LOGIN_FIELD_
                USESECURE_DESC">
                                        <option
                                                value="0">JNO</option>
                                        <option
                                                value="1">JYES</option>
                                </field>
                        </fieldset>
                        <fieldset
                                name="advanced">
                                <field
                                        name="layout"
                                        type="modulelayout"
                                        label="JFIELD_ALT_LAYOUT_LABEL"
                                        description="JFIELD_ALT_MODULE_LAYOUT_
                DESC" />
                                <field
                                        name="moduleclass_sfx"
                                        type="text"
                                        label="COM_MODULES_FIELD_MODULECLASS_
                SFX_LABEL"
                                        description="COM_MODULES_FIELD_
                MODULECLASS_SFX_DESC" />
                                <field
                                        name="cache"
                                        type="list"
                                        default="0"
                                        label="COM_MODULES_FIELD_CACHING_
                LABEL"
                                        description="COM_MODULES_FIELD_
                CACHING_DESC">
                                        <option
                                                value="0">COM_MODULES_FIELD_
                VALUE_NOCACHING</option>
                                </field>
                        </fieldset>
                </fields>
        </config>
</extension>
```

The opening lines set out the type of file and the associated Joomla! version number. Immediately following is a series of tags that indicate:

Module's name	Author's e-mail
Author's name	Author's website URL
Creation date	Module's version number
Copyright	A short description
Module's license agreement terms	

The remainder of the code defines the parameters that appear to the site administrator inside the Module Editing workspace.

Module template

The /tmpl directory contains the templates for the module. The template file takes the data that has been generated by the primary module file and displays it on the page. The Login module includes two templates, one for the normal login form and another to be displayed if the user is logged in. The key file that defines the normal module state is default.php, and is listed here:

```php
<?php
/**
 * @package     Joomla.Site
 * @subpackage  mod_login
 *
 * @copyright   Copyright (C) 2005 - 2012 Open Source Matters, Inc.
   All rights reserved.
 * @license     GNU General Public License version 2 or later; see
   LICENSE.txt
 */

defined('_JEXEC') or die;

JHtml::_('behavior.keepalive');
JHtml::_('bootstrap.tooltip');
?>
<form action="<?php echo JRoute::_('index.php', true, $params-
    >get('usesecure')); ?>" method="post" id="login-form"
    class="form-inline">
    <?php if ($params->get('pretext')): ?>
        <div class="pretext">
        <p><?php echo $params->get('pretext'); ?></p>
        </div>
    <?php endif; ?>
    <div class="userdata">
        <div id="form-login-username" class="control-group">
            <div class="controls">
                <div class="input-prepend input-append">
```

```
                            <span class="add-on"><i class="icon-
user tip" title="<?php echo JText::_('MOD_LOGIN_VALUE_USERNAME')
?>"></i><label for="modlgn-username" class="element-
invisible"><?php echo JText::_('MOD_LOGIN_VALUE_USERNAME'); ?></
label></span><input id="modlgn-username" type="text"
name="username" class="input-small" tabindex="1" size="18"
placeholder="<?php echo JText::_('MOD_LOGIN_VALUE_USERNAME') ?>"
/><a href="<?php echo JRoute::_('index.php?option=com_
users&view=remind'); ?>" class="btn hasTooltip" title="<?php echo
JText::_('MOD_LOGIN_FORGOT_YOUR_USERNAME'); ?>"><i class="icon-
question-sign"></i></a>
                    </div>
                </div>
            </div>
            <div id="form-login-password" class="control-group">
                <div class="controls">
                    <div class="input-prepend input-append">
                        <span class="add-on"><i class="icon-
lock tip" title="<?php echo JText::_('JGLOBAL_PASSWORD') ?>"></
i><label for="modlgn-passwd" class="element-invisible"><?php echo
JText::_('JGLOBAL_PASSWORD'); ?></label></span><input id="modlgn-
passwd" type="password" name="password" class="input-small"
tabindex="2" size="18" placeholder="<?php echo JText::_('JGLOBAL_
PASSWORD') ?>" /><a href="<?php echo JRoute::_('index.
php?option=com_users&view=reset'); ?>" class="btn hasTooltip"
title="<?php echo JText::_('MOD_LOGIN_FORGOT_YOUR_PASSWORD');
?>"><i class="icon-question-sign"></i></a>
                    </div>
                </div>
            </div>
            <?php if (JPluginHelper::isEnabled('system', 'remember')) :
?>
            <div id="form-login-remember" class="control-group
checkbox">
                <label for="modlgn-remember" class="control-
label"><?php echo JText::_('MOD_LOGIN_REMEMBER_ME') ?></label>
<input id="modlgn-remember" type="checkbox" name="remember"
class="inputbox" value="yes"/>
            </div>
            <?php endif; ?>
            <div id="form-login-submit" class="control-group">
                <div class="controls">
                    <button type="submit" tabindex="3"
name="Submit" class="btn btn-primary btn"><?php echo JText::_
('JLOGIN') ?></button>
                </div>
            </div>
            <?php
                $usersConfig = JComponentHelper::getParams('com_
users');
```

```
                    if ($usersConfig->get('allowUserRegistration')) : ?>
                    <ul class="unstyled">
                            <li>
                                    <a href="<?php echo JRoute::_('index.
    php?option=com_users&view=registration'); ?>">
                                    <?php echo JText::_('MOD_LOGIN_
    REGISTER'); ?> <i class="icon-arrow-right"></i></a>
                            </li>

                    </ul>
            <?php endif; ?>
            <input type="hidden" name="option" value="com_users" />
            <input type="hidden" name="task" value="user.login" />
            <input type="hidden" name="return" value="<?php echo
    $return; ?>" />
            <?php echo JHtml::_('form.token'); ?>
    </div>
    <?php if ($params->get('posttext')): ?>
            <div class="posttext">
            <p><?php echo $params->get('posttext'); ?></p>
            </div>
    <?php endif; ?>
</form>
```

This file plays the key role in the display of the login form. The majority of the code in this file is HTML used to create the various form fields needed by this form. The PHP supplies the logic and the variables that relate to the language strings and the URL paths.

> **NOTE**
>
> The root module directory and the /tmpl directory both contain an index.html file. This file does not serve any purpose other than to block users from accessing the directory index by typing into their browsers the URL of the directory. If a user enters the directory path as a URL, she is served the index.html file, which displays only a blank page. You will see these files used throughout the directories of your Joomla! installation.

Creating a new module

A detailed tutorial on all the aspects of module creation is outside the scope of this chapter, but you should understand the basics of creating a new module. If you want to explore this topic in more detail, you can find a number of excellent resources on the topic in the official Joomla! Developer documentation.

> **TIP**
>
> Don't forget that the Joomla! core includes the module type Custom HTML. This is a blank module that allows you to insert whatever content you want. If you only need to create a module to hold content, there may be no reason for you to go through the process of coding a new module; instead, try creating a new module by using the Module Manager and select the type named Custom HTML. I discuss the use of the Custom HTML module in Chapter 17.

Meeting the minimum requirements

The basic structure you must create parallels what you saw in the earlier discussion of the Login module. You need to follow the structure of that module to create the necessary directories and files. Make sure that you follow the naming requirements for the module elements:

- The naming convention for module directories is `mod_modulename`. For front-end modules, the directory should be placed inside the `/modules` directory at the root of your site. For back-end administrator modules, the directory is placed inside `/administrator/modules`. All module files must be located inside the module directory.

- The primary module file must be named `mod_modulename.php`.

- The naming convention for the module's XML file is `mod_modulename.xml`.

- The helper file should be named simply `helper.php`.

- The template file should be named `default.php` and placed inside a subdirectory named `/tmpl`.

> **CAUTION**
>
> Make sure your XML file is created in UTF-8 format.

Conceptually, building a module means creating a `helper.php` file to do the heavy lifting — that is, the logic and the data access — and then creating a template to render the data. You have to add a file to tie it all together, as well as a file to supply the information needed to get the module into the system. Put another way, you create a new module by accomplishing the following tasks:

- Put the logic in the `helper.php` file.

- Use the `mod_modulename.php` file to include the helper file, grab the parameters from the module configuration, get the items from `helper.php`, and then include the template for display.

- Format the template files to render the data as you see fit.

- Create an XML file to make the module installable and help the system discover all the necessary elements. If you want to offer configurable parameters to your site administrators, add them to this file as well.

> **NOTE**
>
> For a good discussion of working with module parameters, visit `www.vergegraphics.com/blog/joomla/58-extending-joomla-modules-with-parameters`.

- Package it all for installation.

Looking at the Login module discussed earlier in this chapter, you can clearly see each of these elements in action and how they fit together to create the module.

Packaging a module

Proper packaging may not be an issue if your module is only intended for your own use, but if you intend to give your module to others, or if you want to install it again elsewhere, you should create a proper installation package for the module. Proper packaging allows you to manage module installations through the default Joomla! Extension Installer.

Packages are archives that contain all the necessary elements of a module, along with an XML file containing the information needed by the Joomla! Installer. The XML file must be modified to include a list of all the files that need to be installed. You already have an XML file for your module, so you can simply add in the declarations needed by the installer. Each file is listed inside the `<filename>` element. All filename elements are wrapped by the `<files>` tag.

Reference the `mod_login.xml` file shown earlier in this chapter for an example of the syntax and the included elements.

An example will make this simpler: Looking at the `mod_login.xml` file listed earlier in this section, you will note the following lines of code:

```
<files>
        <filename module="mod_login">mod_login.php</filename>
        <folder>tmpl</folder>
        <filename>helper.php</filename>
        <filename>index.html</filename>
        <filename>mod_login.xml</filename>
</files>
```

Note that it is not necessary to list the directory for the module files because the system automatically places the module in the proper directory.

After this change is made to the XML file, all you need to do is zip up the files and name the archive something descriptive, preferably `mod_modulename-version.zip`.

NOTE

Although I have used the ZIP format for this example, you can use your preferred archive format: ZIP, gz, tar, or tar.gz.

CAUTION

Make sure that you are careful about what you zip up into the archive. Do not accidentally include system files generated by your local machine. This is an easy mistake to make and it can sometimes cause problems for module installation.

Working with Plug-ins

Joomla! plug-ins are helper applications that work by detecting and responding to events. Technically they are an observer class that looks to a global event dispatcher. The result is that you, as a developer, are able to create a plug-in that executes some code when an event occurs. This is most useful to you as a way to supplement your work on a component or module.

Plug-ins are the simplest extensions to write from scratch. The directory structure is very simple and there are only two required files. Conceptually, creating a plug-in is a matter of extending the core JPlugin class and then writing methods for each event you want the plug-in to handle.

In the following section, I look at plug-in architecture and an example of one of the core plug-ins. I then look at the basic process for creating and packaging a new plug-in.

> **NOTE**
> At the time this was written, the plug-in documentation had yet to be updated for Joomla! 3. As a result, many of the official documentation resources discuss older versions of the system. Plug-in architecture remains little changed from Joomla! 2.5, and plug-ins written for 2.5 will work in the current version. For a discussion of how to use a plug-in with another extension, see http://docs.joomla.org/Tutorial:Using_plugins_in_your_own_extension.

Understanding plug-in architecture

Joomla 1.5 added the observer class JPlugin, and plug-ins follow the Observer design pattern. The core also includes the JEventDispatcher class, which calls all registered plug-ins when an event is triggered. When you create a plug-in, you extend the core class JPlugin and register your plug-in with JEventDispatcher. Put another way, creating a plug-in is a two-part process whereby you create a class to extend JPlugin, and then write a method for each event you want the plug-in to handle.

> **NOTE**
> Joomla! includes a variety of core events. For a complete list, organized into groups and listed alphabetically, see http://docs.joomla.org/Tutorial:Plugins.

Creating a new plug-in

The system includes a number of plug-ins. The plug-ins are grouped into 11 categories and kept in the /plugins directory. Plug-ins require, at a minimum, two files: pluginname. php and pluginname.xml. The PHP file contains the primary code, while the XML file contains the descriptive information needed for the plug-in to be recognized and used by Joomla!.

Given that most plug-ins are relatively small and narrowly tailored units of code, it is unlikely that you will modify existing plug-ins. If you want to make changes, it's actually easier to create a new plug-in and add it to the system. Your first step in plug-in creation is to determine how you will classify the plug-in. The default classifications in Joomla! 3 are

Authentication	Content
Captcha	Editors

Editors-xtd	Search
Extension	System
Finder	User
Quickicon	

Pick the classification that best fits your new plug-in, as your plug-in files will go into that directory inside the /plugins folder on the server and the classification will be reflected in the Plug-ins Manager workspace.

> **NOTE**
>
> If you want to step outside the default plug-in classification schema, you can create your own classification by adding another subdirectory inside the /plugins directory.

The structure of the plug-in files is best shown by looking at examples. If you open the /plugins/finder directory on your server, you will find the following files inside that directory:

- finder.php
- finder.xml
- index.html

The structure of this plug-in is typical for the system and the comments in the code of this plug-in make it particularly useful as an example. The finder.php file does all the work, extending the JPlugin class. The finder.xml file handles describing the plug-in and telling the system where the resources are located. The index.html file is there to block users from directly accessing the directory.

Here's the code from the finder.php file:

```php
<?php
/**
 * @package       Joomla.Plugin
 * @subpackage    Content.finder
 *
 * @copyright     Copyright (C) 2005 - 2012 Open Source Matters, Inc.
 *   All rights reserved.
 * @license       GNU General Public License version 2 or later; see
 *   LICENSE.txt
 */

defined('_JEXEC') or die;

/**
 * Finder Content Plugin
 *
 * @package       Joomla.Plugin
 * @subpackage    Content.finder
```

```
 * @since       2.5
 */
class plgContentFinder extends JPlugin
{
    /**
     * Finder after save content method
     * Article is passed by reference, but after the save, so no
    changes will be saved.
     * Method is called right after the content is saved
     *
     * @param    string        The context of the content passed to
    the plugin (added in 1.6)
     * @param    object        A JTableContent object
     * @param    bool          If the content has just been created
     * @since    2.5
     */
    public function onContentAfterSave($context, $article, $isNew)
    {
        $dispatcher    = JEventDispatcher::getInstance();
        JPluginHelper::importPlugin('finder');

        // Trigger the onFinderAfterSave event.
        $dispatcher->trigger('onFinderAfterSave', array($context,
    $article, $isNew));

    }
    /**
     * Finder before save content method
     * Article is passed by reference, but after the save, so no
    changes will be saved.
     * Method is called right after the content is saved
     *
     * @param    string        The context of the content passed to
    the plugin (added in 1.6)
     * @param    object        A JTableContent object
     * @param    bool          If the content is just about to be
    created
     * @since    2.5
     */
    public function onContentBeforeSave($context, $article, $isNew)
    {
        $dispatcher    = JEventDispatcher::getInstance();
        JPluginHelper::importPlugin('finder');

        // Trigger the onFinderBeforeSave event.
        $dispatcher->trigger('onFinderBeforeSave', array($context,
    $article, $isNew));

    }
    /**
     * Finder after delete content method
```

```
 * Article is passed by reference, but after the save, so no
changes will be saved.
 * Method is called right after the content is saved
 *
 * @param     string          The context of the content passed to
the plugin (added in 1.6)
 * @param     object          A JTableContent object
 * @since     2.5
 */
public function onContentAfterDelete($context, $article)
{
      $dispatcher     = JEventDispatcher::getInstance();
      JPluginHelper::importPlugin('finder');

      // Trigger the onFinderAfterDelete event.
      $dispatcher->trigger('onFinderAfterDelete', array($context,
$article));

}
/**
 * Finder change state content method
 * Method to update the link information for items that have been
changed
 * from outside the edit screen. This is fired when the item is
published,
 * unpublished, archived, or unarchived from the list view.
 *
 * @param     string    $context  The context for the content passed
to the plugin.
 * @param     array     $pks      A list of primary key ids of the
content that has changed state.
 * @param     integer   $value    The value of the state that the
content has been changed to.
 * @since     2.5
 */
public function onContentChangeState($context, $pks, $value)
{
      $dispatcher     = JEventDispatcher::getInstance();
      JPluginHelper::importPlugin('finder');

      // Trigger the onFinderChangeState event.
      $dispatcher->trigger('onFinderChangeState', array($context,
$pks, $value));
}

/**
 * Finder change category state content method
 * Article is passed by reference, but after the save, so no
changes will be saved.
 * Method is called right after the content is saved
 *
```

```
 * @param    string    $extension  The extension whose category has
been updated.
 * @param    array     $pks        A list of primary key ids of the
content that has changed state.
 * @param    integer   $value      The value of the state that the
content has been changed to.
 * @since     2.5
 */
public function onCategoryChangeState($extension, $pks, $value)
{
        $dispatcher  = JEventDispatcher::getInstance();
        JPluginHelper::importPlugin('finder');

        // Trigger the onFinderCategoryChangeState event.
        $dispatcher->trigger('onFinderCategoryChangeState',
array($extension, $pks, $value));

}
}
```

Look at what happens in the code:

- The first line is there for security purposes only and is standardized across extensions.

- The second line of code sets up the new class `plgContentFinder`, an extension of `JPlugin`. Note the naming convention here, as it is mandatory: `plgNameofdirectoryNameofplugin`.

- What follows afterwards are five methods, each tied to a specific event. Note the naming convention: The name of the method is the same as the event that triggers it. The comments accompanying each of the methods explain the purpose of the code.

- For a breakdown of the various parameters listed in the preceding code, see the discussion on creating a content plug-in at `http://docs.joomla.org/How_to_create_a_content_plugin`.

> **NOTE**
> To learn more about when events are triggered, view the API Execution Order page at `http://docs.joomla.org/API_Execution_Order`.

The `finder.xml` file is even simpler:

```
<?xml version="1.0" encoding="utf-8"?>
<extension version="3.0" type="plugin" group="content">
    <name>plg_content_finder</name>
    <author>Joomla! Project</author>
    <creationDate>December 2011</creationDate>
    <copyright>Copyright (C) 2005 - 2012 Open Source Matters. All
    rights reserved.</copyright>
```

```
<license>GNU General Public License version 2 or later; see
LICENSE.txt</license>
<authorEmail>admin@joomla.org</authorEmail>
<authorUrl>www.joomla.org</authorUrl>
<version>3.0.0</version>
<description>PLG_CONTENT_FINDER_XML_DESCRIPTION</description>

<files>
        <filename plugin="finder">finder.php</filename>
        <filename>index.html</filename>
</files>
<languages>
        <language tag="en-GB">en-GB.plg_content_finder.ini</
language>
        <language tag="en-GB">en-GB.plg_content_finder.sys.ini</
language>
</languages>
<config>
        <fields name="params">
        </fields>
</config>
</extension>
```

This file's key function is to provide the information necessary for installation of the plug-in, though it can also be used to activate parameters that can be set by the administrator from inside the Plug-in Manager.

> **CAUTION**
> Make sure your XML file is created in UTF-8 format.

When you set out to create a plug-in, follow the structure shown here. All the files shown in the example are required. Once you have created the files and populated them with the logic you desire, you can package them for installation.

Packaging a plug-in

Proper packaging may not be an issue if your plug-in is only intended for your own use, but if you intend to give your plug-in to others, or you want to install it again elsewhere, you should create a proper installation package for the plug-in. Proper packaging allows you to manage plug-in installation through the default Joomla! Extension Installer.

Packages are archives that contain all the necessary elements of a plug-in, along with an XML file containing the information needed by the Joomla! installer. The XML file must be modified to include a list of all the files that need to be installed. Because you already have an XML file for your plug-in, you can simply add in the declarations needed by the installer. Each file is listed inside the <filename> element. All filename elements are wrapped by the <files> tag.

An example will make this simpler. Looking at the `finder.xml` file listed earlier in this section, note the following lines of code:

```
<files>
        <filename plugin="finder">finder.php</filename>
        <filename>index.html</filename>
</files>
```

Note that it is not necessary to list the directory for the plug-in files because the system automatically places the plug-in in the proper directory according to its group attribute in the installer tag. Declaring the `finder.xml` file is also not necessary.

After this change is made to the XML file, all you need to do is zip up the files and name the archive something descriptive, preferably `plg_pluginname-version.zip`.

NOTE
Although this example uses the ZIP archive format, you can use your preferred archive format: ZIP, gz, tar, and tar.gz.

CAUTION
Make sure that you are careful about what you zip up into the archive. Do not accidentally include system files generated by your local machine. This is an easy mistake to make, and it can sometimes cause problems for plug-in installation.

Summary

In this chapter, I covered the basics of how Joomla! components, modules, and plug-ins work and what you need to create your own. The topics included

- Finding the right tools to help you with development
- Understanding the architecture of components
- Building a new component with Component Creator for Joomla!
- Understanding module architecture
- Creating a new module
- Understanding plug-in architecture
- Creating a new plug-in

In the next chapter, I cover how you can extend your Joomla! site and take a look at some of the most popular extensions that supply commonly requested functionality.

Extending Your Site

IN THIS CHAPTER

Finding extensions for your site

Installing extensions

Uninstalling extensions

Finding extensions to meet common needs

One of the strengths of the Joomla! system is the availability of a large number of extensions. You can find a Joomla! extension for just about any purpose you can imagine. An extension can be as simple as a plug-in that improves your search capability, or as complex as a complete e-commerce catalog management and shopping cart system. An extension may merely enhance existing functionality or it may add completely new functionality; extensions can also be purely aesthetic in the case of templates.

This chapter covers how to find extensions as well as how to install and uninstall them. In the last half of the chapter, I also look at some of the most popular extensions for Joomla! 3.

Finding Extensions

You can find Joomla! extensions in a number of locations, from the developers' websites to various extension directories. Two officially maintained directories are JoomlaCode and the Joomla! Extensions Directory; the Extensions Directory is the most popular and easiest to use source of Joomla! extensions. The directory was purpose-built by the Joomla! team to provide a listing of extensions that you can browse; it currently contains over 10,000 extensions that you can download and install on your Joomla! site. The Joomla! Extensions Directory is shown in Figure 22.1.

> **NOTE**
> The Joomla! Extensions Directory is located at `http://extensions.joomla.org`.

FIGURE 22.1

The official Joomla! Extensions Directory website offers thousands of extensions. Note the directory tree in the left column.

Each extension in the directory is classified and described. Information includes user reviews and ratings as well as indications of download volume and popularity, as shown in Figure 22.2. The additional information and feedback provided with the listings are invaluable, given the large number of options you face.

All the extensions in the Joomla! Extensions Directory are released under the open source GPL license. The majority of the extensions are free of charge, although some charge fees in some fashion, often by subscriptions. The listings in the Joomla! Extensions Directory identify the developer or company behind the extension, and provide links to the developer's website as well as to any available support and documentation resources.

FIGURE 22.2

A typical listing on the Joomla! Extensions Directory

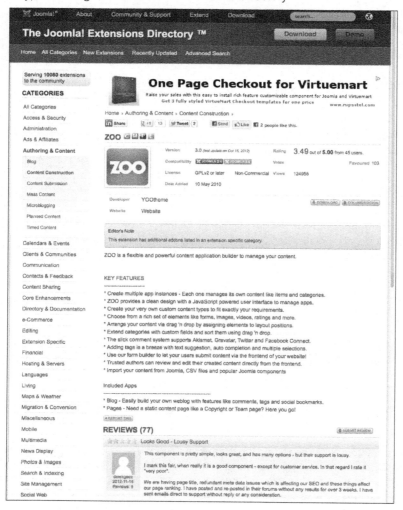

The Joomla! Extensions Directory is organized like most directories, with a tree of categories and subcategories that you can browse by topic. You can also browse the extensions based on ratings, views, and popularity, or you can view the newest or most reviewed extensions. Additionally, the site includes both a basic and an advanced search feature at the top-right corner of each page. The advanced search is particularly useful because it allows you to filter by version compatibility.

Finding Joomla! Templates

Both JoomlaCode and the Joomla! Extensions Directory contain a wide variety of components, modules, plug-ins, tools, and Language Packs; however, neither of these official sites includes templates for your Joomla! site. As a result, a large number of template providers have jumped in to fill the gap. Following is a list of some of the more popular template sites. The list includes both commercial and noncommercial templates, but you should note that many of the sites that offer free templates typically expect promotional exposure on your site by means of links back to their websites on the template.

DreamTemplate

www.dreamtemplate.com

DreamTemplate provides thousands of design templates, including templates for websites. They provide only a small selection of ready-to-use Joomla! templates, but also have a much wider assortment of generic designs you have to convert yourself. Prices vary widely, depending on whether you are a member and whether you want exclusive rights to the design.

Template Monster

www.templatemonster.com

With a catalog containing thousands of designs, Template Monster is perhaps the largest of the commercial template providers. Template Monster includes more than 1,000 ready-to-use Joomla! templates. Prices vary widely, depending on whether you want exclusive rights to the design.

RocketTheme

www.rockettheme.com

The RocketTheme group specializes in ready-to-use templates for the most common content management systems, including Joomla!. The number of designs in their catalog continues to grow, and some of their templates are among the most flexible and functional on the market. RocketTheme also provides the Gantry theme framework.

YOOtheme

www.yootheme.com/themes/joomla

YOOtheme offers over 60 templates based on the Warp Framework. Their products emphasize HTML5 and CSS3, and they specialize in creating responsive design templates. Of special note is their Master Theme product, which you can use as the basis for creating your own themes using the Warp Framework.

CAUTION
Make sure that you download only extensions that are compatible with your version of Joomla!. Extensions written for earlier versions of Joomla! are typically not compatible with Joomla! 3. Joomla! version compatibility is shown in the heading of each extension.

Note that unlike JoomlaCode, the Joomla! Extensions Directory does not host any of the downloads. Therefore, when you click to download an extension, you are taken to a different site. Sometimes, the downloads are hosted on JoomlaCode, but often the files are hosted on the developer's website. Note also that some developers may require you to register on their site before you can download the extension files.

The JoomlaCode site serves as a code repository and distribution point for noncommercial extensions. The site hosts over 2,000 extensions, organized into categories and subcategories that you can browse or search. JoomlaCode does not include reviews or ratings and can be difficult to use. The structure of the site makes it a challenge to find extensions, unless you already know what you are looking for!

NOTE
The JoomlaCode website is located at www.joomlacode.org.

 I discuss JoomlaCode.org at length in Chapter 2.

Working with the Extension Manager

Extensions are handled through the admin system, by way of the Extension Manager. The Extension Manager provides an interface for dealing with components, modules, plug-ins, templates, and Language Packs. It enables you to install, uninstall, enable, and disable all the extensions on your site. The Extension Manager handles not only the third-party extensions that you install on your site, but also the core components, modules, plug-ins, Language Packs, and templates.

In this section, I look at the various functions of the Extension Manager, with an emphasis on how to add new extensions to your system.

Introducing the Extension Installer

To access the Extension Installer, you need to click the Extension Manager option under the Extensions heading on the main admin navigation bar. The Extension Installer workspace loads in your browser, as shown in Figure 22.3.

FIGURE 22.3

The Joomla! Extension Installer workspace

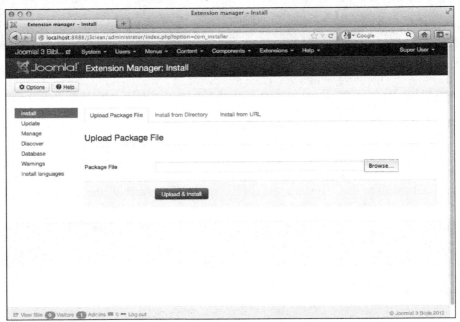

The toolbar at the top of the Extension Installer provides two buttons: Options and Help. The Options button opens the Installation Manager Configuration workspace. There are only two options for configuring the installer: the Preferences tab lets you set the frequency with which the system checks for updates to the extensions, and the Permissions tab allows you to determine which user groups have permission to use the installer.

Under the toolbar in the left column are seven links, which provide access to the following functionality:

- **Install.** Click to access the Extension Installer. I discuss this page in more detail shortly.
- **Update.** Click to check for any available updates to your installed extensions; this page also includes the option to install the updates.
- **Manage.** Click to view a list of all extensions in the system, control their publication state, and clear an extension's cache. This page also provides the option to uninstall extensions. I discuss this page in more detail later in this chapter.
- **Discover.** Click to find extensions that you have added manually. Use this page to discover those extensions and add them to the Extension Manager.
- **Database.** Click to see if there are any problems with the database tables used by the various extensions. This page provides a maintenance function.

- **Warnings.** Click to see if there are any error warnings related to your extensions. Typically, error messages relate to possible conflicts or dependency failures. This page provides a maintenance function.

- **Install languages.** Click to access the Language Pack installer.

 I cover working with Language Packs in Chapter 11.

The Installation Manager workspace includes three tabs:

- **Update Package File.** This tab shows you the Install screen.

- **Install from Directory.** This tab shows you the components installed on your system.

- **Install from URL.** This tab shows you the templates installed on your system.

These tabs provide three alternative methods for installing extensions for your site. You only need to use one method to install an extension, and the method you choose depends largely on the nature and location of the extension files you need to install.

Installing an extension from a package file

The normal way to install an extension is from a package file. Most users find that this method handles all their needs. To install a new extension from a package file, follow these steps:

1. **Download the extension's archive file to your local computer.**

2. **Log in to the admin system.**

3. **Access the Extensions Installer dialog box by clicking the Extension Manager option under the Extensions menu.** The Extensions Installer loads in your browser window.

4. **Click the Browse button.** The File Upload dialog box opens.

5. **Locate the extension's archive file on your local computer.** Click the file and then click the Open button. The pop-up menu closes, and you see the name of the extension archive file in the Package File field.

6. **Click the Upload & Install button.** The system attempts to install the extension, and if it is successful, you see a confirmation message.

Adding an extension from a directory

Use this installation option if you need to unarchive the files before you move them to the server, or if you have been given the files in an unarchived form. To install a new extension from a directory, follow these steps:

1. **Download the extension's archive file to your local computer.**

2. **Unarchive the files locally.**

3. **Log in to your server via FTP or your web host file manager.**

4. **Move the extension directory and files up to your server, noting the location.** A safe place to put these files is in the /tmp folder.

5. **Log in to the admin system of your Joomla! site.**

6. **Access the Extensions Installer dialog box by clicking the Extension Manager option under the Extensions menu.** The Extensions Installer loads in your browser window.

7. **Click the Install from Directory tab.** The tab comes to the front.

8. **Type into the Install Directory field the address of the directory on the server where you have placed the extension files.**

9. **Click the Install button.** The system attempts to install the extension, and if it is successful, you see a confirmation message.

Installing an extension from a URL

Use this installation option in situations where you can access the archive file directly on another server and do not need to download it to your local machine first. For example, you can use this method to install archives directly from the JoomlaCode website. To install a new extension from a URL, follow these steps:

1. **Locate the extension's archive file on the remote computer, noting the URL.**

2. **Log in to the admin system.**

3. **Access the Extensions Installer dialog box by clicking the Extension Manager option under the Extensions menu.** The Extensions Installer loads in your browser window.

4. **Click the Install from URL tab.** The tab comes to the front.

5. **Type the extension archive file's URL into the Install URL field.**

6. **Click the Install button.** The system attempts to install the extension, and if it is successful, you see a confirmation message.

The installation process is the same for all types of extensions. In the next section, I look at how to uninstall extensions.

Uninstalling extensions

Though the Joomla! system provides specific interfaces for components, modules, plugins, templates, and Language Packs, it also provides an interface dedicated to giving you a global view of all the extensions in one screen: the Extension Manager's Manage workspace, shown in Figure 22.4. The Manage workspace not only provides a convenient view of what's installed on the site, but also gives you access to controls that refresh the extension's cache, disable the extension, or even uninstall it.

FIGURE 22.4

The Manage workspace of the Extension Manager provides a global view of the system's extensions.

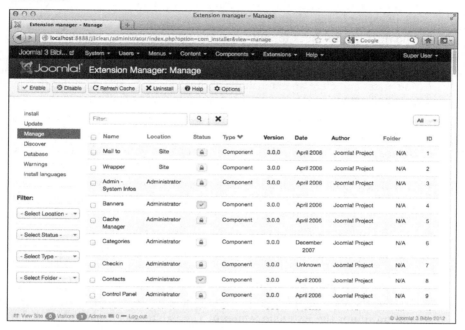

The toolbar at the top of the page provides the following six commonly used controls:

- **Enable.** Select an extension from the list and then click this button to enable the extension.

- **Disable.** Select an extension from the list and then click this button to disable the extension. Note that disabling an extension is not the same as uninstalling it.

- **Refresh Cache.** Select an extension from the list and then click this button to refresh the cache for that extension. This option is most useful if you have made changes to an extension and the changes are not showing up on the front end of the website.

- **Uninstall.** Select an extension from the list and then click this button to uninstall the extension. I discuss this topic in more depth shortly.

- **Help.** Click to view the Help files for the active page.

- **Options.** Click to open the Installation Manager Configuration workspace. There are only two options for configuring the installer: the Preferences tab lets you set the frequency with which the system checks for updates to the extensions, and the Permissions tab allows you to determine which user groups have permission to use the installer.

Under the toolbar in the left column are seven links, which provide access to the following functionality:

- **Install.** Click to access the Extension Installer. This page is discussed in more detail earlier in this chapter.
- **Update.** Click to check for any available updates to your installed extensions; this page also includes the option to install the updates.
- **Manage.** Click to view a list of all extensions in the system, control their publication state, and clear an extension's cache. This page also provides the option to uninstall extensions. I discuss this feature in more detail later in this chapter.
- **Discover.** Click to discover extensions that you have added manually, and add them to the Extension Manager.
- **Database.** Click to see if there are any problems with the database tables used by the various extensions. This page provides a maintenance function.
- **Warnings.** Click to see if there are any error warnings related to your extensions. Typically, error messages relate to possible conflicts or dependency failures. This page provides a maintenance function.
- **Install languages.** Click to access the Language Pack installer.

To uninstall an extension, follow these steps:

1. **Log in to the admin system.**
2. **Access the Extensions Installer dialog box by clicking the Extension Manager option under the Extensions menu.** The Extensions Installer loads in your browser window.
3. **Click the Manage link in the left column.** The Manage workspace loads in your browser.
4. **Click the check box next to the name of the extension you want to uninstall.**
5. **Click the Uninstall button on the toolbar.** The system attempts to uninstall the extension. If it is successful, you see a confirmation message.

> **CAUTION**
>
> There is not a confirmation warning prior to deletion! Deleting an extension is permanent and cannot be undone. Uninstalling also typically wipes out any data on the extension from the database. If you want to use the extension again, you must reinstall it.

The uninstallation process is the same for all types of extensions. As a matter of caution, you should disable extensions prior to uninstalling them, in order to avoid disruption for site visitors and to make sure you are not also impacting other content or functionality. If an extension is needed for another extension to function, you may be blocked from uninstalling it until you remove the dependent extension.

Finding the Right Extension for the Job

Perhaps one of the most daunting parts of exploring extensions is finding the right tool for the job. Thousands of extensions are available, and sometimes you are faced with multiple options that appear to address your needs. Although there is really not a substitute for downloading extensions and trying them out yourself, in this chapter I provide a list of extensions that are a good starting point for addressing common needs.

Note that I am not endorsing one particular extension over another; I am simply listing resources to help you get started. The list includes both commercial and noncommercial extensions. Note also that this list was created for Joomla! 3 and that you must always be certain that the extensions you download and install on your site are compatible with your version of the core.

> **CAUTION**
>
> The rate of change in the open source world can be daunting. Developers change, some projects fork, and other projects are abandoned. It's impossible to say what will be here in 12 months' time. One thing is certain: The extensions provided in this list will change over time. You should always keep this in mind when you are selecting extensions, and if business risk is an issue for you, then you need to do your own research and consider carefully which extensions you adopt.

Improving content management

The extensions listed here all expand upon the default content management functionality of Joomla!. The list includes extensions to enhance existing articles as well as several powerful tools for changing the nature of the articles and the article-editing functionality.

Content Versions

    http://extensions.joomla.org/extensions/authoring-a-content/content-
        submission/18166

The Content Versions extension adds content versioning to your Joomla! site. Once installed and enabled, the extension adds a versions button to your site's WYSIWYG editor. You can click the button to view the past versions of the article. You can also restore previous versions. This is a very useful component if your site has frequent content changes, sensitive content, or multiple administrators. This is a noncommercial extension.

Editor Switcher

    http://extensions.joomla.org/extensions/edition/editor-buttons/9912

Editor Switcher is a simple extension that does one thing: It adds a combo box below the text field in your Article Editing workspace that allows you to select from the available WYSIWYG editors. This provides a quick shortcut; without this extension, the user has to leave the article page, go to his user profile, change the editor choice, and then go back to the article page.

JCE

`www.joomlacontenteditor.net`

JCE is an third party WYSIWYG editor for your Joomla! site. If you are looking for an alternative to the default editor, JCE is one option. The editor is extendable, allowing you to add in a file manager, a media manager, and an image manager. This is a noncommercial extension; however, some of the enhancements offered for this extension do incur a fee.

JCK Editor

`http://extensions.joomla.org/extensions/edition/editors/90`

JCK Editor is an alternative WYSIWYG editor that you can install on your site. The primary advantage of this editor is its compatibility with the iPad and iPhone. It also adds an enhanced file manager functionality for file uploads, giving each user her own folder. This is a noncommercial extension. There are a number of related extensions that you can install to add more functionality.

K2

`http://getk2.org`

K2 is a content construction kit for Joomla!. With this extension installed, you can create custom content types with custom fields. This extension also supports tagging as well as the inclusion of a variety of media formats. K2 is a noncommercial extension.

MetaMod

`www.metamodpro.com`

The MetaMod extension enhances module management. It allows you to add additional rules and logic for displaying modules on your pages. You can set start and end dates for module publication and trigger module display according to the appearance of text or metadata in an item. MetaMod also has geo-location filtering, making it possible to show visitors different content, based upon their IP address. One of its more useful features is the ability to hide modules after a user has logged in. This is a noncommercial extension.

RokPad

`http://extensions.joomla.org/extensions/edition/editors/9427`

RokPad is a replacement WYSIWYG editor whose strength lies in its ability to handle code editing. If you like having a WYSIWYG editor but want to have better access to working with the article's code than what is offered by the default editors, then this extension is a good choice. It's particularly useful during site construction or initial content creation. This is a noncommercial extension.

Search & Replace for Joomla!

`http://extensions.joomla.org/extensions/edition/replace/9496`

Search & Replace for Joomla! provides site-wide search-and-replace functionality, making it easy to find and change text throughout your entire site. If you have ever wanted to make a change across multiple articles and got tired of editing each individual article, then you know the value of this extension. This is a noncommercial extension.

Widgetkit

`www.yootheme.com/widgetkit`

Widgetkit provides site administrators with access to a variety of functions, called widgets. Widgets include galleries, slide shows, maps, accordion content panels, and much more. You can build the widgets inside the admin system without having to write code. The Widgetkit extension also includes *shortcodes* that you can use to place widgets inside of your articles. This extension comes in both a free and a premium commercial version.

ZOO

`http://extensions.joomla.org/extensions/authoring-a-content/content-construction/12479`

ZOO is a content construction kit that allows the administrator to quickly roll out custom content types with a wide variety of attributes. The system includes commenting, ratings, tagging, and a form builder. It's a useful extension for creating a blog, a directory, or even a product catalog. Though it requires a fair amount of configuration to set up your site, the ZOO extension makes it possible to create complex content types without programming. Additional extensions are available that can extend the functionality of ZOO. This extension comes in both a free and a premium commercial version.

Improving site administration

The extensions listed in this section are all intended to make managing the administration of your Joomla! site easier. They provide functionality that you may already have from other external tools, but with these extensions you are able to do the job directly from within the Joomla! admin system, thereby saving time and effort.

Admin Tools

`www.akeebabackup.com`

Admin Tools provide an entire suite of utilities that can help you perform common maintenance tasks and improve site security. The tools include enhancements to update notifications, the ability to edit your `.htaccess` file, an automator that uses `cron` to schedule common tasks, and utilities to make your admin login more secure. Admin Tools comes in two varieties: a free version and a commercial version with extended functionality.

Akeeba Backup

www.akeebabackup.com

Akeeba Backup is a flexible and customizable backup component for Joomla!. It creates a full backup of a site in a single archive and can be restored by any Joomla!-capable server, thereby providing not only basic backup functionality, but also an aid for site migration. This is a noncommercial extension.

Cookie Monster

http://extensions.joomla.org/extensions/site-management/cookie-control/20831

The Cookie Monster extension was built specifically in response to the new cookie disclosure regulations in place in the European Union. You can install this extension to add the required notifications and consent elements to your site. This is a noncommercial extension.

JSN PowerAdmin

http://extensions.joomla.org/extensions/administration/admin-navigation/20267

The JSN PowerAdmin extension represents a rethinking of the way the Joomla! admin interface works. The emphasis here is on usability, and it features a number of shortcuts and design enhancements that make working inside the admin system more effective. While some of the issues this extension was created to address have been dealt with in Joomla! 3, you may still appreciate having an alternative to the default admin system. This is a noncommercial extension.

OSE Security Suite

http://extensions.joomla.org/extensions/tools/security-tools/7032

This extension is an all-in-one suite that combines file security with site security and antivirus protection. It includes two-stage firewall screening of requests, as well as file scanning of all uploads. Scanning and blocking discretion is given to the administrator, who has the option to block a user's IP, show the user a 503 error page, or simply filter out the user's inappropriate behavior while leaving the IP active. It offers a lot of features and options, but it is a commercial extension.

Reset Admin Password

http://extensions.joomla.org/extensions/tools/security-tools/13785

The Reset Admin Password extension serves only one function: It allows you to reset a lost admin password. While the same result can be achieved by other means, this extension is an easy solution if you are not comfortable running queries against the database. Note that you have to have FTP access to the site to install Reset Admin Password. This is a noncommercial extension.

Chapter 24 contains a discussion of alternative methods for regaining admin access to your site.

Enhancing search functionality

The Joomla! search function sometimes needs a little help. Even with Smart Search enabled, the Joomla! site search does not extend to outside files or third party sites. If you want to expand the search capabilities of your site, here are two extensions you can add that will improve the site search experience for your users.

OS PDF Indexer

```
http://extensions.joomla.org/extensions/search-a-indexing/site-
     search/11620
```

If you carry PDF files on your site, the OS PDF Indexer extension adds indexing of those files so that their contents show up in your site search. This extension also supplies limited indexing of Word documents. This is a commercial extension.

RokAjaxSearch

```
http://extensions.joomla.org/extensions/search-a-indexing/site-
     search/9011
```

RokAjaxSearch is a module that you can use to enhance the basic search functionality of your Joomla! site. Using this module, you can offer a search functionality that includes not only your site, but also Google Web search, Google Image search, Google Blog search, and Google Video search. This module also improves search performance and allows you to apply a variety of skins. This extension is noncommercial.

NOTE

Solr is an enterprise-level site-indexing and search engine. It is an open source product based on the Apache Lucene project. Solr can be integrated with Joomla!, though at the time of this writing there was not a Joomla! 3-compatible release available. If your site is large or you require extensive indexing of your site and documents, then you will want to look at Solr as an alternative to the Smart Search functionality in Joomla!. You can learn more by visiting http://lucene.apache.org/solr/.

Enhancing menus and navigation

Although Joomla! provides some flexibility in the creation of menu layouts, these two extensions make it easy to create great-looking menus in a variety of formats and styles.

Extended Menu

http://de.siteof.de/extended-menu.html

Extended Menu extends the functionality of the Menu module in Joomla!. You still have to use CSS to achieve the styling, but the configuration options make it very easy to change the menu orientation and to split and reorder the menus. This extension also enhances your ability to work with parent-child menu item relationships. This extension is noncommercial.

swMenu

www.swmenupro.com/

swMenu is a set of menu creation and management extensions. You can create and integrate unlimited menu modules and achieve a wide variety of styling. Commercial and noncommercial versions are available on the developer's site.

Building complex forms

The default Joomla! system offers extremely limited options for form creation. The extensions listed here address this issue by providing you with the ability to create complex forms on your Joomla! site.

bfForms

www.forms-for-joomla.com

The bfForms extension uses an AJAX admin interface that makes it easy to create complex forms. This extension supports unlimited forms and fields and is Smarty Templates–enabled. Forms created with this extension support the Akismet and Mollom anti-spam systems, as well as IP banning and blacklists. Submit buttons and validation are also configurable. This is a commercial extension.

ChronoForms

www.chronoengine.com

ChronoForms is a great choice if you have HTML skills and want more control over your forms. By using this extension, you can create the form in your favorite HTML editor and then copy and paste it into the ChronoForms component. There is also a drag-and-drop form creation interface if you don't want to do the work in HTML. This extension also gives you the ability to create database tables and connect those tables to forms, thereby allowing you to capture form data in the database. This extension is a noncommercial component, but does include a back-link to the developer's site. You can remove the back-link for a fee.

Adding a gallery

Galleries are one of the most requested extensions to Joomla!. It is therefore not surprising that a large number of options are available in this area. The following list includes both full-featured galleries and simple slide-show components.

Art Gallery

```
http://extensions.joomla.org/extensions/photos-a-images/galleries/
    photo-gallery/10775
```

Art Gallery is a full-featured image gallery extension that supports automatic thumbnail creation, slide shows, and a lightbox display. This extension uses CSS3 for rotation, giving good support across multiple browsers. This is a commercial extension.

Frontpage SlideShow

```
http://www.joomlaworks.net/extensions/commercial-premium/frontpage-
    slideshow
```

Frontpage SlideShow creates JavaScript and CSS-based slide shows. One of the most powerful features of this extension is its ability to integrate text with images to create PowerPoint-type slides. Configuration options give you a great deal of control over the timing, display triggers, and transitions. This is a commercial extension.

Quick Gallery

```
http://extensions.joomla.org/extensions/photos-a-images/galleries/
    content-photo-gallery/22070
```

Quick Gallery is a Joomla! plug-in. After you install and enable this plug-in, you can add your galleries into either articles or modules using the plug-in's parameters. Quick Gallery includes a selection of themes and over two dozen transition effects for use with the slide show. This is a commercial extension.

RapidGallery

```
http://extensions.joomla.org/extensions/photos-a-images/galleries/
    photo-gallery/20371
```

The RapidGallery extension is a jQuery-based photo gallery with extensive use of Ajax. It includes 12 different gallery skins and a number of layout features. This extension is compatible with tablets and phones and is able to work in both module positions and in the main content area of your pages. This is a commercial extension.

SIGE

```
http://extensions.joomla.org/extensions/photos-a-images/galleries/
    content-photo-gallery/13762
```

Simple Image Gallery Extended, or SIGE, is a gallery content plug-in. It adds a SIGE button to your content editing interface to make it easy to add galleries to your articles. SIGE includes automatic thumbnail generation and supports the integration of a variety of slide shows. This extension provides a number of features, including watermarking of images. It is noncommercial.

sigplus

```
http://extensions.joomla.org/extensions/photos-a-images/galleries/
    content-photo-gallery/11426
```

The sigplus extension makes it easy to add lightbox images or a complete gallery to your articles. It also supports sliders and carousel rotation. This extension is noncommercial.

Adding a forum

Threaded discussion forums have moved way past the old bulletin board format. At the time of this writing, there was only one company that had announced plans to release a version compatible with Joomla! 3.

```
www.kunena.com
```

The Kunena extension is a fork of the popular FireBoard Forum component. This forum supports all common features, including threaded discussions, multiple categories, user management, moderation, avatars, and much more. This extension is noncommercial.

Enhancing SEO

Joomla! provides search engine friendly URLs as part of the Global Configuration options, but if you want to do more to improve your site's search engine optimization, you should consider these extensions.

 For a discussion of creating a search engine-friendly site, see Chapter 25.

Easy Frontend SEO

```
http://extensions.joomla.org/extensions/site-management/seo-a-
    metadata/17926
```

Easy Frontend SEO gives you control over your site's metadata. With this extension installed, you can edit your metadata fields while viewing the pages on the front end of the website. The metadata is edited from the front end of the site instead of from the admin system. Title tag management is also possible. This is a noncommercial extension.

RSSeo

```
www.rsjoomla.com/joomla-extensions/joomla-seo-sef.html
```

The RSSeo Suite provides a wide variety of metrics, tools, and tips. This extension is designed for the site owner who wants to handle the SEO for his own site. The suite includes an SEO dashboard that provides you with access to Google, Alexa, Bing, and Compete data inside your admin interface. This extension provides metadata and title management, and can also "grade" your pages and provide you with recommendations for improvements. This is a commercial extension.

SEO-Generator

```
http://extensions.joomla.org/extensions/site-management/seo-a-
    metadata/meta-data/7171
```

The SEO-Generator extension is an automated metadata generator for Joomla!. This extension works by identifying the most commonly used words in an article — less common parts of speech, and other words you have included in a blacklist — and then adds the top words to the keywords field for the article. SEO-Generator also gives you the ability to set title configurations, robot meta tags, and Google Webmaster verification tags. This is a commercial extension.

Xmap

```
http://joomla.vargas.co.cr
```

Xmap produces frontend user site maps and XML site maps. The options are few, but it does exactly what you need it to do and is very easy to use. This extension is noncommercial.

Adding Web 2.0 functionality

Web 2.0 functionality is now considered standard for websites. This section lists several extensions that help you build your web community and stimulate user interaction.

Community Builder

```
www.joomlapolis.com
```

Community Builder is an entire suite of components and modules that enable you to turn Joomla! into a community website with user pages and a high degree of user interactivity. Many modules and plug-ins are available for Community Builder, and integration of the extension is widely supported by other common extensions. This extension is noncommercial, but it does require registration to download.

Facebook-Google-Twitter+1

```
http://extensions.joomla.org/extensions/social-web/social-share/
    social-multi-share/18072
```

This extension adds buttons that allow users to cross-post your site's content to Twitter, Facebook, and Google +. It also supports Facebook comments, giving you threaded comment functionality, with a social twist. To use this extension to its fullest, you need to have accounts on the various services, and you need to set up a Facebook application to be used by the extension. This is a noncommercial extension.

JReviews

```
www.reviewsforjoomla.com
```

JReviews is a powerful extension that lets you create a reviews and ratings website with Joomla!. This system is customizable and can even be used as an alternative method for handling your Joomla! content items, with a customized structure and fields. This extension is commercial.

plugin Googlemaps

```
http://joomlacode.org/gf/project/mambot_google1
```

The plugin Googlemaps extension is a Joomla! plug-in that integrates Google Map functionality. It enables users to view Google Maps and also includes support for KML files and marker placement. Directions are integrated and can appear in pop-up menus or in a lightbox. This extension is noncommercial.

Improving Ad Management

If you want to run ads on your site at anything more than a basic level, you need an extension that provides you with greater functionality than the basic Joomla! Banner Manager. The two extensions listed in this section gives you more options for controlling the advertising space on your site.

ProJoom Multi Rotator

```
http://extensions.joomla.org/extensions/ads-a-affiliates/banner-
    management/6303
```

ProJoom Multi Rotator is a full-featured banner rotator. This extension integrates with the core Joomla! Banner component but also supports banners uploaded through the extension, text ads, and mixed content. It also supports banner transitions, delays, and scheduling. ProJoom Multi Rotator is compatible with a wide variety of browsers, as well as tablets and mobile devices. This is a commercial extension.

Carousel Banner

```
http://extensions.joomla.org/extensions/ads-a-affiliates/banner-
    management/3114
```

Carousel Banner is a simple banner rotator that adds more features than are offered in the default Banner component. This extension provides banner transition effects using the jQuery library. This extension is noncommercial.

Summary

In this chapter, I looked at how you can extend the functionality of your Joomla! site. I also looked at some of the most popular extensions available for Joomla! 3. The topics included

- Finding extensions for Joomla!
- Installing new extensions
- Uninstalling extensions
- Reviewing popular extensions that address common needs

In the next chapter, I look at techniques to help you maintain your Joomla! site and keep it secure.

Part V

Overseeing Website Maintenance and Management

P art V covers the ongoing maintenance of a Joomla! website. This final section of the book is focused more on website ownership issues and will be of more interest to webmasters and website owners. The first chapter in the section looks at implementing a security regimine and at the related topic of patch management. The second chapter looks at how you can enhance the performance of your website and how to improve accessibility of your content. The final chapter in this section looks at techniques for enhancing the search engine friendliness of your Joomla! website.

Keeping Your Site Secure and Up to Date

S ite security and upgrade management are two critical issues for site owners and administrators. Keeping your site patched and up to date is the key to maintaining your site's integrity and protecting it against hackers. Unfortunately, instead of budgeting for ongoing maintenance of their sites, many site owners think that once it's built, the work is done. The truth, however, is quite the opposite: Like any complex software package, you need to periodically install updates and patches, both to enhance functionality and to plug holes in the site's security. Management of upgrades and patches can be time consuming, particularly for complex sites with numerous extensions. The investment of time and energy is worth it, however, as a compromised site can cause huge headaches for both the site's owners and users.

In this chapter I look at security best practices for Joomla! and provide advice and tips on how to set up your Joomla! site in a secure manner and thereafter keep it secure. I also cover the related topic of managing upgrades.

Implementing Security Best Practices

Creating and maintaining a secure website requires attention to a variety of issues. The process starts at server setup and continues throughout the life of the site. There is no such thing as a site you can build and forget, or one that takes care of itself. To keep your site safe, you must take preemptive steps and develop an awareness of security and maintenance issues. Although you cannot protect yourself from every conceivable threat, you can reduce the vulnerability of your site to a manageable level with a reasonable amount of effort.

Adherence to a few simple principles dramatically decreases your threat profile and lays the foundation for manageable recovery in the event of a crisis. In this section, I look at security best practices and how you can apply them to your site.

> **TIP**
>
> The single most important factor in maintaining the integrity of your site over time is the creation and maintenance of a backup and recovery process. The effort it takes to regularly back up your system is more than offset by the time and stress it saves in the event of a site crash!

Securing the Joomla! core

Security is not one single thing; it is a process, a set of steps that you need to take to achieve a result. The process begins with your server settings and the Joomla! core files. If you fail to make this base level of the system secure, then additional steps won't be very effective; at the very worst, they will be pointless.

> **TIP**
>
> The first step toward assuring your site's integrity is also one of the easiest: Only install the most recent version of the Joomla! core file packages found at the official download site, JoomlaCode.org. Do not download and install core file archives from other sites, because you cannot be certain of their origins, completeness, or integrity.

Protecting directories and files

In the process of installing the system on your server, you create a number of new directories and files. The permissions you set for these directories determine who has access to them. While the Joomla! installer takes care of most of this for you, and implements permissions that are appropriate, there are several steps you can take to enhance the security of the directories and files on your server.

The first step to enhancing the security of your directories and files is to adjust the permissions to be as strict as possible without impairing use of the site. The key issue is to implement write-protection for your critical directories. As a general rule, you should set the directory permissions to 755 and the file permissions to 644; you can do this using either FTP or the file manager on your web-hosting control panel. Note that the best time to do this is after you have completed your installation of the core and all extensions. You may have to make these settings more permissive if you need to install extensions in the future.

> **TIP**
>
> You will find a good discussion of how to set file permissions, and what they all mean, on the Joomla! docs site at `http://docs.joomla.org/Security_and_Performance_FAQs - How_do_UNIX_file_permissions_work.3F`.

There are a number of other steps you may want to consider taking; however, you should note that each of these steps has a trade-off, either in terms of increased admin overhead or other limitations:

- **Move the** `configuration.php` **file outside of the public HTML directory on your server and rename it.** The `configuration.php` file is a common target of hackers. The default placement of the file inside the public HTML directory presents an opportunity for hackers; they know the file is likely to be there and the location is accessible. You can avoid this threat by moving the file to another location. If you take this approach, you must edit the `/includes/defines.php` file to point to the new configuration file location or your site will not work.

> **CAUTION**
>
> Technically, moving the `configuration.php` file and altering `defines.php` is a core hack and therefore frowned on by many. You must remember that if you implement this approach, that you may lose your changes on upgrade. You will need to document this for yourself and your predecessors.

- **Use** `.htaccess` **to block direct access to critical files.** You can edit your `.htaccess` file to include instructions to block access to key files. Note this only applies to servers using the Apache web server and web hosts that allow you to modify `.htaccess`. Make sure you back up your old `.htaccess` file before you try this in case you experience problems and need to restore the old file. Looking at two examples, if you want to block access to your `configuration.php` file, you can add the following lines of code to your `.htacess` file:

```
<FilesMatch "configuration.php">
Order allow,deny
Deny from all
</FilesMatch>
```

To block access to the `.htaccess` file, add these lines of code to the `.htaccess` file:

```
<Files .htaccess>
Order allow,deny
Deny from all
</Files>
```

- **Change the default log path.** Hackers sometimes look to the log files of a site as a way to identify what extensions are installed, in hopes of finding an extension that has a known vulnerability they can exploit. To help deter this bit of information-fishing, alter the log path settings in the Global Configuration Manager.

- **Change the default temp directory.** The contents of the temp directory can also provide information you may not want to disclose about your site. You can alter the temp directory settings in the Global Configuration Manager.

- **Use SEF URL rewriting.** The default Joomla! URLs often carry with them information that indicates the extensions used on the site, making them another source of information for those who might be looking for vulnerable URLs. Implement an SEF URL extension to avoid this problem. In addition to providing search engine benefits, the SEF URL rewriting obscures your original URLs and masks this information.

23

I discuss working with the Global Configuration Manager in detail in Chapter 4.

Protecting your site from unauthorized access

Humans are your most common source of security policy failure. Admin passwords should be changed often. Don't use "admin" as your default username, as this name is too commonly used. If your username is "admin," then you've given a hacker one-half of the answer to the puzzle he needs to solve to gain access to your site. Passwords are also key. You should strive to make your passwords as varied and as secure as practicable.

> **CAUTION**
> A good administrator password should be at least seven characters long and employ a combination of upper- and lowercase letters, numbers, and nonalphanumeric characters. Never, under any circumstances, use words that can be found in the dictionary! For example, "4tG~9fU#ss3" is a lot harder to crack than "tinytoons." If you shy away from obscure letter and number combinations, go for length. A long password is much harder to crack.

In addition to controlling the access to your admin system, you need to be sensitive to the access issues that relate to your database. If you have control over the access privileges to the user accounts on your MySQL database, make sure that all accounts are set with limited access.

Joomla! also provides you the option to use SSL for your administration system. This is a recommended enhancement and you should use it if possible. Joomla! supports SSL for both the admin system and the entire site. While using it for the entire site may not be desirable due to performance issues, using it for the admin system most certainly is. If your web host supports it, use SSL for the admin system.

 I cover enabling your site to employ SSL via the Customizing Server Settings in Chapter 4.

Removing unnecessary files

Unnecessary files simply create unnecessary risks. If you don't need it now and you don't intend to use it, get rid of it. Keep your installation as lean as possible to decrease your threat profile.

Logical targets for deletion include

- Unused templates
- Extensions you have installed on your server and then decided not to use
- Unused third-party applications you have installed on your server
- Archive files copied to your server during installation

Another good idea is to disable all unused core components that cannot be uninstalled. Disabling unneeded core components shuts down one more avenue of attack and has the added advantage of cleaning up the administration interface. This option is not available for all core components. Only the following can be disabled:

- Banners
- Contacts
- Newsfeeds
- Search
- Smart Search
- Weblinks

To disable core components in Joomla!, follow these steps:

1. **Access the admin system of your site.**
2. **Click the Extensions menu.** The Extensions Manager opens in your browser.
3. **Click the Manage link.** The Manage Extensions workspace opens in your browser.
4. **Identify the components you want to disable and then click the green arrow next to them in the Status column.** The Status column indicator changes to show a red X, and the selected components are now disabled.

Maintaining a sensible server setup

In an ideal world, we would all have our own dedicated servers where we could control every aspect of the system. In the real world, shared hosting is the reality for many users. Although certainly more cost effective than a dedicated host, shared hosting involves trade-offs in terms of security and access privileges.

> **NOTE**
>
> The move to PHP5 has brought about a number of changes that have removed several security threats. However, if you are using earlier releases of PHP, you may need to be concerned with items like Safe Mode, Register Globals, and Magic Quotes GPC. Make sure Safe Mode and Register Globals are set to Off, and set Magic Quotes GPC to On.

Your goal should be to make the host setup as secure as possible, regardless of whether it is dedicated or shared. Exactly what you are permitted to do with your server varies, but you should consider the following:

- **Use Secure FTP, if available.** This helps avoid the possibility that someone can determine your username and password while you are in the process of a file transfer.

- **If the** `mod_security` **module is installed on your Apache web server, use it.** It acts as an embedded web application firewall and provides significant protection against many common attacks. You can learn more about how to use it at www. modsecurity.org.

- **Don't use PHP allow_url_fopen.** Set this option to Off.
- **Use PHP open_basedir.** Set this option to On.

TIP

Contracting with a web host solely on the basis of price is a bad idea. Moreover, as competition has increased in the hosting market, it is becoming more of a commodity business and price points have narrowed. Instead of simply going with the cheapest host, make your selection based on service levels, quality of hardware, access privileges, software installed, and backup policies.

Securing third-party extensions

From a security perspective, every extension you install on your Joomla! site increases the risks you face. Each extension comes with its own set of files and potential vulnerabilities. Moreover, the fact that extension quality varies wildly is a serious issue for site owners.

Each extension you install brings with it a need for due diligence and ongoing maintenance. Given these issues, the first point of concern for site owners should be the issue of trust: Do you trust that the developer is capable of producing solid, secure code, and do you trust this developer to keep it patched and to keep users updated about risks as they arise? Never forget that, just like the core files, extensions have to be maintained, patched, and upgraded.

The wide variety of Joomla! extensions means that you have choices. Accordingly, before you decide to adopt a particular extension, you need to do your research. Not only should you be concerned with whether it works and looks like you want it to, but also you need to be convinced that the extension is of good quality and comes from a reputable source. There are no guarantees; it is up to you to do your homework and make a judgment call. Visit the developer's site. Is it professional? Is it up to date? If this is a project-based extension, check for levels of project activity and issues that have been reported but remain unfixed. Extensions listed on the Joomla! Extensions Directory include ratings and reviews — read them!

TIP

Joomla! maintains a Vulnerable Extensions List. You should always check this list before you finally decide to adopt a particular extension. The list is maintained at `http://docs.joomla.org/Vulnerable_Extensions_List`.

Next, before you install a new extension on a live site, test it locally. Check to make sure it installs cleanly and without error messages. Test all the various functionalities, regardless of whether you intend to use them. It's also a good idea to check and see if the extension comes with a README file; if it does, read it! Finally, before installing the new extension on your live site, back up the live site. That way, if a problem occurs, you can roll back and restore from the backup.

If at some point you decide that the extension is no longer necessary and you uninstall it, make sure that the extension has uninstalled cleanly and has not left any files on your server. Often, extensions leave directories and files behind on a server, despite being uninstalled.

Keeping Up With Security Notices

Things change. New vulnerabilities are discovered and new hacks are created to take advantage of them. Sometimes the rate of change is quite impressive, and it becomes a challenge to keep up and maintain all aspects of your site. The Joomla! Security Strike Team was formed by the community to address the dynamic nature of threats to the Joomla! system. As new issues are discovered, the community reports them to the Strike Team. The team formulates responses, works to learn more, and, when needed, sends patches out to the users.

Keeping up with the announcements from the Joomla! Security Strike Team is one of the ways you can stay informed of important news that may impact your Joomla! site. Important notices are always published on the home page of Joomla.org. Of course, if you rely on these default notifications, you only discover new alerts when you visit the site. If you want more immediate notices, then you should consider either subscribing to the RSS feed with a separate newsreader or joining the mailing list so that notifications are sent to you by e-mail. The URLs for both services are included in Table 23.1.

The way you prefer to receive alerts is entirely up to you, but the simple fact is that the only way to keep your site secure is to keep it — and its extensions — up to date. When new versions are released, do not delay in upgrading. New releases require immediate action. If you fail to upgrade your site after a security release is announced and your site is subsequently hacked, you really have no one to blame but yourself.

The Joomla! team and community have created and now maintain a number of useful security resources, which are listed in Table 23.1.

TABLE 23.1   Joomla! Security Resources

Name of resource	URL
Security Checklist: Getting Started	`http://docs.joomla.org/Security_Checklist_1_-_Getting_Started`
Security Checklist: Hosting and Server Setup	`http://docs.joomla.org/Security_Checklist_2_-_Hosting_and_Server_Setup`
Security Checklist: Testing and Development	`http://docs.joomla.org/Security_Checklist_3_-_Testing_and_Development`
Security Checklist: Joomla! Setup	`http://docs.joomla.org/Security_Checklist_4_-_Joomla_Setup`

continued

23

TABLE 23.1 *(continued)*

Name of resource	URL
Security Checklist: Site Administration	`http://docs.joomla.org/Security_Checklist_5_-_Site_Administration`
Security Checklist: Site Recovery	`http://docs.joomla.org/Security_Checklist_6_-_Site_Recovery`
Joomla! Security Strike Team General and Contact Information	`http://developer.joomla.org/security.html`
Security and Performance FAQs	`http://docs.joomla.org/Security_and_Performance_FAQs`
Automatic Email Notification System	`http://feedburner.google.com/fb/a/mailverify?uri=JoomlaSecurityNews`
Security RSS Feed	`http://feeds.joomla.org/JoomlaSecurityNews`
Joomla! 3 Security Forum	`http://forum.joomla.org/viewforum.php?f=714`
Vulnerable Extensions List	`http://docs.joomla.org/Vulnerable_Extensions_List`
Security Announcements for Joomla! Developers	`http://developer.joomla.org/security/news.html`

Managing Site Maintenance

Whenever a new patch or update is released, you need to install it on your site without delay. Sometimes, particularly in the case of extensions, the patch can be a small matter; in other cases, particularly with a new version release, installation of the new files can involve a significant amount of work. In either event, having an established process for dealing with the upgrades is useful as it helps ensure that you won't miss something during the upgrade only to discover problems later on.

Two tools that are built into Joomla! ease the burden of patch management: the Joomla! Update component and the Extension Manager. The Joomla! Update component can help you keep track of new releases for the Joomla! core and then manage the upgrade process. While the Joomla! Update component is a significant time saver, it does not help you with updating and patching your extensions; you have to manage these tasks via the update function in the Extension Manager.

> **NOTE**
>
> Support for automatic extension updates via the Extension Manager is still inconsistent. While a number of extensions support this functionality, it is not universal at this time. You need to make sure that your extensions employ this function before you rely on it exclusively.

In this section, I look at the upgrade process and how to use the Joomla! Update component and the update function of the Extension Manager.

Taking a site offline

Prior to undertaking any major upgrade on a live site, you should take the site offline, that is, hide it from public view. Joomla! makes it possible to take a site offline with one click, while still retaining access to the admin system. After the site is offline, you can perform whatever maintenance you need and check your work prior to taking the site live again.

To take your site offline, follow these steps:

1. **Log in to the admin system of your site.**
2. **Access the Global Configuration Manager either by clicking the Global Configuration link on the control panel or by clicking the Global Configuration link under the Site menu.** The Global Configuration Manager loads in your browser.
3. **Click the Yes option next to the Site Offline label.**
4. **Adjust the Offline Message text, if you so desire.**
5. **Click the Save button.** The system takes the front end of the site offline and displays the Offline Message to site visitors.

While the site is offline, visitors are not able to see the front end of the site, but the administrators can access the back end of the site. You can run upgrade processes for both the core and extensions while the site is offline.

To put the site back online, follow these steps:

1. **Log in to the admin system of your site.**
2. **Access the Global Configuration Manager by either clicking the Global Configuration link on the control panel or clicking the Global Configuration link under the Site menu.** The Global Configuration Manager loads in your browser.
3. **Click the No option next to the Site Offline label.**
4. **Click the Save button.** The system puts the front end of the site back online.

Backing up your site

Before you begin any significant maintenance process, make sure that you have a current backup of your site. If something goes wrong, you need to be able to roll the site back to the previous version. While it may be time consuming to follow this advice, it is worth it. Trust me, you aren't doing this for the 99 times out of 100 that you don't have a problem; you are doing it for the one time that you do! If you are dealing with your personal site, this may seem inconvenient, but if you are handling a client's or employer's site, it is unprofessional not to take the appropriate precautions to protect their site and their data.

Backing up a Joomla! site involves making copies of the files on the server as well as the data in your database. A complete backup encompasses both tasks.

How frequently you need to back up your site depends on the frequency with which your site changes. If your site changes daily, then perhaps daily backups are in order. If your site changes only sporadically, then weekly backups will probably do the job.

Make sure that you don't keep all your backups in one location. If there is a fire or other problem that results in the loss of one backup, you want to increase your chances that the second copy is protected. If your web-hosting contract provides for backup services, make sure you periodically download the files to keep a local copy as your failsafe.

To make a complete backup of your site, you need to access the files on the server and make a copy of them. Typically this is done via FTP or through your web-hosting control panel's file manager. You also need to use a tool such as phpMyAdmin to make a copy of the database for the site. As an alternative to using multiple tools and doing this manually, you can install additional extensions to your Joomla! site to enable you to do this from within the admin interface. As I discuss in Chapter 22, several tools can help you create and manage your backups.

Restoring from a backup

Manually restoring your site files from a backup is a simple process; you only need to copy your backup files onto the server, replacing the files on the server. If you have used full backups, this is a one-step process. If you are using incremental backups, you first need to copy the full backup and then copy the incremental backup files.

Manually restoring your database is slightly more complicated. Your database backup will typically be in the form of a ZIP or SQL file. In either event, you need to run a SQL query on your database to update the database tables. For most people, this means using phpMyAdmin to import the backup files to overwrite the existing database tables.

Just like creating backups, you can restore from a backup manually, but the process can be made much simpler by using one of several third-party extensions that are available.

> **TIP**
>
> If you have never restored a site from a backup, I highly recommend that you try the process once before you deploy your site. The process is not difficult, but you don't want to be doing it for the first time on a live site that you need to get working without delay!

Regaining access to your administration system

Sometimes a site administrator loses his password, or a hack attempt results in the loss of the administrator's password. If you have access to the Password Reset functionality on the Login Form, you can try to use it to get a new password. If that does not work, then you need to go to the database to solve the problem. Although you cannot recover a lost admin password, you can reset it in the database and thereby gain access to the account.

Passwords are stored in the database along with the user data. The passwords are not human-readable, because they are stored as MD5 hashed values. By way of example, follow these steps to reset a user's password to the value "admin":

1. **Use phpMyAdmin to access the database on your server.**

2. **Select the database for your Joomla! site from the combo box on the left side of the page.** The list of database tables in the database is displayed in the left column, below the combo box.

3. **Click the table named (database-prefix)_users in the list of tables.** The users table screen appears on the right side of the page.

4. **Click the Browse button on the top toolbar.** The screen shows all of the users that are set up for this site.

5. **Find the user whose password you want to change, and click the Edit icon next to the user's name.** The Edit screen appears.

6. **Type the following value into the field named Password: 433903e0a9d6a712e0 0251e44d29bf87:UJ0b9J5fufL3FKfCc0TLsYJBh2PFULvT.** This is the MD5 hash value that equates to the string "admin."

7. **Click the Go button.** phpMyAdmin saves the new value for the password and returns you to the users table.

The value entered into the password field in this example changes the user's password to "admin." The user should now be able to log in to the site by typing his username along with the password "admin." He should change his password immediately to his preferred value.

An alternative workaround is to create a new super administrator account and use it to regain access to the back end of your Joomla! website. You can add the new user account directly to the database by executing an SQL query, as follows:

1. **Use phpMyAdmin to access the database on your server.**

2. **Select the database for your Joomla! site from the combo box on the left side of the page.** The list of tables in the database appears in the left column, below the combo box.

3. **Click the SQL tab.** The SQL query tab comes to the front.

4. **In the text field provided, enter the following code:**

```
INSERT INTO `jos_users`
  (`name`, `username`, `password`, `params`)
VALUES ('NewAdmin', 'newadmin',      '433903e0a9d6a712e00251e44d29b
    f87:UJ0b9J5fufL3FKfCc0TLsYJBh2PFULvT', '');
INSERT INTO `jos_user_usergroup_map` (`user_id`,`group_id`)
VALUES (LAST_INSERT_ID(),'8');
```

Note that in the example query, you should replace the prefix 'jos_' with your site's database table prefix.

5. **Click the Go button.** The query runs and the new user is created.

When this process is complete, you have a new Super Administrator named NewUser. You should be able to log into the site using the username *newuser* and the password *admin*.

Upgrading the core with Joomla! Update

The Joomla! Update component is provided to help you discover and install updates to the Joomla! core. The component is enabled by default and you can access it at any time by clicking the Joomla! Update option under the Components heading on the main admin menu. When you select this option, the Joomla! Update Manager workspace opens in your browser, and if any updates are available, they appear. Figure 23.1 shows the Joomla! Update Manager workspace.

To install the update, simply click the Install the update button. The Installation Method combo box gives you two choices for handling the update: If you want to allow the installer to install the update directly, leave the default option, Write files directly; if you prefer to use FTP to update the files, then select the option, Write files using FTP. If you elect to use FTP to install the files, you need to provide the FTP access details.

The toolbar at the top of the Joomla! Update Manager includes two options: Purge Cache and Options. Click the Purge Cache button to remove updates from the list and force the list to refresh. Click the Options button to go to the Joomla! Update Configuration workspace. Figure 23.2 shows the Joomla! Update Configuration workspace.

The configuration options for the Joomla! Update component are very limited. The only choices relate to where the system looks for its updates. The Update Server combo box contains the following values:

- Long Term Support (recommended)
- Short Term Support
- Testing
- Custom URL
- Currently Configured (no change)

FIGURE 23.1

The Joomla! Update Manager displays an update that is ready to install

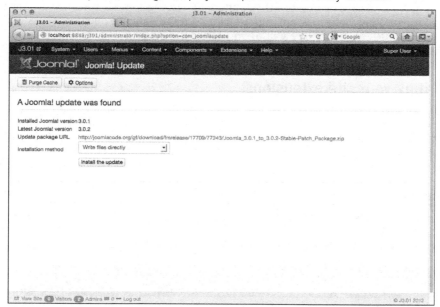

FIGURE 23.2

The Joomla! Update Configuration workspace

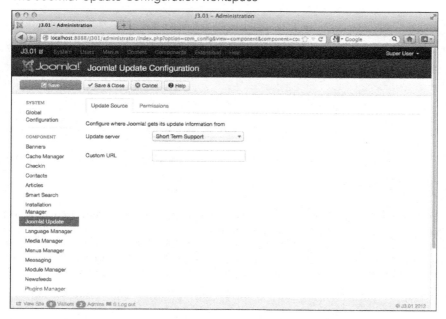

If you are running a Long Term Support release of the Joomla! core, select Long Term Support; otherwise, select Short Term Support. The Testing option is for when you are testing new releases. The Custom URL option allows you to set a specific URL for updates, an option you may want to use if you are behind a firewall and need to access updates from a local URL inside the firewall. If you select the Custom URL option, enter the URL in the field immediately below.

Updating your site extensions

The Joomla! Extension Manager includes automated update management. To access this feature, simply click the Extension Manager option under the Extensions heading on the admin menu. When the Extension Manager loads in your browser, click the Update link in the left column. Figure 23.3 shows the Extension Manager Update workspace.

FIGURE 23.3

The Extension Manager Update workspace shows that there aren't any updates available.

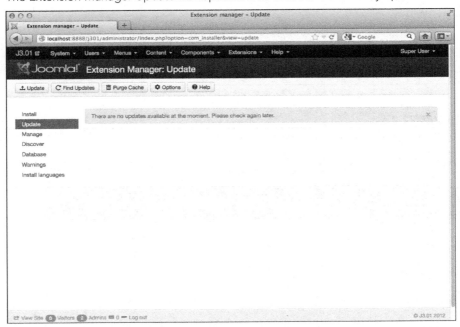

Any available updates appear on the screen. To update one or more extensions, select the updates you desire and click the Update button on the toolbar. If you want to force the system to check for updates, click the Find Updates buttons on the toolbar. Click the Purge Cache button to remove updates from the list and force the list to refresh. Click the Options button to go to the Extensions Update configuration workspace.

The Extension Manager Update functionality offers only one option: the ability to specify how long the update data is cached. Shorter cache times mean that the system checks more frequently for updates.

> **NOTE**
> The Extension Manager Updates feature looks for updates to components, plug-ins, templates, and Language Packs.

Summary

This chapter looked at Joomla! security and site maintenance issues. I covered the following topics:

- Implementing security best practices
- Securing the Joomla! core and extensions
- Keeping up to date on security notifications
- Backing up your site
- Installing patches and upgrades to your site

In the next chapter, I take a look at how you can improve the performance and accessibility of your site.

23

Managing Performance and Accessibility

IN THIS CHAPTER

Managing caching in Joomla!

Improving the performance of your site

Creating content that performs well

Evaluating the default Joomla! templates for accessibility

Enhancing the accessibility of your site

S ite performance and accessibility should be common concerns for all website owners. Although performance tuning may not appear to be related to website accessibility, the opposite is true. Many of the items that improve the performance of a website also improve website accessibility. Indeed, the features that many owners include in their websites can limit both the site's performance and its accessibility. This chapter looks at how you can optimize Joomla! for better performance and improve site accessibility. The topics covered range from optimizing configuration for enhanced performance through management of templates and content items to boost site speed and promote accessibility.

Employing Effective Cache Management

Cache files are temporary files created and stored on the server to help reduce server load and improve performance times. When a file is cached, the server can display the cached version instead of having to call up the file from out of the database and assemble it for display. When site traffic is heavy, the efficiency gained through caching can result in dramatic performance improvements.

Joomla! includes multiple caching options, including support for component view caching, page caching, and individual module caching. You can configure the caching controls to limit the length of the time data is cached and tell the system how long to hold content before refreshing it. In some situations — for example, when you install an updated component — you may want to dump your cached data in order to force the system to update the information in the cache. The Joomla! admin system gives you the ability to flush the cache either completely or selectively.

The Joomla! cache management controls are split between the Global Configuration Manager, the System - Cache plug-in, and the individual module parameter controls. In the sections that follow, I discuss all three options, as well as how to clean and purge your site's cache.

> **TIP**
>
> If you are looking for more cache control, consider installing a third-party extension to expand this functionality. The Joomla! Extensions Directory includes a subcategory dedicated to enhanced caching, at `http://extensions.joomla.org/extensions/site-management/cache`.

Setting the site cache

Global caching of Joomla! component views is handled by the Cache Settings options found in the Global Configuration Manager. This caching option is limited, as it only applies to viewing component output. Nonetheless, it is worth enabling, as it will give you some performance improvement. How much it will help you depends largely on how many of your components support this feature.

The Cache Settings controls are located on the System Tab of the Global Configuration Manager, as shown in Figure 24.1. In the default configuration, site caching is turned off.

There are three caching controls on the System tab. Here's what they do:

- **Cache.** This combo box allows you to turn caching on or off. There are two options for enabling caching: Conservative Caching and Progressive Caching.

> **TIP**
>
> Conservative caching shows each site visitor the same content. Progressive caching caches the content for each user individually. Progressive caching overrides conservative caching, so if you want maximum flexibility, set the global caching to conservative, then vary the cache settings per module when you desire progressive caching. Since progressive caching creates cached copies of pages for each individual user, it can actually cause a performance decrease on your site if used inappropriately. Progressive caching is most appropriately used in situations where you are serving specific content to specific users; in all other cases you are better off to use conservative caching.

- **Cache Handler.** If caching is enabled, then this combo box allows you to specify how the cached files are stored, either with File caching or with XCache. The default setting is File, which results in the system using a directory on the site as a temporary storage space for cached files. XCache is a more aggressive cacher that is focused on enhancing PHP performance.
- **Cache Time.** If caching is enabled, then this field allows you to specify how frequently the cache is refreshed. The value you enter here represents the number of minutes.

FIGURE 24.1

The Joomla! Global Configuration Manager's System tab contains the Cache Settings controls.

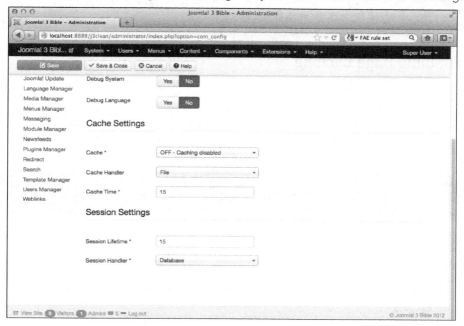

To enable site caching, follow these steps:

1. **Log in to the admin system of your site.**
2. **Access the Global Configuration Manager by either clicking the Global Configuration link on the Control Panel or by clicking the Global Configuration link under the Site menu.** The Global Configuration Manager loads in your browser.
3. **Click the System tab.** This tab comes to the front.
4. **Set the Cache option to On - Conservative Caching.**
5. **Click the Save button.** The system enables caching.

> **NOTE**
>
> The Global Configuration Manager provides view caching, which applies mostly to component views. Support for this feature must be built into components by the component developers. Sadly, this is often not done.

Enabling page caching

While the site caching options in the Global Configuration Manager are the most obvious, they are not necessarily the most useful. As noted previously, the site cache option provides view caching, which applies to the components. For many sites, page caching provides a more significant performance boost. Page caching focuses on the articles in your site. Enabling caching for the articles delivers performance gains for users who are viewing your content items.

> **NOTE**
>
> The page caching functionality in Joomla! only caches pages for site visitors, not for logged-in users.

Page caching is supplied by the System - Cache plug-in, which is disabled by default. You can access the plug-in by going to the Plug-in Manager under the Extensions menu. Clicking the System - Cache option opens the plug-in for editing, as shown in Figure 24.2.

FIGURE 24.2

The System - Cache plug-in

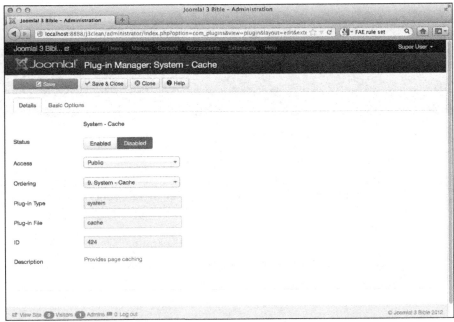

To enable page caching, follow these steps:

1. **Log in to the admin system of your site.**

2. **Access the Plug-in Manager by clicking the Plug-in Manager link under the Extensions menu.** The Plug-in Manager loads in your browser.

3. **Click the System - Cache plug-in.** The System - Cache workspace opens in your browser.

4. **Set the Status option to Enabled.**

5. **Click the Save button.** The system enables page caching.

> **NOTE**
>
> You can also enable browser-side caching for your site's pages by displaying the Basic Options tab and setting the Use Browser Caching option to Yes. Browser-side caching stores some of your commonly used page elements on the user's computer inside the user's browser cache. Support for this option depends on whether the user is permitting items to be cached by the browser; most people do. The downside of browser-side caching is that changes on the server may not immediately update to the browser.

> **CAUTION**
>
> Page caching is the most aggressive form of caching offered by the default Joomla! system. You should test your site after enabling page caching; in particular, you should test its impact on front-end functionalities such as the Random Image module, the Newsflash module, and the login and logout process. If you have installed any third-party extensions, make sure that you also test them after enabling the System - Cache plug-in. If you observe problems, disable the plug-in and test again.

Caching module output

A number of the site modules include caching options. The caching controls are typically located on the Advanced Options tab of the module. You can configure most, but not all, of the site modules to cache their output. Caching is available for the following modules:

Archived Articles	Articles Category	Latest News
Articles - Newsflash	Banners	Latest Users
Articles - Related Articles	Breadcrumbs	Menu
Articles Categories	Custom HTML	Most Read Content
	Feed Display	Search
	Footer	Weblinks
	Language Switcher	Wrapper

24

Caching is not an option for the following modules:

Login

Random Image

Smart Search

Syndication

Who's Online

Module caching parameters typically include two options: First, you can choose to use the Global Cache settings, as defined in the Global Configuration Manager, or you can exempt the module from that setting. The second option allows you to set the cache time for the module, though this option is not available for all modules.

Clearing the cache

Clearing the cache wipes out the cached files and forces the system to refresh the cached information. If you have updated an important content item, or installed a new module or component, you may want to clear the cache and get the updated information to appear on the site.

Joomla! includes a cache cleaner that you access from within the admin system. Simply click the Clear Cache option under the System menu. The Clear Cache workspace loads in your browser, as shown in Figure 24.3.

The toolbar at the top of the Clear Cache workspace provides quick access to the following functions:

- **Delete.** Select one or more items from the list and then click this button to delete them. In this context, deleting an item means deleting only the cached files.
- **Options.** Click to access the configuration options for the Cache Manager. The only configuration option available is permissions management.
- **Help.** Click to access the online Help files related to the active screen.

Below the toolbar, in the left column, are three links: The Check-In link leads to an unrelated function, the Global Check-In workspace. The Clear Cache link takes you to the screen shown in Figure 24.3. The Purge Expired Cache link leads to the Purge Expired Cache workspace, where you can delete all expired cache files.

FIGURE 24.3

The Clear Cache workspace

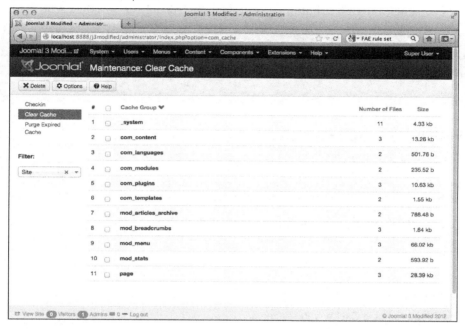

The main content area of the workspace contains a list of all the cached files for your site. The columns provided are

- **#.** This is an indexing number assigned by Joomla!; it cannot be changed.
- **Check box (no label).** This column allows you to selectively delete items from the cache. Click a check box to select an item.
- **Cache Group.** This is the type of item being cached. Note that the name here reflects the name of the subdirectory where the cached item is kept on the server.
- **Number of Files.** This is the number of files in the cache group.
- **Size.** This is the total size of the files cached in this group.

To clean up your site's cached files, follow these steps:

1. **Log in to the admin system of your site.**
2. **Click the Clear Cache option under the System menu.** The Clear Cache workspace loads in your browser.

24

3. **Select the check box next to the items you want to delete, or click the top check box to select them all.**

4. **Click the Delete button.** The system immediately deletes the cache files.

Purging the expired cache

The system's caching mechanism retains expired cache files on the server. When you use the Clear Cache option, you clean both the current cache and the expired cache files. The system also provides you with a separate option to clean up, or purge, only the expired cache files, leaving the current cache files intact.

To use this alternative cache-cleaning tool, click the Purge Expired Cache option under the System menu. The Purge Expired Cache workspace opens in your browser, as shown in Figure 24.4.

FIGURE 24.4

The Purge Expired Cache workspace

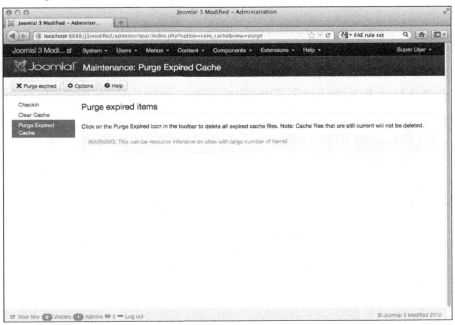

The toolbar at the top of the workspace provides quick access to the following functions:

- **Purge expired.** Click to instigate the purge.
- **Options.** Click to access the configuration options for the Cache Manager. The only configuration option available is permissions management.
- **Help.** Click to access the online Help files related to the active screen.

The main content area of the screen contains only the instruction text and a warning that the process may take a while.

To purge the expired cache files, follow these steps:

1. **Log in to the admin system of your site.**
2. **Click the Purge Expired Cache option under the System menu.** The Purge Expired Cache workspace loads in your browser.
3. **Click the Purge expired button.** The system immediately deletes the cache files.

> **NOTE**
>
> Using the Purge Expired Cache option has the advantage of not causing a decrease in the front-end site performance. If your site experiences heavy traffic, using the Clear Cache function can cause a performance decrease because the system must rebuild the cache after you force it to dump the files. Purge Expired Cache only deletes the expired files, leaving the current cache files untouched. Typically this is only an issue if your site has a lot of active users when you decide to clear the cache.

Improving Content Performance

Everything that is on the pages of your website has an impact on the site's performance. If you build large pages with large files, the pages load more slowly than smaller, lighter pages. While the pages your Joomla! site generates from components are largely beyond your control, you can have a significant impact on the size of your articles' pages. If you work smart and keep in mind the need to build lean pages, you can serve web pages to your visitors more quickly and also reduce the burden on your system. Never forget, it all adds up. If you have multiple visitors on your site simultaneously, the page each visitor is viewing contributes to the load. Saving a few kilobytes in file size here and there can add up to a large savings very quickly.

In this section, I explain the issues you should consider when creating content for your site.

Avoiding large files

Excessively large file size is usually an issue with graphics inserted into the body of articles. You should always make an effort to optimize your images to keep file sizes down to reasonable levels. As image file size is at least partially a byproduct of the physical dimensions of the image files (width and height), it is hard to say what is right for your site;

however, a reasonable goal is to keep your display images under 100KB and your small images below 30KB in size. If your images are too large to achieve that goal without a loss in quality, you may want to consider whether you need to display large images on the page; perhaps a better course would be to display a smaller image, such as a thumbnail, that a user can click to open a larger image. Note also that for the web, an image resolution of 72 dpi is sufficient; any higher resolution is excessive and unlikely to be noticed in the user's monitor.

> **TIP**
>
> If you are using the Firefox web browser, two free add-ons can help you diagnose and solve performance problems. The YSlow and Firebug add-ons include tools that help you identify the sizes of all the files on any particular web page. This is a great way to identify problem areas and bottlenecks. YSlow also provides suggestions for improving performance. You can get both extensions from `https://addons.mozilla.org`.

Saving images in the right format

Image format is also important when considering image file size. You should use the correct image format for the content you need to display. The most common formats for web use are JPEG, GIF, and PNG. Use JPEG for photos and any images that require a smooth transition from one color to another or that include large amounts of detail. Use GIF or PNG for any images that contain large blocks of color or black and white. For example, photos are best saved as JPEGs, while a chart or a graphical illustration is best served as a GIF or PNG. Given a choice between GIF and PNG, I prefer PNG because it often produces a better quality image and is copyright-free.

> **TIP**
>
> PNG files can be either interlaced or non-interlaced. Interlaced files provide progressive rendering — that is, they render little by little on the screen, starting out fuzzy and becoming clearer. You should avoid interlaced PNGs because they are larger in size, and they confuse some users. Also, note that there are three types of PNG files: 8-bit, 24-bit, and 32-bit. The 24-bit and 32-bit formats offer full transparency, whereas the 8-bit PNG offers a lower quality transparency, approximately on par with a transparent GIF.

Optimizing images

Upload the image in the actual size at which it will appear. Do not upload files larger than are needed and then force them to resize into a smaller display by setting smaller width and length values for the image in the code. Forcing the images to a new size not only fails to save file size, as the file size remains constant, but it also forces the system to do additional work to resize the image dimensions. Uploading a smaller image and forcing it to resize into a larger display results in poor image quality.

Keeping your code clean

If you are copying and pasting text into your WYSIWYG editor, pay careful attention to the code that results. Although the Joomla! system does its best to eliminate unneeded tags and redundant code, you should switch to the plain text editor and look at it yourself to ensure that redundant tags and inline style definitions have not found their way into your page formatting. One of the worst culprits for producing redundant code is text copied from older versions of Microsoft Word. The cleanup option on the default WYSIWYG browser can help, but a manual check is always the best solution. Note also that valid code renders faster, so it is always a good idea to validate your HTML and CSS.

 I discuss the cleanup code option in more detail in the discussion of WYSIWYG editors in Chapter 6.

Avoiding tables

When possible, use Cascading Style Sheets (CSS) instead of tables to format your page layouts. Tables slow down the display, as the whole table needs to be assembled before the contents are rendered. Tables must also be carefully constructed to maintain accessibility. Complex tabular data may require the use of tables, but as a general rule, CSS is the better way to go.

> **NOTE**
>
> If you are not familiar with CSS, a good starting point is the W3C site: www.w3.org/MarkUp/Guide/Style.

Using image rotators

Image rotators are extensions that provide a rotating image inside a module position on your page. A popular technique on many websites today is the use of a rotating image on the header of the page. The rotator works like a slide show, displaying a series of images as the visitor is looking at the page. The problem is that many of the extensions that provide this functionality require all the images to load before the rotation occurs. Therefore, a large amount of data is loaded for the page, some of which may be completely pointless as the user has already clicked and moved on before the image displays. If you have to use an image rotator, keep the image sizes small and do not load too many images into the sequence; three images in rotation perform much better than four, five, or six images. If front-page performance is a key concern, keep image rotators off the front page.

Using wrappers

Wrappers are used to display a web page inside of your web page. This means that the wrapper contents have to be fetched and displayed inside your page. By definition, this increases the number of HTTP requests that have to be made to complete the page, thereby increasing the loading time of the page. If the web page you are wrapping is

24

located on another server, the display of the wrapper content depends upon the performance of the remote system and upon the quality of your connection to that server. All of these factors add up to a greater risk of disruption and to increases in page loading time. If, on the other hand, the wrapped content is kept on your server, the risk decreases dramatically, but the delay factor remains. If front-page performance is a key concern, keep wrappers off the front page.

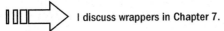 I discuss wrappers in Chapter 7.

Limiting use of animation

Animation files tend to be larger in size and must completely load before they function properly. Accordingly, limit the use of animation on your page to keep the page's file size down.

Restricting use of Flash

Flash files can be quite large, and they keep your visitors waiting as they spool in to play. If you must use Flash on your pages, use only Flash elements inside the page, rather than using Flash for the entire page content area. Also, plan your Flash so that your viewers do not experience long delays.

Limiting streaming

If you want to give users access to video files, do not stream the video until requested by a user. While this does mean that users who want to view the video have to wait for it, it does not force all the users to endure slow page loading while a file they may never view eats up their bandwidth.

Tuning Joomla! Performance

This section looks at various techniques you can use to tweak the performance of your Joomla! site. Some of the tips in this section are simple to implement and available to anyone, while others require more work or depend upon support from your web host. Effective performance tuning requires an understanding of the hosting environment of the website. Because there are many different types of web hosts, not all of the suggestions in this section may be suitable for your site, but certainly some of them are.

If you are not sure where to begin, start with the simplest tuning tips. Every little bit helps, and just because a technique is more complex does not necessarily mean it will deliver a greater benefit. If you have the time, the ability, and the support of your web host, implement as many of these techniques as you can. Your site visitors will appreciate the improvements in performance, and increasingly, the search engines are rewarding better-performing sites with an advantage in search engine rankings.

Enabling server-side compression

Joomla! supports the server-side compression protocol GZip. If your server supports GZip, you should enable this feature in the Global Configuration Manager as it can result in significant performance improvements. The GZip page compression options are located on the Server tab in the Global Configuration Manager.

 See Chapter 4 for more information on using the Global Configuration Manager.

Disabling unnecessary features

Disable all components, modules, and plug-ins that you are not using. Even if you are not displaying the output on the page, the system is likely doing at least some of the processing associated with the feature.

> **TIP**
> As I discuss in Chapter 23, unneeded components, modules, templates, and plug-ins can also have site security implications!

Minifying your CSS and JavaScript

Minification is the process of reducing the size of CSS selectors and JavaScript by removing unnecessary spaces and characters. Although minifying a single selector saves only a small amount of file space, it all adds up, and minifying all of your CSS can result in a meaningful savings. This is a tedious manual process, so if you want to employ this technique, I suggest using one of the many tools designed to make this easier. Run a Google search for "minify CSS" and "minify JavaScript" for lists of options.

> **TIP**
> The Joomla! Extensions Directory also lists several extensions that can compress your CSS and JavaScript.

Implementing Google Analytics

Google Analytics, though a wonderful and useful service, can slow down your site. Every page that includes the Google Analytics code increases your load time as the Google Analytics script causes the system to wait while it contacts the Google servers. The impact of this service varies greatly, depending on the time of day, the traffic on your site, and the location of your servers.

Optimizing your template

Your template developer can have a significant impact on your Joomla! site performance. Many of the lovely templates I see in circulation rely heavily upon images to achieve their look and feel. As a result, the size of the templates and the number of HTTP requests they

24

generate are not optimal. Select your template carefully. Look at the file size and the quality of the code. You want to select templates that use CSS, not tables, and those that prefer system text to images. Be particularly careful of templates that use images for the menus, rather than system text and CSS. Not only do these templates have a negative impact on site performance, but they also tend to be less than optimal in terms of both SEO and accessibility.

Being selective about extensions

Some third-party extensions are incredibly resource-intensive. When you are comparing components, modules, or plug-ins, use YSlow to compare their impact on your page performance and to check resource usage on your server. Don't forget that small differences in performance can balloon into big differences when the site experiences spikes in traffic.

Skipping live stat reporting

Components or modules that produce live, real-time statistics on your site can be significant drains on site performance. If you don't have a compelling need for real-time statistics, skip them.

Disabling SEF URLs

Though this may not be an option for you, if your goal is performance above all else, disable the SEF URLs option. The conversion of your native URLs into aliases causes a performance hit.

Optimizing your database

One of the main performance bottlenecks for any content management system is the database server. To improve performance, you should periodically optimize the database tables. You can perform optimization from within phpMyAdmin. To learn more about this process, visit the MySQL website at `http://dev.mysql.com/doc/refman/5.0/en/optimize-table.html`.

> **TIP**
> If you have a large site and are using Smart Search, performance during indexing can be an issue, as can the maintenance of very large Smart Search index tables. You can find good advice on the Joomla! Docs site for managing this particular issue by visiting `http://docs.joomla.org/Smart_Search_on_large_sites`.

Maintaining Accessibility

Accessibility refers to the extent to which the largest number of users with different physical capabilities are able to access the contents and functionality of your website. This topic is often a point of focus in discussions concerning persons with disabilities and their rights to access. The right to access has been the subject of legislation in North America and in other jurisdictions and is widely considered to be an issue of best practices in web design. In the U.S., this right is codified in Section 508, an amendment to the Rehabilitation Act. In web design circles, the standards are outlined by the World Wide Web Consortium's Web Content Accessibility Guidelines, also known as WCAG.

NOTE

You can find the Section 508 guidelines at `www.section508.gov`. The WCAG guidelines can be found at `www.w3.org/TR/WCAG10/`.

Creating an accessible website can be a challenge. Although basic levels of compliance can be achieved with a modicum of work, the more stringent requirements of Section 508 impose many limitations on the way that you can display content and on the way the functionality behaves. Before you begin work on a site, determine what level of compliance is necessary, because the limitations imposed by the standards will impact template and extension selection. Going forward, awareness of the required standards should inform your content management decisions and the ways in which your content creators work.

In this section, I look at how Joomla! measures up in the accessibility department and offer a number of tips on how to build more accessible websites.

TIP

One of the best resources for information on website accessibility is the Web Accessibility Initiative (WAI) from the W3C. The site includes a lot of information about how to build accessible sites, as well as links to tools that can help you test your site's compliance with various standards. Visit WAI at `www.w3.org/WAI`.

Accessing the accessibility of Joomla!

The default Joomla! system comes with two templates for the front end of the website. Both templates produce valid CSS and XHTML, but the degree to which they comply with various accessibility standards is less clear. I set out to test both of the Joomla! 3 default templates for compliance with entry-level accessibility standards.

For testing, I used the WAVE Accessibility Evaluation tool, provided free of charge by WebAIM. For this test, I initially checked the home page both with and without the sample data installed. Unfortunately, the sample data included a number of accessibility problems and generated significantly higher error numbers. Accordingly, I restricted the final report to the errors and warnings generated by the templates without the sample data installed. Table 24.1 shows the results.

TABLE 24.1   Testing the Default Templates for Accessibility with WAVE

Template	Test Results
Beez	5 failures, 8 warnings
Protostar	6 failures, 2 warnings

Both templates meet the entry-level standards for creating accessible websites, though not without some issues. This analysis shows that the default Joomla! system is capable of performing well in basic accessibility scenarios. The errors displayed during the testing process also emphasized the vital role of templates and the importance of creating accessible content as the content items generated many minor problems.

NOTE

To obtain a copy of the WebAIM testing tool, visit `http://webaim.org/`.

Note also that the impact of extensions on accessibility can be substantial. If you are concerned with creating and maintaining a compliant site, then you can retest the site after installing each of the extensions.

TIP

The Joomla! Extensions Directory provides a specific category for these extensions at `http://extensions.joomla.org/extensions/style-&-design/accessibility`.

Improving template accessibility

The results of the WebAIM tests in the previous section demonstrate the key role that templates play in Joomla! accessibility. The creation of accessible templates is a broad topic, but you need to follow certain basic principles. I cover these principles in this section.

Support semantic structure

The H tags in HTML were intended to allow the people who create content to impose hierarchical ordering on that content. The proper use of these tags makes it easy for users and search engines to determine the information structure and the relationship between the various parts of the document. When designing the site's CSS selectors, make sure that you provide for the use of H tags in proper sequence by your content managers.

Avoid tables

By now, avoiding tables should be a well-established rule. Tables are not optimal and should be avoided. The exception to this general rule is when you have to display complex tabular data. If you must use tables, use the TH element to make the table headings separate from the data.

Do not rely on JavaScript

A number of users disable JavaScript on their browsers. If you build your template so that it relies on JavaScript for functionality, you need to make sure that the template degrades gracefully and that alternatives are provided. Always test to make sure that the page is navigable with only a keyboard.

Use system fonts for your nav menus

Use of image files for your navigation can cause accessibility problems unless you consistently provide for text alternatives. Note that the use of images is also disadvantageous because they decrease the search engine friendliness of the site while increasing the page file size.

Use a suitable color scheme

Make sure that your color selection maintains an appropriate level of contrast for viewers with visual acuity problems. Also remember to test your system in black and white to make sure that it remains navigable with the colors turned off.

Order elements on the screen logically

Place the page elements in a logical order inside your code. If the visitor views the site without the benefit of the CSS, the logical structure you have created in the code helps to maintain the integrity of the page. The use of *skip to* or *jump* links can also help make the page more navigable and enable users to jump to interim points on the page.

Make sure your text resizes

Use proper CSS coding to ensure that the user's browser can resize your text; typically this means using ems or percentages for font size in the CSS.

Use jump links

You should place jump links at the top of the page to allow visitors to jump directly to key content or functionality.

Make forms accessible

Forms need to be useable by all visitors. If necessary, use assistive technologies.

Provide alternatives to applets and plug-ins

If the page requires the use of an applet or plug-in, provide a text link to the download of the applet or plug-in, or provide an alternative for the display of the content.

Avoid requiring timed responses

Avoid forms or other functions that require timed responses. If this is unavoidable, make sure that it is clear that there is a time limit, make the limit generous, and make sure that the time markers are clearly communicated to the user.

Creating accessible content

If the developer has done a good job of creating an accessible template and you have assembled accessible components, you have half of the problem solved. Unfortunately, if your content creators aren't mindful of what accessibility means and how to create accessible content, all of your efforts may have been wasted! Creating accessible content items is a key success factor. Following the tips in this section can help keep your content items accessible to the widest audience of users.

24

Testing Accessibility

As a web developer or a site owner, you need to be able to test your site to identify accessibility issues. Table 24.2 lists several free tools that you can use online or download and run locally. In addition to the tools listed here, the Web Developer Toolbar add-on for the Firefox browser also provides some useful information and links to testing resources.

TABLE 24.2 Free Tools for Testing

Tool	URL
EvalAccess 2.0	`http://sipt07.si.ehu.es/evalaccess2/index.html`
Web Accessibility Inspector	`www.fujitsu.com/global/accessibility/assistance/wi/`
WAVE	`http://wave.webaim.org`

For a complete and maintained list of accessibility testing tools, visit `www.w3.org/WAI/ER/tools/complete`.

Format headings correctly

Just as the developer should make sure that the CSS provides the formatting to support the creation of semantic content, the content manager must make sure that headings are used properly to convey the structure of the content. Do not use strong, bold, or italic tags to make headings stand out; instead, use the proper H tags.

Use lists correctly

Do not use the ordered list and unordered list tags for purposes other than the creation of lists inside content items.

Use alt image attributes

The `alt` attribute for images allows you to provide text equivalents for images. If a visitor has the images turned off in her browser, proper use of the image `alt` attribute can help the user better understand the role the images play on the page and help improve understanding of the content.

Summarize graphs and charts

Provide a summary of graphical and chart data along with the chart or use the `longdesc` attribute to link to a separate description and data set.

Summarize multimedia

Provide summaries or transcripts of multimedia or use the `longdesc` attribute to link to a separate description and data set.

Summary

In this chapter, I looked at two related topics: improving Joomla! performance and maintaining website accessibility. I covered the following:

- Implementing view caching, page caching, and module caching
- Creating content that performs well
- Assessing the accessibility of the default templates
- Improving the accessibility of your site

In the final chapter, I turn to building a search engine–friendly site and the basics of search engine optimization.

24

Making a Site Search–Engine Friendly

IN THIS CHAPTER

Creating search engine-friendly URLs

Creating custom error pages

Working with metadata

Creating custom page titles

I f I build it, they will come — or so goes the old way of thinking. On today's web, that sort of thinking is the recipe for failure. The amount of noise and competition is nothing short of spectacular, and it can easily drown out your site, even if the quality of your content is excellent. If you want to get traffic and be seen, you need to make an effort to create a search engine-friendly site and you need to engage in at least some basic search engine optimization.

Joomla!, like most content management systems (CMS), faces some challenges to create a truly search engine–friendly site. You will hear some commentators say that you cannot achieve good search engine optimization (SEO) with a CMS, but that is not entirely correct. You can create a search engine–friendly site; however, you may not achieve the level of optimization that a highly trained SEO specialist can get from a pure HTML website. That said, given the competitiveness of search marketing these days, your use of a CMS is not likely to be fatal to your SEO goals. Effective site optimization has an important role, but it should be only one part of your broader search-marketing efforts.

This chapter looks at various SEO techniques that you can apply using only the default Joomla! features. Of course, if you want to do more and if you really want to be competitive, you must do more. There are numerous third-party extensions that you can add to your site to address various SEO issues.

Creating Search Engine–Friendly URLs

The default Joomla! system produces messy URLs. A default URL contains query strings and other characters that are hard for humans and search engines to read. Accordingly, the first step in any effort to make Joomla! more search engine friendly is to get rid of the messy URLs and get your system to use search engine–friendly (SEF) URLs.

What is a search engine–friendly URL? Generally speaking, a search engine–friendly URL is a human-friendly URL. The default Joomla! system produces a URL that looks something like this:

```
http://www.joomla3bible.com/index.php?option=com_
    content&view=article&id=27:the-joomla-community&catid=30:the-
    community&Itemid=30
```

This is not search engine friendly because some search engines will have difficulty with the odd characters and query strings. It is also not human friendly because it is long, hard to remember, and even harder to type accurately. URLs like this are even difficult to e-mail because their length often forces a line break and causes people to make mistakes when they cut and paste the URL into their browsers.

A better URL would look like this:

```
http://www.joomla3bible.com/the-community
```

This URL is search engine friendly and human friendly.

The process for enabling SEF URLs depends on the web server that your web host is using. SEF URLs are simplest to enable on the Apache web server, but they depend upon the `mod_rewrite` package being installed and your ability to create an `.htaccess` file. This is not as hard as it may sound because `mod_rewrite` is typically installed on most systems and Joomla! actually bundles in the default distribution an `.htaccess` file that is ready to go — all you have to do is rename it.

If you are running Apache, you can enable SEF URLs on your Joomla! site by following these steps:

1. **Access the files of your Joomla! installation on the server.**

2. **Find the `htaccess.txt` file, create a duplicate of it, and rename the new file `.htaccess`.** You can then exit the server; you are done here.

> **NOTE**
>
> On some servers, once you rename the file to `.htaccess`, the file seems to disappear from the file structure. (It doesn't really disappear; the file is still there, just "hidden" from the file view.)

3. **Log into the admin system of your Joomla! site.** The Control Panel loads in your browser.

4. **Click the Global Configuration link in the left column.** The Global Configuration Manager loads in your browser.

5. **Set the Search Engine Friendly URLs option to Yes.** This is located on the right side of the site page in a section named SEO Settings.

6. **Set the Use URL Rewriting option to Yes.**

7. **Click the Save button.** The system saves your changes and enables SEF URLs.

CAUTION

You must use the `.htaccess` file provided by Joomla!. Do not attempt to modify the file or create your own file, unless you have experience with this process. Definitely do not try this on a live site without first testing it!

If your site is using Microsoft IIS web server, instead of the Apache web server, the process is different and more involved. Note that the process requires you to install the ISAPI filter on the server. You will probably not be able to install this filter if you are on a shared web host. Accordingly, I have not described the steps here in detail. If you have access to your IIS installation, or you can convince your web host, then it is possible to set up SEF URLs on IIS. To learn more about this process, see the dedicated page on this topic on the Joomla! documentation site at `http://docs.joomla.org/SEF_URLs_on_IIS`.

NOTE

The Joomla! SEF URLs functionality is enabled by the System - SEF plug-in. This plug-in must be enabled for SEF URLs to work. Although it is enabled by default, if you are having problems, check the Plug-in Manager to ensure it is enabled in your system. I discuss plug-ins and the Plug-in Manager in Chapter 19.

Creating Your Own URL Aliases

In the earlier SEF URLs example, the last part of that URL, `the-community`, is referred to as the alias. It is possible to achieve a degree of control over the alias that is created by Joomla!.

Categories, articles, and individual menu items include options to set a specific alias. When creating or editing a category, article, or menu item, you can specify an alias for the system to use to construct the SEF URL. You do this by typing the string you want to use into the Alias field. Note that the Alias field only accepts lowercase letters, numbers, and the hyphen character; it does not accept spaces, upper-case letters, or unusual characters. If you do not specify an alias, the system automatically converts the item's title into an alias.

Pay attention when creating aliases in order to avoid creating multiple, conflicting aliases. This is primarily an issue where you are setting the alias for an article, and then linking directly to the article from a menu. In this case, the menu item also has an alias field. You should try to make the article alias and the menu item alias consistent, for simplicity's sake. Note that where there is a menu item linking directly to an article, the menu item alias takes precedence over a conflicting article alias.

Note also that categories have aliases. If you are linking directly into the category list pages, then you need to pay attention to those aliases, as well.

In some cases, use of SEF URLs in Joomla! results in the creation of duplicate article content. If you are concerned about this and want to avoid it, you must manage closely and carefully the aliases between the articles and the menu items.

25

Creating Custom Error Pages

You can create custom pages to handle common errors, such as 404 (page not found) errors. This step is optional, and while it has little direct benefit for search marketing, it is very helpful for your site visitors. It can help keep visitors on your site and can improve the perception that the site is professional and useful.

Error pages in Joomla! are handled by this file: `/templates/system/error.php`. You can override the default file by copying it to your active template directory and then making your changes on the copy; if there is an `error.php` file in the active template directory, it is shown instead of the default system file. If you want to work on the styling of the file, you also need to copy the CSS files, located at `/template/system/css/`, and move the relevant files to your default template directory. Remember to update the `error.php` file to point to the new location of the CSS.

Working with Metadata and Page Titles

Your site's metadata and page titles play important roles in search engine optimization. Key metadata fields, like the meta description and meta keywords fields, are sometimes used by search engine spiders to classify your content, and in some cases for the description that is associated with your site in the search results output. Page titles not only appear on the browser for the users, but are also indexed by the search engines and appear in the search results.

Setting the metadata

Joomla! provides multiple metadata options. You can set metadata for the entire site using the options in the Global Configuration Manager. You can also override the global settings for individual articles and for menu items. The default system does not, unfortunately, provide options for individual component metadata.

See Chapter 4 for more information on the Global Configuration Manager.

The hierarchy followed by the system prefers article metadata over menu item metadata, and menu item metadata over the metadata set in the Global Configuration Manager. If metadata has been specified in the article's parameters, it appears inside the code for that page, regardless of the other metadata values that are set elsewhere. If article metadata has not been specified, the menu item metadata appears; if there is not any menu item metadata, then the default global metadata appears in the page's code.

NOTE

The default system supports a limited set of metadata fields. If you want to add expanded metadata sets, either edit the template files to add more metadata fields into the head of the template, or consider adding a third-party extension that provides this facility.

 For a discussion of useful extensions for enhancing SEO in Joomla!, see Chapter 22.

Setting the page titles

By default, the value you specify for the title field of an article becomes not only the title you see on the page above the article's text, but also the resulting web page title. The web page title appears on the title bar of the browser and also as the page title in the search results of most of the popular search engines, including Google.

Many search engine specialists believe that the page title has a direct impact on the site's search engine effectiveness. By default, the browser page titles in Joomla! are generated dynamically, which is not optimal. Displaying the same value for the title of the text and for the title of the resulting web page restricts your ability to create optimal page titles that are in line with your search marketing efforts.

You can create a separate browser page title for articles, if there is a menu item linked to the article. By setting the Browser Page Title parameter in the Menu Item workspace, you can specify the page title for the item connected to the menu item. The Browser Page Title value takes precedence over the title specified in the article.

To set this up in Joomla!, follow these steps (note that for this example, I assume that you already have an article set to display the article title [the default setting] and that there is an existing menu item linking to that article):

1. **Access the admin system of your site.**
2. **Click the name of the menu where the menu item you want to change is located.** The Menu Item Manager opens.
3. **Click the name of the menu item you want to change.** The Menu Item Editing workspace opens in your browser.

25

4. **Click the Advanced Options tab.** The tab comes to the front.

5. **Click the Page Display Options heading.** The Page Display Options panel opens.

6. **In the Browser Page Title field, enter the text that you want to appear as the page title for the target of the menu item.**

7. **Click the Save button.** The system saves your changes.

This example results in the title given to the article appearing above the text of the article, but the Browser Page Title value specified in the menu item is used for the web page title tag.

> **TIP**
>
> If you also set the menu item parameter named Show Page Title to Yes, then the string you entered in the menu item Browser Page Title parameter is used both as the web page title tag and as the title above the article text.

> **NOTE**
>
> These approaches work equally well on menu items that link to components.

The Global Configuration Manager includes one other option for enhancing your browser page titles: the ability to append the site name to the page title. Adding the site name can improve the usefulness of bookmarks for your pages, making it easier for the person who bookmarked the page to later remember that the page came from your site. It can also give the pages of your site a boost in relevancy rankings for searches done for your site name. To enable this feature, follow these steps:

1. **Log into the admin system of your Joomla! site.** The Control Panel loads in your browser.

2. **Click the Global Configuration link in the left column.** The Global Configuration Manager loads in your browser.

3. **On the right side of the site page is a section named SEO Settings; set the Include the Site Name in Page Titles option to After.**

4. **Click the Save button.** The system saves your changes.

> **TIP**
>
> While the SEO Settings control gives you the option to add the site name either before or after the page title, I recommend placing the name after the page title, as the total length of the page title is a concern with some search engines and it is better to keep the information specific to the page on the front end of the string.

Remember these tips when you create your page titles:

- Ensure that the title reflects the page contents.
- Use key phrases in your page title.

- Start the title with the key phrase.
- Don't over-optimize the title by trying to cram in too many keywords.
- Keep the page title length to less than 70 characters.

Summary

This chapter covered the basics of creating a search engine–friendly Joomla! website and touched on some search engine optimization fundamentals. You learned how to:

- Enable search engine–friendly URLs
- Create a custom error page for your site
- Control site, menu item, and article metadata
- Create effective page titles

25

Part VI

Appendixes

Part VI contains the Appendixes, which provide supplemental information, including a look at all the sample data installation options, and a guide to finding all the key files in your Joomla! installation. I also cover how to install the XAMPP and MAMP server packages on your computer, thereby allowing you to create a local development installation. In the final appendix, I look at using the VirtueMart extension to add e-commerce functionality to your website.

IN THIS PART

Appendix A
Choosing a Sample Data Set

Appendix B
Locating Key Files

Appendix C
Installing XAMPP

Appendix D
Installing MAMP

Appendix E
Implementing e-Commerce with VirtueMart

Choosing a Sample Data Set

IN THIS APPENDIX

Understanding the various sample data options

Working without sample data

Creating a blog site

Deploying a brochure site

Installing the default sample data set

Using the Learning Joomla! sample data

Installing testing data

J oomla! comes bundled with sample data files you can elect to include when you run the Joomla! installer. There are six options you can choose from, including an option to install Joomla! without any of the sample data. While setting up the site without sample data provides you with a clean slate, there are circumstances where installing the sample data is desirable. If you are new to Joomla!, you will even find a sample data set tailored to helping you find your way around the system for the first time. Even if you are an experienced Joomla! user, you may want to install the sample data in some cases, as it can jumpstart your site-building efforts by providing common modules and menu items that are ready to use. You can either keep the structures that are created by the sample data or edit them to suit your needs; in either event, it may be faster than creating everything from scratch. Finally, Joomla! also includes a sample data set created specifically for testing purposes, to assist with ongoing development of the Joomla! CMS.

In this appendix, I explain the purpose of each sample data set and provide screenshots of the output created by each one. The six variations discussed in this appendix are

- **None.** Does not include any sample data at all
- **Blog.** Implements a possible blog site structure
- **Brochure.** Implements a possible brochure site structure
- **Default.** Provides a full set of modules
- **Learn Joomla!.** Installs a sample data set tailored to the needs of new users
- **Test.** Provides a sample data set purpose-built for Joomla! development testing

Installing No Sample Data

If you are experienced in Joomla! and want a clean slate to start your work, you should choose the None option when prompted to choose a sample data set during installation. As the name implies, you get a completely empty site; there are not any articles, extraneous modules, or menu items. Figure A.1 shows the front end of the site without any sample data installed.

FIGURE A.1

A Joomla! site without any sample data installed

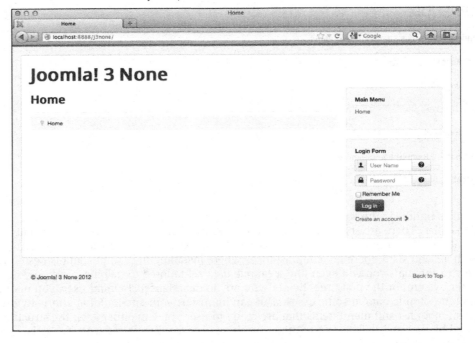

Creating a Typical Blog Site

If you want to use Joomla! to run a blog, then the Blog sample data will fast-track your site configuration. The Blog sample data set includes instances of the most popular blog modules, as shown in Figure A.2, including the following:

- **Older Posts.** This is a module showing the most recent posts.
- **Blog Roll.** This is a links module for use as a blog roll.
- **Most Read Posts.** This is a module showing the most read blog posts.
- **My Blog.** This is a syndication link for your site visitors to follow your posts; it is shown with the RSS icon.
- **Author Login.** This is a dedicated login module, located in the bottom-right column.
- **Archive.** This is an archives module that is available to use, although it is not shown in the figure, as there are not any articles set to the status archive.

The home page layout is also tailored to blog usage, with the menu item type set to Category Blog. The layout is configured to show the four most recent articles in a column, with links to the previous four articles underneath that. Figure A.2 demonstrates the front-end output as it appears with the Blog sample data installed.

Deploying a Brochure Site Structure

The Joomla! sample data offers a sample data set tailored to fast deployment of a typical brochure site. A brochure, or marketing, website is one of the simplest site structures. These informational sites often have similar elements: an About Us page, a contact form, and a few content pages.

When you choose to install the Brochure sample data, you end up with the result shown in Figure A.3. The module selection is limited to a login form and a Custom HTML module. There is an article for use as an About Us page, and there is a contact setup for use as the Contact Us page. The News choice on the Main menu is created using the Category Blog menu item type so that you can assign articles to the designated category and automatically display the most recent items.

FIGURE A.2

The output of the Blog sample data

FIGURE A.3

The front end of the site with the Brochure sample data set installed

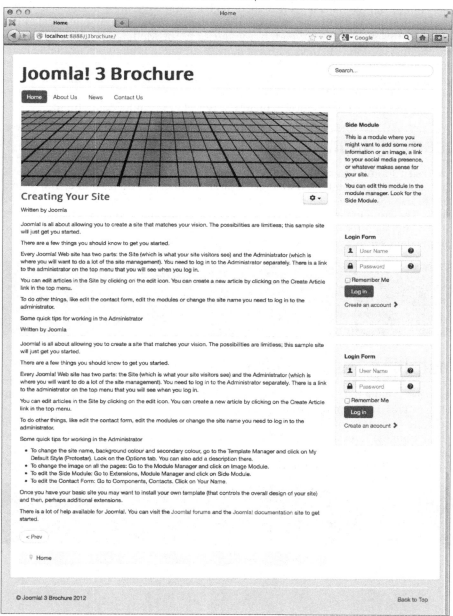

Installing the Joomla! Default Data

The Default sample data set is designed to give you the greatest flexibility while still providing resources to fast-track your site development. There's only one article here, and very little to see on the front end, but if you go to the Module Manager, you will discover that the installation is loaded with versions of all the module types available in the system. The various module types have been created, but are not published; that step is up to you. The Main menu includes only a home link. The installation is also designed to accommodate front-end users, with both a Login Form module and a User menu already in place and published. Figure A.4 shows the Default sample data output.

Learning Joomla! Sample Data

The Learn Joomla! sample data set is intended to help you if you are new to the system. This sample data installation includes a large number of articles and examples explaining how to use the system. This set also includes the sample sites, Fruit Shop and Australian Parks. The contents are extensive, so this is probably not your best choice for starting to build a site, as it requires a lot of cleaning up. If you are new to the system, however, this sample data set is a great way to start. See Figure A.5.

TIP

If you are new to the system, trying installing the Learn Joomla! sample data. Explore the site and kick the tires. Once you feel comfortable, wipe out the installation and re-install using one of the more efficient sample data sets to construct your actual site. It's a bit more work, but it is worth it.

Installing Testing Data

The Test sample data option is purpose-built to assist with the testing of the Joomla! release. This variation of the sample data contains active examples of all the system's menu item types, modules, and functionality. It also contains content items providing instructions on how best to test the system. Install this sample data set if you intend to help the Joomla! development team; otherwise, it is probably better not to install the sample data, as it requires a lot of cleaning up to use for any other purpose. See Figure A.6.

NOTE

If you plan to install this sample data set for the purpose of testing, do not delete the installation directory during installation. Leave the installation directory in place, as it will assist in testing.

FIGURE A.4

The Default sample data output

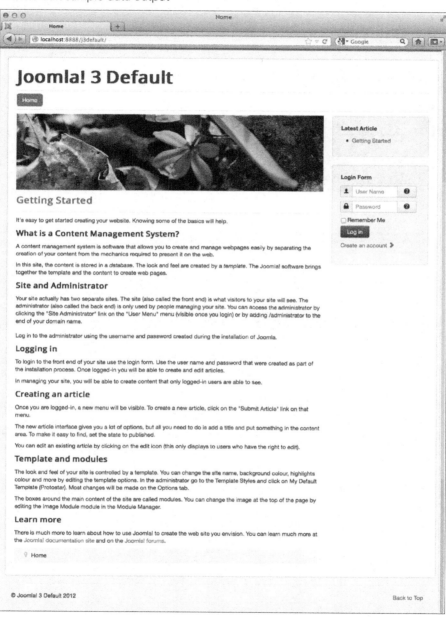

FIGURE A.5

The Learn Joomla! sample data provides extensive examples and tutorial content.

FIGURE A.6

The front end of the default Joomla! site with the Test sample data installed

Locating Key Files

IN THIS APPENDIX

Locating the key files in your system

Though the Joomla! mantra states, "Do not modify the core files," there are times when it is useful to know where to find key elements, either for the purpose of overriding them, or to simply crack open the file and look at it to better understand how things work. In this appendix, I've assembled a quick guide to where you can find all the key elements of the system, in hopes that it might save you from spending your time digging through directories and hoping you have found the right file.

Table B.1 shows the locations of most the critical files in the system. The table's contents include the key files used by the front-end components and modules, as well as the locations of the Language Packs, the default images, and perhaps most importantly, the front-end and admin templates and CSS files.

Note that the location I have included is the path to the files on your server, relative to the directory where you have placed your Joomla! installation.

TABLE B.1 Key Files

Item	Location
Configuration Settings	
Configuration file	`configuration.php`
Components (front-end output)	
Banner	`components/com_banners`
Contacts	`components/com_contact`
Newsfeed	`components/com_newsfeeds`
Search	`components/com_search`
Weblinks	`components/com_weblinks`
Wrapper	`components/com_wrapper`

continued

TABLE B.1 *(continued)*

Item	Location
Site Modules (front-end output)	
Archived Articles	`modules/mod_articles_archive`
Articles - Newsflash	`modules/mod_articles_news`
Articles - Related Articles	`modules/mod_related_items`
Articles Categories	`modules/mod_articles_categories`
Articles Category	`modules/mod_articles_category`
Banners	`modules/mod_banners`
Breadcrumbs	`modules/mod_breadcrumbs`
Custom HTML	`modules/mod_custom`
Feed Display	`modules/mod_feed`
Footer	`modules/mod_footer`
Language Switcher	`modules/mod_languages`
Latest News	`modules/mod_articles_latest`
Latest Users	`modules/mod_users_latest`
Login	`modules/mod_login`
Menu	`modules/mod_menu`
Most Read Content	`modules/mod_articles_popular`
Random Image	`modules/mod_random_image`
Search	`modules/mod_search`
Statistics	`modules/mod_stats`
Syndication Feeds	`modules/mod_syndicate`
Weblinks	`modules/mod_weblinks`
Who's Online	`modules/mod_whosonline`
Wrapper	`modules/mod_wrapper`
Language Files	
English (default en-GB Language Pack)	`language/en-GB`
Any language overrides	`language/overrides`
Site Templates	
Beez3 template	`templates/beez3`
Protostar template	`templates/protostar`
CSS (front-end)	
Stylesheets	`templates/[active template name]/css`

Item	Location
Admin Template	
Hathor	`administrator/templates/hathor`
Isis	`administrator/templates/isis`
CSS (admin system)	
Stylesheet	`administrator/templates/` `[active template name]/css`
Image Files	
Default banner images	`images/banners`
Default header images	`images/headers`
Sample data images	`images/sampledata`
System images	`images/`

B

Installing XAMPP

IN THIS APPENDIX

Setting Up XAMPP on your Windows machine

X AMPP is a unified software package that bundles all the elements necessary to create a fully functional server environment on your computer. The system includes not only the basics, like the Apache web server, the MySQL database, and PHP language support, but also useful management tools such as phpMyAdmin. If you want to build a local development or testing server, XAMPP is an easy way to get up and running quickly. XAMPP is cross-platform compatible and can be installed on almost any computer running Windows, Linux, or Mac OS.

> **TIP**
>
> If you are using Mac, you will probably prefer to use MAMP instead of XAMPP. I cover MAMP in Appendix D. If you are using Linux, you may not need a package like this at all, as many Linux distributions already have the necessary tools installed.

This appendix provides a step-by-step guide to installing XAMPP on a Windows machine. At the conclusion of this process, you will have a functional server on your Windows machine that allows you to run Joomla! locally.

Follow these steps to acquire the XAMPP installation package and set it up on your local machine.

1. **Connect to the Internet and open your browser.**
2. **Direct your browser to** www.apachefriends.org. The web page loads in your browser.
3. **Click the XAMPP button in the Main menu.** The XAMPP page loads.
4. **Click the XAMPP for Windows link.** The XAMPP for Windows page loads.
5. **Scroll down the page to the list of installer options, and click the version you prefer.** Your browser is redirected to the Sourceforge.net downloads page. The download begins automatically.
6. **A pop-up menu prompts you to save the file; click OK.** The software installer downloads to your computer. After it is complete, you can continue to the next step.
7. **Locate the downloaded installer package on your local machine.**

8. **If you downloaded an archive file type, double-click it to extract it; if not, continue to the next step.**

9. **Double-click the new file.** Select the language you prefer. Click OK. The installer takes you to the next screen.

10. **Click Next.** The installer takes you to the next screen. Select the installation location. Click Next. The installer takes you to the next screen.

11. **Change any settings you want on the Options page.** All choices are optional. Click Install. The installer takes you to the next screen and completes the installation.

12. **Click Finish.** The installer closes.

The installation is complete and the software is ready to run.

To begin, simply start XAMPP by choosing Start ⇨ Programs ⇨ XAMPP. Use the start/stop buttons to control the servers.

To create a new website, simply copy the files into a directory placed inside the /htdocs directory. You can then access your new site by opening the URL in your browser, as follows: http://localhost/sitedirectoryname.

Installing MAMP

IN THIS APPENDIX

Setting Up MAMP on Your Mac

MAMP is a unified software package that bundles all the elements necessary for creating a fully functional server environment on your local computer. The system includes not only the basics, like the Apache web server, the MySQL database, and PHP language support, but also useful tools like phpMyAdmin. If you want to build a local development or testing server, MAMP is an easy way to get up and running quickly. MAMP is cross-platform compatible and can be installed on almost any computer running Windows, Linux, or Mac. That said, MAMP is most often used on Macs, with many PC users preferring XAMPP, which I discuss in Appendix C.

> **NOTE**
> Linux users often do not need these packages, as many Linux distributions have all the necessary elements already installed.

This appendix provides a step-by-step guide to installing MAMP on a Mac machine. At the conclusion of this process, you will have a functional server on your Mac that allows you to run Joomla! locally.

Follow these steps to acquire the MAMP installation package and set it up on your local machine.

1. **Connect to the Internet and open your browser.**
2. **Direct your browser to** `www.mamp.info`. The web page loads in your browser.
3. **Click the Downloads tab in the Main menu.** The Downloads page loads.

4. **Click to download the software package named MAMP & MAMP PRO.** Note that the basic free MAMP is often bundled together with commercial MAMP Pro.

5. **A pop-up menu prompts you to save the file; click OK.** The software installer downloads to your computer. After it is complete, you can continue to the next step.

6. **Locate the downloaded archive (ZIP) package on your local machine.**

7. **Double-click the archive package.** The software unpacks and leaves a new file on your desktop.

8. **Double-click the file.** The file opens a new window showing the installer icon.

9. **Drag the MAMP icon into the Applications directory shown in the installer window.** The system immediately begins to copy all the necessary files to your computer's Applications directory. When it is done, you hear a confirmation beep.

10. Close the installer window.

The installation is complete and the software is ready to run.

To start the servers, simply double-click the MAMP icon inside the new MAMP directory. The MAMP controller opens. If the servers fail to start when you open the application, click the Start Servers button. You should see two green lights, one for the Apache server, and another for the MySQL server. You need two green lights to use the application! When both green lights are visible, the system automatically opens the MAMP welcome page in a browser window. Note that this page contains links to all the information and utilities you need, including the phpMyAdmin tool. Typically, this page URL is `http://localhost:8888/MAMP/?language=English`.

To shut down the servers, click the Stop Servers button.

To create a new website, simply copy the files into a directory placed inside the `/applications/MAMP/htdocs` directory. You can then access your new site by opening the URL in your browser, as follows: `http://localhost:8888/sitedirectory name`.

Implementing e-Commerce with VirtueMart

IN THIS APPENDIX

An introduction to using VirtueMart

How to obtain and instal VirtueMart

First steps with VirtueMart

I f you want to create an online catalog or sell products on your Joomla! site, you can do so easily by installing the VirtueMart system. VirtueMart turns your Joomla! site into a powerful and full-featured e-commerce framework.

You can either add VirtueMart to an existing site, or obtain an all-in-one installer that provides Joomla! plus VirtueMart and a selection of additional extensions. Once installed, you can configure VirtueMart to handle multiple products and categories and support a wide range of shipping and payment options.

At the time of this writing, VirtueMart was not yet compatible with the Joomla! 3 series. This appendix introduces VirtueMart as an option for implementing e-commerce on your Joomla! site.

Introducing VirtueMart

VirtueMart is an open source e-commerce plug-in for the Joomla! CMS. The system interfaces with all the most common shipping programs and payment gateways to offer a turnkey e-commerce solution for Joomla! users. The VirtueMart project has been around for a number of years — indeed, longer than Joomla! — and is the most popular e-commerce plug-in for Joomla!. The VirtueMart team has created a full-featured system that provides all the most common functionality that you would expect from an online shopping site.

VirtueMart is designed for two purposes:

- Online catalog management
- Online sales

It is equally suited to either task, and these two functions are typically combined into one site — that is, the system is used to manage an online catalog from which items are sold. VirtueMart is capable of handling either physical or virtual products, meaning that you can either carry inventory that is physically delivered, or provide digital products that are delivered by download directly from the site.

> **NOTE**
> You can test-drive a live VirtueMart installation at the demonstration site that the project maintains. This site allows you to check out both the front end and the back end of the system. Try the demonstration online at `http://virtue mart.net/home/demo`.

The default VirtueMart system supports a wide range of features for both site visitors and administrators. Note that these features are in addition to the standard Joomla! site features, and further, that you can extend your VirtueMart site by adding extensions to the installation.

Front-end visitors, or *shoppers* as they are referred to in the system, have access to a number of features that enable them to find items and track their orders. They can

- Quickly search for products with filters for features and discounts
- Manage their account (registered users only)
- Manage their shipping details (registered users only)
- View their order history (registered users only)
- Pick their preferred currency
- View and rate products
- Receive automatic notifications when a product is back in stock
- Browse and sort products by relevance, price, newest additions, and so forth

Site administrators can manage the catalog and the users. The VirtueMart system is intended to cover the most common needs of an online shop manager, including currencies, taxes, shipping, discounts, and order management. Features include

- Unlimited number of products and categories
- Multiple images per product
- Catalog management only, or catalog plus shopping cart
- Customizable product attributes
- Grouping shoppers to show different prices and payment options
- Support for downloadable products
- Support for multiple currencies and multiple payment gateways
- Flexible pricing

- Support for SSL connections
- Support for multiple delivery methods and shipping modules
- Support for multiple discount systems and "specials"
- Management of stock levels and display of product availability
- Support for multiple tax calculations
- Support for order status management
- Shop statistics

NOTE

Like Joomla!, VirtueMart is extendable. The VirtueMart site includes an Extension directory with more than 150 entries. You can browse the directory at `http://extensions.virtuemart.net/`.

Obtaining and Installing VirtueMart

The first step to setting up your online store is to obtain the VirtueMart code. There are multiple versions of the package available, so make sure you obtain the proper version for the version of Joomla! you have installed. You should obtain the VirtueMart installer package only from the VirtueMart site, `http://virtuemart.net`, or from the JoomlaCode site at `http://joomlacode.org/gf/project/virtuemart/`.

If you want to create a fresh installation, you should obtain the all-in-one installer that bundles Joomla! with VirtueMart and additional related extensions. This package is created by VirtueMart and is called the eCommerce Bundle. If you are creating a fresh installation, this is the easiest way to get VirtueMart up and running with minimal effort.

CAUTION

Because the eCommerce Bundle is maintained by VirtueMart, not the Joomla! team, you need to make sure that your Joomla! installation is up to date. Immediately after installation, you should check if there are any upgrades or patches for the Joomla! core, and if so, install them without delay.

The installation process applicable to the VirtueMart eCommerce Bundle is identical to the installation process for the Joomla! core.

 See Chapter 2 for a full explanation of how to install the Joomla! core files on your server.

E

TIP

Note that the bundle installer includes the option to install sample data. If this is your first time working with VirtueMart, then you should install the sample data to grasp the system's capabilities and see various modules in action.

If you already have an installation of Joomla! and you need to add VirtueMart to the site, you can do so by installing the VirtueMart component. This approach does require a bit more work.

Getting Started with VirtueMart

When you access the VirtueMart component, you first see the default VirtueMart Control Panel. The Control Panel is intended to give you quick access to the most common functionalities needed by a shop administrator. The first time you visit the Control Panel, you should go directly to the shop configuration, as this is critical to getting your shop up and running.

In addition to providing information about your store, you need to configure payment and shipping options and then set up all your products. The VirtueMart system is capable of supporting a wide range of product attributes. By default, you can classify products by manufacturer, vendor, type, or category. For larger shops, the various options are useful, but for a small shop, they can be overwhelming. To work in the simplest configuration, you need only to create products. That said, as a shop owner, if you have more than a few products, you may find that product management is significantly improved if you also create categories for grouping your products. Categories are not required, but they are very useful.

Once your shop is up and running, VirtueMart can also help you keep track of your shoppers, your transactions, and your inventory. VirtueMart includes a number of features that are intended to make administering an online shop easier. The back office feature of VirtueMart is one of the areas where the system has seen significant improvements over the years, and it now contains a number of useful features.

VirtueMart also provides snapshots of activity in the system. You can use the report generation function to display a summary of the number of customers, products, and orders. The system's ability to generate reports is somewhat limited and is focused on transactions. You can also tailor it to display activity data by date range, and to include not only orders, but also a summary of the products sold.

Index

Index